Rob Dielenberg's research on Ted Bundy is complete and thorough. This book, an assimilation of his findings, is a major step towards understanding the mind of one of the world's most puzzling serial killers. Every person who seriously wants to understand the criminal mind should read it.

- Al Carlisle (PhD Clinical Psychology) - Author of *I'm Not Guilty*

Dr. Dielenberg has done an exhaustive study of the life and crimes of Ted Bundy. When dealing with matters of which I have personal knowledge he is extremely accurate, and I trust that the rest of his book exhibits the same high quality and adherence to fact. Although one can disagree with some of the conclusions he draws, no one can disagree that he has produced an invaluable reference for anyone wishing to research serial killers in general and Ted Bundy in particular.

- George R. Dekle Sr. (Law Skills Professor) - Author of *The Last Murder*

Rob Dielenberg's book is well-planned out, and accuracy of information is spot on. Good reading. I recommend that anyone who is or is going to be a homicide investigator read this book. I also recommend that any Criminology Professor requires their students to read this book.

- Don Patchen (AAS Law Enforcement, Ret. Homicide Investigator) -

It has always struck me as odd that after the death of Albert Einstein, his brain was assiduously and aggressively studied to determine the neurological correlates of intelligence, and yet Bundy's brain, which perhaps held clues to the depraved mind, was fried in the electric chair. Granted, this is the curious view of a student of neuroscience, and ignores many historical, legal, and social concerns, but the ultimate goal of understanding this other crucial dimension to humanity is just as valid, and perhaps even more critical. Here, Dielenberg meticulously recreates a neurological model that would make Bundy's brain blush, artfully blending modern neuroscientific scholarship with the known behavior and autobiographical statements of one of America's most notorious serial killers. This is a powerful and provocative addition to the field of neurocriminology.

- Jack Pemment (MS Biology) - Author of the essay 'Blame the amygdala'

TED BUNDY: A VISUAL TIMELINE

A geographical and psychological road map through Ted's crimes

Rob Dielenberg

Updated edition, November 2016.
2nd updated edition July 2017.
3rd updated edition, April 2018.
4th updated edition September 2018.

First edition, December 2016.
First updated edition, April 2018.
Second updated edition September 2018.

National Library of Australia Cataloguing-in-Publication entry
Creator: Dielenberg, Robert A., author.

Title: Ted Bundy : a visual timeline / Robert A. Dielenberg.

ISBN: 978-0-9945792-1-8 (paperback)

Subjects: Bundy, Ted.
Serial murderers--United States--Biography.
Criminals--United States--Biography.
Murder--United States--Case studies.

For enquiries or feedback, please visit:
https://www.facebook.com/Ted-Bundy-A-Visual-Timeline-1780367725516517/

Cover art, copyright Rob Dielenberg 2016.
Back cover art: Chevron road map excerpt, 1972.

This book is dedicated to all the families, victims and authorities that were impacted by the deeds of Ted Bundy.

Contents

Acknowledgements

I started this book alone, not realizing what I was getting myself into. As I progressed and dug deeper into the Ted Bundy story, I realized that if I was to go forward I would need help.

I am very fortunate in that I encountered three individuals that not only jumped at the chance to make this book better, but openly embraced the often frustratingly detailed work that it involved: Chris Mortensen, Chuck Meeks, and Dave Woody. Mike Dicianna and Drew Bales also contributed to specific cases making them more accurate. The book in its present form would not exist without the enthusiasm of all these people. Concretely, they provided photos, many of which required driving interstate, interviews with original sources, and documents (scanned and photographed). They also played a vital role in shaping some of the speculations developed in the book by visiting locations where Ted was active and researching topographical information.

I also want to thank the many contributors of photographs. These range from the official archives (Florida State, King County, Von Drehle), to local libraries and university collections. In particular I wish to thank Detective Don Patchen (retired), Vincent Tan, John Young (Colorado Maps), Randy Stilson (Evergreen State College), Marty Blackson (Central Washington University), Dave Woody (Susan Rancourt, Issaquah, Taylor Mountain research), Mike Dicianna (Kathy Parks, OSU documents), Drew Bales (Donna Manson, Evergreen State College research) and Kristina Erickson. George Dekle Sr. in particular was extremely helpful in providing information and guidance during the later stages of the book.

I also want to thank Al Carlisle for his help and feedback as the book progressed. Al was always there when I needed him.

I would also like to thank Chris Eskridge for his reflections on the Laura Aime case and Stéphane Bourgoin for his information on Gerard Schaefer.

Lastly, I want to thank Michael Debono for his erudite editing services and our facebook and other contributors who have sent in additional information that had previously not been made publicly available.

Image copyright

Electronic Version

The images in this book have been acquired from diverse sources, including the Internet, book scans, eBooks, magazines, archives, photographers' personal collections, authors, newspapers and film media. In all relevant cases, a sincere attempt has been made to track down the copyright holder of the image; copyright permissions have been requested and money paid.

Not all copyrighted images could be tracked down. The provenance information of some images appears to have been lost or misplaced. If a copyright holder sees an image they think has not been properly credited in text, or if a copyright holder seeks financial reimbursement for an image that was originally for sale, then contact me via the address provided in the disclaimer section of this book. Hopefully a fair negotiation can be reached.

Ideally, in the good world, I would prefer that people feel they have paid me for the information I have structured and produced, not the images. This ideal has inspired a two-tiered business model. US$9.99 for the 100 dpi resolution version and US$29.99 for the 300 dpi resolution version. It is argued that if someone is prepared to pay 30 dollars for a good copy, then they are not going to pirate the images. If someone wishes to pirate the 100 dpi version, the original copyright holders can still sell high-resolution versions. It is additionally argued that the images contained in this book will actually promote sales of the works referenced herein.

In summary, it is hoped that readers will appreciate what a monumental task it is to gather so many images and organize them in the correct sequence. Taken from this perspective, the author would prefer the book to be received more as a public offering than an exercise to solely benefit himself. One way that this can happen is if a percentage of the money generated by this version goes out to the research assistants as points in the book (they also share some costs of course), and some of it is put aside for the 2nd edition, meaning that other people could join the team, invest a little, and improve the product and get some gain.

Paperback Version

The paperback version contains a slightly different image list than the electronic version. New images added to this version have been acquired from contributors and copyright remains in their hands. In parallel to a two-tiered model for the electronic version, a two-tiered model has been deployed for the paperback version: a collector's edition and a standard edition. The collector's edition is printed on high quality paper and has a robust perfect bound finish; the standard edition is printed on standard paper and a standard perfect bound finish. Paper quality affects image quality. A diligent attempt has been made to adjust image color and levels to compensate for this difference. The copyright argument presented for the electronic version applies equally to the paperback version as does cost, which is reflected in the printing costs for the two versions. Thus, the collector's edition will retail for US$99.95; the standard for US$39.95 (the cost of international shipping is built into the price).

Abbreviations

Books:

Holmes & Holmes 2008: (H&H 2008).
Keppel & Birnes 2004: (K&B 2004).
Keppel & Michaud 2012: (K&M 2012).
Michaud & Aynesworth 1983/2000: (M&A 1983/2000).
Winn & Merrill 1980: (W&M 1980).

Archives:

King County Archives: KCA.
Florida State Archives: FSA.
David Von Drehle Archives: DDA.

Reports:

State of Utah Adult Probation and Parole Presentence Investigation Report, March 22, 1975: (PIR 1975).
Ted Bundy Multiagency Investigative Team Report 1992: (MTR 1992).

Acronyms:

Prefrontal cortex: PFC.
Florida Department of Law Enforcement: FDLE.
Law School Admission Test: LSAT.
Registered Nurse: RN.
Tallahassee Police Department: TPD.
Violent Criminal Apprehension Program: ViCAP.

Place names

Florida State University: FSU.
University of Puget Sound: UPS.
Salt Lake City: SLC.

Miscellaneous:

[ref]: means a reference is needed.

Preface

This book is intended for mid- to high-level university students studying criminology and forensic psychology. This prescription is not because any one single data point in the book is complex, or requires great understanding, but because the totality of the data must be absorbed, processed, and then understood at the level of pattern and mechanism.

When I was studying psychology, we received a lecture on serial killers including Ted Bundy. I didn't know it then, but that lecture was somehow unsatisfactory, even if it might have sparked an interest in Bundy that I then forgot about. A lot of time passed, then I came upon Bundy again accidentally while researching Australian pathological killers for a historical project about the 1970s. I got interested in all things 70s and I inevitably bumped into Bundy again. This time I read a little more and I learned he spent time in Seattle. A friend of a friend lived there and I began to wonder if I should not learn more about Ted in Seattle. Pretty soon I got hooked. It was his monstrously inflated sense of self, that he was driven to seek out self-gratification at any expense, that intrigued me. He appeared to be very happy with his "achievements." We do not conceive of him as a person gripped by abject horror during the act of killing even as he goes on to kill anyway, a so-called split personality. No, Ted was high as a kite when he killed. Only afterwards, and only after the first kills did he feel any guilt and remorse. Except he soon stamped that out. What kind of consciousness would ever drive that kind of behavior?

I quickly ran into difficulties. I learned that childhood trauma and obsessional fantasies are often cited as causative factors. But I wasn't satisfied. It seems that those factors are necessary, but not sufficient. How did the violence start? How does a person break down their barriers of morality? Were they born that way, or were they self-made? So many questions.

This book is an attempt to unravel some of them, and revisit the university lecture I wished I had received. Accordingly, it is intended as a one-stop-shop for students to examine the life of Ted Bundy and discover for themselves the problem that he posed to society, namely: How do you know the person standing in front of you is the person they represent themselves to be? While this problem has existed ever since humanity became self-conscious and evolved civil societies, Ted in particular highlights this problem because he was the quintessential wolf in sheep's clothing of the modern era.

In studying Ted you will often hear the complaint, "Not enough about the victims, too much glorification of the killer."

This book does not glorify Ted. However, it does not pretend to answer the complaint, because the complaint is unrealistic. Firstly, most victims of Ted have barely more than a paragraph written about them in some form or another. Even if you cobbled together the thirty-odd victims that Ted is claimed to have murdered you would not have enough to write a book. The only partial counter-example to this is Janice Ott and maybe the interviews of Belva Kent, Debbi Kent's mother. (Rhonda Stapley's 2016 the "second Ted survivor" stepping out of the closet is an autobiography, not a biography, and a dubious one at that.) Police unfortunately are reluctant to give up their inside files on Ted's victims. I have put as much as feasibly possible about victims and their families in the timeline, but it is clearly insufficient. Secondly, most of the victims were snatched from life before they could become interesting people. It takes an entire life to build up the sufficient and necessary human complexity to become worthy of consideration to biographers. This is the cruel truth.

This does not automatically mean Ted is a worthy candidate for biographers. If anything, writing about Ted is a nasty and dirty business. There is hardly a single redeeming feature about him. It would serve biographers much better to write about the constructive and inspirational luminaries of this world.

Also, let us not pretend that writing about Ted will save the world. Even if we learned everything there is to learn about what makes serial murderers tick, that would not rid the world of these destructive deviants. The best thing that has come along to mitigate the problem is mobile devices and CCTV. Also, to a certain extent, the ViCAP system (Violent Criminal Apprehension Program in the United States and others like it around the world). ViCAP helps authorities coordinate their efforts to capture and prosecute these individuals. In Ted's time, none of these technologies existed. If Ted existed now, he wouldn't have gotten away with more than a few murders, at most.

What makes Ted an interesting study then, are not the sensational and macabre stories that swirl around him like so much detritus, but the little things, the small details that reveal something unexpected and surprising about him. In some cases, the details paint a more human picture of the man, not the 2-dimensional monster of our imaginations. From a neuroscientific perspective, we also want to know what drove Ted to do the things he did. The goal is to reverse engineer his brain to help us better understand how it gave rise to his particular cognition and behavior. Specifically, this means to not only open the black box on the dark and devious world of the homicidal necrophiliac, but take what we learn from that and apply it to humanity in general. In a very real sense, learning about deviant cognition & behavior teaches us more about the range and dynamics of consciousness itself. Some people—perhaps most—will conclude we ought to banish this type of behavior (if not cognition) from our species. We have no way of knowing what type of genetic makeup that would be, whether we would be fit to survive long-term as a species if that ever came about. Perhaps not all psychopathic and/or personality disorder traits are redundant.

Another aspect of this study is the appreciation of the historical context that Ted existed in. In particular, the physical space that he moved through. This book makes use of numerous maps at varying levels of detail, often historically accurate to the time. This allows readers to enter a kind of virtual yesteryear where they can imagine what happened and how it happened. In quite a few cases, this informed the speculations of myself and my two side-kicks (Chris Mortensen and Chuck Meeks) with a greater sense of practical reality. All too often our team encountered highly fantastical theories spun by police and lay people alike. The mapping work therefore serves as an antidote to these fantasies.

This leads to another important aspect of this book: accuracy. The general information about Ted is mostly consistent. While most approaches to Ted's life are chronological, different people focus on different parts of his life depending on how much they know about that part. Also, biographers often put an image from one era of Ted's life next to a description of another part of his life. In other words, a mismatch between data and image. As you dig deeper, you find more instances of data that don't match up. One author says this, another says that. They can't both be right. In some film depictions, the locations, props, and dialogue are wrong and have been put out of sequence. This is because film is designed to rouse emotion more than reason. It is interesting that some writers attempt to tell Ted's story partly like a film.

This book levels the playing field because it provides a very comprehensive chronology of the most important events in Ted's life and if an image is found that links to that event, it is added to the story. Some of the images are era-correct. Some are modern day. Some are composites. There is a lot of variety. As you go through the timeline a new narrative forms in your head, slightly different one from the one that is available to date. Some parts are the same, but in other areas, new information and images opens the door to further speculation, sometimes a better understanding of what Ted may have done.

If by chance an entry in this book happens to contain an error, we hope to be notified so we can correct it for the next edition. We say this because this project has grown from its initial aim to something much bigger than a first edition alone could adequately encompass. Even as I write, new data is flowing in.

Robert A. Dielenberg (PhD Neuroscience)
May 27, 2016.
Newcastle
Australia

Preface to the updated edition

The pdf version of the "first edition" went out on May 10, 2016. This updated started development on June 1, 2016. It is now November 2, 2016, and the final draft of the updated pdf is nearing completion. A lot of time has been invested in maintaining facebook and gathering new data. We noted that a synergistic effect occurs between facebook and our own pro-active efforts. The usual pattern is we kick off with a topic, and facebook contributors respond. Sometimes a facebook individual pops up out of nowhere with an offer. Some of these individuals are time-wasters; some are curious and just want to throw stuff out there (some of their content is interesting, some inappropriate); and some have a genuine interest and want to contribute to the history. A select few of this last group has made it onto the contributor list.

New contributors (not limited to facebook)

Lyndon Prist: research into Ted's VW.

Dave Woody: Susan Rancourt - CWU, Taylor Mountain, Issaquah maps.

Mike Dicianna: Kathy Parks - OSU documents and maps.

Marian Stauffer Fowden: a new timeline entry, placing Ted at a specific location at a specific time.

Spencer Wallace: additional photos of 4143 12th Ave N.E. Seattle, WA.

Drew Bales: Donna Manson - Contemporary photographs of Evergreen State College campus.

Carol Culver: special thanks go to Carol for her brave retelling of Lynnette Culver's life. Carol also contributed a previously unpublished photo of Lynnette.

Cass Hardy: contributed an alternative account of the day of Denise Oliverson's disappearance.

New historical data

Most of the historical data that has been added to this updated version has been initiated by myself and the tight-knit group of " free-lance research assistants" (as I like to call them). The following is a list of topics that we delved more deeply into:

- Utilization of more historical aerial maps. Part of our team effort is to create accurate historical maps of Ted activity. This is a complex undertaking, because it involves sourcing the correct latitude and longitude on the globe, and getting aerial photography as close to the key dates (1974-75), as possible.

- Gathering more historical images. Finding new photos of individuals and locations in the story. Chris Mortensen has done a terrific job covering the Salt Lake City area. Chuck Meeks has continued to lend his image analysis expertise. Dave Woody and Mike Dicianna, apart from contributing new material provided feedback on theories raised by the new data.

- Tables. I have made a big effort to tabulate patterns in Ted's behavior. The M.O. table reveals the way he acquired victims; the Abduction-Rape interval table provides insight into his timing, where we were able to derive some new ideas about how he went about his rape and murders.

- Chapter updates: a significant amount of new material and analysis has been added to the Adult chapter. Other chapters have also been modified, some with new material. Numerous corrections have been made throughout the book, from minor typos to major arguments. We have reversed our position on Ted holding live victims for extended periods of time. We believe Ted kept victims only as long as he feasibly could, which was usually limited to the secluded location where he murdered them. If Ted did stay with a victims for any extended period of time, it would be at these secluded locations and the hours would typically (but not always) be after midnight into the early morning hours. We have changed other things too, the astute reader will pick these up. One section of the Introduction, for example, has been re-written to clarify and expand on the analysis of Ted's brain.

- The epilogue has been mostly re-written to form a tighter conclusion for the book.

- Two new appendices have been added. The first is a portfolio of images that support chapters within the book. The second is a list of all the missing west coast girls for the period in question so that readers can determine for themselves how many people Ted might have been involved in.

Robert A. Dielenberg (PhD Neuroscience)
November 2, 2016.
Newcastle
Australia

Preface to the paperback version

Approximately three-and-a-half months have gone by and the paperback version of this book is nearly complete. It would have taken me much longer to do the layout for this version if I did it all by hand. Fortunately I was able to write some automation JavaScripts that allowed me to speed up the process and take out much of the stress.

This paperback version went through several iterations before it found its footing. I realized that with all the maps we needed a format that would allow discernment of detail with the naked eye, so I chose a magazine layout (11 x 8.5 inch). This provides just enough real estate to do the job.

Due to the requirements of a 2-column design, some new images have been added, and a couple have been removed in comparison with the electronic form.

In a few places, text has been modified since the "updated" electronic version.

Note: throughout the book, American spelling has been mostly adopted. There are some exceptions, for example "racquet" and "manoeuver." These spellings have been retained for aesthetic purposes.

Robert A. Dielenberg (PhD Neuroscience)
February 21, 2017.
Newcastle
Australia

Preface to the 2nd updated edition. Some minor errors have been fixed in a few places through a combination of contributor discovery and our own revision. The major change is the entire timeline for September 1–6, 1974, has been re-written. In the first edition a theory as to what happened during this time window was erected, but in this version a modified approach was taken that puts less stress on creating a fixed itinerary and more on a range of possibilities given the corrupt data. A new image and an inset have been added in support of this new version.

Robert A. Dielenberg (PhD Neuroscience)
July 25, 2017.
Newcastle
Australia

Preface to the updated paperback version

This updated version came about because MT7 Productions issued a take down notice to our publisher over the following images drawn from *Terrible Secrets* (2012):

Donna Manson Poster: Page 87
Brenda Ball Flyer: Page 96
Denise Naslund: Page 107
Hand Drawn Map: Page 118
Michael Fisher: Page 187
Terrible Secrets Cover Page (includes an AP photo licensed by MT7) Page 292

This updated edition has removed these images at the request of Mike McCann who represents MT7 Productions. I sent him several emails (provided by my publisher via his take down notice) asking why he did not want to negotiate licensing these images. In fact, I tried numerous pathways to contact MT7 Productions *before* the publication of the first edition of this book, but I could not find anything leading to an address or an email contact. MT7 Productions did not provide any contact information in *Terrible Secrets* or any other place where the book was promoted. It was for this type of case that I wrote a copyright disclaimer in the front matter of this book in the hope that anyone finding an image that they believed was their copyright to contact me directly (my contact details are provided in the front matter of this book), whereupon I would gladly and sensibly negotiate monies for copyright. In black-and-white terms, using someone's image without permission is contra-indicated, and there is no denying that. However, the purpose of this book is educational and the visual timeline concept predetermines its format. As such, there is equally no escaping the inclusion of images in the timeline that serve that educational purpose. The intention is not to steal, as it has been done up-front with full transparency, with the promise of retro-dating reimbursement. The fact is, this book has cost me considerably more to produce than any money I make from it. The number of images is unprecedented for this type of subject. Who would be crazy enough to try and pull it off? It was hoped that owners of any copyright would recognize my diligent and honorable intentions, rather than just issue a knee-jerk reaction.

Mike McCann did eventually respond to one of my emails and uncompromisingly stated that there was nothing to negotiate and that he would institute legal action against me. So much for transparency. I responded by reiterating that "his" images will be removed.

The use of inverted commas here is intentional. The first three images—Manson, Ball and Naslund—are derivatives of original images that are publicly available at the King County Archives. The only difference is that they are embedded in missing posters in *Terrible Secrets.* I'm not an expert on copyright, but claiming copyright over identical images embedded in a missing poster seems to me to be a little bit of a stretch.

The second item of concern is McCann's uncompromising attitude regarding the use of his *Terrible Secrets* cover image in my bibliography. The reason why I put it there is that many of the books in this study have different versions and seeing the cover aids the reader in identifying which version was used. One would think that this constitutes a promotion of *Terrible Secrets*, but I suppose it's not up to me to promote someone else's product.

This leaves just two images that can be legitimately claimed by MT7: the Mike Fisher screen grab and the Ted hand-drawn map. Both of these were shown in small format, and both are part of the overall canon of Bundy material disseminated through various publications and the web. Once again, I would have been happy to pay a nominal copyright fee for their inclusion.

This business aside, we—by which I mean Chris Mortensen and myself—have taken the opportunity in this update to re-write the Wilcox narrative. We have been able to put a few more myths to bed. We also updated the Melissa Smith case on discovery of the actual police report which provides some information as to where her body was found. This information is not explicit, but we did our best anyway to modify the body location map so that readers can have the latest available information. Elsewhere, we updated the Debbie Smith case, and in other places added a couple of new photos so that overall, this update is quite significant. We'd also like to thank Aleksander H. Fiskum for spotting several typos, and Mark Ulrik for his help in ironing out numerous small errors and omissions, as well as providing data to significantly update the Appendix in this version.

Robert A. Dielenberg (PhD Neuroscience)
September 21, 2018.
Newcastle
Australia

Introduction

> **According to Bodiford, "He (Bundy) said *I passed a girl on the street. I had a feeling I had never had. I wanted to possess her* — and he used the word 'possess' — *by whatever means was necessary. I just had to have that girl.*"**

- *St Petersburg Times*, July 23, 1979 -

Questions

In delving into Ted Bundy, the most common questions asked are: How did he become a serial murderer? Why did he chose death over life, and how many people did he really murder?

To be honest, none of these questions will ever be satisfactorily answered. This book, however, has for the first time assembled pretty much everything of importance there is to know about Ted and has put those items into their correct sequence covering his life from cradle to grave. This gives us an unprecedented database from which to draw our inferences. If in the last analysis our inferences prove to be false, this is not due to our logic, but the validity of the available data. We have made the best effort to triple check our data; in more than a handful of cases, there are conflicts and contradictions. At all times original sources are given priority over hearsay and anecdotal evidence. But in some cases, hearsay and anecdotal evidence is all we have. In other cases, we have nothing at all; we have to interpolate, or extrapolate as the situation demands. In assessing these situations we ask the reader to test our speculations against the most probable, as opposed to automatically assuming the possible (and sometimes, the implausible).

The standard model of psychopathy

The standard model of psychopathy, as all scientific models, is an evolving construct. The history of its evolution is long and detailed, and we shall not explore it here. For our purposes, the modern concept of psychopathy

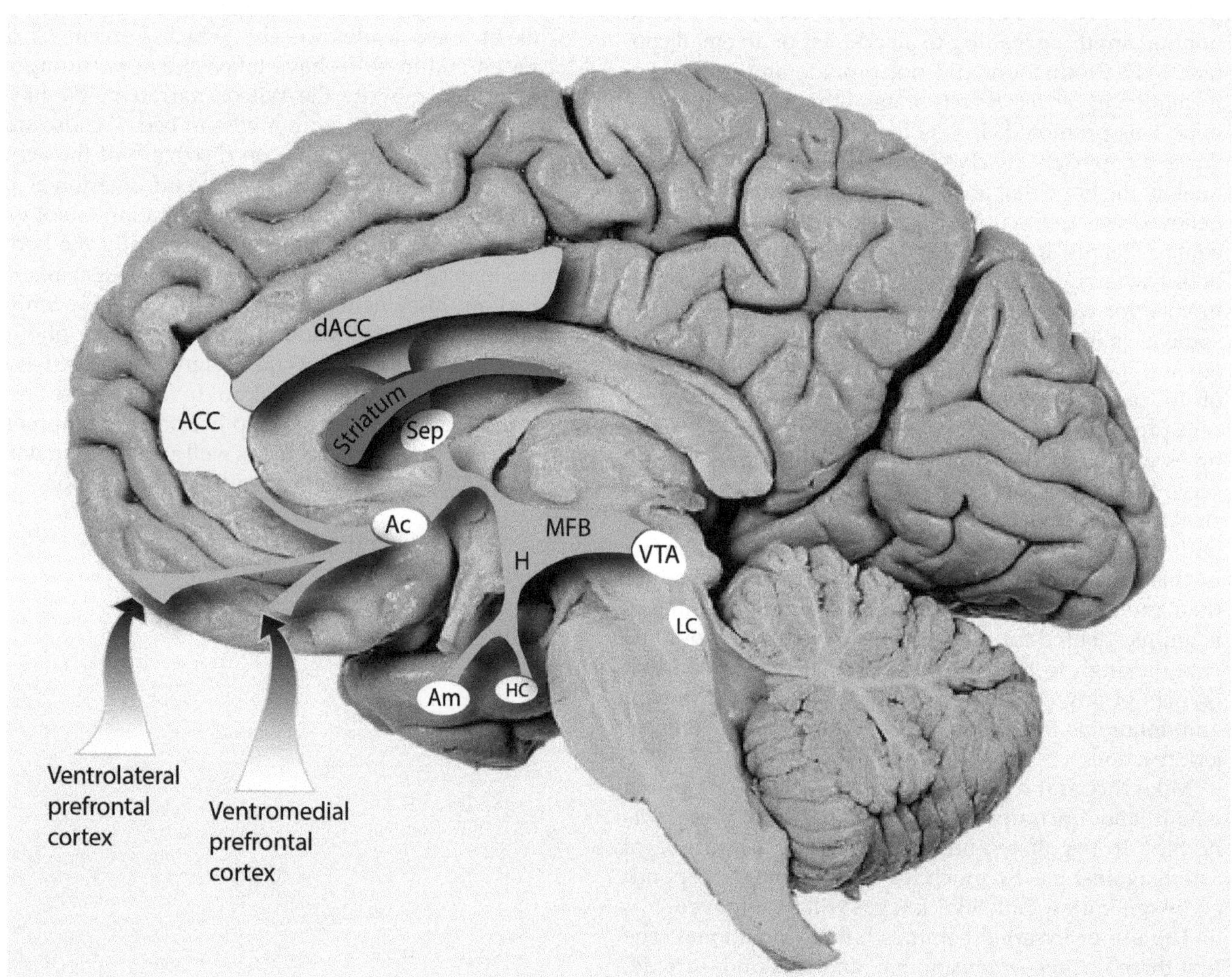

Primary brain areas discussed: ACC (anterior cingulate cortex); dACC (dorsal anterior cingulate cortex); Sep (septum); Ac (nucleus accumbans); MFB (medial forebrain bundle); H (hypothalamus); VTA (ventral tegmental area); Am (amygdala); HC (hippocampus); LC (Locus coeruleus). Brain image public domain.

evolved out of Hervey Cleckley's clinical descriptions, insights, and speculations which he detailed in *The Mask of Sanity* (1941/1976). Cleckley identified 16 distinct clinical criteria for a diagnosis of psychopathy, among them: hot-headed, manipulative, exploitive, irresponsible, self-centered, shallow, unable to bond, lacking in empathy or anxiety, likely to commit a wide variety of crimes, more violent, more likely to recidivate, and less likely to respond to treatment than other offenders (Tanay 2010, 127-8). Clinical instruments were subsequently developed, culminating in the all-pervasive Hare Psychopathy Checklist-Revised (PCL-R; Hare 1991). The PCL-R is comprised of four dimensions: *Interpersonal* (glibness/superficial charm, grandiose sense of self worth, pathological deception, conning/manipulative); *Affective* (lack of remorse or guilt, shallow affect, callous/lack of empathy, failure to accept responsibility for actions); *Lifestyle* (need for stimulation/proneness to boredom, parasitic lifestyle, lack of realistic long-term goals, impulsivity, irresponsibility); and *Antisocial* (poor behavioral controls, early behavior problems, juvenile delinquency, revocation of conditional release, criminal versatility). Two other items (promiscuous sexual behavior, many short-term relationships) do not load on any factor but contribute to the total PCL-R score.

This author is unaware whether the first version of the PCL was ever applied to Ted. However, Cleckley did assess Ted and found he was "capable of understanding the charges against him and of participating in his defense" (*Sarasota Herald-Tribune*, June 12, 1979). Ted opted not to use Cleckley's assessment of himself in his defense, so we have no way of knowing what the details were, although we can imagine that Cleckley must have observed some signs in Ted's character that loaded on dimensions later refined in the PCL-R. Note: Cleckley admitted his interview with Ted was far from comprehensive (Dorothy Lewis court transcript, December 15, 1987, p. 279, DDA). We could expand on the four dimensions of the PCL-R as it applies to Ted, but we will be taking a different tack and focus more on constructing a neurobehavioral model of Ted. In doing this, we hope to open the lid on a number of mysteries that are still very much in the air in explaining the evidence he left behind, for which labeling him a psychopath serves as a signpost pointing toward what seems like an ever receding horizon. We hope to bring that horizon a little closer.

A neurobehavioral model of Ted

The discussion that follows focuses on three areas: the prefrontal cortex (PFC), the reward circuit (ventral tegmental area, medial forebrain bundle, nucleus accumbans, amygdala), and the insular cortex (anterior and dorsal anterior aspects). Each of these areas in Ted's brain was perturbed – either through genetics, epigenetics or intrauterine influences, or conditioning (both willfully and through unconditioned environmental influences).

After drawing together evidence spanning Ted's entire life, we have come to the conclusion that Ted's primary problem was a developmental disorder of the prefrontal cortex (PFC). Developmental disorders cover a wide range of expression, including among others, autistic spectrum disorders, antisocial behavior, schizophrenia and Attention Deficit Hyperactivity Disorder (ADHD). PFC disorders are the most difficult to diagnose when they are borderline symptomatic as was in Ted's case.

The prefrontal cortex (PFC)

In laymen's terms, the PFC is the seat of the soul and creativity. In neuroscientific terms it is defined as the executive center of the brain (Fuster 2001; Goldman-Rakic et al 1996). Its principal function is the temporal organization of actions towards biological or cognitive goals (Luria 1966; Fuster 1997). Higher order control rather than more specific abilities such as spatial cognition and theory of mind (see "empathy" below) has been proposed as the core trait selected during evolution (Christensen 2007), and the PFC is the area of the brain that has most benefited from this development. To execute control, the PFC essentially functions as a comparator and bias generator.

Broadly speaking, the PFC can be divided into two areas: medial and lateral. Medial portions have reciprocal connections with brain regions that are implicated in emotional processing (amygdala), memory (hippocampus), and higher-order sensory regions (temporal cortex). Lateral portions have reciprocal connections with brain regions that are implicated in motor control (basal ganglia, premotor cortex, supplementary motor area), performance monitoring (cingulate cortex), and higher-order sensory processing (association areas, parietal cortex). In addition to this, the medial and lateral aspects of the PFC are reciprocally connected to each other allowing for information exchange and integration of their broader connections (Grossmann 2013). Because of the diffuse interconnectivity of the PFC, it is able to compare inputs from diverse regions of the brain and then send back bias signals to those areas that then influence further processing in those areas. This enables it to establish the proper mappings between inputs, internal states, and outputs needed to perform a given task. However, even though the PFC is massively parallel in its connectivity, it operates serially. The cost of operating serially is high. Recent research has shown that, contrary to popular belief, humans regularly "goof off" which in operational terms is the PFC going off-line to conserve and consolidate the energy needed for serial processing. This is known as the *default mode network* theory (Raichle et al 2001). Since the PFC has diverse connections to most parts of the brain, even the slightest perturbation of its operation can lead to behavioral symptoms in other parts of the brain which are often mistakenly interpreted as mental disorders in their own right (Coolidge et al 2004).

What kind of developmental disorder did Ted have?

It appears Ted suffered from what can be loosely described as *stress-induced PFC decompensation.* "Decompensation" normally refers to a functional overload of an organ due to fatigue, stress, illness or old age. Applied to the PFC, it means the same thing. Under minimal load, Ted's PFC was able to operate normally. He was able to distribute his energy to working memory and sequential tasks in an effective and timely manner. However, compared to normal individuals, whose PFC had fully matured and established the necessary connections needed to sustain functional operation, Ted's PFC was somewhat compromised in its connectivity and therefore required a greater amount of energy to perform comparable work vis-a-vis his peers for social processing tasks. Here, an important concept enters the story: *ego-depletion.* The theory states that the PFC has a finite amount of energy to perform serial tasks (Baumeister et al 2000). Over the course of the day, this energy dissipates. Sleep is an important restorative factor, whereupon a person is able to wake up fresh and start the day over. However, a person with compromised functional connectivity of the PFC can succumb to ego-depletion more easily and this can lead to decompensation, which in turn precipitates a *regression* in behavior. At its most subtle, in normal people this might express as the feeling of "I need to reward myself" which usually means consuming fat, sugar, nicotine and alcohol, or it might express as a sudden explosive burst of anger such as road rage. In Ted, however, it was more specific. As he put it:

> You take the individual we're talking about—a unique personality with certain defects, if you will—and then you subject him to stress. Stress happens to come up randomly, but its effect on the person is not random; it's specific. That results in a certain amount of chaos, confusion, and frustration. That person begins to seek out a target for his frustrations (M&A 2000, 69).

It was when Ted's ego was depleted that he was particularly vulnerable to triggering stimuli, things that would set him off in search of a means to replenish himself. Depletion cannot be depicted as depression. But because depletion-replenishment occurs in a cyclic manner (due to the natural pattern of life stressors), it can take on the appearance of mood swings, which led psychiatrist Dorothy Otnow Lewis to theorize that Ted suffered from bipolar disorder. However, Ted knew better:

> ... 'mood swings' isn't accurate. It's just changes. It's harder than hell to describe, but all I want to do is lay (sic) around. I'm not motivated to do anything! I just consume huge volumes of time, really, without doing anything. I'm not particularly depressed. There's just no momentum. There's no desire to do anything. It's just blaaaah! It cannot be characterized by depression or deep sadness (M&A 2000, 26).

No human is immune to ego-depletion, but Ted was particularly vulnerable to it because of his PFC deficit. The key concept here is that ego resources do not get used up just through serial tasks but also through emotional insults. When the integration function is sub-optimal, as was in Ted's case, not only does it incur a higher energy cost to integrate content, but it also incurs more energy wastage through inefficient processing. This invariably leads to "chaos, confusion, and frustration."

What evidence do we have for Ted's developmental disorder?

As in all cases of developmental disorders, researchers look to genetic inheritance. Lewis found that Ted's grandfather, Samuel Cowell "spoke aloud to unseen presences" (Nelson 1994, 154). This is very suggestive of schizophrenic-like behavior. Apparently, Sam Cowell was also a violent and frightening man. According to Ted's aunt Virginia "Ginny" Bristol, his family and employees feared and hated him. His brothers even "wanted to kill him" (Brennan 1989). Under duress of Ted's impending execution, Ted's mother Louise Cowell admitted that "... her father had been violent and probably beat her mother" (Nelson 1994, 158). Eleanor Cowell, Ted's grandmother, had been diagnosed with agitated depression (suggestive of manic episodes) and incorrectly received shock therapy (M&A 1983, 314). These clues point toward inappropriate acting out, possible schizophrenia and bipolar disorder in the family. There is also the implication that deleterious inherited genes may have skipped a generation as there is no reported evidence that Ted's mother Louise or her sisters ever suffered from neurobehavioral problems.

The second clue in support of Ted's developmental disorder is Michaud & Aynesworth's observation that Ted was a case of arrested development:

> From all that he said and all that we now knew about his past, he might as well have been a twelve-year-old. His apparent emotional retardation resulted in a diseased pre-adolescent mind directing the actions of an adult male body (M&A 1983, 17).

Our third clue comes from Polly Nelson who acted as Ted's defense lawyer during the last three years of his life. In her book *Defending the Devil* she writes:

> Ted had real deficits in judgment, awareness, and deeper thinking. He could talk and write, but he couldn't comprehend or respond. [...] He was incapa-

> ble of independent thought or elaboration. If I probed his statements, he was unable to explain himself or take an idea deeper (Nelson 1994, 61).

Finally, and perhaps most poignantly, we have Ted's own account:

> In junior high school, everything was fine. Nothing that I can recall happened that summer before my sophomore year to stunt me, or otherwise hinder my progress. But I got to high school and I didn't make any progress. How can I say it? I'm at a loss to describe it even now. Maybe I didn't have the role models at home that could have aided me in school. I don't know. But I felt alienated from my old friends. They just seemed to move on, and I didn't, I don't know why, and I don't know if there is an explanation. Maybe it's something that was programmed by some kind of genetic thing. In my early schooling, it seemed like there was no problem in learning what the appropriate socials behaviors were. It just seemed like I hit a wall in high school (M&A 1983, 58).

All of these clues invariably point to a developmental disorder of the PFC. Of particular note to our theory is that the PFC is one of the last cortical regions to undergo full myelination during adolescence in humans (Fuster 1997). It would seem that Ted's inkling that he was genetically programmed to stop developing in his teens has some basis in fact. The pre-adolescent brain has a chaotic proliferation of neural connections in the PFC. As the brain matures, connections in the PFC undergo *differential myelination*. Connections that supported childish behavior and their emotional reactions get pruned, while connections that support mature socialization (learning the adult world of social rules, reciprocation) become more myelinated; they develop long-term arteries of information flow ending in finely fenestrated river deltas of inter-connection at their termini. A recent finding demonstrated that versions of a gene within the major histocompatibility complex (MHC) called complement component 4 (C4), helps control synaptic pruning (Sekar et al 2016). Too much C4 can cause excessive pruning. A surplus of synaptic pruning, particularly during adolescence, could disrupt elaborate neural connections needed for proper socialization – effectively lead to insufficient development of those river deltas.

Meanwhile, as Ted was having this brain problem, the other parts of his body matured normally; he was becoming a young adult. The failure of Ted's PFC to mature, to cross-link and reach all the important parts of his brain, meant that he was in effect a child trapped in an adult's body. We hear the same story repeated time and time again: that Ted loved sneaking out from behind bushes and other hiding places to scare women. A kind of child's hide-and-seek, but with sinister trappings. There are many other examples of Ted's childishness that can be found in the timeline. Paradoxically, children are good at acquiring "dots," but they haven't got the adult perspective to join those dots together to form a cohesive narrative that adults are capable of (even if sometimes there are mysteries in life). A normal mature adult has the ability to hold a bird's eye view of a problem, but then additionally zoom down to the level of individual trees. A child by analogy stands at the base of large trees in the forest looking up through the canopy, but is unable to soar above the forest and look down on it and see the "big picture." Children live at the level where everything is still local detail but with little awareness of how all the localities interrelate. As a result, they are fantastic at collecting things, a skill they get better at as they grow older—and which can give them the outer appearance of maturity—but this is exposed as soon as their cognitive ability is comprehensively challenged. While Ted had the cunning of a child to evade authorities when he was free, once he was apprehended his inability to see the big picture is revealed as a common pattern in his behavior.

Inner speech and "voices"

In analyzing Ted, we have to acknowledge that he had a mind like us, with thoughts, memories and emotions. And like all of us, he had *inner speech*. Inner speech is most commonly experienced by the person as speaking in his or her own naturally inflected voice but with no sound being produced (Hurlburt et al 2013). Inner speech is distinct from hearing voices; the latter is referred to as *auditory hallucinations*. Inner speech has been found to consistently activate brain regions that subserve speech production such as the medial PFC and left inferior frontal gyrus (McGuire et al 1996). Inner speech occupies a significant amount of our conscious experience (both waking and sleep). The case of Jill Bolte Taylor, however, provides a dramatic example of what happens when it shuts down (Taylor 2008). Following a stroke she lost conscious awareness of her inner speech:

> Without a language center telling me: 'I am Dr. Jill Bolte Taylor. I am a neuroanatomist. I live at this address and can be reached at this phone number,' I felt no obligation to being her anymore. It was truly a bizarre shift in perception, but without her emotional circuitry reminding me of her likes and dislikes, of her ego center reminding me about her patterns of critical judgment, I didn't think like her anymore (Taylor 2008, 67–8).

This passage suggests that inner speech may play an important role in constructing the experience of self-identity. It has even been argued that Dr. Taylor lost consciousness of her self-identity *because* she lost her inner speech (Morin 2009). Because Taylor's PFC was still functional after her stroke, it appears that her awareness of her own inner speech did not fail because her PFC failed, rather, she lost awareness of her inner speech because the language centers of her brain were silenced after the stroke. This is important for our discussion, because it shows that awareness of inner speech can be decoupled from its production, something one would expect with a prefrontal cortical model which acts as the executive center of the brain. [Note, the other important part is the thalmo-cortical loop, which acts as a gearbox between the PFC and the other parts of the brain.] Other parts of the brain and body can be damaged, but so long as there is no damage to the PFC, a person has a reasonable chance of recovery. In stark contrast to this, when the PFC itself is damaged, there is very little that can be done to fix it.

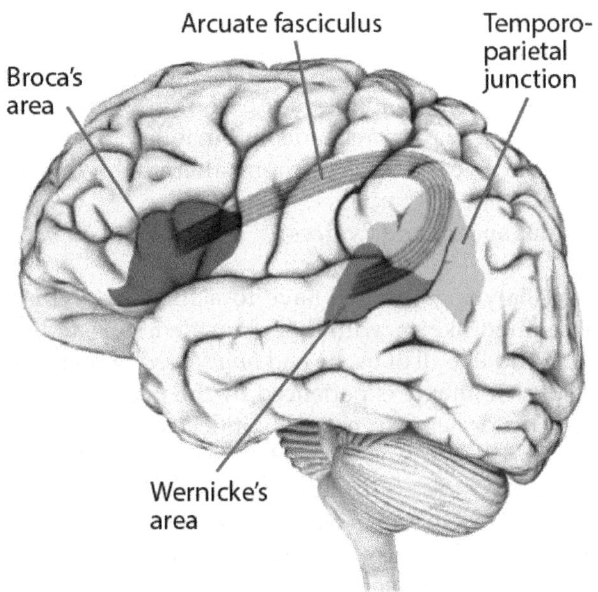

The primary language centers linked by the arcuate fasciculus.

Thought insertion

For the average person who does not suffer from major thought distortions, inner speech tends towards cohesion. This is to say, it is experienced as belonging to oneself; it is not normally experienced as alien or "other." Given this state of affairs one can imagine how frightening it must be to hear voices that are experienced as not belonging to oneself. This is referred to as *thought insertion* (Schneider 1959). There are two types of experience at this level: internalized and externalized. The externalized type is experienced as auditory hallucinations. The internalized is harder to identify. In internalized thought insertion, the individual hears the voices as coming from inside their own head (but disowns them). This type of experience is more typical for Obsessive Compulsive Disorder (OCD). True schizophrenics, by comparison, ordinarily experience voices as an externalized phenomenon, as coming from outside their body and somewhere in the near vicinity. Hence the association with hallucinations. The experience is complicated by the fact that embodiment itself is not completely cut-and-dried. Even though our body boundaries are circumscribed by our skin, our sense of self can extend across those boundaries into the objects we interact with (Clark & Chalmers 1998). Our sense of self can also be "leaky," in that we can never be completely sure that the totality of our selves always remains within the boundary of our bodies. For example, we can sometimes give away what we are thinking through facial expressions and body language. High speed cameras these days pick up micro-expressions. Technology can also peer into our brains via electroencephalography (EEG) or brain scans. The embodiment problem therefore complicates anything we might say about voices, and we have to be careful not to box schizophrenics in on the issue of externalization. What is external to one individual may not be so clearly demarcated in another individual. Moreover, as the schizophrenic grows accustomed to their voices, their character and locus may shift.

The core issue of thought insertion, of course, is the mysterious process where the normally cohesive stream of inner speech suddenly and inexplicably splits into two streams; the original and the "other." To date, no one has actually provided a convincing explanation for how this happens, or indeed, if it happens at all (Merckelbach et al 2002). Intuitively, there appears to be a dissociation, however, it may be that nothing is actually dissociated. It may be that what has changed is the individual's perspective of their inner speech. It may be that inserted thoughts are created by the self, but due to some sort of self-monitoring failure are perceived as coming from an other self. In one theory, self-monitoring is intimately linked to predictive states and comparator functions (Frith et al 2000; Jones & Fernyhough 2007; Seal et al 2004)*. The attractiveness of this theory is that it has generalizability. It appeals to the notion that our brain acts in some ways like a virtual reality machine, that it generates goals for which it predicts outcomes, assesses those outcomes and uses that information to make guidance corrections on current behavior or the next iteration of some planned behavior. If the comparator is not provided with a prediction, or if it is provided with one but the outcome is so bizarre that it falls outside the realm of expectation, or if the comparator itself has a fault, any or all of these failures can produce a mismatch between a person's self-concept and their ongoing experience. Admittedly "self-concept" is still something of a mystery, but here it is used to mean the narrative a person produces to explain oneself to *oneself and to others*, which has a past that can't be changed, a present which is sometimes changeable, and a future that assumes the best but doesn't always work out. We can relate to this admittedly circular but simple definition because we understand that people who suffer from depression often don't like their past, feel powerless to change the present, and expect the worst of the future.

Currently, there appears to be an increasing acceptance

* There are other theories but this one is sufficient.

of the idea that we are composed of multiple selves, each with its own mode of existence contingent upon context. So for example, a father can be a good parent at home with his wife and children, but then frequent prostitutes whom he treats as second-class citizens. What this illustrates, however, is that the self is modal; it doesn't prove the self is divided. By "modal" we mean rather than fragmenting into separate selves, the self is able to develop specialized role identities (Donahue et al 1993).

Having said this, there is evidence that supports some sort of *compartmentalization* of the self. This is because the brain is fundamentally a hybridized entity, with some areas that specialize and other areas that generalize. The specialized areas are often deeper within the brain (or lower in the hierarchy), have specific connections, and support innate behaviors, whereas the generalized areas are situated in the neocortex, have more diffuse connections to widespread parts of the brain, and support higher level integration of information. It is not possible for higher cortical areas to access all deeper specialized area, leading to an abrupt transition from conscious to unconscious processing. As mentioned earlier, the brain basically operates in parallel fashion (because of its simultaneous multiple connections), but self-monitoring is limited to serial operation. It seems to act like a searchlight, casting its beam on a narrow area during focused cognition, but spreads out like moonlight during non-focused tasks. However, because of the abrupt transition between the conscious and unconscious, there are still many areas that cannot be cross-accessed, leading to some parts of the brain operating relatively independent of one another.

In the strictest sense, compartmentalization can lead to individuals holding totally contradictory attitudes. In the more general sense, every human is doomed to some degree of compartmentalization throughout their life because the self is fundamentally a finite construct. We can never become all-aware (the myth of enlightened beings is just that, a myth). However, even though many processes operate independent of one another, a proportion of them can reach the light of consciousness through willful effort – or, according to one theory, through faulty *gating* of the PFC. The latter could account for thought insertion. Under normal conditions, when the gating mechanism operates properly, there is no problem. In other cases, when it is put under stress, or if it has an intermittent fault, then content from previously unaccessed areas of the brain could potentially "leak" into the field of consciousness and disturb the individual (Shimamura 2000).

The intuitive appeal of this model is that often those contents that do leak into conscious awareness are usually fragmentary or not fully formed, suggesting that they indeed originate from parts of the brain that process ongoing experience unconsciously in episodic fashion and have stored the fragmented results in memory in distributed locations. Therefore, more often than not it is up to the conscious function to try and make sense of these fragments, which it often initially fails to do, but over time may grow accustomed to and develop its own weird interpretation of. This in turn can become a *cause* of new behavior as the person integrates these fragments with their inner speech.

What evidence do we have that Ted experienced thought insertion?

The main, but not only, source of information about Ted's voice is Polly Nelson's *Defending the Devil.* Nelson and Lewis visited Ted the day before his execution and conducted one final interview (note: Ted's attorney Jim Coleman was responsible for getting him to speak to Lewis in his final days). The story unfolds after Lewis expressed the firm opinion that with only a day left to live Ted needed to be real, not waste time performing a charade by claiming incompetency. Lewis had reread Michaud & Aynesworth's *The Only Living Witness* on the plane on the way down to Florida State Prison, and broke the discussion open with a direct question about the "entity," fishing as it were, for a Multiple Personality Disorder diagnosis (MPD; note currently referred to as Dissociative Identity Disorder). Ted deflects Lewis' "imaginary companion" telling her Michaud & Aynesworth's entity was somewhat different in his estimation. Right from the start, Ted is at pains to formulate an explanation of himself in the best terms he is capable of. It is as much an intellectual exercise as a cathartic release for him.

Ted begins by saying: "A portion of my personality was not fully – it began to emerge ..." (Nelson 1994, 276). What he is telling us is that he conceived of himself as whole, to which new elements were added. The essence of these new elements, of course, was the rapist-killer. "In my high school years ... I would fantasize about coming up to some girl sunbathing in the woods ...." This little ditty about the bikini girl in the woods was something Ted came back to time and time again. Particularly the woods. Ted loved the woods. He'd prance around them naked and masturbate. We know that the nascent voyeur was already there, because he described looking out of his upper bedroom window down into the neighbor's bathroom, where we are invited to imagine the neighbor's daughter undressing ....

So Ted was actively into fantasy before his teens. He probably discovered masturbation to ejaculation in his very early teens, so he almost certainly masturbated to the neighbor's daughter (and his own maturing half-sisters most likely). Was Ted over-sexed? According to one report he was a compulsive masturbator (MacPherson 1989, 190). But in other ways he was a normal teenager, except his fantasies increasingly became macabre. When he said he fantasized about coming up to some girl, he meant by surprise, to gain control over her and rape her. This theme runs through Ted's life like Ariadne's thread. The surprise attack was the core element of his M.O. – as he got more sophisticated, he tried various ruses, but always behind it was the surprise.

Ted then goes on to explain that in his mid-teens, he began to get interested in morbid things, like dead bodies in detective magazines. What drew him to death is a mystery; it may have started out as an innocent curiosity, since normal people also get drawn to images of carnage and mutilation. What separates Ted from normal people however, is he may have also masturbated to these images (although he denied doing that). At the same time, he was looking for books in the library that had descriptions of sexual activity. So we get the first hint that he is beginning to fuse sex-and-violence with the orgasm.

Meanwhile, Lewis presses Ted to tell her more about the entity. A somewhat amateur move, revealing a hint of desperation, as if this was the only way to trick Ted into talking. If she listened to Ted, she might have got him to describe an image from one of those magazines he was talking about – describe it in as much detail as possible, because Ted would have been talking about something he didn't create and therefore would have been relatively objective and we'd get our first glimpse of a *specific* image that influenced him (we can generalize from the archives what he may have got into, but we have no specific images to work from). In that sense, Lewis missed an opportunity.

Then came the big high, his obsession with Diane Edwards in 1967 that ended in failure when he bombed out of Chinese and was dropped by Diane for not being mature enough, not man enough (no doubt this was also a class struggle, in that Ted was also not rich enough for her either). Shortly afterwards he admits to having passive rape fantasies involving her, where he watches someone else doing it. There is a sense of disingenuity here, but we have to take it for what it is. Ted then goes on to talk about the sequence of events leading to his first murder, possibly that of Kerry May Hardy on June 1, 1972. At this point, Lewis pursues her MPD theory again:

> Lewis: Did you ever have a sense of another Ted, or another person? Did you ever actually talk to the other?
> Ted: Oh, yes. In fact – oh, yes – I'd have this dialogue.
> Lewis: I don't mean thinking, "gee, you're nuts to do this." I mean, did you ever feel like another person? [Lewis here is starting to sound like a cracked record. Her line of questioning is most unhelpful and in fact biases Ted to produce interpretations of his voice that favors her interpretation.]
> Ted: It reached a point, I would say in '74, where ... it would have conversations. And I'm not saying I was a multiple personality. I don't know. All I know is that this other part of myself seemed to have a voice, and seemed to have a need (Nelson 1994, 284-5).

Ted goes on to say that the voice became particularly strong when he was intoxicated. It worked like a steam kettle whistle. There was a "force which energized" the entity inside him. It had to be expended. Once it receded, the other normal part of his self could take the forefront again. Lewis continues to press forward and Ted replies: "I know there was this kind of dialogue going on, not just talking to myself innocently. Really a *'Give in to me'* kind of thing." After some more probing, Lewis comes up with a statement that reveals the key criteria for her theory:

> Lewis: Have you ever been told that you did something you don't remember? The reason I'm asking is that I am wondering, because you raised the issue of multiple personality, to what extent are you, who I'm talking to now, really separate from the other entity, and to what extent it's just a variant of a mood you get.
> Ted: Yeah. I hear what you're saying. I think that there's more, an integration there, an interrelationship, which when the malignant portion of my personality or consciousness, call it what you will—the entity—is more or less directing the mood and the action, I'm still on another level conscious of this, I'm not totally unconscious of, or unaware of it (Nelson 1994, 287; punctuation modified).

In fact, Lewis was the one pursuing the MPD diagnosis; Ted only raised it in response to her leading questions. Lewis seems to think she can make Ted own the disorder, but he deftly quashes that idea. The issue of the "voice" therefore is not whether he was a divided self; he was not. It is about how his PFC might have failed in some way allowing previously inhibited material to enter his field of conscious awareness.

What evidence do we have of faulty gating in Ted's PFC?

One region of the PFC that is particularly relevant for our discussion is the orbitofrontal cortex (in our first diagram the ventromedial PFC). Damage to the orbitofrontal cortex results in socio-emotional deficits, including emotional outbursts, impulsivity, risk-taking, difficulty with goal-directed behavior, and a failure to abide by social rules and norms (e.g., Bechara et al 2000). Obviously these examples are at the extreme end of the scale. Ted didn't suffer trauma; his deficit was developmental and therefore much more subtle. Interestingly, psychiatrists and psychologists mostly deferred their diagnosis of him, ostensibly due to this subtlety. They also had a hard time extracting anything more than generalities out of him, which was just as much a function of his passive aggressive behavior in the face of authority as his inherent superficiality. Another problem for psychiatrists and psychologists was that they did not observe Ted while he was under extreme duress. Their tests were conducted in a controlled environment and followed a protocol that fostered cooperation and prevented confrontation. This played directly into Ted's hand because under those conditions his PFC could function relatively normally.

As a comparator and bias generator, the PFC needs to effectively gate emotional responses which would otherwise perturb the system. Based on this definition:

> It is of interest that the defendant displayed marked signs of hostility when asked about his early childhood. Specifically, when he was asked about his "real father's whereabouts," his face became quite contorted and reddened and he paused momentarily. He then gained composure and replied rather succinctly and appropriately: "You might say that he left my mother and me and never rejoined the family" (PIR 1975).

The interviewer inadvertently put Ted in a situation where his PFC gating mechanism was put under stress. The result was that previously compartmentalized emotional content flooded his field of conscious awareness. For a brief moment, the interviewer saw a part of Ted that he normally kept hidden. However, because Ted was in a controlled environment he was able to regain his composure. But suppose this had happened in an uncontrolled environment? How would he have dealt with the situation then? Our prediction is that it would have depleted some of his ego resources. This in turn would have initiated a PFC decompensation event leading to further ego-depletion. While in this state he would have been highly vulnerable to ...

> ... all kinds of triggers, internal triggers, external triggers. I mean, sometimes, sometimes just the sight of a particularly attractive young woman, or sometimes it would be something I'd read or seen in a magazine or on TV. And sometimes it would be spontaneous, just feel like I've got to go out now and start looking for something [...] In fact, what would happen would be a series of downs and disappointments together with one of these triggers ... (Nelson 1994, 289-90).

Ted's last observation, that it would happen after "a series of downs and disappointments" invariably led him to act out premeditated *displaced aggression* (Geberth 1990; email to author January 11, 2016). In other words, actively find a target to vent his frustration and anger on. No matter what that victim did, comply or not comply, Ted would make sure to find an excuse to exact his punishment.

The role of cannabis and alcohol

Ted repeatedly stressed to anyone who cared to listen that alcohol played a crucial role as a disinhibitor prior to the commission of his crimes. He said that it helped steady his nerves. He also admitted to regular cannabis use. However, he never once associated cannabis with his "problem." Here we aim to show that it was integral to his problem, may have in fact precipitated it, and served as a powerful facilitator in the elaboration of his fantasies. It is not our aim to demonize cannabis. It has beneficial as well as detrimental effects. Its effects also heavily depend on individual differences and vulnerabilities.

The first reference we have of Ted using cannabis is April 1968, when he worked at the Queen Anne Hill Safeway in Seattle and lived for a short time with a thief and drug user (Kendall 1981, 34). He was 21 going on 22. Was this the first time Ted used cannabis? Probably not. It was the late 60s, Washington State was deeply steeped in the counter-culture movement as was its neighboring southern west-coast states. Interestingly, Ted distanced himself from the counter-culture movement. Rather than rock'n'roll, he preferred classical music. He also offered to spy on student dissidents. Nevertheless, there is an enigmatic clue contemporary to this period of his life. According to an un-named "intimate" friend of Ted's who wanted the story told:

> Ted believed that he was demonically possessed. It began in college. He called it 'the Beast.' It was not your typical demon. It spoke to him, but it had no human emotion, no conscience. At first, he was afraid. The demon was totally contrary to his make-up. But then he conditioned himself to it and got so he could tolerate it. Finally, Ted gave himself over. He joined the demon and got to like pornography. He believed that other serial killers were also possessed. He struggled with the demonic influence, marked by lust and feelings of violence, even in prison. But through prayer and reading God's word, he subdued the demon somewhat. However, he never felt that the Beast ever left him entirely (Nobile 1989, 45).

Putting aside theological connotations, the key line is: "It began in college." This could mean University of Puget Sound, or it could mean University of Washington. It could mean Stanford, California. It could mean Temple University, Philadelphia. It's hard to say where college ends and "university" begins. If you count his second stint at University of Washington, the "college" years span from September 1965 - June 1972, with a Bachelor of Science (psychology) course started in January 1971. Somehow Ted crammed a 2-year course into 1.5 years. We assume he was able to do this because he was motivated to find out about his "problem" (he would later say psychology didn't help). So maybe we can exclude "college" during his second stint. In which case we can assume his earlier years were from 19 to 21. This would place the emergence of the "Beast" around this time, or who knows, maybe even earlier.

Cannabis is a well-known precipitator of psychosis in vulnerable individuals (e.g., Arendt et al 2008). The core symptom is auditory hallucinations. Paranoia is also common. The active ingredient of cannabis, Δ9-tetrahydrocannabinol (THC), has been shown to increase activity in the PFC, but lower activity in the striatum, leading to aberrant salience attribution (Bhattacharyya et al 2012). The mechanism of action is dysregulation of the neurotransmitter dopamine. Salience attribution is the process whereby the brain engages in increased cue reactivity to certain stimuli compared to others. There is strong evidence that dopamine is critical in producing the motivation of "wanting" something (as opposed to "liking" or "learning" something) (Berridge 2007). Disruption of the PFC-striatal network via drugs can lead to wanting something more than normal by sensitizing networks responsible for stimulus associations. In practical terms, if Ted was masturbating to concurrent pictures of cheerleaders and dead bodies while high on cannabis, he would not only increase his wanting of them, but draw them into a tighter associational relationship. But that is not the real kicker. The problem is that THC increases activity in the PFC, leading to more integrated cognitive processes, something that is desirable *in-and-of-itself* for someone who normally experiences sub-optimal neural integration of the PFC. However, this is at the expense of disruption of PFC gating. In other words, the gain is a more interconnected thought process but at the expense of increased intrusion of memory fragments that are normally compartmentalized. This is then exacerbated by alcohol, which causes further disinhibition of the PFC. Ted's use of these two drugs in conjunction with his vulnerability and conditioning turned him into time-bomb.

Addiction

It has often been said that Ted was addicted to killing. In the last days of his life he tried to stress the importance of hardcore violent pornography as a major contributor to the genesis of his problem. Pornography, of course, was just a facilitator for his masturbation fantasies. It would be more appropriate to say he was addicted to masturbation, of which pornography and killing became an extension. A recent study has shown that addiction is generic. It doesn't choose type; the brains of addicts, no matter what type, appear to look the same. This has been verified in a study comparing the brains of people who engage in compulsive sexual behavior with those of normal individuals (Voon et al 2014). Sex addicts showed increased activity in the dorsal anterior cingulate, ventral striatum and amygdala, three key regions associated with the brain's reward circuit and addictive behavior. The paradox of the addict is not the imbibing behavior itself, but the approach behavior to the addictive substance, the willfully placing of themselves in situations where they know they will encounter a triggering stimulus. They continue to do this long after the behavior has lost its hedonic value and has become self-destructive. It appears that the anticipation of the event before it happens charges up the system with nervous energy, a state which is desirable in itself because it replaces the boredom and frustration that preceded it. Ted knew this well. The anticipation was the best part! He even went so far as to say that the "... fantasy that accompanies and generates ... the anticipation that precedes the crime is always more stimulating than the immediate aftermath of the crime itself" (M&A 2000, 84). This accords well with Robinson & Berridge's incentive sensitization theory of addiction which posits a dissociation between wanting and liking (Robinson & Berridge 2008). Voon's study also supports this where she found compulsive sex addicts displayed increased desire when shown sexually explicit images, but registered the same levels of liking as shown by normals. A two-speed neural economy appears to have been instantiated in the addict's brain. When they encounter their target stimulus, their desire increases, but cognitively they do not feel more excited. The picture we form is of a person having sex because they want it, but they do not feel like they are getting a great deal of pleasure out of it. Maybe that is why Ted referred to the sex part as "obligatory."

Why did Ted become addicted to sex and violence? There is no clear answer to this question. Some would argue he was born that way; others believe he learned it. The truth probably lies somewhere in between. Notwithstanding, we have one piece of anecdotal evidence that allows us to at least speculate on a mechanism. The theory rests on the generally accepted observation that children before the age of five are highly susceptible to imprinting. In Ted's case, there is a report that as a *four year-old* he perused his grandfather's stash of porn in the old man's garden shed (a claim we have no way of verifying). If true, this may have potentiated two consequences: increased cue reactivity (more sensitivity to sexual triggers in the environment); and stimulus habituation (the addict seeks out increasingly more explicit content compared to age-matched peers because they have become habituated to less explicit content). We have ample evidence that Ted did have heightened cue reactivity to sexual stimuli in the environment – he said so himself. We also have one anecdotal report supporting habituation. Sometime during his preteens, Ted showed one of his friends a photo of a man and woman performing oral sex (Morris 2013, 83-4). The friend claimed to be shocked. When asked where he found it Ted lied and said he found it on the sidewalk. Whether just a rumor or true, it illustrates that Ted at the time seems to have had more exposure to sexually explicit content compared to his age-matched peers, and suggests that he had already undergone a degree of habituation to such content.

Fantasy

So much has been written about the role of fantasy in the genesis of serial killer behavior that we will not repeat it here (e.g., see Geberth 1990; Carlisle 1993; Carlisle 2013). What is more interesting for us is: why did Ted reify his fantasies? That is, take the fantasy out of his head and project it onto the world. The short answer is that humans have done this ever since they had the spark of self-awareness. However, in civilized societies people don't go around willy-nilly projecting their murderous fantasies onto innocent victims. They might let their frustrations out via displaced aggression onto their dog, or simply dissipate it in an alcoholic haze. But for Ted that was not enough. Something drove him to cross the line.

The remarkable thing is that it took a great deal of planning and effort. Ted didn't just wake up one day and kill. He worked his way toward it step-by-step, as methodical as someone learning a musical instrument or a new language. For someone who supposedly had a developmental disorder of the PFC, which implies a person that has sub-optimal stamina and endurance, this is not only remarkable, but contradictory. The answer to this conundrum may be addiction to various risk-taking behaviors that excite. This pattern is intensified by cannabis and released by alcohol. More specifically, cannabis allowed Ted to elaborate his fantasies to a greater level of intensity than normal, particularly visual and auditory stimuli. It doesn't explain why Ted crossed the line. But it is well-known that animals and humans alike are prepared to work hard for highly salient rewards such as drugs and sex. When they are combined, as in Ted's case, and with his vulnerability, they provide ample attractive value, giving him a context that focused his mind. This was a process that could be enjoyed in-and-of-itself, a feeling that everything was coming together, leading to sustained sequences of behavior: "... when I was really going all out and took my time, yeah, ..." as Ted described it to Robert D. Keppel a couple of days before his execution on January 24, 1989.

As for why Ted crossed the line, we have two plausible and inter-related possibilities: the first is that masturbation only took him so far; the second is habituation. In Ted's own words:

> I don't like some of the, some of the things I've done and that uh, that I don't like it, but yet I do it. And, as I say, uh, I've searched around inside before. And I talked to Joe [Aloi] about some things today. About a process that I went through and, and that the process of conditioning, so to speak, self conditioning and I thought there was a time when I could counter condition myself, desensitize myself. See, I made myself the way I was. I uh, I mean bit-by-bit and step-by-step and day-by-day. I don't know why, I don't know what spurred me on to do it. You see, I, there was a time, way back, when I felt deep, deep guilt about even the very thought of, of harming someone else. And yet for some reason I had desire to, to condition that out of me. And I did, day-by-day-by-day. Conditioned out on an abstract level and then when it got down to actual cases, it was guilt. I conditioned that out of myself too. And I always thought, well, you let this thing grow inside you or you, you allowed yourself to be conditioned, if that's another way to term it. I don't know whether we're dealing with an organic problem or behavioral problem or a combination of the two. But in any case I thought it's possible to counter condition myself. Well that uh, takes a process of years and I don't know if the damage was, is irreparable but in any case, it appears that by myself I'm not capable of doing it (Leon County Sheriff's Office, February 20, 1978, FSA).

Ted doesn't explain what the conditioning process involved, but in Polly Nelson's book he says:

> ... there was still, in essence, a barrier there to that kind of conduct. [...] in essence, my other erotic behavior—masturbation fantasy—was a way of deconditioning feelings of inhibition against engaging in conduct. At the same time it was a way of dealing with remorse, I mean, repressing any kind of remorse or guilt because the fantasy became more graphic each time it was aroused (Nelson 1994, 282).

Ted could be saying that he tried to sublimate his killing urge into sex, but it didn't always last. Eventually he had to go on and kill, because it gave him a guaranteed high. The mechanism whereby reality and fantasy merge (as opposed to being dissociated) is that Ted would often masturbate not just alone in his room, but in his car, in a forest, and while peeping into the windows of unsuspecting victims. The outdoor scenarios, due to their location, involve random environmental stimuli that could potentially intrude on the masturbation fantasy, however the masturbator becomes so involved in their autoerotic activity that all but the most alarming environmental stimuli are thresholded out of consciousness. This is the crux of Ted's conditioning. For Ted did not only have to overcome internal moral barriers, but the constant environmental signals that attenuated the positive feedback needed to attain sexual climax. At this level, there is a sense of pre-adolescent hide-and-seek mentality at play, a state of mind that may have mitigated any unwanted intrusions and fostered heightened arousal through the excitement of concealment and voyeurism. Eventually sex and killing would merge.

Lack of empathy

Another aspect of Ted's conditioning relates to claims that he lacked empathy. There are several theories of empathy. We shall use a tri-part system: cognitive, emotional, and motor (Blair, 2005). The cognitive part has been referred to as "theory of mind" because it is the part that allows us to imagine what another person is thinking. It has been called theory of mind because when we imagine what another person is thinking, we assume they *actually* have a mind. Theory of mind only refers to relations between genuinely cognitive creatures. If there was a rock and we imagined what it was thinking, that would be a case of *projection.* Projection is tricky, because it is hard to deny that when we imagine someone else's thoughts, we are also projecting our imagination into that person as well. The more we find out what that person is really thinking, the more we can withdraw our projection from them. The fascinating thing about projection is that it can never be completely withdrawn. There will always be a vestige of our imagination that lingers between us and the other person.

This is important, because it sweeps aside the popular assumption that a good empathiser is someone who is able to "step into someone else's shoes." It would be more appropriate to think of someone else's thought processes as a topography. A good empathiser is someone who shares a similar topography and is able traverse that topography in like fashion, giving the impression of sharing the same mental space. In truth, no topography is identical, and no navigation of it is the same. However, if there is a strong mapping between topographies, then the recipient feels they are being understood. If there is a weak mapping, then they feel they are not being understood. It might be this definition, of strong versus weak mapping, that differentiates empathy from sympathy.

Cast in terms of topography, we might say that the cognitive part of empathy can be likened to the contents of the landscape, the flora and fauna, the rocks and soil, the rivers and lakes. The emotional component would then be its weather, calm or stormy, and also the roughness of the terrain, the peaks and valleys, lush or desert. Finally, the motor component of empathy could be likened to the movement through the landscape, fast or slow, cumbersome or agile.

Naturally, we would say a good empathiser is someone who maps strongly onto our topography, who shares key features, and who moves through it with grace and agility. The dangerous thing about psychopaths is that they move through our landscape in all these ways by trickery. How are we to distinguish them from true empathisers? Often, by the time (we) the victim finds out it is too late.

The current consensus is that psychopaths have empathy when it is directed at themselves (narcissism), but no empathy for others. We might shake this definition up a little in relation to Ted because Liz (Kloepfer, aka "Kendall") mentions "all the strays Ted had brought to my house, the hamsters and guinea pigs and kittens" (Kendall 1980, 76) and the time Freda Rogers and Ted had coffee in her kitchen and an outsized fly began to buzz around them; Frieda started to swat it, but Ted jumped up, exclaimed, "Don't kill it!" and chased the fly out the window (M&A 1983, 67). And we recall Herb Swindler's daughter saying how it was impossible not to love Ted (in the Platonic sense) for he was a champion of the down-trodden and dispossessed. Were these behaviors of Ted put on, or were they real? The orthodox model of psychopathy is the triad of bed wetting, animal cruelty and fire starting. Ted doesn't seem to fit into this model at all.

If Ted's empathy system was impaired, that impairment must have been extraordinarily specific and contextual. Adrian Raine has developed a model that separates psychopaths into "successful" and "unsuccessful" (Gao & Raine, 2010). While this distinction is highly idealized, unpacking it provides some pointers for further discussion. Raine suggests that serial killers may fall in between these two categories and calls then "semi-successful." More research needs to be done, but it appears semi-successful psychopaths have somewhat enhanced cognitive capabilities compared with other apprehended violent offenders. Because semi-successful psychopaths share some overlapping abilities with successful psychopaths, there is a possibility that this group may share superior cognitive empathy – the ability to understand another's perspective without necessarily feeling any level of emotional empathy (Ishikawa et al, 2001). It is this overlapping ability that we will now turn our focus on.

What does it mean to possess superior cognitive empathy but no emotional empathy? Is this how people misinterpreted Ted's behavior, believing he was a gentle soul, wouldn't hurt a fly? In one study successful psychopaths were found to have increased frontal white matter but less gray matter that has been observed in pathological liars (Yang et al., 2005a, 2005b). On the one hand, this increased white matter—the fiber tracts that connect different regions of the brain—suggest greater integration, but due to the decreased gray matter—the processing areas—there is a paucity of properly thought through ideation, and in all likelihood, an increase of stereotypical thinking. In effect, the fiber tracts lead to lots of places, but those places are predominantly dead-ends. This very much supports the generally accepted observation that the fabrications of pathological liars when examined closely generally reveal a degree of absurdity and child-like logic. How many times have we seen Ted's ruses fall into this category? True as this is, it doesn't explain his apparent ability to fool people into thinking he was a caring individual. One may be able to fool people for a short period of time, but not over long periods in different contexts. Eventually people start to smell a rat.

Some psychopathic individuals may get away with superficial charm because they constantly shift to new social groups, never hang around long enough to be exposed. To a degree, this partially describes Ted, but he also had some long-term relationships (his family of course, but also Ann Rule, Liz Kloepfer, and the Rogers to name a few). One would think they would have detected some kind of abnormality in his emotional responses, but it seems that the problem is more complex than researchers of empathy would have us believe. The notion of specificity and context keeps rearing its ugly head. One study appears to have made an attempt to address this issue. Drawn from a population of incarcerated psychopaths (therefore perhaps representative of Raine's "unsuccessful" group), researchers using brain scans showed that psychopaths were able to "switch on" their empathy areas when asked to do so, but when no instructions where given they showed the typical blunted affect and lack of neural activation of empathy areas that has been consistently shown in a variety of other tests (Meffert et al 2013). The investigators did not come up with an explanation for this switching ability, but nevertheless identified the possibility that it may not be a broken empathy system as such but an attentional problem.

In support of this, another study found dramatic difference between psychopaths and normals in response to tasks that required affective processing. Psychopathy was measured using the Psychopathic Personality Inventory (PPI). Developed in 2005, the PPI is not identical to the PCL-R, but shares common conceptual areas. In general, the PCL-R is used more in criminal/forensic settings, whereas the PPI is intended more for sampling the community at large. Broadly speaking, the PPI loads onto 3 factors: fearless-dominance, impulsive antisociality, and coldheartedness. The average psychopath is said to have fearlessness and focus. These traits have traditionally been attributed to deficits in emotional processing. The results of the study demonstrated that psychopaths primarily used their right dorsolateral PFC, an area consistently associated with performance on working memory tasks, whereas the normals used a distributed general emotion network that includes the amygdala, and inferior frontal, medial prefrontal areas (Gordon et al., 2004).

Which is to say, psychopaths compensated for their emotional processing deficit by recruiting parts of their brain normally used for working memory tasks (which in our discussion is hypothesized to lead to more rapid ego-depletion than normals in situations where emotional recognition is required). The upshot of these studies suggests that psychopaths have the ability to recognize emotions, but do so without understanding what it often feels like to have those emotions. It may be that the reason why they are unable to experience any proper feelings behind the emotions of others is that all their neural resources are tied up in the task of simply recognizing what the emotion is, and by the time they have done that they have already fallen behind. No wonder Ted always felt like he needed to be one step ahead.

Because we cannot make the blanket claim that Ted *never* understood emotions, we are still left without a mechanism for why his empathy system failed when it did. It may be that the emotional component of his empathy system was susceptible to being hijacked by certain environmental stimuli and sent into a *positive feedback loop* (Buckholtz 2010; note: normal individuals are able to exert PFC control and interrupt the loop). In terms of an empathy breakdown, we would say a psychopath is a person who is able to stop at a traffic signal under normal circumstances when the light is red. However, if they are distracted by a triggering stimulus as they approach the intersection—one that they are vulnerable to—they may shift their attention and drive through the red light with little awareness of wrongdoing (or willful wrongdoing as the case may be). In essence, the emotional component of their empathy system has undergone a *stimulus-dependent failure.* It is quite possible that they could still function perfectly normal at the cognitive and motor level.

Thus, a serial killer might recognize his victim has a mind, but he treats them like a symbolic object. He may mimic the expressions of pain in a victim's face in his own face, thereby showing his motor empathy is functioning. He might listen to the pleading of his victim, show he understands logically and analytically that what he is doing is wrong by offering excuses or apologies, but he will go on and kill his victim regardless because the emotional component of his empathy system has been hijacked and sent into a positive feedback loop and his need for gratification exceeds what he feels for them.

In his last interview Ted described how after a murder he would wake up in the morning with a clear mind, with all his "essential moral and ethical feelings intact at that moment," and be absolutely horrified at what he had done – that he was capable of doing something like that (James Dobson interview, January 23, 1989). As much as we would like to think he is a "cold-hearted son of a bitch" through and through, what this illustrates is that once the individual has been sated and the energy levels are reset, normal function resumes, and with it, normal empathic responses – until the next PFC decompensation event occurs.

Necrophilia and the anterior insula

Our neurobehavioral model of Ted would not be complete if we did not explore the necrophilic side to his character. From all that we know it appears Ted was a homicidal necrophiliac. According to one influential study examining necrophilic behavior, up to two thirds of perpetrators are motivated by the desire to possess an unresisting and unrejecting partner (Rosman & Resnick 1989). Other motivations include a desire to be reunited with their dead romantic partner, sexual attraction to corpses, a desire to attain comfort or overcome feelings of isolation, and/or a need to gain self-esteem by expressing power over a homicide victim. The closest Ted came to revealing the psychological motivations for his necrophilic behavior was that he apparently said "he was preoccupied with the cyanotic hue of a corpse's fingernails, discoloration of the skin after death" (K&B

2005, 513). He also told FBI agent Bill Hagmaier that:

> If you've got time, they can be anything you want them to be. [...] after a while, murder isn't just a crime of lust or violence. It becomes possession. They are part of you. After a while, when you plan these, that person becomes part of you and you are forever one. [...] even after twenty or thirty [...] it's the same thing, because you're the last one there. You feel the last bit of breath leaving their body. You're looking into their eyes and basically, a person in that situation is God! You then possess them and they shall forever be a part of you. And the grounds where you kill them or leave them become sacred to you, and you will always be drawn back to them (M&A 1983, 317).

Ted obviously studied death. He became a master of knowing the threshold between life and death. He would have been a keen observer of vital signs. Which means that for him death was not over just because the person was clinically dead. Ted hinted that he would often return to interfere with his corpses until advanced putrefaction prevented him from doing so (note that in some cases, he disappeared for days, so we do not know all the time relationships involved). Ted's additions to the FBI serial killer questionnaire are revealing. He expanded a whole section vis-a-vis "site where body was found" (Nelson 1994, 160-171). His detail is unquestionable. He expressed an area of knowledge that he was extraordinarily proficient in and he expressed it quite systematically. This leads directly to questions about hygiene, putrefaction odors, and serious deviancy. Normal people experience disgust reactions at situations involving lack of hygiene, putrefaction odors (e.g., *cadaverine* and *putrescine* – the smell of rotting flesh). All of these reactions, and more, are linked to the anterior insula. The insula has both social and biological circuits. This is demonstrated by its behavior: the observation of disgust in another and olfaction of a disgusting odor activate a similar neural representation of those emotions in its circuits (Wicker et al., 2003). The anterior insula has also been shown to light up when subjects viewed images of contamination and mutilation (Wright et al., 2004). The insula is an old structure, has diverse connections, and among its various facets is involved in the processing of norm violations (Sanfey et al., 2003), empathy (Singer, 2006), sexual arousal (Karama, 2002) and orgasms (Ortigue, 2007), showing that it has a broad range of connections with complex behavior.

The obvious question is: did Ted condition his anterior insula in some way so that it didn't bother him, or was it broken from the start? He once admitted sometimes he wished he didn't kill his victims so quickly so he could spend more time with them (while they were alive). Suggesting that he sometimes got himself into a position where he lost control, leaving him with a corpse too early. Inevitably, he'd end up spending more time with them when they were dead.

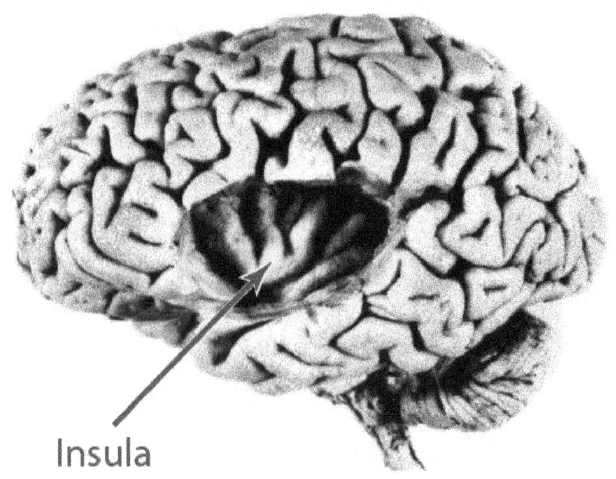

The insula is tucked deep within the folds of the cortex under, and inward, toward the central ventral area of the brain. You can only see it by pushing the temporal lobe down and cutting away part of the lateral cortex to peer inside.

Intriguingly, the anterior insula has also been implicated during tests of self-awareness. Specifically, it appears to be central to two processes: subjective feelings from the body and emotional awareness. These processes are described by the James-Lange theory of emotions and Damasio's 'somatic marker' hypothesis (Craig, 2009). In these descriptions emotions are the result of a physiological reaction to events. For example, the olfactory pathway in the human brain is a rapid response system. Odor molecules enter the brain and directly connect to the limbic system, the emotional engine of the brain. Olfactory processing only receives PFC input after-the-event (the body reacts before the mind is aware of it). Activation of the limbic system is highly correlated with physiological reactions (heart rate increase, respiratory interruption, fight-flight etc). Ted would have surely been aware of putrefaction odors, but it seems he had a higher threshold for disgust. His body certainly reacted, but it appears his mind was disconnected in some way, leading us to question whether he would have felt as disgusted viscerally as we normals would have had we been in the same situation. The caveat of course is that Ted habituated himself step-by-step, he didn't plunge in de novo. It shows awareness of disgust can be decoupled from its emotional reaction. We know this because disaster recovery health workers can become habituated to overwhelming numbers of cadavers ... albeit leaving some to develop PTSD later on.

Trolling

In his final public interview with James Dobson, Ted said: "I led a normal life except for this one small but very potent, very destructive segment of it that I kept very secret, very close to myself, didn't let anybody know about it ..." And to Lewis the day before he said:

"We're talking about less than 10 percent of my consciousness, my waking hours, during maybe the ten-year period were occupied with this kind of thing. I think that's one thing people have a hard time understanding. They think that somehow, this predilection, this kind of thinking that goes along with this kind of violent behavior more or less permeates every aspect of your life and thoughts, and it's not true – it doesn't. It's episodic and very compartmentalized, in some way." Ted then contradicts himself and says: "inherent in its need to survive is secrecy" (Nelson 1994, 289).

The following list reveals a man whose life, from the time he began killing, significantly revolved around thinking about, planning and executing murder, then engaging in necrophilia and covering up the evidence of his crimes:

> He constantly played "mind chess" with people, wherein he prepared dialogue in advance of a social situation so that he would feel in control.
> He compulsively lied.
> He bit his nails to the quick.
> He allegedly consumed detective magazines depicting eroticized females bound, gagged, strangled, and molested by sexual perverts.
> He was a big fan of junior-ed magazines (showing scantily clad teenage female cheerleaders).
> He compulsively stole all manner of items from shops and people.
> He had a sock obsession; he uncontrollably purchased more socks than he needed.
> He compulsively followed women around at night without their knowledge.
> He prowled neighborhoods and peered into windows, masturbating as he watched young females undress and go to bed.
> He sometimes raped women without murdering them.
> He prepared elaborate ruses using plaster casts, crutches, fake mustaches, different hair styles, fake identities, and changed license tags.
> He carried a murder kit with him in his VW (handcuffs, binding, gloves, masks, ice-pick, flashlight and crow bar).
> He removed the front passenger seat so he could carry his "cargo" on the floor next to him where he could control it.
> He drove many miles for long hours in search of prey.
> He staked out abduction sites and body locations in advance of his murders.
> He collected flyers and pamphlets containing information about prospective abduction sites.
> He followed the police reports of his murders in the newspapers and on TV.
> He took several women on driving dates close to the areas where he discarded the bodies of his murder victims.
> He constantly topped up the petrol tank of his car to ensure that he would never run out of gas in case he had a victim with him at the time.
> He was a fastidious cleaner (in order to conceal his crimes).
> He returned to the locations where he left the corpses of his victims, often interfering with them.
> He took Polaroids of his victims and kept them in a shoebox so he could masturbate to them afterwards.
> He decapitated/separated at least five heads of his victims post-mortem, transported them to a new location where he discarded them.
> In Utah he appeared to change his M.O. insinuating himself into the life of at least one victim before abducting, raping and murdering her.

Most of these activities take planning and preparation. Once you exclude normal activities such as daily chores, sleep, work and pro-social behavior, it is clear that Ted's 10 percent figure is not tenable. If we include the entire envelope of activities associated with hunting, killing and concealment, in his prime we would have to allocate at least 10-15 days a month, which pushes the figure closer to 50 percent, which is still probably an under-estimate.

Number of victims

> They have no idea what it takes to do one, what it takes out of you (Nelson 1994, 257).

Ted's final victim count was most likely somewhere in the vicinity of 30-34 (see victim tables). This corroborates his last confession to Lewis and contradicts Bob Keppel's and Seattle attorney John Henry Browne's claim of more than 100 (Browne claimed that Ted's first murder was a man). It most definitely contradicts the assessment of Ronald M. Holmes who quotes Don Patchen as saying Ted did 300. Of course, there were also many Ted survivors. It could be safely assumed there were at least as many survivors as the dead, or more, so in total Ted was involved in 70 or more attacks at the most conservative estimate. In other words, what we are really saying, is Ted spent a lot of time thinking about sex and killing, and when he had his mind on other matters, he couldn't wait till he could get back to thinking about sex and killing.

Table 1: Victims and suspected victims, Seattle base, Washington.

D/M/Y	Days	Name	Age	Description	Taken from	Miles
23/06/66	0	Lisa E. Wick	20	Survived	Seattle, WA	N/A
23/06/66	0	Lonnie Trumbull	20	Body found	Seattle, WA	N/A
1/02/69	954	Unknown	?	Survived	Ocean City, NJ	N/A
30/05/69	118	Susan Davis	18	Body found	Ocean City, NJ	64
30/05/69	0	Elizabeth Perry	18	Body found	Ocean City, NJ	64
16/09/70	474	Jeanette Rose Miller	17	Missing	Arlington, WA	96
1/06/71	258	Unknown	?	Survived	Seattle, WA	N/A
1/07/71	30	Unknown	?	Survived	Seattle, WA	N/A
19/07/71	18	Rita Curran	24	Body found	Burlington, VT	N/A
22/07/71	3	Joyce LePage	21	Body found	Pullman, WA	583
1/01/72	163	Unknown	?	Survived	Seattle, WA	N/A
25/05/72	145	Beverly May Jenkins	16	Body found	Eugene, OR	564
1/06/72	7	Kerry May Hardy	22	Body found	Seattle, WA	166
1/06/72	0	Geneva Joy Martin	19	Body found	Springfield, OR	566
3/03/73	275	Kathleen Edna Rodger	16	Missing	Oroville, CA	1368
1/05/73	**59**	**Unknown hitchhiker**	**?**	**Missing**	**Tumwater, WA**	**122**
20/06/73	50	Allison Lynn Caufman	15	Body found	Portland, OR	380
29/06/73	9	Rita Lorraine Jolley	17	Missing	West Linn, OR	374
1/07/73	2	Laurie Lee Canaday	18	Body found	Portland, OR	352
20/08/73	50	Vicki Lynn Hollar	24	Missing	Eugene, OR	566
15/10/73	50	Deborah Lee Tomlinson	16	Missing	Creswell, OR	584
4/11/73	20	Laura A O'Dell	21	Body found	San Francisco, CA	1616
5/11/73	1	Suzanne Rae Justis	23	Missing	Portland, OR	346
25/11/73	20	Lulaida Morales Sejalbo	17	Missing	Santa Clara, CA	1616
4/01/74	**40**	**Karen Lee Sparks**	**18**	**Survived**	**Seattle, WA**	**N/A**
31/01/74	**27**	**Lynda Ann Healy**	**21**	**Skull found**	**Seattle, WA**	**66**
2/03/74	30	Unknown	20	Survived	Seattle, WA	N/A
12/03/74	**10**	**Donna Gail Manson**	**19**	**Missing**	**Seattle, WA**	**?**
17/04/74	**36**	**Susan Elaine Rancourt**	**18**	**Skull found**	**Ellensburg, WA**	**280**
6/05/74	**19**	**Roberta Kathleen Parks**	**22**	**Skull found**	**Corvallis, OR**	**553**
1/06/74	**3**	**Brenda Carol Ball**	**22**	**Skull found**	**Burien, WA**	**77**
12/06/74	**11**	**Georgeann Hawkins**	**18**	**Femur found**	**Seattle, WA**	**38**
1/07/74	19	Sandra Jean Weaver	19	Body found	Salt Lake City, UT	2294
14/07/74	**13**	**Janice Ott**	**23**	**Bones found**	**Issaquah, WA**	**23**
14/07/74	**0**	**Denise Marie Naslund**	**19**	**Bones found**	**Issaquah, WA**	**40**

Blue = victims that Ted confessed to; **Blue bold** = victims that Ted murdered; Red = increased probability that Ted was involved; Green = decreased probability that Ted was involved; Days = number of days between victims (not necessarily Ted's); Miles = these figures are summed, where applicable, from 1) the distance from Ted's home to the location of abduction; 2) the distance from the location of abduction to the body location; and 3) the distance from the body location back to Ted's home.

Table 2: Victims and suspected victims, SLC base, Utah.

D/M/Y	Days	Name	Age	Description	Taken from	Miles
2/09/74	**1**	**Unknown hitchhiker**	**?**	**Missing**	**Boise, ID**	**N/A**
2/10/74	**30**	**Nancy Wilcox**	**16**	**Missing**	**Holladay, UT**	**18**
18/10/74	**16**	**Melissa Smith**	**17**	**Body found**	**Midvale, UT**	**61**
31/10/74	**13**	**Laura Ann Aime**	**17**	**Body found**	**Lehi, UT**	**77**
8/11/74	**8**	**Carol Ann DaRonch**	**18**	**Survived**	**Murray, UT**	**13**
8/11/74	**0**	**Deborah Jean Kent**	**17**	**Missing**	**Bountiful, UT**	**228**
4/12/74	26	Laurie Lynn Partridge	17	Missing	Spokane, WA	1442
12/01/75	**39**	**Caryn Eileen Campbell**	**23**	**Body found**	**Snowmass, CO**	**790**
15/03/75	**62**	**Julie Cunningham**	**26**	**Missing**	**Vail, CO**	**870**
6/04/75	**22**	**Denise Lynn Oliverson**	**24**	**Missing**	**Grand Junction, CO**	**568**
15/04/75	9	Melanie Suzanne Cooley	18	Body found	Nederland, CO	1088
6/05/75	**21**	**Lynnette Dawn Culver**	**12**	**Missing**	**Pocatello, ID**	**330**
27/06/75	**52**	**Susan Curtis**	**15**	**Missing**	**Provo, UT**	**269**
29/06/75	2	Shelley Kay Robinson	24	Body found	Golden, CO	1086
4/07/75	5	Nancy Perry Baird	23	Missing	Layton, UT	48
1/02/76	212	Debbie Smith	17	Body found	Seattle, WA	36

Table 3: Victims and suspected victims, Tallahassee base, Florida.

D/M/Y	Days	Name	Age	Description	Taken from	Miles
15/01/78	714	Cheryl Rafferty	?	Survived	Tallahassee, FL	N/A
15/01/78	**0**	**Margaret Bowman**	**21**	**Body Found**	**Tallahassee, FL**	**N/A**
15/01/78	**0**	**Lisa Janet Levy**	**21**	**Body Found**	**Tallahassee, FL**	**N/A**
15/01/78	0	Kathy Kleiner	21	Survived	Tallahassee, FL	N/A
15/01/78	0	Karen Chandler	21	Survived	Tallahassee, FL	N/A
15/01/78	0	Cheryl Anne Thomas	21	Survived	Tallahassee, FL	N/A
8/02/78	24	Leslie Parmenter	14	Survived	Jacksonville, FL	126
9/02/78	**1**	**Kimberly Diane Leach**	**12**	**Body Found**	**Lake City, FL**	**176**

The suspect would have to fall into the rapist category. I have divided the rapists into five classifications: the show-off; the verbal abuser; the physical verbal abuser; and the last group, the necrophiliacs, who commit murder as part of their sexual gratification. They either have sexual intercourse just prior to the murder or possibly a single ejaculation, or else they have an ejaculation after the murder either by penetration or otherwise.

Excerpt from a letter written by Edward E. Shev, a consulting neurologist and psychiatrist, to Sonoma County, California, April 20, 1974, in relation to the murders that happened there during the early 1970s. Shev provided a detailed list of traits he thought the killer would possess, among them this description of homicidal necrophilia. Source: KCA.

Table 3: Abduction Modus Operandi

	Victim group	Abduction type			Ruse type	Injury type	Request help type	Skull
	Hardy †	Blitz?	?	?				
	Sparks *	Blitz						
1.	Healy	Blitz						✔ rts
2.	Manson	Ruse/Blitz?	?					✔ rts
3.	Rancourt	Ruse + Blitz			Injury	Sling		✔ rts
4.	Parks	Ruse			Companionship		Student	✔ rts
5.	Ball	Ruse			Companionship		Student?	✔ rts
6.	Hawkins	Ruse + Blitz			Injury	Crutches		✔ rts
7.	Ott	Ruse	?		Injury	Sling		✔ rts
8.	Naslund	Ruse	?		Injury	Sling		✔ rts
9.	Wilcox	Blitz			Acquaintance?			? rts?
10.	Smith	Blitz						
11.	Aime	Ruse			Acquaintance		Student?	rts?
	DaRonch *	Ruse + Blitz			Request help		Police officer	
12.	Kent	Blitz	?					?
13.	Campbell	Ruse + Blitz?			Injury/ Request help	Heart problem?	Car trouble?	
14.	Cuningham	Ruse + Blitz			Injury	Crutches		rts
15.	Oliverson	Ruse/Blitz?	?		Request help?		Car trouble?	
16.	Culver	Ruse	?		Request help		Authority figure?	
17.	Curtis	Ruse/Blitz?	?		Request help?		Car trouble?	
18.	Bowman	Blitz						
	Kleiner *	Blitz						
	Chandler *	Blitz						
19.	Levy	Blitz						
	Thomas *	Blitz						
	Parmenter *	Ruse			Request help		Fireman	
20.	Leach	Ruse		?	Request help		Authority figure?	

†= unconfirmed. * = survived. rts = returned to site.

Table 4: The abduction-rape location interval

Victim	Abduction location	Rape location	Travel time (mins)
Sparks	4325 8th Ave NE, Seatl	*4325 8th Ave NE, Seatlle*	0
Bowman	Chi-Omega House	*Chi-Omega House*	0
Levy	Chi-Omega House	*Chi-Omega House*	0
Kleiner	Chi-Omega House	*Chi-Omega House*	0
Chandler	Chi-Omega House	*Chi-Omega House*	0
Thomas	Dunwoody Street	*Dunwoody Street*	0
Culver	Alameda Junior High	Pocatello Holiday Inn	3
Wilcox	Arnett Drive, Holladay	Millcreek-Holladay area	5
Campbell	Wildwood Inn	*Owl Creek Road**	5
Parks	Oregon State Univ.	OSU boathouse	5
Oliverson	Grand Juntion rail overpass	West Grand Junction?	8
Kent	Viewmont High	Farmington Bay - Centerville?	10
Ott	Lake Sammamish	*Issaquah*	10
Naslund	Lake Sammamish	*Issaquah*	10
Ball	Flame Tavern	Sea-Tac?	10
Manson	Evergreen State College	Delphi Road SW?	15
Aime	Robinson Park?	Timpanogos Cave?	15
Hawkins	Greek Row	*Issaquah*	25
Rancourt	Central Washington Univ.	Yakima River-Taylor Road?	30
Curtis	Brigham Young Univ.	Thistle?	35
Leach	Lake City Junior High	*Suwannee River State Park*	45
Smith	Wasatch - I-15 overpass	*Timberline Subdivision?*	45
Healy	5517 12th NE, Seatl	*Taylor Mountain?*	60
Cunningham	Vail	*Rifle*	65

Italics represents same body disposal/victim abandonment location as rape location. * Rape body location close enough to be the same. Excluding zero values, the average abduction-rape interval is 16.7 mins +/- 19.7 mins. The data shows that Ted generally raped his victims as soon as practically possible after abduction.

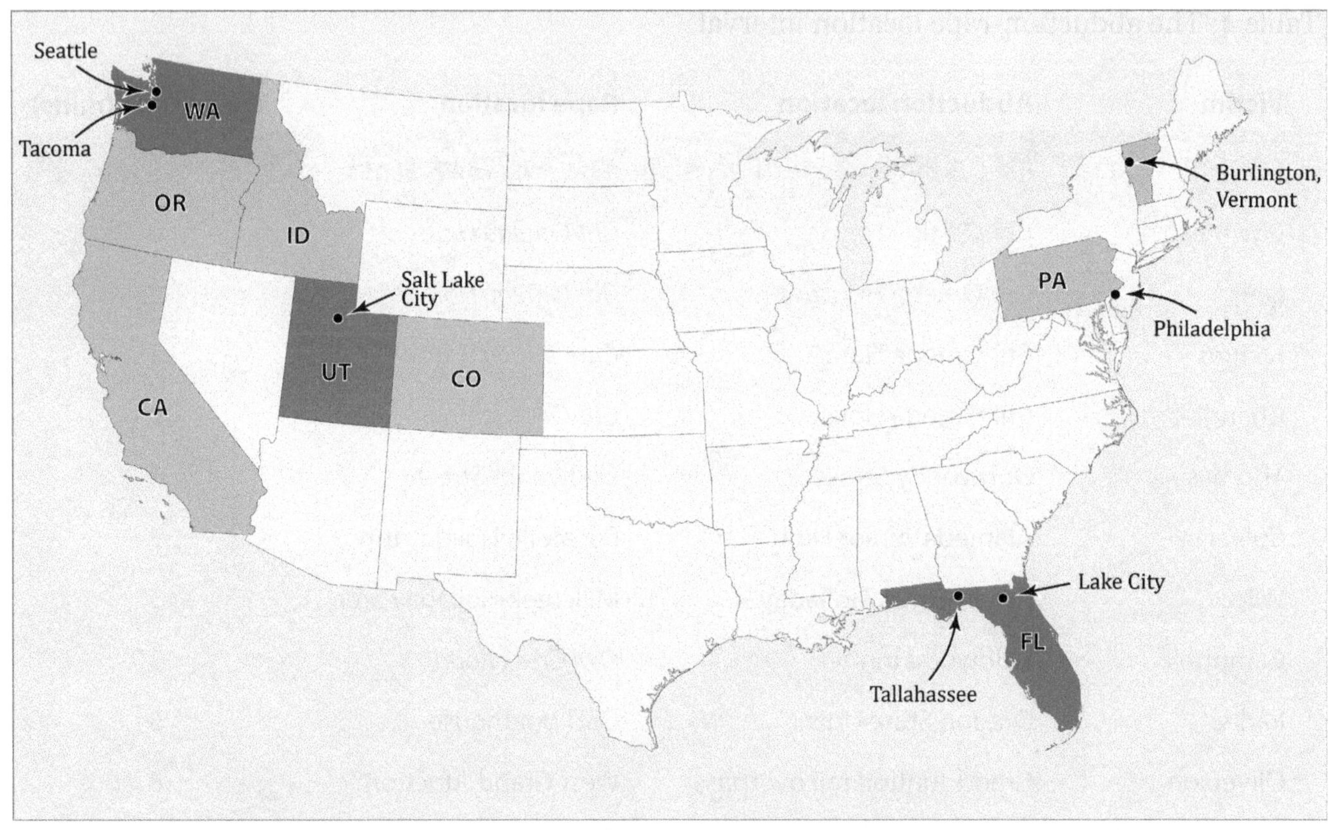

The Bundy footprint. Washington: confessed 11, 8 identified. According to Ted the unidentified cases were south of Seattle. Oregon: confessed to 2, 1 identified. California: confessed to 1, none identified. Idaho: confessed to 2, 1 identified. The other is the Boise hitchhiker. Colorado: confessed to 3, 3 identified. Utah: confessed to 8, 5 identified. Florida: confessed to 3, 3 identified. Map courtesy © Free Vector Maps.

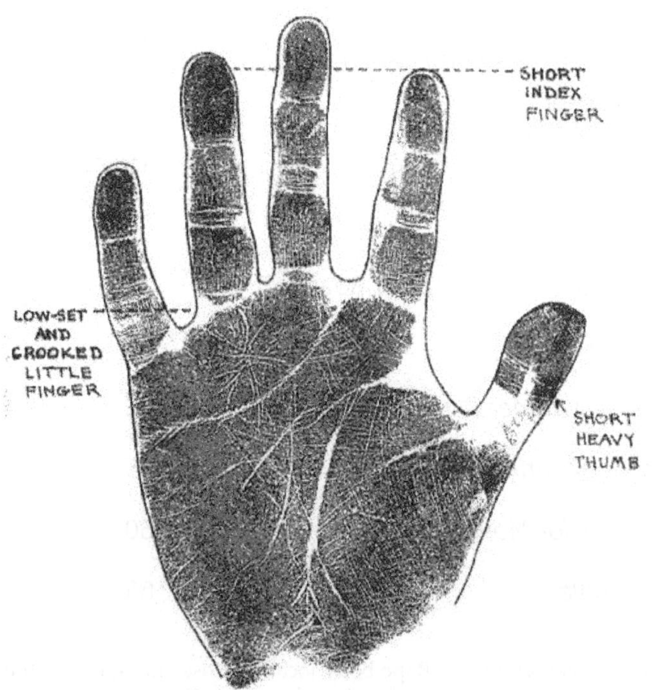

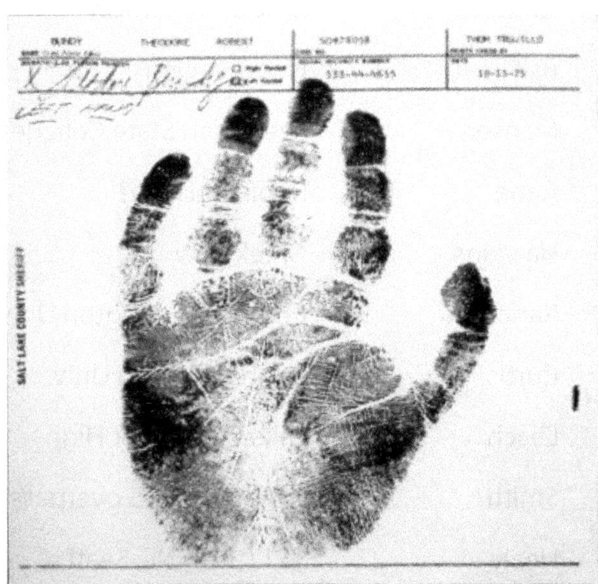

Ted's actual palm print. FBI 1975.

Ted's left hand idealized palm print. His digit ratio (2D/4D) is approximately 0.9508 (somewhat in the lower range), suggesting high levels of intrauterine testosterone. Low second-to-fourth digit ratio has been associated with more aggressiveness and risk-taking in males, e.g., (Perciavalle et al 2013).

References

Arendt, M., Mortensen, P. B., Rosenberg, R., Pedersen, C. B. & Waltoft, B. L. (2008). Familial predisposition for psychiatric disorder: Comparison of subjects treated for cannabis-induced psychosis and schizophrenia. *Archives of General Psychiatry*, 65(11), pp. 1269-74.

Baumeister, R. F., Muraven, M. & Tice, D. M. (2000). Ego-depletion: A resource model of volition, self-regulation, and controlled processing. *Social Cognition*, 18(2), pp. 130-50.

Bechara, A., Damasio, H. & Damasio, A. R. (2000). Emotion, decision making and the orbitofrontal cortex. *Cerebral Cortex*, 10(3), pp. 295-307.

Bell, V. (2013). A community of one: Social cognition and auditory verbal hallucinations. *PLoS Biol*, 11(12), p. e1001723.

Berridge, K. C. (2007). The debate over dopamine's role in reward: The case for incentive salience. *Psychopharmacology*, 191(3), pp. 391-431.

Bhattacharyya, S., Crippa, J. A., Allen, P., Martin-Santos, R., Borgwardt, S., et al. (2012). Induction of psychosis by Δ9-tetrahydrocannabinol reflects modulation of prefrontal and striatal function during attentional salience processing. *Archives of General Psychiatry*, 69(1), pp. 27-36.

Blair, R. J. R. (2005). Responding to the emotions of others: Dissociating forms of empathy through the study of typical and psychiatric populations. *Consciousness and Cognition*, 14(4), pp. 698–718.

Brennan, K. (January 25, 1989) Violent Childhood Twisted Killer, Doctor Says. philly.com. (http://articles.philly.com/1989-01-25/news/26122339_1_bundy-louise-cowell-violent-childhood). Accessed March 2, 2015.

Buckholtz, J. W., Treadway, M. T., Cowan, R. L., Woodward, N. D., Benning, S. D., et al. (2010). Mesolimbic dopamine reward system hypersensitivity in individuals with psychopathic traits. *Nature Neuroscience*, 13(4), pp. 419-21.

Carlisle, A. (1993). Toward an understanding of the dark side of the serial killer. *American Journal of Criminal Justice*, XVII(2), pp. 23-33.

Carlisle, A. (2013). *I'm Not Guilty* (2nd ed.). Encino, CA: Genius Book Publishing.

Christensen, W. (2007). The evolutionary origins of volition. In D. Spurrett, H. Kincaid, D. Ross & L. Stephens (Eds.), *Distributed Cognition and the Will: Individual Volition and Social Context* (pp. 255–88). Cambridge, MA: MIT Press.

Clark, A. & Chalmers, D. (1998). The extended mind. *Analysis*, 58, pp. 7-19.

Cleckley, H. M. (1941). *The Mask of Sanity: An Attempt to Clarify Some Issues About the So-Called Psychopathic Personality*. St. Louis: MO: Mosby.

Coolidge, F. L., Thede, L. L. & Jang, K. L. (2004). Are personality disorders psychological manifestations of executive function deficits? Bivariate heritability evidence from a twin study. *Behavior Genetics*, 34(1), pp. 75-84.

Craig, A. D. B. (2009). How do you feel – now? The anterior insula and human awareness. *Nature Reviews Neuroscience*, (10), pp. 59-70.

Donahue, E. M., Robins, R. W., Roberts, B. W. & John, O. P. (1993). The divided self: Concurrent and longitudinal effects of psychological adjustment and social roles on self-concept differentiation. *Journal of Personality and Social Psychology*, 64(5), pp. 834-46.

Frith, C. D., Blakemore, S.-J. & Wolpert, D. M. (2000). Explaining the symptoms of schizophrenia: Abnormalities in the awareness of action. *Brain Research Reviews*, 31(2), pp. 357-63.

Fuster J. M. *The PFC: Anatomy, Physiology and Neuropsychology of the Frontal Lobe*. New York: Lippincott-Raven; 1997.

Fuster, J. M. (2001). The prefrontal cortex – an update: Time is of the essence. *Neuron*, 30(2), pp. 319-33.

Gao, Y., & Raine, A. (2010). Successful and unsuccessful psychopaths: A neurobiological model. *Behavioral Sciences & the Law*, 28(2), 194-210.

Geberth, V. J. (1990). Serial killer and the revelations of Ted Bundy. *Law and Order*, 38(5), pp. 72-7.

Goldman-Rakic, P. S., Cools, A. & Srivastava, K. (1996). The prefrontal landscape: Implications of functional architecture for understanding human mentation and the central executive [and Discussion]. *Philosophical Transactions of the Royal Society B: Biological Sciences*, 351(1346), pp. 1445-53.

Gordon, H. L., Baird, A. A., & End, A. (2004). Functional differences among those high and low on a trait measure of psychopathy. *Biological psychiatry*, 56(7), 516-521.

Grossmann, T. (2013). Mapping prefrontal cortex functions in human infancy. Infancy, 18(3), pp. 303-24.

Hare, R. D. (1970). *Psychopathy: Theory and Research*. New York: Wiley.

Hare, R. D. (1991). *The Hare Psychopathy Checklist — Revised*. Toronto: Multi-Health Systems.

Harlow, H. F., Dodsworth, R. O. & Harlow, M. K. (1965). Total social isolation in monkeys. *Proceedings of the National Academy of Sciences of the United States of America*, 54(1), pp. 90-7.

Hurlburt, R. T., Heavey, C. L. & Kelsey, J. M. (2013). Toward a phenomenology of inner speaking. *Consciousness and Cognition*, 22(4), pp. 1477-94.

Ishikawa, S. S., Raine, A., Lencz, T., Bihrle, S., & Lacasse, L. (2001). Autonomic stress reactivity and executive functions in successful and unsuccessful criminal psychopaths from the community. *Journal of Abnormal Psychology*, 110(3), 423.

Jones, S. R. & Fernyhough, C. (2007). Neural correlates of inner speech and auditory verbal hallucinations: A critical review and theoretical integration. *Clinical Psychology Review*, 27(2), pp. 140-54.

Karama, S., Lecours, A. R., Leroux, J. M., Bourgouin, P., Beaudoin, G., et al. (2002). Areas of brain activation in males and females during viewing of erotic film excerpts. *Human Brain Mapping*, 16(1), pp. 1-13.

Kendall, E. (1981). *The Phantom Prince: My Life with Ted Bundy*. Seattle, WA: Madrona Publishers.

Keppel, R. D. & Birnes, W. J. (2004). *The Riverman: Ted Bundy and I Hunt for the Green River Killer*. New York: Pocket Books.

Luria A. R. *Higher Cortical Functions in Man*. New York: Basic Books; 1966.

MacPherson, M. (1989). Ted Bundy: Anatomy of a serial killer. *Vanity Fair*, May, pp. 144-198.

McGuire, P., Silbersweig, D., Murray, R., David, A., Frackowiak, R., et al. (1996). Functional anatomy of inner speech and auditory verbal imagery. *Psychological Medicine*, 26(01), pp. 29-38.

Meffert, H., Gazzola, V., den Boer, J. A., Bartels, A. A., & Keysers, C. (2013). Reduced spontaneous but relatively normal deliberate vicarious representations in psychopathy. *Brain*, 136(8), 2550-2562.

Merckelbach, H., Devilly, G. J. & Rassin, E. (2002). Alters in dissociative identity disorder: Metaphors or genuine entities? *Clinical Psychology Review*, 22(4), pp. 481-97.

Michaud, S. G. & Aynesworth, H. (1983). *The Only Living Witness*. Authorlink Press, Irving, Texas.

Michaud, S. G. & Aynesworth, H. (2000). *Ted Bundy: Conversations with a Killer*. Authorlink Press, Irving, Texas.

Morin, A. (2009). Self-awareness deficits following loss of inner speech: Dr. Jill Bolte Taylor's case study. *Consciousness and Cognition*, 18(2), pp. 524-9.

Nelson, P. (1994). *Defending the Devil*. William Morrow and Company. New York.

Ortigue, S., Grafton, S. T. & Bianchi-Demicheli, F. (2007). Correlation between insula activation and self-reported quality of orgasm in women. *Neuroimage*, 37(2), pp. 551-60.

Perciavalle, V., Di Corrado, D., Petralia, M. C., Gurrisi, L., Massimino, S., et al. (2013). The second-to-fourth digit ratio correlates with aggressive behavior in professional soccer players. *Molecular Medicine Reports*, 7(6), pp. 1733-8.

Raichle, M. E., MacLeod, A. M., Snyder, A. Z., Powers, W. J., Gusnard, D. A., et al. (2001). A default mode of brain function. *Proceedings of the National Academy of Sciences of the United States of America*, 98, pp. 676–82.

Robinson, T. E. & Berridge, K. C. (2008). The incentive sensitization theory of addiction: Some current issues. *Philosophical Transactions of the Royal Society B: Biological Sciences*, 363(1507), pp. 3137-46.

Robertson, J. & Bowlby, J. (1952). Responses of young children to separation from their mothers II: Observations of the sequences of response of children aged 18 to 24 months during the course of separation. *Courrier du Centre International de l'Enfance*, 2, pp. 131–42.

Sanfey, A. G., Rilling, J. K., Aronson, J. A., Nystrom, L. E. & Cohen, J. D. (2003). The neural basis of economic decision-making in the ultimatum game. *Science*, 300(5626), pp. 1755-8.

Schneider, K. (1959). *Klinische Psychopathologie*. New York/Stuttgart : Thieme Verlag.

Seal, M., Aleman, A. & McGuire, P. (2004). Compelling imagery, unanticipated speech and deceptive memory: Neurocognitive models of auditory verbal hallucinations in schizophrenia. *Cognitive Neuropsychiatry*, 9(1-2), pp. 43-72.

Sekar, A., Bialas, A. R., de Rivera, H., Davis, A., Hammond, T. R., et al. (2016). Schizophrenia risk from complex variation of complement component 4. *Nature*, 530(7589), pp. 177-83.

Shimamura, A. P. (2000). The role of the prefrontal cortex in dynamic filtering. *Psychobiology*, 28(2), pp. 207-18.

Singer, T. (2006). The neuronal basis and ontogeny of empathy and mind reading: Review of literature and implications for future research. *Neuroscience & Biobehavioral Reviews*, 30(6), pp. 855-63.

Taylor, J. B. (2008). *My Stroke of Insight: A Brain Scientist's Personal Journey*. Viking.

Voon, V., Mole, T. B., Banca, P., Porter, L., Morris, L., et al. (2014). Neural correlates of sexual cue reactivity in individuals with and without compulsive sexual behaviours. *PLOS ONE* 9(7), p. e102419.

Wicker, B., Keysers, C., Plailly, J., Royet, J.-P., Gallese, V., et al. (2003). Both of us disgusted in my insula: The common neural basis of seeing and feeling disgust. *Neuron*, 40(3), pp. 655-64.

Wright, P., He, G., Shapira, N. A., Goodman, W. K. & Liu, Y. (2004). Disgust and the insula: fMRI responses to pictures of mutilation and contamination. *Neuroreport*, 15(15), pp. 2347-51.

Yang, Y., Raine, A., Lencz, T., Bihrle, S., Lacasse, L., & Colletti, P. (2005a). Prefrontal white matter in pathological liars. *The British Journal of Psychiatry*, 187(4), 320-325.

Yang, Y., Raine, A., Lencz, T., Bihrle, S., LaCasse, L., & Colletti, P. (2005b). Volume reduction in prefrontal gray matter in unsuccessful criminal psychopaths. *Biological psychiatry*, 57(10), 1103-1108.

Childhood Years (1946-1959)

- 1921 -

April 23, 1921: Johnnie Culpepper Bundy born, Tacoma.

- 1924 -

September 21, 1924: Eleanor Louise Cowell born, Philadelphia.

- 1927 -

December 10, 1927: Harvey Murray Glatman born in The Bronx, New York City.

- 1939 -

January 31, 1939: Jerome Henry "Jerry" Brudos born in Webster, South Dakota.

- 1940 -

November 7, 1940: Collapse of the Tacoma Narrows Bridge, Pierce County.

- 1945 -

May 4, 1945: Glatman attacks Eula Jo Hand (17) while on her way home from the movies in the Capitol Hill neighborhood of Denver. He puts a gun to her back, takes her to an alley, ties her to a telephone pole, molests her, and steals 18 streetcar tokens and $14.95. Hand tells police she recognized her attacker as a fellow East High student.

May 18, 1945: Glatman is arrested in Denver for the first time for the "robbery" of Eula Jo Hand and two other women.

May 21, 1945: Ophelia Glatman bails her son out of jail for $2,000.

July 15, 1945: While out of jail on bond, Glatman binds, gags, molests, and robs Norene Lauer (age ?) in Boulder, Colorado, of $2.

July 17, 1945: Glatman is arrested in Denver for the second time for the assault on Norene Lauer.

July 31–September 8, 1945: Glatman is confined in the Colorado Psychopathic Hospital.

September 2, 1945: Official surrender of the Japanese, thereby ending WWII. Sam Lusky, writing for the *Rocky Mountain News,* described the Denver scene: "... servicemen kissed their girls and they kissed somebody else's girl and pretty soon everybody was kissing everybody else, and nobody was complaining" (Newton 1998, 45).

September 27, 1945: While out of the hospital and out on bond from both the Denver and Boulder county jails, Glatman bound, gagged, molested, and robbed two women in the Park Hill neighborhood of Denver. He also molested another Denver woman, who screamed and ran out of her house.

Harvey Glatman Colorado prison photo, December 5, 1945. Photo public domain.

September 30, 1945: Glatman is arrested in Denver for the third time, for the Park Hill neighborhood assaults.

December 5, 1945: Glatman begins his first prison term at the Colorado State Penitentiary.

- 1946 -

March 25, 1946: Gerard John Schaefer born in Wisconsin.

July 27, 1946: Glatman is paroled from the Colorado State Penitentiary after less than eight months of his one-to-five-year sentence.

July 27–August 25, 1946: Glatman returns to his mother in New York State. There, he commits several more robberies and assaults on women.

August 25, 1946: Glatman is arrested and confined in jail, Albany, New York.

October 10, 1946: Glatman is sentenced to one-to-five-years for the first of his New York robberies and assaults.

Louise Cowell sometime around Ted's birth. Photo public domain.

Elizabeth Lund Home for Unwed Mothers (circa 1940s). Photo source http://www.lundvt.org.

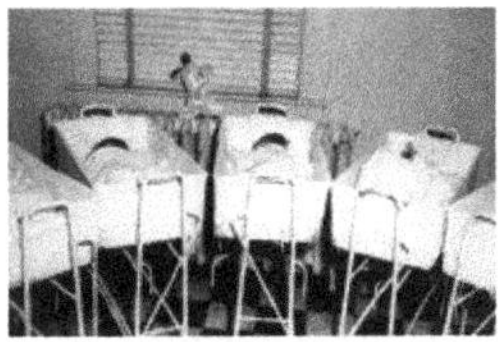
Lund cribs (circa 1940s). Photo source http://www.lundvt.org.

November 24, 1946: Theodore Robert Cowell born at The Elizabeth Lund Home for Unwed Mothers in Burlington, Vermont, on Lake Champlain. Louise spent a total of 63 days at Lund, presumably up until, and a short while after, Ted was born. He weighed 7 lbs, 9 oz. and there were "no complications" (MacPherson 1989, 145). Louise left Elizabeth Lund alone, leaving Ted there for adoption. Ted spent 3 months motherless at Elizabeth Lund before Ted's grandfather Samuel F. Cowell insisted that Louise take him home to Roxborough (on the Schuylkill River). Louise claimed she was seduced by a war veteran; nothing has been found on the man. In the end, Louise was just as secretive about who Ted's father was as Ted was about his murders. According to Ted's great-aunt Virginia Bristol: "When I heard Louise was 'not home' I knew things were not right. Next thing I heard was that Sam and Eleanor had adopted a boy. I was smart enough to know damn well they weren't adopting this baby. No adoption agency would've given them one; Eleanor wasn't well enough to take care of one! I knew it had to be Louise's baby. But they wanted to cover up. All we ever got was evasions. I had a very secretive brother" (MacPherson 1989, 145).

- 1947 -

1947: William E. Cosden Jr. born in Maryland.
February 1947: After spending 3 months alone at Lund, Louise brings Ted home to the "middle-class" rural suburb of Roxborough, Philadelphia (Brennan 1989). Ted was "adopted" by grandfather Samuel F. Cowell and wife Eleanor. Ted was led to believe his grandparents were his parents, his mother his sister.

- 1949 -

1949: Ted's 15-year-old aunt Julia supposedly wakes up to find 3-year-old Ted had placed kitchen knives in her bed (*Deseret News*, January 25, 1989).
1949: Warren Leslie Forrest born in Vancouver, Washington.

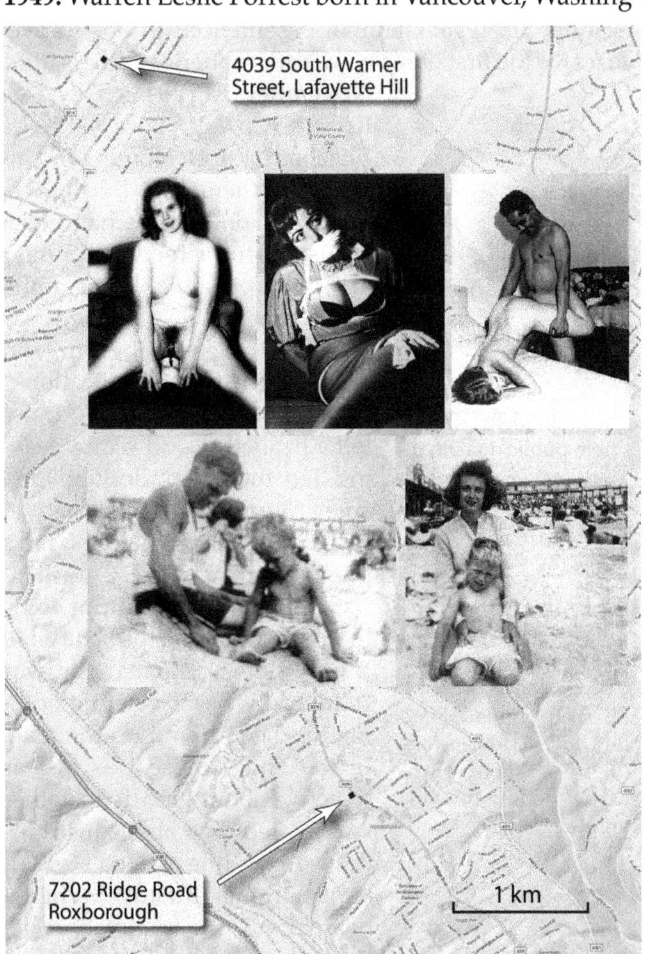

Map showing Roxborough in relation to Lafayette Hill, where Ted stayed in December 1968. Map courtesy OpenStreetMap contributors 2015. Photo insets (top row): A sample of 1940s pornography. Photo insets (bottom row): Samuel Cowell (left) and Louise Cowell (right) with Ted. Photos public domain.

February 18, 1949: Gary Leon Ridgeway born in Utah. In his mid-teens, he stabs a six-year-old boy in the liver. The boy fortunately survives.

- 1950 -

1950: Story has it Ted sneaks into grandfather Samuel's greenhouse with Cousin "Bruce" and secretly peruses his stash of pornography. Samuel incorporated "Roxborough Nursery" on March 22, 1950, at 7202 Ridge Road, Roxborough.
October 6, 1950: Louise Cowell goes to local court in Philadelphia and changes Ted's name to Theodore Robert Nelson.

- 1951 -

Jack Cowell (undated). Photo public domain.

1951: Moved to Tacoma and briefly stayed at uncle John "Jack" R. Cowell's on Alder Street, before moving to Browns Point. Started kindergarten (4 years old). Becomes friends with "Bill" and "Richard." As to why Louise moved, Ted's grandaunt Virginia Bristol put it this way: "We felt Louise had to be rescued" (M&A 1983, 313).

Left: Tacoma, looking east on 9th Street, circa 1953. Photo from an old postcard, public domain. Right: Brown's Point, Tacoma, circa 1950. Photo courtesy U.S. Coast Guard.

May 2, 1951: Glatman returns to Denver, where his parole stipulates that he be put under the care of psychiatrist Franklin G. Ebaugh.
May 19, 1951: After meeting at a Methodist church adults' night (singles dance) Louise Cowell (27) marries Johnnie Culpepper Bundy (29), a mustered out Navy man. Ted sticks his hand in the wedding cake. Parents move to 1620 South Sheridan Avenue, Tacoma. Attends Stanley Elementary school (1712 S 17th St., Tacoma). Attends Methodist church every Sunday.
September 12, 1951: Gerald Eugene Stano born in Schenectady, New York.

- 1952 -

1952: The term "psychopath" was officially replaced with "sociopathic personality" (Tanay 2010, 128). Glatman's father, Albert Glatman, dies.

A typical street scene on South Sheridan Avenue. Photo courtesy Vincent Tan © 2015.

Johnnie Culpepper Bundy with Ted (dated 1953). Photo public domain.

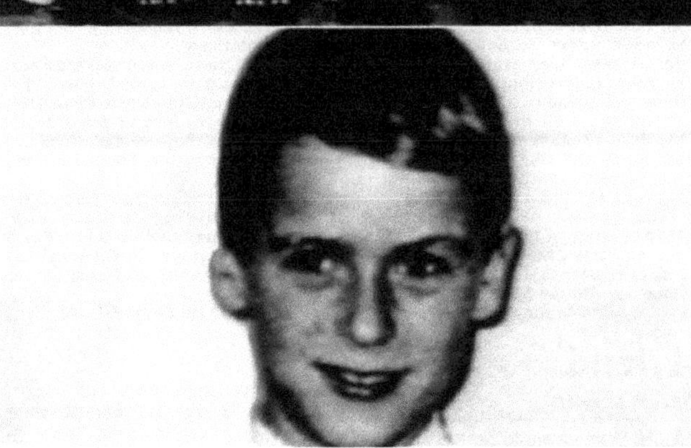

A Geiger Elementary class photo with Ted (circled above), perhaps circa 1955-6. Photo public domain.

Late 1952: Linda Bundy is born. Ted is no longer permitted into his parents bed when he grows frightened in the middle of the night.

- 1953 -

658 North Skyline Drive, Tacoma. Photo courtesy Vincent Tan © 2015.

1953: Glatman's psychiatrist, Franklin Ebaugh, retires leaving Glatman unattended.

1953: Ted attends Geiger Elementary school (621 South Jackson Avenue, Tacoma). Aged 7, Ted's second grade teacher Miss Geri breaks a ruler over his knuckles for having socked a classmate in the nose during a playground scuffle. Around this time Ted began to feel a vague sense of "uneasiness" within himself (M&A 1983, 53). Parents move to 658 North Skyline Drive.

- 1954 -

February 1954: Glen Bundy is born. Ted becomes friends

Ted the Boy Scout, farthest right. Doug Holt center, holding the puppet up to the camera. Photo courtesy Rebecca Morris (2013). Photo original source Beverly Burr.

with Doug and Sandi Holt (Morris 2013, 80). Sandi and Doug lived on North Howard Street, about a block from Skyline Drive where Ted lived. Ted joins the Boy Scouts. He hits a kid named John Moon on the head with a stick "from behind." In an unverified story, on a Boy Scout camping trip one summer, the other troop members—including Doug—caught Ted and Doug Holt's father naked together in a tent in the middle of the day. Doug believed that something "kinky" had happened between his father and Ted. The other boys teased Ted; that may have been the outing when Ted hit John Moon. A father of one of the other boys berated Mr. Holt for being in the tent with Ted, but beyond that there were no repercussions. Ted abruptly stopped going on Boy Scout camping trips but wouldn't explain why. Remarkably, Sandi said her father sexually abused her and Doug throughout their childhood (Morris 2013, 81-82). In other unverified stories, Sandi said she saw Ted use a pocket knife to cut open animals, douse them with gasoline, and set them on fire; Ted and Doug used knives to slash the leather seats of expensive cars in the neighborhood; Ted would try to "pants" young girls, lure them into the woods, pull down their pants, and urinate on them; Doug Holt was a little smaller than Ted, but he hit Ted once when he tried to drag Sandi into the woods (Morris 2013, 82).

Dorothy Gay Howard, aged 15. Photo public domain.

Warren Dodge, 1965 *Nova* Yearbook.

April 8, 1954: The body of Jane Doe is found west of Boulder. She was identified as Dorothy Gay Howard (18) on October 28, 2009. Police believe she may have been a victim of Glatman. The theory is she was hit by a car while running away from him. Boulder detective Steve Ainsworth tracked down a 1951 Dodge Coronet like the one Glatman bought in Denver and was driving when arrested in California, and calculated where that car would have hit Howard's body. The locations match Howard's injuries.

April-May 1954: *Crime SuspenStories* was a bi-monthly anthology crime comic published by EC Comics in the early 1950s. The first edition came out October/November 1950, the last February/March 1955. The issue pictured is number 22, April-May 1954. This cover is often trotted out in reference to Ted's appetite for detective magazines. Ted was 7 ½ when this appeared. Photo public domain.

Ellensburg Daily Record - Jan 24, 1989

One friend, Terry Storwick, recalled a time when Bundy attacked another boy during a Boy Scout outing.

"It was easy to see when Ted got mad," Storwick told the authors of "The Only Living Witness," a book about Bundy. "His eyes turned about black with anger."

- 1955 -

1955: Becomes friends with Terry Storwick and Warren Dodge. Enters second grade at Geiger Elementary school.

Gainesville Sun - Jul 6, 1986

Boyhood friend glad Bundy was granted a stay

The Associated Press

TACOMA — Ted Bundy once had a friend named Warren Dodge. On the eve of Bundy's scheduled execution last week, Dodge could not believe in his heart that the shy and clever young man from his boyhood could be a killer.

Dodge, 39, is a drug store manager who still lives near the Tacoma neighborhood where he and Bundy grew up. As boys, they were inseparable. As men, they celebrated their common 21st birthday together.

"He had a bit of a temper, but so did a lot of other people who turned out all right," Dodge said. "The Ted Bundy sitting on death row is not in any way the same person."

Bundy was convicted in Florida in 1979 of killing a 12-year-old Lake City girl and two Chi Omega sorority sisters at Florida State University in Tallahassee. Police believe Bundy may be responsible for at least 36 slayings around the country.

King County police describe Bundy as the prime suspect in the unsolved 1974 slayings of eight young women.

Bundy, who was sentenced to death for the Florida slayings, won a two-month stay of his execution, which had been scheduled for last week.

Although he believes Bundy committed the murders, Dodge was glad Bundy won the stay.

"(Killing him) would serve no purpose," he said. "Granted, I wouldn't like to see him running around free, but I don't want him to die. I really don't.

"Deep down inside, I hope he never dies," he said.

Dodge has known Bundy since the two were in the second grade. After high school, they saw each other only rarely. Dodge stayed in Tacoma to attend the University of Puget Sound,

See FRIEND on page 4D

Friend

From page 1D

while Bundy went to Seattle to attend the University of Washington.

They last spoke in 1972 when Bundy was working on then-Gov. Dan Evans' re-election campaign. "He showed up one day and helped us move," Dodge said. "He seemed just like the Ted I knew before — maybe a little more sophisticated."

He did return to visit Dodge while out on bail after his 1975 arrest in Utah, but only Dodge's wife was home. By that time, suspicions about Bundy were well-known.

"Her only reaction was absolute fear," Dodge said. "She would not allow him in the house." She told Bundy that Dodge would be back the next day, but Bundy never returned.

Dodge later learned Bundy wanted to communicate with him, but Dodge couldn't find it within him to write.

"What would I say after all this time and everything that's happened? I have no idea how I would word a letter to him. How could you just erase those 12 years and talk about high school?" he asked.

- 1956 -

1956: Sandra Bundy born. October 1975 – Ted (then aged 29) had been visiting home one evening when he noticed his 19-year old half-sister Sandra was preparing to go out on a date. Ted said, "You know, Mom, she looks like all those other girls." Her hair was long and parted in the middle. (Larsen 1980, 90). In defense of Ted after his first arrest, Linda Bundy wrote: "I remember one time when he was home I understood my sister was going out. My brother asked who was she going with and where was she going because he was concerned" (PIR 1975). That Ted had a "type" cannot be denied, but many girls wore their hair long and parted in the middle in America at that time. So too did some men. What we do know was Ted was obsessed with cheerleaders, dancers, and athletic-looking girls. Many of them just happened to wear their hair long and parted in the middle. Their attractiveness, their willingness to help him, turn their backs on him was equally—if not more—important.

- 1957 -

Glatman's photo of Judith Ann Dull. Photo public domain

August 1, 1957: Harvey Glatman murders Judy Ann Dull (19) in Riverside County (Los Angeles), California. During his senior year in high school, 1944-5, he started binding, gagging, and molesting Denver women, while robbing them of small amounts of money. He was arrested several times for assault and robbery before he committed his first murder.

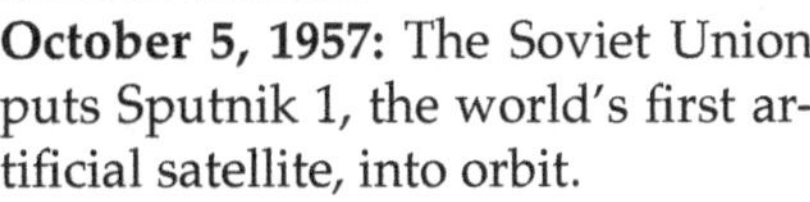

October 5, 1957: The Soviet Union puts Sputnik 1, the world's first artificial satellite, into orbit.

- 1958 -

1958: Ted enrolls at Hunt Junior High. For six years, from seventh grade at Hunt Junior High until he graduated from Wilson High in 1965, Ted sat behind Jerry Bullat in homeroom. The two boys formed a friendship based on

A class photo of Ted (circled) from Hunt Junior High (circa early 1960s). Photo public domain.

Hunt Junior High library, circa 1961. Can we imagine Ted here, exactly as it is? Photo accessed from Hunt Junior High facebook page.

their shared love of skiing, especially night skiing at Snoqualmie Pass, Washington (Morris 2013, 83-4). One day, Ted took Bullat aside at school and showed him a B&W photo of a man and a woman having oral sex. Bullat was shocked. Ted said he found it on the sidewalk, but Sandi Holt says Ted discovered it at her father's: he hid his porn outside in a bag under grass clippings on their North Howard Street property. Meanwhile Ted adopts the role of Vice President of the local Methodist Youth Fellowship. It was reported that on several occasions, Ted was caught masturbating by his peers in the broom closet of his classroom at Hunt Junior High. Rumor has it, some fellow classmates would, on these occasions, open the door and throw cups of water on him and tease him (since when do junior high students carry around cups of water in class?). When asked about this for his PIR, Ted denied the allegation. According to Rule, after gym class Ted showered alone in a private stall. Inevitably, his peers, who showered in the open stalls, bullied him by throwing cold water over him (this sounds more plausible).

Shirley Ann Bridgeford (circa 1958). Photo public domain.

March 9, 1958: Glatman murders Shirley Ann Bridgeford (24) in San Diego County, California.

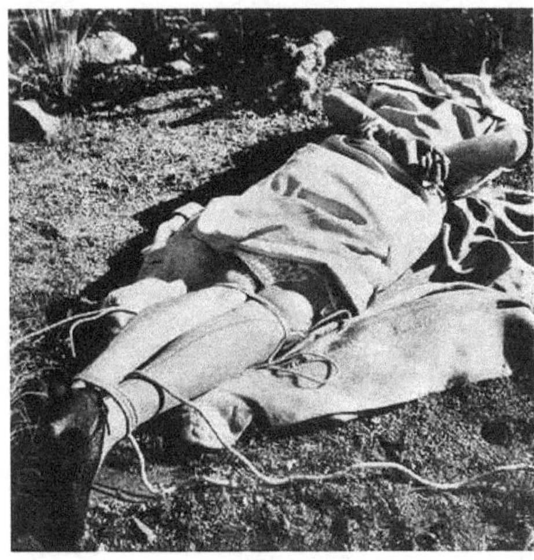

Photo of Shirley Ann Bridgeford Glatman took shortly before strangulating her to death. Photo public domain.

Ruth Mercado. (circa 1958). Photo public domain.

Lorraine Vigil (October 1958). Photo public domain.

Harvey Glatman, taken shortly after his arrest in October 1958. Photo public domain.

May 8, 1958: "Dracula," starring Christopher Lee, debuts.

July 24, 1958: Glatman murders Ruth Mercado (24) in San Diego County, California.

October 27, 1958: Glatman is arrested in Orange County, California, while assaulting Lorraine Vigil (27).

October 31, 1958: Glatman is arrested for the murders of Bridgeford and Mercado, but not Dull.

December 16, 1958: Glatman is sentenced to death for the murders of Bridgeford and Mercado. According to one interpretation of Glatman, it was all about the "rope" (Newton 1998, 177). "I would make them kneel down. With every one it was the same. With the gun on them I would tie this 5-foot piece of rope around their ankles. Then I would loop it up it up around their neck. Then I would stand there and keep pulling until they quit struggling."

NOTES

If you count back 9 months from Ted's birth, you get February 24, 1945. The Japanese surrender occurred on September 2, 1945. For several months or more after the surrender, servicemen slowly filtered back into society. Many of them felt lucky to be alive. There was a general feeling of jubilation in the air that lasted like an extended honeymoon.

Did Ted have an idyllic childhood? From the point of view of freedom, yes. He wasn't sheltered. He could go out into the neighborhood and muck up with kids his own age. But the freedom stopped there. Psychologically Ted was cast off his moorings from the day he was born. There are different versions of Ted's birth and his relationship with his mother. In Louise Bundy's own words she said, "... she had gone with a young man for a short period of time and that after she became pregnant he left and she has not seen him since" (PIR 1975). That man, according to one account was Jack Worthington, "a rakish veteran of the recent war" (M&A 1983, 51). Another version is she was "left pregnant" by "a sailor" (Rule 2006, 7). The veteran and the sailor are probably the same man. According to Rebecca Morris, Rule never believed that story. She speculated that Louise was a victim of incest by her father Samuel F. Cowell (Morris 2013, 25). Morris also quotes Ted's defense attorney Polly Nelson as believing Louise "had made her decision when she left Vermont [...] that she never intended to keep Ted" (Morris 2013, 26). What Nelson actually said was "Ted was three months old by the time his mother retrieved him from the foundling home where she'd placed him for adoption after his birth (Nelson 1994, 155). No one actually knows if leaving Ted for adoption was something Louise willingly did, or whether it was driven by shame and fear of returning home with a child out of wedlock, since accounts generally paint a picture of the home run by Sam Cowell as a fearful place. What we do know for sure is that on the morning of his execution, Louise said, "You'll always be my precious son" (*The Telegraph*, January 24, 1989). In retrospect, it was too little, too late. Louise was just as secretive about her life as Ted was about the part of him that "was hidden, all the time" (*Ogden Standard Examiner*, 24 Jan. 1989). Few people, even in our modern age, fail to recognize the corrosive nature of secrecy. So we cannot hold that against Louise. We just wish it didn't have to be that way.

Secrecy made Ted a stranger in his own house. His half brothers and sisters, whom he often had to baby sit, were aged 7 years younger than him. When first-born Linda was a toddler, Ted was already 10-years old. By the time Linda first started taking shape as a little girl, Ted was entering puberty. No wonder Louise made sure to lock the door (and probably guard it) when Linda was taking a bath (Carlisle 2103, 33). It's tempting to see a connection between this prohibition and rumors of Ted's early sexual proclivities, one of which was to pull the pants down on young girls, drag them into the woods and urinate on them (Morris 2013, 16). One wonders why such behavior was never reported back to Ted's parents. It would have presented one of the many opportunities to intervene and suggests that this story may be more fiction than fact. In any case, in June 1987, Nelson learned that psychologist Arthur Norman "was out in Tacoma and had burst in on Ted's mother [...]. Apparently he had attempted to interview her, but ended up browbeating her, telling her she must have been a bad mother not to have seen the signs in Ted as he was growing up" (Nelson 1994, 172). Despite this, we never learn much else from Louise except her saying: "We did everything parents of the '50s and '60s did", even down to reading *Parent* magazine and Dr. Spock (*Sarasota Herald-Tribune*, February 20, 1989). They were devastated when Ted began confessing days before his execution. Louise said:

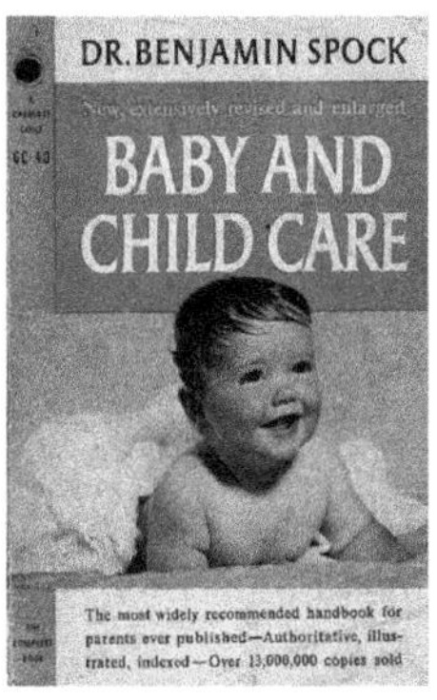

> I don't mean to say he was perfect. I mean, he would do things that would make us angry, and so forth – but what son doesn't? All I can say is, he was the light of our lives. I wouldn't say that if he had been a problem child or constantly misbehaving. We just cannot, in any way, figure what would have [...] caused it (*Ellensburg Daily Record*, January 23, 1989).

On entering junior high (aged about 12) Ted listened to "KGO in San Francisco, a talk show from about 10 p.m. into the early morning hours" (M&A 1989, 21). Ted really got into it. He learned a lot about how different people talked. He would then try out accents on people he knew. He soon became adept at taking on the subtle idiosyncrasies of various characters, a skill that would serve him well when hunting victims. Talkback radio provided Ted with a level of intimacy that he lacked in his home and school life. The late-to-early-morning hours of the show also established a different diurnal pattern in Ted's life. It fostered the nascent vampire in him.

Whether it's something that people pick up after-the-fact, finding faces in clouds, or whether it is a genuine theme running through Ted's childhood, sex-gone-wrong seems to constantly loom large in his life. There is the story about Ted being found naked with a friend's father in a tent during the day while on a Boy Scout outing; the story about Ted masturbating in a schoolroom broom closet and getting caught; of Ted finding porn in the neighborhood trash and showing it to his school friend; of Ted getting pushy and shovey anytime anyone would mention sex or girls. In general, these events tell us more about ourselves and our biases as to what we think might cause serial murder rather than what they actually tell us about Ted. In other words, it takes a lot more than a few isolated incidents to define a pattern.

Similarly, there is a tendency to blame Ted's early home environment for what he became. Near the end of his life, Lewis learned about Sam Cowell and his violence and hypocrisy. It is not known if Ted bore the brunt of this behavior or was just an accidental witness. At the same time, Ted apparently perused Sam's stash of porn in the old man's garden shed as early as the age of three. (Note: this report came from Ted's slightly older cousin Brian. How did Brian know about it? He would have had to see it himself. Why wasn't he adversely affected?) Ted adored Samuel Cowell (M&A 1989, 18), so we have to imagine however warped Sam's world was, it was all Ted knew.

Which raises the specter of the absent father syndrome as another cause of Ted's malaise. All too often, Ted's illegitimacy is blamed as a significant force in his maladaptive development. When questioned by Donald M. Hall for his PIR Ted "displayed marked signs of hostility when asked about his early childhood. Later, in an interview for *Vanity Fair* magazine Lewis said, "many of Bundy's last thoughts and words were about his deep confusion and anger toward his mother" (MacPherson 1989, 142). So what are we to make of this? That Ted murdered young women because he was angry at his mother for not telling him the truth about his biological father? An appealing theory for those inclined to believe unanswered questions of paternity are sufficient to cause someone to become a serial murderer. Freudians would say Ted killed a symbolic image of his mother – in his eyes she was a whore, unfaithful. Ted presumably heard this from Sam, who probably called Louise a whore, a common term in those days. The sense of abandonment looms.

So perhaps the anger was directed more specifically at his early maternal abandonment. Harry Harlow's experiments on Rhesus monkeys in the 1950-60s established for the first time that infant maternal deprivation leads to a raft of behavioral problems later in life (Harlow et al., 1965). The problem here is that Harlow's experiments were conducted at the extreme end of the scale. Ted may have been temporarily motherless, but he received sufficient care to sustain good health. Childhood amnesia would have prevented any conscious recollection of the experience. And within a reasonably short period of time he was back in his mother's care, who, according to Ted's childhood friend Terry Storwick, "loved him very much" (M&A 1983, 57). Moreover, 5.1 percent of births by white women between 1945-49 in America were premarital (Bachu, 1999), and of those a percentage involved paternal abandonment, yet it can be safely said that most of the children from those abandoned conjunctions did not turn into murdering psychopaths. This is not to say that those first 3 months did not leave a lasting impact on Ted. The subtle signals of mimicry that build object relations in the newborn infant may been left partially undeveloped in Ted as a result of that early isolation. One just has to think of those poor Romanian orphans discovered after the fall of the Communist government in 1989. This could partly explain why he had trouble understanding human relations as an adult.

But if this is not enough, we still have to add stories of grandfather Sam talking to unseen presences and his grandmother suffering from (manic) depression and agoraphobia (M&A 1983, 314; Nelson 1994, 154). And to top it off, Ted was taught from an early age that his mother was his sister ... although family members remember Ted calling Louise "Mommy" when he was three (MacPherson 1989, 188). It would seem that not one thing but a row of dominoes was at play. When you add it all up, it's hard to see how the little boy who had potentially inherited schizophrenic-type genes, had been maternally deprived, lied to, witnessed domestic violence, uprooted, isolated and shamed, could ever turn out to be anything but normal. It seems too much for one person to bear.

Should we feel sorry for little Ted? Perhaps we should. But Ted eventually went on to become a man. And to boot, someone who even studied psychology. We will learn about that in subsequent chapters. What are we to make of his decisions then?

References

Bachu, A. (1999). Trends in premarital childbearing. U.S. Department of Commerce, Economics and Statistics Administration, U.S. CENSUS BUREAU.

Brennan, Kathy, Violent Childhood Twisted Killer, Doctor Says, Philly.com, January 25, 1989 (http://articles.philly.com/1989-01-25/news/26122339_1_bundy-louise-cowell-violent-childhood) (Accessed, June 21, 2015).

Carlisle, A. (2013). *I'm Not Guilty* (2nd ed.). Encino, CA: Genius Book Publishing.

Franscell, R. & Valentine, K. B. (2013). *The Crime Buff's Guide to Outlaw Pennsylvania.* Guilford, CT: Globe Pequot.

Hall, D. M. (1975). Presentence Investigation Report. The State of Utah Adult Probation and Parole: Salt Lake City.

MacPherson, M. (1989). Ted Bundy: Anatomy of a serial killer. *Vanity Fair,* May, pp. 144-198.

Michaud, S. & Aynesworth, H. (1989). *Ted Bundy: Conversations with a Killer* (Paperback ed.). New York: Signet.

Michaud, S. G. & Aynesworth, H. (1983). *The Only Living Witness: The True Story of Serial Sex Killer Ted Bundy.* Laguna, TX: Authorlink.

Morris, R. (2013). *Ted and Ann: The Mystery of a Missing Child and Her Neighbor Ted Bundy.* Seattle, Washington: True Books.

Nelson, P. (1994). *Defending the Devil.* New York: William Morrow and Company, Inc.

Newton, M. (1998). *Rope: The Twisted Life and Crimes of Harvey Glatman.* New York: Simon and Schuster.

Rule, A. (1989). *The Stranger Beside Me* (revised edition). London: Warner.

Tanay, E. (2010). *American Legal Injustice: Behind the Scenes with an Expert Witness.* Plymouth, U.K.: Jason Aronson, Inc.

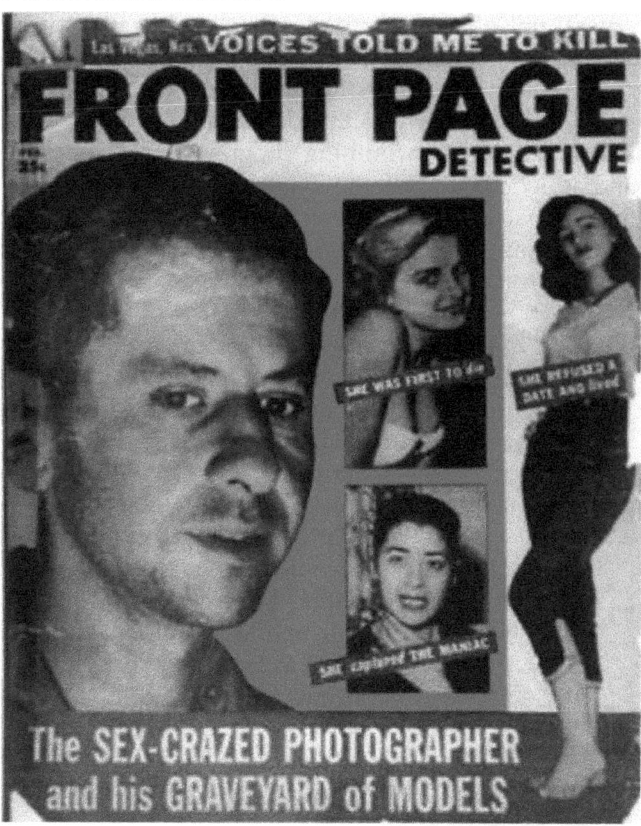

Boulder County Sheriff's Detective Steve Ainsworth used this cover of the 1959 edition of *Front Page Detective* as the front of an evidence file on Harvey Glatman. Photo public domain.

- 1959 -

September 18, 1959: Glatman, aged 31, is executed at San Quentin State Prison, California, in the gas chamber by sodium cyanide. It took him approximately 10 minutes to die.

1959 Nash Rambler (model 6), the kind that Johnnie Bundy drove. Ted despised them. Photo public domain.

- 1960 -

1960: In a conversation with Lewis the day before his execution, Ted told her that as a teenager of about 12-13, "over a two- or three-year period, I would go out at night, a warm night—we had some woods in the back of our house—I would take off my clothes and run around the woods" (Nelson 1994, 277). Explaining this behavior of himself, he said, "… I wasn't flashing on anybody or trying to imagine me stalking anybody, but it was just an innocent kind of sport. So there's nothing at this point that's bad, but I see what was happening, I was beginning to get involved in what they would call, developed a preference for what they call, autoerotic sexual activity. And that's exactly what it was."

When he'd get home, he'd listen talkback radio into the early hours. As people called in to speak their minds, he would formulate questions as if they were talking to him personally (M&A 2000, 21).

Photo from the back dust cover of *The Phantom Prince*, 1981.

From left: Sandra, Glenn, Louise, Linda and Ted. Circa 1960. Photo public domain.

- 1961 -

1961: Richard Bundy born. According to the PIR, Ted said he was closest to his mother and Richard.

Ted enrolls at Wilson High (1202 North Orchard Street, Tacoma). Also according to PIR, Ted advised "that he discontinued dating throughout high school and when queried about this, [...] was unable to offer an explanation. The fact that [...] he didn't date in high school is not necessarily all that unusual; however, what is unusual is his mother's statement that he dated throughout high school, and she was particularly aware of girlfriends who 'surely liked him, because they were always calling him'."

Woodrow Wilson High School. Photo from *Nova* yearbook, 1961.

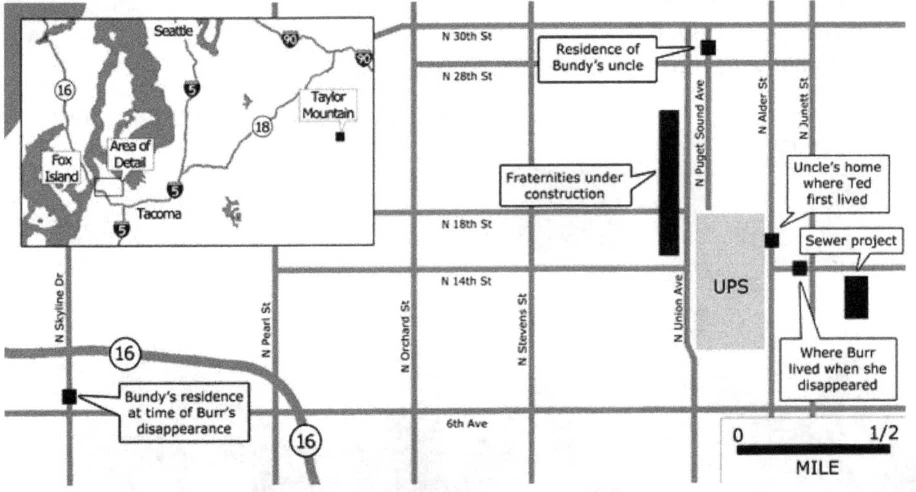

Map showing the relationship between the Burr family and the Bundy family, 1961. Map courtesy Rebecca Morris © 2013.

August 31, 1961: Ann Marie Burr is abducted from her Tacoma home, North 14th Street, just off Alder between Cedar and Junett, next to Gustafson's apple orchard. Ted delivered the *Seattle Post-Intelligencer* or *The Tacoma News Tribune* depending on your source. The paper route was only about 40 customers and was spread out over several miles. Often there were several blocks between subscribers. At the time, Tacoma was a much more innocent city, and it was not unusual for kids to ride bikes all summer, particularly to the University of Puget Sound with its summer swimming program open till 9 p.m. and athletic fields where kids played pick-up games of flag football and fly-up. Univ. Puget Sound is about four blocks from the Burr house, and the campus bisected the paper route. To apply for the route, Ted would have had to travel to 6th Avenue and N. Fife Streets, where the office manager was. In August, the sun usually rose at about 5 a.m. (around time when the kidnapping occurred). It wasn't total darkness, but a time before people got out of bed. After Ann Marie's disappearance, Mr. and Mrs. Holt immediately kept a closer rein on Sandi, and Doug was ordered to walk her to Geiger Elementary school when the new school year began (Morris 2013, 93).

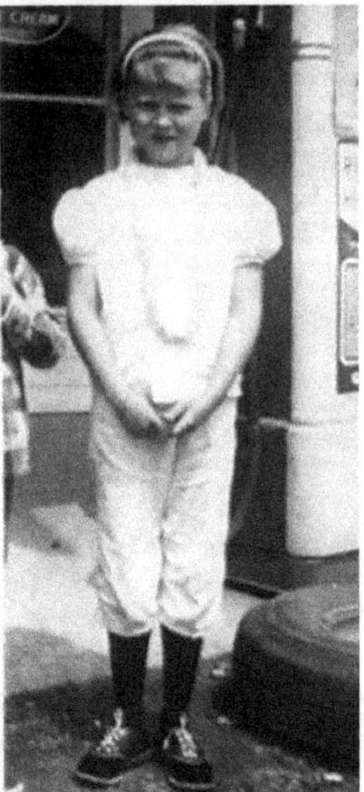

8 year 8-month-old Ann Marie Burr. Photo source: 'Remembering Victims of Ted Bundy' facebook page.

- 1962 -

1962: Ted's sophomore year at Wilson High. Started noticing a perplexing halt to his social development.

October 16-28, 1962: Cuban Missile Crisis.

- 1963 -

November 22, 1963: President John F. Kennedy assassinated by Lee Harvey Oswald in Dealey Plaza, Dallas, Texas.

- 1964 -

March 2, 1964: Harvey Louis Carignan is released on parole from Minnesota State prison. He moves to Seattle, Washington. From late 1972 till his final arrest in Minneapolis on September 24, 1974, he killed at least 5 women, however, he is suspected of killing many more. At least two of those victims were in Washington State around the same time Ted first started killing.

October 27, 1964: Albert Henry DeSalvo is arrested and later confesses to being the Boston Strangler. Ted once told Hugh Aynesworth that his story "was more important than the Boston Strangler's" (M&A 1989, 197).

Left: Harvey Carignan. Right: Albert DeSalvo, 1967. Photos public domain.

A 1963 Wilson High yearbook photo showing Ted, center, leaning at the camera. Photo public domain.

- 1965 -

1965: Ted picked up in Pierce County for suspicion of auto theft and burglary. Record expunged. There is no indication that he was ever confined, but his name was known to juvenile caseworkers (Rule 2006, 11). It is remarkable that Ted's parents never said anything about this in later interviews, since police would have surely consulted them over their suspicions.

February 21, 1965: Malcolm X (40) assassinated by Nation of Islam members, Manhattan, New York.

March 1965: Graduates Woodrow Wilson High School with a 3.02 average out of 4.0 (awarded scholarship to the Univ. Puget Sound). In a classmate's copy of the school magazine *Nova*, he wrote an unusual note:

Ted in graduation robes. Photo public domain.

> Dearest V.,
> The sweetness of the spring time rain runs down the window pain [sic].
> (I can't help it. It just flows out)
> Theodore Robert Bundy
> Peot [sic].

Left: Ted's 1965 Wilson High *Nova* yearbook portrait. Right: Ted in a Political Science class from the same yearbook. Photos public domain.

March 29, 1965: Reported being in a car wreck the previous Friday night (March 26, 1965); said he had a headache and had scratches on his face.

June 1965: Worked for Tacoma City Light as a forklift operator. At night volunteered in a campaign for the House of Representatives.

September 1965: Ends work with Tacoma City Light.

1933 Plymouth Coupe. Photo Public Domain.

September 26, 1965: Bought a 1933 Plymouth Coupe. Enrolled Univ. Puget Sound. To Al Carlisle Ted said he had only one relationship with a girl while at this university. He did say he may have been somewhat hurt by her but could not remember her name nor many details about the event (Psychological Evaluation by Al Carlisle, June 2, 1976, FSA).

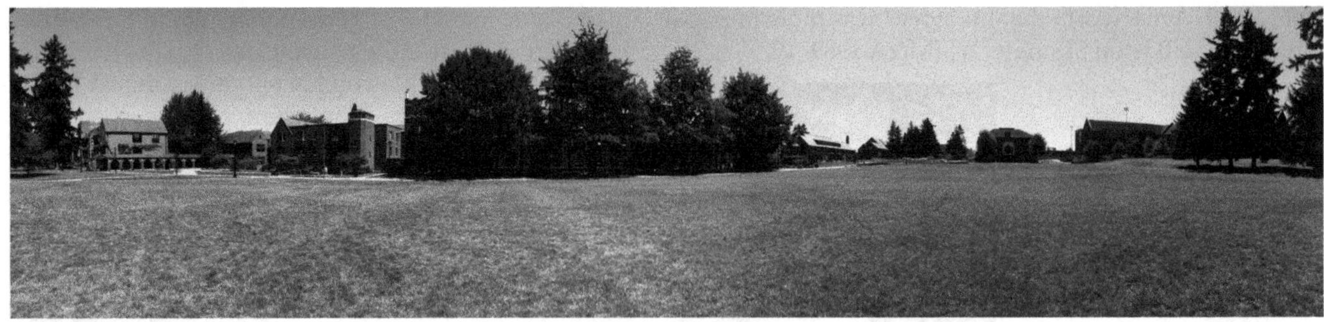

University of Puget Sound. Photo courtesy Vincent Tan © 2015.

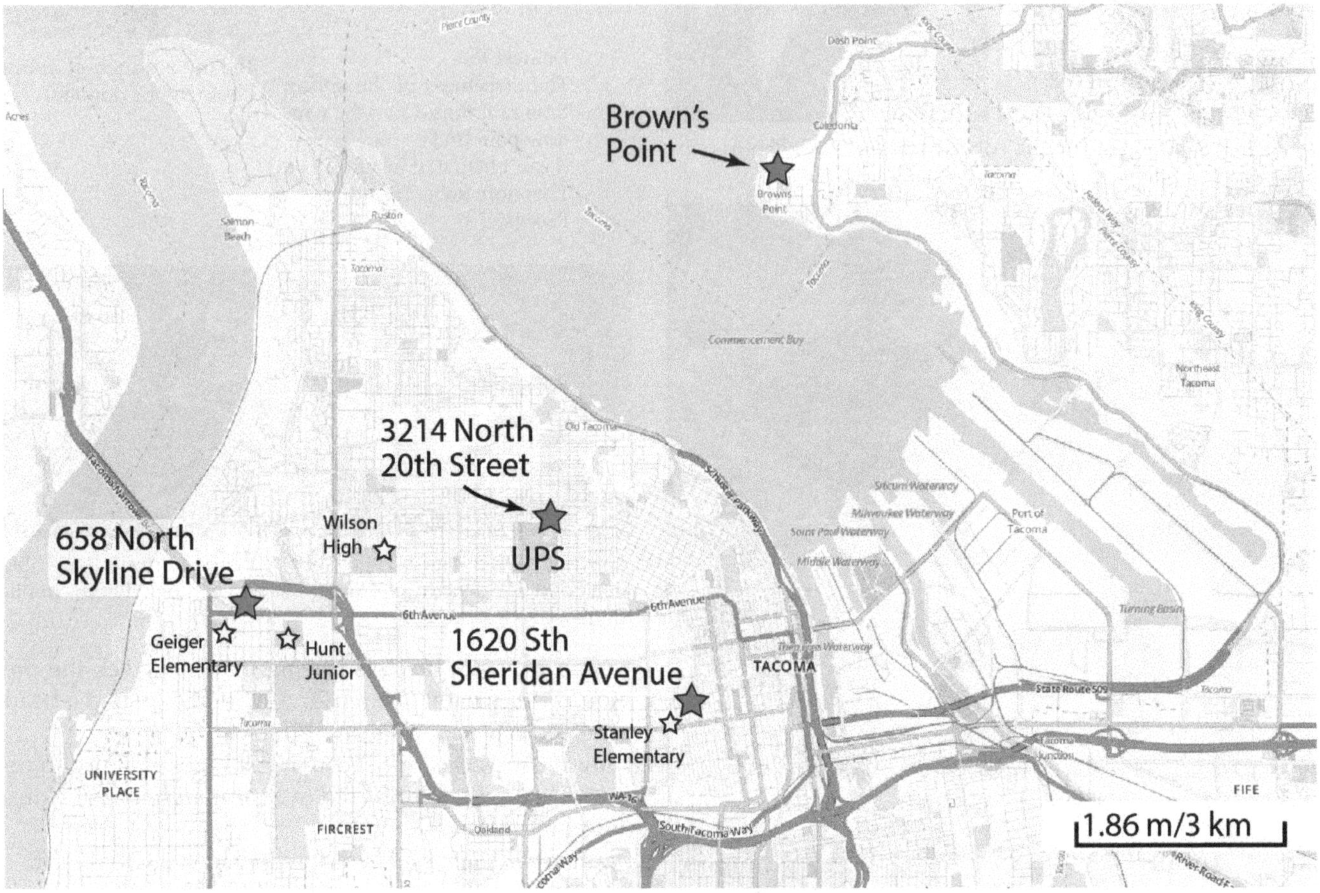

Brown's Point
3214 North 20th Street
Wilson High
UPS
658 North Skyline Drive
Geiger Elementary
Hunt Junior
1620 Sth Sheridan Avenue
Stanley Elementary
TACOMA
UNIVERSITY PLACE
FIRCREST
FIFE
Commencement Bay
Port of Tacoma
6th Avenue
State Route 509
South Tacoma Way
1.86 m/3 km

Tacoma Bundy residences and schools. Map courtesy OpenStreetMap contributors, 2015.

NOTES

Not much is known about Ted's teenage years. By his own admission, he felt somewhat traumatized over not getting chosen for various team sports. But that would pale into insignificance compared to a more profound awakening in him:

> In junior high, everything was fine. Even went to some parties. Nothing I can recall happened that summer before my sophomore year to stunt me or otherwise hinder my progress. But I got to high school and I didn't make *any* progress (M&A 1989, 23).

The progress that Ted is talking about is the maturation of emotions, a sense of growing into adulthood, of understanding the complex and often arbitrary rules of the adult world. This perplexing halt to his social development foreshadowed the prefrontal cortical deficit that would plague him for the rest of his life. In normal teenagers, the prefrontal cortex usually struggles with suppressing the tumultuous hormonally driven behavior of the limbic system, but this eventually settles down as teenagers become adults. Ted never went through this process properly. His prefrontal cortex failed to completely mature, leaving him exposed to more vulnerable teenage-like symptoms even as his body matured into an adult.

Two activities during Ted's teenage years usually receive attention. The first is skiing. Ted described how it enabled him to temporarily join a social group. He engineered his way into their circle by master-minding a crude forgery scheme by bleaching and dying color-coded ski-lift passes. No one ever found out. Nor did anyone find out that Ted had stolen his ski equipment. We will never know, but we can reasonably assume that these two cases represent just the tip of the iceberg when it comes to Ted's thievery. In support of this, we have Rule's discovery that Ted was picked up at least twice in Pierce County on suspicion of burglary and auto theft in 1965 (Rule 2006, 11). Since there are no reports from his school mates regarding this behavior we can also assume that Ted kept it totally secret. Thus, Ted had learned from a very early age to keep a part of himself hidden from those who personally knew him.

The second activity is that during his senior year at Woodrow Wilson High School, Ted worked as a volunteer in a local political race. Ted's under-developed prefrontal cortex, while it hindered his emotional development, did provide him with the benefit of being constantly open to tangential learning. In Ted's own words:

> [...] politics gave me a lot. It gave me a direction and an education in a lot of things tangential to politics – things I needed to know. In politics you can move between the various strata of society. You can talk and mingle with people to whom otherwise you would have absolutely no access (M&A 2000, 25–6).

Ted's statement reveals an enormous amount about himself, things that he himself was aware of. His acute sense of class, his desire to move among the affluent and respected, and the nature of political gatherings and their formal communication structures that contrasted with the unstructured and spontaneous communication patterns of everyday social interactions – interactions that on the whole, baffled Ted. In politics, Ted learned that he could be in control.

With the practice of listening to talkback radio, and now his immersion in politics, Ted had discovered two sources of inspiration that would help him construct what he thought was the right persona to move into adulthood. We will later learn that this first attempt at building a persona would fail when it came to intimate relationships, since talkback radio and politics lack opportunities for the actor to spontaneously inject their inner world into the exchange, something that one-to-one intimate relationships fundamentally expose.

Unfortunately, we have no way of knowing what Ted's inner world was like at this time. All we can do is surmise, based on what clues are available. We know he often engaged in theft behavior. The objects he desired were generally things that he could not afford, but more importantly, they were things that he felt raised his class status. Superficiality is the key to understanding this aspect of Ted's personality. His prefrontal cortex, with its under-developed emotional connections (but facility for tangential learning) meant that Ted could acquire many separate instances of civilization's outer trappings but never integrate them into a coherent whole. Acquisition without comprehension. A perfect recipe for loneliness. For loneliness is not a disease of being alone, but of not knowing one's place in the world.

Terry Storwick relates one story that captures the essence of Ted's loneliness at this time. According to Storwick, "We'd be standing in the hallway [at school] and someone would come up to me and say, 'Hey, we're going to have a party Friday. Can you come over?' Ted would be standing there and he wouldn't be asked. It wasn't that he was singled out for ridicule, but you have to remember that Ted was a very sensitive person – very sensitive" (M&A 1999, 59). Typical for school boys at this age, there'd be lewd and exaggerated claims of sexual desire and conquest, but according to Ted, all of that "went over my head" (ibid). Yet, in interviews later on, Ted admitted that around this time he was also delving into pornography (e.g., Dobson interview, January 23, 1989), so we have to assume that he was more familiar with the machinations of sex than he let on. In terms of his inner world, we might be inclined to conclude that Ted probably had a confused idea about sex, but plenty of desire. His mind was full of images of explicit sex scenes, which fueled that desire, but without the confidence or the experience to express himself, to chat a girl up sociably, he would have turned that energy back onto himself. A self admission during his final interview with Lewis supports this argument (Nelson 1994, 276-7):

> Ted: In my high school years I was really out of touch with my peers—really out of touch. I mean, my old neighborhood friends went on to groups, and high school, being [part of] a bigger community—and I was sort of just stuck. I spent a lot of time with myself.
> Lewis: Why were you out of touch?
> Ted: I don't know. The summer—something happened, something, I'm not sure what it was ... Well, I would think that, at the time I wasn't thinking about anything illegal or criminal or aggressive necessarily. I would fantasize about coming up to some girl sunbathing in the woods, or something innocuous like that.
> Lewis: And what, and you're doing what?
> Ted: I'm just watching her ... It was basically voyeuristic. I mean, among my sexual activities was to look out of my bedroom window, which looked down into the neighbor's bathroom ... Nothing really harmful or threatening, but things which, because I was totally on my own and wasn't sharing this with anybody—nobody could say, "Gee, that's weird, don't do that" you see. I mean, for instance, over a two-or three-year period, I wold go out at night, a warm night—we had some woods in back of our house—I would take off all my clothes and run around the woods.
> Lewis: When you were thirteen, fourteen?
> Ted: Yeah, again, I wasn't flashing on anybody or trying to imagine me stalking anybody, but it was just an innocent kind of sport. So there's nothing at this point that's bad, but I see what was happening. I was beginning to get involved in what they call, develop a preference for that they call, autoerotic sexual activity. And that's exactly what it was.

And "even more inflammatory" as Ted put it, is that around this time—when he was running around the woods naked, masturbating—he was simultaneously getting deeply into detective magazines, absorbing pictures of dead bodies. So we can speculate with relative confidence that this is where Ted's fascination with sex and violence had it genesis, at least in its conscious form.

What Ted does not talk about until much later, is that behind this exposure to sex and violence, lay a deeper strata to his psyche, a driving factor that neither he, nor anyone else will ever adequately explain, namely, his "voices." They must have been present during his teens, otherwise he would not have developed into a serial murderer. But by "voices," we are not implying schizophrenia. As discussed in the introduction, true schizophrenics generally hear voices *external* of their bodies. It would be more appropriate to consider an obsessive compulsive (OCD) pseudo diagnosis for Ted, because his voices were most probably an amplified version of the internal dialogue that every normal human being has. Ted said that these voices became particularly strong when he was drinking heavily, and although he would not admit it, when he was smoking cannabis. Cannabis in particular is linked with the amplification of internal dialogue, and in some cases—in vulnerable individuals—it can lead to psychosis, with the temporary hearing of voices external of the body. Ted never admitted to this experience, so we have to assume his phenotype was an internally driven phenomenon. We do not know if Ted smoked cannabis during his teens, but there is a possibility given that he was living at a time when psychotropic agents in general were becoming more available and accessible. Certainly, by the time he graduated from high school in 1965 at the age of 18, from then on, or shortly afterwards, we can assume Ted was a regular user. Accordingly, we should not underestimate the role cannabis played in facilitating the elaboration of Ted's fantasies vis-a-vis his "voices." By marrying sex and violence during his teenage years, once he started using the drug in early adulthood, his brain was ripe for expressing ideas about women "in a very hateful manner, in a very angry, in a very malicious manner" (Nelson 1994, 286-7).

In presenting a prefrontal cortical model of Ted, then adding OCD, there is a danger of building up a multi-layered cake of diagnoses. We are not specifically adding OCD to Ted's neurological model. What we are suggesting is that his prefrontal deficit expressed a heterogeneous phenotype, which includes the expression of OCD-like components. In support of this, numerous studies show clear linkages between prefrontal cortical dysfunction and OCD (e.g., Huey et al., 2008, Saxena and Rauch, 2000). Recent research demonstrates the role of the orbitofrontal cortex in reward, the anterior cingulate cortex in error detection, the basal ganglia in affecting the threshold for activation of motor and behavioral programs, and the prefrontal cortex in storing memories of behavioral sequences. Notable is that two of these areas, the prefrontal cortex and anterior cingulate gyrus, form the foundation for our neurobehavioral model of Ted. In explaining Ted's steps to becoming a serial killer, we have the difficult task of explaining why he persisted in pursuing the singular line of murder when at any given time along the branching path of his life he could have chosen otherwise. Our brief discussion about Ted's teenage years leaves us with little choice but to consider the very real possibility that Ted was already contemplating murder by the time he finished high school. Bill Hagmaier, who knew Ted better than anyone, said:

> If Ted Bundy is to be believed, and evidence from very hard-working detectives is accurate, he didn't kill his first victim until he was 27 years old. Most serial killers would have struck long before that. Bundy was killing people psychologically, he didn't want to get caught, he recognized [...] the risk at hand, but then when he lost his temper and killed his first victim at 27, then all the things he had dreamed about doing, started to materialize (ViCAP, 2002).

Hagmaier suggests that Ted began "killing people psychologically" a long time before he actually acted out the desire. How long we cannot be sure, but since he obliquely admitted to starting his voyeuristic activities during his teens (looking down into the neighbor's bathroom), and was reading pornography around the same time, we can safely assume his rape fantasies, however immature they were, were already well underway. When you add the detective magazines into the mix, it seems reasonable to assume he may have first started thinking about murder around the time he left school in 1965, aged 18. If that slip of the tongue he made to Keppel in his final interview before his execution is anything to go by, then he first killed in 1972, which more realistically gives him an age of 25 and a period of 7 years of incubation, a period we will examine more closely in the young adult chapter. The key point here is that Ted pursued his agenda methodically for at least that 7-year period. Such extraordinary application calls for an equally extraordinary motivation. From this perspective, it seems that somewhere behind his behavior lay an obsession, and perhaps a compulsion. Something that was sufficiently powerful to swamp any ethical considerations and make Ted choose murder over life.

References

Dobson, J. (1989). Fatal Addiction. www.focusonthefamily.com.

Huey, E. D., Zahn, R., Krueger, F., Moll, J., Kapogiannis, D., et al. (2008). A psychological and neuroanatomical model of obsessive-compulsive disorder. The Journal of Neuropsychiatry and Clinical Neurosciences, 20(4), pp. 390–408.

Michaud, S. & Aynesworth, H. (1989). *Ted Bundy: Conversations with a Killer* (Paperback ed.). New York: Signet.

Michaud, S. G. & Aynesworth, H. (1999). *The Only Living Witness: The True Story of Serial Sex Killer Ted Bundy*. Laguna, TX: Authorlink.

Nelson, P. (1994). *Defending the Devil*. New York: William Morrow and Company, Inc.

Rule, A. (1980). *The Stranger Beside Me*, 2006 revised edition. London: Time Warner Books.

Saxena, S. & Rauch, S. L. (2000). Functional neuroimaging and the neuroanatomy of obsessive-compulsive disorder. Psychiatry Clinical North America, 23(3), pp. 563–86.

ViCAP. (2002). VICAP: On The Trail Of Violence.

- 1966 -

April 1966: Univ. Puget Sound last session ends. Sometime shortly before May Ted sold his Plymouth Coupe and bought a '58 VW bug.

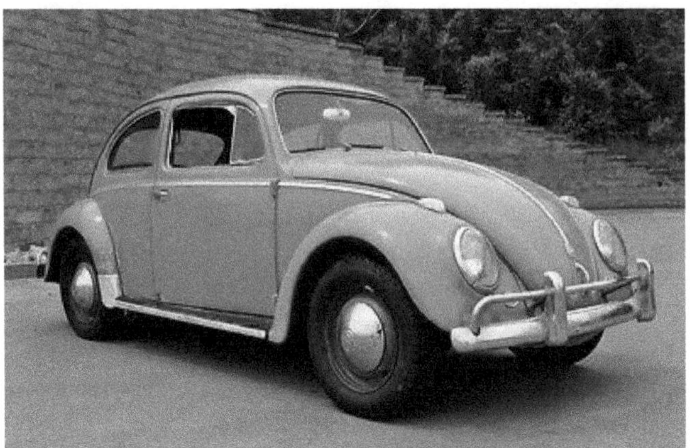

Original 1958 VW bug. Photo public domain.

June 23, 1966: Queen Anne Hill, Seattle, Lisa E. Wick (20) and Lonnie Trumbull (20, deceased) were bludgeoned as they slept in their basement apartment. Wikipedia incorrectly states that Ted worked at the nearby Queen Anne Hill Safeway at the time. Ted did not start working at the Queen Anne Hill Safeway until April 12, 1968. Detective Sergeant Herb Arnold said a bloodstained piece of wood three inches square and 18 inches long, apparently taken from a nearby garage, was found in a nearby vacant lot and was believed to have been the weapon used in the beatings. Purses of the two girls were found but police declined to say where. Both girls were found in their nightclothes in their beds, the walls spattered with blood, when their roommate, Joyce Bowe, came home in the morning around 9:30 a.m. When she returned the front door was unlocked and a light was on. Neither girl was sexually assaulted. Both had been repeatedly clubbed on the head. Evidence led detectives to believe the attack may have occurred as late as 3:00 a.m. instead of before midnight as was first estimated. An employee of United Airlines said he telephoned Miss Wick about flight plans around 11:45 p.m. The employee said Miss Wick took the information and said she would relay it to Miss Trumbull, who was asleep. Lisa Wick, barely alive, was taken to the King County Hospital. She had multiple fractures of the skull and was listed as critical. There was the suggestion the only reason Miss Wick survived the attack was she was wearing hair rollers to bed, which may have cushioned some of the blows. Police were using "every available man" in the manhunt Police Chief Frank Ramon said.

Lisa E. Wick (left) and Lonnie Trumbull (right) as they appeared for United Airlines. Photo source *The Owosso Argus-Press*, June 24, 1966 .

June 24, 1966: Police develop a "vengeance theory" of the stewardess attack saying they have no evidence the crime was committed by a casual prowler.

June 25, 1966: Terry Allman, a deputy sheriff who lives on Vashon Island, said he had been with Miss Trumbull on Wednesday, leaving the apartment about 5:00 p.m. He talked with her by phone around 10:00 p.m. A neighbor George Stoss said he heard an automobile roar away from the apartment building shortly after midnight and "at the same time I heard someone scream." One neighbor said she heard a car; others heard nothing. Police questioned a 17-year-old youth about the attack Friday, but released him after he passed a lie-detector test.

June 29, 1966: At least six lie detector tests were conducted but no clues were turned over to help solve the case, according to Captain Paul Lee, Chief of Seattle Homicide Division.

June 30, 1966: A bartender, Homer Sims, told police a man "about 30 years old" was in his tavern about 8:00 or 9:00 p.m. asking directions on June 15. Sims said the man had a city map and asked how to reach the 2400 block on 8th Avenue where Trumbull and Wick were attacked. According to Lieutenant Frank Moore, investigators were not that "excited about this lead."

July 15, 1966: Police develop a composite sketch of the assailant and a witness who could identify him. Miss Wick told detectives *she was awake* when the intruder bludgeoned Miss Trumbull to death in her sleep. He then turned on her. According to Wick, the assailant was white, about 30 years old, 5 feet 10 inches tall and weighed about 165 pounds. He had thinning blond hair. She could not say whether she had ever seen the man before, however, she said she could identify the man if she saw him again.

July 20, 1966: Lisa Wick is shown photos of suspects, including one of Richard Speck, a suspect in the slaying of eight student nurses in Chicago.

September 1966: Ted accepted for transfer to Univ. Wash..

September 3, 1966: Lisa Wick leaves hospital.

September 26, 1966: Ted enrolls and attends University of Washington. Studies Chinese. Lives in McMahon Hall dormitory. Larry Foster, one of Ted's clustermates and a senior that year said: "[He was a] normal guy, good dresser, very personable. [...] His [quirks] were no greater than those of others." Foster remembers his roommate as a staunch Republican, with a love of skiing but as yet undecided on a career path. Foster would occasionally offer Bundy words of advice about his future after graduating. "I suggested the military as a place to get some

Univ. Wash. campus entrance coming in from 12th Avenue NE. Photo courtesy Vincent Tan © 2015.

McMahon Hall, circa 1967. Photo courtesy Univ. Wash. Campus Photograph Collection.

further skills and then see what he wanted to do," Foster said.

October 2, 1966: Nancy Leitner (21) and Pamela Nater (20) disappear from a skin diving club picnic in the Alexander Springs Recreation Area of the Ocala National Forest in Lake County, Florida. Gerard John Schaefer would be later linked to their murder. The bones of Leitner and Nater were found in Ocala National Forest in 2007, twelve years after Schaefer was murdered in prison on December 3, 1995.

Nancy Leitner (undated, left) and Pamela Nater (undated, right). Photos public domain.

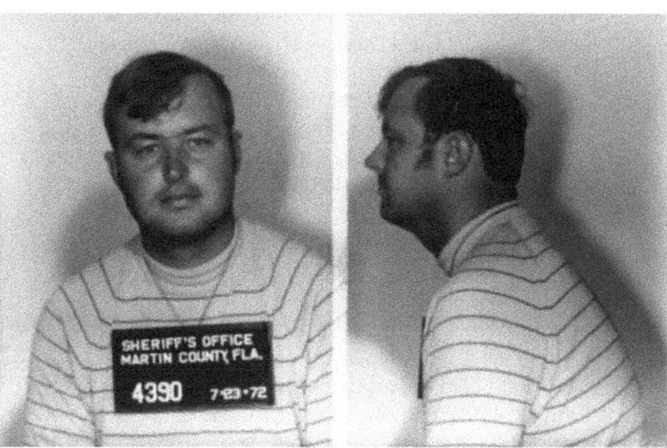

Gerard John Schaefer, July 23, 1972 mugshot that led authorities to the belated realization they had caught a serial killer. Photo public domain.

December 31, 1966: Last attendance Univ. Wash. for the year. Moves out of McMahon Hall into 5015 16th Northeast, Seattle.

- 1967 -

March 1967: Meets Diane Edwards at Snoqualmie while skiing. Snoqualmie opens at start of December. According to Rule, Ted met her in Spring 1967, perhaps last snow – February-March. The relationship develops through the Summer of Love – August 1967. In a personal communication to Carlisle in 1975, Diane Edwards said of Ted:

> He was pitifully weak when we argued. This was my main criticism of him after a year and a half of our relationship. He kowtowed to me. He wasn't strong. He wasn't real masculine. If I got mad at him because of something he did he felt apologetic about

it. He wouldn't stand up for himself. There was no use getting mad because he didn't react. And, the things I primarily got mad at him for were that he lied when it wasn't necessary that he had to. He would say something he knew would sound good to me rather than telling me the truth (Carlisle 2014, 48).

Seattle skyline, circa 1967. Photo public domain.

Ted talked about Diane on February 20, 1978, after his final arrest.

Patchen: Tell us about Diane Edwards.
Bundy: We were incompatible. […] she wanted a great deal more. […] she was a perfectionist of a kind. She wanted everything just right. She was the only child of her father who I never got to know that well. [I met him only] on two or three occasions. […] I think we were both about the same age, she maybe a few months older. […] She could dance good. […] She was a model at one time. […] We were thinking about getting married. […] We talked about children. […] I think she had reservations about having children. She wanted other things at the time. […] The last time I saw her was, I think it was January 1st, 1974, because after that she lived in San Francisco. […] Diane knew about Liz. […] She was a tall girl, she was about five ten. Uh, she had dark hair, long dark hair. Very beautiful.
Chapman: […] you called [Diane] and she rejected you?
Bundy: Diane was very subconscious about being married. […] the engagement situation falling through […] it had her upset. Okay? She rejected me. I don't care how it turned out. […] it was a relief. (Florida State Archives, Tape #2, Side # 1, Part D, February 20, 1978).

Stanford Univ. library, San Francisco. Photo courtesy Liam Quin: "March/April 2006 – Redwood City, America" (2006).

March 17, 1967: Withdraws from Univ. Wash.
June 1967: Attends summer school Stanford Univ. on a scholarship, does intensive studies in Chinese. Compulsive voyeurism starts around this time.

Ted and Diane, presumably circa late 1973. Photo public domain.

Yearbook photo of Diane Marjorie Jean Edwards (undated). Source unknown. Photo public domain.

Diane drove a 1967 Ford Mustang. Photo public domain.

June 25, 1967: Ted arrives San Francisco. Address Palo Alto.
June 26, 1967: Attends Stanford.
July 1967: Attends Stanford.
July 8, 1967: Ted has dinner in San Francisco with Diane Edwards. When Ted drops Diane at the airport for her return to Seattle and studies at Univ. Wash. the next day, he still feels he cannot give up on the relationship.
Later in July, 1967: Ted flies to Seattle for one night to try and salvage his relationship with Diane. The effort fails and they break up.
August 1967: Stanford studies end; attains a "C" grade. In Seattle, Ted is befriended by an elderly lady, Mrs. Fer-

ris, a pastry chef at the Seattle Yacht Club. She helps him get some menial jobs. In a personal communication to Carlisle in 1975, Mrs. Ferris had this to say about Ted:

> I'm a woman 70 years old and I know what goes on but he doesn't have it. I don't know if he was high on dope or liqueur, but he was sure a peculiar person. He was going with a girl from San Francisco. He would portray himself to be a really big politician to try to get in good with her family. He sometimes used a British accent. He borrowed Havilland China and sterling silver and linen from me and had her there for dinner and he was going to show her what a fine cook he was, and what a man he would be around the house. He got her drunk and they spent the night there.
>
> He borrowed my car several times to go out on night trips. I was scared to death when he was gone. Something was up because he just wasn't running true to form of where he was going or what he was doing.
>
> He got him a job [sic] at the Olympic Hotel and went through the men's employee lockers and found some old tuxedo waiter's clothes (pants, coat, etc.). He got them fixed up and would dress himself up as if he were the headwaiter in some restaurant. He lived for a short while with an elderly couple and they were going to go to Norway. They finally had to ask him to move.
>
> I helped him get a job at Safeway for a short while and he just quit, not even going back to work to tell them he was leaving.
>
> He borrowed $100.00 from me. I tried to get it back but he always had some reason why he couldn't pay me back right then. He never did pay me back. I talked to his mother once and asked her if she would appeal to him as a man to return the $100.00 I loaned to him. His mother said, "He doesn't live here anymore and we're not responsible for anything he does."
>
> He is a very, very peculiar boy. He was just kind of sneaking around. He'd be on the telephone when you'd least expect him to be. He would tell you he was going to be one place and he would be somewhere else. He left the city on a plane and he said he was going to Colorado to be a ski instructor there. Something happened and he came back.
>
> He went to Pennsylvania and drove his uncle's Cadillac and came back flat broke looking for a job. All in all, he's just a very weird boy.
>
> I worked with him at the Seattle Yacht Club when he was a busboy and I got him a job at the Olympic Hotel. Then he got a job at Safeway. Then he got into politics and I called and told [his supervisors] he was a strange boy and a little on the crooked side.
>
> He was six weeks at the Yacht Club and they let him go. He wasn't supposed to eat the food, but he was always in the pantry eating all the fresh foods and whipped cream he could get and all the fancy foods he could eat. He would grab them and take them to his locker.
>
> He had kind of a running game of his own. He didn't have too much to do with his family. He borrowed my car a couple of times saying he was going home. Ted never talked about his family or showed much affection for them. He spent quite a bit of time at a friend's house, an antique dealer who had been in prison and this guy went back at least once after Ted knew him.
>
> Ted told me he was studying Chinese at the University of Washington. When the staff seemed to get close he told me he was going to skip out and go to Taiwan.
>
> I have been suspicious from the day those two girls were killed at Lake Sammamish with that "Ted." I remember seeing him in an Albertson's store in Green Lake with a cast on his arm. I was going to do something about it, but living alone I was afraid to do more than what I had already done.
>
> He seemed to have mental problems. He had ways of getting money. He had a very expensive overcoat with a fur collar that came from the Yankee Peddler, one of the men's best dress shops in the University District. He had a key to the men's dormitory at the University of Washington long after he was no longer a student there. He carried the key with him and used to go in there and sleep on the lounge couches when he didn't have any place to go and he would

Seattle Yacht Club (July 20, 2015). Photo courtesy Vincent Tan © 2015.

> take clothing and things from the dorm.
>
> I was willing to give him the benefit of the doubt because I felt he needed help. I felt there was something very, very wrong in his life and it seemed that he was quite an unloved child. That's the way that it hit me. I just kind of felt I could help him, but I finally decided I was just knocking my head against a wall and I just had to stop it and I couldn't have him taking my car and keeping it out until 3:00 am or 4:00 am in the morning and telling me, "I'll be back at midnight" and me sitting up waiting.
>
> He told me he was going on trips. He would be gone all these hours and would come back all hepped up. He did this two or three times. I thought he might be trafficking dope (Carlisle 2014, 44-47).

In a separate report Mrs. Ferris informed investigators that Ted would often befriend older people, gain their confidence, then as an apparent favor, take items to the junkyard to sell, or take their shopping lists to the store, often not returning with food or money (KCA, February 21, 1978). In the same report, claims are made that Ted experimented with bisexuality around this time.

September 1967: Starts studying Urban Planning and Sociology at Univ. Wash. but is failing. Ted informs the university he will not be attending the winter semester of 1968. Continues work at Seattle Yacht Club. Ted's job description was he "parked cars." He often drove people from the club home who were too drunk to drive. Lives at 5015 16th N.E. Has 873 N. 16th on registration card for Univ. Wash..

End 1967: Ted starts considering himself the actor rather than spectator in his violent sexual fantasies according to Polly Nelson and Dorothy Lewis (Nelson 1994, 279). According to an un-named "intimate" friend of Ted's who wanted the story told:

> "Ted believed that he was demonically possessed. It began in college. He called it 'the Beast.' it was not your typical demon. It spoke to him, but it had no human emotion, no conscience. At first, he was afraid. The demon was totally contrary to his make-up. But then he conditioned himself to it and got so he could tolerate it. Finally, Ted gave himself over. He joined the demon and got to like pornography. He believed that other serial killers were also possessed. He struggled with the demonic influence, marked by lust and feelings of violence, even in prison. But through prayer and reading God's word, he subdued the demon somewhat. However, he never felt that the Beast ever left him entirely" (Nobile 1989, 45).

- 1968 -

1968: Ted's parents move to 3214 North 20th Street, Tacoma. The term "sociopathic personality" gives way to "personality disorder, antisocial type" (Tanay 2010, 128).

January 1968: Ends works at the Seattle Yacht Club.

January 18, 1968: Registered for Winter quarter Univ. Wash. but withdrew. Travels to San Francisco. Flew to Denver, skied Aspen and Colorado. Then went on to Philadelphia, Pennsylvania and Fayetteville, Arkansas, to see his musical professor uncle Jack Cowell who had moved there to take up a position at the Univ. Arkansas. Ted's cousin Edna remembers his stop in Fayetteville: "He asked my parents for money. I don't remember if they gave him any," she said. Ted stayed a few days, Edna Cowell took him out for a meal, to a 1950s-style drive-in, and then he continued his trip east. Ted went on to NY and Burlington, Vermont, where, according to Rule, he got an extract of his birth certificate and learns for certain that his mother is Louise and that he is illegitimate (Rule 2006, 16). Spends two nights in New York and pays his first visit to a strip joint. He then drove back to Philadelphia, Arkansas and Tacoma.

3214 North 20th Street, Tacoma. The Bundy family was still living here when Ted was arrested in 1975. Photo courtesy Kristina Erickson © 2016.

Louise and Johnnie Bundy at their Tacoma residence (circa 1989). Photo public domain.

Linda Slawson (undated). Photo source: findagrave.com.

January 26, 1968: Linda Kay Slawson (19) of Aloha is last seen selling encyclopedias in the Portland, Oregon, in the neighborhood where Jerome Henry Brudos lived with his wife, Ralphene, and their two kids. Brudos lured her into his garage, bludgeoned her senseless, then strangled her to death. Afterwards he told his wife to take the kids out to eat hamburgers. While his family was out, he dressed Slawson in high heels and lingerie, cut off one of her feet and put it in the freezer. That night as his family slept, he tied her body to an automobile transmission and dumped her in the Willamette River. Slawson's body was never recovered, but Brudos would later tell police he killed her and threw her body into the Willamette from the Wilsonville bridge on Interstate 5, Oregon. He had a fetish for women's shoes from the age of five and reportedly attempted to steal the shoes of his first grade teacher. He also had a fetish for women's underwear and claimed he would steal them from neighbors as a child. He spent his teens in and out of psychotherapy and mental hospitals. He began to stalk local women as a teenager, knocking them down or choking them unconscious, and fleeing with their shoes.

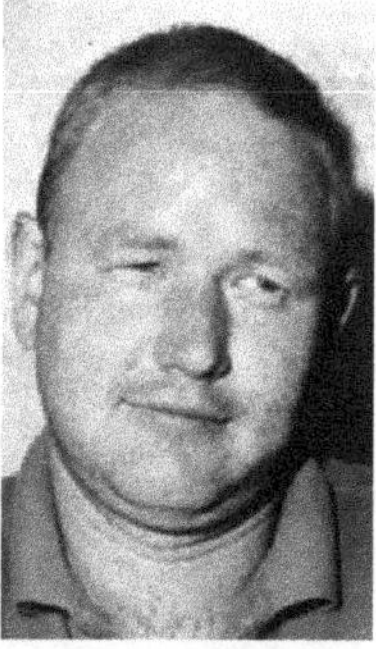

Jerry Brudos (undated). Photo public domain.

February-March 1968: Ted back in Seattle. Gets a job at the Seattle Olympic Hotel as a bus boy, but is let go for suspected thievery after only one month.

The Olympic Hotel, Seattle (now the Fairmont-Olympic Hotel). Photo rights obtained. Image dated October 10, 2010.

March 1968: Diane Edwards totally breaks off relationship with Ted after she discovered he used her money and credit cards to buy things for himself.

Captain Herb Swindler. Photo source: *The Stranger Beside Me* (Rule, 2006).

April 1968: Appointed Seattle chairman and assistant chairman of the New Majority for Nelson Rockefeller, and wins trip to Miami for the Republican National Convention. Dates and pets Cathy Swindler, Seattle Police Crimes Against Person's Unit Captain Herb Swindler's daughter. Sometime later, Richard Larsen quoted Cathy as saying: "Ted Bundy was a figure that people met and loved. I mean, I thought I loved Ted Bundy. Not totally in a romantic way ... but in terms of being moved by what he said and his feelings for other humans beings ... if you know him, you can't help but have a great deal of affection for him as a human being" (Larsen 1980, 7).

April 4, 1968: Martin Luther King Jr. assassinated by James Earl Ray in Memphis, Tennessee.

April 12, 1968: Starts work as a "stocker" at Queen Anne Hill Safeway, 2100 Queen Anne Avenue North. Befriends 'Richard,' an ex-con, drug dealer and thief. First reference to Ted's use of cannabis (Kendall 1981, 34).

June 1968: Diane Edwards graduates at the Univ. Wash.

July 1968: Stephanie Vikko (16, no image) is reported missing in Portland, Oregon. Brudos is the leading suspect. There are no photos or further information relating to Vikko until her remains are found on March 18, 1969.

July 26, 1968: Stops going to work at Safeway.

Art Fletcher (undated). Photo public domain.

September 1968: Works as driver for Art Fletcher, a Republican nominee for lieutenant governor. By his own account, loses virginity to an older woman (just before turning 22) while totally inebriated.

October–November 1968: Works in a Seattle department store selling shoes.

November 25, 1968: Brudos victim Jan Whitney (23), a Univ. Oregon student of McMinnville, is last seen in Eugene, Oregon. Her car was later found abandoned at

Panorama of Queen Anne Hill Safeway, Seattle. Ted worked here for a while then stopped abruptly, without explanation. Photo courtesy Vincent Tan © 2015.

a rest stop along Interstate 5 between Salem and Albany.

December 1968: Ted arrives in Philadelphia, takes a room at 4039 South Warner Street, Lafayette Hill, Sam Cowell's new residence. Starts visiting New York porn houses along 42nd Street.

Jan Whitney (undated). Photo public domain.

4039 South Warner Street, Lafayette Hill, Philadelphia. Photo courtesy Karen Valentine © 2013.

42nd Street New York, 1966. Photo public domain.

- 1969 -

January 1969: Enrolls for one semester Temple University, Philadelphia. According to Al Carlisle, Ted chose Temple because a person could get a law degree there without first needing a bachelor's degree. The university was located in an area that had a lot of street crime and gang violence. The new buildings had no windows. There was a guard by some of the doors, and playgrounds had barbed wire around them. Ted's goal was to study the nature of student populations to find a way to get the community involved in change. But Ted couldn't concentrate. He skipped classes, claiming he was depressed. In fact, he had hoped the change of place would solve his "problem" but he quickly realized it wouldn't. He would often go out in the evenings and stalk women. By this time he'd learned to do it without

Campus scene at Temple University, circa 1960s. Photo public domain.

arousing suspicion. He is reported to have stayed with an aunt on his mother's side while he studied.

Through February 1969: Continues studies at Temple University. In his last interview with Lewis and Nelson on January 23, 1989, Ted relates how he bought a fake mustache, fake hair, hair dye, and registered in a seedy motel under a false name in New York while visiting the famous flesh spots on 42nd Street. He worked up a plan to follow some woman in some hotel to her room and rush in on her and rape her (Nelson 1994, 281).

Late February 1969: Approaches a woman in Ocean City, New Jersey, tries to abduct her but she escapes.

March 1969: Returns to Washington State. Leaves Univ. Wash., rents a room at 4143 12th Avenue N.E. University District. Landlords, Freda Rogers, an elderly woman who, along with her husband Ernst, owned a neat, white two-story frame house. Ted rented a large room in the southwest corner of the house. He ended up living there from March/May 26, 1969 – September 1, 1974. In that time he helped Ernst who was ailing with the heavy chores and gardening, a promise he kept. The house is only a few blocks from the Univ. Wash. campus.

Rogers' rooming house (4143 12th Avenue N.E. 19 July 2015). Ted lived on the second floor in the southwest corner (top right). Photo courtesy Spencer Wallace © 2016.

March 18, 1969: Stephanie Vikko's remains are found in a wooded area northwest of Forest Grove, Oregon.

March 27, 1969: Brudos victim Karen Sprinker (19) is last seen alive in the Meier & Frank parking lot, downtown Salem, Oregon. Sprinker was a medical student studying at Oregon State University. The cause of her death was determined to be asphyxiation. Both her breasts had been sliced off and, although she was still wearing the clothing she had on the last time anyone saw her alive, her bra had been changed to a black one that was too big for her. The cups had been stuffed with paper.

Karen Sprinker. (undated). Photo source: findagrave.com.

April 21, 1969: Brudos encounters Sharon Wood (24) in a parking garage at Portland State University. Sharon attempted to fend off Jerry's attack by biting his thumb. Jerry beat her unconscious but an oncoming car caused him to flee the scene of the crime. Police failed to draw a connection between this event and the previous disappearance of women in the area.

Sharon Wood (undated). Photo public domain.

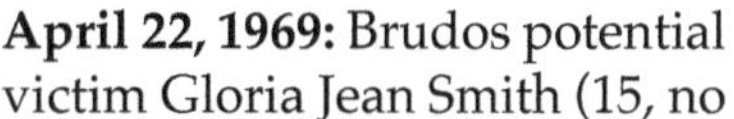

April 22, 1969: Brudos potential victim Gloria Jean Smith (15, no image) is nearly abducted while walking near Parrish Middle School, Salem, Oregon. Smith eventually identifies Brudos as the man who attempted to kidnap her and take her to a green Volkswagen Karmann Ghia, a car later identified as belonging to Brudos' mother. Jerry also encountered Liane Brumley (14). He attempted to abduct her into his car but she screamed and escaped. There are no known photos of these girls.

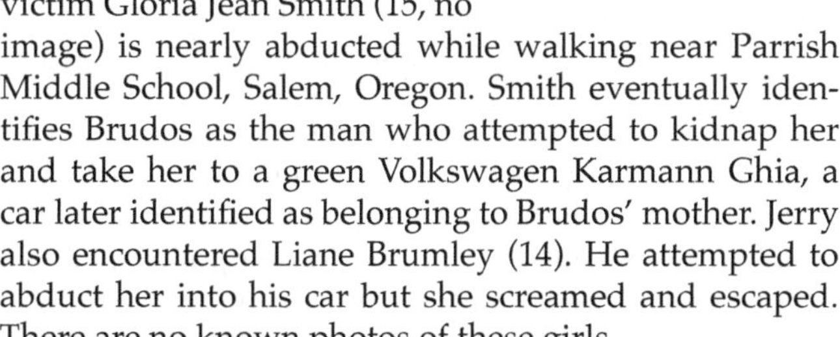

April 23, 1969: Brudos victim Linda Dawn Salee (22) of Beaverton is last seen alive at the Lloyd Center parking lot in Portland, Oregon.

Sometime in May 1969: Ted drove down and stayed with friends for 2-3 weeks in San Francisco. According to Rule, Ted sneaks up behind Diane Edwards in San Francisco and surprises her.

May 10, 1969: The body of Brudos victim Linda Salee is found in the Long Tom River near Monroe, Oregon, weighted down. She had been strangled and raped and a cloth was tied around her neck.

Linda Salee (undated). Photo public domain.

May 12, 1969: The body of Brudos victim Karen Sprinker is found in the Long Tom River weighted down. An autopsy revealed she had been "smothered or choked."

May 18, 1969: Brudos is identified as a possible suspect after a tip from an Oregon State University student.

May 26, 1969: Brudos' home on the 3100 block of Center Street Northeast, Salem, is searched by police who find copper wire, rope, and pictures of female victims.

May 29, 1969: Brudos is arrested on a charge of armed assault related to the April 22 incident with Gloria Smith.

May 30, 1969: Susan Davis (19) and Elizabeth Perry (19) were stabbed to death near Somers Point, New Jersey. The bodies were found by Parkway employee Wood Faunce 20 feet apart hidden under a bed of leaves in dense pine and oak woods 200 yards from Milepost 31.9 on Garden State Parkway in Egg Harbor Township, just by the bridge over Patcong Creek, north of the Somers Point/Ocean City exit. Susan Davis was nude, and her clothes were in a pile near her. Elizabeth Perry was dressed except for her underwear, which was missing. The coroner said the bodies were too decomposed to determine whether they had been sexually assaulted, but did determine they had eaten breakfast about an hour before they were murdered. Both had been stabbed with a penknife. Perry died of a penetrating stab wound to her right lung; she also had stab wounds in her abdomen and side of her neck. Davis died of a wound in her neck that cut her larynx; she also had wounds on the left side of her abdomen and right side of her neck. Police found a skin diver's watch near the scene believed to belong to the murderer. A jacket bearing the name 'Susan Davis' was also found nearby.

Top: Elizabeth Perry (undated). Bottom: Susan Davis (undated). Photos public domain.

The girls had stayed in Syben House, Ocean City, since the Tuesday before. They drove off at 04:30 "to beat Friday traffic." Had breakfast at Somers Point Diner. A state trooper found their powder-blue convertible abandoned by the Parkway two miles north of the Somers Point interchange around noon. The car keys were found tossed a short distance away from the bodies. There was one witness who says that they may have picked up a young man with his arm in a sling, who was hitchhiking. Others think they may have left with two young men who they had met earlier at Somers Point Diner. The bodies were located about 150 yards from the abandoned car at about 1:30 p.m.

Richard Larsen, author of *The Deliberate Stranger*, believes Ted made the trip in a car borrowed from a Temple University faculty member. Larsen also learned that one of the victims had been tied to a tree with her hair. Larsen obtained a tape made in October 1986 wherein

Ocean City, New Jersey, 1969. Photo public domain.

Ted talked about his life in Philadelphia in 1969 with forensic psychologist Arthur Norman. Ted explained to Norman that around that time he was getting more and more into violent pornography. He repeated the same story to Lewis the day before his execution, in January 1989. Where his story differed, however, was his description of what happened next.

> "Talk about being pushed to the edge," Ted said on the tape. He began referring to himself in the third person. "So, after being more or less detached from people for a long period ... didn't have any friends, didn't really go anywhere, just more or less had school and then sort of entertained himself with his pornographic hobby and drove the shore and watched the beach and just saw young women lined up along the beach," he said. "You know, it's like an overwhelming kind of vision, eventually found himself tearing around that place for a couple of days. And eventually, without really planning anything, he picked up a couple of young girls. And ended up with the first time he had ever done it" (*The Enquirer*, May 31, 1993).

Investigator Major Thomas Kinzer, one of the original detectives on the murders, said that two New Jersey detectives tried to interview Ted in 1988 about the Somers Point slayings but he would not discuss the case. Kinzer said he did find Ted's aunt in Philadelphia, who told him that her nephew could not have gone to the Jersey Shore that weekend because he had been in an auto accident and had a cast on his leg. No record of the accident was found. Kinzer said Ted was such a loner at Temple that no one even remembered him. "All we had was his records," he said. Some people believe Ted was responsible for the double murder but provide no evidence tying him to the crime, including placing him in Ocean City on the day that it happened or how he did it.

Ted is not the only suspect. Another candidate is Gerald Stano who gave details of at least 41 murders on the east coast when he was captured in 1980. He often stabbed his victims. According to one policeman, "He thinks about three things: stereo systems, cars, and killing women." Tommy Ray, a homicide detective with the Polk County Sheriff's Office in the 1980s, said Stano exaggerated his record of killings, thinking the resulting investigations would indefinitely delay his execution. Nevertheless, police took Stano's confession serious enough to send two detectives down to Florida State Prison to interview him, but he didn't know any of the specifics of the case, had the murder taking place on the wrong side of the Parkway, and got all of the details wrong. Stano was basically a coward before men and a thug against women. In his own words: "As for the question, 'What made me kill and kill again,' I can't really answer that, except like this. I would be drinking, and lonely, and thinking about all the couples having fun together, and here I am single having no fun at all. Then I would go out riding around, and I would find a girl walking, and hopefully she would get into my car, but she would end up making some kind of remark about my weight, music or looks. That would turn me into a different person, altogether" (Montane & Kelly 2011, 5).

Map showing where the bodies of Susan Davis and Elizabeth Perry were found in relation to Ocean City, New Jersey. Bing Aerial Map image courtesy USGS Earthstar Geographics SIO © Microsoft Corporation.

Murder Probe Focus Shifted Out Of Area

Ann Arbor News, June 4, 1969

Washtenaw County police officials, stymied in their investigation of the murder of five young women in this area in the past two years, were looking today toward New Jersey and Midland, Mich., in the quest for new information.

Ann Arbor police say they are in contact with officers in Egg Harbor Township, N.J., who are investigating the stabbing deaths of Susan Davis of Camp Hill, Pa., and Elizabeth Perry of Excelsior, Minn. The partially nude bodies of the two 19-year-old girls were found yesterday about 150 yards from their abandoned 1966-model car on the Garden State Parkway near Somers Point, N.J. The bodies, covered with leaves, had been stabbed repeatedly.

Local officers say they are also having conversations with Midland County Sheriff's Department detectives who are holding a former Ann Arbor man in the kidnapping, rape and attempted murder of a 24-year-old divorcee. Frank James Anderson, 31, now of Bay City, was arrested shortly after the woman, also of Bay City, was found wandering nude along a country road north of Midland, her body slashed and stabbed.

Assistant Prosecutor Robert Fraser of Midland said Anderson, who lived in Ann Arbor some years ago, followed the woman from a tavern where she works near the Bay City State Park about 3:30 a.m. Sunday. A short time later when the victim left her home to drive to West Branch, her car was forced into a side road where she was struck on the jaw and carried to another car.

Fraser said she was driven into Midland County where she was raped and stabbed numerous times. She remains in critical condition today with eight stab wounds, including a severed trachea and a broken jaw.

After being raped and stabbed, the woman was dragged 100 feet down an old trail and dumped in a clump of bushes, Midland County sheriff's detectives say. She managed to crawl to a gravel pit and later to a Larkin Township road where a motorist spotted her and called deputies.

Ann Arbor police said the attack on the woman resembles the fatal assault on Marlynn Skelton of Romulus, one of two murder victims whose bodies were found in Ann Arbor. Her body was found last March. The body of Joan E. Schell of Plymouth was found in June of last year.

Sheriff's detectives here say the attack also is similar to the one on 13-year-old Dawn Basom of Ypsilanti Township, whose nude and stab-riddled body was found on Gale Rd. in Superior Township last April 16. The first of the five local murder victims, Mary Fleszar, 19-year-old Eastern Michigan University coed, was stabbed more than a dozen times and left on a private dump in July, 1967.

Anderson was paroled from Southern Michigan Prison at Jackson only three months ago after serving 11 years for a rape he committed in Arenac County in 1957. Ann Arbor police say they are checking the possibility that Anderson was in this area at the time of the Skelton or Basom murders as well as the killing in March of U-M Law School Student Mary L. Mixer.

In the New Jersey murders an autopsy has revealed that both Miss Davis and Miss Perry died of multiple stab wounds probably inflicted with a small knife, possibly a pen or a paring knife. The girls, vacationing in Ocean City, N.J., left their rooming house at 4:30 a.m. Friday to drive to the Davis home in Camp Hill, Pa., 135 miles away. The girls had been classmates at Monticello Women's Junior College in Godfrey, Ill. They apparently were ambushed by their killer less than 30 minutes after leaving Ocean City.

New Jersey police have found only a pair of eyeglasses and a watch in their search for clues near the murder scene, and were using electronic detectors today in a further check of the area.

Ann Arbor police and Washtenaw County sheriff's detectives say the method of murder in the New Jersey cases has "remarkable" similarities to the Fleszar-Schell-Skelton-Basom slayings. Local officers say while they are keeping in touch with the New Jersey authorities, there is no plan to send detectives to that state at this time.

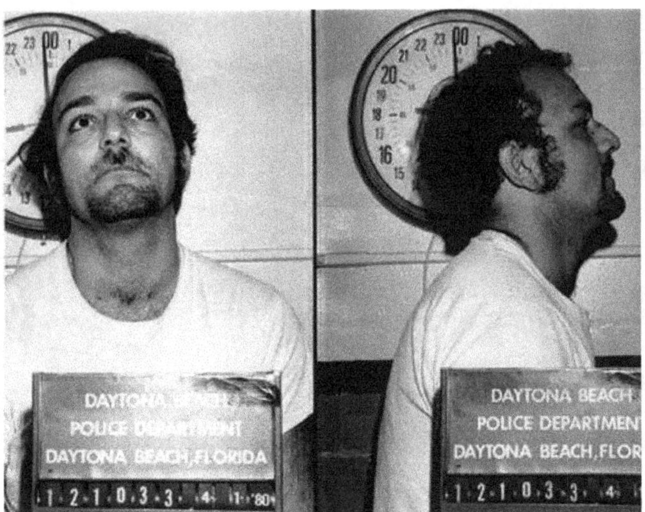

Gerald Stano mugshot after his arrest April 1, 1980. Photo public domain.

May-June 1969: Ted works at Export Pacific (otherwise known as Griggs Lumber Mill) in Tacoma, hauling lumber.

1969 aerial view of Export Pacific Co. Headed by Chauncey L. Griggs, the firm dealt in the lumber export business. Photo courtesy Tacoma Public Library.

June 3, 1969: Brudos is indicted in Salem, Oregon, on three counts of murder for the deaths of Karen Sprinker, Linda Salee and Jan Whitney.

June 27, 1969: Brudos pleads guilty to three counts of murder in the deaths of Sprinker, Salee and Whitney three days before the scheduled start of his trial. Judge Val Sloper hands down three consecutive life sentences. Brudos is transferred to the Oregon State Penitentiary. He died in prison on March 28, 2006.

July 20, 1969: 20:18 UTC. Americans Neil Armstrong and Buzz Aldrin become the first humans to land on the moon.

July 27, 1969: The body of Jan Whitney is found tied to a piece of railroad iron in the Willamette River near Independence, Oregon.

Early September 1969: Starts work for Attorney Messenger and Process Service, Seattle.

Charles Manson (circa 1969). Photo public domain.

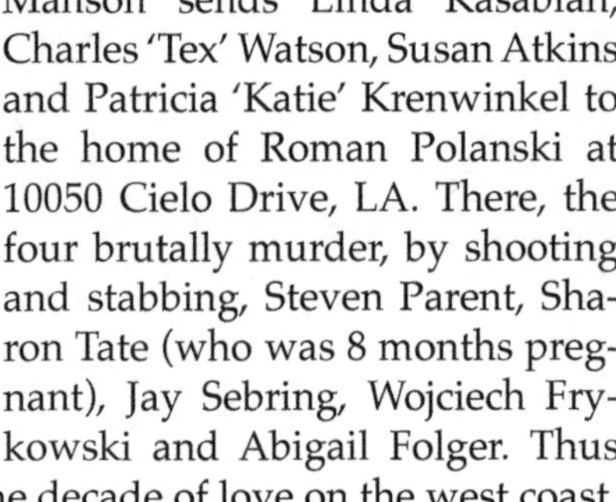

August 9, 1969: Charles Milles Manson sends Linda Kasabian, Charles 'Tex' Watson, Susan Atkins and Patricia 'Katie' Krenwinkel to the home of Roman Polanski at 10050 Cielo Drive, LA. There, the four brutally murder, by shooting and stabbing, Steven Parent, Sharon Tate (who was 8 months pregnant), Jay Sebring, Wojciech Frykowski and Abigail Folger. Thus ends the decade of love on the west coast.

Leigh Bonadies (undated). Photo public domain.

September 8, 1969: Leigh Hainline Bonadies (25) disappears from Boca Raton, Florida. Gerard Schaefer had complained of her "taunting" him by undressing with her curtains open, so he murdered her. A locket belonging to Bonadies was found among his belongings in his mother's house after his arrest. Bonadies' body was found in Boca Del Mar, Florida in 1978, nine years after her disappearance. However, it was not identified until 2004.

September 30 - October 1, 1969: Ted meets Elizabeth Kloepfer [née Hirst, 25, retained name from divorced husband], University District Bar, Sandpiper Tavern, Seattle. They start seeing each other more regularly soon after and a serious relationship develops.

This nondescript building was formerly known as the Sandpiper Tavern in 1970. Photo courtesy Vincent Tan © 2015.

October 12, 1969: Ted shows Liz Kloepfer his Rogers' rooming apartment. Liz notes that it was "orderly and spotless." Around this time attends traffic school for bad driving record (unverified).

Carmen Hallock (undated). Photo public domain.

November, 1969: Ted takes Liz and daughter Tina (pseudonym) to his parents' house in Tacoma for dinner.

December 18, 1969: Carmen Marie Hallock (22) was last seen by her sister-in-law in Fort Lauderdale, Florida. Hallock said she had an appointment with a male teacher from the local junior college that evening. Schaefer had a job as student teacher at Stranahan High School, Fort Lauderdale, but his stay there was short-lived due to indecent behavior.

December 24, 1969: Arrives at Liz's parents' place in Ogden, Utah after obtaining lift with friends of Mary Chino, Liz's best friend.

December 26, 1969: Ted back in Seattle with Liz.

December 29, 1969: Peggy Rahn (9) and Wendy Brown Stevenson (8) vanish from Pompano Beach, Florida. Schaefer confessed on April 19, 1989, to cannibalizing them. Kenneth Guy Shilts (42), a drifter and known child molester was also a suspect.

Left: Peggy Rahn (circa 1969). Right: Wendy Brown Stevenson (circa 1969). Photos public domain.

End of 1969: According to Liz:

> "Not long after we started spending time together, he came over one night and said he had something very important to tell me, something that might change my opinion of him. Shaking with nervousness, he told me that he was illegitimate. His mother gave birth to him in a home for unwed mothers in the East, he said, and they moved to Tacoma to live with relatives when he was very small. Then she married Johnnie Bundy and had four more children. Johnnie Bundy had adopted him, but Ted knew nothing about it until he was a teenager. It had come as a terrible shock. A cousin had been teasing him about it, and Ted had refused to believe it. The cousin had taken Ted up to the attic and showed him proof: his birth certificate. Ted was upset by his cousin's cruelty and furious with his mother because she had left him unprepared for humiliation at the hands of his cousin. 'She never even had the decency to tell me herself,' he said bitterly. He asked if I thought he should confront his mother about it. I told him no. I could sympathize with her. She had made a mistake when she was young, as I had, but had overcome it and had gone on to make a life for herself. It could not have been easy that many years ago – harder, I was sure, than it was for me when I was pregnant with Tina. 'I'm sure it's a source of a lot of pain for her,' I said, 'and that's probably why she didn't talk about it. It's not important anymore. What's important is that you've got a lot going for you. I love you because you're wonderful.' Ted put his head in his hands and cried."

The only contemporary photo available of Liz taken sometime between 1970-1974, as shown on the back cover of *The Phantom Prince.*

- 1970 -

1970: According to the MTR, Ted spent time at 1252 15th Avenue, Marin County (just north of San Francisco), California, during 1970. The closest address this can be associated with is 1252 15th Avenue, San Francisco, opposite the San Francisco Botanical Gardens. There is also a dubious report which can be found on the Internet saying he worked at Electro Vector in Forestville (just northeast of Santa Rosa) for a short while in 1970, but no dates are supplied. It could not be January 1970 as Liz said they spent most nights together that month.

January 1970: Ted helps Liz find a new apartment on Green Lake, Seattle.

February 1970: Ted and Liz obtain wedding license for $5. But before the month is over, Ted tears the license up.

March 1970: Liz finds out Ted was lying for the past six months. He never mentioned that he did not have an undergraduate degree yet.

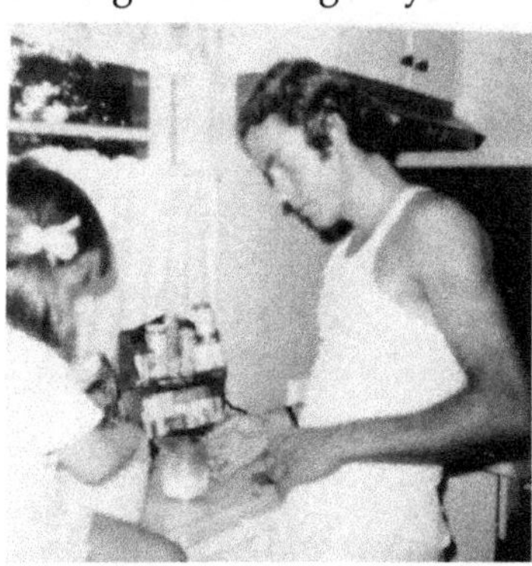

Ted with Tina Kloepfer as shown on the back cover of *The Phantom Prince.*

May 1970: Fired from Attorney Messenger and Process Service because of absence from work (he claimed he was looking after Tina while Liz was at work). Returns to Univ. Wash., contacts campus police and offers his services as an informant. Concurrently, all through May, students protest against the Vietnam war. Seattle in turmoil.

Around this time, Ted takes up work as a delivery driver for the Pedline Surgical Company, a family-owned medical supply company. According to Michaud & Aynesworth, Ted once stole a photograph from a doctor's office and was caught. His boss let him off with a "stern lecture." The company didn't know that he was stealing from them too. Among things he took was a container of plaster casting material.

May 4, 1970: Members of the Ohio National Guard fired into a crowd of Kent State University demonstrators, killing four and wounding nine Kent State students.

May 28, 1970: United Airlines Stewardess Eileen Condit (23) is stabbed to death in her Lake Washington cottage. Condit rented a small house not far from Madison Park near the shores of Lake Washington, several miles east of Seattle's downtown section. The houses were built very close together there because it was a very desirable location, and her next-door neighbors could see into her living room if her drapes weren't pulled, which she seldom did during daylight hours. She was a gamine-like girl with a short "pixie" haircut, friendly and approachable. She was wearing jeans and a sweater over a shorty nightgown when her body was found lying beside a 10-inch long serrated butcher knife taken from her own kitchen. She was stabbed six times. Neighbors said they heard screaming on the night she was murdered but mistook it as roughhousing between friends. Another neighbor saw lights go out and a man leaving Condit's small cottage about 11:30 p.m. wearing tennis or boat shoes.

Eileen Condit. Photo source *Palm Beach Post*, May 31, 1970.

June 1970: According to Liz, Ted takes "summer classes" (assumption is Univ. Wash., Far East studies?).

July 1970: Ted saves Terry Storwick's 3 ½-year-old niece, Wendy, from drowning in Green Lake.

The East Green Lake Playground, May 1969. Photo courtesy Seattle Municipal Archives.

August 1970: Schaefer graduates from Florida Atlantic University (BA Geography).

August 20, 1970: Detective Jerry Thompson of Salt Lake City police logged a call from Detective Pat O'Neil from the Sheriff's Office in Sacramento, California, on October 21, 1975. He informed Thompson that Mr Bundy had a traffic citation on August 20, 1970, in Marin County, the Bay Area, and he was driving an old white Ford pick-up truck. Liz stated that "he purchased a white ford pickup which he has presently in the SLC area about one year ago just before he left for SLC" (Ira Beal report post Liz Kloepfer interview, September 17, 1975). In 1970, however, Ted was still living in the U-District in Washington. Moreover, Liz states that they spent most days together through the summer of 1970, a pattern which continued on into Autumn. At the time authorities were trying to tie Ted into the Santa Rosa hitchhiker murders [ref].

August 29, 1970: Goes on trip with Liz to Wasatch Mountains, Utah. Then Ogden, Utah. Yakima, Washington. Baker, Oregon. Ogden, Utah. Smoked cannabis with "Richard," Ted's ex-con friend (Kendall 1981, 34).

Downtown Ogden, May 1973. Ted visited often while he was in a relationship with Liz. Photo public domain.

September 4, 1970: Returns with Liz to Seattle.

Jeannette Miller (undated). Photo public domain.

September 16, 1970: Jeannette Rose Miller (17) was last seen on the Lincoln Bridge, Arlington, Washington State, a little over an hour north by car from Seattle. She was wearing a brown suede jacket with fringe, a long-sleeved white blouse, a white-yellow-blue-black plaid skirt, a gold chain belt and dark blue shoes. She has a three-tooth denture plate on the left side of her upper jaw.

September 24, 1970: Changed major from Far East to Psychology at Univ. Wash..

Christmas Day to New Year's 1970: Liz back in Ogden, Utah, alone with her parents.

January 1971: Ted back again at the Univ. Wash., takes up studies in psychology. Ronald E. Smith taught Bundy in two psychology courses. "He distinguished himself academically in both courses," Smith said. "He was extremely bright, always well-dressed, very mature." Smith remembers Bundy coming to him with an interest in pursuing an honors thesis on the topic of mental illness and conditional decision making. "He was a tormented soul in a lot of respects, and psychology would appeal to a person like him," Smith said. "He was not unusual for a very clever psychopath individual. He was able to inspire confidence in others and provide a very good front. Nobody who interacted with him actually suspected what was going on." Smith once wrote a reference for Ted which read in part:

> Mr. Bundy is undoubtedly one of the top undergraduate students in our department. Indeed, I would place him in the top 1% of undergraduate students with whom I have interacted both here at the University of Washington and at Purdue University (Rule 2006, 19).

Ronald Smith. (A&E Television Networks, 2007, originally broadcast on A&E's television program *Biography* in 2002.)

March 1971: Liz tells Ted she's getting interest from another man. Ted acts nonchalant, but later follows her to The Walrus Tavern. Liz finds him "shaking like a leaf." He leaves without her.

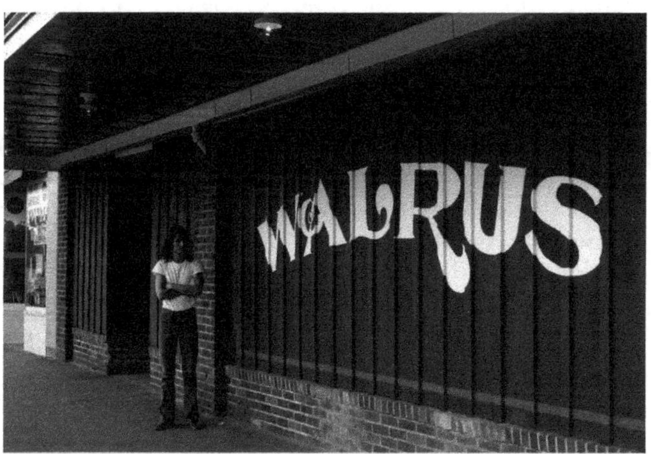

The Walrus Tavern, 1970. Photo public domain.

June-July 1971 (this date is interpolated): Seattle. According to Nelson and Lewis, Ted follows a woman, picks up two-by-four in a lot, lays in wait, but the woman enters her house before she reaches his hiding spot. A few nights later he saw a woman park her car, walk up to her door, and fumble for her keys. He walked up behind her and struck her with a piece of wood he was carrying. She fell down screaming. He panicked and ran.

July 1971: Liz moves into an apartment closer to Ted's on a tree-lined street close to Univ. Wash. campus (5208 18th N.E.). However around this time she also reports that she and Ted were "out of sync."

July 7, 1971: *Two-Lane Blacktop*, a road movie, is released in New York. A female hitchhiker known only as "the girl" says, as she gets into a car driven by two dudes: "You guys aren't like the Zodiac killers or anything, right?"

Rita Curran (undated). Photo public domain.

July 19, 1971: Rita Curran (24), second grade school teacher at Milton elementary, was found lying nude on the bedroom floor of an apartment on 17 Brooks Avenue, Burlington, Vermont. Two other girls shared the house for the summer (adjacent to the Elizabeth Lund Home for Unwed Mothers). She also worked as a chambermaid at a local motel. Curran was beaten, raped and strangled. Her body was discovered at about 1:00 a.m. when one of the girls returned from a date. According to police, she was beaten on the head and face. Detective Lt. Richard Beaumont said his men were checking for a connection between the girl's slaying and several assaults on Univ. Vermont Milton coeds and other women in the Burlington area last winter. Municipal records note that a person named "Ted" was bitten by a dog that week (Rule 1980, 508). There are no records of Ted traveling to the east coast for July 1971. Liz makes no mention of it in her book. The "son of a very prominent Burlington family" is the prime suspect (unverified).

Joyce LePage (undated). Photo public domain.

July 22, 1971: 10:00 p.m. Joyce LePage (21) disappears on the way to her apartment near Stevens Hall at Washington State University, Pullman.

September 1971: Works at Seattle Crisis Clinic, Capitol Hill, "an old Victorian house." According to Rule, Ted saved lives while working there (Rule 2006, 25).

September 3, 1971: Gerard Schaefer is hired by Wilton Manors Police Department.

December 7, 1971: Jamie Rachel (Rochelle) Grissim (16) was last seen walking home from Fort Vancouver High School, Washington State. Lara Starr, Jamie's younger 14-year old sister, recalled the day she last saw her sister alive: "Jamie was outside, waiting for the school bus to come pick her up. She waited for a few minutes, then came back inside to get warm. We had a brief conversation, and she told me she was going to walk home from school later that afternoon. [...] The walk was four miles, but she felt it would be better than waiting around for a school bus." Investigators allege Grissim is the first victim of serial killer

Warren Leslie Forrest.
December 17, 1971: Gerard Schaefer graduates from the police academy at Broward Community College.
December 31, 1971: Ted leaves Pedline Surgical Company.

Jamie Grissim (undated). Photo public domain.

Warren Leslie Forrest upon his arrest in October 2, 1974. Photo public domain.

NOTES

Ted's one-year stint at the University of Puget Sound in 1966 was a doldrum in his life, a no-man's land between the age of 19 and 20. He finished up work at Tacoma City Light shortly before enrolling, and it appears he saved just enough to buy a second-hand car (a 1933 Plymouth coup). Ted continued to live at home during his freshman year, a decision that was most likely part convenience, due to the proximity of his parents' house to the university, and part necessity, since he had no income and his family was not wealthy enough to support him living away. As a way of disguising his poverty, he probably stole text books and clothes, a pattern of behavior that continued from his teenage misdemeanor thefts. The happiest moment of the year came when he sold his Plymouth coup for a '58 Volkswagen beetle, a style of car he would favor for the rest of his life.

Without a steady income, Ted could not afford to get involved in fraternity or sorority activities. The most often quoted phrase for this period of his life is that he "had a longing for a beautiful coed [but] didn't have the skill or social acumen to cope with it" (PIR 1975). Ted's self-description, truthful as it is, conceals the deeper psychic hunger he had for love and affection. Concurrent with finishing up work at Tacoma City Light, he also wound up nightwork as a campaign volunteer for the House of Representatives. Ted would later comment that politicking gave him access to hitherto inaccessible stratas of society. It also offered something else, an environment where social interactions were structured, where he could hone a repertoire of behavior that enabled him to construct what psychiatrist Hervey M. Cleckley termed "the mask of sanity" (Cleckley 1941).

Behind the facade, he continued to consume pornography and detective magazines, his primary respite from loneliness. This changed somewhat when he moved away from home at the end of 1966 and transferred to the University of Washington. Around this time he met and fell in love with Diane Edwards. The 1967 Summer of Love had arrived. But Ted didn't dress like a love child or behave like one. It seems he also didn't listen to contemporary pop music either, but preferred classical (Kendall 1981, 19). His relationship with Diane did not last. She found him immature and a liar. Ted's first attempt at constructing a mask had failed. He decided to go on a soul searching trip in the hope that the change of environment would hand him a new perspective on life. He ended up in his birthtown of Burlington where he obtained an abstract of his birth certificate and learned for sure that he was illegitimate (Rule 2006, 16). Defeated, he returned to the west coast and worked his way through a string of menial jobs. Aged 22, with two failed years behind him, he immersed himself ever more deeply in his rape fantasies.

In September 1968 he worked briefly as a driver for

Art Fletcher during Fletcher's campaign for lieutenant governor of Washington State. By his own account, Ted lost his virginity around this time to an older woman while totally inebriated. Fletcher's campaign subsequently failed and Ted lost his job, so he decided to return to the east coast again, this time enrolling for a semester at Temple University, Pennsylvania. He began frequenting the flesh spots of New York. It was sometime around late February 1969 in Ocean City, New Jersey, according to his own testimony, that he attempted his first rape. Even though it was unsuccessful, he felt he had finally reached the point of no return. From now on, he would pursue the double life with total commitment.

Feeling the east coast wasn't conducive for the kinds of acts he intended, and with the summer approaching, Ted returned to Seattle and moved into an apartment near the University of Washington. He continued to support himself through menial jobs. Meanwhile, throughout the remainder of 1969, he proactively escalated his predatory experimentation. It was around this time that he discovered instrumentation afforded him the best chance of success (that is, the use of a club or some physical item to over-power the victim). Then, at the end of 1969, he met Elizabeth Kloepfer, a young divorcee and single mother of a young daughter. Thus began a relationship that continued, off-and-on, for the next seven years. It was the type of relationship that he could exploit: a woman with low self-esteem and a young child with whom he could role-play a father figure. He would repeat this pattern with at least two other women during his life.

Liz encouraged Ted's dream of becoming a lawyer. However, because Ted had not yet completed his undergraduate degree, he needed to go back to university. This time he enrolled in psychology at the University of Washington (at the start of 1971), a decision that appears to be driven by his need to understand himself, and also, in retrospect, to improve his mask of sanity. Psychology appears to be the one subject that he excelled at. Many of his teachers heaped praise on him. Little did anyone know that Ted was about to embark on his first murders.

References

Cleckley, H. M. (1941). *The Mask of Sanity: An Attempt to Clarify Some Issues About the So-Called Psychopathic Personality.* St. Louis: MO: Mosby.

Hall, D. M. (1975). Presentence Investigation Report. The State of Utah Adult Probation and Parole: SLC.

Kendall, E. (1981). *The Phantom Prince: My Life with Ted Bundy.* Seattle, WA: Madrona Publishers.

Montane, Diana; Kelly, Kathy (2011). *I Would Find a Girl Walking.* N.Y.: Penguin.

Tanay, E. (2010). *American Legal Injustice: Behind the Scenes with an Expert Witness.* Plymouth, U.K.: Jason Aronson, Inc.

Adult Years (1972 - August 15, 1975)

Sometime early 1972: Entered a Seattle woman's house for the first time, attempted to suffocate her with a pillow; she struggled, he fled the scene. She was a waitress who worked at a cafeteria near campus who would get off at midnight and walk home and Ted would follow her—she lived in a basement apartment—and he would look in her bedroom window (and masturbate). According to Ted: "Well, anyway ... I rushed in there, still somewhat inept, dealing with images that came out of movies, and movies are not real, so I ran in there and hopped on top of the bed and tried to put a pillow on top of the girl's face. She struggled and started to scream and I ran away. End of story. Even this is a step further. I mean, going to somebody's house is really ..." (M&A 2000, 113; Nelson 1994, 284).

Early 1972: Liz pregnant by Ted. Has abortion. Major Nick Mackie, Commander of the Seattle Criminal Investigation Commission, in his February 21, 1978 report to Captain Jack Pottinger of the Leon County Sheriff's Office, Tallahassee, incorrectly stated: "Without emotions or regard to the girl's thoughts about having a child, Bundy informed her to abort the child." In contrast to this Liz wrote:

> Both of us knew it would be impossible to have a baby now. He was going to start law school in the fall, and I needed to be able to work to put him through. I was distraught. I knew I was going to terminate the pregnancy as soon as I could. Ted, on the other hand, was pleased with himself. He had fathered a baby. I didn't want to hear about it. I didn't want to think about what I was going to do. I wanted to sleep most of the time, while Ted did most of the cooking and looked after Tina. As soon as a doctor confirmed what we already knew, I made an appointment for an abortion, which had just been legalized in Washington State. It was awful. Ted took me home and put me to bed. He lay down beside me and talked about the day when I wouldn't have to work and we would have lots of kids. He fixed me food which I couldn't eat and did all he could to comfort me. Within a few days I was feeling better and determined never to think of it again (Kendall 1981, 39).

January 4, 1972: Belinda Hutchens (22) gets in a stranger's car in Fort Lauderdale, Florida, never to be heard from again. Schaefer confirmed as her abductor on April 7, 1973.

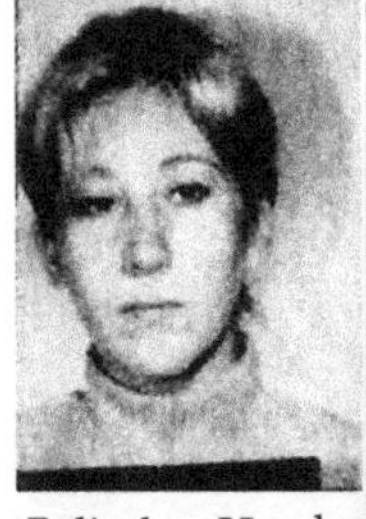

Belinda Hutchens (undated). Photo public domain.

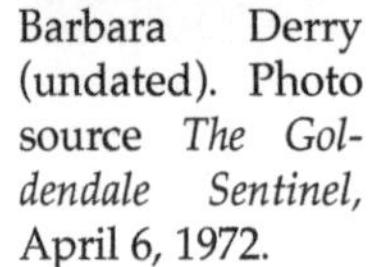

Barbara Derry (undated). Photo source *The Goldendale Sentinel*, April 6, 1972.

February 11, 1972: Barbara Ann Derry (18) last seen hitchhiking along State Highway 14, East from Vancouver, Oregon. Suspected victim of Warren Leslie Forrest.

February 22, 1972: Sent application to Univ. Utah law school.

Debora Lowe (undated). Photo public domain.

February 28, 1972: Debora Sue Lowe (14) last seen walking to James S. Rickards Middle School, Oakland Park, Florida. Schaefer the prime suspect in her abduction.

March 19, 1972: Starts his internship at Harborview Mental Health Center, Seattle. According to Rule he carried a full caseload of twelve clients during a four-month internship in Harborview Hospital's Outpatient Clinic. Held periodic sessions with clients; entered progress reports in hospital charts, continually re-evaluated psychiatric diagnoses, and referred clients to physicians for medical and psychotherapeutic medication evaluations. Participated in numerous training sessions conducted by staff psychiatrists (Rule 1983, 37).

Harborview Medical Center. Photo courtesy Vincent Tan © 2015.

March 29, 1972: Barbara Derry's body was found at the bottom of the silo at the Grist Mill, in Northern Clark County. It was covered with boards and debris, partially disrobed, missing a bra. Mode of death was discovered to have been caused by one stab wound to the heart, with a narrow bladed instrument.

April 15, 1972: Buys gas in Seattle (tag # unknown). Buys gas in Neah Bay, Washington (tag # unknown).

April 22, 1972: Meets Sandy Gwinn, a co-worker, for the first time at the Harborview Hospital Mental Health Center. Later on has an affair with her. She claimed Ted was not capable of being emotionally responsive to patients. Ted was also suspected of engaging in inappropriate conduct with one female client at the center.

April 28, 1972: Buys gas in Seattle (tag # unknown).

May 5, 1972: Buys gas in Seattle (tag # unknown).

May 12, 1972: Ted receives a rejection from Univ. Utah law school.

May 18, 1972: Buys gas in Coeur d'Alene, Idaho (just east of Spokane).

June 1972: Kerry May Hardy (22) disappears from Capitol Hill, Seattle. Her remains were found in a shallow grave at Suncadia Resort, Washington, September 2010, but not reported until June 3, 2011. At the time the area was forest but later underwent logging. On June 1, 2011, the Center for Human Remains told the Sheriff's Office that it had matched DNA from a bone sample to DNA from May's mother, which was obtained by the King County Sheriff's Office in 2004 as part of the investigation into the Green River killer. Hardy was found wearing a size five or six 14-carat gold ring, and blue-colored clothing, and had straight teeth with extensive dental work. We will never know if Ted killed Kerry, as he usually removed all clothing from the victim. However, in a slip during his last interview with Keppel, he may have admitted that he took his first victim in 1972. A possible further corroboration comes from a confession he made to Nelson sometime in April 1987:

Kerry May Hardy (undated). Photo public domain.

> Then he described the steps leading up to one of his first murders, a blonde in the vestibule of her apartment building. He stopped after recounting his still clear vision of her unconscious body laid out on the floor, after he had hit her with a club, her long hair spread out like a fan above her head." [...] After a moment, he skipped ahead and talked about pulling the woman's body into the weeds at the back of the building ... (Nelson 1994, 172).

We cannot say whether Ted was talking about Hardy, but his first series of abductions took place in houses or apartments. According to the MTR, Ted's first murder involved beating and manual strangulation (i.e., using hands, not a ligature which he later used). We do not have access to Hardy's autopsy, nor DNA tests, so we have no way of knowing if Ted was involved. What we do know is the body was located on Ted's I-90 axis, and the time frame is within range.

June - September 1972: Works shifts at Harborview Hospital Mental Health Center.

June 4, 1972: Buys gas in Seattle (tag # unknown).

June 9, 1972: Buys gas in Seattle (tag # unknown).

June 10, 1972: Graduates B.S. Psychology (2-year course), Univ. Washington. According to Rule, he achieved mostly A's with a sprinkling of B's in courses such as physiological psychology, social psychology, animal learning, statistical methods, developmental psychology, deviant personality and deviant development. He was liked by three professors: Patricia Lunneborg, Scott Fraser and Ronald E. Smith. Finishes work at Harborview Hospital Mental Health Center.

June 17, 1972: Bought gas driving Seattle (tag # unknown).

Sometime in July 1972: Ted tells Liz he has a "date" outside their relationship [Sandy Gwinn?]. Big fight. Edna Cowell (Ted's cousin) visits Karen Covach [?] (who once

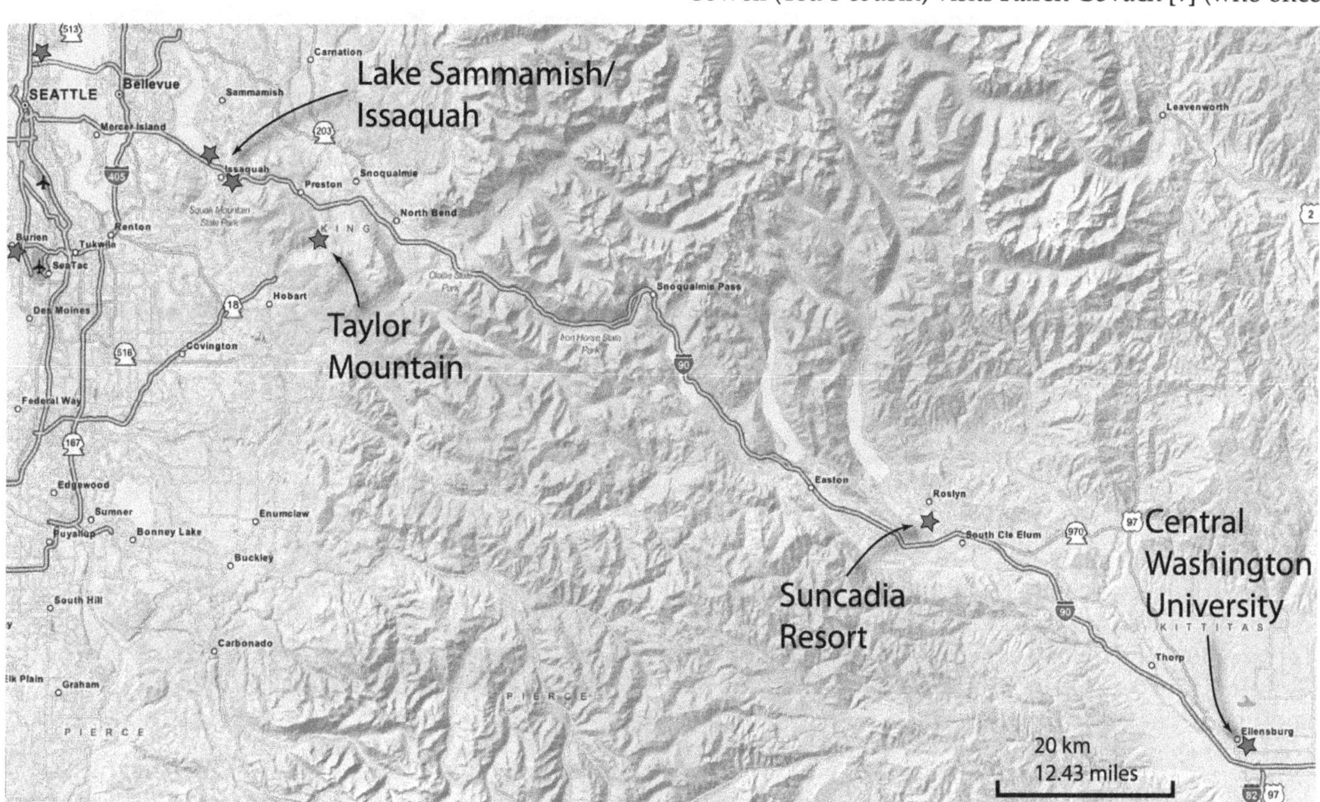

Red stars indicate abduction/body locations in relation to the I-90 corridor: Seattle, Burien, Lake Sammamish, Issaquah, Taylor Mountain, Suncadia Resort (golf course), Central Wash. Univ., Ellensburg. Map courtesy OpenStreetMap contributors, 2015.

roomed with Lynda Healy).
July 4, 1972: Bought gas driving, Hoquiam, Washington (tag # unknown). Ted continues to date Sandy Gwinn who said their relationship lasted from May - June 1972. Had sexual intercourse with her once at Humptulips River west of Seattle near the coast. On that occasion he attempted to drown her. She said she also drove Ted around the Lake Sam area aimlessly looking for a relation of Ted's:

> Ted was supposedly looking for an aunt or some old woman who was family. He said he was trying to find her place. I'll never forget it because it was my car and my gas and I was not exactly pleased to do this. I kept driving and driving and I kept saying to Ted, 'What does the place look like? At least tell me what the place looks like, so I can help!' There was never any description. We just drove around (M&A 2000, 70-71).

In 1975, for his presentence report, Ted depicted Gwinn as a disturbed girl. There is an unsourced report that Liz threatened suicide over the affair which led Ted to end it. His experience working on a suicide hotline was in his recent past.
July 10, 1972: Bought gas driving, Seattle (tag # unknown).
July 16, 1972: Bought gas driving, Seattle (tag # unknown).
July 21, 1972: Schaefer, now a Martin County deputy, picks up Paula Sue Wells (17) and Nancy Ellen Trotter (18), warns them of the dangers of hitchhiking, then lets them go.
July 22, 1972: Schaefer picks up Paula Wells and Nancy Trotter again, this time abducts them. Balances them on ground surface tree roots and puts nooses around their necks so they risk hanging if they slip and fall. He departs the scene and leaves them there. The girls escape and are found by authorities later that day.

Nancy Ellen Trotter and Paula Sue Wells leave court. Photo source *The Palm Beach Post* September 25, 1973.

July 23, 1972: Schaefer telephones his superior, Sheriff Richard Crowder and admits his crime. Fired on the spot, he is charged with false imprisonment and two counts of aggravated assault. He is released on $15,000 bond.
July 24, 1972: Bought gas driving, Seattle (tag # unknown).
August 19, 1972: Bought gas driving, Issaquah, Washington (tag # unknown).
August 23, 1972: Bought gas driving, Seattle (tag # unknown).
August 25, 1972: Bought gas driving, Tacoma (tag # unknown).
August 28, 1972: Bought gas driving, Seattle (tag # unknown).
September 1972: Starts works in Governor Dan Evans' re-election campaign. Shadows Evans' opponent former governor Albert Dean Rosellini and records his speeches for analysis by Evans' team. Sometime later is exposed and interviewed on TV. Mary Lynn Chino spots him around 2:00 a.m. roaming through the backyards of the houses opposite her rear window (this is in the University District near where Ted lived). On September 17, 1975, Liz told Detectives Jerry Thompson, Ira Beal and Dennis Couch that Ted would follow her and her girlfriends and seemed to like to jump out at them from behind the bushes just to scare them (PIR 1975).

Left: Governor Daniel J Evans (circa 1973). Right: Ted the politician (circa 1973). Photos public domain.

Rosellini, campaign HQ, November, 1972. Photo © AP.

September 1, 1972: Bought gas driving, Seattle (tag # unknown).
September 2, 1972: North Cascades Highway opening

day. "He certainly wasn't driving my car ... It's totally bogus. They even had him babysitting our boys. It's just absolutely nonsense. It never happened" (Evans interview, *Methow Grist*, August 27, 2012).

September 3, 1972: Bought gas driving, Cle Elum, Washington.

September 7, 1972: Bought gas driving, Seattle (tag # unknown).

September 15, 1972: Bought gas driving, Seattle (tag # unknown).

September 16, 1972: Bought gas driving, Seattle (tag # unknown).

September 17, 1972: Bought gas driving, Cle Elum, Washington.

September 19, 1972: Bought gas driving, Seattle (tag # unknown).

September 24, 1972: Bought gas driving, Seattle (tag # unknown).

September 26, 1972: Bought gas driving, Seattle (tag # unknown).

September 27, 1972: While out on bail Gerard Schaefer abducts and murders Georgia Crystal Jessup (16) and Susan Place (17) at Fort Lauderdale, Florida. These are the only murders for which he received a conviction.

Top: Susan Place (undated). Left: Georgia Jessup (undated, best available image). Photos public domain.

September 28, 1972: Bought gas driving, Seattle (tag # unknown).

October 1972: Hired by Seattle's Crime Prevention Advisory Commission. Worked up a preliminary investigation for the Commission into assaults against women and "white collar" (economic) crime.

October 5, 1972: Bought gas driving, Seattle (tag # unknown).

October 7, 1972: Bought gas driving, Seattle (tag # unknown).

October 10, 1972: Bought gas driving, Seattle (tag # unknown).

October 19, 1972: Bought gas driving, Seattle (tag # unknown).

October 20, 1972: Bought gas driving, Seattle (tag # unknown).

October 23, 1972: Bought gas driving, Richland, Washington (tag # unknown). Bought gas driving, Seattle (tag # unknown). Also on this day, Mary Alice Briscolina (14) and Elsie Lina Farmer (13) were last seen hitchhiking to a local restaurant in Fort Lauderdale. Schaefer implicated in their disappearance.

Left: Mary Briscolina (undated). Right: Elsie Farmer. Photos public domain.

October 24, 1972: Bought gas driving, Seattle (tag # unknown).

October 26, 1972: Bought gas driving, Seattle (tag # unknown).

November 1972: Finishes work with Dan Evans. Starts work at Seattle Crime Commission. Assists in developing issues regarding crime.

November 7, 1972: Bought gas driving, Seattle (tag # unknown).

December (sometime): Ends work with Seattle Crime Commission. Upset he was rejected from the prestigious Univ. Washington law school.

December 16, 1972: Attends Crisis Clinic Christmas party with true crime writer Ann Rule.

December 24, 1972: Schaefer sentenced to 6 months county jail followed by 3 years probation for the Trotter-Wells crime.

December 26, 1972: Bought gas driving, Spokane, Washington.

December 27, 1972: Bought gas driving, Seattle (tag # unknown).

December 30, 1972: Bought gas driving, Seattle (tag # unknown).

- 1973 -

January 1973: Failed to make director of Seattle's Crime Prevention Advisory Commission; resigns. Is contracted to King County Office of Law and Justice Planning to identify recidivism rates for offenders found guilty of misdemeanors and gross misdemeanors in the twelve county District Courts. Governor Evans Inauguration Ball. Liz a fish out of water when it comes to social events. Ted continues to steal even though he's earning good money.

January 8-14, 1973: Barbara Ann Wilcox (19, no image) and Collette Marie Goodenough (19, no image) vanish while hitchhiking in Florida. Schaefer is falsely connected to this case through spurious evidence.

January 8, 1973: (Night time) Northgate Shopping Center, Seattle, Ted apprehends a purse-snatcher while shopping with Liz. Article from *The Seattle Times* on this date: Ted, 26, who was assistant director of the Seattle Crime Commission caught a man who had snatched a woman's purse in the Northgate Mall parking area Monday night. Police said Ted chased the man on foot on First Avenue Northeast and caught him as he was stuffing the purse into a garbage can. The suspect was turned over to the police and is being held on suspicion of robbery. The suspect, police said, grabbed the purse of Darlene M. Covey as she walked toward her car with her two children. Police said Ted recovered from the suspect the $34 that had been taken from the purse. Ted would later receive a commendation from the Seattle Police Department.

January 10, 1973: Buys gas in Seattle (OPM-001).
January 15, 1973: Schaefer starts his jail sentence for the Trotter-Wells crime.
January 17, 1973: 9:00 a.m. LSAT penned in Ted's 1973 diary. Also on this day, Elsie Lina Farmer's skeletal remains were found at a construction site near Plantation High School.
January 19, 1973: Buys gas in Seattle (OPM-001).
January 29, 1973: Buys gas in Seattle (OPM-001).
February 1973: Reapplies to Univ. Utah law school.
February 10, 1973: Buys gas in Seattle (tag OPM-001). 08:30 LSAT penned in Ted's 1973 diary.
February 15, 1973: Mary Briscolina's remains were found about 200 yards away from Elsie Farmer's. Both girls were identified via dental records. The girls' teeth had been pulled and scattered around their grave sites, a precaution investigators said Schaefer took because he knew it would make identifying the bodies more difficult.
February 27, 1973: 8:30 a.m. "Olympia" penned in Ted's 1973 diary.
February 28, 1973: 8:30 a.m. "Seattle" penned in Ted's 1973 diary.
March 1973: Arrested for ticket warrants according to MTR. According to Rule, she sees a bearded Ted briefly at a meeting in a Seattle Public Safety Building (Seattle Police).

Photo supposedly taken by Liz in March 1973. Ted looks like he had just shaved his beard off (maybe that's why she took the photo?). Photo public domain.

March 1, 1973: 8:30 a.m. "Seattle" penned in Ted's 1973 diary. Also penned in on the afternoon is "Public Safety."
March 2, 1973: Liz's VW bug stolen. She suspected Ted stole it.
March 5, 1973: Buys gas in Seattle (OPM-001).
March 9, 1973: Buys gas in Seattle (C-26464). 10:00 a.m. Has "Ross Davis, Olympia" entry in 1973 diary.
March 16, 1973: Turned in progress report for King County Office of Law and Justice Planning. Ted wrote: A number of rape offenders do not seem to be "sick people." Still wearing beard.
March 26, 1973: Buys gas in Seattle (OPM-001).
March 29, 1973: Buys gas in his VW, Washington (tag # IBH-521).
March 30, 1973: 1:30 p.m. Ted has his VW repaired, and has key made for Liz's VW.
March 31, 1973: (Morning) "Yakima" entered in 1973 diary.
April 1973: Ted and Liz in a hardware store, Ted gathers up tools and puts them in a tool chest. Liz says, "You're not going to steal those, are you?" Ted lies and says "No." But several days later Liz notices the tool chest in Ted's car.
April 1, 1973: Georgia Jessup and Susan Place skeletal remains found near Blind Creek, on Hutchinson Island, Florida.
April 3, 1973: Bought gas driving his VW, Seattle.
April 5, 1973: First acceptance into Univ. Utah law school.
April 7, 1973: Search warrant issued on Doris Schaefer's home where Schaefer lived. Found: a stash of women's jewelry, writing, sketches depicting mutilation-murders of young women, newspaper clippings of Schaefer-linked cases, bootleg pornography, Barbara Wilcox's driver's license, Collette Goodenough's passport, a purse owned by Susan Place, two gold crowned teeth and a shamrock pin belonging to Carmen Hallock, photographs of a nude male body in female underwear (Schaefer's), rope, a rifle, and a hunting knife.
April 8, 1973: Bought gas driving his VW, Seattle.
April 12, 1973: 12:30 p.m. Ted has gas leak repaired in his VW in Seattle. Bought gas driving his VW, Seattle.
April 13, 1973: Ted in Seattle.
April 16, 1973: Bought gas driving his VW, Seattle.
April 18, 1973: Ted in Seattle.
April 19, 1973: Bought gas driving his VW, Seattle.
April 20, 1973: Bought gas driving his VW, Seattle. Bought gas driving his VW, Tumwater.
April 22, 1973: Bought gas driving his VW, Seattle.
April 23, 1973: Ted in Seattle.
April 24, 1973: Purchased gas driving his VW in Dupont, Washington. Takes plane from Seattle to Spokane. Checked into Fiesta Motel, room #8, Colfax, Washington. Entries in 1973 diary: 3:00 p.m. Colfax. 4:15 p.m. Northwest 116. 5:02 p.m. Spokane.
April 25, 1973: Entries in 1973 diary: 9:00 a.m. Spokane. 11:20 a.m. Northwest 305. 12:09 p.m. Seattle.
April 26, 1973: Ted in Olympia. Bought gas driving his VW, Seattle.
April 29, 1973: Bought gas driving Seattle (OPM-001).
April 30, 1973: Ted in Olympia.
May 1973: According to Keppel, Ted picked up his first victim, a teenage hitchhiker at Tumwater, Olympia. Unconfirmed, but the timeline suggests that Ted will have progressed to murder around this time.
May 1, 1973: Ted in Olympia. Bought gas driving his VW, Seattle.
May 2, 1973: Evening. "Ross' cats" entry in 1973 diary. [Ted was working as an aide to Ross Davis]
May 4, 1973: Ted in Olympia.

Tumwater, looking towards Olympia, 1973. Photo public domain.

May 7, 1973: Bought gas driving Seattle (tag # unknown).
May 8, 1973: Ted in Seattle.
May 9, 1973: Ted in Olympia. Bought gas driving his VW, Tacoma.
May 10, 1973: 8:00 a.m. "Camera" entry in 1973 diary. Ted in Olympia. Bought gas driving his VW, Tacoma.
May 12, 1973: Bought gas driving his VW, Seattle.
May 14, 1973: Bought gas driving his VW, Seattle.
May 15, 1973: 10:25 a.m. "Spokane" entry in Ted's 173 diary.
May 16, 1973: 9:00 a.m. "Davenport" entry in Ted's 1973 diary.
May 17, 1973: Ted in Davenport Hotel, Spokane, Washington.
May 18, 1973: Ted in Olympia. Afternoon. "Yakima" in Ted's 1973 diary.
May 19, 1973: Ted driving his VW Enumclaw, Washington. [Picked up and murdered hitchhiker?] Bought gas driving his VW, Seattle.
May 21, 1973: Schaefer flown to Chattahoochee Mental Facility for psychiatric evaluation.
May 22, 1973: Ted in Olympia. Bought gas driving his VW, Seattle.
May 25, 1973: Ted in Seattle. 10:30 a.m. "News Conference" entry in Ted's 1973 diary.
May 26, 1973: Ted in Olympia. Bought gas driving his VW, Seattle. 2:00 p.m. "Snoqualmie Pass Cascade Conference" entry in Ted's 1973 diary.
May 29, 1973: 9:00 a.m. "San Francisco" entered in 1973 diary.
May 31, 1973: Bought gas driving his VW, Seattle.
June 1973: Liz has affair with 'Greg.' Around this time Marlin Vortman, a law student who knew Ted from the 1972 Evans campaign recalls Ted once explained that he often came and went from his second-floor room at Rogers' rooming house by means of a ladder, "because he didn't want to disturb his fellow roomers" (M&A 1983, 73).

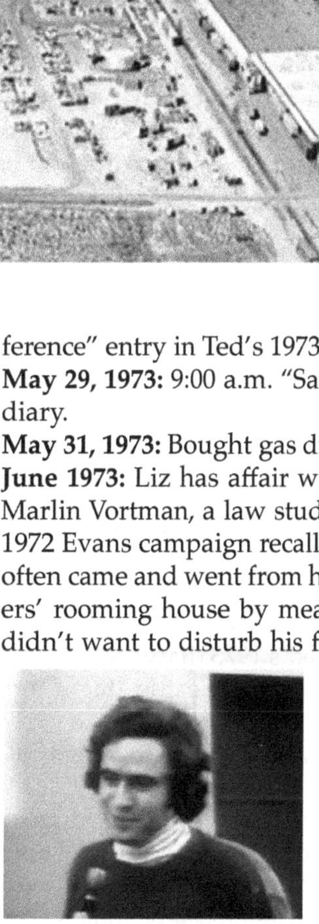

Ted being interviewed on TV for spying on Rosellini (sometime 1973). "It's hard for to me to believe that what I did was newsworthy, in [sic] my part of the campaign was so insignificant I'm embarrassed that I should be taking this publicity from it, really embarrassed." Photo public domain.

June 1, 1973: Ted in Olympia.
June 2, 1973: Bought gas driving his VW, Seattle. Ted rents unknown make of vehicle from National Rental Car, Seattle.
June 4, 1973: Ted in Olympia. Bought gas driving his VW, Seattle.
June 5, 1973: Ted in Olympia. Bought gas driving his VW, Seattle.
June 6, 1973: Bought gas driving Seattle (tag # unknown). 11:00 a.m. "San

Francisco" entry in Ted's 1973 diary.
June 9, 1973: Bought gas driving his VW, Seattle.
June 10, 1973: Ted in Olympia.
June 11, 1973: Ted in Seattle.
June 12, 1973: Bought gas driving his VW, Seattle.
June 13, 1973: 8:30 a.m. "San Francisco" entry in Ted's 1973 diary. Ted stayed at Mark Hopkins Hotel, San Francisco.
June 14, 1973: Ted stayed at Mark Hopkins Hotel, San Francisco. Ted's application received at UPS law school.
June 15, 1973: Ted in San Francisco, left for Seattle.
June 18, 1973: Bought gas driving his VW, Seattle.
June 19, 1973: Bought gas driving Seattle (tag # unknown).
June 20, 1973: Ted travels Seattle, Tumwater, Olympia. Bought gas driving his VW, Tacoma.
June 25, 1973: Ted in Olympia. Ted bought gas driving his VW, Tumwater.
June 27, 1973: Ted in Seattle & Olympia.
June 30, 1973: Ted buys gas in Seattle (tag # unknown).
July 1973: According to Michaud & Aynesworth (1983, 73), Ted flies to San Francisco to see Diane Edwards (Diane now sees a "man of action"). Every day of July except 21-22 is covered by a gas receipt in the Seattle area, so if Ted went to San Francisco it was either a day trip or occurred between 21-22 July 1973.
July 2, 1973: Ted in Olympia and Seattle (I-229).
July 3, 1973: Ted in Seattle and Olympia.
July 4, 1973: Rents room at Edgewater Inn, Seattle. Bought gas driving his VW Seattle.
July 5, 1973: Ted in Olympia.
July 6, 1973: Ted in Seattle. Date circled in Ted's 1973 diary.
July 7, 1973: Bought gas driving Seattle (OPM-001).
July 8, 1973: Ted in Seattle & Olympia.
July 9, 1973: Bought gas driving Dupont, Washington (OPM-001). This date circled in Ted's 1973 diary.
July 10, 1973: Ted in Olympia.
July 12, 1973: Bought gas driving his VW, Dupont, Washington. This date circled in Ted's 1973 diary.
July 13, 1973: Bought gas driving Seattle (tag # unknown).
July 14, 1973: Bought gas driving his VW, unknown city, Washington.
July 16, 1973: Date circled and "Pick UPS law directory" entry in Ted's 1973 diary on this day. Evening. "Feed Ross's [sic] animals" entry. [Ross Davis].
July 17, 1973: Bought gas driving Seattle (tag # unknown).
July 18, 1973: Ted in Seattle.
July 19, 1973: Ted in Seattle.
July 20, 1973: Ted in Seattle.
July 23, 1973: Ted in Seattle. Bought gas driving his VW, Tumwater. This date circled in Ted's 1973 diary.
July 24, 1973: Ted in Olympia.
July 25, 1973: Ted in Seattle. Has lunch with Dick Schrock, lobbyist.
July 26, 1973: Ted parked a vehicle, Seattle.
July 27, 1973: Ted in Seattle. 8:30 a.m. "UPS deposit $100" entry in Ted's 1973 diary.
July 28, 1973: Ted in Seattle & Ellensburg, Washington.

Rita Jolly (undated). Photo public domain.

July 29, 1973: Ted in Seattle & Olympia. Rita Lorraine Jolly (17) left her apartment on Horton Road in West Linn, Portland, Oregon, at 7:15 p.m. to go for a walk. She was last seen between 8:30 p.m. and 9:00 p.m. walking uphill on Sunset Avenue wearing a brown Pendleton shirt, army fatigue pants or blue jeans, and blue, low-cut tennis shoes with buckskin heels. Her body has never been found.
July 30, 1973: Bought gas driving his VW, Tumwater.
Early August 1973: Liz's VW stolen. Found soon after. The oriental knife that Ted said he received from a friend and had put in the glove compartment a couple of weeks earlier was missing. "Three days later" Ted borrows Liz's car and has auto accident.
August 1973: Diane Edwards spends a week in Seattle. She and Ted spend a week in Marlin Vortman's apartment while he and his wife Sheila are away on vacation in Hawaii. Afterwards, Diane flew home to San Francisco thinking she was engaged to Ted to be married.
August 1, 1973: Ted in Seattle.
August 2, 1973: Bought gas driving his VW, Tumwater.
August 3, 1973: Ted in Seattle.
August 4, 1973: Ted in Seattle. Bought gas driving, Tumwater (tag # unknown).
August 6, 1973: Bought gas driving his VW, Seattle.
August 7, 1973: Ted parked a vehicle, Seattle.
August 10, 1973: Ted in Olympia.
August 11, 1973: Ted in Seattle & Tumwater.
August 15, 1973: Bought gas driving his VW, Seattle.
August 16, 1973: Ted in Seattle.
August 17, 1973: Bought gas driving his VW, Seattle.
August 18, 1973: Bought gas driving Tacoma (tag # OYU-149).

Vicki Lynn Hollar (undated). Photo to public domain.

August 20, 1973: Vicki Lynn Hollar (24) was last seen 5:00 p.m. by a co-worker as she walked to her black 1965 Volkswagen Beetle with Illinois license plates GR 7738 and running boards removed after getting off work at the Bon Marche store (now Macy's) in downtown Eugene, Oregon, where she had been employed as a seamstress for about two weeks. She was seen getting into her car but was not seen driving from the parking lot at 8th Avenue and Washington Street. She was possibly heading home to her apartment that she shared with five other people on the 600 block of West 27th Avenue in Eugene because she planned to meet up with a friend that night to attend a party in the neighborhood. She had a habit of

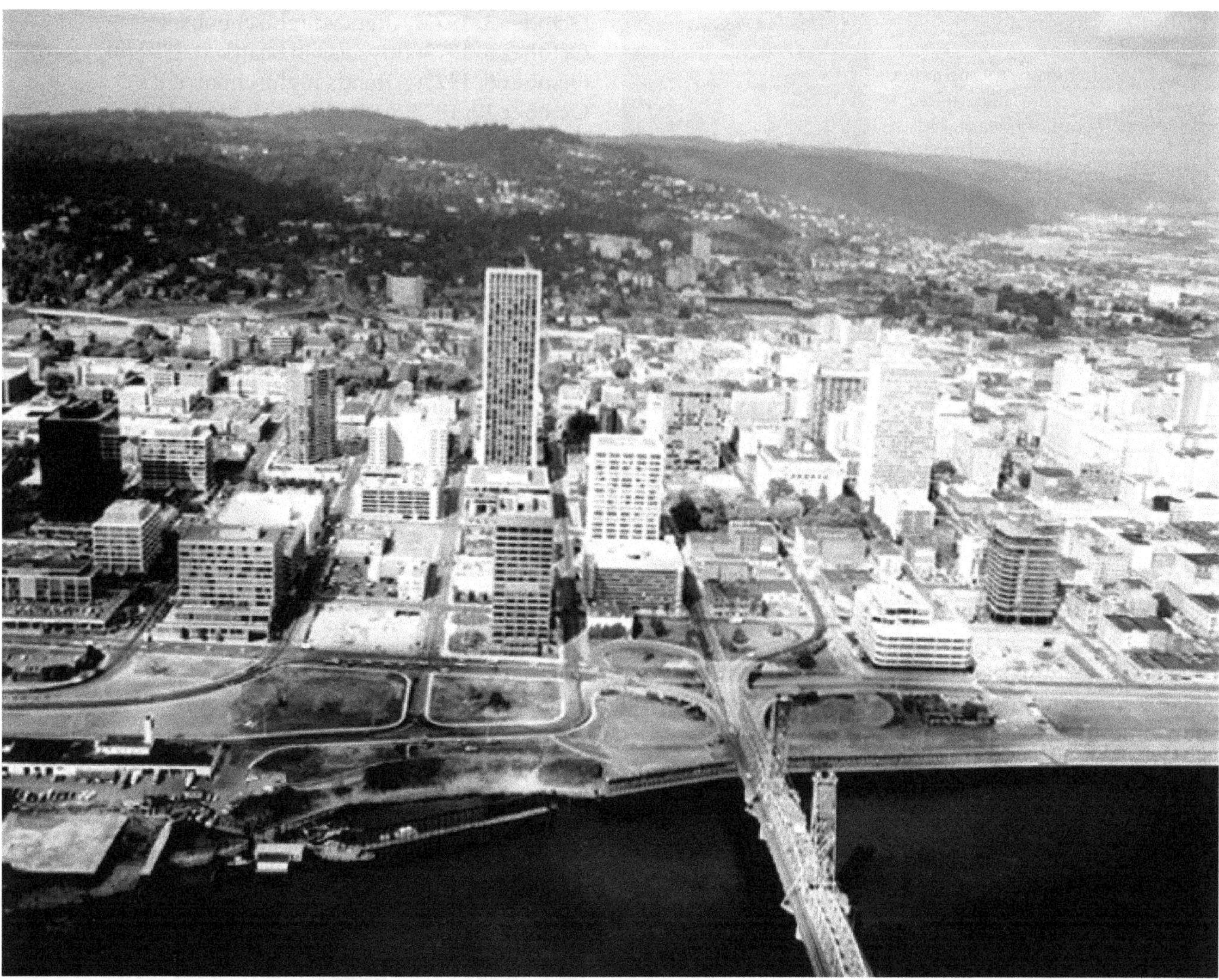

Portland, Oregon, 1975. Photo public domain.

picking up hitchhikers and had moved to Eugene from Illinois the previous June after graduating from college there. Her car and purse have never been recovered. It takes at least 4 hours 40 minutes to drive from Seattle to Eugene. While possible, due to time discrepancies, the window of opportunity here seems too narrow to realistically speculate.

August 22, 1973: Ted in Seattle.

August 23, 1973: Buys gas in Tumwater (tag # unknown).

August 24, 1973: Ted in Olympia. Has accident with Liz's VW, Seattle.

August 28, 1973: Bought gas driving his VW, Dupont, Washington.

August 29, 1973: Bought gas driving, Tumwater (tag # ICI-418).

August 30, 1973: Bought gas driving Tumwater (tag # 17241V). 12:00 p.m. Drove Hertz rental truck, Olympia. 8:00 p.m. returned rental truck, Olympia.

August 31, 1973: Ted in Seattle. (PM) Ted at Sea-Tac airport, Seattle Washington. Diane Edwards arrives.

End August 1973: Ross Davis notices pair of handcuffs in Ted's VW trunk.

September 1973: Gets well-paid position as assistant to the Washington State Republican chairman. Second accepted into the Univ. Utah law school.

September - November 1973: Lynda Healy moves into 5517 12th Avenue Northeast, Seattle.

September 1, 1973: Ted parks a vehicle, Seattle.

September 2, 1973: Diane Edwards and Ted officially engaged. Bought gas driving, Issaquah, Washington (tag # BTR-416).

September 3, 1973: Buys gas in Seattle (tag # unknown).

September 4, 1973: Starts night classes UPS law school. Diane Edwards returns to San Francisco. Ted in Olympia.

September 5, 1973: Ted in Seattle.

September 6, 1973: Bought gas driving his VW, Seattle.

September 7, 1973: Attends nightschool, UPS.

September 9, 1973: Enters UPS law school according to MTR. Youtube video submitted August 9, 2013 by Kansas Police in which Elaine Crafton revealed the following encounter with a Ted-like suspect sometime in the

1970s:

Elaine Crafton, August 9, 2013. Photo public domain.

"I did have an encounter with a young man when I was about 19-years old. I was walking down the street near the University of Puget Sound campus when I was approached by a young man driving a Volkswagen Beetle, pulled up to a curbside, and wanted to talk to me, waived me over to his Volkswagen, and said, 'Hi, I'm not from around here. Can you tell me where there are any parks near here?' I found out after his arrest that the individual who actually waived me to his car that day was Ted. My inner voice had told me even though I was looking at a very nice-looking individual, who's very nice and clean-shaven, clean-cut, my inner voice kept saying to me, guys like him don't talk to you, guys like him don't stop and pick you up."

September 10, 1973: Attends nightschool, UPS.
September 11, 1973: Ted in Tumwater. Driving '72 Ford, ¾-ton [pickup] truck. "Operation Peace of Mind" is opened after Texas State Police is flooded with inquiries on missing children during the discovery of the Houston mass murders.
September 12, 1973: Attends nightschool, UPS.
September 13, 1973: Shaved off beard.
September 14, 1973: Attends nightschool, UPS.
September 17, 1973: Had sprained ankle checked at an orthopedic clinic, Seattle. Also on this day, Schaefer's trial begins in Florida.
September 18, 1973: Attends nightschool, UPS.
September 19, 1973: Attends nightschool, UPS.
September 20, 1973: Ted parks vehicle, Seattle (tag # unknown).
September 21, 1973: Attends nightschool, UPS.
September 24, 1973: Attends nightschool, UPS.
September 25, 1973: Bought gas driving his VW, Tukwila, Washington.
September 26, 1973: Attends nightschool, UPS.
September 27, 1973: Attends nightschool, UPS.
September 25, 1973: Bought gas driving his VW, Seattle.
September 27, 1973: Schaefer pronounced guilty for the murder of Place and Jessup. Receives two life sentences.
October 1973: Liz finds a brown paper sack in the middle of the floor just inside Ted's apartment door. She noticed one of the items in the sack was a woman's bra, however, she did not go through the sack any further. This was in the Fall of 1973 (Ira Beal notes from Kloepfer interview September 17, 1975). Rape victims' clothing? Snow-dropping? Also around this time Ted is involved in political campaigning with Bob Santos and Jim Mattingly.
October 1, 1973: Attends nightschool, UPS.
October 3, 1973: Attends nightschool, UPS.
October 4, 1973: Ted parks a vehicle, Seattle.
October 5, 1973: Attends nightschool, UPS.
October 6, 1973: Buys gas in Seattle (tag # unknown).
October 8, 1973: Attends nightschool, UPS.
October 10, 1973: Attends nightschool, UPS
October 12, 1973: Attends nightschool, UPS
October 13, 1973: Ted bought gas driving his VW, Seattle.

Deborah Tomlinson (undated). Photo public domain.

October 15, 1973: Deborah Lee Tomlinson (16) from Creswell, Oregon, ran away from home with another female teen whose identity is unknown. Both have never been seen again.
October 17, 1973: Attends nightschool, UPS. OPEC Oil Embargo begins.
October 18, 1973: Parked a vehicle, Seattle.
October 19, 1973: Attends nightschool, UPS.
October 21, 1973: Bought gas driving Seattle (IBH-521).
October 24, 1973: Attends nightschool, UPS.
October 23, 1973: A 17-year old Pocatello girl is taken from her home while babysitting and raped. No arrests are made.
October 26, 1973: Attends nightschool, UPS.
October 29, 1973: Attends nightschool, UPS.
October 31, 1973: Attends nightschool, UPS.
November 1, 1973: Visits unemployment office in Seattle.
November 2, 1973: Attends nightschool, UPS.

Suzanne Rae Justis (circa 1968). Photo public domain

November 5, 1973: Suzanne Rae Justis (23) lived in Eugene, Oregon, but was last heard from when she telephoned her parents from outside the Memorial Colosseum in Portland. She said she would be back in Eugene the following day to pick up her son from school. Her mother (Mrs Seay) reserved a room for her at a nearby motel, but Justis never used the room. Her car was found in Eugene, leading police to believe she hitchhiked to Portland, as she was known to do. She hasn't been heard from since.
November 7, 1973: Visits unemployment office in Seattle.
November 9, 1973: Attends nightschool, UPS.
November 13, 1973: Visits unemployment office in Seattle.
November 14, 1973: Attends nightschool, UPS.
November 16, 1973: Attends nightschool, UPS.
November 19, 1973: Attends nightschool, UPS.
November 25, 1973: Had beard and moustache. Kather-

ine Merry Devine (14) last seen standing at a north Seattle intersection.
November 26, 1973: Attends nightschool, UPS.
November 27, 1973: Has birthday party, Seattle.
November 28, 1973: Attends nightschool, UPS.
November 30, 1973: Attends nightschool, UPS.
December 1973: Ted secretly reapplies to the Univ. Utah law school. According to Liz, he picks up a copy of a book called *The Joy of Sex* (Rule 1989, 157).

The original 1972 cover. Photo public domain.

December 2, 1973: 12:30 p.m. – 4:30 p.m. Had car repaired at Freeway VW. Set points and fixed gas leak. Chris Sharpe saw a ski mask in Ted's car. Around this time Ted had access to Marlin Vortman's VW bug.
December 6, 1973: Attends nightschool, UPS. Wrote check to Ernst Rogers.
December 6, 1973: Ted wrote check Univ. Washington bookstore. Also on this day Katherine Merry Devine's body found in McKenny Park (3.6 miles west of the city of Olympia). She had been strangled, sodomized, and her throat was cut. On March 8, 2002 prosecutors using DNA were able to determining that William E. Cosden Jr. murdered her. Cosden had been released from a mental hospital in 1973 where he was confined for the murder of a woman in 1967. On November 30, 1975 he raped a woman in rural Thurston County (Olympia-Tumwater area). He was arrested for that rape in 1976 and has been imprisoned ever since.

Top: Kathy Merry Devine (circa 1973). Bottom: William Cosden 1975 mugshot. Photos public domain.

December 8, 1973: Attends nightschool, UPS. Wrote check to University Auto Parts.
December 12, 1973: Has VW Washington tag IBH-521 in for gas repairs, Seattle.
December 15, 1973: Attends Crisis Clinic Christmas party again with Rule. This time brings Liz along. According to Rule, "She seemed very small, very vulnerable, and her long light brown hair overpowered her facial features. Clearly she adored Ted, and she clung to him ..." (Rule 1989, 40). Ted tied Liz up spread-eagle during sex and nearly choked her around this time. Liz said he also tried anal intercourse with her a few times but she put a stop to it after the choking incident (Ira Beal, Bountiful Police Department report, September 17, 1975).
Mid-December 1973: Quits UPS law school before end-year exams.
December 18, 1973: Kathy Devine's family seeks initiative to put hitchhiking issue on state ballot (*Spokane Daily Chronicle*).
December 19, 1973: Visits unemployment office in Seattle. Writes check to Safeway.
December 24 1973: Liz goes to parent's home in Ogden. Diane Edwards comes up to Seattle and spends time with Ted. They affirm their marriage plans. During a conversation about abortion he yelled at Diane and frightened her (Kendall 1981, 100). Around this time Ted injures his head skiing at Crystal Mountain, Washington.
December 28, 1973: Ted bought gas Tukwila, Washington (which is next to the King County International Airport). Wrote a check to the UPS. Wrote check to Safeway.
December 29, 1973: Writes check to Fidelity Ticket Office, Seattle.
December 31, 1973: (Day) Writes check to Thriftway, Seattle. Writes check to Tai Tung's. (New Year's Eve) Liz cleaning oven when Ted suddenly appears. He beguiles her. They go out to the Sandpiper Tavern where they first met and neck in a back booth. [One problem with this date is that Diane Edwards is still in Seattle according to other accounts. How could Ted leave her on such an important day?] Bought a chess set for Marlin Vortman, showed it to Edwards.

- 1974 -

Early 1974: Buys gallon of regular gas: $0.53. Jeanie Packer reports on 1 March 2014, that when she was 6 years old, she was nearly abducted from her Seattle home front yard:

> "A man walked up to the side of me and said, hi, then he asked what I was doing and I told him. He then asked me if I wanted to go meet Jesus. I told him, yeah, and then he held out his hand and helped me to my feet. He did not say anything more to me after that. We had walked just past my house and were in front of my next door neighbor's house, when my friend's mother called out to me, Jeanie – where are you going? I turned slightly to answer her and the man let go of my hand abruptly and took off running into the Navy woods. This place was connected to Fircrest Hospital. [...] I remember the man was thin. He had medium brown hair. He was not tall, I think looking back on it now that he was probably in the 5'6" to 5'7" range. I feel this because they asked if he was as tall as my dad and I said, no – shorter. My dad was 5'11". I knew he was taller than my mom though. She was 5'2". His hair was curly, but they were large round curls. They asked me what color he was, and I could not figure it out at first. He was not black, white, Asian or brown. Then they showed me pictures of skin tones and I picked out what was called swarthy. His voice was very soft but he did not have an accent. He seemed the way he spoke to be

very safe at the time" (Packer 2014).

January 1, 1974: Writes check to Thriftway, Seattle. Nick Mackie's February 21, 1978 report to Leon County Sheriff's Office has Diane Edwards flying back to San Francisco on this day. 5:00 p.m. "Airport" entry in Ted's 1973 diary. In his February 1978 interrogation, Ted also said he last saw her January 1, 1974. These three pieces of information make it likely that Ted last saw Diane on this day.

January 2, 1974: Ted visits unemployment office in Seattle wearing a beard.

Chevron gas card, 1975. Photo public domain.

January 3, 1974: Chevron card gas purchase, Seattle, $3.75.

January 4, 1974: Shortly after midnight Karen Lee Sparks (21) turned off the TV in the living room of her home (4325 8th Avenue NE, Seattle), and retired to her bedroom set up in the basement of the house. She was a dance student at Univ. Wash. in Seattle and rented a room in the house along with three men. A small window on the south side of the house was undraped and looked down on Karen's bed. There was also a tree outside the window that would have concealed a voyeur. Further information given by a roommate indicated one of the doors on that south side of the house was always left unlocked. This was probably the entry and exit point. Sometime after 2:00 a.m. Ted stole into the basement bedroom and bludgeoned Karen while she slept. From the police photos it appears that Karen slept on a mattress on the floor. There are blood stains on the wall at the level of the mattress. This contradicts Rule's report of Ted ripping a rod from Sparks' bedframe (Rule 2006, 49). The three men living in the house told police they thought a piece of steel rebar they had seen lying outside the house was missing (Larsen 1980, 15). In another account, after battering her with the rebar Ted assaulted her with a speculum which he left in her vagina after leaving her for dead (K&M 2012, 46). Why would Ted leave behind such incriminating evidence? This also doesn't make sense. Around 2:30 p.m. the next day, one of the young men Karen lived with poked his head into her bedroom, saw her in bed, and assumed she was sleeping in, or napping. However, at 7:30 p.m. on January 5th, when it was realized Karen had still not risen from her bed, her roommates rushed

We cannot confirm that this is a 1974 photos of Karen Sparks' house (4325 8th Avenue NE, Seattle), however, examination of 1937 aerial maps leads us to this best guess. Photo courtesy KCA.

Karen Sparks' room showing the bloody mattress on the floor (in situ, January 5, 1974). Where is the bedframe? A picture from a different angle showing the chair in the foreground is on the web and incorrecly attributes the room to Lynda Healy. Photo courtesty KCA.

to her bedside and found her bloody and barely alive. She remained unconscious for ten days, suffered severe internal injuries and permanent brain damage, but she survived. After Karen recovered, doctors put her under sodium pentothal in the hopes that she recollected some information about her attacker, but to no avail.

January 7, 1974: Writes check to UPS bookstore, Seattle.

January 8, 1974: Writes check to Book store, Seattle.

January 9, 1974: Writes personal check on Rainier Bank to Rogers' rooming house. Chevron card gas purchase, Seattle, $4.15.

January 10, 1974: Writes check to Department of Motor Vehicles, Seattle.

January 11, 1974: Attends evening classes at UPS.

January 12, 1974: Writes check to Aurora Plumbing, Seattle.

January 14, 1974: Attends evening classes at UPS.

January 15, 1974: Chevron card gas purchase, Seattle, $2.78.

January 16, 1974: Attends evening classes at UPS.

January 17, 1974: Picks up unemployment check in Seattle. Writes personal check on Rainier Bank to UPS bookstore.

January 18, 1974: Attends evening classes at UPS.

January 19, 1974: Writes check to the Office of the Attorney General for a workshop, Seattle.

January 20, 1974: Attends evening classes at UPS. Shaves off beard.

January 21, 1974: Deposits money in bank, Seattle.

January 22, 1974: Parks a vehicle at the Oly Hotel, Seattle, Chevron card $1.50.

January 23, 1974: Chevron card gas purchase, Seattle, $3.00.

January 25, 1974: Attends evening classes at UPS.

January 28, 1974: Deposits money in bank, Seattle. Receives letter from Diane Edwards (probably confirming anger at final breakup).

January 29, 1974: Chevron card gas purchase, 1200 Block Denny, Seattle, $3.46. Picks up unemployment check in Seattle.

January 30, 1974: Attends evening classes at UPS.

January 31, 1974: Ted wrestling with midterms. Wrote check at Safeway store, 49th and Brooklyn, close to Lynda Healy's residence.

Lynda Healy (circa 1973). Photo public domain.

February 1, 1974: (Sometime in the early hours after midnight, Friday) Ted abducts Lynda Ann Healy (21) from 5517 12th Avenue NE, Seattle (University-District). He takes her while she is semi-comatose to an undisclosed location where he rapes and strangles her, then deposits her body (most probably) above ground where animals are able to devour it. (Morning) Ted deposits money in his bank, Seattle. Chevron card gas purchase $2.15 at 43rd and Roosevelt. Then class at UPS, Tacoma. (Afternoon) Lynda reported missing.

Dante's Tavern (undated). Photo public domain.

Lynda's house, 5517 12th Avenue Northeast, (February 1974). Photo courtesy KCA.

On normal days, 7:00 a.m. radio listeners heard Lynda's friendly voice announce the ski conditions for the major ski areas in western Washington:

> "Hi, this is Lynda with your Cascade Ski Report: Snoqualmie Pass is 29 degrees with snow and ice patches on the road; Stevens Pass is 17 degrees and overcast with packed snow on the roadway ..." (Rule 2006, 49).

The product of a good family and an upper-middle-class environment, she was an excellent singer and a senior at Univ. Wash., where she majored in psychology. Ted's cousin Edna Cowell knew of Lynda, and Ted

Healy residence, showing side entrance door (February 1974). Photo courtesy KCA.

Top left: View showing the side door open leading down to the basement rooms. Top right and bottom left: View of stairs from basement. Bottom right: View looking into Lynda Healy's room at bottom of stairs (February 1974). Photos courtesy KCA.

was enrolled in the same psychology course as Lynda in 1972. Lynda loved working with children who were mentally handicapped.

Lynda walked home from Dante's Tavern with her housemates, Joanne Testa and Ginger Heath and a mutual friend Pete, around 9:30 p.m. Pete caught a bus home at 9:41 p.m. Back home, Lynda received a call from her ex-boyfriend. They talked for about an hour. The girls then watched TV until around just before midnight, when Lynda went to bed. Her alarm went off at 5:30 a.m., when she was supposed to get up and ride her bike to the radio station to do her ski report. The radio station rang at 6:00 a.m. to ask why Lynda wasn't at work. Karen Skavlem's bedroom lies next to Lynda's in the basement. She was awoken at 5:30 a.m. by Lynda's alarm but went back to sleep. She woke up again to her own alarm at 6:00 a.m. She got up, went past Lynda's room, assumed she was lying in bed listening to the radio, and presumably had breakfast. At 6:30 a.m. Northwest Ski Promotions rang asking why Lynda wasn't at work. Karen went to her room and called her. When she didn't answer, she turned the light on and found her absent. Not realizing the full extent of what happened, but unsettled, the girls went about their day.

It was around 4:00 p.m. in the afternoon when the girls got back home. Lynda had a dinner planned for her parents and her boyfriend that evening. That plan was now in disarray. Between 5:00 and 6:00 p.m. Lynda's brother and father arrived. Lynda's father talked to Lynda's mother on the phone. She was worried and after some back-and-forth called the police. According to Monica Sutherland, a single officer came around at about 6:00 p.m. and took a missing person's report (Officer Marshall). After the officer left, the girls began ringing their friends, asking after Lynda. Lynda's brother and father left around 8:00 p.m. Concern mounted and by midnight a second police unit arrived; detectives Wayne Dorman and Ted Fonis. Joanne Testa's police report provides the following information:

> Before the police went to Lynda's room I had gone in it. I found her curtains to be closed. I believe it was usual for her to open them during the day and close them at night. I noticed that her room was neat and her bed was also neatly made. To my knowledge it was not customary for Lynda to make her bed on those mornings that she had to work. It also seems to me that she did not always put her pillow under the bedspread – rather sometimes placed it on top. She had two pink satin pillowcases. I was there when the policeman pulled back the spread for the first time. I saw that the pillow case was gone and that there were blood stains on the pillow as well as one fairly large blood stain on the sheet – near the pillow. As far as I know, Lynda always kept a pillowcase on her pillow.

Ginger Heath's report is even more revealing:

> On showing them the room they went through the waste paper basket and pulled back the bedspread and blankets on Lynda's bed finding blood. The first thing I immediately noticed was the missing pillowcase. Also the bed was made differently from the way Lynda usually makes it. The bedspread was tucked under the pillow whereas usually she just throws it over the pillow without a crease under the pillow. Also the bedspread was so perfect, in that there were

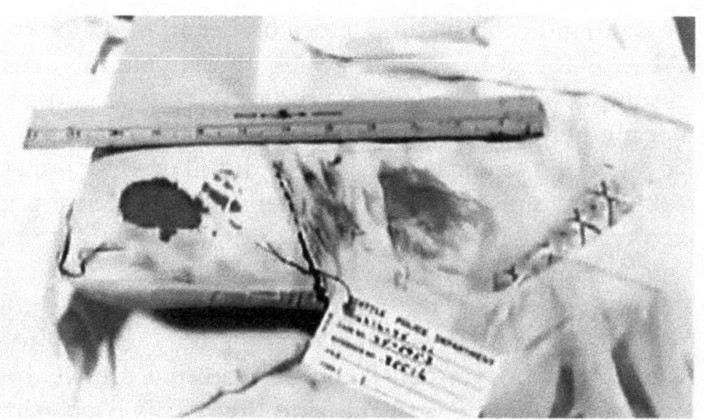

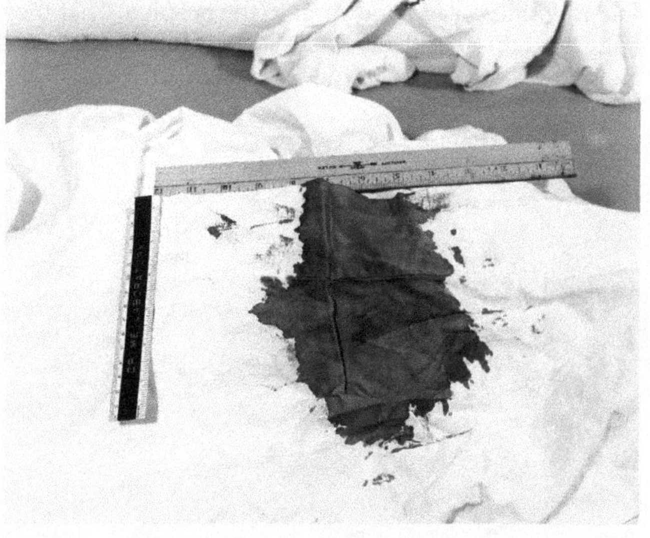

Top and right: Close-up of the bloodstained pillow and sheet (February 1974). Photos courtesy KCA.

> no wrinkles on the bed. I thought too, that when the officers pulled back the blankets, the sheets were folded in such a fashion that the blood wasn't as visible.

The detectives concluded that there was enough blood to indicate serious injury, but not death. The accepted story is the detectives then searched Lynda's closet and found her nightie. But Heath wrote the following in her police report:

> I later went down to her room to see about clothing missing—this is still on Friday night and early Saturday morning—I then found her nightie draped across the bottom pole in her closet, finding a smear of blood on the shoulder.

This means that Heath must have pointed out the nightie to the detectives. There are no known photos of it, but it has been described as "pink." The housemates helped police conclude that Lynda's white peasant blouse, her old jeans with a funny triangular patch on the back, her two turquoise rings—distinctive round flat rings with tiny, turquoise nuggets "floating" on top silver circles—and her boots she had worn the previous evening, were gone. So too was her red backpack that had gray straps. The officers initially concluded that Lynda had suffered a

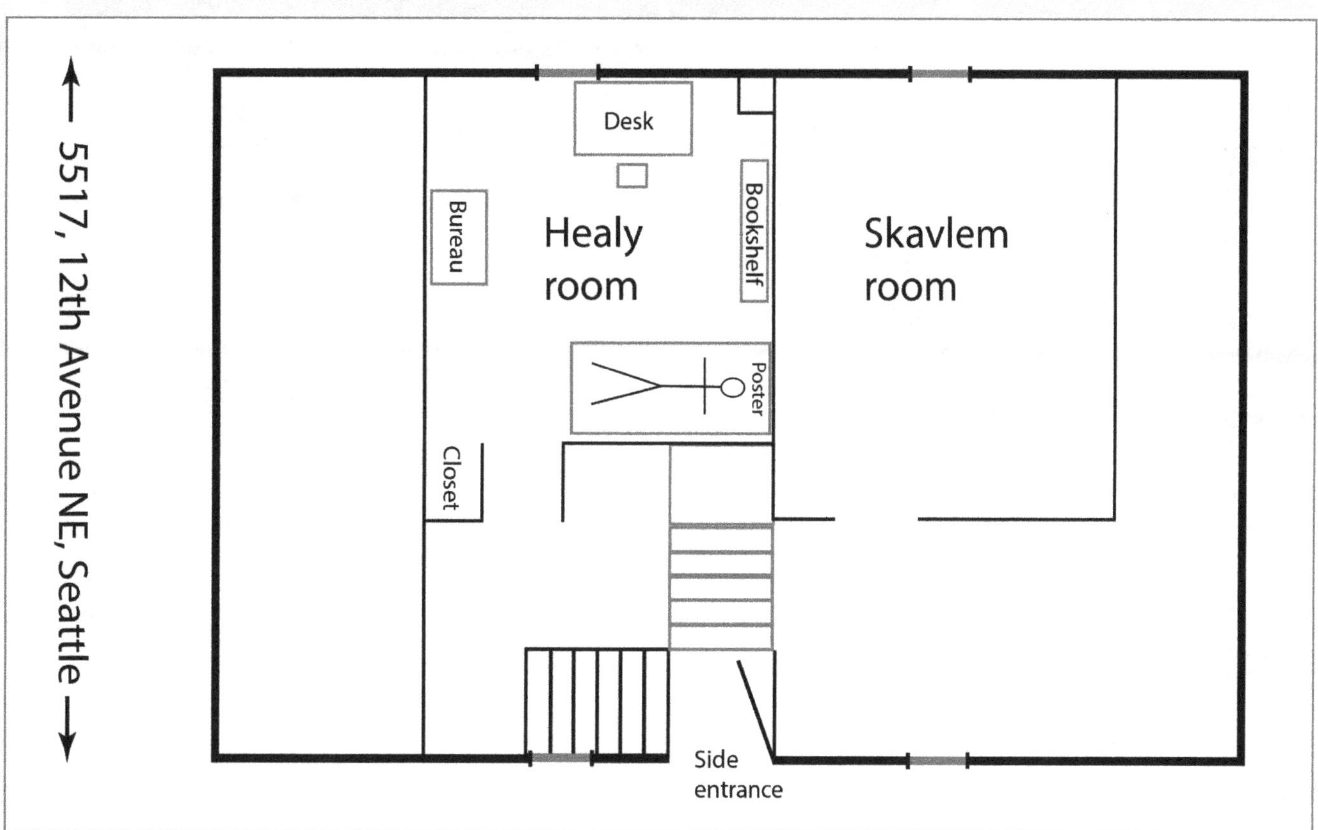

Plan of Healy's basement room based on a contemporary police diagram (courtesy KCA). There is no information about Skavlem's room, so it is not clear where her bed was positioned.

late-night nosebleed and went to the hospital. That they suggested this (a full day after she had still not contacted anyone) indicates incompetence on behalf of the police. When that argument didn't stick, they made the usual assumption that Lynda was a runaway. But according to her mother Joyce, not Lynda. Still, the police would not be moved. As a consequence, they didn't dust for fingerprints, vacuum the room for hair and fiber evidence, and according to Michaud & Aynesworth, failed to test for a semen stain found on Lynda's bed sheet (1983, 27).

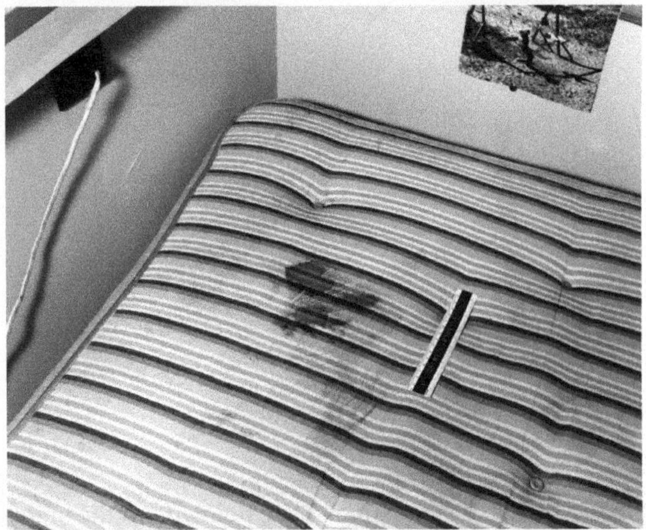

Close-up of the bed mattress (February 1974). Photo courtesy KCA.

As time passed, the police were forced to conclude that Lynda had been abducted. The theory was put forward that whoever had taken her had first dressed her before carrying her out the side door. This conclusion was based on the fact that her backpack and clothes were missing. There is no evidence for this theory; it is based on emotional reasoning rather than practical logic. If anyone actually tried to dress a semi-comatose person in a blouse, jeans and boots, they would quickly discover that a substantial amount of manhandling is required. Sitting up, pulling, laying down again. This amount of handling would have resulted in a significant amount of blood transfer beyond the circumscribed area it was

Lynda's bed in situ (February 1974). Karen Skavlem's room lies behind the wall with the poster of Seattle. Photo courtesy KCA.

found in. The nightie only had a blood "smear" around the shoulder area. We know he removed it because it was later found in the closet.

Ted said he found the front door open (M&A 1983, 114). More likely, he stole Lynda's keys (she "lost" them sometime before the abduction). He claimed he gagged Lynda and carried her out, put her in the back seat of his car and covered her with something, then drove her out to a "secluded" location (presumably Taylor Mountain). The initial question is: did Ted plan the abduction ahead of time? We recall what he did to Karen Sparks. In that incident, it appears he left her lying there thinking he killed her. That, of course, is an assumption. We learned that Sparks was battered in her sleep, so there was no opportunity for her to recognize her attacker. Ted knew this, so we cannot be completely sure he intended to kill her. He knew he was safe the moment he bashed her. However, it doesn't account for the speculum he left behind; a most incriminating piece of evidence. Even though no finger prints were recovered, it was later linked to his job at Pedline. Ted would not make the same mistake again.

Given the Sparks experience, it still does not allow us to assume Ted planned to abduct Lynda. His M.O. could have been the same. Silently enter the house, bludgeon the young lady unconscious, rape her, and leave. Even if he left semen evidence, so long as he was not linked to the crime, he was safe. The difference appears to be the amount of blood. In the Sparks case there was more blood, primarily because the victim had lain in bed for a day allowing greater transfer. The limited amount of blood in the Healy case does not suggest a lesser trauma; rather, it may indicate more rapid removal of the victim from the scene after the beating. Police also learned that Ted's checking account records showed he had cashed checks at the Safeway food store at 47th and Brooklyn in

Healy's housemates (March 1974). From left to right: Ginger Heath, Joanne Testa and Monica Sutherland. Karen Skavlem not shown. Karen once met Ted at Sandy Gwinn's parent's place. Keppel claimed that after Lynda's disappearance Ted "would go over to her apartment frequently to visit her roommates" (Aspen Seminar, November 13-14, 1975). Photo public domain.

the heart of the U-District only eight blocks from Lynda's residence on the very date she disappeared. They also found Lynda had cashed a check at the same Safeway store on the same day and at virtually same time. They contacted the clerk whose initials were on the check and asked her to tell them how long she worked that day. "Only four hours" was the answer. So the margin was relatively narrow. If they were both in the store at the same time there is the possibility that Ted may have actually stalked Lynda on the day he abducted her. More incriminating was that Ted and Lynda were in the same psychology course, even though they may have not attended the same classes. And finally, Ted's cousin, Edna Cowell, was friends with one of Lynda's roommates (Karen Covach?). The weight of evidence, therefore, suggests that Ted probably planned the whole thing.

Following this assumption, the next branching question is: did he remove her and return to clean up the crime scene, or did he clean up the crime scene and remove Lynda in a single action? The higher probability lies with the latter. Firstly, because from all accounts, this was Ted's first abduction from a home. As such it represents an escalation of behavior, and with it, comes an increased risk, and therefore nervousness on Ted's part. Secondly, it is hard to imagine Ted leaving a semi-comatose victim in his car on the street while he is out of visual and auditory range cleaning up a crime scene. The only exception to this rule appears to be the Kent case, but this happened at a time when Ted was at an all time high in confidence, with at least fourteen successful abductions under his belt. So it is highly unlikely that he would have left Lynda alone in his car once he had her there. Most likely, he would have wanted to high-tail out of there as fast as possible.

As an interesting aside, Joanne Testa, one of Lynda's roommates, said that two nights before the abduction an unidentified man fled when he was found in the basement of a home two doors away. And earlier in the week, a prowler was reported outside a nearby apartment house testing a locked door with a knife. We do not know if these reports are linked to Ted, but they suggest an increased level of crime in the area at the time. Also, on February 6, 1974, Monica Sutherland gave a report to Seattle Homicide. A month after Christmas (which placed it about a week before Lynda's abduction) Sutherland had just come home and undressed for bed (the assumption being that it is late in the evening). She went on to relate the following:

> Our neighbor dog started barking considerably, much more so than usual and [so I] grabbed a robe and ran downstairs not being fully dressed and looked through the door, and saw a young man standing on our lower step and holding this little dog around the neck shaking it fiercely. I rushed out—and found many neighbors already outside, and yelled at him—he replied something like this dog was attacking me and then fled on foot and [I] believe he was dressed in dark blue sweatshirt and pants – white male – 21-25.

Given these reports, it makes Ted's success even more unlikely. It would seem that despite all his planning and preparation, luck was on his side.

Going with the single action theory, and knowing he made the bed, we have no option but to conclude that he must have put Lynda temporarily on the floor. But if he did that he risked the possibility of transferring blood. According to Keppel:

> We noticed in the crime scene photographs that her photos had been pinned on the wall above the headboard of her bed. It appeared as though some were askew and, from the empty spaces, that some were missing from their place on the wall. We figured they might have been dislodged and fallen down between the wall and the bed during the assault. If so, we wanted to process those for latent fingerprints. The crime scene photos didn't show the floor, so we didn't know if there was a rug, which is often a magnet for the kind of physical evidence—hair or fibers—we were in search of. As it turned out, there was a rug (K&B 2005, 88).

It would make sense to roll her up in the rug and carry her out that way, but there is a surprise. Keppel continues:

> One roommate who had let Lynda borrow the rug had retrieved it from Healy's apartment after the crime and had given it to her father. He had rolled it up and placed it in a storage closet. Lucky for us, he had never bothered to clean it. So when we asked him for it, he simply turned it over in the same condition it was right after the crime, and Kay Sweeney [our crime lab expert] quickly figured out which part had been underneath Healy's bed. We found several light brown human hairs in the rug that did not belong to Lynda or her friends (K&B 2005, 89).

All very interesting, but in the end, nothing came of the rug evidence it seems. No further mention is made of it by Keppel. So how did Ted do it?

He almost certainly brought a rape kit with him. This would have included a torch, bindings, rope, and maybe a club of some sort. It is hard to say whether he brought a knife; it doesn't appear necessary. Some time after 1:30 a.m. he crept into Lynda's room and clubbed her, following the same M.O. he used with Sparks. We do not know what level of injury Lynda sustained during this first attack, but judging by the blood evidence, it must have been sufficient to disorient her for at least a few minutes. During this time, Ted would have gagged and bound her. He now had options. Rape her there, or take her some place else and rape her. If the semen rumor is true, then he probably performed some sort of sexual activity at her bedside. It is at this stage that he probably removed her nightie. That part of the attack over, Ted now had to decide what to do with her. If we go with our assumption that he planned her abduction in advance, then he would begin the cleaning process, to create obfuscation between himself and potential discovery. This required moving Lynda to the floor, so as to make the bed. To avoid transfer of blood, he probably put the pillow case over her head. This would serve the dual purpose of keeping the victim disoriented, while also reducing the amount of blood transfer. It is at this point that he made the bed. He then grabbed Lynda's ready-to-hand clothes and stuffed them in her backpack. The aim of that move was to lead Lynda's housemates to believe Lynda left on her own volition (and judging the police's thinking process, it worked). As a final flourish, he hid her nightie in the closet. With those steps completed, he put the backpack on, then slung Lynda over his shoulder and carried her out to his car. We do not know if he took a sheet and wrapped her in it before doing this, or whether he carried her out naked with a pillow case over her head. At that time of morning, it may not have mattered. All he had to do was check left and right up and down the street, and finding it clear, quickly manhandle her into his car and drive off. This would be Ted's last known home invasion until Chi Omega in January 1978.

February 4, 1974: Attends evening classes at UPS.

February 6, 1974: Attends evening classes at UPS.

February 7, 1974: Chevron card gas purchase for Liz's VW, Seattle, $2.35.

February 11, 1974: Chevron card gas purchase $4.50 (8.9 gals).

February 12, 1974: Petrol prices rise to unprecedented levels due to the OPEC Oil Embargo. Rationing creates long cues.

February 13, 1974: Picks up unemployment check in Seattle.

February 15, 1974: Uses credit card to buy shoes, Nordstrom university store, Seattle. (Afternoon) Deposits money in bank, Seattle. Attends evening classes at UPS.

February 21, 1974: Heidi Brigit Peterson (4) disappears. She was last seen by her mother, Sally Peterson, playing with her two-and-a-half-year old brother Carl in the front yard of the Peterson home in Capitol Hill, Seattle, around 1:30 p.m. The search for her was one of the most extensive, organized efforts ever launched for a missing child.

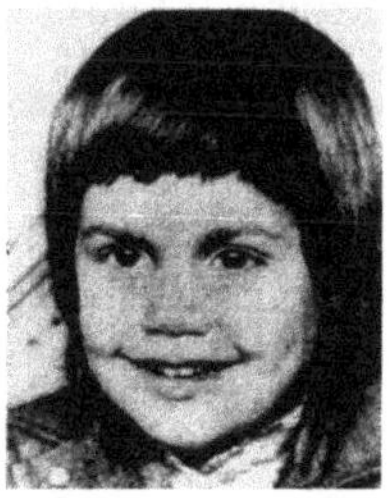

Heidi Peterson (undated). Image source *Boca Raton News*, August 11, 1974.

February 22, 1974: Attends evening classes at UPS.

February 27, 1974: Picks up unemployment check in Seattle. Chevron card gas purchase $4.35.

March 1, 1974: Attends evening classes at UPS.

March 2, 1974: A young woman (20) is raped in her home (4220 12th Avenue N.E.) only a few doors down from Freda Rogers' rooming house where Ted lived. Seattle Morals Detective Joyce Johnson investigated the case. The victim, an attractive twenty-year-old woman, had gone to bed around 1:00 a.m. on Saturday morning. According to Rule:

> "My shades were drawn, but there's a place where one of the curtains doesn't meet the sill and someone could look in and see that I was alone. About three-quarters of the time, I have someone with me. That morning, I'd forgotten to put the wooden slat in the window to lock it. The man took off the screen, and, when I woke up about four, I saw him standing in the doorway. I saw his profile. There was a light shining through from the living room where he'd left his flashlight on. He came over and sat on my bed and told me to relax, that he wouldn't hurt me." The woman had asked him how he'd gotten in and he answered, "It is none of your business." The man had worn a tee shirt, jeans, and had a dark navy watch cap pulled over his face to below his chin. "It wasn't a ski mask, but I think he had made slits in it for his eyes because he could see. His voice was well-educated. He'd been drinking; I could smell it. He had a knife with a carved handle, but he said he wouldn't use it if I didn't fight." The man had taped her eyes, and then he had raped her. She didn't fight him. When he was finished, he'd taped her hands and feet, telling her it was just to "slow her down." She heard him go into the living room and crawl through a window, then heard the sound of footsteps running toward the alley. She heard no car. She told Detective Johnson, "He was so calm and sure of himself. I think he's done it before" (Rule 1989, 174).

Note: Ted's 'oriental knife' was discovered missing from Liz's VW glove box when her car was retrieved after being stolen in early August 1973.

March 3, 1974: Writes check to Northwest Copy, Seattle.

March 4, 1974: Deposits money in bank, Seattle. Attends evening classes at UPS.

March 5, 1974: Chevron card gas purchase, Seattle, $3.00 (6 gals).

March 6, 1974: Attends evening classes at UPS.

March 7, 1974: Chevron card gas purchase, Seattle, $3.10.

March 8, 1974: Attends evening classes at UPS.

March 9, 1974: Uses credit card to buy shoes, Nordstrom Northgate, Seattle.

March 11-12, 1974: Chevron card gas purchase, Seattle, $4.75 (two purchases). Fails to pick up unemployment check, Seattle. Helps Liz Kloepfer move.

March 12, 1974: Approximately 7:00 p.m. Abducts Donna Gail Manson (19) from Evergreen State College, Olympia. Decapitates head at some point. A friend of Donna's, Tom Sampson, used to play racquetball with Ted. Did Sampson talk about Donna to Ted? Donna was a student at Evergreen State College in Olympia in 1974. Tuesday night, was rainy, she planned to attend a jazz concert on campus. Her dormitory mates recalled she changed clothes several times before settling on red, orange and green striped shirt, blue slacks, a fuzzy black coat, an oval-shaped brown agate ring, and a Bulova wristwatch.

Evergreen State College (1976). Yellow dashed line designates path Donna Manson may have taken. Photo courtesy Evergreen State College Archives.

THE THURSTON COUNTY Sheriff's Department has launched an intensive search Saturday for Donna Gail Manson, a 19-year-old Evergreen State College student, who was last seen by her roommate and friends at 7 p.m. Tuesday, March 12, on the Olympia campus. She was wearing green slacks, a red, orange and green-striped top and a fuzzy, black maxi-coat. The daughter of Mr. and Mrs. Lyle E. Manson, Auburn, she is five-foot tall with long brown hair and blue eyes. Anyone having information is asked to telephone 753-8100 or 357-6668. Authorities suspect foul play was involved in the young woman's disappearance.

She then went out to the concert, which was scheduled for 8:00 p.m. in the library lobby. She never made it. She was not reported as a missing person for six days, as she often hitchhiked to nearby locales and could disappear for several days at a time without notice. Friends initially believed Donna was depressed at the time of her disappearance and may have been suicidal, according to one rumor (but see below). Donna was something of a wayward student, spending most of her nights out smoking cannabis and sleeping during the day it had been claimed. Her roommate had asked to be moved to another room shortly before Donna's disappearance due to a clash of lifestyles. Donna was heavily into alchemy. She kept a diary. She was also close to her parents. She spent the weekend of February 23-24 with them, and had called them on March 9, and written a letter to them on March 10, only two days before her disappearance. She was in good spirits and planning a trip to the beach with her mother. These facts suggest she wasn't depressed. How did Ted abduct her? At the time, he was going through a phase where he employed the injury ruse to lure victims to his car. This is one way he may have diverted Donna. Another is he may have parked (ironically) on Hidden Springs Drive, which lies between the dormitory and the library, a perfect place to ambush a student after dark. A third possibility is he may have lured her with pot. The things she left behind in her room—her backpack, her flute, suitcases, her clothing, her camera—were turned over to her parents after it became obvious she was gone.

Ted later told Keppel that he burnt Donna's skull to ashes in Liz's (Green Lake?) apartment fireplace (see entry for March 17, 1974). The following is a detailed transcription of that interview (January 20, 1989):

Keppel: Okay, how about Donna Manson? Gal from Thurston County, Olympia. Where's she?
Ted: Where is she? That was different. That was different.
Keppel: What was different about it? You told me before that she might be buried.
Ted: I won't beat around the bush with you anymore, cause I'm just tired and I just want to get back and go to sleep …
Keppel: Okay.
Ted: So let me just tell you I'm, I know that, this part of the forest, buried up in there but, nothing identifiable, probably just, literally, bones, but, the head however, the—the skull, it wouldn't be there.
Keppel: Where is it?
Ted: It's nowhere.
Keppel: It's nowhere?
Ted: Well, I don't know, I'm not trying to be flippant, it's just, it's just nowhere. It's, it's—it's—it's in a category by itself, in—in that ah, it was … no I just assumed this was, something that you just can't, I don't know, [garbled] see the headlines now, but ah, ah—
Keppel: Ted, there's not going to be any details. Wh—what you told me about Georgeann Hawkins isn't going to be known. I got parents out there that don't even want to know the details—
Ted: Well I know … I know—
Keppel: He [Hagmaier who is present next to Keppel] wants to know, and I want to know for my own good.
Ted: Well it, it was incinerated, and it was, just ah—an exception, ah—a strange exception, but ah—it was incinerated.
Keppel: Where'd you in-

1973 aerial showing hypothetical crime scene location for the Donna Manson case. Aerial photograph courtesy USGS.

cinerate it?
Ted: [Embarrassed laugh]
Keppel: Come on pard'ner.
Ted: [Embarrassed laugh]
Keppel: These are things they don't know about you.
Ted: Well this is, this is probably, the—the disposal method of preference among those who get away with it—
Keppel: Yeah.
Ted: But because ah, gee, um, it's the most bizarre, bizarre thing I ever—ever, ever been associated with, and I've been associated with bizarre shit—
Keppel: Right. [Long pause] It's incinerated—

Hidden Springs Drive heading west out of Evergreen State College. Ted could have parked on the "Emergency and service vehicles" side road that branches off just in the distance on the left and intersects the dormitory path to the library. He could have walked to the dorms with the intention of picking up a victim there and just as he arrived, Donna Manson came out. He could have offered her some pot, walked with her, saying he had to drop some books off at his car on the way to the jazz concert. Photo courtesy Drew Bales © 2016.

Ted: It's incinerated.
Keppel: Tell me about it, what the hell happened?
Ted: Well it, ah, I don't know the address of the place, I never want to tell this incident, but I promised myself I'd never tell this because it would ah, I—I thought, that, of—of all the things I did to this woman this was probably the one she would least likely to forgive me for, poor Liz—
Keppel: Uh-huh.
Ted: ... in her fireplace, ah, it's really not that humorous, but um, in the fireplace in that house—
Keppel: Burned it all up?
Ted: Down to the last ash, in a fit of, you know, paranoia and cleanliness, what have you, just vacuumed down all the ashes. That's the twist.
Keppel: Yeah, it's a slight twist, yeah—
Ted: —twist and ah, it's a lot of work and—and certainly very risky, though under the circumstances [Embarrassed laugh], I mean the kids come home from school and there's a roaring fire in the fireplace and, it's warm outside—
Keppel: Do you ever keep anything in your refrigerator?
Ted: [Long pause] No.
Keppel: No body parts in the refrigerator?
Ted: No, well, that was not—not, that was not something that I ever found any kind of—the body part things, something that—

The only other available image of Donna Manson, presumably dated to around 1974. Photo courtesy KCA.

Postscript: On August 29, 1978, two fishermen came upon a human skull while walking in the foothills of Mount Rainier, southwest of Eatonville, where Washington 7 crosses the Mashel River. Searchers combed the area and found more human bones, hair and a multicolored shirt, which became a key piece of evidence. Donna reportedly was wearing a similar shirt when she was last seen (*Deseret News*, February 28 1998). While one would think that something should have come out of this, a series of bureaucratic blunders and miscommunication resulted in the case being closed. It remained that way until December 2, 1996, when the case was briefly revived around rumors that the skeletal evidence had been lost from the Sheriff's Office, including X-rays and other coroner's records related to the skeleton. Apparently, a check of dental records of missing persons in the state (ostensibly before the loss) produced eight possible identities for the Eatonville skeleton. A forensic dentist hired by the sheriff's department ruled out all but one case – that of Donna Manson. Since then, the case has gone cold again.

March 13, 1974: Ted at school UPS, Seattle.

March 14, 1974: Chevron card gas purchase, Seattle, $3.11.

March 15, 1974: Attends evening classes at UPS.

March 17, 1974: OPEC Oil Embargo ends. Wrote check to Quality Food Centers, Seattle. (Possibly on this Sunday or the next, March 24): Liz finds Ted in "tears" at her place. He looked "haggard." He spoke of dropping out of law school. It was around this time that Ted claimed to Keppel he burned Manson's skull to ashes in Liz' fireplace, a dubious claim as skulls do not completely disintegrate even in a furnace. Maybe Ted crushed it into small pieces once the fire weakened it ...

March 18, 1974: Picks up unemployment check in Seattle.

March 19, 1974: Chevron card gas purchase, Seattle, $4.30.

March 21, 1974: Deposits money in Rainier Bank, Seattle.

March 22, 1974: Attends evening classes at UPS.

March 23, 1974: Safeway foods, Seattle; checking account.

March 25, 1974: Chevron card gas purchase, Seattle, $3.50; checking account: PEMCO, Standard Oil. Two bank deposits.

March 26, 1974: Chevron card parking, Seattle, $0.80; checking account: University Bookstore. Standard Oil credit card: Olympic Hotel.

March 27, 1974: Picks up unemployment check in Seattle.

March 29, 1974: Chevron card gas purchase, Seattle, $3.55.

April 1, 1974: Chevron card gas purchase, Seattle, $4.55 (8.4 gals).

April 3, 1974: Attends evening classes at UPS.

April 5, 1974: Writes check to Rogers' rooming house.

April 9, 1974: Withdraws from UPS law school just two weeks before finals. According to Rule, he dropped out of law school on the 10th of April, 1974.

April 10, 1974: Picks up unemployment check in Seattle.

April 11, 1974: Chevron card gas purchase, Seattle, $6.05 (9.4 gals, two purchases).

April 12, 1974: Chevron card gas purchase, Seattle, $3.56 (6.5 gals). A Central Wash. Univ., Ellensburg, student, Jane Curtis, said she talked to a tall, handsome man in his twenties outside the campus library who had one arm in a sling with a metal brace on his finger. He had trouble managing an armload of books and had dropped several. He asked her to help him carry them to his car. The car, a VW was parked about 300 yards from the railroad trestle near the one of the student parking lots. When she got there she noticed the passenger seat was missing. She put the books on the hood of his car and ran (for more see report April 17, 1974). Around this time, Ted visits Jerry Bullat, an old high school friend who attended Ellensburg campus.

April 15, 1974: Chevron card gas purchase, Seattle, $3.35. Rode in car pool to take UPS law school exam [contradicts report he dropped out before this date]. Wrote check to Freeway Volkswagen, Seattle.

April 16, 1974: Had new muffler put on his VW, Seattle.

April 17, 1974: (Morning) Wrote check to Freeway Volkswagen. Wrote check to QFC. Wrote check to Ernst Rogers, Seattle. (Evening) Bought gas at Standard Station, Seattle. 9:30 p.m. Ellensburg Washington State College girl Kathleen Clara D'Olivo (21) helped him carry some packages wrapped in butcher's paper to his car.

> I was walking from the Boullion Library at approximately 10:10 p.m. at Central Washington State Campus. Behind me I heard someone drop packages. I turned around and saw a man dropping a few boxes and a package of books. I asked if I could help him – I thought he was going into the library. He began walking past the library. I asked where he was going, he said his car was just up a ways. I said O.K. I'd walk there. I was extremely cautious while with him – I never gave him the opportunity of walking behind me. His right arm was in a cloth sling and he had a metal brace on one or two fingers of his right hand. His left hand had a metal plate (bracing his fingers) on the palm side. There were bandages holding the brace on. He had brown hair (I think fairly dark brown). His hair was below the ear. It was dark and I didn't really notice his features. he was about 5'8" - 5'11". Medium build. We walked across Mary Grupe Conference bridge, under the trestle and right, into the alley. It was extremely dark there. His car was parked against the log there. The car was a VW bug. I don't remember color, but the car was a newer VW model and shiny. He walked to the passenger side and started to unlock the door; I set the bag of books down to leave and he dropped the key into the dirt. He tried to feel for it on the ground, but said he couldn't 'cause of his metal brace. He asked

> if I would find it for him. I wasn't about to bend over in front of him, so I suggested we stand back and see if the reflection of the light would let us see the key. Luckily the key did shine, I picked it up handed it to him and left. He told me his bandages were the result of a ski accident and explained how the accident had happened. He might have had a moustache. His hair was the type that was sort of in his face – I think that's why nothing about his face stands out in my mind. I also think he many have had wire-rimmed glasses. I don't vividly remember these things, I just remember his face wasn't clear to see or clean-cut looking. His voice wasn't outstandingly different, he talked fairly softly with – kind of an "inward" voice (Statement taken July 21, 1974, Sheriff's Office, Tacoma, Washington).

Shortly after 10:15 p.m. Abducts Susan Elaine Rancourt (18). Leaves her body at an undisclosed location. Jerry Bullat remembers Ted visiting Ellensburg around this time. Terry Storwick, Ted's boyhood friend, attended Central Wash. Univ., Ellensburg, same time as Susan. Terry and Susan jogged together.

Susan was a freshman at Central Wash. Univ., Ellensburg. On April 17 she pursued an opportunity to get a job as a would-be dorm advisor. At 10:00 p.m. she took

Susan's route with Ted (blue). Her normal route to Barto Hall (green). The red 'X' marks where police believe Ted parked his car.

Bouillon Hall (1963). Brooks library was under construction in 1974, so Bouillon Hall was used as a library. Ted must have employed his injury ruse outside this entrance. However, we do not know what ruse he used to lure Susan. She may not have made it to the library. He may have intercepted her on her way. Photo courtesy Dr. James E. Brooks Library, Archives and Special Collections, Central Washington University.

a load of clothes to a washroom in one of the campus dorms, then walked off to the advisor's meeting at Munson Hall. She planned to see a German film after the meeting back at Barto Hall then get her clothes. But no one saw her after the meeting. She was last seen wearing gray corduroy slacks, a short-sleeved yellow sweater, a yellow coat, and brown "hush puppy" shoes. Police tried to trace her last steps from the advisor's meeting back to the dorm, about a ¼ mile away.

At approximately 10:15 p.m. Barbara Blair reported seeing a white female "wearing a yellow coat going north on the Wallnut Mall" (CWU Security incident report, April 26, 1974). This appears to be Susan just after she exited Munson Hall. Walnut Mall runs alongside the western side of Bouillon Library. If Ted was working his ruse, he could have intercepted Susan as she approached Black Hall. He may have

An undated photo of Susan walking walking north on Walnut Mall near the Language and Literature Building. Photo public domain.

Susan Rancourt (undated). Photo public domain.

1975 aerial of Teanaway, Washington, and the area just east of it depicting a potential location where Ted could have raped and murdered Susan Rancourt. This site meets all the criteria listed in the Epilogue. After taking Rancourt to this site, it appears Ted transported her body to a new site, where he deposited it above-ground, and from where he later removed her skull. Inset courtesy USGS Earthstar Geographics SIO © Microsoft Corporation. Aerial photo courtesy University of Washington Libraries Map Collection 2016.

then walked her the same route as D'Olivo, up Chestnut and under the railway trestle. One policeman said: "If someone watched her, followed her, and meant to grab her, it would have been here – under the trestle; it's dark as hell for about twenty feet" (Rule 1989, 61). She was carrying a folder full of loose papers that would have scattered in every direction if there was a struggle. Susan was short-sighted. She wore neither her contacts, nor glasses that night.

One version of Jane Curtis' report to the Central Washington University campus police:

> About 9:00 p.m. [April 12, 1974] I walked out of the library to go back to my apartment. Right outside of the main entrance a man carrying a large stack of books was having difficulty … A cast-like bandage was on his arm. He dropped the books and was making a noise [pain] as though his arm was hurting him. I went over to offer some assistance. I picked up the books and handed them back to him. But then I said, "Would you like me to help you carry them?" He said, "Yes." We walked past Black Hall and walked under the railroad crossing … I asked him how he hurt his arm. He told me it was a skiing accident. He [said he had] hit a tree … He was grubbily dressed, with a dark wool hat on, and dark, long hair … When he looked at me, it sort of bugged me – two big eyes staring at me weirdly. But I remember the passenger's seat wasn't in the car … It was gone. When we were standing next to the car, he started complaining about his arm: "Oh my arm hurts." He opened the door and told me to start the car. I stood there and said, "No." He then said, "Get in." I said, "No." I dropped the books, turned around, and ran back to my apartment.

Susan Elaine Rancourt IS MISSING

SUSAN ELAINE RANCOURT
WHITE, FEMALE
AMERICAN
DATE OF BIRTH

HEIGHT:
WEIGHT:
EYES: BLUE
HAIR: BLONDE SHOULDER LENGTH
AGE:

$1,000.00 REWARD

FOR INFORMATION LEADING TO HER PRESENT WHEREABOUTS AND RETURN

SUSAN WAS LAST SEEN WEDNESDAY EVENING. SHE HAS NOT CALLED HOME, HER RESIDENCE HALL AT CENTRAL WASHINGTON STATE COLLEGE, ANY OF HER KNOWN FRIENDS. NOR HAS SHE BEEN SEEN WITH ANYONE SINCE WEDNESDAY.

SHE WAS LAST SEEN WEARING A YELLOW COAT, YELLOW SHORT SLEEVE SWEATER, GRAY CORDUROY PANTS AND BROWN HUSH-PUPPY TYPE SHOES.

IF YOU HAVE SEEN SUSAN OR ANYONE CLOSELY RESEMBLING HER PLEASE CALL C.W.S.C. (COLLECT) (509) 963–1111 OR THE NEAREST POLICE DEPARTMENT OR THE WASHINGTON STATE PATROL.

April 18, 1974: Deposits unemployment checks, Seattle. Susan's roommate at Barto Hall phoned Judy Rancourt (Susan's sister) to say that Susan had not come home from a dorm leaders meeting the previous evening.
April 19, 1974: Wrote check to Ness Flowers, Seattle (buys bouquet for Liz). Liz Kloepfer's birthday.
April 22, 1974: Chevron card gas purchase, Seattle, $5.12.
April 23, 1974: Fails to appear at Laurelhurst caucus as elected delegate for the 43rd District.
April 24, 1974: Picks up unemployment check in Seattle. Receives application papers for Univ. Utah law school. Tells Liz with typical melodramatic effect, even though he had planned it 4 months earlier.
April 25, 1974: Chevron card gas purchase, Seattle, $3.75 (7.4 gals).
April 26, 1974: Mails application to Univ. Utah law school from Seattle.
April 29, 1974: Chevron card gas purchase, Seattle, $3.75 (7.4 gals).
May 1974: Leaves UPS law school.
May - June 1974: Liz sees hatchet and crutches in Ted's VW.
May 2, 1974: Chevron card gas purchase, Seattle, $3.62. Ted's boyhood friend Terry Storwick's birthday. Ted had visited him in Ellensburg sometime shortly before this date.
May 3, 1974: Chevron card gas purchase, Seattle, $3.25.

Roberta Parks (circa 1973). Photo public domain.

May 6, 1974: Chevron card gas purchase, Standard Station, Seattle, $2.40 (4 gals, two purchases). Wrote check to Safeway, Seattle. Wrote check to Pay and Save, Seattle. Cashed two checks totaling $20.00 (M&A 1983, 77).
Around 11:00 p.m. abducts Roberta "Kathy" Parks (20) from Oregon State University campus. Kathy, five-seven, 120 lbs, waist length hair, was wearing a white corduroy coat, blue pants and sandals when she went missing. She had just received news that her father had been hospitalized with a heart attack but was stable and recovering. She apparently did not get on that well with him but was just in the process of making amends. She also decided to part from her boyfriend to find her own feet. From the OSU Security Department files we were able to construct the following mini-timeline:

> 9:00 - 9:30 p.m. Kathy goes to Edward Sumida's room (233 Sackett B).
> 10:15 p.m. Leaves Sumida's room.

10:30 p.m. Exercises in the hallway outside her room with Cherrell Smith. Kathy's roommate "Bunny" Schmidt said come over to room 324 afterwards.
10:50 p.m. Returns to her room (325 Sackett).
10:55 p.m. As Schmidt leaves room 325 to go to 324 Kathy says, "Go ahead and I'll be over in a while."
11:00 p.m. Cherrell comes out of her room sees Kathy leaving her room (325) walking down the hallway carrying her purse and wearing her coat. She spoke to Kathy who told her that she was going to the MU to get something to eat. Kathy asked her what time it was and Cherrell said "11 o'clock." Kathy said she still had about half an hour before the MU closed. (The MU commons closes at 11:00 p.m. on weekdays.)
11:00 p.m. (around this time) Lorrain Fargo was returning to Sackett Hall from the library when she sees Kathy walking east on Jefferson at the intersection of College Drive and Jefferson Street (the southwest corner of Memorial Union Hall). Kathy was wearing her corduroy jacket and carrying her purse at the time. They stopped and talked at this location for approx-

Sackett Hall, Oregon State University (undated). Photo public domain.

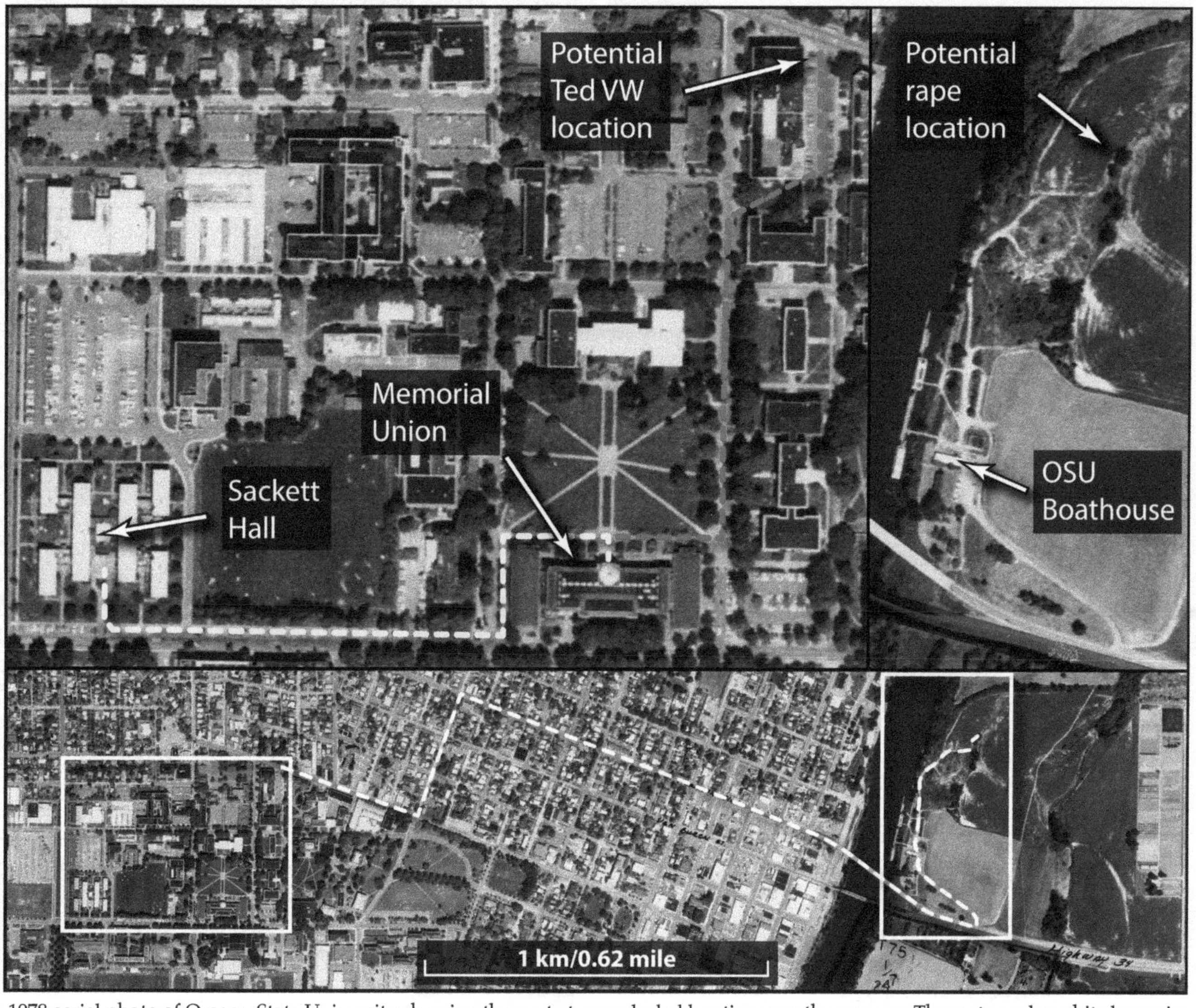

1978 aerial photo of Oregon State University showing the route to a secluded location near the campus. The rectangular white boxes in the lower panel are represented in the upper two panels respectively. The route taken by Kathy Parks from Sackett Hall is shown with a yellow dashed line while the hypothetical route she took with Ted to a potential parking lot location is shown with a red dashed line. Aerial image courtesy OSU Special Collections and Archive Research Center, 2016.

imately 5 minutes. Lorraine last saw Kathy turn the corner walking north up College Drive, toward Monroe Street.

Ted "speculated" that he picked her up in the MU commons cafeteria, she was supposed to be depressed and lonely or something (M&A 1983, 118). Carl Hoffman was a grad-student on sabbatical leave at OSU, aged in his 50s, and had recently lent a sympathetic ear to Kathy. He sensed she seemed to be searching for a friend she could confide in. In Hoffman, Kathy must have seen stability and maturity, just the kind of person she needed to talk to about all the turmoil in her life, and along comes Ted, aged 27, suave, an even better target to confide in. Ted said he drove her out to a remote location, got her to undress, then raped her. Afterwards he said he transported her alive all the way back to Taylor Mountain where he raped her again then killed her. Only her skull (with a missing viscerocranium) was found at Taylor Mountain. How it got to be that way is explored in the NOTES section. For now, what we can say is that we have no way of verifying what Ted said is true. OSUSD William R. Harris doggedly pursued every lead on Parks since she went missing. He even flew to Florida to question Ted in the last days of his life, but he was denied face time. So we are stuck with what he have, and given the total pattern of Ted's behavior, and the evidence we do have, it could be equally argued that Ted deposited Parks whole somewhere for a time, before returning to decapitate her defleshed skull, which he then discarded on the western flank of Taylor Mountain. Of course, this does not accord with the official narrative. But it fits the evidence more plausibly. It is here that we remind ourselves that we know very little in the way of Ted's evolution as a rapist-killer at this stage other than he was growing in confidence daily around the time he took Parks.

MISSING

$500.00 REWARD FOR INFO. LEADING TO A PERSONAL CONTACT WITH KATHY.

KATHY PARKS
5'7" TALL 120 LBS.
20 YRS OLD W/ WAIST LENGTH HAIR
MISSING SINCE 5/6/74
LAST SEEN WALKING NORTH ON THE OSU. CAMPUS WEARING A WHITE CORDUROY COAT, BLUE PANTS AND SANDALS.
ANY ONE WHO HAS SEEN OR DOES SEE HER CONTACT:
O.S.U. SECURITY. 503-754-1473

May 9, 1974: Chevron card gas purchase, Seattle, $4.95.
May 10, 1974: Deposits money in bank, Seattle.
May 12, 1974: Chevron card gas purchase, Seattle, $8.30 (two purchases).
May 13, 1974: Requests readmission to UPS law school. Readmitted, but doesn't show up.
May 14, 1974: Bought Adidas shoes, Nordstrom Northgate, Seattle. Buys gas in Seattle.
May 15, 1974: Buys gas in Tacoma.
May 20, 1974: Chevron card gas purchase, Seattle, $4.77.
May 21, 1974: Deposits money in Rainier bank, Seattle.
May 22, 1974: Chevron card gas purchase, Seattle, $4.32.
May 23, 1974: Liz's parents visit from SLC. According to Rule, on this day Ted was hired to work on the budget for the Washington State Department of Emergency Services, a many-armed agency responsible for quick action in natural disasters, forest fires, enemy attack, and even plague. In 1974, the first of the nation's gas shortages was at its peak. Fuel allocation would be part of the D.E.S. duties. According to Liz, Ted started in June, 1974, Olympia. "Some nights he stayed with a friend in Olympia, some nights with his parents in Tacoma [3214 North 20th Street], some nights at his place in Seattle." Olympia is a 2-hour commute from Seattle.
May 24, 1974: According to the MTR, Ted bought gas in Tukwila, Washington. According to Keppel (K&M 2012, 184), Ted bought gas using his Chevron card in Seattle ($4.05).

High school photo of Brenda Baker (undated). Photo public domain.

Diane Gilchrist (undated). Photo public domain.

May 25, 1974: Brenda Joy Baker (14) of Maple Valley disappears while trying to hitchhike from her home to Fort Lewis, Washington. Possible victim of William E. Cosden Jr.
May 27, 1974: Ted bought dress at Nordstrom Southcenter Mall, Seattle (for Liz or potential victim?). Liz and Ted picnic at Dungeness Recreation Area (which looks directly across the straits at Victoria, British Columbia).
May 28(?), 1974: Bought gas in Seattle.
May 29, 1974: Chevron card gas purchase, Seattle, $4.78 (9.1 gals). Also on this day, Diane Sue Gilchrist left home in Vancouver to run away and was never seen again. She was last seen getting into a van driven by an unidentified man. She is a suspected victim of Warren Leslie Forrest.
May 30, 1974: Works in Seattle accord-

ing to the MTR. It is unclear what kind of work, whether connected to Emergency Services in Olympia or not.

May 31, 1974: Chevron card gas purchase, Seattle, $3.32 (6.1 gals). Deposits money in Rainier Bank, Seattle. Receives acceptance from the University of Utah College of Law. Dined out, dropped Liz off at her parents before 9:00 p.m. According to the MTR Ted bought gas in Olympia.

Also on this day, Gloria Nadine Knutson (18) was at The Red Caboose bar in downtown Vancouver, celebrating her impending graduation from Hudson's Bay high school the next day. Gloria tried to hitchhike home. She was never seen again. Suspected victim of Warren Leslie Forrest.

Gloria Knutson high school senior photo. Photo provided by her family on July 23, 2015.

June 1974: On a warm summer night in 1974, a woman sat in the passenger seat of her date's car as he drove her home after an evening together in the U-District. The woman, who prefers to remain anonymous, recalls him seeming nearly perfect – a handsome, articulate recent Univ. Wash. Psychology graduate with future plans of attending law school. The two chitchatted as they drove down the road in his light brown 1968 Volkswagen Beetle. At the time, only one thing about him struck her as a bit unsettling. "I remember looking down at his hands, and his fingernails were chewed down to the quick," the woman said. "It struck me as kind of odd, that somebody who was that charming and handsome would have fingernails like that." The woman also recalls her second and final date with Ted. As the two drove to a location just past Issaquah toward Tiger Mountain to go river rafting, the woman said he seemed withdrawn and became oddly angry about some nearby road construction. "It was a beautiful Saturday morning, and there was no traffic on the road and no construction going on, and he went on this big tirade about traffic construction," she said.

June 1, 1974: 2:00 a.m. Abducts Brenda Carol Ball (22) from (outside?) the Flame Tavern, Burien, near Seattle Airport. Ted frequently made deposits at a bank in White Sands area close to the tavern. According to the MTR, he began working on a budget for Olympia Emergency Services Department. He missed the King County convention held at the Seattle Center. 3:20 p.m. Belatedly attends Tina Kloepfer's baptism. Tired, he stays at Liz's until 11:00 p.m.

Brenda Ball, 1974. Photo public domain.

Brenda had been a Highline Community College student until two weeks before her abduction. She lived with two roommates in the South King County suburb of Burien. On the night of May 31, she went to the Flame Tavern in Burien, south of Seattle. Her roommates last saw her at 2:00 p.m. that Friday afternoon. She told them that she planned to go to the tavern, and mentioned that she might catch a ride afterwards to Sun Lakes State Park in eastern Washington and meet them there. She was seen at the tavern by several people who knew her, but no one remembers exactly what she was wearing. Her usual garb was faded blue jeans and long-sleeved turtleneck tops. She stayed until closing time 2:00 a.m., tried to get a lift from a musician but he explained that he was going in the other direction. Brenda was last seen in the parking lot with a handsome, brown-haired man who had one arm in a sling.

Ted would elaborate: "He was interested in varying his M.O. in such a way as not to fan the flames of community outrage or the intensity of the police investigation. This is why this Ball girl found herself to be the next victim" (M&A 1983, 124). He claimed he took her home to his apartment at the Rogers' rooming house where he had sex with her then strangled her, a most dubious story:

> The initial sexual encounter would be more or less a voluntary one, but one which did not wholly gratify the full spectrum of desires that he had intended. And so, after the first sexual encounter, gradually his sexual desire builds back up and joins, as it were, these other, unfulfilled desires, this other need to totally possess her. After she'd passed out, as she lay there somewhere in a state between coma and sleep, he strangled her to death (M&A 1983, 125).

Given that he once said he used a ladder to come and go from the apartment so as not to disturb his neighbors, we can reasonably assume he did not take Ball to his apartment. Michaud and Aynesworth claim the skull had an enormous crack in it which is at odds with Ted's explanation of her murder (M&A 1983, 125). However, a close examination of the skull shows it was missing the left temporal bone which is best explained by animal predation, not blunt forced trauma. What we do know is that when Ball's skull was found it was also missing vertebrae, just like Rancourt's and Parks'. From this we can surmise that Ted most probably removed the head from an already decayed body at an unknown other site after he had deposited it there above ground and where animal predation would have partially disarticulated the remains.

A week or so after Brenda vanished, a young woman (25) spent the evening at a tavern just down the street from the Flame, Brubeck's Topless Bar. She was petite, had long brown hair parted in the middle. She drove there in her convertible and left before midnight, however, her car wouldn't start, so she accepted a ride home with friends. At 4:00 a.m., just as the sun was climbing over the horizon, she went back to start her car. She

Fiesta Del Mar, formerly the "Flame Tavern", 12803 South Ambaum Blvd in Burien, near Seattle airport. Photo courtesy Vincent Tan © 2015.

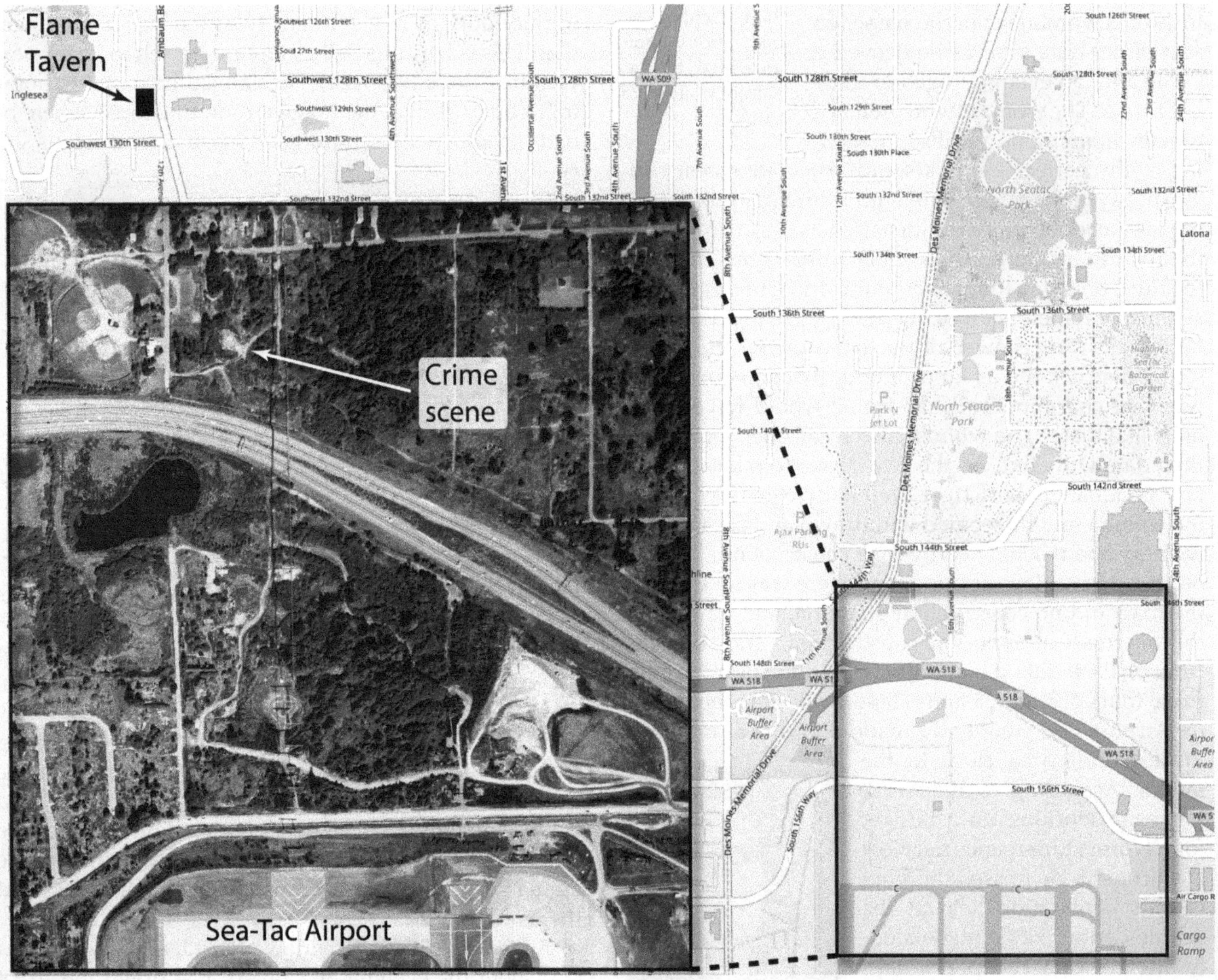

1977 aerial inset showing hypothetical rape and murder location of Brenda Ball. In this scenario, rather than taking her to his apartment at 4143 12th Avenue N.E., he took her somewhere relatively secluded that was not far from the Flame Tavern and raped and murdered her there. This accords more plausibly with Ted's M.O. which was to rape and murder his victims as soon as practically possible after the abduction. An examination of aerial imagery for the area around the northern side of the airport offers at least two locations. Here we show the one furthest north (and therefore closer to the Flame Tavern). This area would have been deserted and was sufficiently secluded from nearby houses to make it a good location to act out his murderous fantasies. Map courtesy OpenStreetMap Contributors 2016. Aerial photograph courtesy USGS.

didn't want to leave it vulnerable and open in the tavern lot.

> I was fiddling with the car, trying to get it started—and it wasn't responding—when this good-looking man walked out from behind the tavern. I don't know what he was doing there at that time of the morning, and it didn't occur to me then that he might have deliberately disabled my car. He tried to start it, and then told me that I needed jumper cables. He didn't have any, but he told me he had friends in Federal Way who did. We went to this store and he sent me in to get some. The guy inside thought I was nuts, and said he didn't have any jumper cables. Well, this man who was 'helping' me said, "I know someone who has jumpers." Before I could say no, we hit the freeway in his car, heading someplace north – toward Issaquah. We were driving along, and I thought he knew where he was going, but I was worried because my five-year-old daughter was home alone. All of a sudden, the guy said, "Do me a favor," and I looked at him and he pulled a switchblade from between his legs and held it to my neck. I started to cry, and he said, "Take your top off," and I said, "It's coming off," and he said, "Now your pants," and then he made me take off my underclothes. I sat there stark naked, and I tried to talk to him – use psychology. I told him he was a nice-looking guy and he didn't need to do

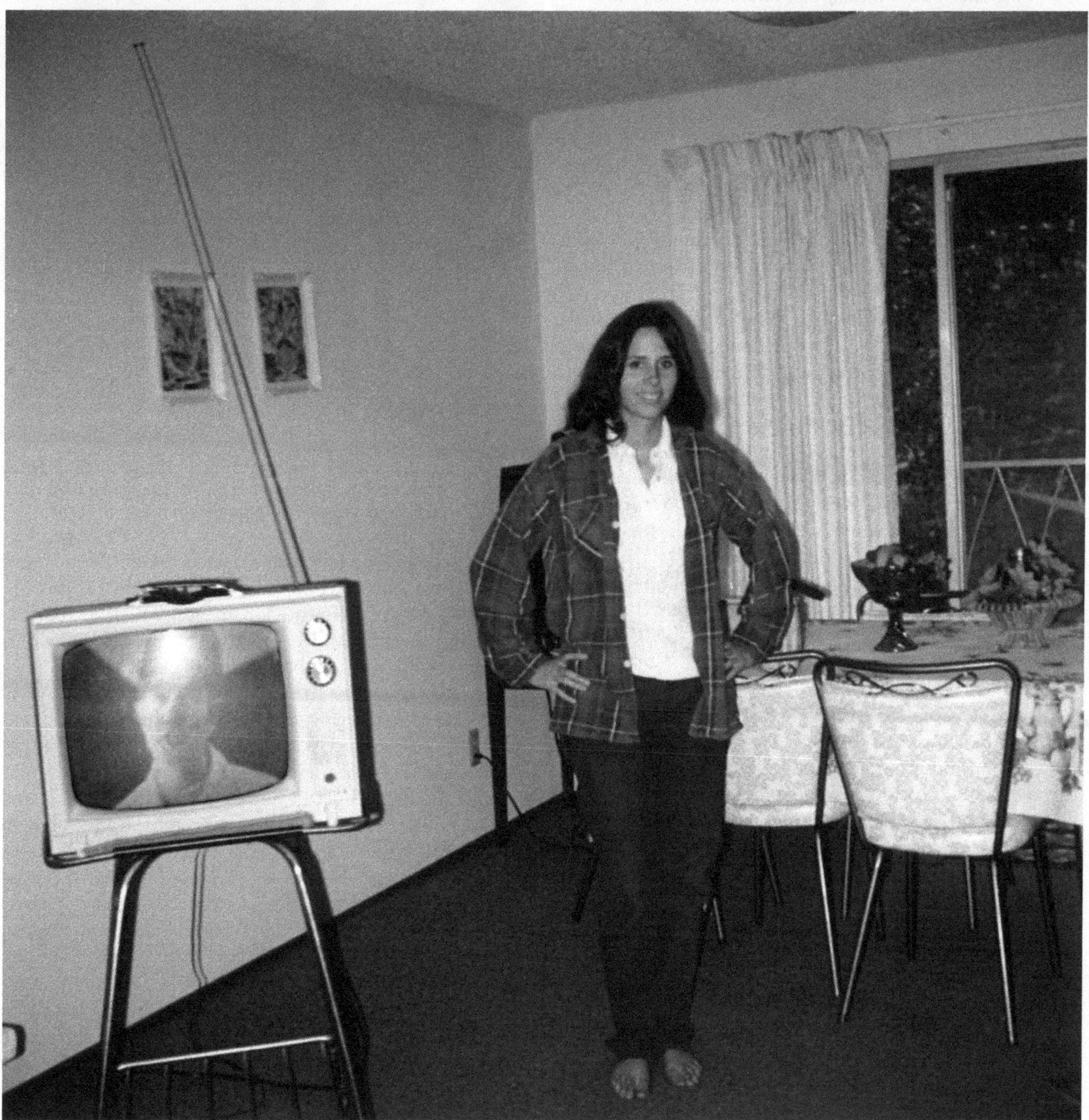

Brenda Ball (undated, location unknown, but presumably circa 1974). Photo courtesy KCA.

> something like this to have a woman. He said, "I don't want that – I want a little variety." I grabbed for the knife, and he was furious. He shouted, "Don't do that." Finally, I said, "My five-year-old's home alone, and she's going to wake up and she'll be all alone." He changed all of a sudden. Just like that. He drove onto a street with tall trees. He said, "This is it – this is where you get out." I shut my eyes, thinking he was going to stab me, and said, "Not without my clothes." He threw my clothes out of the car, but he kept my purse and shoes. I got to a house and they let me in, and called the police. They found that someone had pulled the distributor cap on my car. They never located the guy who pulled a knife on me. But a year or so later, I was watching the news on television and I saw the man on the screen. I yelled to my friend, "Look! That's him. That's the guy who almost killed me." When they said his name, it was Ted Bundy (Rule 1989, 496-7).

June 3, 1974: Chevron card gas purchase, Olympia, $5.36.
June 4, 1974: According to the MTR Ted bought gas in Olympia. According to Keppel (K&M 2012, 185), Ted bought gas using his Chevron card in Seattle, $0.95.
June 5, 6, 1974: Chevron card gas purchase, Olympia, $4.66. Ted in Tacoma. Absent from state convention as elected delegate for the 43rd District.
June 7, 1974: Chevron card gas purchase, Olympia, $5.03. Around 11:00 p.m. a male college student saw a man with a briefcase and crutches outside the Beta Theta Pi fraternity house on the alley between 45th N.E. and 47th N.E. University District. "A girl was carrying his case for him, and, later on, after I'd taken my girl home, I saw the girl again, walking alone" (Rule 1989, 71).
June 8, 1974: Writes check to Rogers' rooming house. Visits relatives in Tacoma. 12:00 (noon) Ted pays overnight visit to a friend, Seattle.
June 9, 1974: 5:00 a.m. Ted departs friend's house, Seattle. Wrote two checks in the Univ. Wash. area.
June 10, 1974: Chevron card gas purchase, Olympia, $4.45 (6.1 gals)
June 11, 1974: Chevron card gas purchase, Standard Station, Olympia, $5.21 (7.5 gals). 1:00 a.m. Abducts Georgeann Hawkins (18) from Seattle University District. (Noon) Bought gas Standard Station, Olympia. Returns to body location to remove potentially overlooked evidence and perform necrophilia with the body (decapitates head perhaps to bury it elsewhere). 5:00 p.m. Returns to abduction site on bicycle to collect a shoe and pierced ("little hoops") earrings.

Univ. Wash. student, Daffodil Princess, cheerleader, long brown hair, brown eyes, Georgeann was known simply as 'George' to her friends. Straight-A student, entering her finals week, she was studying for an up-coming Spanish test. She disappeared while walking in an alley between her boyfriend's dormitory and her sorority house, as if into thin air. The alley that runs along the back of the Greek Row sorority houses from 45th N.E. to 47th N.E. was well-lit, it was a warm night, windows were open, few were asleep, even at midnight; most were cramming for finals. 12:30 a.m. on June 11, she visited her boyfriend for an hour or so at the Beta Theta Pi fraternity house, borrowed some Spanish notes, and then said good night, left the back door to walk the ninety feet (27 m) to the back door of her Kappa Alpha Theta House. Wearing blue slacks, white backless tee-shirt, and a sheer red, white and blue top, she exchanged goodnight with Duane Covey from the 2nd story window of the Beta Theta Pi house, walked a few more feet and was never seen again. A very thorough search by Seattle Police of the alley found no evidence at all. Police later learned that she was shortsighted but wasn't wearing her glasses or contact lenses after a long day of study.

Hawkins walks into the Washington state Legislature in Spring 1973 on the arm of a state representative. She spoke there as a Daffodil Festival princess. Photo public domain.

They also learned that a student had been walking in front of the Beta Theta Pi fraternity house, University District, about 12:30 a.m. on June 11 and encountered a man on crutches carrying a briefcase. One leg of his jeans had been cut up the side and he appeared to have a full cast on the leg. He was having a lot of trouble and was dropping the briefcase every few steps. The student helped him carry the case as far as her boyfriend's fraternity house and told him she would be out in a few minutes and could help him to his car if he needed it. She stayed over an hour; when she came out he was gone. A male college student had also seen the man with the briefcase and crutches [this must have been the previous Friday]. "A girl was carrying his case for him, and, later on, after I'd taken my girl home, I saw the girl again, walking alone." So it wasn't George.

In his confession to Keppel, Ted explains how he abducted Hawkins. The following transcript is from *Riverman* (K&B 2005, 454-466) and has been truncated in places to remove extraneous material:

> Ted: I can't remember what night of the week it was – Thursday night, I believe, I don't know. Eleven to twelve, probably closer to twelve on a warm Seattle May night, I mean it was, I think it was clear. The weather had been fairly good. At about midnight that day, I was in the alleyway behind the sorority and fraternity houses that would have been Forty-fifth, Forty-sixth, Forty-seventh Street, somewhere in there. In back of the houses across the alley and across the other side of the block, there was the Congregational church, I believe, and some parking lots in back of the sorority and fraternity houses. I was moving up the alley, using a briefcase and some crutches, and a young woman walked down. I saw her round the north end of the block into the alley and stop for a moment and then keep on walking down the alley toward me. And about halfway down the block I encountered her and asked her to help me carry the briefcase, which she did, and we walked back up the alley, across the street, turned right on the sidewalk in front of the fraternity house on the corner there, and rounded the corner to the left going north of Forty-seventh. Well, midway in the block there used to be one of those parking lots they used to make out of burned-down houses in that area. The university would turn them into instant parking lots. There was a parking lot, dirt surface, no lights, and my car was parked there. We were to [sic] the car. All right, basically when we reached the car, what happened was, I knocked her unconscious with the crowbar.
>
> Keppel: Where did you have that?
>
> Ted: By the car
>
> Keppel: Outside?
>
> Ted: Outside, in back of the car.
>
> Keppel: Did she see it?
>
> Ted: No, and then there were some handcuffs there, along with the crowbar. [Whispering] And I handcuffed her and put her in the passenger's side of the car and drove away.
>
> Keppel: Was she alive or dead then?
>
> Ted: Oh no. No, she was unconscious, but she was very much alive.
>
> Keppel: Okay, what happened next?
>
> Ted: We drove down the alley to Fiftieth, I believe,

The rear lane behind "Greek Row." Photo public domain.

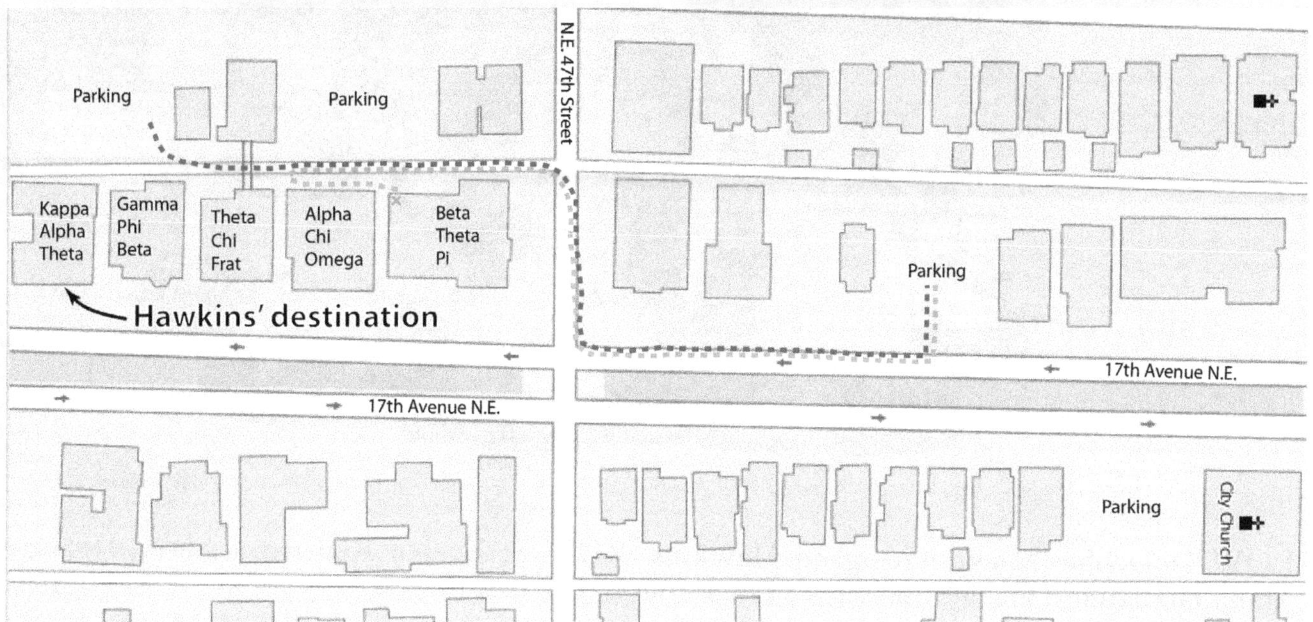

The route that Hawkins took (blue dashed line), showing where Duane Covey talked to her from the 2nd floor window of the Beta Theta Pi house, and where Ted moved up the alley with his briefcase (red dashed line). The final destination parking lot on 17th Avenue N.E. is the best guess from historical maps. Map modified to match historical data, courtesy OpenStreetMap contributors, 2015.

Northeast Fiftieth or, you know, the street going east and west, and turned left. Went to the freeway. Five, is it? It's been a long time. Anyway, and then [we] went south on the freeway to turn off on the old floating bridge, I-90. She was conscious at this time. I mean, she had regained consciousness at this time, basically. Well, there's a lot of incidental things that I'm just not getting into, you know, not talking about, 'cause they are just incidental anyway. We went across the bridge, across Mercer Island, east past Issaquah, up the hill, down the road, and up to the grassy area. [Ted had previously talked about the grassy area, describing the Issaquah body location and crime scene as if he was reliving it]

ROW 1: Debbie Moore, Georgann Hawkins. ROW 2: Evelyn Robertson, Sheryl Drummon
Mona Hernandez, Debbie Spitzer. ROW 3: Sue Gee, Cheri Pierce.

A 1973 photograph of Georgeann as a cheerleader. Mona Hernandez kept a scrapbook of everything written about Georgeann since her disappearance. "I was a year younger and I looked up to her … She made you feel comfortable." Cheri Pierce said, "I tried for 15 years to imagine what happened to her. The last couple of days with the Bundy thing I had nightmares." Photo public domain.

Keppel: Okay, what happened after that?
Ted: Well, I parked, took her out of the [car] and took the handcuffs off her and – [...] And, gee, this is probably the hardest part. I don't know. I don't know, we're talking sort of abstract, not abstractly before, but, well, we're getting right down to it. And I will talk about it. I hope you understand it's not something I find easy to talk about after all this time. One of the things that makes it a little bit difficult is that at this point she was quite lucid, talking about things. It's not funny, but it's odd the kinds of things people will say under those circumstances. And she said that she had a Spanish test the next day, and she thought that I had taken her to help tutor her for her Spanish test. It's kind of an odd thing to say. Anyway. The long and short of it, I mean, I'm going to try and get there by degrees. The long and short of it was that I again knocked her unconscious, strangled her, and dragged her about ten yards into the small grove of trees that were there.
Keppel: What did you strangle her with?
Ted: Cord.
Keppel: Cord?
Ted: An old piece of rope.
Keppel: Is this something you brought there with you?
Ted: Yeah. Something that was in the car.
Keppel: Okay, then what happened?
Ted: [Ted's now omits the most personal, intimate part of the 'encounter' – the time between 1:00 a.m. and dawn] Then I packed the car up. By this time, it was almost dawn. The sun was coming up. And I went through my usual routine. On this particular morning, I went through a frequent routine where I was just absolutely shocked, kind of scared to death, and horrified. I went down the road throwing everything that I'd had—the briefcase, the crutches, the rope, the clothes—just tossing them out the window. I was in a sheer state of panic. Just absolute horror, you know. At that point in time, the consciousness of what has really happened is like you break out of a fever or something. I drove east on 1-90 at some point, throwing articles out the window as I went, articles of clothing, shoes, et cetera.
Keppel: When did you remove those?
Ted: What?
Keppel: The shoes, clothing?
Ted: Well, after we got out of the car, initially. I skipped over some stuff there, and we'll have to get back to it sometime, but it's just too hard for me to talk about it right now.
Keppel: Do you remember what clothes she was wearing that night?
Ted: Yup. A pair of white patent-leather clogs, blue slacks, some kind of halter top of which she had a shirt tied in a knot. [Ted remembers it as if it was yesterday, but this is 15 years after the event]
Keppel: Okay. And where were these deposited?
Ted: Along the roadside. I mean, not right along 1-90. 1 went east to the infamous Taylor Mountain Road. What highway is that?
Keppel: 18.
Ted: At 18, turn right. Went south again and at some point, south of Taylor Mountain a lot of that stuff went out of the car. Down the embankments and what have you.
Keppel: Embankments?
Ted: Yeah.
Keppel: Did you have to pull over to do it or...?
Ted: I would stop, pull over to the side of the road. At this time, it was pretty light out, and just tossed it out. There were sometimes I would do that and sometimes I wouldn't. At this point in time I was so frantic, so panicked, so whatever, about what had happened that I just had to get every reminder of that incident out of the car as quickly as possible. I didn't want to take it home, didn't want it to be around.
Keppel: Did you throw away some of your own stuff?
Ted: Oh, sure. I threw away the briefcase and the crutches, all that stuff. And the crowbar, everything. The handcuffs, everything. I'd get mad at myself a few weeks later because I'd have to go out and buy another pair. I mean, it's not comical but that's what would happen.
Keppel: Now that you've had a while to think about Georgeann Hawkins, is there something you can tell me about her that probably only you know and we know?
Ted: Well...
Keppel: I mean, the Spanish test is pretty darn good, if you ask me.
Ted: That's what she said, unless she was hallucinating. She said everybody called her George. Or how about that she used a safety pin to pin her blue slacks because apparently they were a bit too big.

[The exchange continues, with Ted being evasive about when he removed Hawkins' head. We cannot say whether he did it the same day or the next day. Based on his final confession, if we are to believe him, he said he buried it somewhere at the Issaquah site.]

Keppel: The next day. What did you do the next day?
Ted: Just went back to check out the site, make sure nothing had been left there. See, you know, the feeling is, I reached the point and half expected that she

SEATTLE *POLICE* BU LETIN
OFFICIAL POLICE DEPARTMENT PUBLICATION
CITY OF SEATTLE, WASHINGTON
CHIEF'S OFFICE, PUBLIC SAFETY BUILDING, 610-3rd AVENUE, 98104

JULY 9, 1974 C.I.D. NUMBER 74-16

MISSING PERSON
HAWKINS, GEORGEANN, W-F-18

DOB 8-20-55, 5'2", 120 lbs., shoulder-length brown hair, brown eyes, well sun tanned, moles on back of neck.

Last seen wearing white backless "Tee" shirt, red, white and blue flower print, sheer, long sleeved shirt, navy blue cotton bell-bottom pants, white open toed wedgie sandals; wearing rectangle black onyx ring with small diamond set in light gold triangle setting in center, onyx framed by yellow gold worn on middle finger left hand, also wearing a single cultured pearl set in a low Tiffany setting with a slender gold band worn on third finger right hand.

GEORGEANN HAWKINS, 18 years old, disappeared from an alley behind the 4500 block, 17th Ave. N. E., Greek Row, just off the campus of the University of Washington, around 0100 hours, June 11, 1974.

A reward of $5,000 for information leading to her safe return has been posted by her parents.

Any information regarding Georgeann should be directed to Dets. G. Jelberg or T. Fonis or G. Cuthill, Seattle Police Department: Phone (206) 583-2346, or your local police department.

Case 74-31075

Ted's Seattle crimes and their geographical location relative to his place of residence.

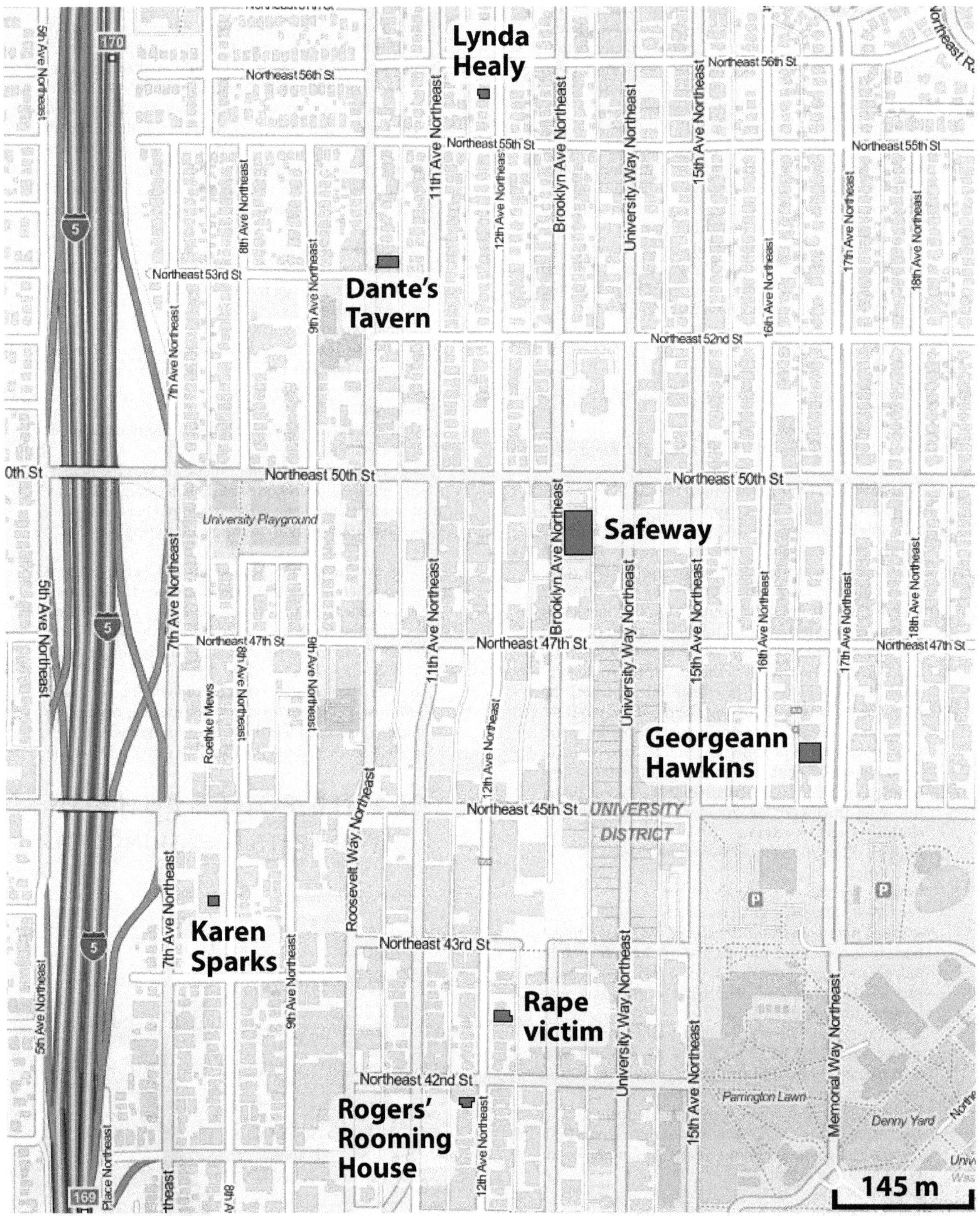

Seattle University District. January 4, 1974, Karen Sparks. January 31, 1974, Lynda Healy after she returns from Dante's Tavern. March 2, 1974, possible rape victim in her home. June 12, 1974, Georgeann Hawkins. All incidents occurred within a 0.68 mile (1.1 km) radius. Map courtesy OpenStreetMap contributors, 2015.

might not even be there. That somehow, I hadn't even killed her, if you will. So I went back – oh, yeah. Removed things like the rope. I – no, no, I had already done that. Can't remember if I found anything there or not. But I wanted to make sure. Oh, that's what it was. Talk about details coming back. I couldn't find one of the shoes, so I thought it was there. But it wasn't. So I went back—this was the next day—got on my bicycle, and rode back to that little parking lot. I knew there were police all over the place by that time, but I was kind of nervous – and I'll tell you why in a minute. 'Cause I'd left and my car had been parked there. Somebody may have seen it. Now, if something was found there, it might connect me. So I went back to that parking lot at about five o'clock in the afternoon and found both pierced earrings and the shoe, laying in the parking lot. So I surreptitiously gathered them up and rode off.

Keppel: After the police had checked that area?

Ted: Well, you can tell me. I'd seen whole streams of them driving around all over the place, but they were concentrating on places like the nearby parks. I bet you they couldn't have looked in that parking lot and missed the white patent-leather clog and two white pierced earrings – little hoops.

Keppel: That was discovered by you the next day?

Ted: Yeah. Around five o'clock, six o'clock.

Keppel: Okay, so what happened in the next couple days?

Ted: Well, again, and this might be something you could plug into, if that's what you want to do. The reason I was so nervous about anything like that being found in that parking lot was that no more than two weeks before, I had been using the same modus operandi in the same neighborhood. In front, now, of the same sorority house that Georgeann Hawkins disappeared from, I encountered a girl going out the door and asked her to help me. I walked her all the way to that lot, eleven o'clock on a Friday night. And I was drunk, and I was just babbling on. Told her I worked in Olympia, that lived in a rooming house. I mean, I was just horrified later on.

Keppel: Were you drunk when you got Hawkins?

Ted: Yes, more or less, but yes. That was basically part of the M.O. at that time. Yeah. But I reached all the way to the car—and this would happen sometimes—and just said, 'No, I don't want to do it.' I said, Thank you. See you later.' And she walked away. But after the Hawkins thing, I was just paranoid as hell that this girl would say, 'You know, something weird happened to me a couple weeks ago. This guy came along with crutches and asked me to help him. He took me to a Volkswagen and said he worked in Olympia and lived here in the university district.' How many people could that apply to? So, there you are.

June 12, 1974: Chevron card gas purchase, Olympia, $3.33.

June 13, 1974: Chevron card gas purchase, Olympia, $3.26 (5.7 gals).

June 14, 1974: Chevron card gas purchase, Olympia, $3.20 (5.4 gals).

June 15, 1974: Returns to Hawkins Issaquah body location, engages in necrophilia, removes more evidence.

June 16, 1974: 12:34 p.m. Rents power mower, Seattle.

June 17, 1974: Chevron card gas purchase, Olympia, $4.75 (8.3 gals). Brenda Ball first reported missing on this day. Brenda Joy Baker's body found near Millersylvania State Park, Thurston County, Washington. When found she was partially clad in a tan corduroy jacket, red bell-bottom pants, white socks and brown leather shoes. Investigators also took two bracelets, a set of earrings and a ring into custody as evidence and for identification purposes.

June 19, 1974: Chevron card gas purchase, Olympia, $4.15. (Evening) Had dinner with friend in Tacoma.

June 21, 1974: Chevron card gas purchase, Tumwater, $5.00.

June 22, 1974: Returns to Hawkins body location, performs necrophilia, removes more evidence.

June 23, 1974: Attends brunch and a day-long party. "Shows up" at Susan Reade's place, where he meets Becky Gibbs. Spends night with Liz.

June 24, 1974: Chevron card gas purchase, Olympia, $4.69. Calls in "sick" to Department of Emergency Services, Olympia.

June 28, 1974: Chevron card gas purchase, Olympia, $5.15. (Evening) Dinner with Larry Voshall, Susan Reade and Becky Gibbs at the home of Reade and Diane Barrick in Bellevue, Washington.

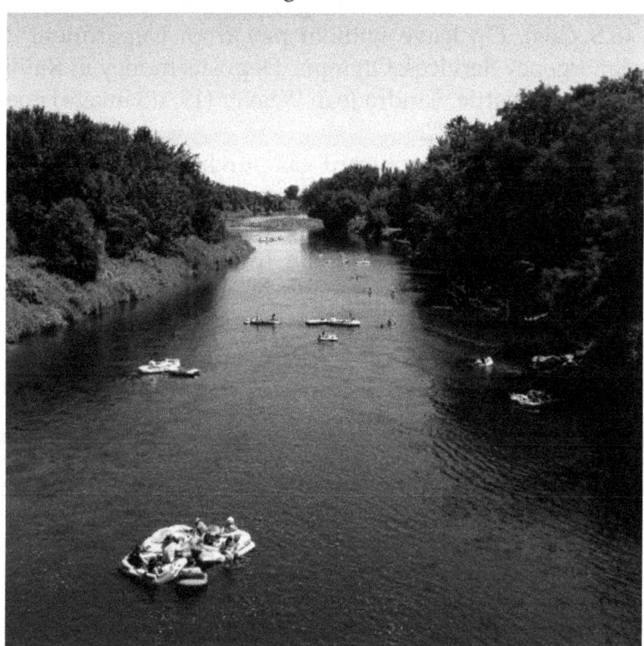

Yakima River, Horn Rapids (undated) Photo public domain.

June 29, 1974: Chevron card gas purchase, Seattle, $1.35. Raft trip with Susan Reade, Larry Voshall and Becky Gibbs down Yakima River. Put raft in at I-90 & Highway 97, Ellensburg, Washington. Acts callously and licentiously friends claim. 10:00 a.m. Voshell finds woman's pantyhose in Ted's VW glovebox. (Evening) Dinner at North Bend, Washington. According to Larry Voshall:

> "We started down the river, with three of us in the raft and the fourth person in an innertube tied on behind the raft. Well, all at once, Ted, who's behind Becky, unties the string of her halter top. The halter top fell off, exposing her breasts. We were all just flabbergasted, embarrassed. You know, we didn't really know each other at all. Ted seemed to get some strange kick out of that. Later on we we're in a pretty swift current, and Becky was behind the raft in the innertube. Ted reached for the rope and said, 'What'll you do if I untie this rope?' Well, Becky's screaming. Just scared to death. And I looked at Ted's face, and I couldn't believe it. He had a look on his face as though he was enjoying subjecting her to that terror—hearing her scream. He had untied the rope. And I really got upset. I got hold of the rope and tied the innertube back to the raft. And I told him we'd better be more careful because the girls can't swim. But Ted was in this grim mood, as though he was angry at all of us ... Later Susan and I talked about it, and we both agreed we'd seen a side of Ted we never knew was there. I'll never forget how he seemed to enjoy subjecting that girl to terror" (Larsen 1980, 96-97).

July 1974: Seen by Mrs. Ferris at Albertson's store at Green Lake in July sporting a cast on his arm. Ted obviously trolling.
Early July, 1974: Removes ski rack from Liz's VW and puts it back on his VW.
July 1, 1974: Chevron card gas purchase, Seattle, $4.52 (8.8 gals). On leave without pay from Department of Emergency Services, Olympia. Deposits money in Rainier Bank, Seattle. Sandra Jean Weaver (19, no image) goes missing from SLC.
July 2, 1974: Chevron card gas purchase, Seattle, $4.85. Sandra Weaver's nude and strangled body is found in DeBeque Canyon along the bank of the Green River about 18 miles east of Grand Junction, Colorado. She had only a tiny wooden cross on a gold chain around her neck.
July 3, 1974: Bought gas in Olympia.
July 5, 1974: Chevron card gas purchase, Tumwater, $5.82.
July 6, 1974: Chevron card gas purchase, Yakima and North Bend, $4.47. Rafting. Ted pushes Liz into the icy waters of the Yakima river. According to Liz:

> About an hour later, I was sitting on the edge of the raft, paying attention to nothing in particular, when suddenly and without warning, Ted lunged at me, put his hands on my shoulders and pushed me into the river. The plunge into the icy water took my breath away. I came up sputtering and grabbed the rope on the edge of the raft, too dazed for the moment to do more than hang on. I looked up at Ted and our eyes locked. His face had gone blank, as though he was not there at all. I had a sense that he wasn't seeing me. I struggled to pull myself into the raft. He didn't move, he didn't speak. I could find no expression on his face.
>
> "Why do you have to ruin everything?" I began when I could finally talk. "That's not funny at all."
>
> He still looked at me as if I were a stranger. Then he looked away and said, "It was no big deal. Can't you take a joke?" (Kendall 1981, 52).

July 7, 1974: Chevron card gas purchase, Seattle, $4.20. Ted scopes out Lake Sammamish. Seen by some people wandering alone along the edge of the lake. Bought gas Mercer Island, Washington. (Afternoon) Ted came over to Liz's to unload the raft which was still in his car.
July 9, 1974: Chevron card gas purchase, Olympia, $3.40 (5.9 gals).
July 10, 1974: Chevron card gas purchase, Olympia, $4.85. (Evening) Dinner with Liz.
July 11, 1974: Chevron card gas purchase, Seattle, $6.35 (two purchases). Absent from Department of Emergency Services, Olympia. This time Ted had phoned to say he was "sick".

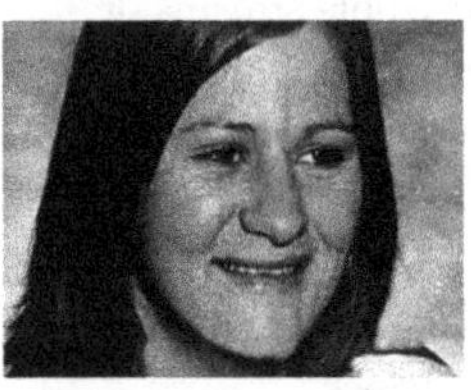
Krista Blake (undated). Photo public domain.

Also on this day, Krista Kay Blake (19) was last seen getting into a blue van driven by a white male in the area of 29th and K St. in Vancouver, Washington. She was a known hitchhiker. Later two other witnesses observed the victim, suspect and blue van together in the area of Lewisville Park sometime before the date of her disappearance. Warren Leslie Forrest was later convicted of her abduction and murder.
July 12, 1974: Calls in sick, continues absence from work Department of Emergency Services, Olympia.
July 13, 1974: Wrote check for cash, Seattle. Liz calls Ted at his parent's house in Tacoma asking if they might do something together the next day.
July 14, 1974: (Sunday morning) Turns up at Liz's. They have a "big fight." Ted leaves. Chevron card gas purchase, Seattle, $3.40. 12:30 p.m. Lake Sammamish. Abducts Janice Anne Ott (23) and Denise Marie Naslund (19).

Ott knew Susan Rancourt while attending Spokane public schools in the 1960s. Ott's high school sweetheart was Dennis Rancourt, Susan's brother. Janice's father in Spokane, Washington, was an assistant director of public schools in that city and had once been an associate of the State Board of Prison Terms and Paroles; the family orientation was decidedly toward public service (Rule 1989, 82). Her father would later say: "She thought that some people were sick or misdirected, and felt that she could help them through her training and personality" (ibid). Patty, a co-worker at the time had this to say about Janice: "I didn't know Janice Ott well. She was a relatively new employee, a juvenile probation caseworker at the King County Juvenile Court in Seattle. She was 23 years old, five-one and a hundred pounds. She had long blond hair and an effervescent smile. I worked in detention on the opposite side of the court system, but we both encountered some pretty tough kids" (Smiley, 2014). Her husband Jim was 1,400 miles away in Riverside, California, completing a course in the design of prosthetic devices for the handicapped at the time she vanished. A former schoolmate remembers Janice Ott as "Janny." Gina Ralph Kelly described her as "one of those people everybody liked. Janny always trusted people were going to do the right thing. It was easy to be friends with her" (*The Spokesman-Review*, January 25, 1989).

Ott rode her Tiger ten-speed bike from her Issaquah home, arrived at Lake Sam around noon. She wore cut-off jeans and a white shirt tied in front. Beneath it, she had a black bikini. She stripped down to that and lay in the sun on a blanket, about 10 feet from three other groups.

Janice (on left) wearing the same cut-off jeans she wore the day she was abducted (undated). Her younger sister on the right. Photo courtesy KCA.

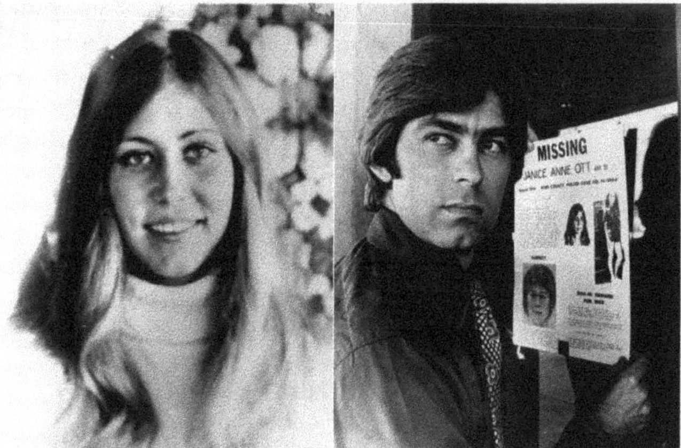

Left: Janice Ott (undated). Photo courtesy KCA. Right: Janice's husband Jim (late July 1974). He came under police scrutiny in the early stages of the investigation. Photo public domain.

The following is a mini-timeline of the events as they were witnessed by various people at the lake that day:

> Janice Ellen Graham (22) arrived at the park after 11:30 a.m. Not finding an empty picnic table she went to the bandstand to watch the races. A guy came up and said hello and she said hello. She kind of moved away at this point. The guy asked her if she could help him for a minute. She said, yeah, what do you want? He said he was waiting for friends but couldn't find them. He said he wanted to load his sailboat on his car. She told him sure. She described him as 5'8" to 5'10", sandy blond hair, curly sort on sides, longer in back, 150-160 lbs, about 24-25 years old, dressed in a white T-shirt with red trim (the neck line was crew-type), with short sleeves, blue Levi's type jeans (long length she thought). She didn't notice his shoes. They walked up to the car which was parked in the parking lot between the bandstand and restrooms. He asked her what she was doing. She told him she was waiting for her husband and parents. He said, "This is out of sight, there are so many people." He stopped many times to hold his arm against his body, as if it were hurting. That was when she first noticed he did not have a cast on the arm. He said he hurt it playing racquetball. He asked her if she ever played it, he said it was a lot of fun. He asked if she lived in the area and she told him Bellevue, where she worked. Approaching the car now, she noticed there was no trailer on the car or sailboat anywhere around. The car was a newer looking Volkswagen bug, metallic brown in color. She asked where the boat was. He replied, "It's at my folks house; it's just up the hill." She said she really couldn't go with him because she had to meet her folks. She asked him the time, and he told her 12:20 p.m. She told him she was late already, she had to meet her folks at 12:15 p.m. He said, "Oh, that's okay, I should have told you it wasn't in the parking lot. Thanks for bothering to come up to the car." He walked her back about halfway through the park, where they separated. He went right towards the bandstand, and she went left to the concession stand. On parting, he said again, "Thanks for coming with me; I should have told you it was not in the parking lot." He was very polite at all times, very sincere, easy to talk to. He did not get upset when she told him she couldn't go with him. At the concession stand, she bought a snowcone. She stayed at the stand eating it. About 10 minutes later, she saw him walking with a girl to the parking lot. The girl had a yellow bike. It looked 10-speed and it had curved handlebars. She thought to herself it didn't take very long for him to find someone else to go with him (King County Department of Public Safety, July 17, 1974, KCA).
>
> At about 12:30 p.m. Sylvia Maria Valint (15) was at the park with Kathy Veres and Pam Okada. They were sitting on the beach close to the water. Ott came near with her bike, laid her towel down, stripped off and sun-baked for about half an hour before a guy came up to her from the west. Valint estimated him to

Lake Sammamish Park aerial showing where Ott and Naslund were taken in relation to where witnesses say Ted parked his car (circa July 1974). Photo courtesy KCA.

be about 5'6" to 5'7", medium build, blondish brown hair down to his neck parted on the side, dark tan, and left arm in a sling with a case that started at the wrist and bent around the elbow. He said, "Excuse me, could you help me put my sailboat onto my car, because I can't do it by myself because I broke my arm." Ott said, "Well sit down and let's talk about it." She asked, "Where's the boat?" He said: "It's up at my parents' house in Issaquah." Ott said, "Oh really, I live up in Issaquah." Then added, "Well, OK." She stood up and put on her clothes. She picked up her bike and said, "Under one condition, that I get to ride in the sailboat." He said: My car is in the parking lot." She said something to the effect: "Well, I get to meet your folks then." He asked her who she knew in Issaquah. They walked towards the parking lot. He had a small English accent (kind of like a fag thought Valint). He had tiny sideburns. He was smooth talking. His clothes looked good, like he was rich and dressed to go sailing. After she said, "My name's Jan," he said, "Ted." (King County Department of Public Safety, July 17, 1974, KCA).

Jerry Snyder (30), a Drug Enforcement Administration agent, was there with his wife around 12:30 p.m. He was positioned about 15 feet from Valint and consequently only heard "portions of the conversation" between Ott and the stranger. He did however enjoy the sight of Ott taking her clothes off. He watched her as she applied cocoa butter to her skin and positioned herself on her towel, facing the sun. He estimated the man's height as 5'8" to 5'10". He was of medium build, had blondish-brown hair, wavy down to the back of his neck, and tanned skin. He wore white tennis shorts, a white T-shirt, white socks, and white tennis shoes, "looked at the laps of the girls as he walked down the beach." Ott and the man talked for about 10 minutes. He did not detect an English accent (K&B 2005, 27; Keppel, Lake Sammamish summary notes, case # 74-123376, KCA).

Theresa Marie Sharpe (26) arrived at the park about 11:45 a.m. She was positioned about 10 feet from Valint. Approximately fifteen minutes after arriving a girl (later identified as Ott) sat down near her after laying her 10-speed bike down on the sand. At 12:30 p.m. a guy came up to her. He looked about 6'0", 180-185 lbs, about 25-30 years old. His hair was about collar length, wavy. He had a tan. He wore a white shirt, white shorts similar to a swim suit. His left arm was in a beige colored sling. She felt it wasn't really hurt—he took his arm from the sling and moved it around. He said something about a sailboat—will you help me with my boat or would you like to ride in my boat.

The girl sort of hesitated then said, "Can I bring my bike with me?" He said, "Sure, OK." The girl thought the boat was at the lake, but he said, no, it was at his parent's house. She looked like she wasn't going, then said, " ... under one stipulation, that I meet your parents." He said, "Sure." She said, "I don't know how to sail." He said, "That's OK, it will be easy for me to teach you." She asked him if there was room in the car for her bike. He said it will fit in the trunk. Then she got up, got dressed, and the two walked away (King County Department of Public Safety, July 17, 1974, KCA).

Approximately 12:30 p.m. Jackie M. Terrell (47) arrived at the park with her daughter Becky (5). By the time Terrell found a parking spot it was 1:00 p.m. She parked across from the Ranger Station entrance in the grass parking area and walked through the wooded area toward the beach, past the concession stand. They put down their towel about 10 feet from the lifeguard stand and stayed in that area for the entire afternoon. "Later in the afternoon" she observed a man walking from the area of the small peninsula north of her. He had his arm in a sling. She paid particular close attention as he walked towards her, then passed her at a distance of about six feet, because she had suffered four broken arms in the past and the sling the man had on was "very unusual." She estimated him to be about 20-26 years old, 5'6" to 5'7", medium suntan, brown hair ("short" by 1970s standards). The hair appeared to be combed back from the forehead, neatly groomed, exposing his ears. No moustache or sideburns. He was wearing an ordinary white short-sleeved T-shirt and red boxer swim trunks, with maybe some white piping on the seams. He was barefoot. He casually glanced from side to side as he passed. As for the sling, her impression was that it was suspicious, not professionally done, without a cast. The time at this point was 4:00 p.m. (King County Department of Public Safety, July 17, 1974, KCA).

Cindy Lynn Galloway (15) rode to the park to participate in the Rainier Beer picnic. During a break (around 2:30 p.m.) she went to check on her bike which was located 60 yards north of the concession stand. As she walked south on the sidewalk she noticed a man with his right arm in a sling. He was standing just north of the life guard's picnic table and was doing nothing out of the ordinary. She estimated his height at about 5'8", with sandy colored hair that was shoulder length. His face was tan but lighter complexion. He wore no shirt, had cut-offs on that appeared to be corduroy that were frayed around the bottom, and was tanned all over. The sling was canvas of muslin color, with leather trim and a supportive strap, no cast or bandage. She thought it was for a broken collar bone (King County Department of Public Safety, July 18, 1974, KCA).

Jacqueline Craven (45) arrived at the park 3:30 p.m. with her family. Between 4:00 and 4:30 p.m. she went to the women's restroom with her 22-year old daughter. The restroom was located in the middle of the park by the concession stand. As she waited for

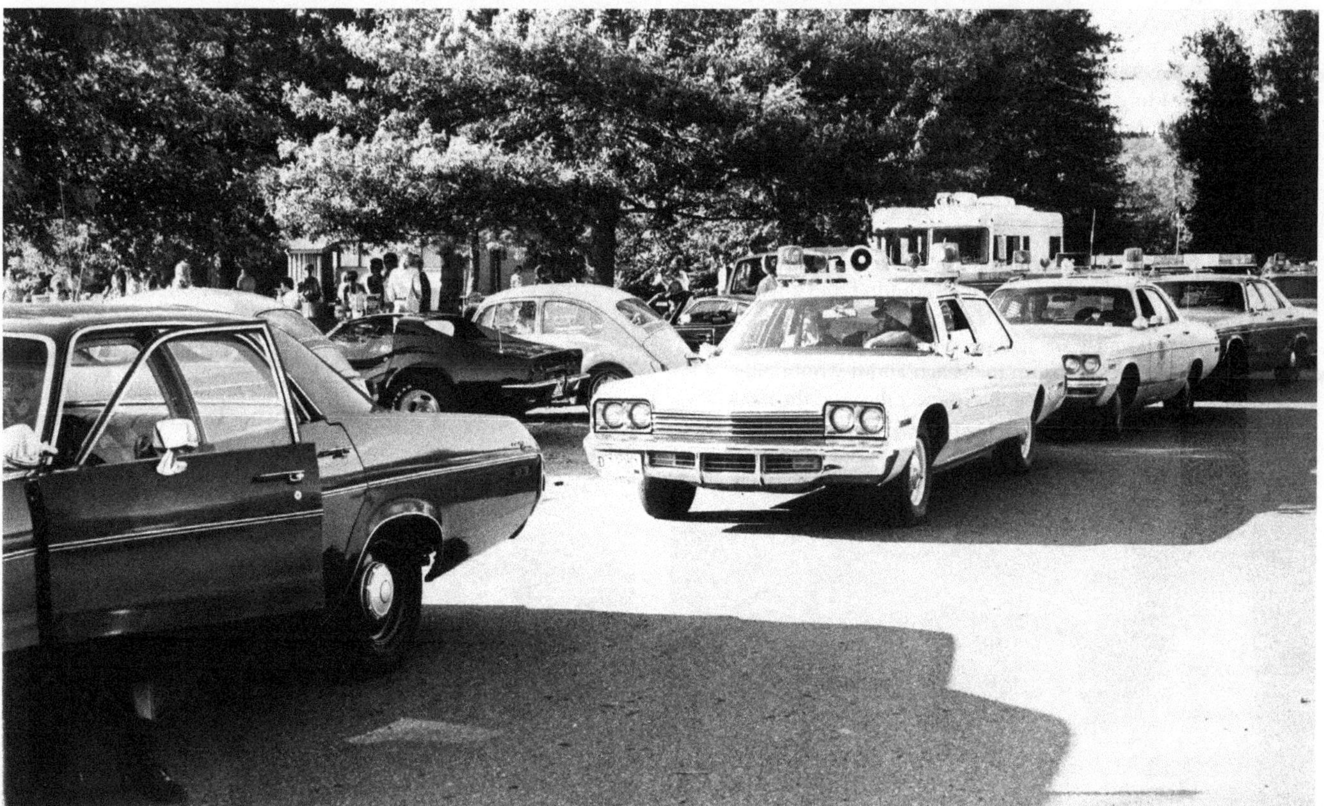

July 14, Keppel thought Ted was sitting in the VW pictured here parked at Lake Sam car park, however, there is no one in the car (it is a reflection of a tree on the window pane) and the engine lid does not have a pair of air intake vents as does Ted's car viewed in photos taken August 1975. The VW bug two cars to the left, likewise, is not Ted's car. Photo courtesy KCA.

her daughter, she noticed a man with a sling on his left arm. He walked back and forth in front of the restroom. Craven described him as 5'7" to 5'8", good build, tan, but fair complexion. He wore boxer type swim trunks with Hawaiian print with possibly a white waist band. No shirt. The sling was a regular triangular bandage, beige in color, but soiled; it had a safety pin on the outside left elbow. His hair was dark brown, clean-cut, sideburns to the middle of his earlobe (King County Department of Public Safety, July 18, 1974, KCA).

Patricia Ann Turner (18) arrived at the park around 3:00 p.m. with friends and boyfriend. Around 4:15 p.m. she didn't feel good, so she got up and walked toward the concession stand. As she walked a man came up to her. He had a sling on his left arm. The sling was bleached white, clean. He had on white shorts, a white T-shirt and white tennis shoes. He was about 5'8", 160-165 lbs, well built. His hair was dishwater blonde, neck length, cut in a shag, no sideburns, parted more or less in the middle, messy. He was good looking, aged about 24-25. He said, "I need to ask a really big favor of you. You can see I'm not very useful of hand, would you please help me launch my sailboat?" She looked at him as if she didn't understand. He said, "I normally wouldn't ask this favor but my brother is busy and is unable to help." He sort of pointed in the direction of the parking lot. She said, "Well, I am sort of in a hurry to go." He said, "That's OK." She walked on to the concession stand glancing off into the crowd and saw him walk away (King County Department of Public Safety, July 19, 1974, KCA).

Sindi Jae Siebenbaum (16) approximately 4:00 p.m. was heading back from the restrooms towards the point where her friends were. About a 100 yards from the restrooms, a man walked towards her and said, "Excuse me, young lady, could you help me launch my sailboat?" His left arm was in a sling and it appeared to be the type a doctor would put on someone. She asked him what had he done to his arm. He stated he sprained it and that he couldn't find anyone to help him. She told him she was sorry, she couldn't help him because she had people waiting. He told her that his sailboat was up the beach and it would only take a few minutes. She interpreted this that the boat was up towards the restrooms. She again told him she couldn't help. However, he kept on asking. She talked to him for about 5 to 10 minutes. She finally told him she was sorry and left. The last time she saw him he was walking towards the restrooms. She estimated his height at about 6'0" or 6'2", really skinny, small bony frame, hair salt and pepper colored about 2" below ears. Hair was parted in the middle with bangs over the forehead. Curly like it had been styled. Eyes were either "green or blue and he looked bug-eyed and set back. His pupils were real small." She guessed his age in the 30s. Clean shaven. Appeared to be nervous. He spoke rapidly and gestured with his hand. He was wearing sort of bleached white boxer swimming suit with elastic waistband. Body full tan, but not real dark. Sort of pointed nose and thin lips (Bothell Police Department, July 17, 1974). Keppel's summary (#74-123376) includes that the man tugged on Sindi's arm. His shirt was long-sleeved, unbuttoned, left arm rolled up, in a sling. It is unclear if the sling or the shirt was faded light green. He pointed with his elbow.

Jacqueline Marie Plischke (20) arrived at the park on her bicycle at about 4:00 p.m. She was there about 20 minutes. She went down to where people water ski from and a white male approached her, 5'8", medium build, dark blond hair, length to about the middle of his ear, average skin tone, left arm in a not very neat beige colored sling with maybe a cast or wrap over his arm. His speech was smooth, clear. The first thing he said was, "Hello, I was wondering is you could help me put my sailboat on my car." She said, "I'm not very strong." He said, "It's better that I asked someone who was alone." He answered her comments right away. She said, "I'm waiting for someone." He said, seemingly not interested in her, "Oh, I see," and turned away and walked toward the bathhouse. He did not act nervous. He was not pushy. He didn't seem disappointed when she told him she was waiting for someone. She was about 2 feet from him. In fact, she noticed him about 15 minutes prior to him making contact. About 10 minutes after he left, she looked at her watch. It was 4:30 p.m. (King County Department of Public Safety, July 17, 1974, KCA).

4:40 p.m. Abducts Naslund (19). Naslund was also known to frequent the Flame Tavern in Burien according to police. Denise was at the park with her boyfriend Ken Little and friends. They took Valium. She wore a pair of cut-off jeans, a dark blue halter top, and brown Mexican-style sandals. Apparently she had an argument with Kenny and went off to the toilet block on the eastern side of the park by herself. A woman saw Denise talking to another woman in the cinderblock structure, and

The toilet block "restroom" where Denise was last seen. Photo public domain.

Denise Naslund circa 1974. Photo courtesy KCA.

Denise Naslund (undated, location unknown, presumably 1974). Photo courtesy KCA.

then saw them walk out together around 4:30 p.m. That was the last time Denise was seen alive.

Several more witnesses came forward after that day but their descriptions were inconsistent. One woman said Ted wore jeans, several others were sure he wore tennis shorts. Accounts of his height and hair color differed. And his sling, they said, was beige, faded green or bleached white. The timing of the encounters posed another difficulty for investigators. One woman said she was approached at the edge of the lake at 5:15 p.m. (45 minutes after Denise' abduction). Was this the same guy? (W&M 1980, 22-3). The cops' frustration said it all. One of them muttered, "Jesus Christ, what the hell could one guy do with two of them in one day anyway?" (Ibid, 24).

6:00 p.m. Removes ski rack from his VW and puts it back on Liz's VW:

> "I was stepping out of the shower when Ted phoned; I stood dripping on the floor as he asked me to have dinner with him. He was at the door in ten minutes, starving, he said. The university student newspaper had just run a hamburger sweepstakes and declared the hamburgers at a bowling alley – near Green Lake the best in town. Ted flopped in a chair while I got ready to go. He had a cold that seemed much worse than it had been that morning. He was so stuffed up he could hardly talk, and he looked tired. I asked him what he'd been doing. He'd just cleaned his car, he said, and helped his landlord with yardwork. The hamburgers lived up to their reputation – good and big. It was all I could do to finish one of them, but Ted ate two and then wanted to go to Farrell's ice cream parlor for dessert" (Kendall 1981, 53-4).

Eleanor Rose, Denise Naslund's mother (undated). Photo public domain.

8:15 p.m. Goes back to his own home alone.

A news article about two weeks after the abductions reveals that police are honing in on Ted's M.O. In each of the encounters, Ted is wearing a cast on his arm. He spins a story that he needs help and lures the victim back to his car. As for Janice's bike, Ted told Keppel he left it at Washington Park Arboretum (K&B 2005, 483). It was never recovered. Keppel's report hints that all the women Ted actively approached that day were sexually alluring, mostly teens and young adults.

While it is true to say that all parents of abducted and murdered daughters suffer terrible grief, Eleanor Rose, Denise Naslund's mother appears to symbolize the grief writ large. She kept a shrine for her daughter at her house, and did not sell the 1964 tan Chevrolet Impala that she gave her daughter for her 18th birthday wrapped in bow. Since Denise's death, Mrs. Rose has attempted suicide several times, received electroshock therapy and has been under psychiatric care. She wrote to Ted in Glenwood Springs jail (late 1977):

> Theodore Bundy: I ask myself, "What were Denise's last thoughts? How long did she suffer? How frightened was she? How? Why? If you know anything – ANYTHING – at all – please let me know … I am so sick at heart and so unhappy. Everywhere I look I see her face. I visualize her walking in the door, sitting here and talking to me – putting her makeup on and combing her hair … Please if you can give me a lead or know anything about anybody, write and let me know (Larsen 1980, 183-4).

She got no reply. Then she wrote him while he was jailed in Florida, and someone typed a response saying he didn't do it and hopes that "God will give me some sort of peace" (*St. Petersburg Times*, July 7, 1986).

Gerard John Schaefer, if we are to believe him, had a little more luck when it came to finding out what Ted did with Ott & Naslund. According to Schaefer:

> [Ted] went out to some park in Washington and grabbed him a long-haired blonde like Susan Place,

> the victim he saw in the tabloid. He caught her in the morning and killed her, then went back in the afternoon and hunted a brunette in a black bikini to copycat Georgia Jessup, who was shown in an alluring black swimsuit. He selected the one he wanted and waited for her to go to the restroom, and then caught her on the way to the toilet. He took her where he killed the first girl and strangled her too. When he got the cord around her neck and pulled it taut she went off like a rocket. He told me that he'd put the seat of the VW as far forward as possible so the woman's knees would be jammed up under the dash. A large woman would be so cramped she couldn't move, but this one gal was on the small side and as soon as he yanked the cord she popped up and was half over the back seat. Her legs weren't tied and she was kicking so hard Ted thought she was going to kick out the windscreen. After that he'd tie the ankles, shove the seat full forward, then get in the back and get down to business. He was annoyed that she crapped when he strangled her, and said he should have grabbed her coming out of the restroom instead of on her way to it. [...] Both the women figured he had rape in mind. The blonde was some sort of social worker who promised she'd help him if he'd let her go. The brunette was sobbing and begging to be let go because of her widowed mother or something. Ted killed both on the same day, and he told me they were chosen because they looked like Place and Jessup...." (Schaefer 1997, 227).

On a different occasion, Schaefer said:

> [Ted] told me that he had followed my case in the detective magazines, and that he had killed two girls in Washington as a copycat crime – so-to-speak – of [Susan] Place and [Georgia] Jessup ... and I think those were Ott and Naslund ... and he told me that he took them up on a logging road, and strangled them and had sex with their corpses, and went back and had sex with their corpses, and cut off their heads" (Schaefer interview by Stéphane Bourgoin at Florida State Prison, October 1991).

The detective magazines that Schaefer is referring to exist. They are *Inside Detective* (September 1973) and *True Detective* (October 1973). If Ted did indeed read the articles on Schaefer, he would have identified with the subtext, which was that authorities knew very little about Schaefer and had no idea how many people he had killed, although they knew it was a significant number. He would also learn Schaefer took heads. Here was another baby-faced killer responsible for some wicked crimes, including necrophilia.

Schaefer liked to boast that he introduced Ted to "doubles." Once again, the magazines do not explicitly make reference to doubles, but many of the victims are pairs. Because there are a number of pairs, there is the implicit assumption that this killer did doubles. The speculation is, did Ted do Lake Sam because of what he read in one of those magazines? Did it inspire him to do his own doubles?

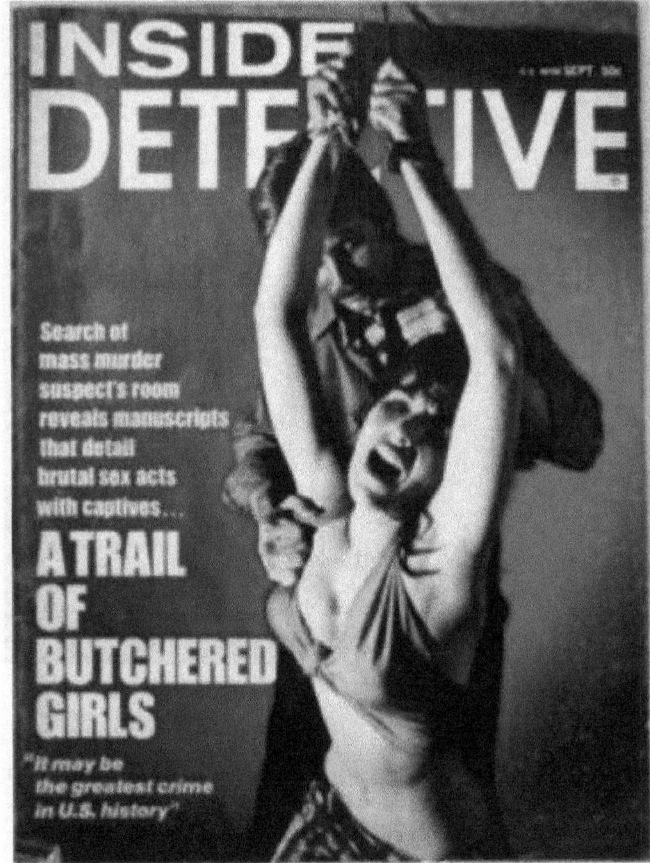

Inside Detective, September 1973 edition (content unknown).

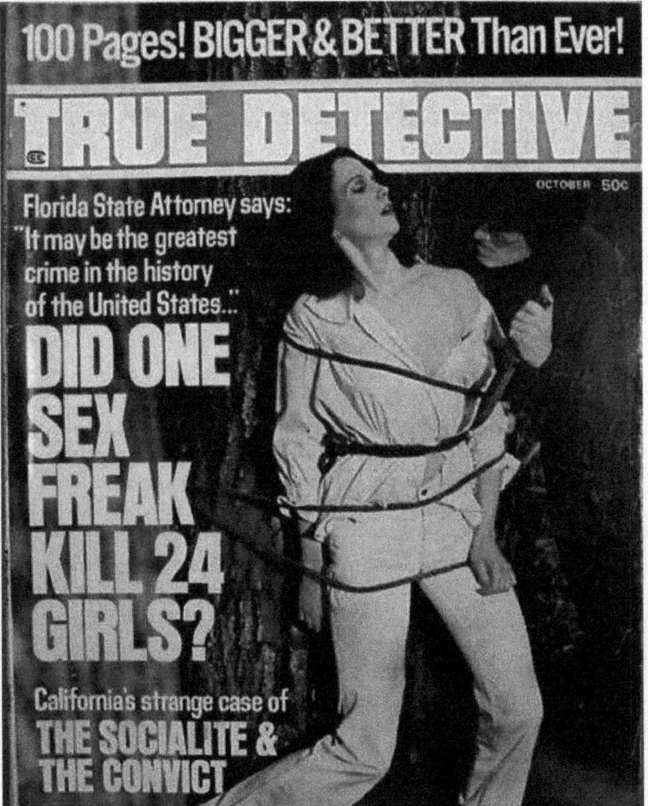

True Detective, October 1973 edition. The article contains a portrait of Susan Place, but not Georgia Jessup.

Keppel was baffled that Ted could take two victims in one day. When he asked why, Ted responded in typical elliptical fashion:

> Well, he just put himself in a position of picking up two at the same time, really not cause he wanted ... it's, it might not be because he wanted to, but because maybe he just got locked into a situation where he was so driven he had to. He saw one, and he, to get one, he had to get two, which is two (K&M 2012, 123).

Not trying to decode this mumbo-jumbo, but is Ted saying that his fantasy could not be found in a single individual? He could only find part of it in one individual, and the other in another individual? So he took two to make up the fantasy, make it whole. In any case, there appears to be no connection to Schaefer's doubles. Not unless we speculate that it wasn't two victims per se, but a plan of doing such-and-such to two people, where two deaths were needed, two bodies to play with at the end of the day.

That aside, at least Schaefer draws us into a another important discriminating factor in characterizing Ted: his degree of wickedness, his level of empathy, or lack of it, during the commission of the crime. It was proposed by Michaud & Aynesworth that Ted's fantasy was to kill one individual in front of the other. They support this contention by adding that it was a "suspicion long held by police" (1983, 127). In his last confession to Lewis the day before he was executed, Ted made it very clear he did not have one girl watch while he harmed the other. When Lewis pushed him on this, saying, "So you made yourself look more callous and cruel," Ted replied: "No, that did not occur to me. Because I knew the police would know, in all likelihood, that there was no such place that I could have done that" (Nelson 1994, 295). Ted is referring to the cabin theory, which we learned about in his Hawkins' confession. A cabin in fact did exist at Issaquah; it was in the southwestern gully (to Ted's left) as he took the dirt road up and across the trestle tracks to the grassy area. It was close to the highway then. Keppel would not have failed to inspect it. We have to assume there was no evidence of murder found there. Alternatively, if it wasn't processed, it is too late anyway. The hut is gone; it went during the construction of the I-90 in 1975.

So Ted murdered the girls up at the grassy area. It was good summer weather, it was private, easy to conceal his activity, and was close to the I-90, easy access in and out. Which means if he did two together, he would have had to leave a living Ott tied up at Issaquah, handcuffed to a tree maybe, for the better part of an hour. Was that a risk he was willing to take? Shouting, calling for help when he was gone? It just doesn't sound reasonable. It wasn't like Ted had done that many victims by this time that he was supremely confident. Just Hawkins the month before, he said he panicked ... so if we are to take that as true, then the extraordinary risk of leaving a conscious bound victim at the site while he went to fetch another—another that he could not be 100 percent certain he'd get—the odds that it played out this way is minimal.

In another scenario he knocked Ott out and left her bound at the site while he went hunting for another. The problem with this modification of the first theory is that he would have had to make sure Ott was totally smashed up, beyond regaining consciousness. What benefit to him would that be? Bring the second victim to show a comatose body? Possible but ....

The third case, which is the most plausible, is he simply just killed Ott at the Issaquah site quickly, either because he was dissatisfied, or premeditatively, then left her there while he went to fetch another. He could still get the shock value out of Naslund. *Look! This is your fate.* We cannot rule that out. We could also consider the softer version, which is he didn't tell Naslund about Ott; he just took her there and killed her alone. This seems less likely than the original theory.

Thus, our measure of empathy for Ted, is possibly not much more than Schaefer's, who we know had a penchant for torturing his victims for long periods of time, taunting them with suggestions that he could kill them while choking them and allowing them to revive. Ted always said his kills were quick. He proved that at Chi Omega. Ted never admits to, and in fact always minimized any suggestion that he was a sadist in the true sense of the word. He denied prolonging the degradation, humiliation and anxiety of the victims, or physically inflicting pain. Of course, the victims, if they were conscious, would have been terrified, something Schaefer lived and breathed for. He explicitly verbalized his fantasies, and they always involved long drawn-out torture sessions. We might be tempted to call Ted a gentleman sadist by comparison. Certainly, the cop who handled Schaefer's case, prosecutor Robert Stone, was under no false pretense: "[Schaefer ...] was the most sexually deviant person I had ever seen. He made Ted Bundy look like a Boy Scout" (Treadway, 2010).

July 15, 1974: Calls in sick, continues absence from work Department of Emergency Services, Olympia. 8:00 a.m. Keppel and Dunn are assigned to the Lake Sam case. 3:30 p.m. Ott first reported missing.

July 16, 1974: Calls in sick, continues absence from work Department of Emergency Services, Olympia. Washington State highway employee stopped his truck on the logging road at the Issaquah body location to have lunch. He immediately detected the unmistakable odor of putrefaction. After walking less than 30 feet, he spotted what he thought was a deer carcass, and decided to move and have his lunch elsewhere. Whether this carcass was Janice Ott, Denise Naslund, or Georgeann Hawkins is unknown.

July 17, 1974: Chevron card gas purchase, Olympia, $5.24. Eleanor Rose formally interviewed about her

1649 Rec'd call from U. of W. professor Joel Kestenbaum, 525-0153 who formerly was a teaching assistant to Ted Bundy, 24-25, 5'8", 160, light parted hair, good student, personable, possible accent, class of abnormal psychology, couple years ago, instructor was Erwin Sarasen. Kestenbaum moving to Ohio on Aug 1, tacoma relatives SK9-1689.

Parent Johnny C. no add.

Theodore Robert Bundy 11-24-46 Burlington, VT B/B in June 10th 1972. 3214 N. 20th Tacoma

Keppel's Joel Kestenbaum note on 25th of July, 1974, one of hundreds of "Ted" calls that came into Seattle police. Document courtesy KCA.

missing daughter.

(4:30 p.m.) Warren Leslie Forrest picks up Norma Countryman (15) sitting on the side of State Highway 501 leading out of Ridgefield, Washington. They drove for 30 minutes then stopped in a field. He grabbed her and put a knife he had used to clean his fingernails at her throat. He forced her into the back of his van, hogtied her, cut off her bra which he used to gag her, and fondled her breasts. He then drove her, crying in the back of the van, stopping several times, at one point slapping her. They arrived at the country park complex of the maintenance sheds at Tukes Mountain, a mile east of Battle Ground. He carried her, still bound, from the van into a wooded area. He tied her head to one tree and legs to another. He punched her in the eye. He then left he saying he would return. While he was gone she escaped, spending the night in another part of the woods.

Norma Countryman shortly after her assault. Photo public domain.

July 18, 1974: Chevron card gas purchase, Olympia, $3.50 (6.4 gals). Norma Countryman is found alive and her assault is reported to the police.

July 21, 1974: Chevron card gas purchase, Olympia, $4.49 (8.3 gals).

July 22, 1974: Liz's co-worker shows her *The Seattle Times* with reference to "Ted" and a "VW." Liz starts to agonize over every little detail, but she can't see the forest for the trees. The news articles describe Ted's VW as "bronze" or "metallic-colored." The tan paint on his VW had weathered and looked sort of dull (Kendall 1981, 58). Liz and her girlfriend Mary Chino, in whom she confided everything: "... went to the university library to read all the newspaper stories and learn everything we could about the disappearances. We paged through all the papers for the last week. One story described "Ted" as five-foot-six or five-foot-seven–several inches shorter than my Ted. The VW was described as metallic gold—Ted's was dull brown—and there was no mention of a ski rack on the back. There was a different composite drawing, too. It gave the suspect curly hair, but the resemblances to my Ted weren't there" (Kendall 1981, 60). These coincidences, or lack of them, spurred Liz to make her first anonymous phone call to Seattle police.

July 25, 1974: Chevron card gas purchase, Tacoma, $4.53. Picks up rug cleaner, Seattle. Joel Mandel Kestenbaum (psychology professor UW) contacts Bob Keppel, "... weird guy in my class who drives a 1968 VW and matches the composite drawing from your office." Kestenbaum mentions that Irwin G. Sarason taught Ted abnormal psychology.

Keppel also received first call from Katherine D'Olivo about her encounter with Ted at CWU (Adams 1981, 205).

Finally, around this time according to Liz:

> I talked to Ted on the phone every day. He was feeling pressured about the budget he was working on and about his move to Utah. I was leaving in a few days to spend a week with my family and bring Tina back; Ted asked me to find him an apartment in SLC. I did as he asked, but it seemed to me that I was doing the work of getting him set for law school without anything in it for me. I spent hours in SLC poring over the rental ads and traipsing up and down stairs of places with pink flamingos on the wallpaper. Finally I found an apartment I knew Ted would like in an old house in a neighborhood called The Avenues, near the University of Utah. The house was being remodeled, but it would be ready by fall. I called Ted to tell him about it, and he was pleased (Kendall 1981, 63).

July 26, 1974: 11:30 Report of a person wearing a cast all the way up to his hip on one leg in 16th N.E. and 50th Seattle U-District.

July 27, 1974: Chevron card gas purchase, Seattle, $3.88 (7.3 gals).

July 28, 1974: Ted went to State Park, Seattle.

July 31, 1974: Buys gas in Seattle.

August 1974: Rule contacts Dick Reed Motor Vehicles Department, Seattle. Ted reported owning a 1968

Ellensburg Daily Record - Aug 2, 1974

Second local encounter with 'Ted'

A second Central Washington State College coed has reported an encounter with a man matching the description of "Ted", said Central Police Chief Al Pickles.

Pickles said the second and similar reported encounter — also with a senior coed — occurred sometime before 9:30 p.m. on the night of April 17, the same night Susan Rancourt was last seen leaving a meeting on campus between 9:30 and 10 p.m.

"Ted" — wanted for questioning is reported to have worn a cast or sling on his arm each time he has had a reported encounter with a woman. He is also reported to drive a Volkswagen.

At Lake Sammamish he is known to have contacted at last five women and asked them for assistance with a boat. One woman accompanied him to the auto — described as being an unusual medium shade of brown. When arriving at the auto and finding there was no boat "Ted" told the woman it was at his parents' place. She left without getting into the auto.

The Central coed told Chief Pickles by phone from her home earlier this week she was coming out of the college library and the man — with a cast on his arm — dropped some books and made a sound like he was in pain.

Pickles said she offered to help him carry the books to his auto.

"I didn't know if she went to the auto," said Pickles. "I didn't go into a detailed discussion with her about the incident because she has been interviewed by the Pierce County Sheriff's office and they are sending us a copy of that report." He said the report had not yet arrived but is expected.

A wire service report of the second reported encounter relates the coed was coming out of the library "about 10 p.m. and was walking toward a parking lot when she heard books drop behind her. A young man wearing a metal brace on his left arm and his right arm in a sling was trying to gather up the books."

The report further says she assisted him in gathering up the books and he asked her for help in taking them to his car in an alley near the lot, which she agreed to do.

When they arrived at the vehicle — described as a brown Volkswagen — the man fumbled with his keys and dropped them. He then asked her to pick them up, the report says.

The girl is then quoted as saying, "I wasn't about to bend over in front of him. I said 'Let's step back and see if we can see them.' " Upon spotting the keys she picked them up and then handed them to the man. She then walked away. The man made no attempt to stop her, the report says.

"It sounds to me to be like the same show the other girl reported to us," said Pickles.

On April 21 a man approached another CWSC coed coming out of the library. He was wearing a "cast like bandage" on his left arm. He dropped books and the girl helped pick them up and carried them to his auto — a yellow Volkswagen — but she balked when he told her to get in and start the auto. She dropped the books and ran when he commanded her to "get in."

In Seattle the King County Police have issued a request for the return of a bike that Janice Ott, 23, was last seen pushing towards a parking lot at Lake Sammamish on July 14 while walking with "Ted" — who had a cast or sling on his left arm. She, and Denise Naslund, 19, disappeared from the lake that day.

Police reports indicate Mrs. Ott was asked by "Ted" to help him unload a boat. She agreed and the pair were last seen walking towards the parking lot with Mrs. Ott pushing the bike.

Six women and four-year-old Heidi Peterson have disappeared in the state since January 31. A total of $31,500 in rewards have been offered in connection with the disappearances. Among that amount is a $1,000 reward for information leading to the whereabouts and return of Susan Rancourt.

"bronze" VW. Ted prepares to move to SLC. Seen by Mrs Ferris on the 'Avenue' where he told her "he was leaving soon to go to law school in SLC."

Early August 1974: Ted cuts his hair short. Liz finds a hatchet under his car seat. Around this time, when Liz announces she'll tell people about his theft behavior, he threatens to break her "fucking neck."

August 1, 1974: Buys gas in Olympia. Deposits money in Rainier Bank, Seattle. (Around midnight) Evergreen State College (Olympia) campus complaint by Joni Dadarion, that she was surprised from behind and frightened by a "schitzy, real wild looking" man at her dormitory laundromat.

Carol Valenzuela (undated). Photo public domain.

August 2, 1974: Carol Platt Valenzuela (19) wife and mother of 10-month-old twins was last seen hitchhiking near downtown Vancouver, Washington. According to Winn & Merrill, Carol was last seen at a welfare office in Vancouver at 11:00 a.m. A caseworker had told her to come back for food stamps. But she never appeared.

August 4, 1974: Bought gas in Olympia.

August 6, 1974: Chevron card gas purchase, Olympia, $1.78.

August 7, 1974: Chevron card gas purchase, Olympia, $5.30.

August 8, 1974: Report out in newspaper, a student had been walking in front of the Beta Theta Pi fraternity house University district about 12:30 a.m. on June 11 (the night that Georgeann Hawkins disappeared) and encountered a man on crutches carrying a briefcase. He was having a lot of trouble and was dropping the briefcase every few steps. The student helped him carry the case as far as her boyfriend's fraternity house and told him she would be out in a few minutes and could help him to his car if he needed it. She stayed over an hour; when she came out he was gone. Liz read the article and, prompted by Mary Chino, makes a tentative call to Seattle Police Department Homicide Unit.

August 9, 1974: President Richard Nixon officially resigns over Watergate.

August 11, 1974: Chevron card gas purchase, Olympia, $4.85.

August 15 1974: Chevron card gas purchase, Tacoma, $5.20. Ted called Liz from his parents' house in Tacoma. According to Liz:

> He was crying and his words came out slowly. He told me that he'd been driving near a shopping center

> in Tacoma, and had seen the police chase a man down the street. 'He was like an animal,' Ted said. 'He ran and ran with the police chasing him in their car, and when they caught him, he urinated all over himself.' I wondered what he was trying to tell me, but when I tried to get him to tell me more about it, he changed the subject and started talking about the budget he was working on (Kendall 1981, 67).

August 16 1974: Liz sneaks into Ted's apartment and rifles through his things. Ted has already started boxing his stuff up ready for the move to SLC. Liz opens some of them and finds an envelope full of canceled checks dated May 1974. She surreptitiously takes it.
August 18, 1974: Chevron card gas purchase, Olympia, $4.10.
August 22, 1974: Chevron card gas purchase, Olympia, $3.00.
August 24, 1974: Chevron card gas purchase, Olympia, $3.87.
August 25, 1974: Chevron card gas purchase, Olympia, $4.22 (7.6 gals).
August 28, 1974: Resigns job at Olympia Emergency Services Department. Leaves bizarre resignation note.

"It is with some regret — not much — that I submit my resignation," he wrote. "Try to bribe me, slash my tires ... but the world needs me. The time I've spent here is without value — it is invaluable."
There was a post script: "Caution: Tears will run the ink."

August 29, 1974: Chevron card gas purchase, Seattle, $5.00.
August 31, 1974: According to Liz:

> Ted was working right down to the wire on his budget. The Sunday before he was to leave, Tina and I went down to Olympia with him for the day. We took my TV set and parked Tina in front of it in a back room, and then I sat at a typewriter while Ted paced up and down behind me, dictating. It was a long day; Ted was way behind in the work and his deadline was Monday. This was the Ted only I knew, I thought. Everyone else thought he was so well organized, but I had spent years helping him out of last-minute jams like this. He had always waited until the last possible moment to write papers and then showed up at my office and asked me to drop everything and type them. He took incompletes in many of his classes and had to make the work up later. Today was typical. It was midnight when we finished, and Ted left his budget on his boss's desk, tied with a big red ribbon (Kendall 1981, 68-9).

Martha Morrison (undated). Photo public domain.

September 1974: Martha Marie Morrison (17) disappeared from her Portland, Oregon home around this time. She is a suspected victim of Warren Leslie Forrest.

University of Utah S. J. Quinney law school classes begin. The modern calender has classes beginning in August 28, with last day to withdraw on September 18. Bruce Zimmer, Dean of the University of Utah College of Law, stated he had known Ted since August 15, 1974. According to Zimmer, Ted attended very poorly during his first quarter classes. Ted's main teacher was Jim Baillin, who reported that Ted attended only two or three days of his class. Despite this, Ted got Bs and Cs during exams at the end of the first quarter.

University of Utah S. J. Quinney Law School. Photo courtesy Chris Mortensen © 2015.

September 1, 1974: Bought item at Nordstrom, Tacoma, WA. (Midnight) Completes budget report for OESD.
September 2, 1974: Labor Day. (Morning) Packs stuff in readiness to leave for SLC, Utah. Has breakfast with Liz, Tina and Mary at the west end of Lake Union. He then heads off for SLC. This is backed up by a photo that re-

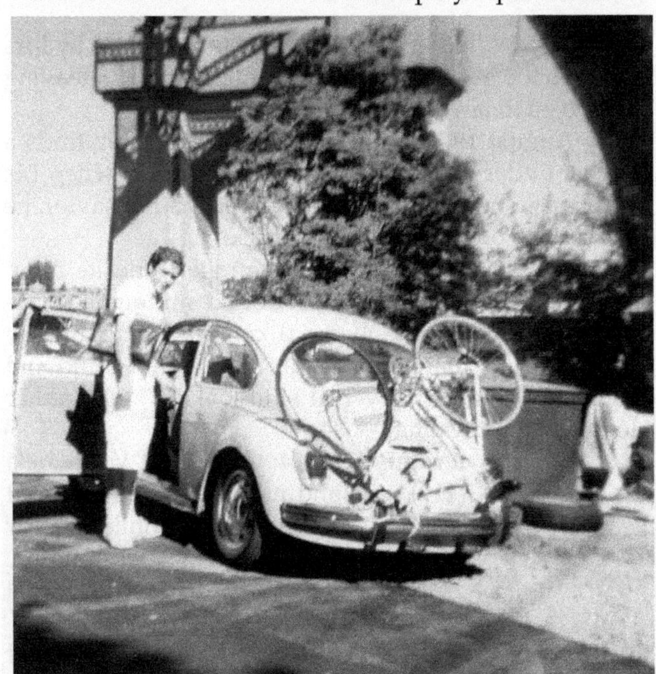

The morning of Ted's departure for SLC (September 2, 1974), the Aurora Bridge a recognizable landmark. The photo appears to have been taken on the north bank on Cheshiahud Lake Union Loop (Burke-Gilman Trail). Photo © 'Theodore the Documentary' Facebook site, May 19, 2017. Original source Mary Chino.

Excerpt from the Multiagency Investigative Team Report 1992

```
Month Day Year
09-01-74 (00:00) BUNDY BOUGHT ITEM AT NORDSTROM, TACOMA,
                 WASHINGTON
09-02-74 (00:00) BUNDY BOUGHT ITEM AT NORDSTROM, PORTLAND,
                 OREGON
         (00:00) BUNDY BOUGHT GAS, SEATTLE, WASHINGTON
         (00:00) BUNDY BOUGHT GAS, YAKIMA, WASHINGTON
         (00:00) BUNDY BOUGHT GAS, PENDLETON, OREGON
         (00:00) BUNDY BOUGHT GAS, BOISE, IDAHO
         (00:00) BUNDY, WHILE MOVING FROM SEATTLE, WASHINGTON, TO
                 SALT LAKE CITY, UTAH, DROVE THROUGH BOISE,
                 IDAHO, AND PICKED UP AN UNKNOWN HITCHHIKER AND
                 KILLED HER. HE THEN DUMPED HER BODY IN THE SNAKE
                 RIVER. VICTIM'S IDENTIFICATION IS UNKNOWN, BODY
                 HAS NEVER BEEN LOCATED.
09-03-74 (00:00) BUNDY BOUGHT ITEM AT NORDSTROM, TACOMA,
                 WASHINGTON
09-04-74 (00:00) BODIES OF JANICE ANNE OTT AND DENISE MARIE
                 NASLUND LOCATED, ISSAQUAH, WASHINGTON
         (00:00) BUNDY BOUGHT GAS, BURLEY, IDAHO
09-06-74 (00:00) BUNDY BOUGHT GAS, SALT LAKE CITY, UTAH
         (00:00) MONEY DEPOSITED IN BUNDY'S BANK ACCOUNT,
                 SEATTLE, WASHINGTON
```

September 1974 (Keppel, Terrible Secrets, 2012)

Second, Monday:	Departs Seattle for Salt Lake City and University of Utah College of Law. GC – Seattle - $3.00 – Yakima, WA. - $2.85 – Pendleton, Ore., - $2.25 – Boise, Idaho - $4.08.
Second, Monday:	Bundy kills an unknown hitchhiker near Boise and throws her body in the Snake River.
Third, Tuesday:	GC – Burley, Idaho - $3.80 (6.5 gallons).
Sixth, Friday:	Buys gas, Salt Lake City.

Ted was working right down to the wire on his budget. The Sunday (Sept 1974) before he was to leave, Tina and I went down to Olympia with him for the day. We took my TV set and parked Tina in front of it in a back room, and then I sat at a typewriter while Ted paced up and down behind me, dictating. It was a long day; Ted was way behind in the work and his deadline was Monday. [...] It was midnight when we finished, and Ted left his budget on his boss's desk, tied with a big red ribbon.

Angie cooked a going-away breakfast for Ted on her houseboat. It was Labor Day weekend, still sunny and hot, and Ted took a last look at the lake and the matching blue sky above it. He would miss Seattle, he said, but he was glad to be starting fresh in Utah and convinced that he would finally be able to concentrate on getting his law degree. He tickled Tina one last time, gave Angie a hug, and then turned to me. We held each other for a long time, then kissed goodbye. Ted waved and honked as he drove off, his Boston fern beside him in the front seat. (Kendall 1981, 68-9)

TED CALLED ME FROM NAMPA, IDAHO, TO TELL me he loved me. We had picnicked there on one of our trips to Utah. He called me again from outside of Salt Lake City to tell me where he was, and he called me from his apartment to tell me how much he loved the place I had found for him.

Note: "Angie" = Mary Chino. (Kendall 1981, 70)

cently surfaced showing Ted standing next to his VW bug under the Aurora Bridge. At this point the timeline goes somewhat pear-shaped. In the original version of this book we failed to put this part of Ted's timeline under sufficient scrutiny. We shall correct that shortfall here. In examining all the available data, we have constructed the inset (below). It reveals several problems. At least three different timelines can be extracted from it. Which one is correct? We have no choice but to work our way through and see where it leads us. They all start with Ted leaving Seattle on the morning of September 2. He makes three gas purchases with his Chevron credit card on this date: Seattle, $3.00; Yakima, Washington, $2.85; Pendleton, Oregon, $2.25; and Boise, Idaho, $4.08. Given the distance involved, it is fair to assume he made the Boise purchase sometime in the afternoon. Prior to driving through Boise, Ted stopped in Nampa to call Liz. Nampa is off the highway about 21 miles before Boise. One wonders what he was doing there? Was it to reminisce on the picnic he had shared with Liz there, or was he casting his eye around for a hitchhiker? In any case, he found what he was looking for in Boise – if his confession can be believed. The girl has never been identified, nor correlated with any missing list. In the desire to raise Ted's body count as high as possible, some pundits like to imagine that Ted had no reason to lie. But can we make that assumption? Ted's Boise hitchhiker confession came hot on the heels of his final failed appeal on Saturday 21, 1989. Early on Sunday morning, he met Russell Reneau, chief investigator for the Idaho attorney general's office. According to Reneau:

> He told me [...] what state she was from [Montana, Wyoming?], she was hitchhiking, and he picked her up outside of Boise [...] he stacked a lot of things in that passenger seat area, so when he picked her up, he had to have gotten out of the car, moved around, opened the door, cleared out that area so she could sit on the floor. He he had very few details to share about this girl - he had so many details about Lynnette, that this really bothered me. I thought ok, one of two things is true here: either, it didn't happen at all and he's making it up, or, as was sometimes his custom, perhaps when he made his move around the car, cleared out the passenger seat, he slammed her on the head with his tire iron, and that's why they never had a conversation. I don't know which one of those is true, and I will probably never know. It could have been [untrue] because there was absolutely no question, when I arrived in Florida, I mean the very first thing I was confronted with, was his attorney. She [Weiner] wanted me to talk to the governor of Florida try to get a stay of execution so that we could spend more time with him to unravel these details about unsolved cases. So it very well could just been a fabrication. I can tell you, based on, what he told me about the area where he said he dumped the body, we patrolled up and down that river - of course it was many years too late - we found nothing, we found no evidence, we found no missing person's report out of whatever state it was he told me that she said she was from, so I'm still up in the air on that. Reneau interview, 15 July, 2015.

Indeed, examining the photo of Ted next to his VW bug one can see the front passenger seat is packed full. One wonders how a hitchhiker could fit in there. If, as Rene-

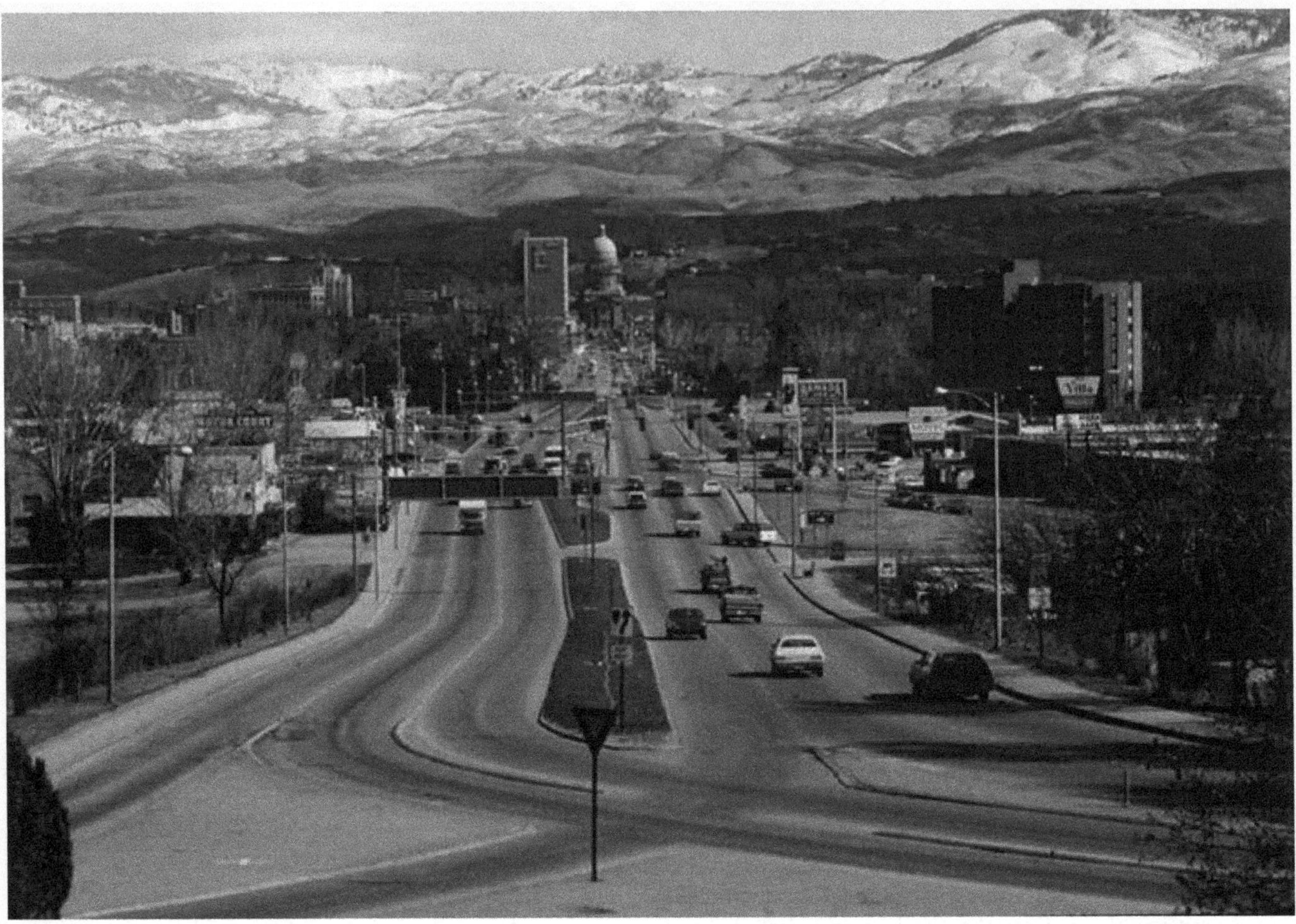

Boise, Idaho (1975). Photo public domain.

au said, she sat on the floor, this would give Ted an opportunity to knock her unconscious and therefore avoid the need for any conversation. That would explain why he imparted so little information about her. She simply did not leave a big enough impression in his mind and the passage of time faded her out. But then Reneau tells us about Ted's 11th hour shenanigans in Florida. A completely different reason could be given for the paucity of information. Maybe Ted was holding back. Dangled the bait so to speak. Or, he could have completely fabricated the victim so as to draw investigators into a quagmire that would stall his execution. We can't eliminate any of these possibilities. In fact, if anything, the latter possibilities bear more weight. For all the confessions Ted made during the last days of his life, not one piece of information he provided led to the physical recovery of any victim or victim parts. Only one item was found that was claimed to belong to a victim and that was Debbi Kent's patella. The Kent family has supposedly had this DNA tested but this has not been verified. Thus, it could be argued that Ted's Boise hitchhiker was a mirage created by a man who was clutching at straws. In the end, we have to conclude we will simply never know – at least not unless someone comes forward with new evidence that might tip the balance the other way.

Having said this, we are given some tantalizing evidence from a different source that, while not conclusive proof of the Boise hitchhiker, raises the speculation stakes:

> He had been driving around the hills of Idaho, getting to know the area, looking for safe sites to take a victim. He was a meticulous researcher. […]
>
> While driving, he spotted a hitchhiker, a girl around fifteen years old. He had not planned to do anything while scouting, but there she was. He checked his rearview mirror for other cars. None. She got in and started talking to him. He had to act fast–he did not like his victims to talk, he did not want to get to know them, he did not want to know they were real. He reached back for his tire iron and hit her over the head. She slumped in the seat, but awoke soon afterwards, moaning.
>
> He knocked her out again. […]
>
> He drove across the across the state line to a secluded place in the woods that he was already familiar with. He led the girl out of the car, assuring her that no harm would come to her. He made her strip and kneel on her hands and knees while he took Polaroid pictures of her. […]
>
> She cried.
>
> He could see the look of terror in her eyes, her eyes begging for mercy. He kept reassuring her. […]
>
> Then he got behind her, slung a noose around her

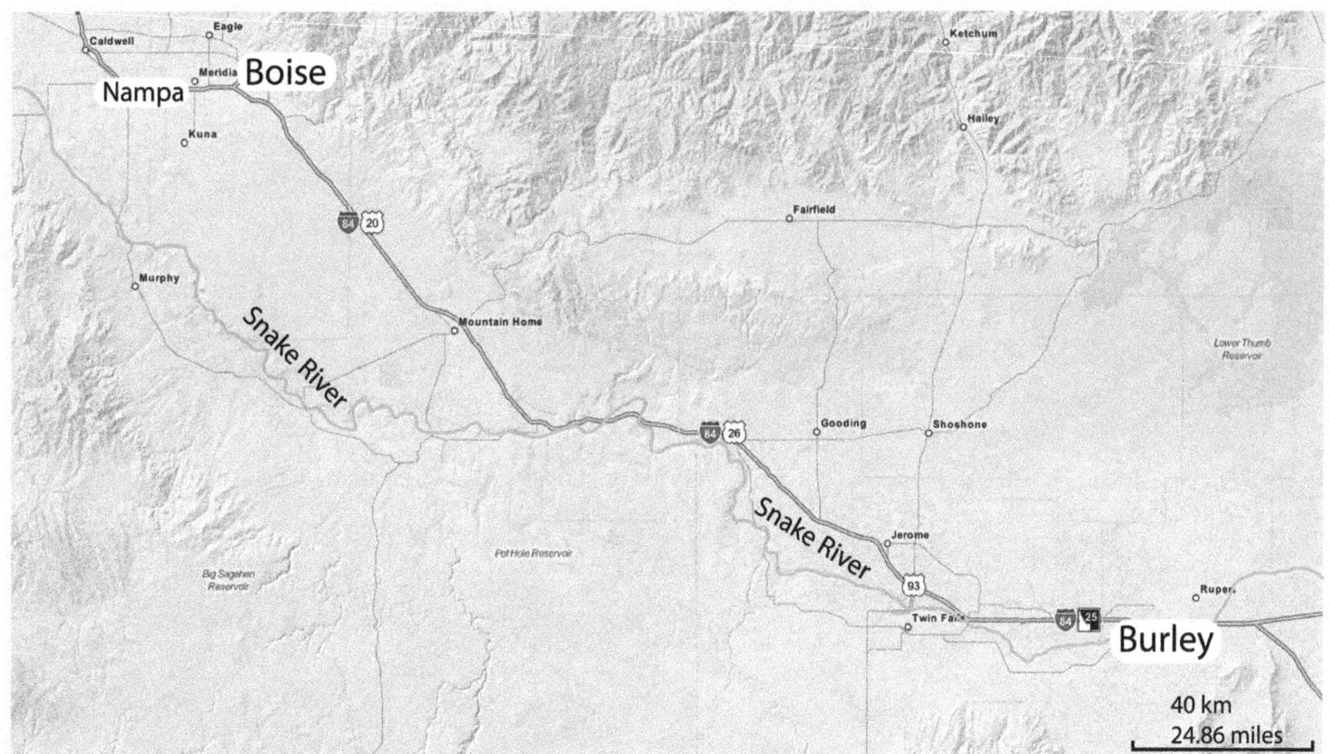

Map showing the Snake River in relation to the Boise and Burley route. Map courtesy OpenStreetMap contributors, 2015.

> neck, and strangled her as he raped her. He continued to reassure her he would let her go, and she had seemed to believe him. He said he'd felt a little sad that he could not let her go, that he had to kill her, but she would be able to identify him, of course. Afterward, he pulled her body deeper into the woods and, the next day, drove back to take more pictures and to cut her body into pieces (Nelson 1994, 257-9); extraneous material omitted.

What are we to make of this? The story contains some striking correlations: Idaho, a 15-year old female hitchhiker, checking his rear view mirror, knocking her out rapidly. Note that Reneau was unaware of this story, yet his speculations seem to intuitively match. On the problematic side, Ted starts the story by recounting that he was driving around the hills of Idaho, that he was a meticulous researcher. This conflicts with the spontaneous, opportunistic nature of picking up a hitchhiker. But then he adds "He had not planned to do anything while scouting." We are left scratching our heads. Could this be a memory distorted version of the Idaho leg of his journey to SLC, or was this an entirely separate event? In any case, we will never know, because this victim, like the phantom Boise hitchhiker, never appeared on anyone's missing list.

Our problems do not end there. According to the MTR timeline, the next day (September 3) Ted is back in Tacoma! This makes no sense. This entry is missing in Keppel's timeline, and reading Liz's account, the impression she gives is that Ted drove straight through, a drive that would normally take him no more than a day. It gets worse. Keppel has Ted buying gasoline in Burley, Idaho, on September 3 while the MTR pegs this event on September 4. Then Keppel and the MTR have Ted buying gasoline in SLC on September 6, the assumption being that this is his arrival day. Even if we have Ted arriving the day before, are we to assume that it took him 4-5 days to travel from Seattle to SLC? This just doesn't fit the normal pattern of Ted's driving activities. Ted was accustomed to driving long distances in short spaces of time. There are no records of him staying anywhere along the route, and he certainly could not have slept in his car, and he didn't have a tent (as far as we know).

The timeline is a mess, and any attempt to reconstruct it will be tenuous at best. But if we take Ted's normal behavior as the rule, then we should posit he left Seattle on the morning of September 2 and arrived SLC on morning of September 3. This is more than enough time to do the journey *and* spend the night with a victim. In this scenario, Ted's purchase of gasoline on September 4 (MTR timeline) would coincide with Ted returning the "next day" to take Polaroids of the hitchhiker's body, cut it up and throw the pieces in the Snake River. In hindsight, this victim, real or not, was never going to be identified.

Depending on which timeline you take, Ted then reaches SLC and moves into his 565 First Avenue apartment. Not only did Liz find the apartment for him, but he was also able to secure the role of property manager of this address, a position which gave him access to parts of the property which were off-bounds to other tenants. One of these locations was the cellar at the back of the

Salt Lake City, Utah, 1975. Photo public domain.

house. According to Dan Lish, who lived on the ground floor eastside with his girlfriend:

> "... right underneath my kitchen window, I had an exit door to go right out on the backside by the parking lot, but there was this little underground storage thing, where you would lift up kind of like an awning thing, and then there were stairs to go down, and Ted would go down there all the time. He'd spend a ton of time down there at nighttime, like in the middle of night, I'd hear, like you could hear it when he'd open the hatch up and stuff, and we'd be in the bedroom sleeping, you could hear him lift that thing up and then close it, it would kind of come down with a bang. [...] I never went down it, because the way it was explained to me is it kind of belonged to the apartment house manager, which was Ted" (Dan Lish interview by Chris Mortensen, 10 August 2015).

The 565 First Avenue house, front view. Ted occupied room #2 on the second floor. Photos courtesy Chris Mortensen © 2015.

Rear of house, inset showing close-up of hatch leading to the cellar (arrow). A careful reading of Jerry Thompson's reports indicates that the cellar was not inspected when Ted's apartment was searched on August 21, 1975. Is this where Ted kept his Polaroids? Or did he use the cellar in other ways?

Top: 565 First Avenue 1978. Photo courtesy Utah Division of State History © 2016. 2nd from top: Stairs leading up to Ted's apartment. Ted's door on right at the landing. 3rd from top: Entrance hall facing north, bedroom straight ahead, bathroom on right. Bottom: Kitchen facing north. Photos courtesy Chris Mortensen © 2016.

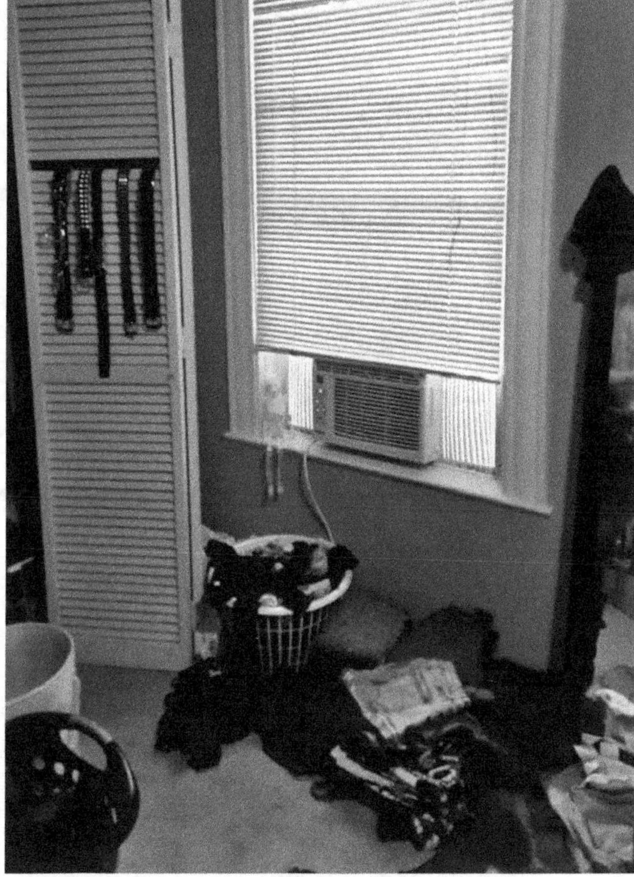

Top: Kitchen facing south. Middle: Dining/lounge on the right beyond. Bottom: Dining/lounge area with the southerly facing windows. The bedroom and the bedroom closet. For a floor plan of the apartment, see Appendix 1. Photos courtesy Chris Mortensen © 2016.

September 3, 1974: (Morning) Calls Liz from 565 First Avenue (this is interpolated). According to Keppel's timeline, Ted makes a Chevron card gas purchase Burley, Idaho, $3.80 (6.5 gals).

September 4, 1974: According to the MTR, Chevron card gas purchase Burley, Idaho.

September 6, 1974: Ted buys gas in SLC. Liz deposits money in Ted's bank account, Seattle.

Issaquah

September 7, 1974: A grouse hunter discovers the remains of Ott, Naslund and Hawkins, one mile east of the old railroad trestle just east of Issaquah. It would appear that it was only a matter of time before the remains would be found because according to Keppel the site was a "multi-use environment" (K&M 2012, 46). In one account it was described as a "lover's lane."

September 8, 1974: First skeletal remains found at Issaquah confirmed as Denise Naslund.

September 10, 1974: Lower jawbone found at Issaquah confirmed by dental records as Janice Ott's.

September 11, 1974: Buys gas, SLC.

September 17, 1974: Buys gas, Tremonton, Utah. It is difficult to explain why Ted was there at this time, but it is probably related to his hunting behavior.

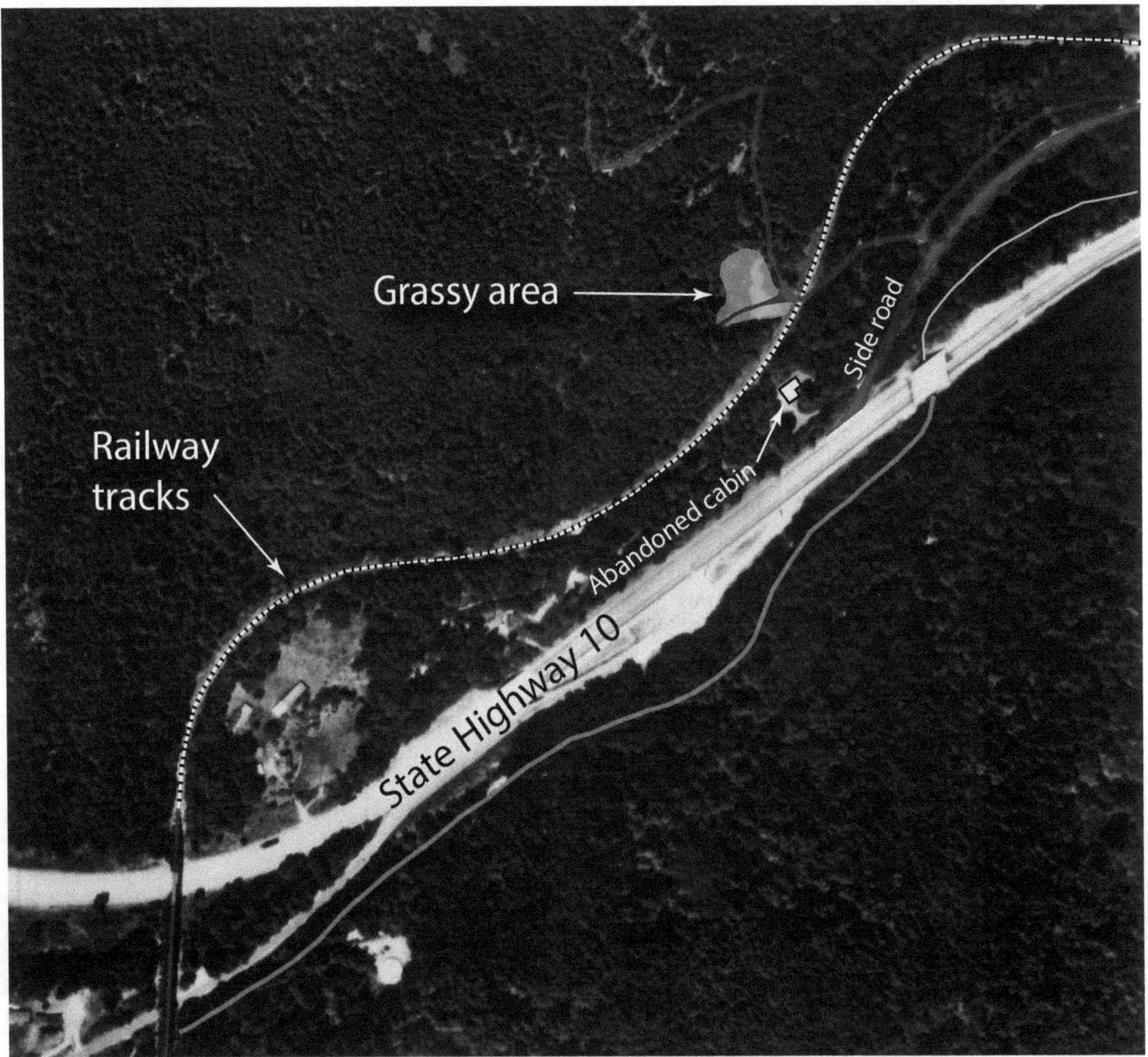

The Issaquah site based on actual police maps. This area has been significantly altered due to roadworks (converting State Highway 10 into the I-90 in 1975). The actual site now lies down an embankment off the Old Sunset Highway, now called Highlands Drive NE. Aerial map (1965) courtesy King County Department of Transportation.

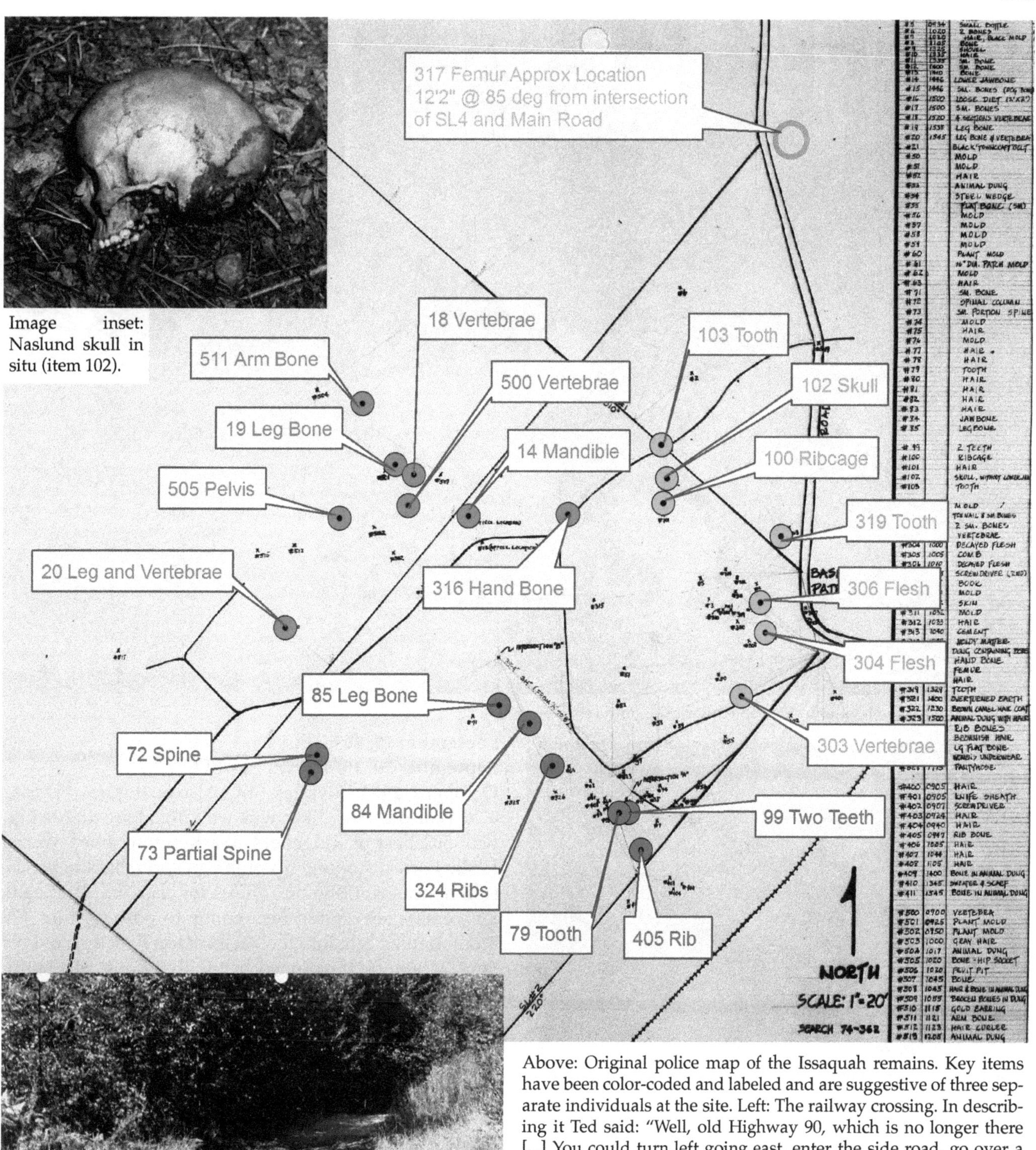

Image inset: Naslund skull in situ (item 102).

Above: Original police map of the Issaquah remains. Key items have been color-coded and labeled and are suggestive of three separate individuals at the site. Left: The railway crossing. In describing it Ted said: "Well, old Highway 90, which is no longer there [...] You could turn left going east, enter the side road, go over a ravine that was between the side road and the highway, turn sort of, go left again, and go back down toward Issaquah. Traveling on the side road you pass underneath some power transmission lines. There was a creek down in the ravine between I-90 and the side road. Maybe a quarter of a mile down this little side road, it would join Ninety again. But if you turned just about the time it reached Ninety again, there's another little dirt road to the right that went up a hill and across some railroad tracks. Just on the other side of the railroad tracks about twenty yards up, there's a little grassy area, some scrub growth and old alders. [...] Also, in the area, maybe fifty yards to the east, down into another ravine, was an old abandoned cabin. Ring a bell?" (K&B 2005, 866-867). Photos courtesy KCA.

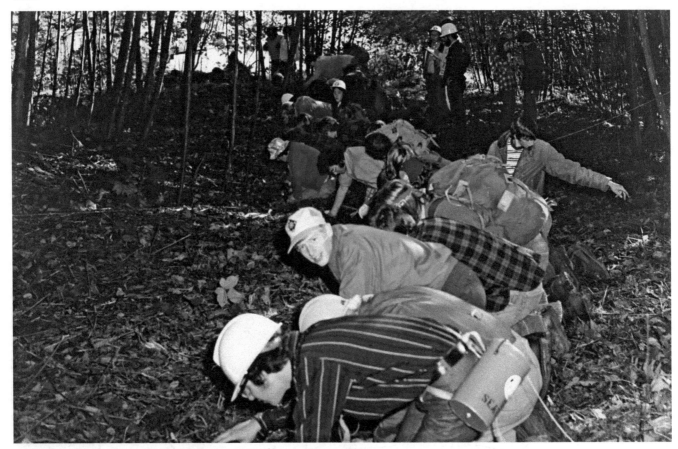

A search line at the Issaquah site, September 1974. Photo courtesy KCA.

Naslund's spinal column and ribcage in situ. Photo courtesy KCA.

September 18-19, 1974: Ted flies back to Seattle to pick up furniture and drives a truck back to SLC with his brother Glen. For obvious reasons, abductions were not possible on this trip.
September 20, 1974: Buys gas, SLC. Around this time Marguerite Christine Maughan, daughter of Supreme Court Judge Richard Maughan, moves into a downstairs apartment at 565 First Avenue.
September 23, 1974: Buys gas, SLC.
September 24, 1974: Buys gas, Murray, SLC.
September 25, 1974: Ted on phone from SLC.
September 26, 1974: Ted Buys gas in Murray, SLC.
September 27, 1974: Buys gas, SLC.
September 30, 1974: Buys gas, SLC.
October 1, 1974: Buys gas, SLC. Also on this day, "Daria," a 20-year old hitchhiker was walking along State Highway 502 East of Ridgefield, Washington, when Warren Leslie Forrest stopped his blue van and talked to her. He said he was working on a thesis for class work at Seattle University. He offered her money to pose for him. She accompanied him into the Washington Park area of Portland, where he threatened her with a knife and bound her with tape. He then transported her about 25 miles to Lacamas Park, a heavily wooded sparsely populated area of Clark County (just east of Vancouver, Washington). There he sexually assaulted her and shot her in the chest with hand honed darts from a .177 caliber dart pistol. Still not finished, he worked her over with a dildo, then led her by a rope around her neck approximately 100 feet down a path, sat her on a log and choked her unconscious before finally stabbing her five times in the chest area with a four-inch knife. Afterwards, he laid her naked body beside the log and covered her with brush and debris, apparently thinking she was dead. He took all clothing from the scene. The victim, however was not mortally wounded, and after about two hours was able to make her way to a public road, where she found assistance. The gun, tape, and baling twine similar to that used on her (and other victims) were taken from a foot locker in Forrest's van. Articles belonging to her were

also found in his house. He had taken leave from work to keep a doctor's appointment in Portland on the day of the kidnap and assault.

Nancy Wilcox (undated). Photo public domain.

October 2, 1974: Buys gas, SLC. Abducts Nancy Wilcox (16) at knife-point from Holladay during the early evening. Ted confessed to sexually assaulting and killing her in a nearby orchard. He said he buried her body in the vicinity of Capitol Reed National Park. It has never been found.

Contrary to reports, Nancy was not a cheerleader (it was her younger sister who was), nor was she last seen riding in a "yellow" VW bug (Sullivan 2009, 92); she left home on foot. She worked part-time at Arctic Circle drive-through (2005 East 3300 South Millcreek). Arctic Circle is famous for its ice-creams, but it also does fast food. When Connie Wilcox reported that she recollected Nancy talking about a good-looking man who liked to come by and flirt, it was previously thought that she was referring to the Highland Drive-in cinema, but this was an error based on the word "drive-in." Reflecting on the event, Connie is quoted as saying, "Now I wonder, 'Was it Ted? Was he stalking out my daughter?' I can't get it out of my mind" (*People Weekly*, February 6, 1989). Connie is not the only person who remembered Nancy talking about the good-looking man at Arctic Circle. Nancy's little sister, Susie Nelson, also remembers hearing her parents discussing this issue shortly after Nancy's disappearance. Furthermore, Nancy's older cousin Jamie Hayden (from Connie's side of the family) also remembers Nancy talking about an older handsome guy approximately Ted's age chatting her up at the Arctic Circle. From these reports, we can surmise that Ted may have seen Nancy working at Arctic Circle and decided to pick her as his next victim.

Nancy had a boyfriend named John Hood who was a year above her at Olympus High School, literally two blocks south of Arnette Drive where the Wilcox family lived. John was popular not least due to his physique and his position on the high school football team. Jamie was around the same age as John and also attended Olympus High. According to her, Nancy and John were a tight couple who kept mostly to themselves. Captain George Q. Neilsen Jr. head of the Juvenile Division (Utah) said, "From our experience, Nancy Wilcox should have been one of those who was gone two or three days before she came home. She had never run away before and there wasn't a history of her being delinquent" (*The Desert News*, December 28, 1974). This account is supported by both Jamie and Susie who described Nancy as generally polite and quiet, and who did not drink alcohol or take drugs (Chris Mortensen interview, October 26, 2017; February 16, 2018). This is backed up by Louisa Paulsen, who was Nancy's best friend and who also worked with Nancy at Arctic Circle (Chris Mortensen interview February 26, 2018).

As for the details of the abduction, Ted provided us

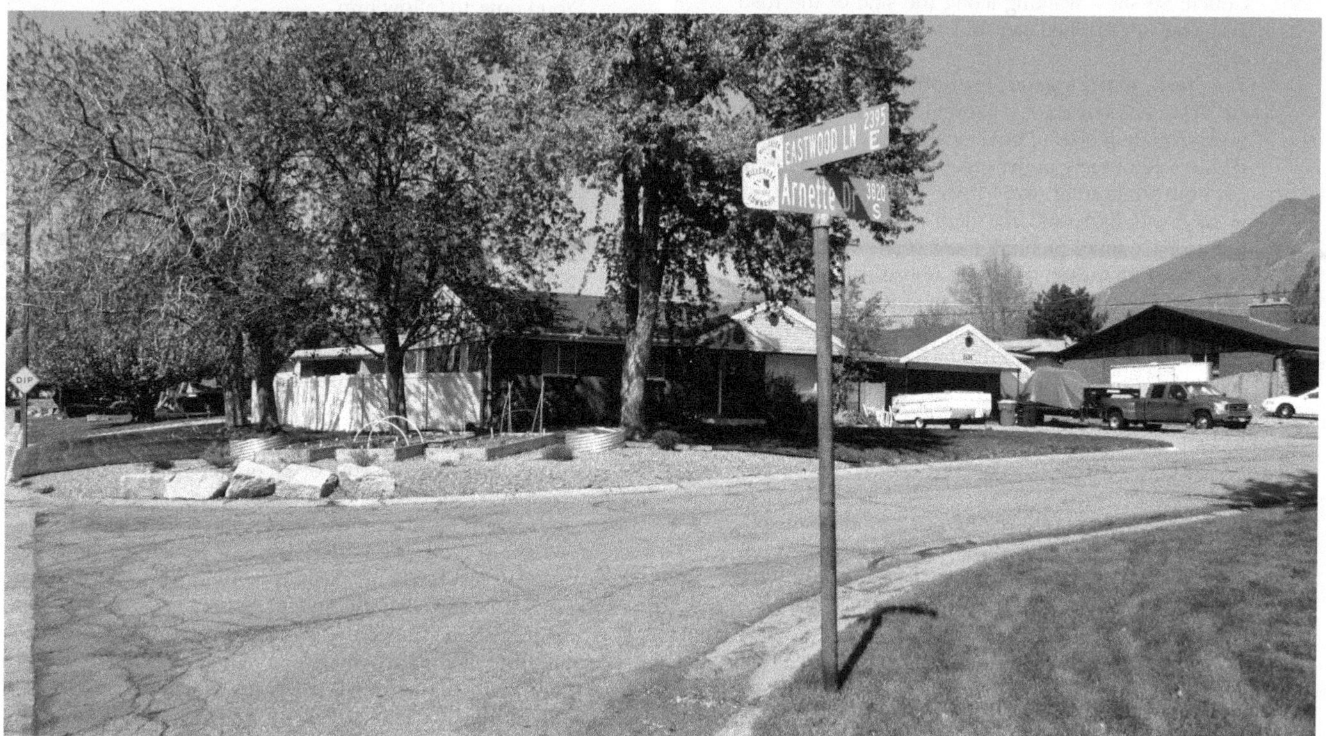

Nancy Wilcox's house. Photo courtesy Chris Mortensen © 2015.

with two accounts. One comes from his 11th hour and tired confession to Detective Dennis Couch of the Salt Lake County Sheriff's Office:

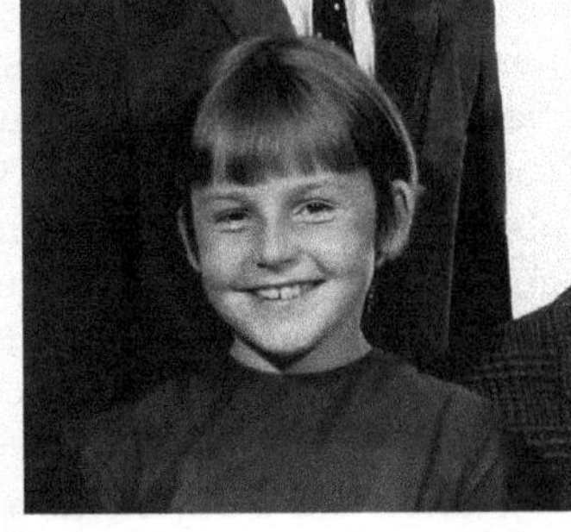

A family portrait of Nancy when she was 7 or 8 years old. Photo courtesy Wilcox family.

> Couch: Do you remember approximately where you encountered Nancy Wilcox? Do you remember what she was wearing, what she looked like?
> Ted: I don't remember exactly what she was wearing – she was wearing like, casual clothes, she wasn't wearing a dress, she wasn't dressed up in a slacks or a dress, or jeans, walking along the side of a road, poorly lit area, suburban, like years ago I think I would have probably had a street map, if I had a street map, there's an outside chance I could show you … you don't happen to have a street map?
> Couch: No.
> [Ted then goes on to describe the area … South of the university and east of State Street.] "By suburban I don't mean 'new' suburban, I mean it looked like older suburban, houses that had been around for a while, wasn't any development, wasn't any sidewalks per se, I think it was just sort of a side area, dark, sewers, curbs."
> Couch: Were you able to have any conversation with her?
> Ted: Not really. Not much. Nothing, not worth …
> Couch: Was she carrying a purse do you recall?
> Ted: Don't recall.
> Couch: So she's walking along the side of the road and you approached her and took her against her will?
> Ted: Yeah, that's a good description, yeah basically. Ah, it was a fairly dark, a particularly dark stretch of, it was a main roadway, but I mean, how can I describe it? But without any bullet streetlight, an old style single bulb street light every three of four poles down it, so it was dark, and ah, there was a, what looked like to be a small orchard, I say very small residential orchard between these two houses, and she was, I [*garbled*] her there, restrained, and placed in the car and taken to the apartment.
> Couch: At what point would she have been killed? In the orchard or your car?
> Ted: The next day. The next day.
> Couch: Are we talking about the same apartment though?
> Ted: Yes.
> Couch: Do you recall anything unusual about her, anything that sticks out in your mind as far as her, any scars, marks, or, obviously did you know her name at that time?
> Ted: No, no I didn't. Ah …
> Couch: Did she talk about, was she able to talk about anything prior to the assault, you say you didn't have much of a conversation with her before
> Ted: No.
> Couch: Where was she taken after the apartment?
> Ted: That's what I'm trying to remember. That's what I'm looking. I need to look over the map, it's unclear to me now. [Ted would later steer Couch to Capital Reef National Park.] (Audio tape courtesy SLC police department).

As usual, Ted avoided any description of what he did sexually to his victim. That he was able to accost Nancy while she was walking along a darkened street suggests he drove up rapidly behind her and jumped out with a knife. Ted also makes it sound like he doesn't know Nancy, but on listening to the tape very carefully, you can hear him add a silent thought after being asked by Couch, almost as if he wanted to contradict himself or add some information.

The other narrative we have from Ted is to Michaud of a girl he raped in an orchard. The implication is that he is talking about Nancy, although her name never comes up (M&A 1983, 133-5):

> Ted: So he, uh, began to just go out driving around the suburbs, uh, in this city, uh, that he was living in, and one particular evening he's driving down a fairly dark street and saw a girl walking along the street. Okay?
> Michaud: Uh-huh.
> Ted: Because the area was dark and she was alone, he decided to select her as the victim for this intended act of sexual assault. He parked his car down the street and, uh, then ran up behind the girl. Just as he came up on her they were at a place where there was an orchid, a number of trees or something. As he came up behind her, she heard him. She turned around and he brandished a knife and grabbed her by the arm and told her to do what he wanted her to do. You know, to follow him.
> Michaud: Yeah.
> Ted: He pushed her off the sidewalk into this darkened wooded area and, uh, told her to submit and do what he wanted her to do. She began to argue with him and he kept telling her to be quiet. She said she didn't believe he would do anything to her, anyway. Then he began to try to remove her clothes and she would, uh, continue to struggle in a feeble manner. And also voice verbally her objections to what was going on. And then, uh, the significance now is that his intent with this victim was not to harm her. He thought this was going to be a significant departure; perhaps even a way of deconditioning himself, to climb down that ladder or, uh, I can't think of a good word, de-, de-escalate this level of violence to the point where there would be no violence at all. Even no necessity for that kind of encounter at all.
> Michaud: I see.
> Ted: But he found himself with this girl who was struggling and screaming. Uh, not screaming, but let's say just basically arguing with him. There were houses in the vicinity, and he was concerned that somebody might hear. And so, in an attempt to stop her from talking or arguing, he placed his hand over her mouth. She stopped and he attempted to remove her clothes and she began to object again. At this point, he was in a state of not just agitation, but something on the order of panic. He was fearing that she

would arouse somebody in the vicinity. So, not thinking clearly, but still intending not to harm her, let's say he placed his hands around her throat.
Michaud: Uh-huh.
Ted: Just to throttle her into unconsciousness so that she wouldn't scream anymore. She stopped struggling and it appeared she was unconscious. But not, in his opinion, to the point where he had killed her.
Michaud: Right.
Ted: Then let's say he removed her clothes and raped her and put his own clothes back on. At about that point he began to notice that the girl wasn't moving. It appeared, although he wasn't certain, that he'd done what he promised himself he wouldn't do, and he had done it really almost inadvertently. Uh, so he took the girl by one of her arms and pulled her over to a darkened corner of this little orchard. And then, in a fit of panic, he fled the scene. He got back into his car and drove back to his house, still not knowing if the girl was alive or dead. But once he returned to the house, upon reflection he began to wonder. He didn't know if he'd left anything at the crime scene. He hadn't thought about publicity and physical evidence. So he decided to return to the scene and if the body was there to recover it and take it somewhere else where it wouldn't be found.
Michaud: Is this the same night?
Ted: Huh? Oh, yeah. But he faced two problems in returning to the scene. First, prior to the incident he was in a state of intoxication and he didn't know the area that well. So he couldn't remember exactly where it was he had to return, couldn't find his way back, as it were. But let's say after a considerable period of time driving about in the general vicinity, uh, he was able to locate the area. It was getting fairly late about this time. Nobody was in the vicinity, so apparently she hadn't gotten up and gone away and the police hadn't returned to the scene. Or she was still there. He parked his car at the curb of this small orchard and walked into it and saw that in fact the body was still in the same position he'd left it. So it was clear that the girl was dead. So he carried the body to his

A 1977 aerial photo of Arnette Drive and the orchard on 3900 S, Holladay (Millcreek area). The red line depicts Nancy's hypothetical route (S 2395 E). The orchard lies between houses exactly as Ted described it. Aerial photo courtesy USGS aerial imagery collection.

> car and put it in and covered it. Then he returned to the general area with a flashlight and scoured it to pick up everything that he may have left there – her clothing, et cetera. He placed that in the car and returned to his apartment.
> Michaud: Did he find everything?
> Ted: I don't know.

Ted would have us believe that he strangled a girl to death unintentionally. This, of course, is just another Tedism. The orchard, however, is problematic. Some commentators have taken Ted's story to be about little Ann from Tacoma. However, this is uninformed speculation. When the two narratives are compared—Couch and Michaud—it is clear that Ted can only be talking about Nancy.

What we have to take seriously, however, is Connie Wilcox's story about the mysterious man who flirted with her daughter. Was it Ted? Given what we now know, that he spent considerable time with Laura Aime before he abducted her, and indirectly knew Lynda Healy, as well as incidentally knew Donna Manson and Susan Rancourt, and maybe even had seen Melissa Smith at the Pepperoni on a prior occasion, we have to err on the possibility that he may have known Nancy before he abducted her. The pattern that emerges is Ted becomes obsessed with certain girls and women. Once this happens, he stalks them and plans their abduction and murder. This explains what he was doing in Holladay that night. Assuming he did see Nancy at Arctic Circle, his usual M.O. was to follow his victims home so he could stake out the abduction. Just like on the day he was first arrested in Granger, he would have spent considerable time parked outside the house after dark and waited for the right moment to strike. As fate would have it, this opportunity would soon present itself.

One newspaper report from the time suggests that "she walked out of her home [...] after a minor family argument" (*The Deseret News*, October 15, 1975). In corroboration of this, we have subsequently learned from Jamie (who lived with the Wilcox family for a few months during this period) that John Hood used to park his pickup truck in the front drive of the Wilcox home whenever he came by to take Nancy out. His car would leak oil onto the driveway which annoyed Herbert Wilcox, Nancy's father, to no end. Understandably, Herbert also took a dislike to John because of his presumptive control over his daughter. On the evening in question, Herbert, who was employed at a Wells Fargo bank downtown, arrived home after work to find Nancy ready to go out. According to Susie, Nancy was wearing brown corduroys, a navy blue v-necked long-sleeved sweater, and a pair of flip-flops made from straw and velvet. Upon asking her where she was planning to go Nancy told him that she was waiting for John to pick her up. This triggered an argument. Nancy responded by walking off, saying she was going to find John down the street.

Nancy Wilcox portrait, 1974. Photo courtesy Connie Wilcox.

An examination of the street layout at this time shows that she almost certainly walked south down S 2395 E towards Olympus High School, most probably in anticipation of finding John finishing up his football practice (since October is football season in SLC). This route would have taken her across 3900 S directly through a narrow lane beside a house that led past an orchard that lays adjacent to the school sports grounds (see map on p. 125). Even though it was already dark, this wouldn't have bothered her, as in all probability it was her regular short-cut to school.

Ted, who was waiting outside and probably observing Nancy leave the house in anger, would have seized on this moment as his opportunity to strike. All he had to do was drive a short way down S 2395 E, park, jump out and follow her across 3900 S. In classic ninja-style, he could have come up to her from behind and grabbed her around the throat while brandishing a knife. Whatever story Ted spun about this rape, what we can be certain of is that due to the proximity of the location to nearby houses, Ted absolutely could not afford to rouse locals by having his victim scream or shout. Therefore, we can safely assume he must have rendered Nancy compliant either through fear by using the knife, or more probably, strangulated her to death right there and then (as he did at Chi Omega where there were close neighbors) and leisurely raped her warm dead body afterwards. Once finished, he could have calmly returned to his car, driven it into the orchard, loaded the body into the trunk, and driven off. Looking at the timeline, we find absolutely nothing for the dates October 3–10, 1975. An entire week ... leading to the possibility that he spent that time visiting Nancy's body somewhere.

Investigators searched Capital Reef National Park, where Ted said he buried her, but no remains were found. Numerous animal bones and a deteriorated "tan-colored blouse with lace" were found (*The Deseret News*, March 19, 1989). The blouse could not have belonged to Nancy as Ted never left items of clothing on victims; the only exception to this rule was that in several cases he left stockings around the necks of some of his victims, perhaps as an identifying mark of some sort.

Even though Nancy's body was never found, she appears to be the first in a new series. It seems that by the time Ted got to Utah he felt confident that he could get close to his victims, linger over their lives longer before taking them. Also on this day, Warren Leslie Forrest is arrested and detained.

October 11, 1974: Buys gas, SLC (twice). Rhonda Stapley

1977 aerial of the final route that Melissa Smith took on October 18, 1974. The yellow circle depicts where the abduction most likely took place. Aerial photo courtesy USGS aerial imagery collection. Photo insets courtesy Chris Mortensen & Rob Dielenberg © 2015/18.

(21) reported she survived being sexually assaulted by Ted in Big Cottonwood Canyon on this day.

October 12, 1974: Carol Platt Valenzuela's and Martha Marie Morrison's skeletons are found in shallow graves near large logs south of Olympia (along Dole Valley Road). The bodies were about 100 feet apart. No identifiable cause of death could be established but police believe Valenzuela was suffocated. No trauma was found on the bones. No clothes were found. The double graves are located near where Jamie Grissim's personal belongings were found. This raises the possibility that Valenzuela and Morrison were victims of Warren Leslie Forrest.

October 13, 1974: 3:24 a.m. Calls Liz from SLC.

October 14, 1974: Ted Buys gas in Murray, Utah.

October 15, 1974: Keppel first alerted regarding Carol Valenzuela's skeletal remains.

October 16, 1974: Buys gas, SLC.

October 18, 1974: Buys gas, SLC. 9:30 p.m. Abducts Melissa Smith (17) from Midvale, Utah. 11:17 p.m. Ted calls Liz from SLC.

The daughter of Midvale Chief of Police Louis Smith, she presumably had heard the stories of street crime and had safety first drummed into her from childhood. Yet this didn't turn her into a conservative or fearful individual. She appeared to have an irrepressible cheeky sense of life. Melissa had planned to leave for an all-night party at a girlfriend's home early in the evening, but when she phoned no one was at home. She was still at home when a friend called her in distress over a lover's spat. The friend worked at a local pizza parlor, the "Pepperoni." Melissa promised to walk over and talk to her. She left wearing blue jeans, a blouse with a blue-flowered patterns, and a navy blue shirt. She departed alone. She knew the route by heart: down the dead-end street which her house was on, along the railway tracks, over a guard rail and down an embankment

Melissa Smith as she appeared posthumously in a 1975 yearbook. Photo scan courtesy Chris Mortensen © 2015.

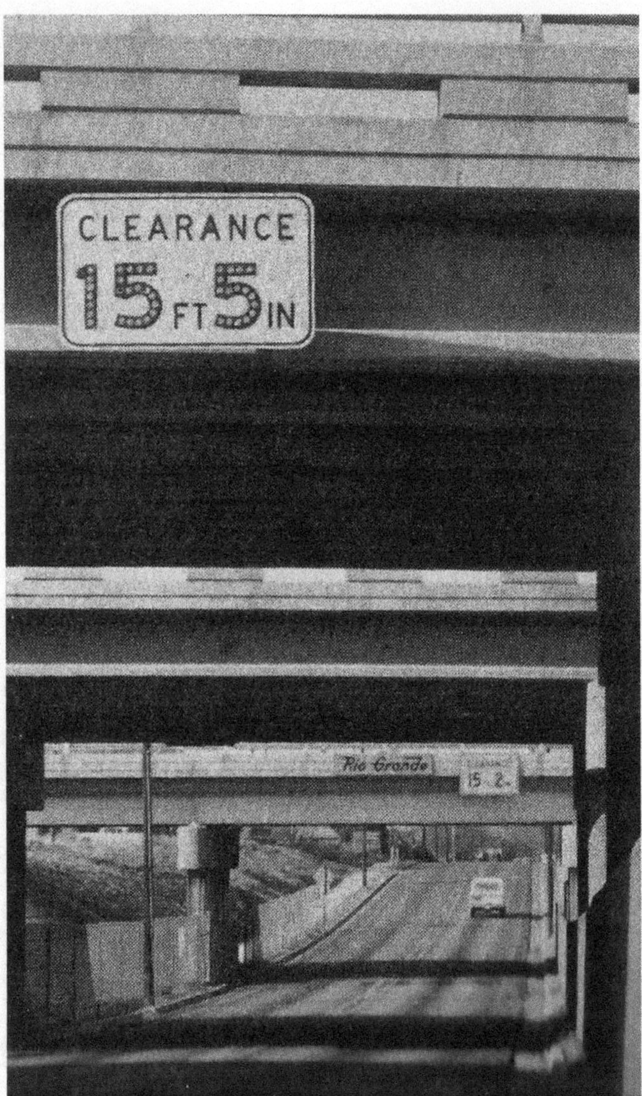

Wasatch overpass, Midvale, taken in 1970, where Ted abducted Melissa Smith in 1974. This view through a telephoto lens from the Oak Street side. The railway line is in the distance. Photo courtesy Midvale Museum, Utah.

Melissa (left) with sister Jolene (now deceased) aged around 14. Photo courtesy Eric Garret © 2015.

to E Wasatch Avenue, under the I-15 highway and railroad overpass, and across the junior-high playing-fields, where she passed through a single cone of light. From there, out onto Center Street, a total of about a mile (W&M 1980, 40).

Melissa stayed with her friend at the Pepperoni until about 10:00 p.m. then left to make her way back home following a similar route. This is where we learned she walked down Oak Street, which runs parallel to the school (interview with family friend Eric D. Garret courtesy Chris Mortensen, 2015). A cousin lived on that street, and Melissa apparently stopped by for about 5-10 minutes. We also learn from Keppel that Ted was seen in the area that night soliciting girls to help with his auto (Aspen Seminar, November 13-14, 1975). Finally, at 10:15 p.m. there is a report from the wife of a police dispatcher raking leaves in her yard near the school saying she heard a scream nearby (what was she doing raking leaves that time of night?). As for why Ted was in the area on this day, we could surmise two scenarios. Perhaps it was a coincidence. He happened to be driving past and saw Melissa leaving the Pepperoni. Alternatively, if we are to believe Keppel's report of Ted soliciting help with his car, perhaps he had been there before and had planned the abduction. In which case, we might speculate that he had previously bought pizza at the Pepperoni and on that occasion happened to see Melissa there and became fixated on her. In any case, once Melissa left the Pepperoni, Ted must have followed her down Oak to Wasatch and under the I-15 overpass. It would be there, under the overpass, dark and claustrophobic, that Ted would have had the best chance of attacking her.

October 19-20, 1974: Buys gas, SLC (twice). Ted goes deer hunting with Liz Kloepfer's father up along Blacksmith Fork Canyon Road, northeast of Ogden.

October 20-21, 1974: Ted returns to SLC from Ogden.

October 25, 1974: Buys gas, SLC.

October 26, 1974: Buys gas, SLC.

October 27, 1974: Ted buys gas Bountiful, Utah. He bought a total of 23 gallons (87 liters) of gas in a four-day period during late October 1974 ... "running the wheels off" his VW. A 1968 bug averages 25 miles to the gallon. A total of 575 miles.

Also on this day, Melissa Smith's body is found. There is conflicting information about where it was exactly discovered. Friends of the family were told it was Lamb's Canyon (communication with Eric Garret, August 11, 2015). Jerry Thompson, who was lead investigator on the case, also seems to remember that it was Lamb's Canyon (personal communication with the author, August 11, 2015). Recently, new information obtained from a Salt

Lake City Sheriff's department forensics officer named Sam Macchione mentioned Lamb's Canyon. Macchione stated that he personally carried the body out with Jerry Thompson (Chris Mortensen interview, March 30, 2018). However, Ben Forbes of SLC Police said she "was found [...] on a hillside up outside of a residential area that we call Summit Park" (Ben Forbes deposition, April 4, 1979). Also, according to the *Salt Lake Tribune* (November 1, 1974) she was found in Toll Canyon.

Melissa had a navy blue sock cinched around her neck. It was entangled with a strand of wooden beads she had worn the evening she left home. It was so tightly wound that her hyoid bone was fractured (Rule 1989, 112). She suffered depressed fractures on the left side and back of the head with massive subdural hemorrhages (initially it was thought to be a gunshot wound). Her back, buttocks and legs had scrape marks. Dirt and twigs were stuffed inside her vagina (M&A 1983, 84). There was evidence of anal and vaginal violation. Reports differ about the state of her appearance. One has her wearing undisturbed makeup and perfect nails (M&A 1983, 94). Another has her hair washed, nails painted and eye makeup reapplied (Sullivan 2009, 97). David Yocom said her body was drained of blood [*Boca Raton News*, April 10, 1978]. The coroner was certain that Melissa had been dead for 48 to 72 hours, implying she had been alive as long as a week after her disappearance. His conclusion would later be hotly disputed. The body was found on a shaded north slope, and even with temperatures between 15-20 degrees Celsius, normal decomposition might have been

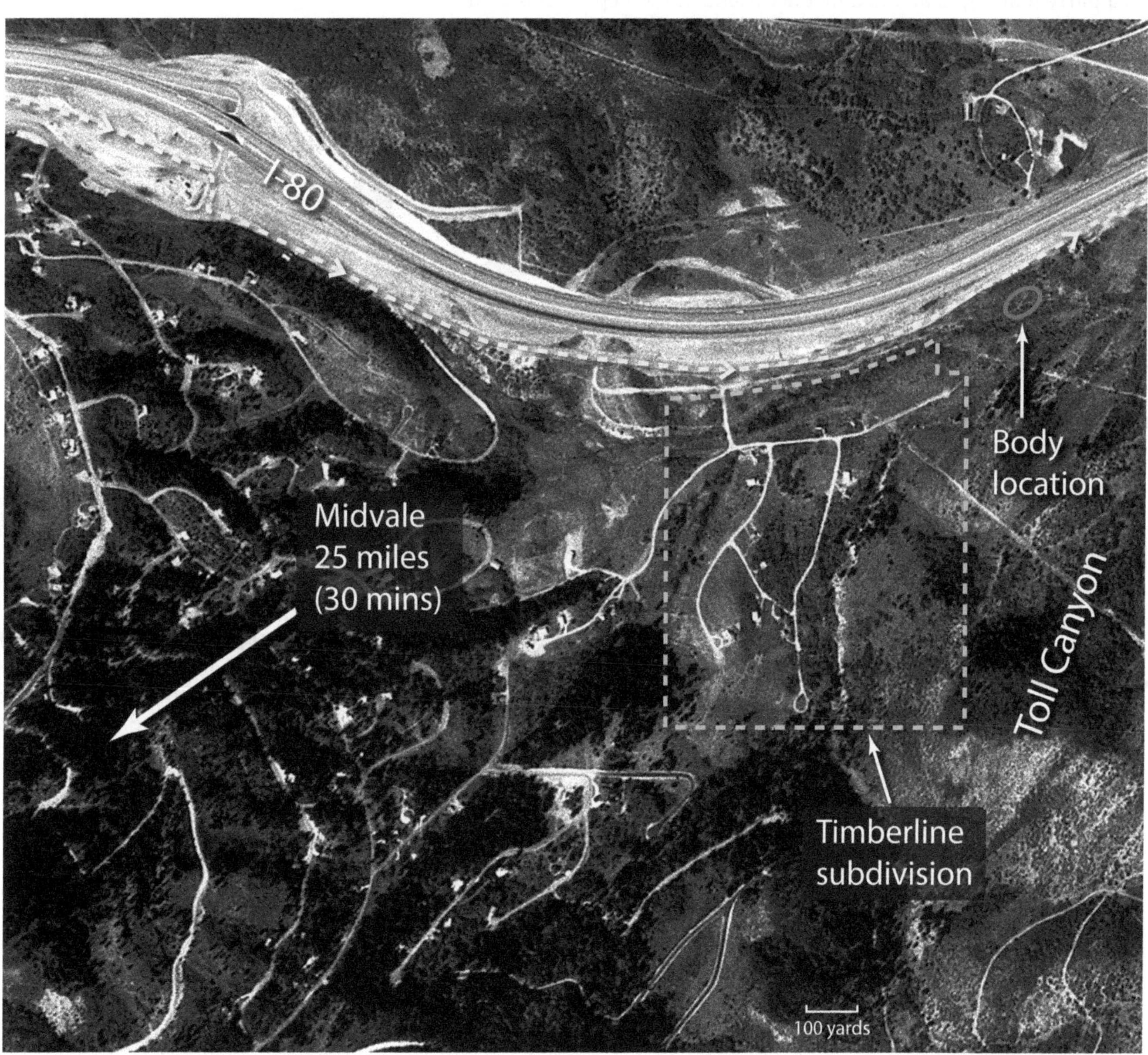

Map dated September 2, 1975, showing the newly created Timberline subdivision and the body location of Melissa Smith. According to the police report signed by Ben Forbes on October 30, 1974, she was found "50 yards northeast of eastern boundary of Timberline" Summit County. Ted drove along Kilby road, stopped, took her out and dragged her down into the "oak brush." Map courtesy USGS.

retarded (W&M 1980, 42). In fact, temperatures for the week she was missing hovered around 0 degrees Celsius during the night and at an altitude of 7000 feet, decomposition would have barely set in. In all probability, Ted discarded her body at Lamb's Canyon in the early hours after abducting her. He had a hunting date with Liz Kloepfer's father Russell Hirst that day, and so would have less time to spend with the body.

Some commentators have assumed that because Melissa was found wearing makeup and nail polish that Ted turned her into a human doll. However, in an interview with Jerry Thompson (courtesy Chris Mortensen, February 15, 2016), Thompson explained that Melissa's parent did not allow her to wear makeup, but her friends let her use theirs. Given that she was planning to go out to a party that night, and had met her friend at the Pepperoni, there is the possibility that she applied makeup there before visiting her cousin on Oak Street. We are not saying this is what she actually did; we simply cannot rule that possibility out. Ted may have applied makeup on her, but given the short amount of time he spent with the body, he may have used his time to do other things than apply makeup and nail polish.

October 28, 1974: Buys gas in Bountiful, SLC. Picks up a flyer for Viewmont High School production *The Redhead* at Bountiful Recreation Center. Also on this day, Liz calls King County Police, Seattle. Major Crimes Unit, Randy 'Hergy' Hergesheimer. Among other things, she repeated her story about finding crutches in Ted's apartment, something she told Seattle police earlier. She was amazed that Hergesheimer didn't associate the crutches with the reports surrounding the disappearance of Georgeann Hawkins. When Hergesheimer asks her name she gave it as "Liz." He made her promise to ring back after he checked with the Seattle police to see if any progress had been made on her previous report. She called back 2 hours later. They agreed to talk again at lunchtime. Liz rang from a pay phone this time. She now learned that police had already checked out Ted based on a tip-off from a university professor (Kestenbaum). Hergesheimer felt Liz's feelings were genuine and asked to meet her in person. They decided to meet in Herfy's (the hamburger joint) parking lot. The assumption is that this meeting occurred on the same day after Liz finished work. While they sat in Hergesheimer's car and talked, Liz related the story about Ted threatening to break her "fucking neck" if she ever told anyone about his thievery. She also told Hergy about their sex-life. Hergy takes away three photos of Ted.

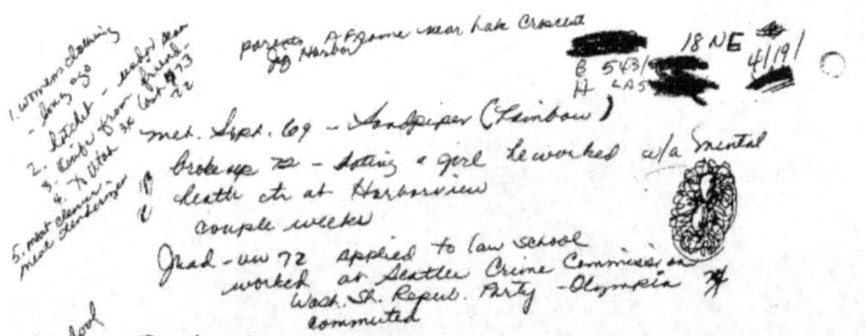

Notes Hergesheimer took while he listened to Liz's story. Image courtesy KCA.

October 30, 1974: Smithsonian Institute Curator of Physical Anthropology J. Lawrence Angel discovers Carol Valenzuela's teeth have a pinkish tinge. This phenomenon occurs when strangulation forces blood into the teeth pulp, leaving the tell-tale sign of discoloration (Adams 1981).

Laura Aime circa 1974. Photo courtesy KCA.

October 31, 1974: (Evening) Abducts Laura Ann Aime (17) from Lehi, Utah. 10:25 p.m. Calls Liz from SLC, then goes out hunting. At six feet tall and weighing 140 pounds (63.5 kg), a horsewoman who enjoyed hunting and the outdoors, Laura was an independent girl. Her mother, scared of the abductions on the news, cautioned her daughter to be safe. Laura replied, "Oh mom, I can take care of myself" (W&M 1980, 43). On Halloween night, Laura dressed like usual: a sleeveless sweater with horizontal stripes, blue jeans, brown tie-shoes, and some silver cross earrings. Her nails were done in black polish with sliver flakes. Friends picked up Laura that evening around 7:00 p.m. The Halloween party at Steven Bullock's trailer home in Orem turned out to be a drag, so Laura got up and left around 10:00 p.m. looking to buy some cigarettes. She hitchhiked north up route 89 to the Jack & Jill Lanes bowling alley in American Fork. Around 10:30 p.m., a friend picked her up in front of that location after Laura had turned down an unknown number of "cowboys" to her outstretched hitchhiking thumb (her intention was to hitchhike to Lehi). She got out at the Knotty Pine in American Fork and went in for a coke (in the literature, colloquially referred to as the "Naughty Pine"). But she got restless again and headed for Robinson Park in American Fork to check if there was some action there. She was last seen there by Thomas Jones around midnight. Her mother didn't call the police until 5 days after she was missing.

In early 1977, Mike Fisher heard a different version of Laura Aime's case from Dick Smith, a sheriff's deputy who worked the case at the time but whose report was ignored. According to Smith, he came across a girl who identified Ted as the guy who had been hanging out over at Brown's Café, at Lehi. Marin Beverige was a girlfriend of Laura and the witness. Smith reported Marin's testimony:

> … an older, good-looking, wavy-haired man, who said he was a university student and who drove a Volkswagen, had first appeared at the small town of Lehi one day in September 1974. Marin remembered that she and Laura were sitting together with some other teenagers on the grass of a high school. He joined them. When a boy teased Laura by putting some grass down her halter top, the "college guy" objected. "This guy came unglued and told him [the boy] Laura was his," Marin said. "He was really weird," Marin continued. She recalled the man kept reappearing in Lehi, always looking for Laura. One night at Brown's Café on the main street of the small town, Marin recalled, "He came in and was sitting there talking and I got up … when Laura said, 'I'm ready to go,' this guy said, 'You can't. I'm going to rape you.'" "Laura just laughed and pushed him away." Marin told her interviewers she had seen the man again and again, once driving his Volkswagen past Marin's house when Laura was there. One night he came to the house and called Laura outdoors where they held a private conversation. Afterward, Marin said, "Laura was really shook up. But she wouldn't say what happened." The night Laura vanished, Marin had a different account of what happened than that concluded by the Utah County Sheriff's Office. Laura, Marin and several other teenagers had gathered at Marin's home for a Halloween party. The boys brought an abundance of vodka and Laura had a lot to drink. "It was about midnight or so, and she was pretty well drunk," Marin said. "And she wanted me to walk downtown with her to get some cigarettes." Marin declined. But, she said, she watched as Laura began to walk in the darkness, toward Brown's, the all-night restaurant, one block away. That was the last they saw of Laura. "Around three or four o'clock some of us went to town to look for her," Marin said, "but we couldn't find her." When shown a photo line-up, Marin chose the picture of Ted. She passed a polygraph test. A woman employee of Brown's Café made a similar identification (Larsen 1980, 197-8).

A collateral to this report comes from the coroner's report:

> There will be testimony that Theodore Robert Bundy knew Laura Ann Aime and they had talked on several occasions. Witnesses will testify that Ted hung around Brown's café, which was frequented also by Laura. Ted drank coffee and flirted with the girls. Ted occasionally sat with Laura and her girl friends. On one occasion as Laura was about to leave, Ted blocked her in a booth and stated, "You can't go, I'm going to rape you". A witness to that will testify that Laura shoved him out of the booth and left. This occurred in late summer or early fall of 1974. On another occasion, in late September or early October, Laura introduced Ted to a group of her friends, including

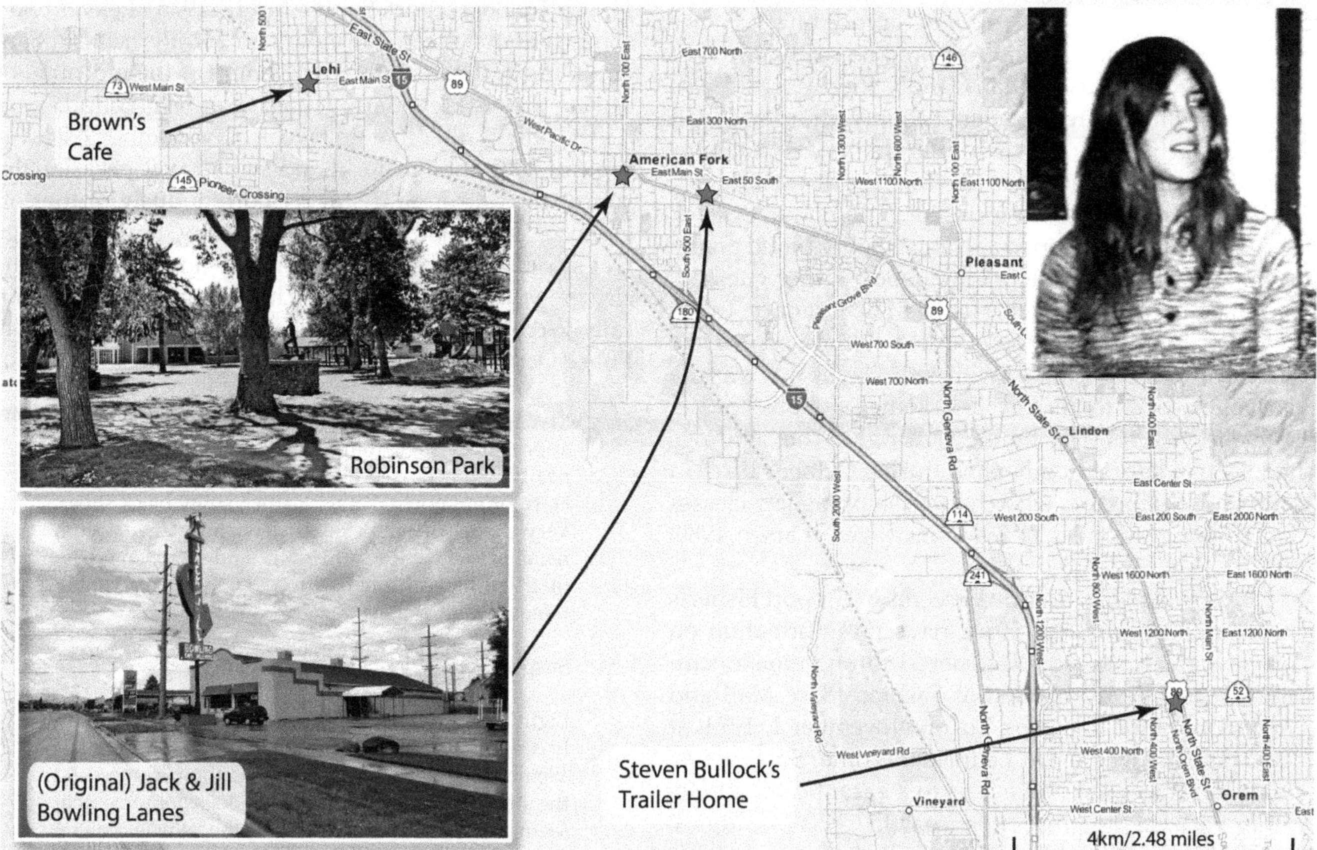

Laura went to Orem after dark, stayed until around 10:00 p.m., then hitched to American Fork, where she was last seen around midnight (undated inset photo of Laura as she might appear in Brown's café). Map courtesy OpenStreetMap contributors, 2015. Original street sign photoshopped into Jack & Jill Bowling Lanes. Photo insets courtesy Chris Mortensen © 2015.

Jerry Bowers. Jerry and Ted got into an argument after Jerry put grass in Laura's halter top. Ted told Jerry to leave Laura alone because Laura was his girl. Laura told Ted to "Get screwed." Ted was left speechless. On another occasion, Ted went to a house where Laura was visiting. Laura went outside with Ted and became quite upset. A witness heard Laura tell him "Get the fuck out of here, I don't want to see you no more." (Excerpt from the coroner's report by Frank G. E. Tucker, District Attorney; signed by Deputy District Attorney Milton K. Blakey, November 27, 1974)

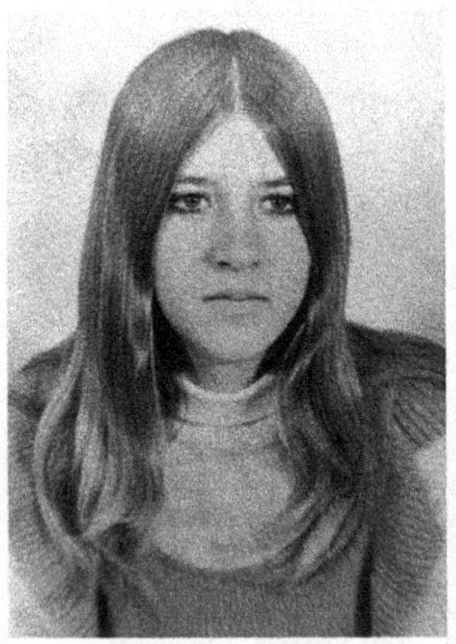

A yearbook portrait of Laura Aime circa 1974. Scan courtesy Chris Mortensen © 2016.

What was it that Ted said to Laura that shook her up? In an earlier version of this book we let our imagination run wild, but we can only speculate. Ted could have said any number of things, most of them, or probably all of them, lies. Mike Fisher said, "Y'know, there's always been something about that Aime case—that one in particular—that bothered Theodore." When several case files were given to Ted in his jail cell, under the discovery procedure, Fisher said, "the first one he went for—and he really tore into it—was the Aime case." Utah County Sheriff's Office later brought in a more aggressive county attorney, Noall Wootton, who had his own well-trained investigator Brent Bullock to dig deeper into the case. It was Bullock who brought Dick Smith to Fisher. And it was Bullock and Fisher who developed a strange theory, based on the new Aime witness evidence. "Maybe," Fisher guessed, "our man departed from his usual M.O. just once. In every other case, the victim became a victim because she had never had any contact with Ted. Maybe this was the one time where there had been some previous contact with the victim." The timing was right. The sightings had been in late September and during October 1974 – a time of stress for Ted, when he was skipping law classes and running up miles in his Volkswagen (Larsen 1980, 198).

Marin Beverige's testimony seems to support Fisher's assertion. The problem is we have no information on Ted's whereabouts from October 31 through to November 8, when he reappeared at Fashion Place Mall and Viewmont High. Ted rang Liz on November 1, 1974, at 12:44 p.m. but where was Laura at this time? Some investigators suspect Ted had access to a vacant cabin in Heber or Park City (correspondence with Chris Eskridge, 6 July, 2015). Another is he may have had a camper trailer up in the foothills of Fairview (Ira Beal telephone interview, 12 July, 2015). It is of interest that Liz's father often took Ted up to his trailer in Flaming Gorge, east of SLC. Interesting speculation. Most probably, however, Ted had already left her up at Timpanogos cave where it had started snowing and made the call when he returned to 565 First Avenue.

November 1, 1974: Buys gas in SLC. 12:44 p.m. Ted calls Liz from SLC.

November 4, 1974: Liz calls Hergesheimer again. No progress.

Carol DaRonch, 1974 yearbook portrait. Photo scan courtesy Chris Mortensen © 2015.

November 8, 1974: Buys gas in SLC. (During the day) Drives past Viewmont High School, Bountiful, and picks up flyer for the school play. 7:30 p.m. Attempted abduction of Carol DaRonch (18) at Fashion Place Mall, Utah. 10:15 p.m. Abducts Debra Jean Kent (17) from Viewmont High School. 11:52 p.m. Phones Liz midnight Seattle time from a pay phone. "It was about 11:00 p.m. here, so it would have been midnight in Utah" writes Liz. She later said that it was unusual for him to call from a pay phone (Ira Beal report, September 17, 1975). Leaves body somewhere between Fairview and Mt. Pleasant in Sanpete County, Utah, in the early hours of the morning, or during the next few days. It has never been found.*

The fall weather that first week of November 1974 was typical: cool enough to herald winter, yet occasionally sunny and warm. SLC still rested tenuously in the soft grasp of an Indian summer. By Friday, however, huge wet storm clouds glided in from the northwest, and the city grew dark early under the hovering sky and misting rain (W&M 1980, 46). The following is the actual Murray Police Department report (taken at 8:30 p.m.):

> MWA, 25 to 30 years, brown hair, medium length, approximately 6'0, thin to medium build, moustache neatly trimmed. Wearing green pants and sports jacket, color unknown. Patent leather, shiny black shoes. Very polite, opened doors for victim. Gave victim name of OFFICER ROSELAND, and seems to victim that first name started with a "D" however, cannot remember the first name.
>
> Suspect Vehicle.
>
> Light blue or white Volkswagen, older model in fairly beat up condition. Victim did not see license plate. Victim stated that the rear seat, the top is ripped and the stuffing is coming out. Victim does not remember seeing any sticker or emblems on the vehicle. Can remember nothing else about the vehicle.
>
> Weapon used.

*Except perhaps for a human patella that is claimed to be DNA tested but records of this have not been verified as yet.

Small handgun, type and caliber unknown. Handgun described as being a little larger than a starter pistol. It is not known by victim if the handgun was a revolver or automatic. Suspect had handgun in his jacket pocket and handgun was described as being all black, believed that suspect held handgun in the right hand. Victim was shown pictures of revolvers and automatics and different type weapons and was still unable to determine exact type model weapon used.

Another weapon used was described as a crowbar, approximately 1 1/2 foot long. This was held by the suspect in the left hand.

Evidence obtained.

One pair of handcuffs. These are Gerocal A. brand, made in Taiwan. Have no serial number or identifying marks on the handcuffs. Detective Joel Riet dusted the handcuffs for prints, obtained some. Also Detective Riet attempted to obtain prints from the door knob at the Laundromat, which will be explained later in the body of the report, with negative results and he will make contact with the complainant tomorrow to try and obtain fingerprints off the right side door of victim's vehicle. Door was wet from rain this evening. Victim's father was going to place the vehicle in his garage, keep it tomorrow until Detective Riet can make contact and obtain prints.

Missing items.

One brown leather purse, has a zipper top, medium sized purse, had a shoulder strap. Also being brown leather which is held by two gold rings. This was an older purse. The stitching along both sides has come unsewn. Value estimated at $20.00. Inside the purse was one woman's gold wallet. This is fold over brushed leather. Value $5.00. Wallet contained approximately $20.00. This will be one five, one ten and some ones and change. Identification on the purse will be Mountain Bell tag, has her name and social security number on it. Victim did not know her social security number but her house keys and car keys. Also two layway slips that would have victim's name and address on them. One is from the Nobby and one is from Rafters which is uptown. There is not other identification in the wallet. No checks or credit cards. Victims was advised to have locks on her vehicle and also her locks on her home changed.

Witnesses.

Victim was picked up on approximately 5800 South 300 East by a Mr. T. Walsh 144 5600 South [phone number]. Mr. Walsh and some of his family picked victim up and brought her into our office. At the time of this report have not had contact with Mr. Walsh, however, dispatcher did talk to him. Mr. Walsh stated they did not see anyone else in the area besides Victim. Detective Riet was given this information for follow up.

Details of investigation.

In talking to the victim she stated approximately 7:00 p.m. this date she went to Fashion Place Mall and parked her vehicle on the west side of Sears and walked into Sears. This being through southwest doors. She then proceeded into the mall through Sears, walked down towards Castletons and down towards Auerbachs. While in the mall she stopped and talked to some cousins for a few minutes. She then turned around and was proceeding back when she was approached by suspect near Waldenbooks. At this time she had been in the mall approximately 10 to 15 minutes. Suspect approached victim and asked her if she had a car in the parking lost on the west side of Sears. She told him yes. He then asked her for her license number. As this time she told him. He then told her that he was a police officer and a suspect had been caught breaking into her car with a pry wire and that he wanted her to accompany him back to her vehicle to see if anything was missing, also to see if she could identify the suspect. The victim walked back through the mall into Sears and out of the Sears doors into the parking lot with suspect. At this time she checked her vehicle by unlocking driver's side and looking in and could see that everything appeared to be O.K. There was no damage to her vehicle. Nothing missing. At this time suspect asked her to open up the passenger side door that he wanted to check inside. She told him no, it would not be necessary, she could see that everything was there, however, suspect did, she believes touch the door handle and try and open the vehicle. At this time suspect stated that he would like her to accompany him to the other side of the mall where he believed the car prowl suspect would be located, that she could identify him and sign a complaint. At this time she proceeded with suspect back through Sears and on into the east parking lot. Suspect looked around, stated that the burglary suspect must have been taken to the Murray Police sub-station. At this time he asked victim to accompany him to the Murray Police sub-station. They then walked through the parking lot, went back into the mall through the main doors on the east side of the parking lot, just north of Casteltons. Proceeded though the mall. Proceeded out into the mall parking lost on the north side to the entrance by Farrell's ice cream, walked across the mall parking lot and across 6100 South to a laundromat which is on the north side of 6100 South. The address of the laundromat is 139 East 6100 South. At this time suspect told victim that this was the Murray sub-station at the mall and he believed the burglary suspect would be located there and she could sign a complaint. He tried the door. This door is on the southeast corner of the laundromat. Appears to be a door to a maintenance room. Has the number 139 just above the door. The door was locked. The suspect did touch this door. Detective Riet later tried to obtain prints with negative results. At this time suspect told victim that they would have to go to the main Murray Police Department and she accompanied him to his vehicle which was parked on the north side of 6100 South facing west, approximately 100 feet east of the Lockhart Company [175 East 6100 South]. While enroute to the supposed Murray Police sub-station, victim asked suspect for some identification. She had asked him once before in the mall. He had just kind of laughed. While walking over she did look at a wallet badge which he produced. Badge is described simi-

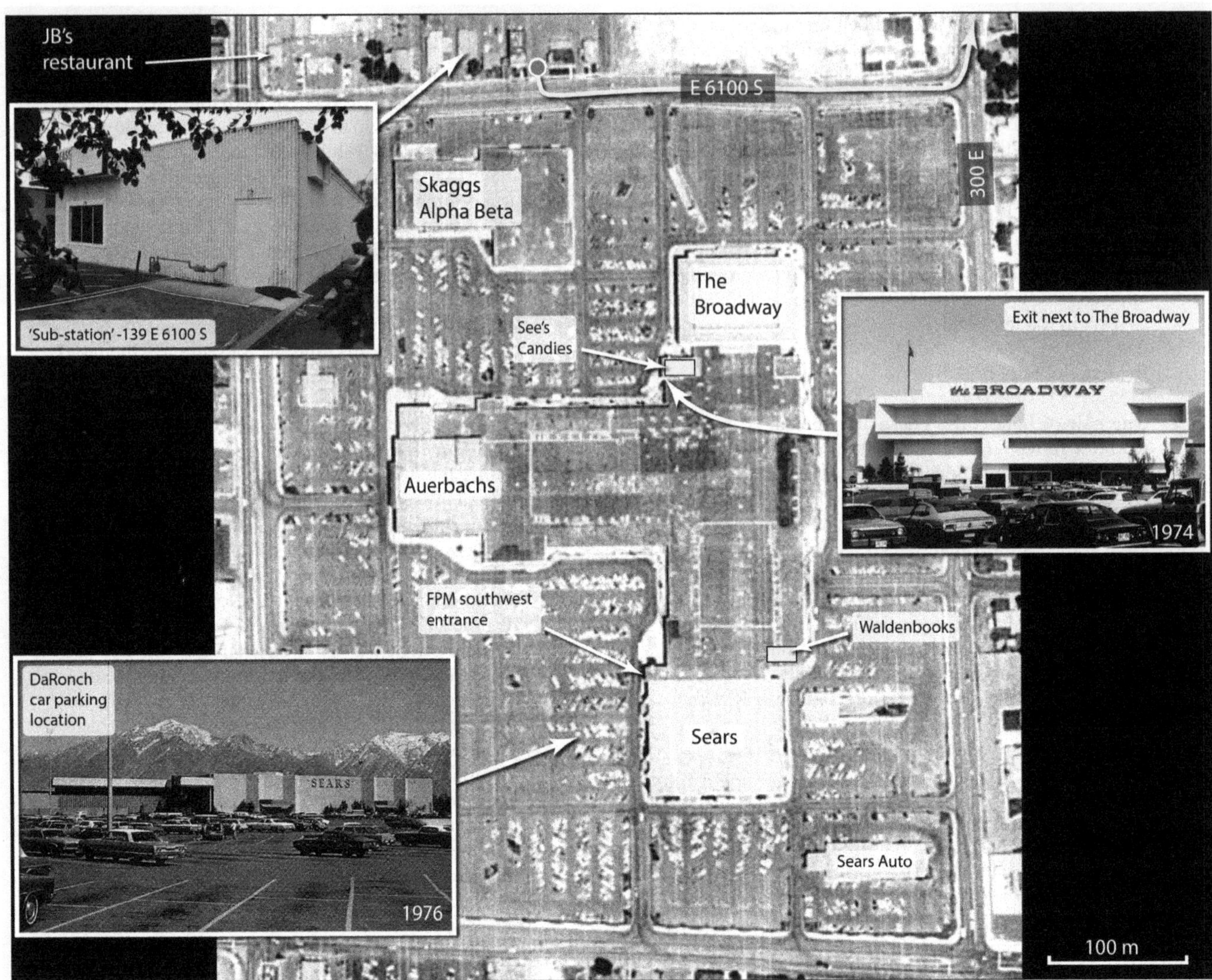

1977 aerial photo of FPM. The red circle is where Ted parked his VW bug. The yellow path marked on E 6100 S designates the route he took to McMillan school. Aerial photo courtesy USGS aerial imagery collection. Historical insets courtesy Murray City Library. Photo inset courtesy Chris Mortensen © 2015.

lar to Murray Police in shape. This was a miniature size badge approximately half the size of our wallet badge. It appeared to be of solid gold. The victim cannot remember engravings, or names or designs on the badge. She later picked out a similar type badge out of the George F. Cake Company book for Detective Riet. [George Cake was not a badge manufacturer, but a police and municipal supply dealer. The badges marked with the Cake hallmark were made by V. H. Blackinton.] After trying the door to the laundromat, both parties then walked to the suspect's vehicle. Suspect opened the door and let the victim in. Suspect then got into the driver's seat, put on his seat belt, told the victim to be sure and put on her seat belt that it made him nervous if people didn't when he was driving. At this time she said no she would not. He also made sure that she locked her door. He then made a turn and proceeded up 6100 South to 300 East where he made a left turn and then proceeded north on 300 East [Fashion Boulevard] to the area approximately 5800 South on 300 East in front of McMillan School. Suspect then pulled his vehicle over. This would be on the east side of the road. The assault that then took place occurred approximately 25 paces from the northwest corner of McMillan School. Occurred in the vehicle which was parked along the sidewalk in the gutter on 300 East [Fashion Boulevard]. Location of assault was determined later by finding victim's shoe laying in the gutter at this location. Victim stated that while in the vehicle she could smell the odor of alcohol beverage about the suspect. As suspect pulled up and parked the vehicle the victim tried to get out at which time suspect reached over and grabbed her, started a scuffle. Suspect got out a pair of handcuffs, grabbed her by the right wrist, put the handcuffs on her right wrist. At this time she started fighting. The suspect was trying to handcuff both hands, however, ended up putting both handcuffs on the right wrist. Victim kept fighting with suspect. At this time suspect reached into his coat pocket, pulled out a pistol which was described above, pointing the pistol at victim and told her if she did not stop struggling he would shoot her. At this time she struggled harder. Got the door open and managed to get outside. At this time suspect also got out of the vehicle and approached her. At this time he picked up a crowbar,

McMillan Elementary School, the infamous curb where the assault took place. The area east of this site at the time was mostly open fields. Photo courtesy Chris Mortensen © 2015.

had the crowbar in his left hand and was raising it as though to strike, at this time the victim grabbed a hold of crowbar and started pushing and shoving with suspect. Victim believed that she scratched suspect, probably on either the hands or arms, that she did notice some blood on her hands that must have come from suspect, that she was not injured herself. However, does not remember actually hurting the suspect. Victim struggled with suspect, finally breaking and running and running out in the middle of the road where she flagged down witnesses [Mr and Mrs Walsh] which were described above who brought her to our office. [Keppel later determined that it was the Walsh's approaching headlights shining on Ted as he fought with Carol that gave her the opportunity to break free.] Witnesses did not remember seeing anybody else in the area (Murray Police Department report, November 8, 1974, 8:30 p.m., by Officer Cummings, courtesy KCA).

John O'Connell it appears believed Ted was not DaRonch's assailant (email to author, November 18, 2015). Against this, we have proven it is physically possible to easily drive the 23 miles to Viewmont High in 30 minutes, the timeframe allotted, which means Ted cannot be ruled out. Regarding the police report, two points are worth commenting on. The first is the approach. It appears Ted relied heavily on role playing to the extent that he tried to maintain the surface validity of his role right to the very last possible moment of the encounter, in this case producing a gun consistent with what he imagined a police officer might do in a situation where a subject was non-compliant. "He would be engaging in the pattern just for the purpose of making the whole encounter seem legitimate" (M&A 1983, 124). It seems he was so wrapped up in this role, "as if seen through a

DaRonch: And then he stopped the car and kind of went up on the curb a litt bit and came back down and I told him "What are we doing" and ther I opened the car door and stuck my foot out and then he grabbed my right arm and he stuck the handcuffs on it and I started screaming and I pulled away and he pulled out a gun and he said he'd shoot m

Riet: Did you see the gun? What kind of a gun do you think it was?

DaRonch: It was a small one, it was all black.

CASE IS:			TYPED BY	DATE	SIGNATURE OF REPORTING OFFICER	NO.
ACTIVE	CLOSED	INACTIVE				
			sp	11-9-74	J. Riet	74-10181

DaRonch's testimony to detective Joel Riet the day after the event. Scan courtesy KCA.

motion picture screen" (M&A, ibid) that he constrained his options. Why didn't he club her as she got in his car? *Suspect opened the door and let the victim in.* One possibility is that he might have stalked her in advance and developed preconceived notions about how she might act. In which case he might not have hidden the crowbar in readiness. Alternatively, he may have prepped the crowbar, but there were witnesses. In which case, as he moved around to the driver's side, he would have needed to surreptitiously recover the crowbar and secret it into the car without DaRonch's knowledge. Once inside the car, he technically had her in his control. Why didn't he simply brandish a knife at this stage? A knife in the confined space of the vehicle would have been a very persuasive instrument – far more adaptable than a crowbar. Another option would have been the gun, although it too would have been inferior to a menacing knife at the victim's throat.

The second is what happened next ... *suspect pulled up and parked the vehicle the victim tried to get out at which time suspect reached over and grabbed her, started a scuffle.* Ted's car was originally parked on 6100 facing west. All he had to do was drive straight ahead, turn right into State Street, head north a couple of blocks and he would have made Murray PD. Instead, he did a u-turn and headed east then north up 300 E. According to DaRonch, "It occurred to me that he wasn't who he said he was and something really bad was going to happen" (*Court TV: Serial Killers - Ted*, November 10, 2000). At this point we can assume she had begun looking for a way to escape. Ted would have noticed this. Perhaps she hovered her right hand by the passenger door handle. Maybe it was this event that triggered him to pull up abruptly and attempt to prevent her from making a desperate lunge out of the vehicle. 18-year-old Laurie Lee Canaday died from head injuries after she fell or was pushed from a speeding car in Portland Oregon in July 1973. Since there is no further information on this victim, we cannot attribute it to anyone in any way, however, it could be given a sinister interpretation. Did Ted sense that DaRonch was desperate enough to leap from a moving car, or worse, from his car as soon as he was forced to stop at an intersection? The problem is, this is where any attempt to raise an explanation goes pear-shaped, not least because DaRonch alters her story along the way. In the original police report and her subsequent interview with Detective Joel Riet the following day, she said Ted clapped handcuffs on her *right* wrist (supplementary report 74-10181, KCA). Then in the 1975 presentence investigation report she says *left* wrist. Finally, in her 2000 documentary interview, she says *left* wrist again. The presentence report incidentally reveals things that do not appear in the original police report:

> She stated that she declined to put on her seat belt but recalled that he did make sure that he had her door locked. She stated that they then drove out of the parking lot and drove to the McMillan School which was located on 1500 East and approximately 5800 South. She stated that he suddenly pulled up over the curb beside the street and then the two tires on the right side came down off the curb. She stated that after he pulled up and parked the car she asked him what he was doing. She stated that he did not reply but lunged at her. She stated that she grabbed for the car door and was able to get it open as he grabbed her left wrist and put a handcuff on it. She said that at that time they fought and she was quite hysterical and was screaming and yelling, "What are you doing? Let me go!" She stated that at that point the assailant reached into his coat pocket and pulled out his pistol. She stated that she did not know what kind of pistol it was but recalled it was black. She indicated that she saw the pistol and struggled harder. She indicated that she managed to get outside of the car and her assailant followed her across the seat and out the car. She asserted at this time that she believed that he tried to hit her with a crowbar. She stated that she had felt her father's crowbar on many occasions and recalls that this is what it was. She admits that the lighting at the time of night (which would have been about 7:30 p.m.), was quite poor. She does recall grabbing his hand just as he was about to lower it. She feels that he was trying to strike her and recalls fighting very violently with him and may have scratched him on the face and hands. She indicated that she was able to tear loose and she ran down the street where a car pulled up. She opened the car door and jumped in (PIR 1975).

Then we have this version by Larsen:

> With his right hand he grabbed Carol's arm and, in an instant, his left hand snapped a handcuff on her wrist. She recoiled, screaming, "What are you *doing?*
>
> "Shut up or I'll blow your head off," he snarled reaching for her other wrist. Terror jolted Carol into a frenzy. Screaming, she struggled away from him. The other handcuff clicked onto the same left wrist, as Carol's right hand clawed for the door handle and found it. Then the door was opening, and she was falling, screaming, outwards. He was lunging towards her, across the passenger's seat. In the darkness Carol could see a metal bar in his hand – a metal bar, raised to strike. She struggled against the blow, reaching up, gripping the steel. In a blur of terror, Carol wrestled free and went screaming, stumbling across the rear of the Volkswagen and out into the wet, dark street, into the headlights of an approaching car (1980, 44).

And finally, we have this interesting snippet from Belva Kent: "... he put one of the handcuffs around her wrist, and tried to put the other on the bar that's on the glovebox on the Volkswagen ...." (mormonchannel.org, accessed 2015; a police theory? Talked to DaRonch?).

Indeed, there is a glovebox handle in Ted's car. This last clue is important because it reveals that this is what Ted may have used during his other abductions. It seems like an ideal place to cuff a wrist. If we continue with the right wrist scenario, then one way of explaining it is that he manages to snap the first cuff on that wrist (the

The interior of Ted's Volkswagen. Indeed, there is a handle above the glovebox on the passenger side of the vehicle. Photo source: Crime Museum, Washington DC.

"lunge") which then caused DaRonch to react in panic. Ted would have tried to pull the right wrist towards the glovebox handle, but DaRonch would have resisted and continued with her goal to exit the car while fending him off with her left hand. At this point, something weird happens. We have to assume that Ted would be using his dominant left hand to perform the cuffing maneuver. What is he doing with his right hand? Most probably he is fending off DaRonch's left hand. As this skirmish takes place, he is pulling on DaRonch's cuffed right hand with his left hand, and as he tries to snap it on the glovebox handle, DaRonch might be using her right hand to stop him, and in that process, Ted snaps the other cuff on her right hand. How this actually happens is a mystery and probably needs to be simulated to figure it out in real life. As soon as this botch-up happens, Ted realizes that he needs to immediately switch to plan B. So he pulls out his gun (maybe it was a starter pistol?). Ted still playing his idea of a cop (albeit a bad one). In performing this action Ted may have given up physical control over DaRonch's hands thereby allowing her to exit the car. He now has no choice but to shift to plan C. Wherein he produces the crowbar (note that we do not know whether it was there all the time, or whether he put it there as he got in the car after being unable to use it earlier). The rest, as they say, is history. Keppel's hypothesis seems to be correct in that it was the approaching headlights that finally saved her. Had they been in a forest somewhere, Ted would have eventually over-powered DaRonch, despite his apparent ineptitude.

The left wrist scenario would have played out in similar fashion except in this case as DaRonch reached for the door handle, Ted grabbed her left wrist and cuffed it. He now has to bring it towards the glovebox handle. DaRonch would have pulled away, and as she did so, Ted snapped the other cuff on the same wrist. Once again, how this happens is a mystery.

However it unfolded, it is clear that Ted never established complete control over DaRonch despite having her in his car. Even more incredible is that DaRonch jumped out of the car after Ted supposedly produced a gun. And to top it off, she survived a crowbar attack. One would think that it would be easy to disable someone with a crowbar, even if they are frontally positioned and aware of your intention. A steel bar crashing into a limb would very quickly render a person compliant. Ted, however, appears to have tried to hit her on the head (in an obvious attempt to knock her out); however, DaRonch had the option of protecting her head with her arms, or better, grabbing the crowbar before it struck. She achieved the latter, and this bought enough time to silhouette the struggle in the headlights of an approaching car, which probably ultimately saved her. Later, when police investigated the scene of the attack, one of DaRonch's shoes was discovered.

The scene now shifts to Viewmont High School in Bountiful, 23 miles to the north. We note here that DaRonch's timeline for her assault must have been slightly dilated. Ted got to Viewmont High by 7:55 p.m. so he must have left FPM area at the latest around 7:30 p.m. to make it comfortably.

The next part of the narrative is best illustrated with a mini-timeline:

Raelynn Shepherd. Source: Viewmont High yearbook, 1974-5. Photos courtesy Chris Mortensen © 2015.

7:55 p.m. Raelynn Shepherd approached by Ted as she was going up the east hall by the auditorium.
8:00 p.m. Kents arrive after dropping their two boys off at a roller skating rink.
8:10 p.m. Shepherd passed him by the east hall, said "Hi" to him, but he said nothing back.
8:45 p.m. Shepherd met him in the east hall.
9:00 – 9:15 p.m. Shepherd saw Ted leave by the west door on front of the school near the auto shop area.
9:50 p.m. Ted approached Kathryn Ricks in the west car park.
10:10 p.m. Dean Kent gives Debbi the keys to the car.
10:20 p.m. Tamra "Tami" Tingey sees Ted acting like an usher at the rear of the auditorium.
10:20 –11:15 p.m. Five witnesses report screams from the west car parking lot.
10:40 p.m. Shepherd sees Ted leaning over the rail at the back of the auditorium. He was breathing heavily, his hair was messed up and he appeared to be very upset. He sat down across the aisle from her and her husband. At this time there were curtain calls in the play. He got up just prior to the end of the curtain calls and left going out the front door.
11:52 p.m. Ted calls Liz from a pay phone at an undisclosed location.
11:55 p.m. The Kents first report Debbi missing.

Piecing together the evidence suggests Ted parked

somewhere in the west car parking lot near the auto shop area. He then quickly entered the lobby and moved to the east side hall adjacent to the auditorium where he first encountered the school's drama teacher, 24 year-old Raelynn Shepherd. Here he employed his familiar car ruse, but Shepherd was too busy preparing for the play and brushed him off. Ted appears to have remained around the east side hall area for about an hour, since Shepherd encountered him two more times there before seeing him exit the west door "on front of the school near the auto shop area" around 9:00 – 9:15 p.m. ('Offer of Proof of Similar Transactions': Report by Frank G. E. Tucker, District Attorney, signed by Deputy District Attorney Milton K. Blakey, Pitkin County, September - November 1977).

We then get a report from Kathryn Ricks. She encountered an individual in the west car park around 9:50 p.m. who asked her if she knew a boy (whose name she cannot remember). She asked him if he (the boy) went to school there. He stated, he didn't know, "I don't keep that good of track of him." He then told her that he had car trouble and he needed her to help him. Whereupon she stated that she didn't know him [presumably this refers to Ricks not being able to trust this individual]. He then asked her if she would come out and hold an item on his car while he attempted to start his car. She told him that she would not and reentered the auditorium ('Offer of Proof of Similar Transactions', September - November 1977). A woman who

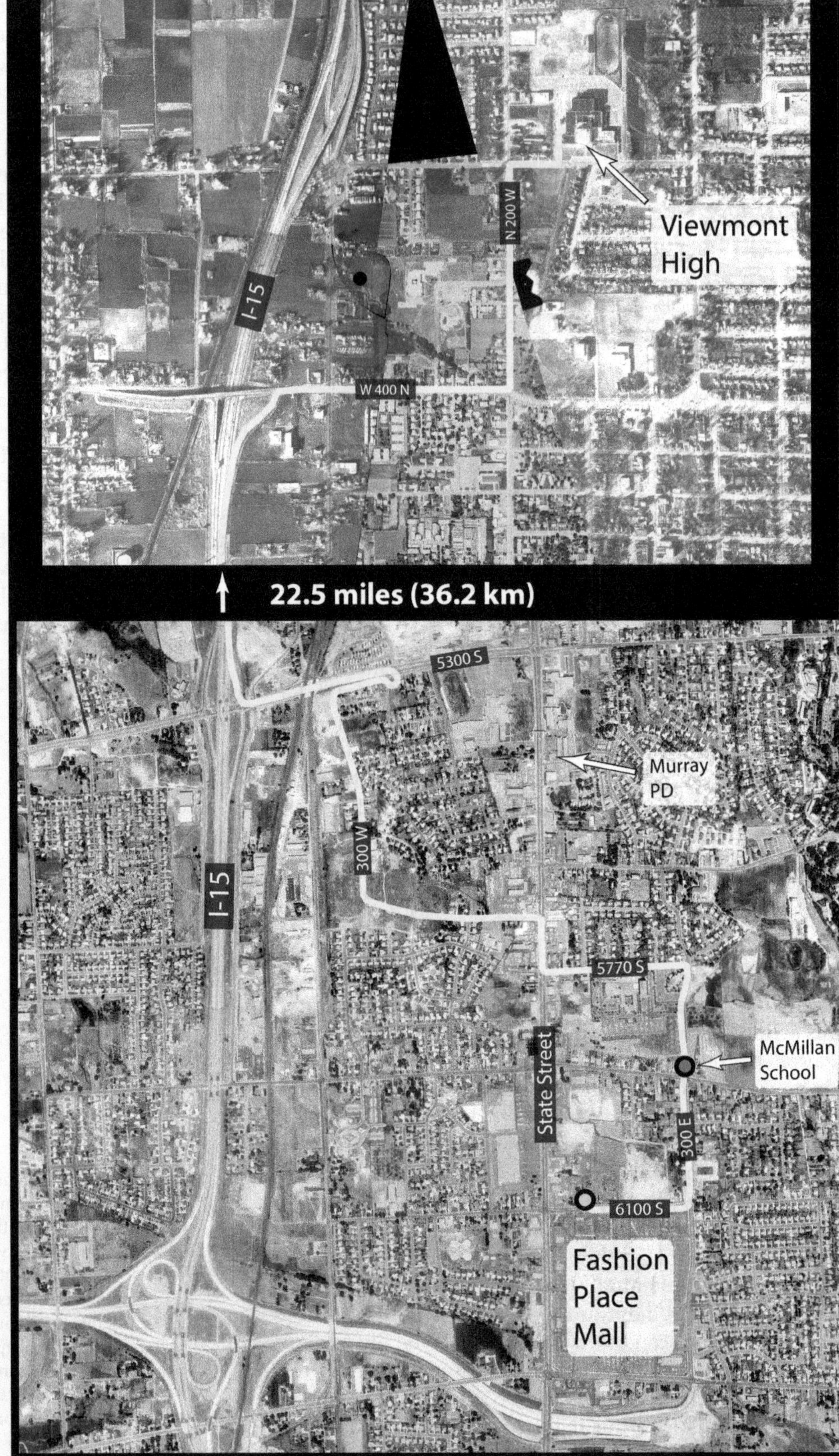

The most likely route Ted took from McMillan Elementary School to Viewmont High. Lower panel 1977. Upper panel 1970 (B&W), 1983 (color). Blue circle represents where Ted parked his VW bug at 175 E 6100 S. Red circle represents where Ted allegedly assaulted DaRonch. Aerial photos courtesy USGS aerial imagery collection.

lived near Ted's 565 First Avenue apartment in SLC said that "Ted always had a couple of pairs of glasses which he used to wear once in a while" (Larsen 1980, 204). She explained that "he had one pair, black rimmed, with just plain glass lenses, which he called his lawyer glasses. Then there was this other pair. They had kind of shaded, tinted lenses. Ted said he wore those because they made him look cool" (ibid).

Kathryn Ricks. Source: Viewmont High yearbook, 1974-5. Photo courtesy Chris Mortensen © 2015.

There is a gap of around 35–50 minutes between the time Ted leaves the lobby and approaches Ricks. We have no idea what he did during that time, but he may have sat in his car and watched and waited for a potential victim. There is no explanation for what Ricks was doing in the west car park at 9:50 p.m. It seems Ted almost succeeded again. But Ricks quickly saw through his ruse. What happens next is not entirely clear. Intermission starts around 10:10 p.m. Dean Kent gives Debbi the keys to the car. The plan was for Debbi to pick the two younger boys up from the roller skating rink. Debbi spends some of that time on the phone. Presumably, this takes 5-10 minutes. Around 10:20 p.m. Tami Tingey reports seeing Ted acting like an "usher" at the back of the auditorium. We do not know where Debbi made the phone call from, but presumably it was from somewhere inside the lobby. Ted may have had a vantage point from the back of the auditorium to spot Dean Kent giving Debbi the car keys. Acting as an usher would allow him to move between the lobby and the auditorium and scan the crowd without raising overt suspicion. Perhaps this is how he was able to monitor Debbi's movement to the phone. As soon as she hung up and went outside, he must have gone out and followed her. Debbi never made it to her parent's car. A handcuff key was found

Tami Tingey. Source: Viewmont High yearbook, 1974-5. Photo courtesy Chris Mortensen © 2015.

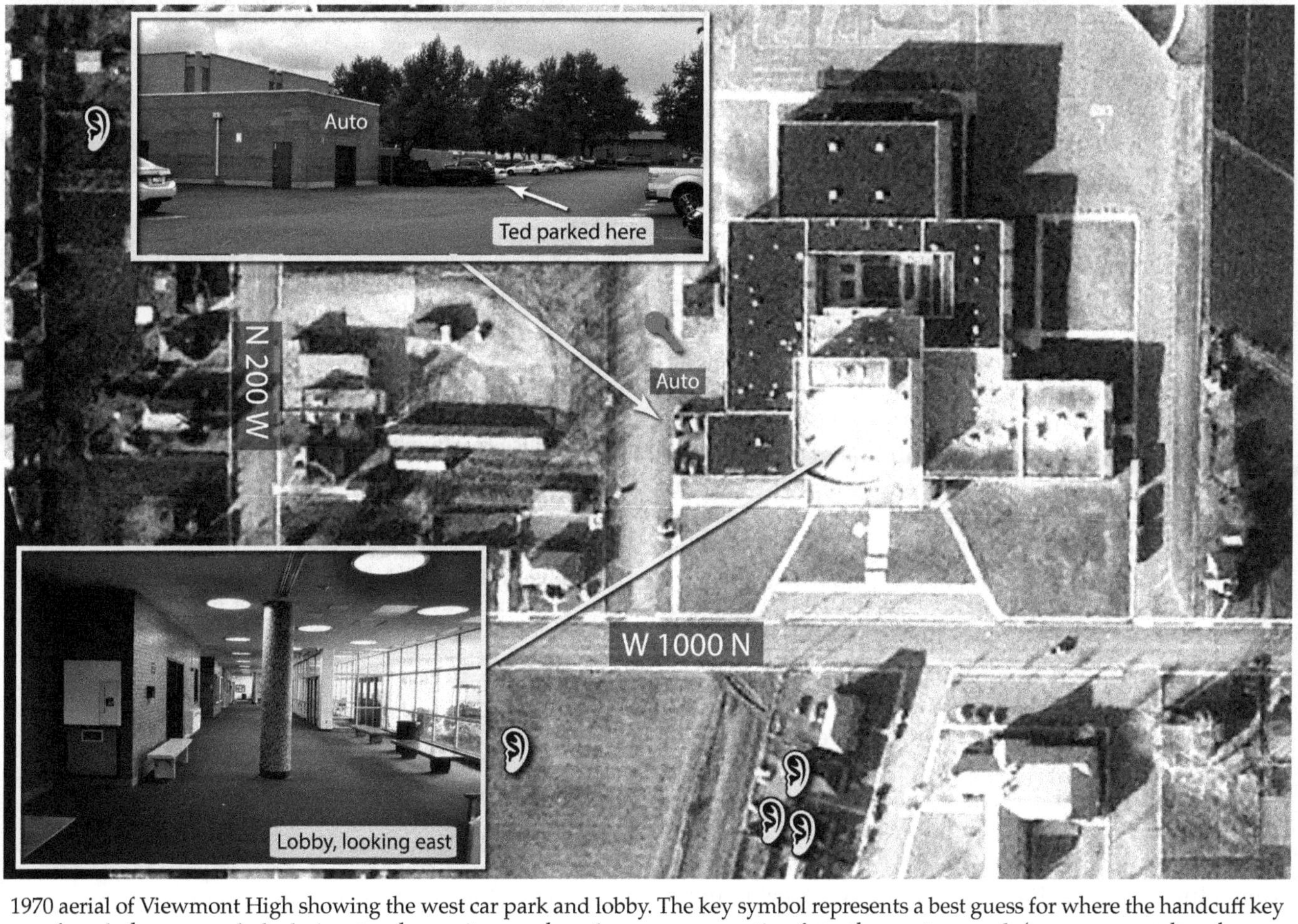

1970 aerial of Viewmont High showing the west car park and lobby. The key symbol represents a best guess for where the handcuff key was found; the ear symbols designate where witnesses heard screams emanating from the west car park (two ears are where houses have not been built yet). Aerial photo courtesy USGS aerial imagery collection. Photo insets courtesy Chris Mortensen © 2015.

Interior shot of Viewmont High auditorium. Photo courtesy Chris Mortensen © 2015.

the next day "outside the sidewalk in front of the east door of the school." The assumption is that Ted must have attacked Debbi there. What doesn't make sense is that Ted lost his cuffs to DaRonch. Are we to assume he had a second pair in reserve? Even so, why would someone need a pair of handcuff keys to cuff someone as opposed to releasing them? It doesn't make sense. In any case, what happens next is even more difficult to interpret. According to Shepherd, she sees Ted inside the auditorium again around 10:40 p.m., however this time his appearance and manner had changed; he looked like he had been in a fight with someone. He stays till the start of the last curtain call at the end of the play then leaves via the front of the lobby.

Examination of the mini-timeline now adds complexity to how we should interpret Ted's behavior. Screams were heard emanating from the west car park between 10:20 p.m. and 11:15 p.m. The most parsimonious explanation is that Ted attacked Debbi sometime after 10:20 p.m., left her bundled unconscious in his car, then returned to the auditorium just before the curtain calls. At first blush it seems like a bizarre strategy. However, if he had driven off with Debbi contemporaneous to her exit from the lobby, given the number of potential witnesses who saw him, people would have quickly drawn a connection between him and Debbi's disappearance. That explains Ted's return to the auditorium post-attack. It doesn't explain the temporally varied auditory witness reports. Of the five reports, only one starts as early as 10:20 p.m. The others range much later. We can only conclude that all time estimates, including the ones given by those in the school, need to be interpreted with some leeway.

The Kents waited in the lobby for Debbi's return until the doors were closed. When they found their car hadn't been used, they went to a nearby friend's house and called their son to get a spare set of keys. They immediately alerted the police, but were told a missing person's report couldn't be filed for 48 hours. Fortunately, a local policeman who knew the family urged his co-workers to promptly start a search the next morning. Over the ensuing days they realized that Debbi wasn't coming back. The psychological toll this had on the family is described by Belva Kent:

Belva Kent in a 1975 Television interview. Photo public domain.

> "Everyone says you're not given more than you can handle, but I've been questioning that a bit lately," she said, wondering when the bitter hand dealt her by Ted will finally play itself out. After Debra disappeared, her brother Bill, who idolized her, blamed himself. His bitterness toward Ted was matched only by his inability to stifle the pain. Five years ago, after his marriage had broken up, he died at 26, in an alcohol-related auto accident. Within months of Bill's death, Dean Kent started drinking, walked out on a 29 year marriage, quit his job as an oil company executive and fathered a child. He lives alone now, trying to come to grips with his shattered life. "I certainly feel he (Ted) was the cancer that destroyed our family," he said. Belva Kent had raised five children and never worked outside the home. Her self-esteem departed with her husband. "But then there comes a point where you see bitterness doesn't get you anywhere," she said (*Boca Raton News*, December 24, 1989).

Only two personal items belonging to Debbi were ever found at the scene. Detective Ira Beal recalls Debbi's purse and keys were discovered in close proximity to her car. Searchers were left frustrated.

The drive from Viewmont High to Ted's apartment would have taken around 15 minutes. If he left Viewmont around 10:50 p.m. and called Liz from a pay phone at 11:52 p.m. where was he during that time? He wasn't at home, yet according to his 11th hour confession to Dennis Couch:

> Couch: If it didn't take place in the schoolyard, did it take place in your car, or …?
> Bundy: No … the place where I lived. [565 First Avenue]
> Couch: You took her home?
> Bundy: Right. […] yeah, it was at the residence.
> Couch: So what, did you take her to your residence and then down here all in the same night? [indicates map location where he buried her]
> Bundy: No.
> Couch: Or keep her there for a period of time.
> Bundy: No, yes. I did keep her there for a period of time, couple, well, day, 24 hours.
> Couch: Is that right? Was she alive during that time period?
> Bundy: Let's see, during half of it.

As for where he discarded the body:

> [Using the map Ted steered Couch to Highway 89

near Thistle and Manti.]

> Bundy: I was driving in the dark, late at night not very conscious of much of anything else. I can kind of remember, I'm trying to remember, remember little turns the road made." [Passes the town of Fairview and head into the mountains.]
> Bundy: Several miles, oh well this should help. There seems to be just on the outskirts of this town ... an iron barrier. It's a gate that swings across the roadway, looks like they closed off that road for some reason.
> Couch: How deep was the grave?
> Bundy: Approximately 3 feet ... 2 to 3 feet maybe.
> Couch: Did her clothes remain with her?
> Bundy: No.

A large-scale search was mounted for Debbi's remains, but she was never found, except for that possible knee cap. The area that was considered to be the most likely candidate location was close to where Ted pointed on the map during his confession. The Kents reported they were satisfied that she ended up in a good burial place. [For further discussion on this case see NOTES section at the end of this chapter.]

MISSING

Missing since Friday, Nov. 8, 1974

DESCRIPTION

Height: 5 ft. 1 in.

Weight: 110 lbs.

Brown, long hair; brown eyes.

Oval face.

When last seen she was wearing white slacks, medium blue sweater, dark blue waist length coat, with navy blue trim.

DEBRA KENT, 17 years

Debra left the Viewmont High School auditorium in Bountiful at 10:10 p.m. on November 8th to get the family car and drive to a local roller skating rink to pick up her brother. She never arrived at the family vehicle and has not been seen or heard from since. Foul play is suspected.

ANYONE HAVING ANY INFORMATION ABOUT THIS GIRL OR HER WHEREABOUTS, PLEASE CONTACT THE BOUNTIFUL POLICE DEPARTMENT, 745 South Main St., Bountiful, Utah. Phone 295-9435.

November 9, 1974: During his Pensacola interviews in February 1978 Ted said he went to Welch Fun Cars in Midvale driving his pickup truck to look for parts for his VW.

November 14, 1974: 9:00 p.m. A report by Marian Stauffer Fowden has Ted eating by himself at JB's restaurant on this date (6099 S State Street, Murray, UT, adjacent to Fashion Place Mall). Fowden stated that she recognized him from a wanted poster. "One evening, my family came in while I was working [as a waitress at JB's]. They were sitting at a large round corner table and there was a man sitting alone at a small table across from them just having coffee. As I was chatting with my family, my sister whispered to me. "Look at that guy. He's creepy looking, staring at women. And he looks like the guy on the poster." I looked at him and realized he did look like the poster. I went over and talked to my friend who was his waitress. She said she'd thought the same thing about him. My family all left, but he stayed for quite awhile after. Not really drinking much coffee, but staring at women there. Finally, we were all so creeped out by him, we went to our manager and told him we wanted to call the police. He asked why and we said "Look. It's the man from the poster!" He told us we were being silly. He didn't think it was the same guy and that if any of us called the police and caused a scene with one of his customers, we would be fired. To this day, I am ashamed that we didn't call for fear of losing a $1.25/hr waitress job. When Ted Bundy was finally arrested and I saw the photos, I was absolutely convinced it was the same man" (Fowden, 28 September, 2016). JB's was frequented by Murray police, so it is not out of the question that he went there to gather local information about his recent failed abduction attempt, or even stalk a new victim.

November 16, 1974: Buys gas in SLC (twice).

November 17, 1974: Buys gas Heber City, southeast of SLC.

November 18, 1974: Buys gas in SLC (twice).

November 19, 1974: 3:36 p.m. Calls Liz in Seattle from SLC.

November 20, 1974: Ted calls Rule, but she is in hospital. Ted then calls Ann's mother, but refuses to identify himself. Kathy McChesney pulled Ted's telephone records in early November 1975 and presented this evidence to Rule. 11:03 p.m. Ted calls Diane Edwards in San Francisco but she is not home. The coroner placed Laura Aime's death on this day.

November 21, 1974: Buys gas in SLC. 11:03 p.m. Calls Liz in Seattle from SLC.

November 22, 1974: Buys gas in SLC. 2:02 p.m. Calls Liz in Seattle from SLC. News article claiming a 29-year old woman was saved by a "slap in the face." The Murray woman "was attempting to put groceries in her car at 5900 S & State Street, when she was approached by a man whose car was parked directly behind hers. After a brief conversation, the man grabbed the woman's wrist. She hit him in the mouth and he fled in his car" (*The Deseret News*, November 23, 1974).

Timpanogos Visitor parking area, 1972. Photo public domain.

November 25, 1974: 12:08 a.m. Calls Liz in Seattle from SLC.
November 26, 1974: 12:00 midnight, Calls Liz in Seattle from SLC.
November 27, 1974: (Around 9:00 a.m.) Laura Aime's body discovered in American Fork Canyon, 500 meters northeast of Timpanogos Cave Visitor's Center, 12 meters from the road below a hill on a creek bank, face down with a stocking knotted around neck. From Larsen (1980, 48):

> … two Brigham Young University students, were hiking along a trail beside a stream tumbling out of the mountains, looking for rocks and fossils which could be helpful in geology class. But mostly they were enjoying each other's company. It was about nine o'clock in the morning.
>
> From where they paused, at the edge of the stream bed, it was about forty feet to the opposite bank. [The female student] gasped, "Oh, God! There's a dead girl over there!"
>
> [The male student] described it: "I looked and I thought, you know, it was a deer or something and … it was a girl … It looked like she had been … she was dead. It was really grotesque. There was blood around her neck and breasts* and she was naked lying on that hill and it was a freak-out and I lost it. I thought maybe the guy was still somewhere around and I just panicked, worrying about my girlfriend … and we ran down the trail … Came down and ran right through the creek and got in the car and just drove like a maniac, I guess as fast as I could, down to the ranger station and I reported it.

The coroner determined that Laura had lain there about a week. Her eyes were intact and there was no evidence of predation. A significant finding in the autopsy report was that the palmer aspect of the fingers was dry and wrinkled and had a dark red-purple appearance, evidence of mummification ('Offer of Proof of Similar Transactions', September - November 1977). Set in the western Wasatch Mountains, Timpanogos Cave area has an elevation of 5739 feet/~1750 meters. For the period October 31-November 27, overnight temperatures continuously trended slightly lower, while daytime highs remained relatively stable, with one slight warming event around November 20-22 followed by a return to average. (Max average: 7.5C/45.5F; Min average -0.9C/30.4F; see NOTES). If she was lying on the north-facing bank of the watercourse, then she would have had little or no sun exposure for the month (even with most of the foliage gone off the trees). Also, according to Utah prosecutor David Yocom on the similarities between the Aime and Smith case, he said:

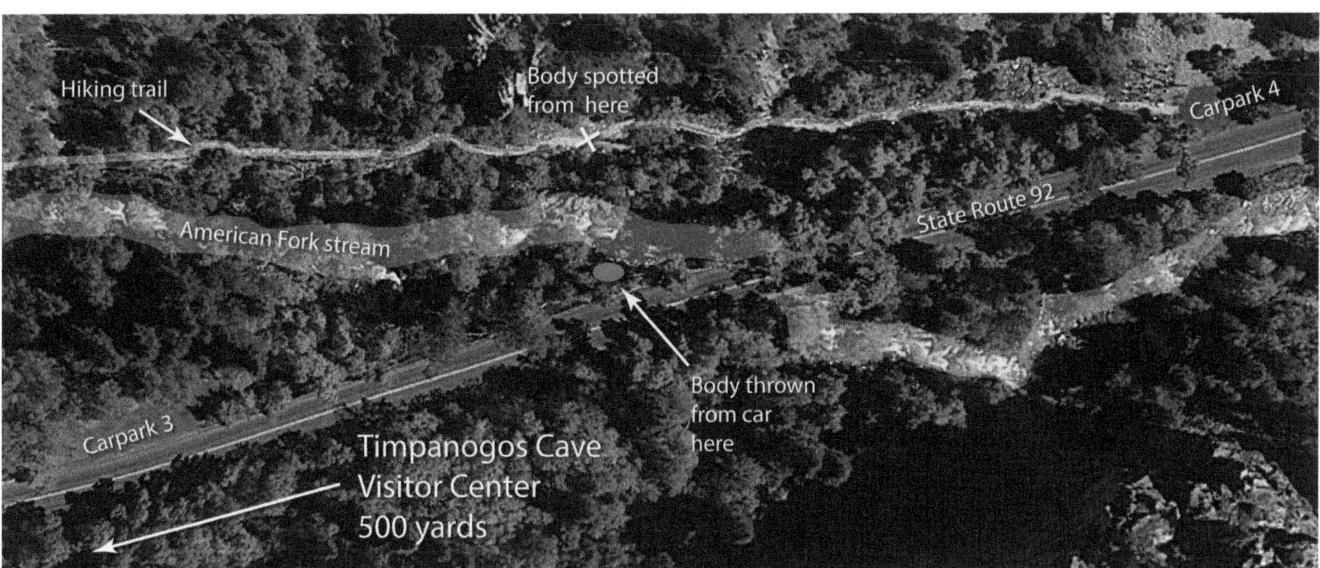

Best guess for Aime's body location (red ellipse). Trail marked in pale yellow is a powerline road. Map image courtesy USGS Earthstar Geographics SIO © Microsoft Corporation.

> Both girls had been killed elsewhere and their lifeless bodies taken to the mountains where they were found. One was drained of blood and the other nearly so. There is no evidence that the draining of the blood had any ritualistic connotations. It's more likely that the girls were simply stored somewhere in a head-down position after death, and the blood drained from the head wounds (*Boca Raton News*, April 10, 1978).

Given that a proportion of her blood was drained, this would additionally delay decomposition. Based on this set of circumstances, we would have to question the coroner's assumption. In the first edition of this book we accepted the coroner's findings, and this led us to conclude Ted had kept Laura alive. There was a frightening possibility that she was alive during Ted's attempted abduction of DaRonch and murder of Kent. However, two other aspects of Laura's autopsy make little sense. She had a blood alcohol reading above the legal limit at the time, and she had no binding marks on her wrists and ankles. One explanation of the alcohol levels is that it could be part of the internal decomposition process, but we also know Laura drank a lot of alcohol in the period leading up to her abduction. If he kept a live victim for an extended period of time, one would think he would need to bind the victim at some point in the timeline. Examining the weather data in more detail also reveals one additional surprise. On the eve of October 31, it snowed 4 inches (~100 mm) up at Timpanogos Cave area. It snowed a further 2 inches on November 1 (~50 mm). Park rangers would have warned prospective visitors not to enter the park at night during these conditions. This leads us to a new hypothesis. It seems more likely that Ted discarded Laura's body either on the same evening that he abducted her, or at the latest, the next morning. We favor the same evening due to the logistics of keeping a dead victim for more than 24 hours. Making our hypothesis more likely, is that a recent study of the decomposition process in high altitudes at two different times of year using pig carcasses, one in August and the other October, shows that in the latter case decomposition is significantly retarded (Parsons 2009). One week after being put down on October 7, at an altitude of around 4,300 feet, there was virtually little change in the state of the carcass. Based on this data, we can safely say that Ted most probably discarded Laura's body down the embankment beside the American Fork watercourse the same night he abducted her, which is to say, during the 4 inches of snow fall. The following night, a further 2 inches of snow fell, which would have covered her and contributed to protecting her from potential predators. As the snow melted / evaporated, her extremities would have undergone the distinctive mummification process.

Laura had numerous lacerations and some deep penetrating wounds to her head, and from which some of her blood must have been drained. Michaud & Aynesworth also reported that her hair had been "freshly shampooed" (M&A 1983, 94). This, of course, makes no sense. It could hardly be fresh given the time she had lain there, whether a week or a month. Pundits of the human doll theory posit that Ted shampooed her hair as part of his ritualistic post-mortem behavior on the body. While Ted almost invariably acted out some sort of post-mortem ritual on his victims, we have no concrete evidence as to what he actually got up to. The shampooing could be interpreted as human-doll work, which invites the image of Ted washing her hair up in the bathroom of his 565 First Avenue apartment, but for reasons we discuss in the NOTES section at the end of this chapter, we discount this idea. The other possibility is that he brought shampoo with him to the body location and applied it there using water from the American Fork stream. The fact that it was thought her hair was freshly shampooed may be because there was sufficient shampoo residue in her hair after snow melt and sporadic rain. It may even be a sign that he visited the body several days after he first put her there. In this case the purpose of the shampoo might serve as a deodorant if he got up close and personal with her body. Partial corroboration of this theory is that Ted's tire-tracks were found at one of the car parks near where the body was located. Over the month we can reasonably assume a number of cars frequented the area, so tire-tread patterns would not last more than a few days or a week (at most) perhaps, and so finding Ted's tire marks there may suggest a more recent visit to Laura's body. Another use of shampoo could be in the initial clean-up process. If we consider the mechanics of exsanguination via head puncture wounds, then we can reasonably assume large amounts of blood would have matted the victim's hair. This makes transport problematic due to transferral of blood to unwanted surfaces. The easiest solution is wrap the head in a containment material (for example garbags). But this method, with the long hair of the victim, is not ideal. Transfer is still possible. Washing the hair therefore presents a logical solution to this problem. However, this means he needed to have access to water. So this explanation only raises more questions. [For further discussion on this case see NOTES section.]

November 28, 1974: Thanksgiving (fourth Thursday November) Liz reads newspapers and becomes alarmed at coincidences. Liz's Bishop offers to call the police on her behalf.

November 30, 1974: Buys gas in SLC.

December 2, 1974: Buys gas in SLC.

Laurie Partridge (undated). Photo public domain.

December 4, 1974: Laurie Lynn Partridge (17) disappears from Spokane. Partridge left Ferris High School at 37th & Havana Streets on Spokane's South Hill early, complaining about not feeling well. Unable to get a ride, she decided to walk the two-plus miles to the home where she lived with her parents and five younger siblings, saying the air might help her feel better. The family reported her missing after she failed to show up for work that evening at Lincoln Heights Theater. The contents of Laurie's purse were located two days later near the location where she was last seen. Initially, based on her unhappiness that the family moved to Spokane from California, sheriff's deputies thought she might have run away from home, but by the time she vanished she had started working on the high school newspaper and was on the drill team. Detectives staked out a Beach Boys concert to which Partridge's father had given her tickets but didn't see her, eventually learning that the tickets had been used but too late to determine by whom.

December 5, 1974: 12:00 (midnight) Calls Liz in Seattle from SLC.

December 6, 1974: Buys gas in SLC. Utah County Attorney-elect Noall T. Wootton calls for the formation of a tri-county task force to tackle missing teenage girls cases (*The Deseret News*).

December 7, 1974: 9:11 p.m. Calls Liz in Seattle from SLC.

December 10, 1974: 8:26 p.m. Calls Liz in Seattle from SLC.

December 11, 1974: 2:42 p.m. Calls Liz in Seattle from SLC.

December 12, 1974: Buys gas in SLC. Inter-Mountain Crime Conference, Stateline, Nevada. Smith, Aime, DaRonch, Kent cases discussed (Rule 2006, 123).

December 13, 1974: 12:54 p.m. Calls Liz in Seattle from SLC.

December 19, 1974: Utah driver's license A957298 issued to Ted. 1:46 p.m. Calls Liz in Seattle from SLC.

Mid-December, 1974: Liz calls her father and tells him of her fears.

December 20, 1974: Buys gas in SLC.

December 21, 1974: 9:14 p.m. Calls Liz in Seattle from SLC.

December 22, 1974: 5:59 a.m. Calls Liz in Seattle from SLC.

December 22 1974: Utah. Ted picks Liz up from airport. Skiing at Snowbird, Utah. While relaxing with some drinks Ted describes a teenage boy getting the attention of some girls as "the James Dean of Midvale."

December 24, 1974: Buys gas in SLC.

December 25 1974: 4:21 p.m. Ted on phone, Ogden, Utah.

December 26 1974: 4:50 p.m. Ted on phone, SLC, Utah.

December 27, 1974: Liz returns to Seattle.

December 29, 1974: Liz calls SLC police, talks to Captain Pete Hayward. Gives Hayward her name.

December 31, 1974: Ted buys gas in Ogden, Utah.

- 1975 -

January 1975: Gallon of regular gas: $0.57. Ted applies for a job as administrative assistant to SLC County Commissioner democrat Ralph McClure. McClure said, "I almost hired him. He had experience in Washington politics, excellent credentials and was an accomplished speech writer."

January 1, 1975: Buys gas in SLC. 9:03 p.m. Calls Liz in Seattle from SLC.

January 3, 1975: (Morning) Ted calls Liz before scheduled morning flight to Seattle. Cries, says: "I just can't seem to connect with people. Sure I can hold doors open for women and smile and be charming, but when it comes to basic relationships I just don't have it. There's something wrong with me" (Kendall 1981, 88). (Evening) Liz picks Ted up from Seattle airport, finds Ted "happy and confident." He was carrying a brochure from a ski resort in Aspen. According to Ted a man sitting next to him on the plane, a salesman for dental equipment, had been on a ski trip to Colorado and had given it to him. Buys gas in SLC.

January 7, 1975: Ted back in Utah. Calls Liz from Provo, Utah, location of Brigham Young University (BYU).

January 8, 1975: 0:31 a.m. Calls Liz in Seattle from SLC.

January 9, 1975: Ted applies for driver's license, SLC.

January 10, 1975: Buys gas in SLC (twice).

January 11, 1975: Purchased gas from Glenwood Springs, Colorado. Stayed somewhere for the night, probably at a Holiday Inn under a false name. Or did he sleep in his car?

January 12, 1975: Purchased gas in Glenwood Springs, Colorado, $3.00. 7:43 p.m. Abducts Caryn Eileen Campbell (23) from the Wildwood Inn, Snowmass, Colorado. Does "his thing" in the car, spends very little time, then discards her. Ted was identified as being in the area just prior to the abduction.

Wildwood Inn, Snowmass, Colorado. Physician Raymond Gadowski, of Farmington Michigan, took his two children and his new girlfriend, nurse Caryn Campbell who worked at the same hospital as him, to the inn for a skiing holiday while he attended a cardiology seminar in Aspen. On the second day of their stay, at 7:43 p.m. Caryn went to the Gadowski room (210) to fetch a

Top right: Caryn Campbell possibly wearing the same woolly beige jacket the night she was abducted. Photo courtesy KCA. Bottom: The Stew Pot restaurant in Snowmass Village, where Caryn Campbell had her last meal about an hour before her abduction. Did Ted happen to see her there? Photo courtesy Chris Mortensen © 2015.

The second floor elevator where Ted may have encountered Campbell. Photo courtesy Chris Mortensen © 2015.

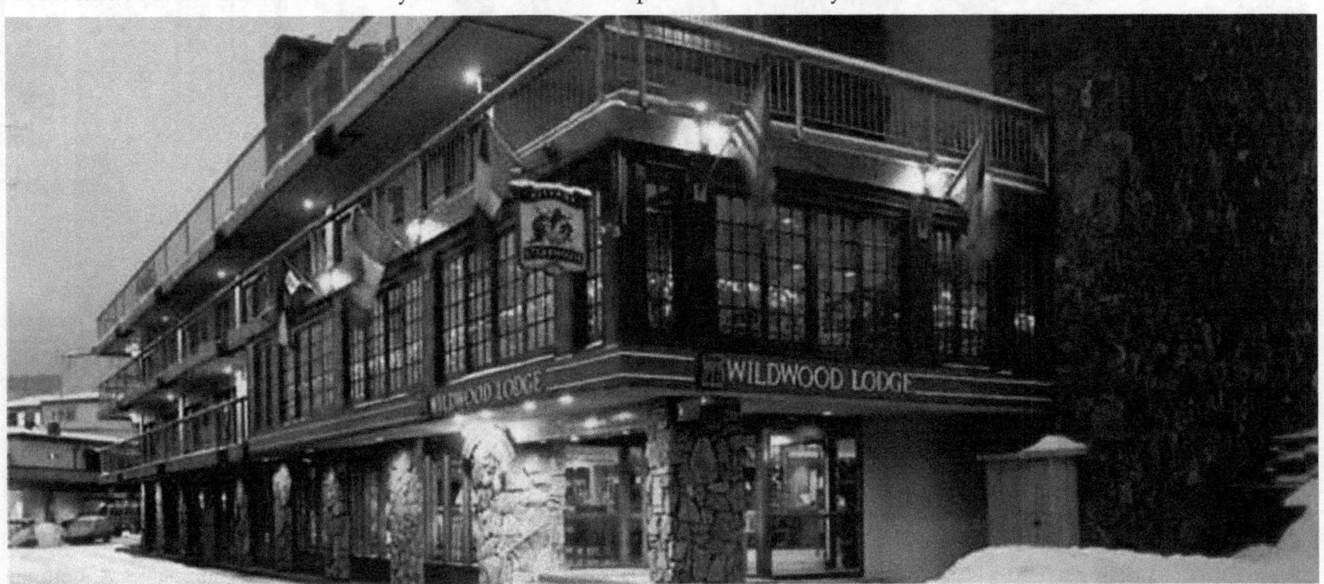

The Wildwood Inn approximately as it would have looked on the night of Campbell's abduction. Photo public domain.

magazine* and never returned. She never made it to the room. Gadowski's daughter later wrote: "Sheila Pierce, a tourist from California, was walking down the second floor hallway when she noticed a handsome man com-

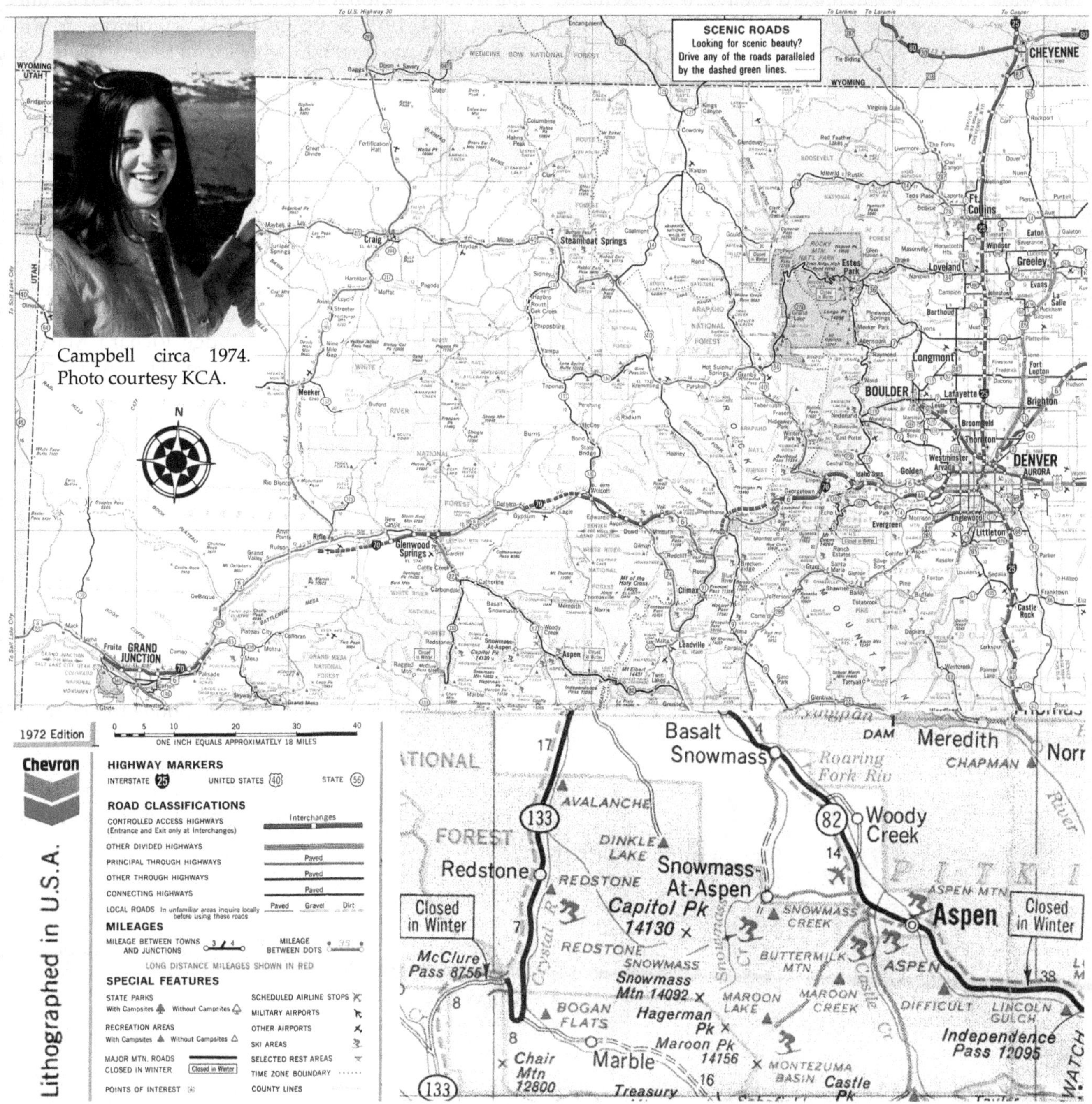

Campbell circa 1974. Photo courtesy KCA.

A road map Ted might have used: Chevron, Colorado, 1972 (excerpt and recombination; inset enlarged). Jan 11, 1975, buys gas at Glenwood Springs sometime in the early evening. Probably drove up to Aspen and Snowmass, practiced a dry run. Drove back to Glenwood Springs in the early hours. Jan 12. Slept in his car till noon. Topped up his tank at Glenwood Springs with $3 of gas—enough to cover the round trip—and headed off for a night of hunting. Abducted Caryn Campbell at 7:43 p.m. No injury ruse. Just charms her with a request for help. She was still wearing her ski boots and could go outside, help him get his car going. They walk down into the parking lot, visually protected by rows of pine trees. He instructs her to hold something, whacks her a few times (autopsy skull damage), throws her in the front passenger seat (transfer of hair), drives on the cross link between Snowmass and Aspen (Owl Creek Road), pulls over about 500 yards short of the summit divide (Sinclair), drags her semi-conscious form into the back seat, starts raping her, but she revives and struggles, scratches his face (marks later observed by witnesses). Still, he rapes and strangles her (or vise versa), then throws her into the front trunk for a drive (transfer of hair), but realizes a few hundred yards up the road that he is bleeding, bad enough to attract attention, not a good idea to keep a body in the car. He makes the decision to throw her out, and heads home. There is a possibility he ran a knife across her neck before he discarded her, but that is pure autopsy speculation. For the next month, rather than hunting, he dated Ann Swenson. Then it started again ... (* Her *Viva* magazine in exchange for a *Playboy*.)

ing towards her. He smiled at her, and she smiled back. [...] three doctors had seen Caryn get out of the elevator and walk down the hall toward room 210" ("Raymond Gadowski," November 12, 2010).

Campbell had shoulder-length brown hair cut in a slight shag, and wore a black flowered blouse, flared jeans, brown boots and a woolly beige jacket. Mike Fisher who later cased the joint found that steam rising from the swimming pool around which the hotel rooms were centered had acted as a cover. Due to the nature of the layout of the inn, he concluded Campbell must have voluntarily followed her abductor down to the car parking lot, a suspicion implied by Ted to M&A (2000, 182).

January 13, 1975: Bought gas in Green River, Utah. 6:23 p.m. Calls Liz in Seattle from SLC.

January, sometime between 13-27, 1975: A Univ. Utah law school classmate Wynn Bartholomew noted that Ted looked "haggard, with bags under his eyes and crimson red scratches branded across his cheeks and neck." He suspected his condition was caused by a woman. Ted lied and said the scratches were caused by tree branches (*Deseret News*, January 24, 1989). More likely, Ted got into a struggle with Campbell, just like the one with DaRonch, only this time he had learned his lesson. Judging from the autopsy report, he may have used a knife.

Wynn and Carol Bartholomew circa mid-70s. Photo public domain.

Carol Bartholomew with Ted at 628, 11th Ave., March 21, 1975. Carol remembered Ted as "polite." Photo public domain.

January 14, 1975: Buys gas in SLC. According to Rule, Ted spent January 14-23 with Liz in Seattle (Rule 2006, 125).

January 23, 1975: Prepares to return to SLC.

January 24, 1975: Heidi Peterson's remains and some of her clothes are found in a blackberry bramble below a scenic bluff two blocks from her Capitol Hill home. Her skull was damaged.

January 27, 1975: 9:14 p.m. Calls Liz in Seattle from SLC.

January 28, 1975: Starts law school, University of Utah. Has possible casual sexual relationship with Marguerite Christine Maughan, resident at 565 First Avenue and daughter of Supreme Court Judge Richard Maughan (dates unknown but possibly linked to law school attendance).

January 29, 1975: Attends Univ. Utah law school.

January 30, 1975: Attends Univ. Utah law school.

January 31, 1975: Buys gas in SLC.

February, 1975: Purchased Utah license plate LJB-088. Ted dates Ann Swenson from February to March, 1975. They went to Mormon Sunday school together. Swenson began working as a legal secretary in John O'Connell's law office several months after she stopped dating Ted. It appears Ann Swenson is the sister of Mark Swenson, a missionary Ted met through Ann. Ted began considering joining the Mormon church around this time.

February 1, 1975: 1:49 p.m. Ted on phone to Liz in Seattle.

February 4, 1975: Attends Univ. Utah law school.

February 6, 1975: Attends Univ. Utah law school.

February 8, 1975: 9:42 p.m. Ted on phone to Liz in Seattle.

February 9, 1975: Buys gas in SLC.

February 10, 1975: Buys gas in SLC. Attends Univ. Utah law school.

February 11, 1975: Attends Univ. Utah law school.

February 13, 1975: 10:04 p.m. Ted on phone to Liz in Seattle.

February 15, 1975: 1:05 p.m. Ted on phone to Liz in Seattle.

February 17, 1975: 1:21 a.m. Ted on phone to Liz in Seattle. Caryn Campbell's body is discovered 2.8 miles from the Wildwood Inn just west of the Sinclair Divide Summit on the south side of Owl Creek Road. There was evidence of at least three separate blows to the head. One to the lower jaw, broke away a molar below the gumline. In addition, it looked like she had suffered deep cuts from a sharp weapon. There was not enough tissue remaining in the neck area to make an exact determination, but her hyoid bone had been cracked, suggesting strangulation at the minimum. Semen residue was found in her vagina, but not anal area. Fingernail scrapings disclosed blue, red and gray synthetic fibers. Later, one of Campbell's hairs was found under Ted's VW floor mat; the other inside the trunk. All in all, Ted spent two days on the road, and probably little more than an hour or two with Campbell before he threw her over the guard rail at Sinclair Divide. Campbell's case clearly illustrates that Ted did not always spend a lot of time with his victims after he murdered them. He never went back to visit Campbell's body. Time of year and terrain are probably the main factors.

February 19, 1975: Buys gas in SLC. Attends Univ. Utah law school.

February 20, 1975: Attends Univ. Utah law school.

February 21, 1975: Attends Univ. Utah law school.

February 22, 1975: 11:48 p.m. Calls Liz in Seattle from SLC.

February 23, 1975: Buys gas in SLC.

February 24, 1975: Attends Univ. Utah law school.

February 25, 1975: Attends Univ. Utah law school.

February 27, 1975: Attends Univ. Utah law school.

February 28, 1975: Attends Univ. Utah law school.

Campbell's body in situ. Photo courtesy FSA.

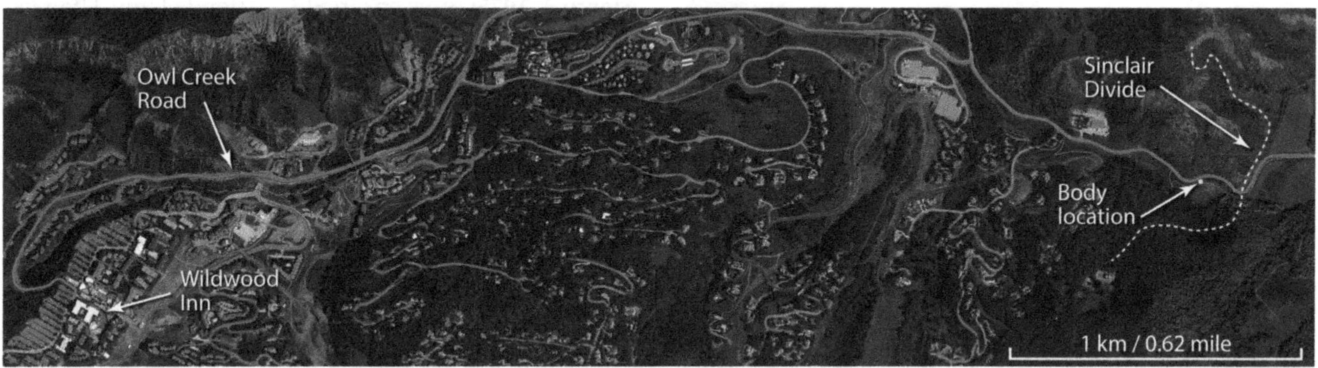

Owl Creek Road from the Wildwood Inn to the best estimate where Campbell was found. Aerial Map image courtesy USGS Earthstar Geographics SIO © Microsoft Corporation.

Caryn Campbell body location estimates based on various sources (local photography, Google Earth, police report including crime scene photos, anecdotal narratives). March 5, 2016. Photo courtesy Jeremy Fleischer © 2016.

Taylor Mountain

March 1, 1975: Buys gas in SLC. Two forestry students discover a human skull on the lower slopes of Taylor Mountain near the town of North Bend. Keppel: "All we found was hair, skull, skull, jawbone, jawbone, and a jawbone." Off Highway 18, where the powerlines cross four miles south of I-90 (1,000 feet northeast of the intersection of the powerline road and Highway 18).

The skulls and jawbones exhibited severe blunt force trauma. Parks' entire viscerocranium was missing. Of the remains, Keppel noted at the time, "... they appeared to have decomposed at the same rate. In other words you had girls basically that were missing in January, April, two in May, but the leaf-fall, the growth of fine maple over the tops of them all kind of had the same look to them. That wouldn't have happened if they were dumped at different times" (*Investigative Discovery*, 2008). If true, considering that Ted murdered Healy on January 31, 1974, and Ball on June 1, 1974, this amounts to at least a minimum period of 121 days – about four months for which he kept Healy's head with successive fewer days for the others. Since he was living at the Rogers' rooming house at the time, how did he keep them without arousing suspicion due to bad odors? One possibility is that he may have skeletonized them. For example bury them or leave them above ground at a secret location where he could easily recover them. But this is pure unsupported speculation.

At the very end, in an interview with Keppel, Ted said he did not keep body parts in the fridge, something that Keppel thought would have been logical if someone wanted to keep human remains fresh. At the end of the day, we know so little about what Ted did to the remains of his victims. The few isolated examples, like Manson's and Hawkins' skull, have never been verified with physical evidence. The remains that have been found, apart from obvious signs of rape and murder provide very little other information about what he actually did, for example, the damage he did to Parks' viscerocranium (see NOTES section at the end of this chapter).

March 3, 1975: Lynda Ann Healy, Roberta Kathleen Parks, Susan Elaine Rancourt and Brenda Carol Ball remains subsequently confirmed according to MTR.

March 4, 1975: Buys gas in SLC. Attends Univ. Utah law school.

March 5, 1975: The MTR has the remains of Healy, Rancourt, Parks and Ball found on this date (which coincides with the newspaper publishing date, but not actual discovery). Despite further searching in the wider area, all that was ultimately found were crania and mandibles.

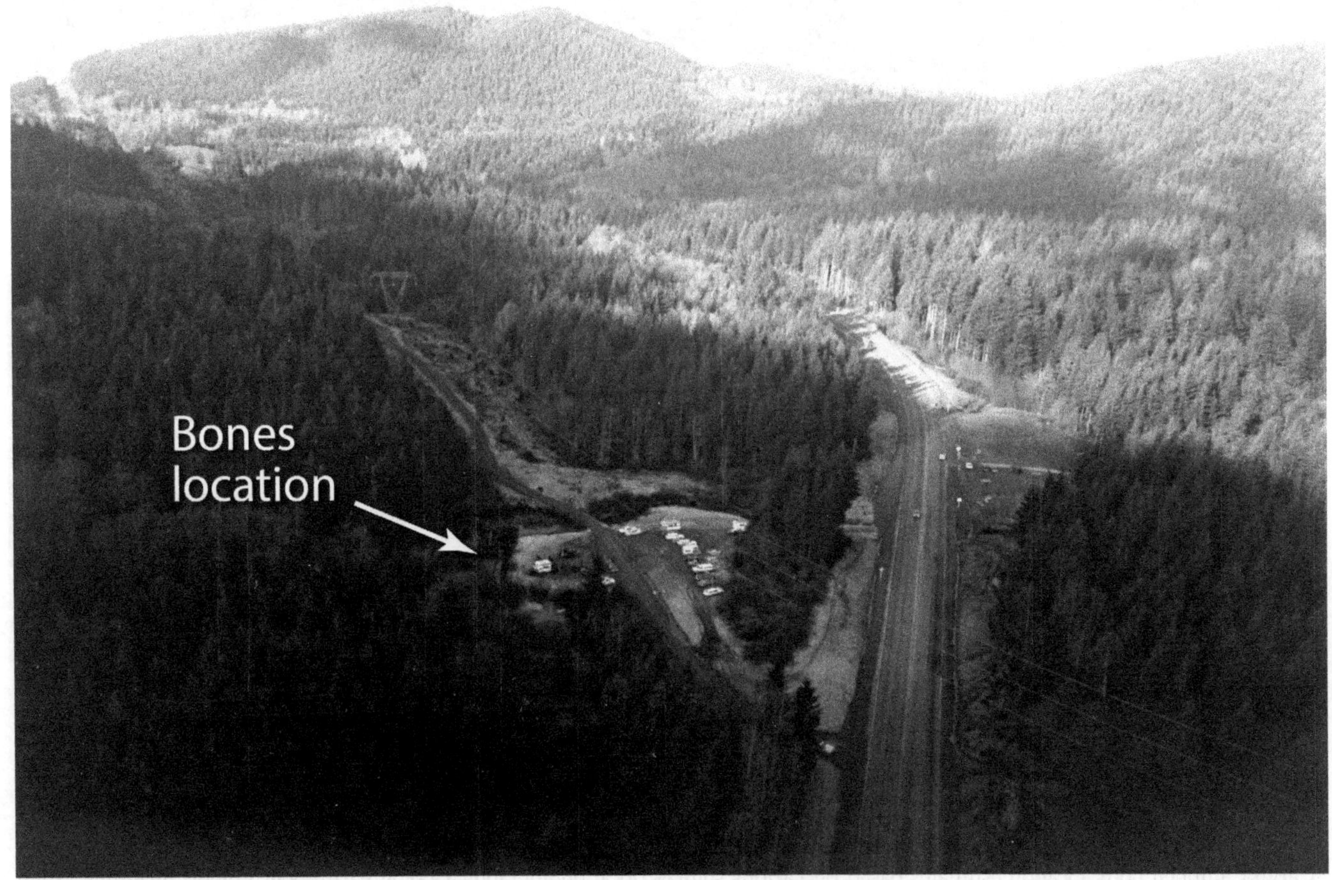

Powerline Road branching off Highway 18 at Taylor Mountain looking south. March 1975 police aerial. Photo courtesy KCA.

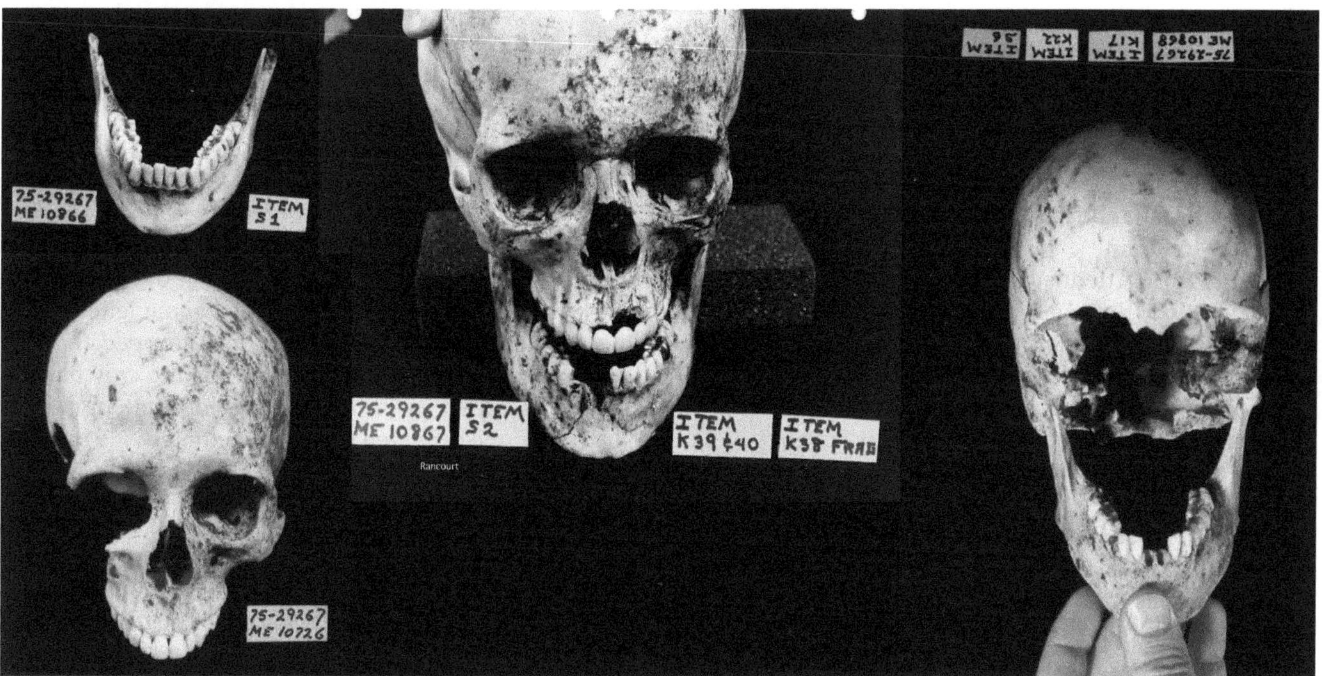

All that was found of Healy (top left), Ball (bottom left), Rancourt (middle) and Parks (right). Photos courtesy KCA.

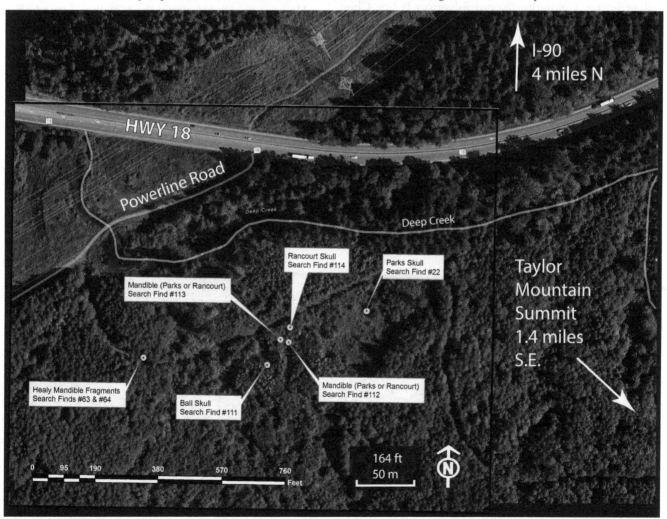

The Taylor Mountain skulls location based on police reports and maps. Map image courtesy USGS Earthstar Geographics SIO © Microsoft Corporation.

March 6, 1975: Attends Univ. Utah law school. 10:11 p.m. Calls Liz in Seattle from SLC. Keppel contacts Crystal Mountain Ski Resort Patrol Office and requests they pull records from January 19, 1974 through April 17, 1974 for any males that injured themselves, as "Ted" suspect had approached Jane Curtis at Central Washington campus and told her that he had injured his arm while skiing at Crystal Mountain.
March 7, 1975: Attends Univ. Utah law school.
March 8, 1975: Buys gas in SLC (three times).
March 10, 1975: Special "Ted" task force reported in *Eugene Register-Guard* (Springfield and Lane County, Oregon). Attends Univ. Utah law school.
March 12, 1975: Attends Univ. Utah law school.
March 13, 1975: Buys gas in SLC. Attends Univ. Utah law school.
March 14, 1975: Purchased gas in Rock Springs, Wyoming. Purchased gas in Laramie, Wyoming. Heads out to the ski fields. Around this time, a ski instructor in Aspen stated that she was approached by crippled guy asking for help carrying his briefcase [ref].
March 15, 1975: Purchased gas in Golden, then Silverthorne, Colorado. (Noon) Silverton Police Chief observes Ted walk into Holiday Inn, Frisco, Colorado (which is near Vail). 4:00 p.m. Ted drives his VW into Vail. 9:00 p.m. Abducts Julie Cunningham (26) from Vail, rapes and kills her near Rifle, Colorado. Returns at least once to the body location, to bury her.

We learn a little about some of the details of Cunningham's abduction from Ted's 11th hour confession to Mike Fisher and detective Matt Lindvall (K&B 2005, 492-506):

> It would have been on the east side of town on the eastern end of the main downtown shopping area [...] pedestrian streets mainly. And [...] around that core is a loop of some sort. And it's on the eastern loop of that by a bridge [where he encountered Cunningham]. I was again using a pair of crutches and a boot bag, a boot tree, and she offered to help me with it, and we walked from that location to the parking lot, which was maybe a distance of one-half to three-quarters of a mile. It was after dark, early evening. We had to climb, actually, to the location where the car was parked, had to climb a rather steep snowbank and descend down into the parking lot where the car was.

As they walked, Cunningham mentioned she had been on her way to either have dinner, drinks, or both with a female friend of hers. She said it didn't matter if she was a little late. She also posted some letters along the way, ran over to a post box and dropped them in. When they got to his car, Ted grabbed the crowbar that he had propped up at the rear beside the engine and struck her once. She fell down immediately. He bundled her into the passenger side, where he had taken the seat out and handcuffed her. He then drove out of Vail on the I-70, through Glenwood Springs where she regained consciousness and began talking ...

> I remember conversation, but I have a hard time coming up with exact words .... She was just asking who I was and all. You know, where I was from.

He kept on driving down the I-70, then turned off at Rifle, onto State Highway 13. He was looking for the usual side road, as he put it:

> ... concerned about houses in the area 'cause I knew it was getting late and I didn't want to turn into somebody's driveway. It couldn't have been that long, we're talking minutes probably, I found a side road, a dirt road, and turned off onto it and drove maybe a quarter-mile off the road to the right.

Ted didn't want to talk about the next part, but Lindvall kept on badgering him until he revealed some details:

> At some point, she'd been asking me to loosen the handcuffs. And I did so. I got out of the car and tried to figure out where things were. Walked from the car

Vail aerial (August 29, 1975) showing the most likely route taken by Ted and Julie Cunningham. Total distance travelled is 0.85 miles. Vail aerial courtesy Colorado Aerial Photo Service © 2015.

Gore Creek Drive, Vail (1975). Ted walked this street in search of a victim. Julie Cunningham came from the left of the frame on this side of the image plane. Photo public domain.

> [...] I noticed her opening the door and getting out of the car [...] apparently she'd slipped out of the handcuffs [...] [we got involved in a struggle and] sometime during the course of the struggle I got a hold of it [the crowbar and knocked her unconscious again].

Ted as usual skipped the rape scene. He went straight on to the murder ...

> I had some links of cord in the car, among other things, [...] and I used a link of that cord, a length of that cord was used to strangle her.

Keppel had prepped Lindvall about Ted's penchant for necrophilia, so Lindvall pressed Ted to reveal what he did with her after killing her. But Ted balked:

> ... I didn't bullshit you. And yet I won't bullshit you now. I'm just having a hard time talking about that one segment of this rather prolonged incident. [...] And I could just say that I've known guys who've just bullshitted their way through this part of it and said, oh, nothing. I'm not going to bullshit you through it. I'm telling you that's a point we're going to, in my case, we will talk about. But not today.

Throughout the interview, Ted reiterated how panicked he was about the abduction, but it is plainly obvious that he is just throwing up a smoke screen. He said he just wanted to get it over with, as if it were some sort of formality. The truth is he spent four hours driving and then wandering around Vail. He said he got stuck in a snowbank behind an apartment complex for a couple of hours and had to dig himself out. He then left his VW in a parking lot and wandered around on foot until it got dark. After dark, he returned to his car and got his crutches and paraphernalia, then took the crowbar out of the car and propped it up by the engine (the same type shown in the photo of his August 16, 1975 first arrest). So he had plenty of time to contemplate what he was doing. At the rape and murder site, when he hit her for the second time, she fell backward, half in and half out of the car, still alive. From that we can surmise he either raped her in the car or on the ground, then strangled her. He couldn't remember whether he did it with her lying face up or face down. He then removed all of her clothes, her suede coat, her boots, her jewelry, and all her other possessions.

How much time he spent with her after he killed her we do not know, but probably till dawn if his Hawkins' confession is anything to go by. He then dragged the body up a slope and hid it under a bush, picked up all the evidence and left the scene. He later threw out her belongings in a Goodwill bin in SLC.

Around six weeks later, he returned to the scene. He had great difficulty finding the location:

> I'd gone to half a dozen different places before I found that one. But seeing it in the day-time was just totally different. I was trying to recreate what it looked like at night. But after the better part of a half a day and getting out of my car half a dozen times, I did locate what seemed to appear to be the spot. [...] it was up the side of this hillside. I mean up the hillside, and this is some scrub trees at the base of a rock, a rocky area, a rocky cliff some fifty, thirty-three to fifty feet high. I wasn't aware of it at the time. And below that little rocky ridge in this little clump of scrub trees was the young woman's body, Julie's body. [...] She was on her back, face-up. But the dry weather and all, it sort of, I don't know what the term would be, 'mummified' her remains. Anyway, I'd gone back to bury her, which is why I had a shovel, a small shovel. And which is what I did.

Lindvall asked why he took the risk of returning to the body:

> [In the case of the Washington body locations] I went back to that scene a day later, two days later, and I don't know how much, how familiar you are, well, about crime scenes. I mean, after a day or two, the body is relatively fresh, after, depending on the climate, animals, humidity, time of year, you name it.

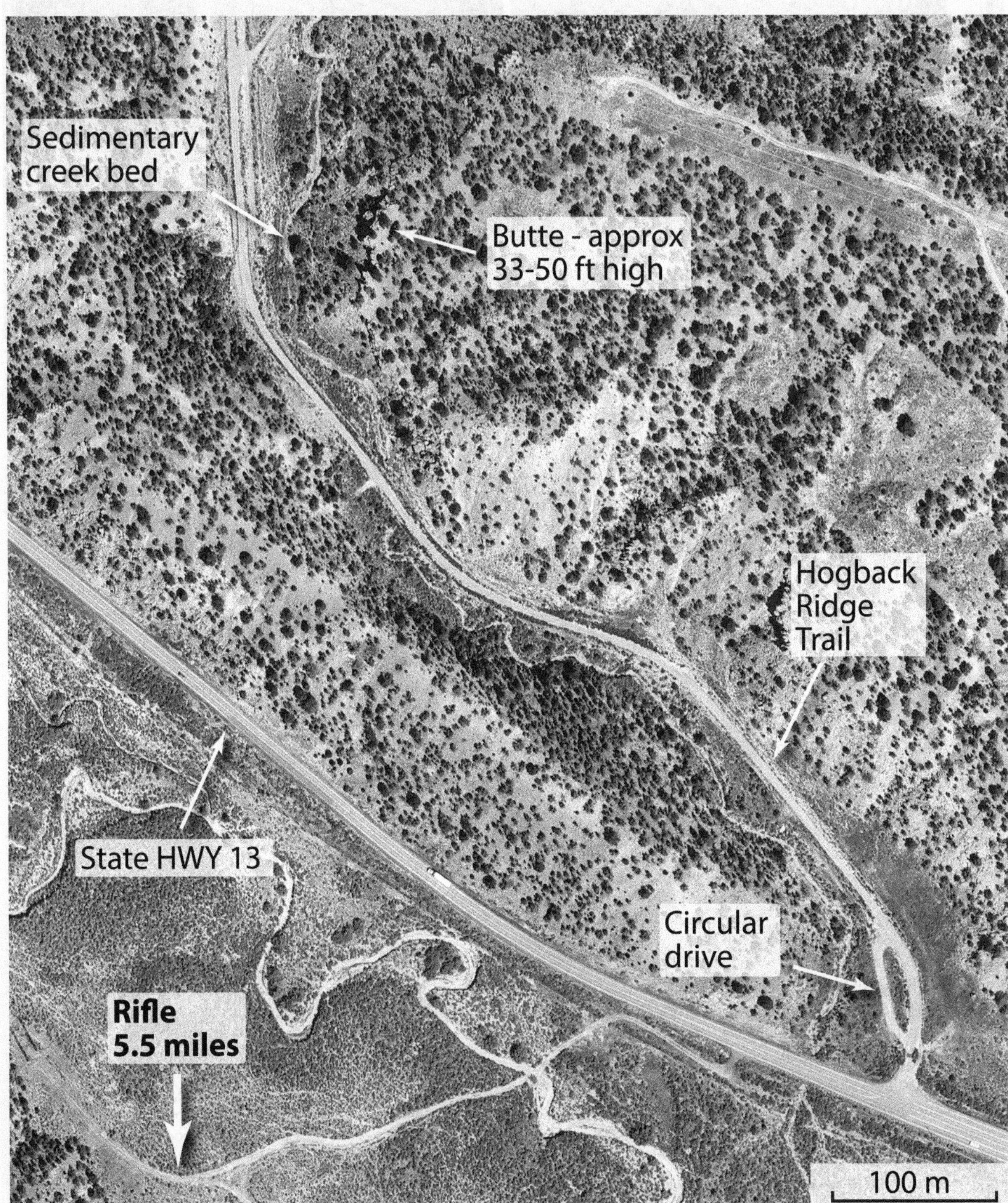

Hogback Ridge Trail. Best candidate location according to the description of where Ted said he buried Cunningham. Map image courtesy USGS Earthstar Geographics SIO © Microsoft Corporation.

> Depends on the decomposition cycle. [In Cunningham's case however ...] I would describe it as being mummified, I had never seen somebody who'd been out that long who was not either eaten, I mean consumed by insects in some way. But the body was basically untouched, but, you know, obviously very different looking than someone who is either alive or just freshly killed. That's not the reason I went back. The reason I went back was twofold. Primarily, for the burial, and secondly, to check the scene to make sure that nothing had been left there.

We do not know if Ted performed any further sex acts on the body when he returned. He may have masturbated over it. Maybe he took some Polaroids.

Perhaps the most remarkable thing about Cunningham's abduction is the distance she walked with Ted from their first encounter to his car. There is a dubious report that Cunningham was seen by several people at a local bar the previous evening with a male she referred to as "Ted," who said he was an attorney in Aspen (Extract from a summary report, Eagle County District Attorney's Office). According to Rule, Cunningham went to Sun Valley, Idaho, in early March with a man who she thought she might settle down with, but it ended abruptly, and she returned to Vail extremely unhappy (Rule 2006, 132-3). It may be that on the night she en-

JULIE CUNNINGHAM, W/F, Age 26, 5'5", 110 lbs., long dark brown hair (parted down the middle), brown eyes (does not wear glasses), has pierced ears, right-handed, DOB 1-10-49.

Miss Cunningham was last seen in Vail, Colorado at her apartment complex at approximately 6:30 p.m. on March 15, 1975. She is believed to be wearing a brown suede jacket with sheepskin lining, blue jeans, mid-calf brown leather boots, and either a brown or white ski hat.

Miss Cunningham was last seen on foot and left all her personal belongings and vehicle behind.

Refer any information to: Chief Gary R. Wall
Vail Police Department
Box 567
Vail, Colorado 81657
Telephone: 303/476-5671

APRIL 11, 1975

2002 S. Colo. Blvd., Denver, Colo. 80222, ph. 303/759-1100

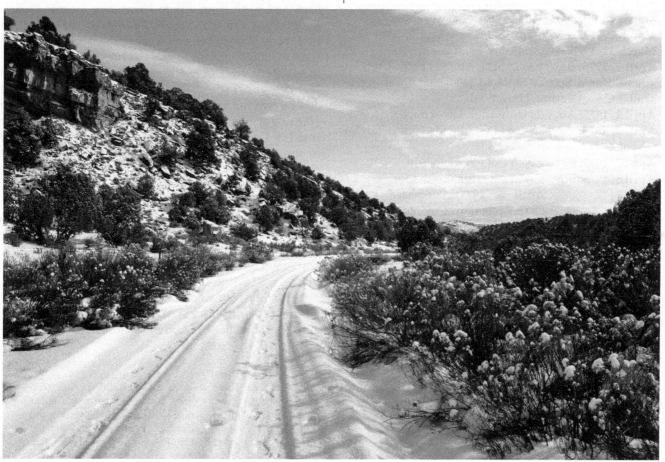

Hogback Ridge Trail looking west beneath the butte that Ted described. Ted may have returned to bury Cunningham on the same trip that he abducted Denise Oliverson. Photo courtesy Chris Mortensen © 2016.

countered Ted she was feeling lonely and walking a mile with a stranger that needed help seemed like a good option.

March 16, 1975: Purchased gas in Dillon, Colorado. 2:47 p.m. Calls Liz in Seattle from SLC. 8:42 p.m. Calls Liz in Seattle from SLC.

March 17, 1975: Seminar held with representatives of police agencies who had missing girls and girls who had been murdered (Adams 1981, 211).

March 18, 1975: 11:01 a.m. Calls Liz in Seattle from SLC.

March 19, 1975: Attends Univ. Utah law school.

March 20, 1975: Buys gas in SLC. Attends Univ. Utah law school.

March 21, 1975: Attends Univ. Utah law school.

March 22, 1975: Buys gas in SLC.

March 24, 1975: Attends Univ. Utah law school.

March 25, 1975: Attends Univ. Utah law school. Ted task force suspect list reaches 2552, with 1000 VW bugs to be examined.

March 26, 1975: Buys gas in SLC.

March 27, 1975: Attends Univ. Utah law school. Keppel is advised by Dr. Donald Reay (King County Medical Examiner) that it would be very difficult to decapitate someone without leaving any vertebrae attached. If there were no vertebrae, then it would indicate that the heads were pulled away from skeletal remains elsewhere.

March 28, 1975: Attends Univ. Utah law school.

March 29, 1975: 3:17 p.m. Calls Liz in Seattle from SLC.

March 31, 1975: Attends Univ. Utah law school.

April 1, 1975: Buys gas in SLC. Attends Univ. Utah law school. Karen Sparks reported recovered from her assault and is attending Univ. Wash.

April 2, 1975: Attends Univ. Utah law school.

April 3, 1975: Buys gas in SLC. Attends Univ. Utah law school.

April 4, 1975: Buys gas in Golden, Colorado.

April 5, 1975: Buys gas in Silverton, Colorado.

Denise Oliverson (undated). Image public domain.

April 6, 1975: Purchased gas in Grand Junction, Colorado. Abducts Denise Lynn Oliverson (24) from Grand Junction, Colorado. [MTR has Oliverson missing since April 4, others have her missing on April 6. Larsen has him buying gas at Grand Junction on April 5.] Denise was riding her bike from 1619 Laveta Street to her parent's place when she vanished. According to Ted's final confession he dumped her body outside of Grand Junction in the Colorado River. Her body was never recovered. Denise supposedly argued with her "common law husband" (boyfriend) on Sunday afternoon and left her house riding her yellow bike and headed for her parents' home. Winn & Merrill take up the story:

> It was three o'clock on a Sunday afternoon, finally warm enough so that Denise could wear just an India print blouse tucked into her Levi's. She turned off Laveta Street, whirring past the pickup trucks and tiny houses in the south end of Grand Junction. She was going to Lincoln Park, she'd told her boyfriend at the end of their spat. The park was across the Colorado River, near her parents' house on the other end of town. He figured she'd go there later to cool off. Normally her route would have taken her over a metal bridge across the river and then over an arched bridge across the railroad tracks. But apparently Denise Oliverson never made it over the gentle bow of the Fifth Street Bridge. The last sign of her was on the tracks underneath. [...] Denise's boyfriend phoned her parents on Monday afternoon to confirm that she was still there. He learned she'd never arrived. Grand Junction police immediately searched Denise's presumed route. It was several hours before anyone thought to look under the bridge, and there, flung across the tracks near an auto salvage yard, was her yellow bicycle; her red exercise sandals were nearby (1979, 74-5).

According to an alternative account by Cass Hardy (email correspondence 9 February 2017), Denise had broken up with her common law husband and lived alone at Laveta Street. Denise babysat Hardy's 6-week old daughter the night before her abduction. "I walked back and forth from where I was 2 or 3 times during the evening and then we sat and talked for at least an hour on her couch before I went home. That is when we were making the plans to meet the next day. [...] She was meeting me around 11 a.m. in the park [Lincoln Park]. Her new [boy] friend that she liked lived in Montrose and he was not around that weekend." However, when Hardy got to the park around 11 a.m. someone there told her Denise had ridden home to change into a pair of shorts as she had come in jeans and it was hot that day. The round trip was about 5 miles. This raises the possibility that Ted might have seen Denise at the park and followed her down to the railway crossing shortcut. Alternatively, he may have already been down there and used his car ruse on her. Apparently the railway crossing shortcut was commonly used by people and Denise would not have been "weirded out" by seeing a stranger there.

Ted's final confession came in a 5-minute tape-recorded conversation with FSP Warden Thomas Barton at 6:15 a.m. Tuesday, about 45 minutes before his execution. Referring to Oliverson:

> Barton: Is that it?
> Ted: No. There is ... Mike Fisher and the Colorado detectives, ah ... the last young woman they wanted to talk about ... Denise Oliverson, I believe, I'm not sure. I hope this is picking up. Can you play some of it back, maybe, just to make sure. [Pause] Referring again to Denise Oliverson, or whoever it was out of Grand Junction that Mike Fisher wanted to discuss, uh, I believe the date was in April 1975. The young

1619 Laveta. Photo courtesty Chris Mortensen © 2015.

The 5th Street Bridge before it was replaced in 1989. Photo courtesy Library of Congress.

Grand Junction aerial photo, March 13, 1975, showing the route Oliverson took (yellow line) and the abduction location (red question mark). Aerial image courtesy Colorado Aerial Photo Service © 2015.

1973 aerial showing the most likely crime scene location for Denise Oliverson. On April 6, 1975, the sun set around 7:40 p.m. so Ted needed tree or shrub cover given he abducted Oliverson well before sundown. Due to the time of year, the river would have been swollen with the winter snow melt. The area today is accessible via Redlands Parkway. Aerial photograph courtesy USGS.

woman's body would have been placed in the Colorado River about five miles west of Grand Junction. It was not buried (*Gainesville Sun*, January 27, 1989).

We are given one more somewhat difficult to interpret clue. Detective James Fromm, who had joined Grand Junction PD just two years earlier in 1973, said: "Oliverson had stopped at a gas station on 5th and Pitkin in Grand Junction within an hour of when Bundy had purchased gas at the same gas station" (*The Denver Post*, February 16, 2013). An interview with retired detective Doug Rushing of Grand Junction police later confirmed that this information had been incorrectly reported (Mortensen interview of Doug Rushing, January 21, 2016). It turns out Ted got gas at 23rd and North Chevron (North Avenue), which is right by Lincoln Park, near where Denise's parents lived. Ted could have come through on route 50 in those days, which was the main highway from SLC; it went right past the gas station at 23rd. (By coincidence it happened to be owned by Rushing's uncle.) According to Rushing, Denise rode down the righthand side of the railway viaduct with the intention of crossing the tracks at that level. It would appear, therefore, that Ted must have seen her and followed her down (or was already waiting), which accounts for why her bicycle and red sandals were found down there the next day. How he abducted her is a mystery. But given that he left her bicycle and sandals down there suggests he used one of his ruses. He could have driven up behind her and past her and scared her off the side of the road (her bicycle was undamaged according to police). He could have passed her and blocked her way. He could have driven past her, stopped and faked a breakdown (which seems probable). In any case, that he left her bicycle there is obvious, but the sandals are harder to explain. One possibility is that by removing them he would make it harder for her to escape if she ever contemplated that action.

April 7, 1975: Oliverson bicycle and sandals found under viaduct near railroad bridge close to the Colorado River on U.S. Route 50. According to Rushing, the sandals are still held in an evidence locker at the Grand Junction police station.

Denise's bicyle and red sandals were found just across the tracks behind the pylon in the foreground (this picture taken looking south). Photo courtesy Chris Mortensen © 2016.

April 8, 1975: (Early hours) Buys gas in Green River, Utah. Attends Univ. Utah law school.

April 9, 1975: Attends Univ. Utah law school. By this date 2200 suspects and 900 vehicles lay before investigators in Seattle. Of those, only 50 had been positively eliminated (KCA). 3:30 p.m. Karen Sparks attends a hypnotic session accompanied by her father at the office of Dr Ralph M. Stolzheise. She was unable to recall anything. Another session was booked for the following week, and when that didn't work, a session with sodium pentothal.

April 10, 1975: Buys gas in SLC. Attends Univ. Utah law school.

April 11, 1975: Notifies Utah authorities that he lost license plates bearing LJE-379. Lie. Attends Univ. Utah law school.

April 14, 1975: Buys gas in SLC. On November 8, 1975, Detective Bob Denning received a telephone call from Detective Dale Getz at the Boulder County Sheriff's Department in reference to possible involvement of Ted in the Melanie Cooley case. Denning advised Getz that Ted purchased gas in SLC and Golden, Colorado, on April 14, 1975 (FSA).

Melanie Cooley, circa 1975. Photo public domain.

April 15, 1975: Melanie Suzanne Cooley (18) vanishes from Nederland, Colorado. The MTR has Ted attending law school in SLC some time during the day.

April 16, 1975: Midnight - 2:30 a.m. worked at Bailiff Hall, University of Utah. Ted's basic job was to run movies, keep the hall open for students late at night, and just generally keep an eye on things. Earns $2.10 per hour. Ted's supervisor Jim Schuster stated that in his opinion:

> ... the individual was a very odd person, in that he thought out every word before he said it to make sure that he was perfect in trying to put over a point. He stated that he felt the individual reminded him of someone that did an awful lot of talking about wanting to change and having different ideas, but in fact he didn't believe in what he was trying to tell you, but he'd do it to try to convince someone something about himself. Ted often turned up drunk or never at all. Schuster's supervisor John Grover demanded that Ted resign or he would fire him (Jerry Thompson police report, FSA).

April 17, 1975: Buys gas in SLC.

April 20, 1975: Buys gas in SLC.

April 22, 1975: Buys gas in SLC. Attends Univ. Utah law school.

April 24, 1975: Carol Booth moves into the apartment directly across the hall from Ted on the second floor of 565 First Avenue. She stays there till May 24, 1975. She stated that she got to know Ted "rather well." She said he was a nice guy, except he "had a phobia for cleanliness." She'd never observed an individual that was as clean as he was with his apartment etc. She stated that some time while they were over there (in his apartment), a sewing machine that she had, she believes she loaned it to Ted, or he came over and got it from her apartment – she hasn't been able to find it since. She asked him about it and he stated "I don't know what you're talking about." She confronted all the other members in 565 First Avenue, and all claimed they had nothing to do with it. Carol Booth believed more strongly than ever after that, that Ted had the machine. After she moved out of 565 First Avenue, she had a party at her new place (which was with Paul Van Dam), and there she introduced Ted to Leslie Knudson in late June 1975 (Jerry Thompson notes, FSA).

April 25, 1975: Buys gas in SLC.
April 28, 1975: Attends Univ. Utah law school.
April 29, 1975: Attends Univ. Utah law school.
April 30, 1975: Buys gas in SLC. Attends Univ. Utah law school.
End of April, start of May, 1975: Ted returns to Julie Cunningham burial-site, Rifle, Colorado, and buries her body (approximately 6 weeks after he murdered her).
May 1975: Carole Ann Boone, Alice Thissen and Joe McLean spend a week with Ted in Salt Lake. Together they visit a homosexual nightclub. According to one source Ted appeared uncomfortable in that setting (uncited). Charles A. Shearer moved into apartment #4 at 565 First Avenue around this time and stayed there until November 1975. According to Shearer, Ted frequented the Sun Lounge, where homosexuals congregate. Regarding homosexuals, Ted said to Shearer: "They are really fun people Charles, happy people who know how to have a good time" (W&M 1980, 119).
May 2, 1975: Melanie Cooley's body found. Detective Thomas Shoemaker of Boulder County Sheriff's Department in talking about Melanie Cooley's case said the victim was found clothed but with her jeans pulled down and unzipped. A blouse was torn in front, and a jean jacket had blood on a sleeve. She had been struck at the base of the skull, probably not going fully unconscious, then struck a second time by a 35-45 pound rock which was dropped on her head. She had scratches on the front of her body where her blouse was ripped open. It was speculated that this might have been the work of a hippie-type individual due to the condition of the pillowcase which was around her neck. Her hands were bound with green nylon cord in front of her body. The pillowcase may have been used as a blindfold, which possibly slipped during a struggle. A portion of the pillowcase blindfold had been torn away. At first her father was a suspect as he had been having sexual relations with Melanie as well as Melanie's girlfriend. The father (Eric "Mountain Horse" Harris) had spent 18 months of a two-year sentence in the state penitentiary for bad checks (Aspen Seminar, November 13-14, 1975).
May 3, 1975: Buys gas in SLC.
May 5, 1975: Buys gas in SLC. (Afternoon) Challenged by security guard in women's high-rise dormitory at Idaho State University, Pocatello. Leaves without being reported to police. Checks into the Holiday Inn, Pocatello.

Lynnette Culver aged 10, 1973. Photo courtesy Carol Culver © 2016.

May 6, 1975: 12:00 noon Abducts Lynnette Dawn Culver (12) from Pocatello, Idaho. Drowns her in a bathtub at the Holiday Inn. Dumps body in Snake River. Lynnette was the second youngest victim after Kimberly Dianne Leach. Lynnette was 12 years 9 months old at the time of her abduction.

The following narrative is derived from an interview between Ted and Idaho Attorney General's Office Chief Investigator Russell Reneau (Mortensen phone interview July 15, 2015 & June 26, 2016). Ted's interview with Reneau took place two days before Ted's execution. It would appear Ted narrowly avoided being reported to police the day before he murdered Culver. As he entered Pocatello driving along the I-15, a high rise women's dormitory on Idaho State University campus caught his attention. Ted admitted to entering the dormitory. However, he soon encountered a male authority figure on the 2nd or 3rd floor. He was immediately stopped; men are not supposed to enter the women's dorms. Ted was asked to leave, and he did so. He admitted to additional attempts to abduct women that evening, but all failed. One reason was the weather; even though it was spring in Pocatello, it was raining and cold and so people were trying to stay indoors. Needing a place to stay, he found a Holiday Inn only a little over a mile down the road and booked a room, signing in with a fake name.

After spending a night alone he woke up the next day and renewed his hunt. Around noon he left the Holiday

Turner Hall, Idaho State Univ.; it is now a mixed dormitory. Photo courtesy Chuck Meeks © 2015.

Inn and headed down Pocatello Creek Road, which runs into East Alameda and then becomes West Alameda (a distance of just under 2 miles from the hotel). There, he came across a lunchtime crowd of kids at Alameda Junior High School, some of whom were leaving school for a small park located south across the road (the park is the most plausible location where Ted picked Lynnette up that we can figure out). The school itself sits at the corner of McKinley and West Alameda. In one report, Lynnette was last seen boarding a bus at Hawthorne Middle School. She was wearing jeans, a red-checkered shirt and maroon jacket with a fur collar. She was seen boarding the bus by the bus driver and several of her friends. The other version is Ted's own confession, wherein he states that he picked Lynnette up from outside Alameda Junior High. In which case, the other sightings of Lynnette are either spurious or conflict with Ted's account. In any account, Ted's confession is the only accurate source we have. According to Russell Reneau:

The former Pocatello Holiday Inn as it stands today. Ground floor rooms conveniently open out on the guest parking lot. Photo courtesy Chuck Meeks © 2015.

> "... she was supposed to meet her boyfriend for lunch when he ran into her, [...] he met her about noon, right outside the school [...] He spent a lot of time talking with her, he had a lot of knowledge about her life, including the fact that they were about to move

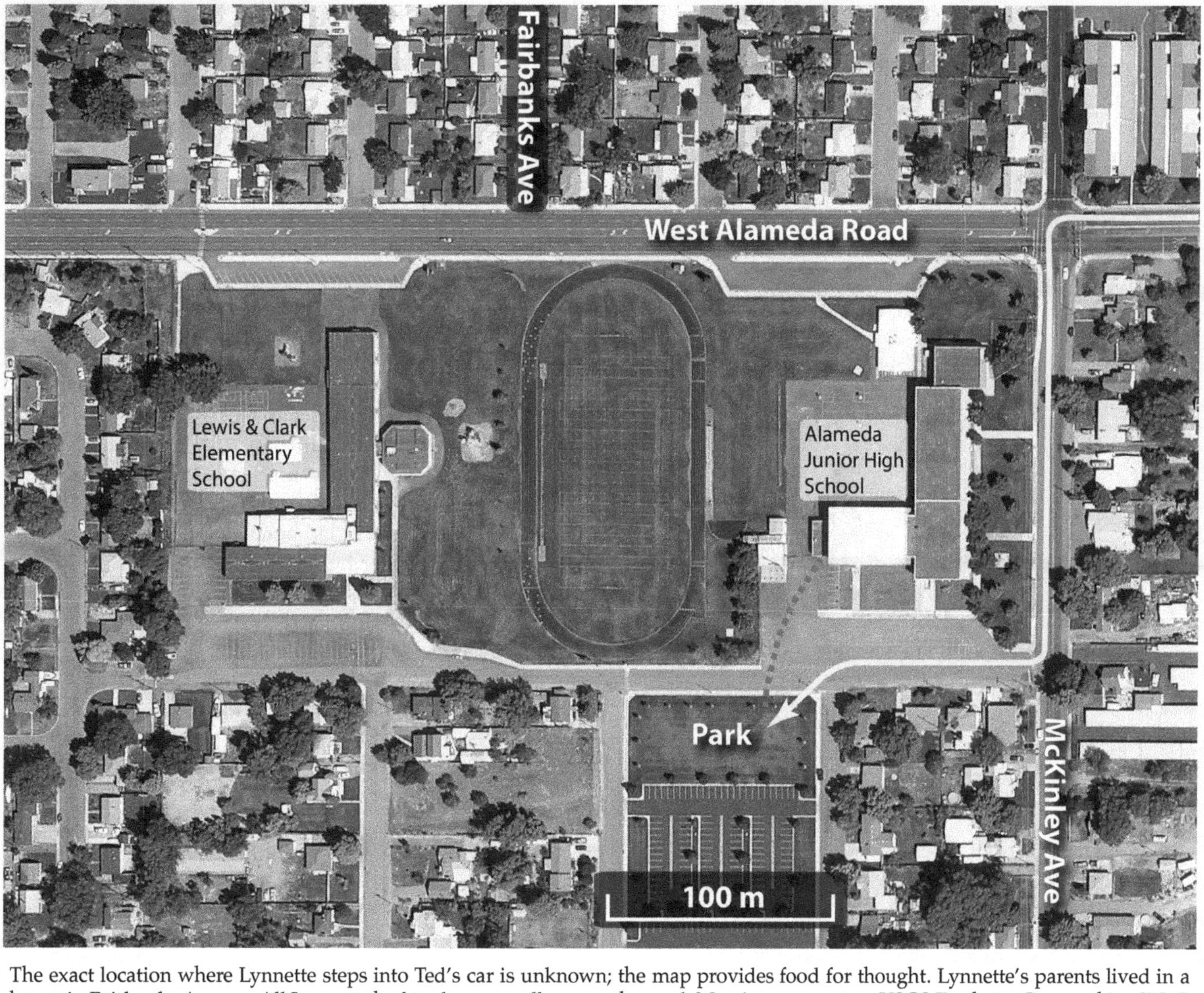

The exact location where Lynnette steps into Ted's car is unknown; the map provides food for thought. Lynnette's parents lived in a house in Fairbanks Avenue. All Lynnette had to do was walk across the road. Map image courtesy USGS Earthstar Geographics SIO © Microsoft Corporation.

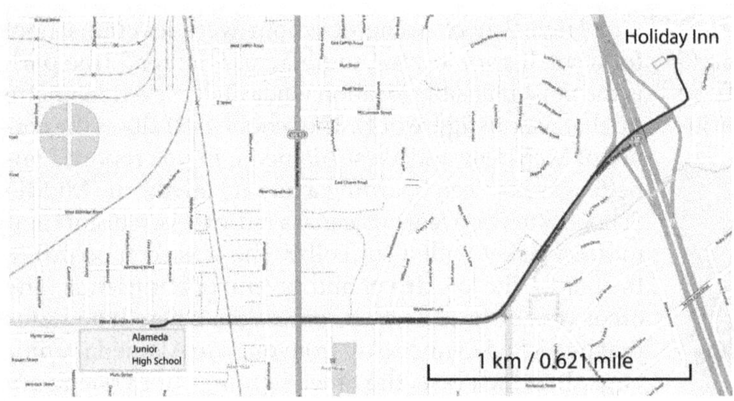

Left: Map showing how close the Holiday Inn is to Alameda Junior High. Map courtesy OpenStreetMap contributors, 2015. Right: An original bath tub in the Pocatello Holiday Inn. Photo courtesy Chuck Meeks © 2015.

> to a larger house so that her grandmother could move in with them, and that turned out to be true. He also said she had a truancy problem at school which the parents denied, but when we checked with the school system that turned out to be true" (January 22, 1989; interview courtesy Chris Mortensen, July 15, 2015).

In a communication with Lynnette's mother, who worked as a high school head mistress herself, the claim that Lynnette had a truancy problem is disputed. Detective Al Kuta, who by fate ended up working the case, was a neighbor and Lynnette had a good relationship with him; she was not rebellious against authority in a bad way.

IDAHO MISSING PERSONS CLEARINGHOUSE

LYNETTE DAWN CULVER

LAST DATE OF CONTACT : 5/6/75

DOB :	7/31/62	**HEIGHT :**	5'02"
GENDER :	FEMALE	**WEIGHT :**	110 lbs
HAIR COLOR :	BROWN	**EYE COLOR :**	BLUE
RACE :	WHITE		

CASE INFORMATION :

LSW RED CHECKARD SHIRT AND MAROON COAT WITH FUR HOODIE AND BLUY JEANS. LAST SEEN WALKING DOWN ELDREDGE RD IN POCATELLO ON 5/6/1975. HAS MOLE ON LOWER LEFT CHEEK.

IF YOU HAVE ANY INFORMATION ABOUT THIS PERSON PLEASE CONTACT :

POCATELLO PD @ (208)234-6100

Russell Reneau, November 4, 2016. Scripps Media © 2016.

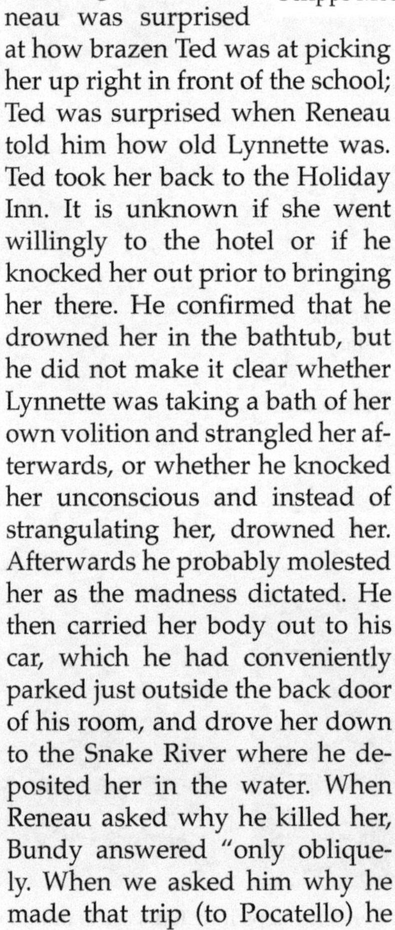

Ted did not tell Reneau what ruse he used to get Lynnette into his car. Reneau assumed he may have used the fake policeman ploy. Another possibility is he may have lured her with cigarettes. Reneau was surprised at how brazen Ted was at picking her up right in front of the school; Ted was surprised when Reneau told him how old Lynnette was. Ted took her back to the Holiday Inn. It is unknown if she went willingly to the hotel or if he knocked her out prior to bringing her there. He confirmed that he drowned her in the bathtub, but he did not make it clear whether Lynnette was taking a bath of her own volition and strangled her afterwards, or whether he knocked her unconscious and instead of strangulating her, drowned her. Afterwards he probably molested her as the madness dictated. He then carried her body out to his car, which he had conveniently parked just outside the back door of his room, and drove her down to the Snake River where he deposited her in the water. When Reneau asked why he killed her, Bundy answered "only obliquely. When we asked him why he made that trip (to Pocatello) he said it was because of 'the madness.' He did not elaborate on that" (*Moscow-Pullman*

Detective Al Kuta (circa 1975). Kuta interviewed hundreds of people. He said Lynnette was reportedly observed by area residents in Fort Hall on the day of her disappearance hitchhiking towards American Falls. All of these sightings, of course, were false; but Kuta didn't know it at the time. Photo public domain.

Daily News, January 24, 1989).

When Lynnette was 5, the Culvers moved to Pocatello, ironically, because they perceived it as a safer environment for children to grow up in. In 1970 the family bought a house in Fairbanks Avenue, just across the road from Alameda Jr High School, which Lynnette started attending in the fall of 1974. Although she was only 11, many people thought she was a teenager. She had dark hair, a long thin nose, and deep set eyes. She had a boyfriend before the first month of school was over. The parents discouraged this, but Lynnette had become quite independent. "The reason I felt that she had run away," wrote Carol, Lynnette's mother, "was, the morning that she came up missing just before she left for school, she said to me, 'What would you do if I didn't come home?' I was in a hurry because of work and I replied something like 'Oh, you will come home. Nothing is going to happen to you.' Well, to this day I wish that I had said, 'If you don't come home my life will be over and my heart will be permanently broken!'"

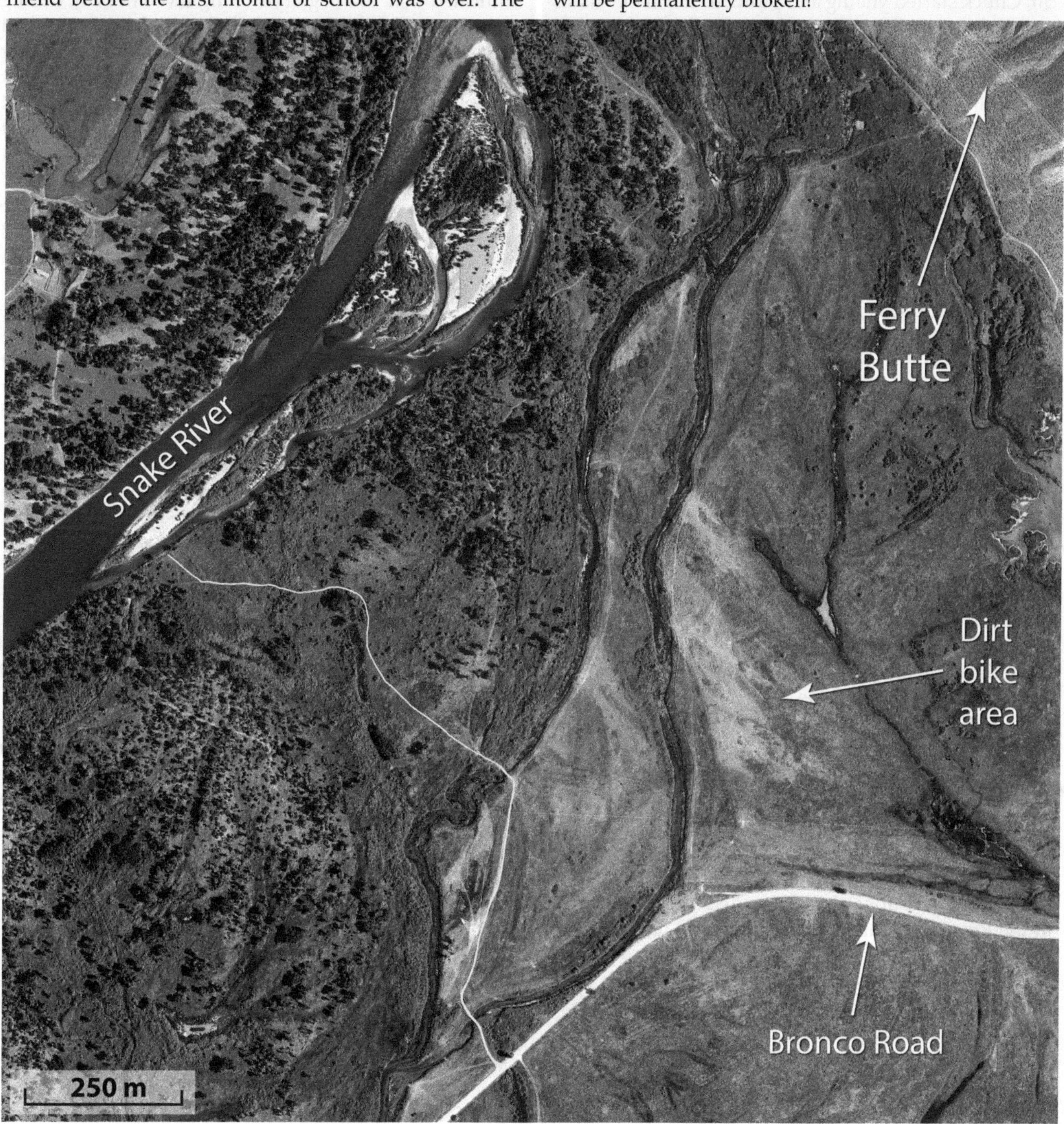

Ferry Butte dirt bike area, 15 miles north of Pocatello, Idaho. This is the best candidate match for the description that Ted gave to Reneau for where he may have put Lynnette's body in the Snake River. The yellow track leading to the river depicts one possible location. Map image courtesy USGS Earthstar Geographics SIO © Microsoft Corporation.

One other curious event may be linked to Ted while he was in Pocatello. Chuck Meeks reported an attempted abduction of his then nearly 9-year-old sister by a man driving a "light blue" VW bug on May 7, 1975, the day after Culver's abduction (personal correspondence April 18, 2015). Chuck, then 12, was walking with his sister when he noticed a man following them in his car. The car screeched to a halt and the man reached out from the passenger side and tried to haul Chuck's sister into the car. Chuck started yelling and punched the man. His sister got away by slipping out of the coat she was wearing, at which point the man drove off. Whether this was Ted, we shall never know, however it is of interest that if Ted was telling the truth about bringing Culver back to the Holiday Inn, then he would have stayed another night as it was already afternoon and past checkout time, which means he was in Pocatello at least two nights. Despite this, we have no information of Ted's whereabouts after Culver's abduction until May 12.

May 12, 1975: Buys gas in SLC.

May 15, 1975: Buys gas in SLC.

May 18, 1975: Buys gas in SLC.

May 22, 1975: Keppel starts work on computerized cross-referencing system to catch "Ted."

May 27, 1975: First working prototype of computerized cross-referencing system ready.

May 30, 1975: Buys gas in SLC.

May 31, 1975: Attends Univ. Utah law school.

June, 1975: Ted grows a beard according to Liz. Liz also reports a strange conversation she had with Ted in June 1975. She said Ted told her there was a report on the radio about rapes which had occurred on 1st Avenue in Salt Lake which is near where Ted lived. The description of the guy involved a beard, and Ted stated "I guess that lets me out."

Sometime during June 1975: Makes a call to Denver, Colorado. [Was this on June 16?]

June 1, 1975: Ted task force reduced to just Keppel & Dunn.

June 5, 1975: Buys gas in SLC. Buys gas in Boise, Idaho (Thompson has this on the 6th of June).

June 6, 1975: Buys gas in Pendleton, Oregon. Buys gas in Ellensburg, Washington. (Friday afternoon) Back with Liz in Seattle. Liz notices Ted's license tag propped up inside the car, but says nothing. Ted puts in a garden at the Rogers' rooming house, a favor he had promised them.

June 12, 1975: Leaves Seattle for SLC. Buys gas in Pendleton, Oregon. Buys gas in Boise, Idaho.

June 13, 1975: Buys gas in SLC.

June 16, 1975: Ted calls the *Denver Post* newspaper (who he spoke to and for what reason is unknown).

June 18, 1975: Attends Univ. Utah law school. Buys gas in Boise, Idaho.

Late June 1975: Carol Booth introduces Ted to her girlfriend Leslie Knudson—a school teacher aged 31 who has a 7-year-old son Josh—at a party hosted by Paul Van Dam, a Salt Lake County prosecutor. Ted and Leslie begin dating about a week later. Ted plays similar role as he did with Liz and her daughter. Regarding Ted, Knudson said she viewed him initially as fairly sociable, although somewhat aloof. She claims that at the party he did not drink much and seemed quite nice. She stated their dates consisted of going to drive-in movies. She said Ted would always include Josh on their dates together. She indicated that Ted began drinking more heavily during the course of their dates together over the summer and that she became very concerned over this. She stated that on one occasion he drank so heavily that he passed out on her living room floor. She claims that other than that he did not seem particularly unusual. She admitted that they had sexual intercourse on several occasions, but she stated, "In my opinion, they were normal relations." She indicated she broke off relations with Ted because he became so moody and depressed that she did not want to continue the relationship. She stated he began wandering around verbally and physically, and told her on one occasion that, "My world is falling apart." She stated that he frequently talked about Liz and how she lost respect for him because he had been dating other girls while engaged to her. She stated that he told her on some occasions that he had political aspirations and wanted to be Governor of Washington State (PIR 1975). Carol Booth made a point of telling authorities that she had never seen someone so obsessed with cleaning their apartment as Ted.

June 23, 1975: Attends Univ. Utah law school.

June 25, 1975: Attends Univ. Utah law school.

Susan Curtis, 1975, women's volleyball team, BYU. Photo courtesy Chris Mortensen © 2016.

June 27, 1975: Abducts Susan Curtis (15) from Provo, Utah, while she was attending the Bountiful Orchard Youth Conference at BYU. Ted said he buried her body along a highway near Clarks Valley area, east of Wellington (near Price) Utah. Curtis coincidentally attended the play at Viewmont High School in Bountiful the same night Kent was abducted.

The following information was obtained from an interview with BYU Lieutenant Arnold Lemmon (Mortensen interview, January 6, 2016). Susan was a sophomore student at Woodscross High, just south of Bountiful, Utah. "… she had agreed with her sister [Barbara] that she would come to the youth conference. […] She rode her bike. She was in pretty good shape. […] It's a Saturday. They're in the Wilkinson Center having dinner, and she had new braces, they'd just been installed. She told her sister that she was going to go back to the dormroom in Helaman Halls to clean her teeth. [...] Her sister was going to the youth conference there, that whole stake was staying in the dormrooms. [...] So this in June of 75, and so she doesn't show up again, and is reported as missing." Examining the BYU campus layout, there is a parking lot between the Wilkinson Center and student housing where the dorms were located. Given that Ted often abducted women in and around carparks, it would appear that this is where he approached her and brought her under control. It would have been a quarter-mile walk along sidewalks and "across a couple of streets" in the fading evening light (*Salt Lake Tribune*, January 27, 1989). The fading light would have given him some, but not complete cover, so it is difficult to say whether he abducted her using stealth or a ruse.

In a last minute confession to Florida State Prison Warden Thomas Barton, (in the BYU Security Police report it states "Assistant Superintendent Turner") where someone had ripped a map out of a book to help with directions, the following exchange occurred:

> Ted: Do me a favor. See that ah ... see that almanac there ah ... open it up ah ... so I'd just like to see a page in it. Well, to ah ... a map of Utah. I think there's something ... that looks like a map of Utah in there.
> Barton: There ain't gonna be one.
> Ted: Oh yeah, there is, ah believe me. You want to look toward the front half. Yeah, all the states are in there. I'll just ... but something to refer to ... Utah ... you can tear the page out or whatever, just so I can ah ... refer to it.
> Barton: You'll have to speak up probably for that little 'mike' to pick up.
> Ted: Is it on?
> Barton: Is the light on?
> Ted: Yeah.
> Ted: January the 24th. 1989. What was the name of that Utah detective, Couch?
> Barton: [Dennis] Couch.
> Ted: There is one more we didn't have time for when

Susan Curtis, 1975 yearbook portrait. Photo courtesy Chris Mortensen © 2015.

1970s aerial of Brigham Young University showing student housing in relation to the Wilkinson Student Center. A large car park was directly on her route. Aerial photo of BYU courtesy BYU archives.

we talked. You should look between ... it's going to be hard ... between Price and Green River. Ten miles south of Price, a road going south ... going south on a road out of Price maybe five miles, 10 miles. There is a side road toward the left or toward the mountains, going east. A quarter of a mile in, this is a dirt road to the left. This is not going to work too well, but I hope we can do something with it. About 200 yards in on the, uh, 100 to 200 yards in on the dirt road ... and to the left, maybe 50 yards, there's the remains of a young woman who disappeared from Brigham Young University in June of 1975. And that's as close as I can get it ... with the map and with what we have here.

Barton: Did you know her name?

Ted: No.

That Ted did not know her name suggests he knocked her unconscious before there was sufficient conversation to learn her name. Susan Curtis' story does not end there. There is a report by a Pat Prine who attended BYU the same year Curtis was abducted. According to Prine:

> It was my first semester back to BYU. It was a cloudy and rainy day and I was walking to my 9 a.m. sewing

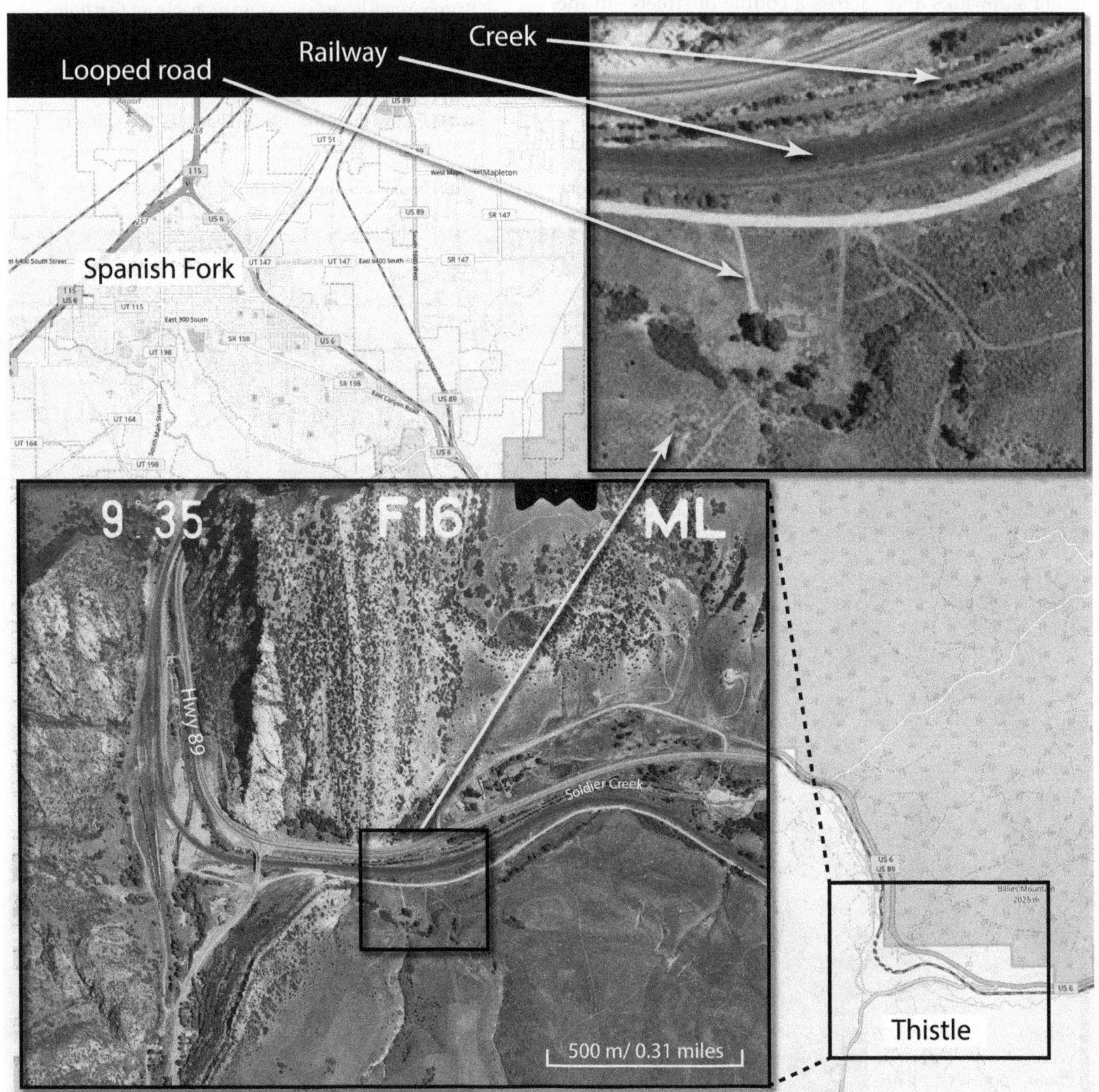

1970 aerial showing hypothetical rape and murder location of Susan Curtis. The location shown (inset, top right) is the first secluded opportunity driving out of Brigham Young University (Provo) via Highway 89. It has all the hallmarks of a Ted Bundy crime scene: a crossing of some description (railway tracks), water (Soldier Creek), a looped side road, and trees. Aerial photograph courtesy USGS.

class. As I approached the Wilkinson Center under the covering on the patio, I saw a handsome gentleman in a nice suit. His eyes were glued to me as he watched me approach. I remember how it flattered me. As I got closer, he said, "Hi, do you go to school here?" I told him yes. "I've seen such good people here," he said. "I'm from out of town and I need to go to downtown Provo to speak," he said, eyeing my umbrella. "Could you walk me to my car so I don't get my suit stained in this rain," he asked. Here was my chance to be a good example of what a member of the LDS church should be. I wanted to be of service to him. I told him, "Yes, I have a few minutes before my class begins." I had a beige three-quarter length rain coat with a wrap-around belt, and a pink umbrella to cover us both on our trip to his car. We walked through three different sections of the parking lot, each taking us farther away from the Wilkinson Center and from my class, so I asked, "Where's your car?" He said that it was just a little bit further. We walked a few more steps, when all of a sudden I felt him grab the belt on the back of my coat. I thought, there's no reason he needs to be doing that. I turned around and jerked hard and got away from him. I ran back quite a ways and then I turned and looked at him. I thought I had made a mistake and had overreacted, shattering my image of a nice BYU student. He said, "Why did you run away – I wasn't going to hurt you! Come back and get your umbrella." I said, "No thank you, you can keep it," and I kept running (*The Spectrum*, July 6, 2015).

Shelley Robertson circa 1975. Photo courtesy KCA.

June 29-30, 1975: Shelley Kay Robertson (24) goes missing from Golden, Colorado. Shelley's father Mr. Elmer B. Robertson stated that Shelley was observed hitchhiking in the vicinity of 34th and Sheridan by one Mel Harvey. According to Mr. Harvey, she was observed getting into a red pickup with a bushy-haired white male. Gary Robertson (Shelley's brother) stated that blue denim cutoffs, a blouse, a brown and white striped dress, and "Earth" sandals were missing from Shelley's wardrobe.
June 30, 1975: Attends Univ. Utah law school.
July 1975: Liz and Ted in Ogden. Liz attempts one last-ditch effort to secure marriage proposal from Ted. Ted promises her for the coming Christmas (1975). Liz tells her parents, but the proposal is met with "silence." Meanwhile Ted continues his relationship with Leslie Knudson and son Josh in SLC. Around this time there is a report of Ted sneaking in on a female neighbor at 565 First Avenue and waking up a female friend staying there – he "pinched her between the legs." Also in July, Ted lost his job as Bailiff Hall Night Manager (for showing up drunk, or late or both) and got a new job as a security guard with the Univ. Utah for $2.50 per hour.
July 1, 1975: Attends Univ. Utah law school. Detective Kathy McChesney assigned to the Sex Crimes Unit.
July 2, 1975: Attends Univ. Utah law school.
July 3, 1975: Attends Univ. Utah law school.

Nancy Baird (undated). Photo public domain.

July 4, 1975: 5:45 p.m. Suspected abduction of Nancy Baird (23) from a Layton service station, Utah. Nancy was working as a clerk for a Fina gas station when she was found to be missing. She was last seen by a patrol officer approximately 15 minutes before her disappearance. She was wearing shorts, halter-top and a smock, all blue in color. The smock had a 'Fina' station logo. Her purse and money were found behind the counter and her car was parked at the station. Baird has small scars on the inside of each wrist, and was known to wear a ring on her pinky finger, with a ruby stone and two smaller rubies on either side, set in gold. Her abduction is associated with a sighting of a truck.
July 7, 1975: Attends Univ. Utah law school.
July 8, 1975: Attends Univ. Utah law school.
July 9, 1975: Buys gas in SLC. Attends Univ. Utah law school.
July 10, 1975: Attends Univ. Utah law school.
July 11, 1976: Collection of bones belonging to Krista K. Blake are found in a shallow grave at Tukes Mountain, Clark County, Washington.
July 12, 1975: Buys gas in SLC.
July 14, 1975: Buys gas in SLC.
July 15, 1975: Buys gas in SLC. Attends Univ. Utah law school.
July 16, 1975: Attends Univ. Utah law school.
July 17, 1975: Keppel picks up the rug that was next to Lynda Healy's bed from Mr Skavlem, father of Karen Skavlem who lived together with Healy and the other girls. The rug had not been cleaned since removal. Keppel hands it over to K. Sweeney for processing.
July 18, 1975: Ted sits for Univ. Utah law school final exam. Sweeny finds no bloodstains on the rug; only blond hairs.
July 19, 1975: Attends Univ. Utah law school.
July 21, 1975: Buys gas in SLC.
July 23, 1975: Attends Univ. Utah law school.
July 24, 1975: Attends Univ. Utah law school.
July 25, 1975: Attends Univ. Utah law school.
July 26, 1975: Attends Univ. Utah law school.
July 30, 1975: Attends Univ. Utah law school.
August 1975: Leslie Knudson breaks off her relationship with Ted. She reported that Ted was drinking more and more heavily. He once passed out in her apartment. Ted often talked about Liz. She felt she couldn't deal with it anymore and made the decision to end it. Also sometime in August 1975, Liz went to Keppel's office in Seattle and made incriminating statements against Ted.

August 1, 1975 (around this date): It appears Ted approached a BYU student around this time. Her name is Susan Crawford (*Detroit Free Press*, March 8, 2015). The event took place in the Wilkinson Center. Crawford had been on the phone signing up for a Spanish class. It was a hot August day, sometime around August 1st. Based on her recollection, Ted had watched her from somewhere around the entrance area while she was on the phone. When she finished, and as she walked for the exit, he placed himself strategically between her and the exit and initiated conversation: "You have such long, beautiful hair, you really are a pretty woman. I love your eyes. They are captivating. May I walk you to your car?" In disbelief that someone could be so complementing to her, and thinking about the diamond ring on her finger which had been in plain sight the whole time, she said: "Thank you, but my husband is going to pick me up shortly," and flashed the ring at him. It was a lie. Her husband wasn't going to pick her up, but at the time she could think of nothing else to say to this alluring man with his "deep," "rhythmic," "poetic voice" and "handsome dimples" as he smiled and spoke. At hearing her rebuttal, he turned and nearly ran out the building. She stood there baffled by his quick and strange departure. There were no explanations like, "I'm sorry, I didn't realize you were married," or "It was nice talking to you." He simply turned, walked away and exited. Fourteen years later, while watching the news on TV regarding his execution she realized that this was the man who had approached her that day.

Susan Crawford, 1974. Photo courtesy Susan Crawford © 2015.

We have no way of verifying if Ted really was the man that spoke to Crawford that day, but everything about his approach and behavior is consistent with his M.O., right down to the response he displayed on finding out she was married. It appears Ted was willing to fish in the same pond on this occasion. Perhaps it was a reaction to his recent breakup with Leslie Knudson. His relationship with Liz was failing, he lost his job as a caretaker at Ballif Hall, and now a single mother who he was dating had dropped him. All of these were potential triggers that could have driven him to go out hunting.

August 8, 1975: Buys gas in SLC.

NOTES

Ted's adult years was a time when he went all out and killed on an almost clock-like schedule. The accepted version of Ted's modus operandi for this period is that he was into stranger killing. This has led at least two Bundy authors to use the word "stranger" in the title of their books. The timeline presented here shows that this interpretation somewhat prematurely puts a stamp on Ted that may not fit the real picture of how he always operated.

Bill Hagmaier in his interviews with Ted learned that Ted was a meticulous researcher. Of his approximately 33 victims, Ted killed only 5 or so spontaneously. The rest he planned in great detail. This included stalking the victim in the days leading up to the abduction, preparing props to gain the victim's trust, entering the victim's property to prepare entry and exit routes, and pre-selecting a rape location as a site to play out his murderous fantasies, including post-mortem activities with the body. Sometimes the rape site and location where he discarded the body were different. While it is true that Ted did not personally know most of his victims, it is not true of all his victims. We now know that he had personal interactions with at least two, and probably knew several others indirectly through friends and acquaintances. Moreover, he didn't immediately clobber all his victims into unconsciousness before raping and killing them, but he also "chatted up" a few of them up as he went along.

Authorities discovered that Ted knew Lynda Healy and stalked her before abducting her. Keppel claimed that "after her disappearance he would go over to her apartment frequently to visit her roommates" (Aspen Seminar, November 13-14, 1975). Ted played racquet ball with Tom Sampson, a friend of Donna Manson's at Evergreen State College. Ted's childhood friend Terry Storwick jogged with Susan Rancourt at Central Washington State College, Ellensburg. Ted claimed he chatted up and entertained Brenda Ball in his apartment before killing her. He claimed he chatted up Roberta Parks before he revealed his true motives to her. And he role-played a police officer in his attempt to abduct Carol DaRonch, spending at least 15 minutes with her before he also revealed his true motives to her. Then came Nancy Wilcox and Laura Aime (note: we have no evidence he previously met or chatted up Melissa Smith). According to Nancy's mother, Ted flirted with her daughter on several occasions before he finally abducted her on the 2nd of October 1974. Laura Aime's case is even more instructive. The accepted narrative is that hers was a stranger killing. But we now know from other sources who witnessed the days and weeks leading up to her disappearance that Ted insinuated himself into her life, and regularly socialized with her before he eventually abducted, raped and killed her. These facts cast new light on Ted's M.O. during this period. It forces us to reconsider his development as a serial killer and points to a more elaborate evolution than previously conceived.

This is not the only re-write of Ted's narrative that we have to consider. We have already covered what may have happened during Ted's failed abduction of DaRonch, but the question of what happened next, after he abducted Debbi Kent, is still very much in the air. Here we examine this crime in greater detail. The first issue that needs to be resolved is Ted's pay phone call to Liz at 11:52 p.m. SLC time. We are now in the position of expanding on this call, since the Dennis Couch confession was recently released (February 18, 2015). In that confession we find the following conversation:

> Couch: If it didn't take place in the schoolyard, did it take place in your car, or …?
> Bundy: No … the place where I lived. [565 First Avenue]
> Couch: You took her home?
> Bundy: Right. […] yeah, it was at the residence.
> Couch: So what, did you take her to your residence and then down here all in the same night? [Indicates map location where he buried her]
> Bundy: No.
> Couch: Or keep her there for a period of time.
> Bundy: No, yes. I did keep her there for a period of time, couple, well, day, 24 hours.
> Couch: Is that right? Was she alive during that time period?
> Bundy: Let's see, during half of it.

In summarizing this conversation, it appears Ted is saying he took Debbi to 565 First Avenue and killed her there. We have the following facts for comparison:

a) Ted abducted Debbi between 10:20–10:30 p.m.
b) He left Viewmont around 10:50 p.m.
c) He called Liz from a pay phone at 11:52 p.m.

It is now time to unpack these items, but before we do, we need to preface our discussion with a disclaimer. In Ted's own words:

> I can see through a guy very quickly. It's fascinating when somebody comes to me, I know when they are bullshitting me, I know when they're not. I know when what they're telling me is real, and when they're telling me is a fantasy. And I've had a guy do both of this. It's a curious, curious situation. I had a guy sit down just tell me stories, I know he's telling me stories, and yet also know, that essentially he'd done what they said he did, but he had a need to tell it a different way, so he'd look different, he'd look better. In his own mind, okay, he wasn't the savage, lust-filled killer, but he was this guy that just … he just got mad. [Dry laugh] "The bitch made him mad." [Dry laugh] It's very curious how guys, some guy, some man will commit a series of murders, over the years, in their own mind, sort of rewrite history, to satisfy their needs, and they will lie (*Terrible Secrets* 2012, date of actual recording unknown).

What this technically means is Ted essentially did what they said he did. So he wasn't lying to Couch when he said Debbi was alive during half of it. It's just that he put his own spin on what actually happened. Did Ted tell the unvarnished truth? Hell no. He told the basic details, that's about it. He never went into specifics. Not even with Hawkins. He confessed to the extent that there was evidence against him, and he *knew* what evidence was stacked against him. He played on that. He always said it didn't affect him, but that was probably just bravado. He knew they had him by the short-and-curlies. But ever a man to keep his image, he painted rosy pictures of his heinous rapes and murders.

If we really want to understand Ted's behavior when he was raping and killing, all we have to do is look no further than Gerard Schaefer. He sets the benchmark for ghoulishness. Schaefer called Ted a ghoul, and he was almost certainly right. But Ted spares us all that. He leaves it to our imaginations. But here enters the problem. If we just run with our imaginations, we'd be just as much victims of Ted's fantasies as he was. The best way out of that problem is to go back and start from first principles, do due diligence to the evidence, keeping in mind Ted's need to rewrite history.

So Ted has Debbi, and he's racing away from Viewmont. Now, in Sullivan's narrative, Ted takes her straight back to 565 First Avenue and from there calls Liz close to midnight. According to Sullivan, Ted's need to call Liz after abducting Debbi was his way of stepping back from the crevasse of complete insanity (Sullivan 2009, 118). In Sullivan's narrative, Ted has Debbi at 565 alive in his car or, as he put it, hauled her up the fire escape ladder. Examine the picture of the eastside fire escape and it is clear that Ted did not carry Debbi up to his room via that route. So Ted is calling Liz in a chaotic state of mind, about to completely break down into a whimpering wreck, or start running around like a madman, shouting and waving his arms. Let the reader observe that these are the general stereotypes of "complete insanity."

In contrast to this, what appears to have actually happened is Ted called Liz from a pay phone at 11:52 p.m. and according to Liz, it went like this:

> November 8 [1974], a Friday. That was the day my parents had left Seattle to go home. Ted had called me late that night. I had tried to reach him earlier but there was no answer. I had fallen asleep on the couch and when he called I had a hard time waking up. He had gotten impatient with me and almost hung up. I kept saying, "Wait a minute, wait a minute," and then when he waited I had nothing to say. He said to call him in the morning. It was about 11:00 P.M. here, so it would have been midnight in Utah. That was almost proof that he hadn't been out abducting women that night, wasn't it? (Kendall 1981, 83).

The eastside fire escape at 565 First Ave. leading up to Ted's room which Sullivan referred to as Ted's "lair" (Sullivan 2009, 87). This is the original that was put on some time late-60s. A climber would have to fit two people through the barely shoulder-width hole in the landing. Note the first rung does not start until practically head-height, so at the very least a person would have to haul up a portable ladder after ascending! Maybe Ted was Houdini? Photo courtesy Chris Mortensen © 2016.

This description of Ted on the phone paints a picture of an impatient man. He does not sound like a man needing to hang on the phone just to hear the voice of the woman who might draw him back from the brink of "complete insanity." But that is not all. It seemed like Ted was so normal during that call that Liz questioned whether he could ever be the rapist and murderer she suspected he was! Is she being sarcastic? If Ted called her from his room at 565 it makes sense to assume he wasn't out monstering; the call from the pay phone, if anything, should have hoisted a red flag in her mind, that he was out and about, and when he was out and about, he was

SUPPLEMENTARY REPORT — Bountiful Police Department

Type of Crime or Complaint	Day of Week	Date of this Report	Case No.
ATTEMPT TO LOCATE	WEDNESDAY	SEPT. 17, 1975	9340-74

She was asked if she could think of anything else unusual. She stated in trying to think back and remember as near as she could recall she had received a phone call that she thought was on a Friday night as near as she could remember which was the same night that one of the girls in the Salt Lake area disappeared, possibly, that of Debra Kent. She stated it was unusual for him to call from a pay phone.

She was asked if he had ever been violent and had ever hit her. She stated he had not. The only time he had hit her they had been out drinking one night, got into an argument and she stated go ahead and hit me and he did.

Typed by	Copies to	Officers Assigned & Writing Report
BRUSCHKE	FILES/INVESTIGATORS	DETECTIVE BEAL (SEE PAGE 5)

Follow up Assigned to	Case Is	Closed	Cleared	Arrest Docket No.	Unfounded
	ACTIVE				

hunting. But Liz doesn't appear to be sarcastic, or even rhetorically ironic. She seems to be genuinely looking for ways to exonerate her man.

So why was Ted calling from a pay phone, and why was he so impatient? This is where we have to draw on a statistical model of Ted, appealing to the most likely things he would do given the task at hand, his state of mind, and his immediate goals.

We know Ted went about his abductions and rapes in a fairly orderly manner. We know he planned many of them well in advance. In this case, after the failed DaRonch abduction he drove the 23 miles to Viewmont High as if he knew where he was going. He chose a location where he could dive into the swirling vortices of a new social scene, enter during maximum social chaos, when people were milling around to see a school production. Yet his pathetic attempts at convincing Raelynn Shepherd to help him, his sexual innuendo, shows just how loose he had become. The DaRonch failure did something to him. It feels like he is throwing everything but the kitchen sink at it. He tries a woman in the carpark. She saw right through him even if she didn't see the more sinister aspects of his scheme. He was reported to have come back disheveled around 10:40 p.m. and was spotted in the auditorium. We have a wealth of information for the time he was at Viewmont High so it is relatively easy for us to draw picture of what happened. Once he has Debbi, however, he is gone for a full hour, a period for which we know nothing about. Making assumptions here is much harder.

We skipped the part where he gets Debbi, because in truth, we have very little evidence of that event. We know he didn't blitz her ninja-style because there were reported screams. These were described as alarm calls, not the innocent cries of a playful teenager. This means Debbi had time to react. It seems that there was a struggle. There are at least two possibilities. He may have propped a crowbar behind one of the wheels of his car and used that to attack Debbi. But if he used this method there would probably be no screams. Additionally, there would be no reason for his dishevelment. The other scenario is he approached her from behind and got her in a choke hold, but she somehow managed to struggle and scream. During the struggle, as he dragged her to his car, he became disheveled (perhaps by her grabbing his clothes). A final possibility is that he did something no one has ever suspected: he strangulated her to death right there and then in the car park and stuffed her in the trunk of his car. The official narrative is that she was very much alive when he sped away from the car park, but it seems that keeping a conscious victim in his car for around 10 minutes while he was in the auditorium is an incredible risk. Assuming there was a struggle after which he knocked her unconscious and left her bound and gagged in his car, how could he be sure of the condition she was in? How much of her state could be accounted for by his attack, and how much by her feigning? Would she wake up and scream or make sounds that could potentially attract help? She had already cried out. Would someone come and investigate? Ted would not want to be thinking about those kinds of things while he was away for those 10 minutes. Thus, there is a very real possibility that he killed her by strangulation before returning to the auditorium, and together with the struggle this accounts for his dishevelment. Moreover, returning to the auditorium temporarily removes him from the scene of the crime while potential witnesses arrived looking for the source of those cries for help as well as creates an apparent continued presence in the auditorium during the time of Debbi's disappearance.

What happened next? We know that at the very latest he probably started hunting as early as 6:00 p.m., so it has taken him a full five hours to finally get what he was looking for, and for that he has exposed himself and taken some serious risks. So what does he do? Assuming Debbi is still alive when he drives out of the car

A hypothetical route that Ted might have taken after abducting Debbi Kent. The Abduction-Rape interval data suggests Ted often raped and murdered his victims as close to the site of abduction as feasibly possible. Sites commonly featured looped sealed gravel roads (e.g., powerline access roads), a crossing (e.g., bridge, railway), water, trees, access to a highway. The site shown here is about 2.5 miles from Viewmont High and meets many of the criteria (inset enlarged). Data composited from 1970, 1972 aerials courtesy geodata.geology.utah.gov. Inset and infill courtesy USGS Earthstar Geographics SIO © Microsoft Corporation.

park, does he drive straight back to his apartment at 565 First Avenue and rape and kill her there, then go to a pay phone and make that impatient call to Liz, or does he do what he statistically used to do every time he got a victim in his control, drive to a secluded pre-planned location and there, in the privacy and comfort of his own fantasy, do what he wanted without a care in the world?

We choose the latter scenario, because that is almost certainly what Ted actually did. If we take Ted's word literally, that he killed Debbi at 565, then we'd have to address a whole raft of practical problems that Ted would have had to face (since he was no evil superhero). We will address these shortly. In the meantime, we will assume the probable, not the fantastical. Therefore, it is most likely that Ted took Debbi to a nearby secluded area as fast as he could once he left Viewmont High, and there acted out his murderous fantasies. The most likely location, given the map at the time, was the Farmington Bay area west of the I-15 about 2 miles north of Viewmont High, 5 minutes drive at most on back roads. Since Ted drove the 23 miles from Fashion Place Mall to Viewmont High directly, as if he knew what he was doing, we can raise the possibility that he probably already scoped out the Farmington Bay area in advance. It makes sense given what we know about his past behavior.

One supporting argument for the straight shot to the Farmington Bay area is Ted's brain. We know he was intoxicated with alcohol that night. We could also suggest cannabis was in that mix, since we know he was smoking a lot of it around that time. He got into an argument with Liz about it. She was concerned about the effect it was having on him (Ira Beal report, September 18, 1975). Charles Shearer, a roommate at 565 said: "He used to come over to our place and smoke dope and drink with us all the time. Then, the next day he'd go to church and not want to have anything to do with us" (Salt Lake County Sheriff's Office, November 30, 1975). So we can reasonably assume cannabis was in his system at some unknown level. Combined with the alcohol that we *know* was in his system, and *his* brain, leaves us with a dangerous mix of heightened fantasy activity and lowered impulse inhibition. This makes it even more likely that he would want to satisfy his lust as soon as possible after getting Debbi in his control. One final corroboration of this supposition is that Ted once admitted to Polly Nelson that he sometimes wished he did not ravage and kill his victims so rapidly after gaining control over them. He wished he spent more time lingering over their lives (Nelson 1994, 294). We see this at Chi Omega, his ability to visit an extraordinary amount of violence and sexual activity on victims in a short space of time. In that instance, he did it right next to the rooms of other people, making it possible that he could have taken Debbi up to his apartment at 565. However, the difference with that scenario was that he did not have to transport a live victim up a flight of stairs undetected, then a dead victim back down again, also undetected.

So one possible scenario is Ted rapes Debbi's unconscious or lifeless body at the Farmington Bay area west of Bountiful. What does he do next? We know he made a phone call from a pay phone at 11:52 p.m. Where? Once again drawing on a statistical model, the most likely location is a service station. The frequency with which Ted visited service stations is nothing short of extraordinary. One suggestion for this behavior is that he was paranoid that he might run out of fuel while on an abduction run. This caused him to frequently stop at service stations to top up his gas tank with small amounts of fuel. Service stations would have been closed around midnight at that time, so he could use a pay phone there relatively undisturbed. However, if he had Debbi in the car somewhere, he would not want to hang on a phone very long in case a suspicious patrol officer happened to drive by. Ted was keenly aware of the possibility of getting picked up for a minor misdemeanor, and this would be no exception.

In any case, Ted says, "Let's see, during half of it." So in our narrative, Debbi is killed in the first half, while in Sullivan's narrative, Debbi is killed in the second half. Let us now explore the complexities of Ted killing Debbi at, or inside 565. The first option is in the car out in the parking lot at the back of the property. The key variables are silence and avoiding detection due to a passerby noticing something via ambient light. Another potential problem is that one of the other four roommates (or their friends or partners) could suddenly walk past. After all, it was Friday night around midnight. So doing Debbi right there in the car is extraordinarily risky, and it is highly doubtful Ted would expose himself to that much risk (unlike the larger more anonymous parking lot at Viewmont High). We know this because he wanted to continue doing his thing, he didn't want to get caught! That pretty much deletes the car option. We could of course insert the body-in-the-trunk scenario here. Ted could have killed her at the Farmington Bay area then driven to 565 and parked his car there with her body in the front trunk. The trunk release handle was inside the car, so locking the car effectively locked the trunk.

The second option is the cellar. This is safer from the point of view of mitigating sound and eliminating visual detection. But carrying a live victim, perhaps still bleeding, down the narrow and cramped stairs, into that cramped environment, poses some major physical challenges. The other alternative is the utility shed on the side of the house, but our investigations reveal that it was originally a gardening shed and very small and cramped (it is now a laundry). One way he might do this is if he dragged her underarm style backward (while her legs dragged along the ground). He could then strangle her from the rear, while she sat in the "L" position. The challenge is doing it in complete silence because the walls around the utility shed conduct sound directly into the east-side downstairs apartment. Once done, he'd have to clean up, remove evidence, then transport

The hatch and steps leading down to the cellar at the rear of 565 First Ave. Photo courtesy Chris Mortensen © 2015.

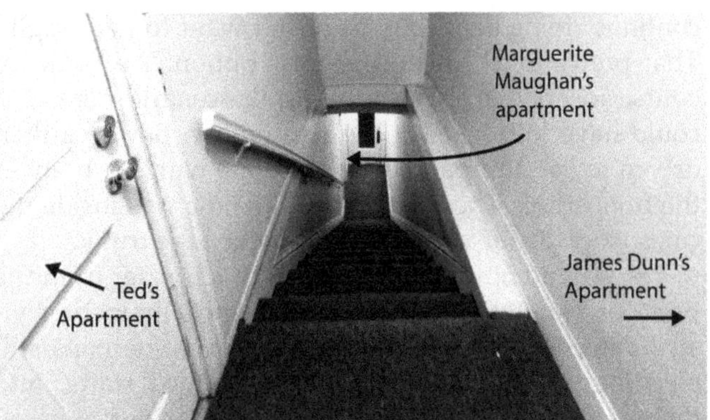

The 2nd floor interior of 565 First Ave. Photo courtesy Chris Mortensen © 2016.

the body back to his car or up to his room.

This last alternative requires further examination. The problem here is that there is only one set of stairs leading to the second floor. It is at the front of the house. It is steep and narrow and does not allow much room for manoeuvering a body. The only viable method here is to carry the victim over the shoulders. But this invites new problems. Her head would be dangling downward and this increases the likelihood of blood dripping, or her head touching the sidewalls. We have to assume this because knocking his victims unconscious was a key aspect of his M.O. in terms of rendering a victim compliant. It would be impossible to carry a kicking and struggling victim the required distance. So once again he'd have to wrap the head in some material; perhaps the victim's own clothing. He could not be seen carrying a victim up the stairs by any residents because there are no reports of Ted ever having had overnight female company, let alone teenage company. In other words, he could not pretend he was carrying a drunk girl if he was caught. If he managed to pull that feat off, carry Debbi all the way from the back of the house (or even from his car parked out front) up to his room, then we should applaud him. Because he now has a new set of problems to solve. To avoid blood transfer or transfer of other fluids such as urine, or excrement, which often accompanies violent strangulation, he needs to do it somewhere that is easy to clean. The obvious location is the bathroom. Real estate records of the property describe it as a Dutch Colonial revival style, five apartments each with their own en suite bathroom. So he takes her into the bathroom. The problem here is bathrooms tend to be noisy places because there is little to absorb sound. So he would have to be extra careful not to make sounds that might imply there was more than one person present. The next problem, after the cleanup, is he has to get her back down to his car again without being spotted. And this time she will be dead, so pretending she is drunk or sick or any of those ruses, can be directly ruled out.

Obviously, taking her up into his room invites an extraordinary amount of risk and a disproportionate amount of work for pleasure. Why would Ted put him-

Ted's old bathroom in 565 First Ave. It lies immediately to the left across the hall from the entrance way. Photo courtesy Chris Mortensen © 2016.

self through so much stress? To lay in the comfort of his own bed for a night with a dead girl in it? The price of this pleasure is the serious risk of exposure during transport, complete silence during the act of rape and murder, and then the clean up during the aftermath. It seems unrealistic. Especially when we add the fact that Ted was property manager at 565, so there was a chance that at any moment someone could knock on his door to pay rent, or ask that something be fixed or whatever. Moreover, James Dunn, who lived next door across the hall was often a visitor at Ted's apartment. He sometimes watered Ted's plants. Ted was best man at his wedding. Given these multiple negative factors, it makes much more sense for him to rape and murder a victim in an unpopulated area, so he could take his time, do what he wanted (with as much noise as he wanted), then dispose of the body in a remote location where he has the possibility of re-visiting it without the headache of having to clean up every last shred of evidence he left behind.

So we can reasonably conclude Ted probably never even dropped by 565 after he abducted Debbi. He may have gone straight to Heber or Park City where it has been suggested he had access to a vacant cabin (correspondence with Chris Eskridge, 6 July, 2015). Alternatively, he could have gone straight down south to the foothills of Fairview where it is claimed he used a camper trailer (Ira Beal telephone interview, 12 July, 2015). He may have even made the phone call from the pay phone at one of those locations (although the call may have also come from within SLC). In which case that would explain why he was impatient to get off the phone with Liz. He would have driven nearly an hour and still not satisfied his lust. We are not stuck fast to the Farmington Bay area west of Bountiful, Heber or Park City, or Fairview. Moreover, we have no dates for Ted's activities for a full week after November 9. The next entry is November 16. This same pattern occurred after Nancy Wilcox; we have no log entries for a full week after her abduction. As a final note, neither Kent nor Wilcox were ever found. There could be any number of reasons for this. In contrast, he left Smith & Aime above ground where they could be potentially found. He said he buried Kent and Wilcox. Could he have done things to Kent and Wilcox that he wanted no one to see?

The 1968 front trunk hood release handle is located inside the glovebox. Once the car was locked, the front trunk was also locked. Photo source Ray Miller 1984, *Volkswagen Bug!: The People's Car.*

It is here that we could introduce the ghoul factor. Perhaps Ted carried only Debbi's head up to his room, which, after all, is a much easier prospect than carrying a whole body. This theory makes Ted's "half of it" a macabre pun. However, even carrying a head is not easy. Ted would have to mitigate leaving any evidence by carrying it inside a garbag, and once up in his room, he would have to wash it in the bathroom. There would be no problem with odors, so he could comfortably spend the night with it in bed if he used something to prevent transfer of biological material to his bedsheets, pillowcase and blankets. The rest of the body could be left relatively safely in his car downstairs. This theory has the added advantage of explaining why he buried Kent and Wilcox, but not Smith and Aime. It doesn't, however, explain

The trunk of a 1968 Volkswagen sedan ("bug"). There is sufficient room to store a body. The tire can also be removed and placed behind the back seat. Photo public domain.

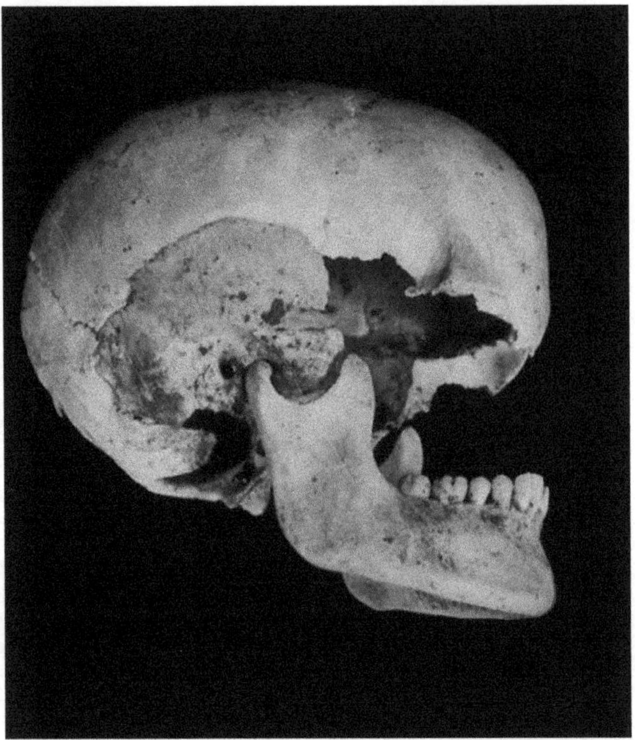

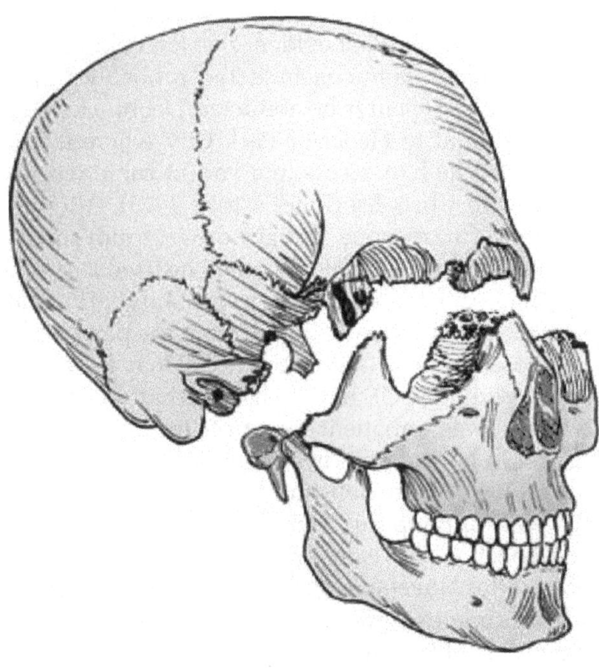

Left: Parks' skull viewed from an inferior lateral aspect. Right: the missing area (viscerocranium) shown in colors. Parks' skull photo courtesy KCA. Skull diagram altered from public domain image.

why he did not also take the heads of Smith and Aime, except in those cases it appears he was short on time. He had a hunting engagement with Liz's father the morning of Smith's abduction, and perhaps he had some other unlogged appointment the morning after Aime's abduction. Finally, in the Wilcox case, Ted also said he brought her back to 565 too. In this case, maybe he did? Either her whole body (dead) or just her head. Each possibility is just as likely. Which means that this same rule could apply to Kent. The conclusion being that our hardest claim is that he most probably lied about bringing live victims up to 565.

While we're on the topic of heads, Sullivan introduces the idea of Ted using them for the purpose of oral sex (Sullivan 2009, 67). He does not introduce it as a hypothesis, but presents it as fact. While we can reasonably expect Ted to have engaged in some sort of ritualistic activity—including sexual activity—with severed heads, what in truth can we really say about his secret behavior with the heads? This is where Sullivan tends towards a biased interpretation of the evidence over a more rigorous approach. For example, he states with respect to Parks' skull: "Investigators noticed that all of her upper teeth were missing" (Sullivan 2009, 128). Having earlier primed the reader with the use of heads for oral sex, is he asking us to imagine that Ted deliberately removed the teeth from Parks' upper jaw so he could insert his penis more comfortably into her ungiving mouth? Why otherwise would he include this detail of her skull to the exclusion of so many other equally important details? For in fact he didn't need to take the investigators' description at face value; detailed photographs of Parks' skull can be obtained from the King County Archives. And these photos reveal the statement that "all of her upper teeth were missing" is actually a gross understatement of the true state her skull was found in. To wit, the temporal bone and zygomatic process were intact (but had a missing styloid processes), while the zygomatic, maxilla, lacrimal, palatine, sphenoid, nasal, and ethnoid bones were all missing. In other words, for all-intents-and-purposes, her viscerocranium (face) was absent. The two possibilities are human versus animal activity. Human activity is more likely as we would see more evidence of scavenger behavior if it was caused by animals, such as teeth punctures, gnawing, cracking of other skull bones, and asymmetry of destruction. Instead, what we find is a very focused symmetrical pattern of damage to the frontal facial area, as if it was done to remove all evidence of Parks' identity. We are not nitpicking here, because this more detailed examination of Parks' skull invites us to think differently about her case compared to what Sullivan would have us believe. Why was her face missing? When did it happen? Post-mortem or pre-mortem? What happened to the missing bones? Ted told Hagmaier that his lashing out at victims' bodies "... was more of an attempt to transport, *conceal*, uh, their remains more than anything else" (Hagmaier interview January 22, 1989; italics added). Ted drove all the way down to Corvalis to get Parks. To Michaud and Aynesworth he said he drove her all the way back to Washington – an extraordinary risk. It is possible he only drove her head back, but given that no vertebrae were found in conjunction with the skull, he may have pulled the skull from skeletal remains elsewhere. This second option makes sense given that her lower jaw was essentially intact, suggesting that he destroyed the viscerocranium with the lower jaw separated. Interestingly, the lower jaw was found intact at Taylor Mountain (with only two teeth missing). However, it was found separated from Parks' skull and in proximity of Rancourt's and Ball's. This suggests that Ted perhaps mixed up Parks' jaw with Rancourt's or Ball's remains. How did this happen? It would appear that the theory that he pulled the skulls at a later date from already mostly skeletonized remains has some plausibility and suggests that Ted had a third, as yet undiscovered, burial site/s for the Washington victims. Keppel noted the vine maple coverage of the skulls was uniform suggesting that Ted threw them there at the same time (note: vine maple falls around October). One theory that can explain this is that Ted went to his third burial site where he deposited Healy, Rancourt, Parks, Ball, and perhaps Manson above ground, but getting there, he found predators had disarticulated some of the remains and dragged them to different locations. In this process, as he hacked off the mostly skeletonized skulls and collected the pieces, he confused Parks' lower jaw with Rancourt's or Ball's, thinking that Parks' lower jaw belonged to Rancourt or Ball. Before taking away the skulls, he smashed Parks' face off using a crowbar, then transported the remains to Taylor Mountain.

In any case, the damage to her skull now takes on a different significance. She was Ted's only known out-of-state victim during his Washington years that we know of (with the exception of perhaps an unknown Oregon case and the mysterious Californian case). It would make sense for him to obliterate her identity because if there was any chance that he was seen with her in Corvalis then he would want to remove any evidence that connected him to that state, and Parks' skull was prime evidence. He would not need to remove such evidence from his Washington victims because he lived in Washington and therefore had an excuse to be there, even if he was coincidentally associated with a victim. Accordingly, we find Ball and Rancourt's viscerocrania intact. We cannot say anything about Healy's skull because only her mandible was found, but we could hazard a guess and say that if her skull was found, it also might have an intact viscerocranium.

We now return to Laura Aime because her timeline overlaps the Debbi Kent abduction. The primary issue is whether Laura was alive or dead when Ted hunted DaRonch and Kent. In our first draft of this book, we took the position that she was alive. However, in lieu of the Kent re-write, we felt it necessary to revisit the Aime case to make sure that our assumptions were founded on good evidence. In the first draft, we went along with the coroner's claim that Aime was killed around November 20, which means that Ted held her alive and captive somewhere while he abducted Kent. Given the reports of Ted accessing a vacant cabin in Heber or Park City, or having a camper trailer down Fairview way, or even using Liz Kloepfer's father's camper trailer up in Flaming Gorge, we concluded that Ted was far more devious than even our wildest expectations. Whichever way we looked at the Aime case, we could not find evidence that the coroner was wrong in his estimate of the time of her death. After all, the coroner was aware of the terrain and climate conditions at the time of her discovery. The ground was frozen, although the snow season had not fully kicked in yet. She was covered in leaves, twigs and caked in mud, and was lying next to a mountain stream. Her eyes were intact and she had undergone relatively little decomposition. Based on this the coroner estimated she had only been there about a week. However, there are some problems with that estimate. The first is that the palmer aspects of the fingers of both hands were dry and wrinkled and had a red-purple appearance. Evidence of mummification. The second is that she had levels of alcohol in her blood that were quite high. While decomposing bodies can produce ethanol for various reasons, and while we cannot rule this factor out in Laura's case, we also know that she was heavily intoxicated the last time she was seen alive. The third is she had no signs of binding marks on her wrists and ankles, something one would expect if Ted was keeping her alive for more than a few days. Even if she was comatose, it would seem logical to bind her in case her condition changed or she made a spontaneous movement.

These three findings challenge the coroner's estimate of her time of death. This opens the door to further research. To this extent, we found an interesting pig study (Parsons 2009) that looked at rates of decomposition in two different scenarios, both at high altitudes (4,300 feet), one in warmer weather (August 6, 2008), and one in colder weather (October 13, 2008). Conducted in west central Montana, the experimental site was primarily covered in conifers and was on a slightly inclined west-facing slope. These conditions favorably match within tolerance the conditions where Laura was found: altitude 5740 feet, conifer forest, date range October 31 - November 27. The main difference was that Laura was found near a water course on a north facing aspect. Also, the pigs were not drained of blood; Laura (and Melissa) were both found partially drained of blood. This last factor is important as it can significantly delay the decomposition process. Naturally enough, the August pig reached advance decomposition within a week of being put down. However, the October pig barely showed signs of decomposition after the first week, and once snow fell, it remained relatively intact through to Spring. This suggests that the coroner's estimates have to be reconsidered. Impor-

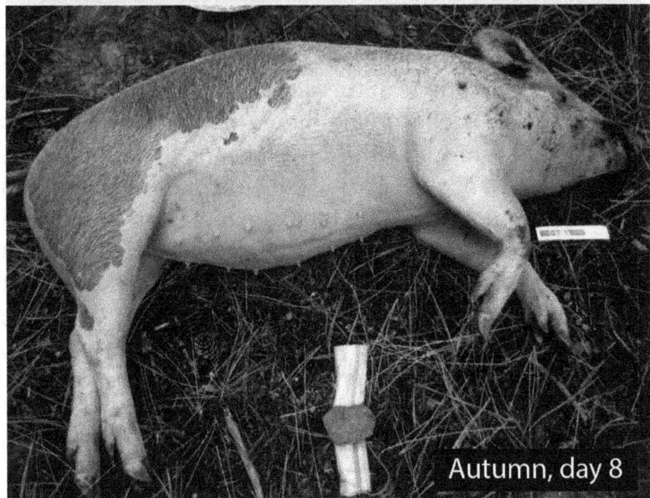

Summer pig weather data

Date	Max T (C)	Min T (C)	Max T (F)	Min T (F)
Aug 6, 2008	37	15	99	59
Aug 7, 2008	37	17	99	63
Aug 8, 2008	30	16	86	61
Aug 9, 2008	32	15	90	59
Aug 10, 2008	26	12	79	54
Aug 11, 2008	27	8	81	46
Aug 12, 2008	30	7	86	45
Average	**31.29**	**12.86**	**88.31**	**55.14**
Stdev	4.39	3.98	7.90	7.16

Autumn pig weather data

Date	Max T (C)	Min T (C)	Max T (F)	Min T (F)
Oct 13, 2008	11	0	52	32
Oct 14, 2008	14	3	57	37
Oct 15, 2008	12	-2	54	28
Oct 16, 2008	11	2	52	36
Oct 17, 2008	20	2	68	36
Oct 18, 2008	16	4	61	39
Oct 19, 2008	16	4	61	39
Oct 20, 2008	12	0	54	32
Average	**14.29**	**1.86**	**57.71**	**35.34**
Stdev	3.30	2.19	5.94	3.95

Parsons' (2009) pig study. Location: the Lubrecht Experimental Forest, west central Montana. Altitude 4,300 feet. "Summer" pig was put down August 6, 2008. "Autumn" pig was put down October 13, 2008.

tantly, bacteria normally enter through the orifices (eyes, nose, ears, mouth, vagina, anus). However, Laura's eyes were intact, and her orifices appeared to be relatively unaffected by bacterial advance. This suggests that Ted could have discarded Laura's body shortly after he abducted her on October 31. In fact, he called Liz at 10:25 p.m. that evening—obviously just before he went out hunting, then called her again at 12:44 p.m.—the two calls being about 2 hours 20 minutes apart. Enough time to abduct and murder Laura.

The official story was that Laura was last seen around midnight at Robinson Park, American Fork. However, a recent interview with Marin Beverige (courtesy Chris Mortensen, July 11, 2018) suggests a more likely scenario is that Ted picked up Laura at Brown's café in Lehi. Marin and her friends actually took to calling Brown's café "Mole Brown's" because the owner had a conspicuous mole on his face. At the time, Brown's café was the only place in Lehi that was relatively immune from Mormon strictures. It was a place where local teens could hang out, smoke cigarettes, drink alcohol, play foosball, pool and generally let their hair down. According to Marin, Ted frequented Brown's café and bought beer for

Weather data for Timpanogos Cave October 31 - November 27, 1974.

Date	Max T (C)	Min T (C)	Rain (mm)	Snow (mm)	Max T (F)	Min T (F)	Rain (inch)	Snow (inch)
Oct 31, 1974	3.89	0.00	37.85	101.6	39	32	1.5	4
Nov 1, 1974	6.11	1.11	6.35	50.8	43	34	0.25	2
Nov 2, 1974	8.89	0.56			48	33		
Nov 3, 1974	6.67	0.56			44	33		
Nov 4, 1974	6.11	0.00			43	32		
Nov 5, 1974	6.67	-2.78			44	27		
Nov 6, 1974	5.00	-1.67			41	29		
Nov 7, 1974	4.44	-1.67			40	29		
Nov 8, 1974	8.89	1.11	5.08		48	34	0.20	
Nov 9, 1974	8.33	-1.11			47	30		
Nov 10, 1974	7.22	-2.78			45	27		
Nov 11, 1974	5.56	-2.78			42	27		
Nov 12, 1974	8.89	-0.56			48	31		
Nov 13, 1974	9.44	1.67			49	35		
Nov 14, 1974	11.1	0.56			52	33		
Nov 15, 1974	11.1	0.56			52	33		
Nov 16, 1974	8.89	-1.67			48	29		
Nov 17, 1974	8.33	0.00			47	32		
Nov 18, 1974	8.89	2.22	1.016		48	36	0.04	
Nov 19, 1974	4.44	-1.11			40	30		
Nov 20, 1974	10.0	0.00			50	32		
Nov 21, 1974	13.8	-3.89			57	25		
Nov 22, 1974	12.2	0.56	8.89		54	33	0.35	
Nov 23, 1974	2.78	-5.00			37	23		
Nov 24, 1974	2.78	-3.33			37	26		
Nov 25, 1974	8.89	0.00			48	32		
Nov 26, 1974	6.11	-2.78			43	27		
Nov 27, 1974	5.55	-2.78			42	27		
Average	**7.53**	**-0.89**			**45.56**	**30.39**		
Stdev	2.78	1.83			5.00	3.29		

Weather data courtesy Cami McKinney, Chief of Resource Management, Timpanogos Cave National Monument (2016).

the kids as an attempt to segue into their group, but he was never accepted. Apparently he smelled because he often slept in his car. At some point he fixated on Laura and began stalking her. He'd sit there and stare at her breasts. Laura responded with "Dude quit, you're burning fucking holes through my chest." Eventually Jerry Bowers intervened to remove Ted from the café. Marin's house was less than a block away and because both her parents worked as truckies and were not home on a regular basis the house became a sort of local hang out in tandem with Brown's café. There was a party at the house that night, and that is when Laura, drunk, said she was going out to get cigarettes (at the café). She was never seen after that again until he body was found up at Timpanogos cave a month later.

By the time Ted took Laura up to Timpanogos cave, just after midnight, snow had started falling. So he probably raped and killed her there immediately and drove back to 565 to avoid getting bogged down (four inches fell that night), just in time to make that call at 12:44 p.m. The only caveat to this new theory is that there appears to be no signs of scavenger behavior on the body. One would expect that a body that had lain next to a relatively unpopulated mountain stream would attract opportunistic carnivores. Perhaps the snow cover protected her; later she was covered in leaves and caked in mud. This could have reduced odors that attracted animals. It is interesting to note that Caryn Campbell who was essentially thrown naked onto snow was soon discovered by coyotes and dragged from her initial resting place. She was discovered a little over a month after her abduction and much of her upper body had been eaten at by scavengers. It had not been disarticulated except perhaps one arm.

The upshot of this new analysis means that we can rule out Ted keeping live victims for extended periods of time before killing and discarding them. Given Ted's recent M.O. with regard to Smith, we can reasonably assume he employed a similar M.O. with Aime and, coupled with the low ground temperatures and blanket of snow, we can safely conclude that her decomposition rate would have been significantly delayed. We are aware that we are contradicting an experienced coroner, however, the coroner did not have contextual data such as Parson's 2009 pig study which demonstrates beyond doubt that decomposition can be delayed by several weeks or more at high altitude and lower temperatures. [Note: air moisture also plays a role. It was very low for the month of October.] Having said this, by extending the time that Laura's body was lying at Timpanogos Cave, we have opened up the door to another possibility, namely, post-mortem visits by Ted. His tire tracks were found at what we guessed was parking area 3. Given the onset of winter, we could assume that visitor numbers were decreasing making it more likely that Ted's tire tracks were preserved for longer before being over-written by others vehicles. If true, then we might assume Ted paid at least one visit to Laura post-mortem. A potential corroboration of this theory is that by leaving her at Timpanogos Cave he had effectively established an alibi for himself. He could walk past, gaze at her body, and if he was seen doing that, he could claim it was a coincidence, that he was in the area hiking.

It should be noted that if the Brown's cafe story is true, and we have every reason to believe it is, then this marks a further shift in Ted's M.O. toward involving himself in the victim's life before abduction. One may well ask, why wasn't a case brought forward identifying Ted as having known Laura before murdering her? There appears to be ample witnesses. We know, according to Fisher's account, that Ted was keenly interested in the Aime case when he obtained her files under the rules of discovery. Perhaps his interest was focused on the same question. Had he been unmasked? The tragedy of the Aime case is that no one pursued this question at the time and represents another missed opportunity to learn more about Ted's M.O. during this period (as well as obtain justice for Laura).

Before we move on, we are left with one other mystery: the draining of the Melissa Smith's and Laura Aime's blood. When Smith and Aime were found, they had tightly wound ligatures around their necks. Both Smith's and Aime's hyoid bones were fractured, showing that the ligature was probably tight enough to occlude bilateral internal carotid arteries. This means that any attempt to perfuse blood from their head wounds would have been seriously impeded. Therefore, it is likely that they were drained prior to the ligature. This presents a problem, because the literature generally assumes Ted enjoyed strangulating his victims. It was part of his sexual thrill. However, by the time half the blood was drained, the victim will have fallen into an irreversible state of unconsciousness, thereby defeating any enjoyment Ted might get from the act of strangulation. How are we to redress this paradox? Are we to argue he strangled the girls to death first then drained their of blood? This means that Ted would have had to loosen the ligature to drain their blood (assuming he angled their bodies in a head down orientation), then re-tighten it before discarding their bodies. Ted the artist making a statement. For obvious reasons we don't find this argument very convincing. The partial answer to the paradox is that the estimates of how much blood was drained from Smith's and Aime's bodies may have been exaggerated. We have to entertain this theory, because so far authorities have been in error on a number of issues, and therefore there is the possibility that they are wrong on this one too. The more realistic conclusion is that Ted strangled Smith and Aime after he had battered and raped them, not for a sexual thrill, but to make sure they were dead when he left them. In all likelihood, he did not want to make the same mistake he made with Karen Sparks. In support of this, we have the Tallahassee case where three victims survived, suggesting that during his earlier crimes Ted probably encountered cases where a heavy battering did not always kill his victims and that manual strangulation was required to finish the job. Despite this conclusion, it still raises other questions. Smith, for example, was found with a deep penetrating wound at the back of her head "approximately 6 inches above the top vertebra" (Ben Forbes police report, October 29, 1974). This was initially thought to be the result of a gunshot wound, but was later revised on autopsy as being caused by blunt forced trauma. The question we have to ask is when did this wound, which would have been the source of her blood loss, occur? If Ted did it at Oak street, he would have had been saddled with the problem of Smith bleeding out in his car. Given that he discarded Smith probably around midnight and had a very early morning appointment with Liz's father in Ogden around 6 hours later (to go on a hunting trip with him), it would seem that the last thing Ted would have wanted was the burden of cleaning the interior of his car. We have to surmise, therefore, that his initial attack on Smith was not fatal, but designed to render her compliant. It leads us to the shocking conclusion that he must have struck the penetrating head wound later on, possibly outside his car but *before* he dragged her by her feet uphill about 150 feet to the location where he discarded and strangled her. On wonders whether this left a blood trail which may have been washed away by rain before the body was found. In any case, until further crime scene evidence is released, we are left with more questions than answers.

Fortunately, in some cases, we have been able to provide answers to some of the Bundy myths out there. A striking example is Keppel's claim that a photo of a parked-in VW at Lake Sammamish on July 14, 1974, showed Ted sitting in the driver's seat, meaning that it was *his* car (top left panel in photo of VW bugs) (Keppel 2012, 44). In a good example of crowd-sourcing, one of our facebook contributors discovered a fatal flaw in Keppel's theory. This came about because we were chasing a different rabbit. We thought it couldn't be Ted's car because it was missing a roof-rack. It turns out we had the wrong image in our minds. It was actually a ski rack. Then we remembered we had read something about Ted mentioning a "ski rack" to Keppel. He said the car in the

Top left panel: Zoom in on the Lake Sam VW. Top right panel: Passenger side on view of Ted's VW. Bottom left panel: Rear view of Ted's VW. Bottom right panel: Front view of Ted's VW. Photos courtesy KCA.

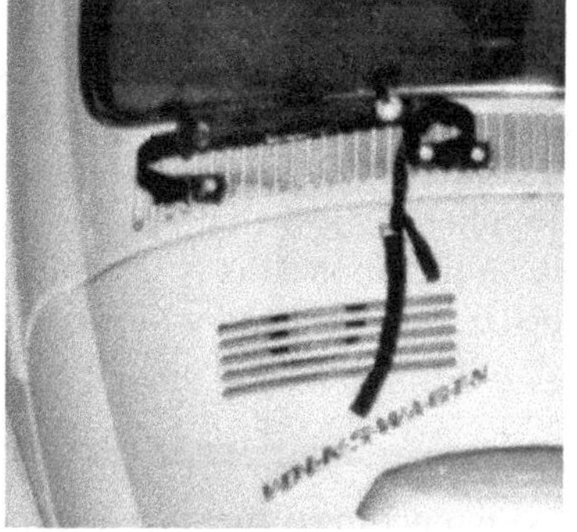

Closeup of the ski rack mounted on the rear of Ted's VW. Photo courtesy KCA.

photo was missing a ski rack, so it couldn't be his car since his car had a ski rack on at Lake Sammamish. But here our contributor pointed out that the VW ski rack was a flimsy affair that clipped on the back of the engine hood. It could be easily taken off and put back on again. Attention now turned to that hood, because it has a particular air intake slot pattern. The contributor discovered that the air intake slots on Keppel's photo and the slots on Ted's actual vehicle were different (Ted wasn't using someone else's VW that day). Further research revealed that the slots first appeared on the 1968 coup but not sedan (they appeared on the sedan in 1970). This raises the possibility that Ted either added a new engine hood after he acquired the car, or he acquired it already in its modified state. For example we know he visited Welch Fun Cars in SLC in November 1974. He may have changed the original engine lid to a 2-slot to improve engine cooling, something he might want to do considering all the driving he was doing. Alternatively, it could have been a reaction to the failed abduction of DaRonch. However, the two rear mounted passive reflectors quash those theories. They come standard on the 1970 body. They mount onto the rear bumper. Not something you would want attached to your car if you don't want it to be visible on a dark side road. Yet Ted didn't remove them. This suggests they came with the original body and Ted was too lazy to take them off. Therefore, it is more likely that Ted bought a hybrid VW: 1968 chassis with 1970 body parts. The most plausible explanation for this is that the original car was probably in an accident and a new engine lid and bumper was installed before it was sold to Ted. As for the claim that Ted was sitting in the vehicle when it was photographed, a more careful look reveals that it is a reflection of a tree branch on the driver-side window. One can also see the bottom half of a man in the distance through the front windshield. All of these items in the image can be made out using a reader's magnifying glass, a common implement that was abundant in the 1970s.

Another example is Ann Rule's claim that Ted had beaten Karen Sparks with "a metal rod wrenched from the bed frame" (Rule 1980, 49). As a coincidence, KCA

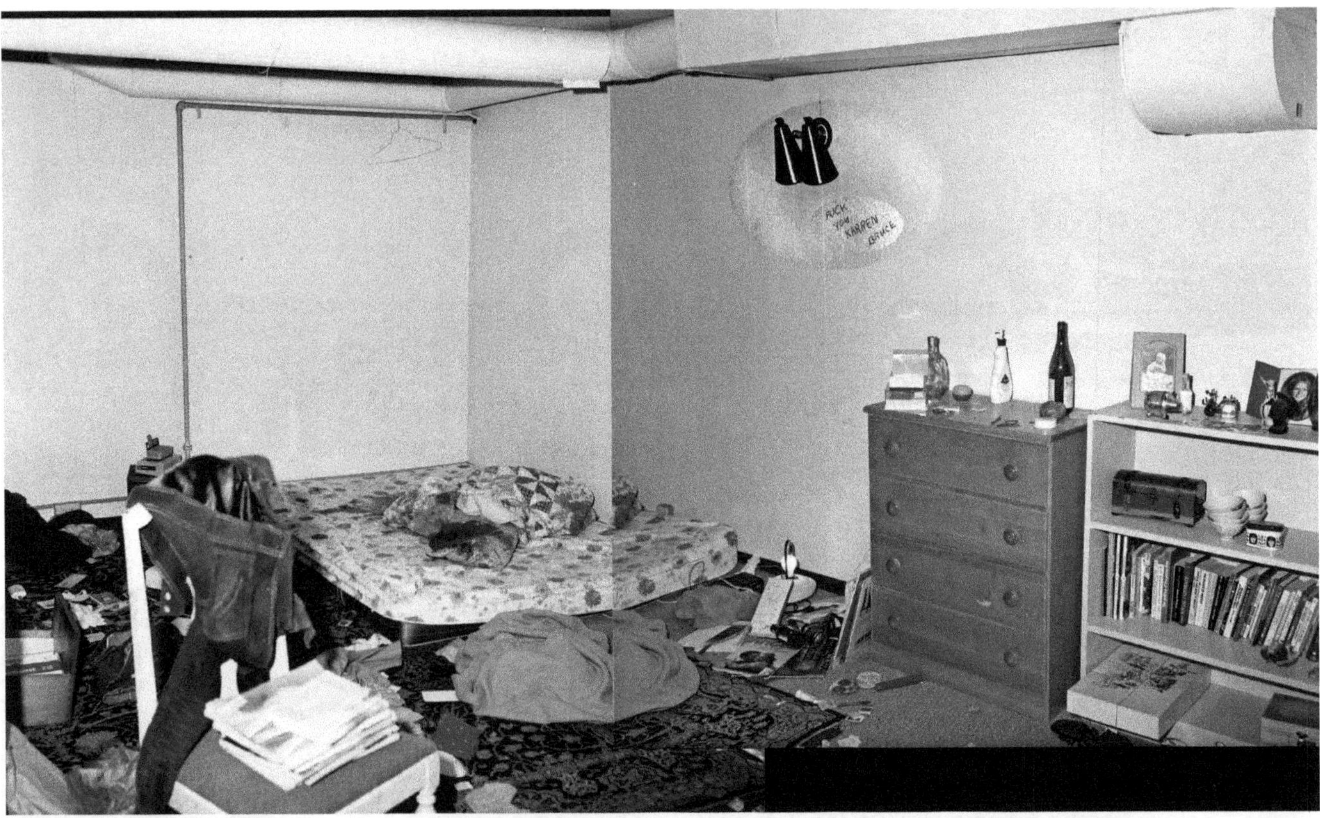

A photomosaic of Karen Sparks' room, showing the mattress on the floor, and enhanced above it, two lamps, just below which is written "FUCK YOU KARREN BRUCE." Note the different spelling of Karen's name. "Bruce" appears to be an angry or playful boyfriend. There is no documentation about the meaning of this graffiti on Karen's wall. Photos courtesy of KCA.

police photos of Sparks' room were mixed up amongst police photos of Lynda Healy's room. This caused some researchers to label Sparks' room as Healy's. The photos however are easily identified as belonging to Sparks because one of them depicts some graffiti scrawled on her bedroom wall. Why researchers overlooked this is a mystery. Nevertheless, the photos show that Sparks actually slept on a mattress on the floor. This is verifiable because the blood transferred from her head wounds are clearly visible on the wall at the same level as her mattress. In other words, the photos are not of a mattress with a bedframe removed. There was no bedframe. So where did the story of Ted wrenching a metal rod from the bedframe originate? In one police report it was noted that Sparks' roommates had observed a length of rebar lying outside the house a few days prior to the assault. Could Ted have placed it there in advance? We will never know. It seems that Sparks' metal rod assault was overshadowed by another report that said she was found with a speculum rammed into her vagina. Why Ted would leave such incriminating evidence behind is another mystery. In any case, it has passed into legend because Ted had worked as a courier for a medical supply company at the time.

Elsewhere, Rule reported that Ted told Diane Edwards at the end of 1973 that Sam Cowell was already dead (Rule 1980, 44), when in fact Sam didn't die until December 19, 1983, in Lafayette Hill, Pennsylvania. Whether Rule believed Sam was dead in 1973, or was just reporting Ted's conversation with Edwards is not clear.

Rule also identified Katherine Merry Devine as a potential Ted victim at the time. We cannot criticize her for making that connection. The circumstances of Devine's disappearance was similar to those of Ted's other victims. However, the discovery of the body and the evidence collected at the scene make it reasonably clear that Ted was not involved (note: we have to remember that Rule published her book in 1980; she may not have had enough time to research Ted fully). Not the same can be said of Keppel. In his *Riverman* book (first published in 1995) he writes the following on presenting the Devine crime scene photos to Ted:

> "Immediately, the contortions of Ted's face told us that he was morbidly transfixed by the Devine scene. His jaw protruded, and his pupils were hideously dilated. His pulse bulged and radiated through his carotid artery like a huge water bump in a garden hose. I felt suddenly as if he were alone with his thoughts, replaying an internal video of his murder, even with us there" (K&B 1995, 415).

Here, Keppel would have us believe he is some kind of serial killer whisperer. In fact, the crime scene evidence for Devine was completely at odds with Ted's M.O. and by 1995, a seasoned investigator should have been able to tell the difference. Completely uncritical, Keppel writes as if he knows Ted is the killer (using hyper-sensationlistic language), when in fact there was no convincing evidence that Ted was involved. Fortunately for the family, the real killer was identified as William E. Cosden Jr. by DNA in 2002.

It is in this context that we have to take other Ted "encounters" with a grain of salt. For example, Rule suggests that Ted may have raped a woman in Seattle near where he lived. In that encounter, he wore a navy watch cap with eye slits cut out, while he taped the eyes of the victim before he raped her, forcing her into submission with a knife that had a carved handle. The knife raises associations of the "curved oriental" knife he claimed was a gift from Marlin Vortman, a UPS law student friend of his. Liz said he kept the knife in her VW glovebox and retrieved it every now and then. It is interesting that Liz's car was stolen while the knife was in the glovebox. When the car was found again, the knife was the only thing she found missing. In one of her interviews with police, Liz said she suspected Ted stole her car (Aspen Seminar, November 13-14, 1975). Did Ted steal the car as a pretext to remove the knife evidence?

In another encounter, Ted started an affair with co-worker Sandy Gwinn at the Harborview Hospital Mental Health Center where he did an internship before graduating with a two-year degree in psychology in June 1972. Sandy related several interesting stories about Ted. One was that on at least two occasions Ted nearly choked her to death with his forearm while they were having sex. It seemed to her that she had to rouse him out of a trance when this happened. And sex was wham-bam thank-you mam. There was no after-play warmth there at all. The other was that she mentioned Ted treated the Harborview patients coldly, and stole patient records. There is a consistency in these two observations.

To this we add the story of Marguerite Christine Maughan, daughter of Supreme Court Judge Richard Maughan, a 565 First Avenue roommate of Ted's. Ted would sometimes "sneak along the side of her first floor apartment and stare through her window without saying a thing until she noticed him" (W&M 1980, 116-7). Even though she thought he was just playing games, she said it creeped her out. Another roommate in the same house once had a female friend stay over. Ted entered the apartment and pinched the girl on the crotch. This report parallels Larry Voshell's account of a rafting trip he and Ted took with two first-time female dates. Ted suddenly and inexplicably undid the halter top of one of the girls, exposing her breasts. Later that day he terrorized the same girl by undoing a rope that secured her to the raft. Ted seemed to gain a perverted pleasure from these antics Voshell noted.

And then there was Leslie Knudson. Leslie met Ted at a party hosted by Paul Van Dam, a Salt Lake County prosecutor in late June 1975. Leslie was introduced to Ted by Carol Booth, a young woman who also lived at the 565 First Avenue house, directly across the hall from Ted's upstairs apartment. At first Leslie found Ted fairly sociable although "somewhat aloof." The pair started dating about a week later. Ted would take Leslie and her 7-year old son Josh out to the drive-in. But gradually Ted's other side began to reveal itself. He began drinking to excess. He began wandering around and told her on one occasion that, "My world is falling apart." Apparently he was referring to his failing relationship with Liz and his failing law classes. She stated that he frequently talked about Liz Kloepfer and how she lost respect for him because he had been dating other girls while engaged to her. Apart from the fact that this story contradicts police accounts of Ted having affairs with a string of women each of whom had no awareness of the other, it shows that Ted was struggling, even if only obliquely, with his inner demons. Leslie, however, stated that her sexual relations with Ted were normal.

Of course the stories that Liz herself related, have now passed virtually into legend. The reader can access those easily from books, so we shall not repeat them here. The more important aspect of Liz's relationship with Ted is her journey from blind devotion to gut-wrenching doubt. Here was a woman living with a man who was systematically raping and killing women in the same city she lived. Some commentators may find it hard to understand how she could have missed the warning signs – and there were plenty. The simple answer is love blinds. But also, of equal importance, is the mid-70s Seattle culture. Male-female relationships were undergoing a revolution. It wasn't just sexual freedom. Many of the normal patterns that moored relationships to middleclass values had begun to erode. People came and went more easily. Curfews were not as strictly enforced. The concept of exclusive ownership of significant others had loosened. It was in this climate that Ted moved. Living in his own apartment, protected by the night, Liz had no chance of knowing where he was or what he was doing apart from the time they were actually together. Seen from this perspective, it is amazing that Liz became suspicious at all.

But she did. She eventually snuck into his apartment when he wasn't there and rifled through his things. One has to imagine the courage (or perhaps desperation) that such an act took. This event represents a significant shift in her trust relationship with Ted. Her description of catching him out in a lie is poignant:

> Liz: Then there was another, a tire iron, I mean, a, I don't know what it was, but he used to sleep in front of my house, and it was sitting there, this is a long time ago but it's just weird, and he left my house late at night and then came back and I opened the door to see what he was doing and he came back to get

> that, and he looked really sick, you know, like he was hiding something, and I says what have you got in your pocket, and he wouldn't show me and I reached in and grabbed it and it was a pair of surgical gloves.
> Thompson: He had them in his pocket? What did he say he was doing with them?
> Liz: I think he turned around and left, I can't …
> Thompson: And this was in the middle of the night?
> Liz: Yeah, it was late at night. It seems incredible as I say all this that I didn't, you know, say you're weird, go away.
>
> (Detective Jerry Thompson's interview of Liz Kloepfer on September 17, 1975, at the King County Sheriff's Office, Seattle. FSA.)

You have to imagine the vibes she is getting from police. Jerry Thompson was onto Ted from day one. At the same time, Liz had built up this pressure of doubt, she needed a release, and the nominally suspicious minds of police provided a perfect sounding board. It was only later, when she found out that police were playing ball with the things she said that she withdrew her support. The police were starved of information themselves, and here was a woman telling them that the man they suspected of murdering dozens of women liked to tie up his girlfriend and have anal sex with her. It was like throwing a match onto tinder. And in the middle of this, Ted was writing long love letters to Liz, taking advantage of her confusion.

But we are getting ahead of ourselves. These events don't unfold until the next chapter. The point is, from a humanist perspective, unless someone has absolute concrete proof that someone has done something wrong, it is very hard to know one way or another from purely social cues what the truth is. It comes back to the fundamental question posed by this thesis: how do you know the person standing in front of you is the person they represent themselves to be? On our own, it is practically impossible to determine. Only when you bring together multiple perspectives from different people can you begin to unravel the truth. Liz didn't have the benefit of numerous perspectives on Ted. She only had her best friend, Mary Lynn Chino. For example, what would she have thought if she had the following observation at her disposal – words that came from the man who supervised Ted from the time he worked as a night manager at Bailiff Hall, Univ. Utah:

> "... the individual was a very odd person, in that he thought out every word before he said it to make sure that he was perfect in trying to put over a point. He stated that he felt the individual reminded him of someone that did an awful lot of talking about wanting to change and having different ideas, but in fact he didn't believe in what he was trying to tell you, but he'd do it to try to convince someone something about himself" (Detective Jerry Thompson's interview with Jim Schuster. FSA).

It is clear that Ted didn't do too well convincing Schuster. One wonders why Liz didn't pick up this obvious trait in Ted, especially if we consider an earlier lie she caught Ted in, the one where he gave her the impression he was applying to law school when he hadn't even finished his undergraduate degree yet. That, by any standards, is a massive red flag. Yet Liz forgave him for it and even helped pay his way through his undergraduate studies when he finally did take them up again.

We have to consider that many women did find Ted exceedingly charismatic. Something that disabled their rational brain when in his presence. We only have to take a look at the way he used his "Officer Roseland" act against Carol DaRonch to see that. In that encounter, Ted followed Carol for at least 10 minutes before approaching her. According to the official police report:

> Suspect approached victim and asked her if she had a car in the parking lot on the west side of Sears. She told him yes. He then asked her for her license number. At this time she told him. He then told her that he was a police officer and a suspect had been caught breaking into her car with a pry wire and that he wanted her to accompany him back to her vehicle to see if anything was missing, also to see if she could identify the suspect (Murray Police Department, November 8, 1974, 8:30 p.m., FSA).

Logic says the first thing that should have come to Carol's mind was: *How did you know I was the owner of the car?* Car breaking information, if it is to be relayed to victims in a shopping mall, would normally be done via a public announcement system, otherwise how would police know *where* the owner of the vehicle was? The only way for a policeman to know that information is if he *followed the victim the whole time*. But DaRonch had already spent at least 10 minutes in the mall when "Officer Roseland" approached her. For the plan to work properly, it would take a second policeman (which Ted ingeniously conjured up) to observe the break-in, while the other policeman ran after the victim. Yet DaRonch believed Ted's phony story! If that is not an example of emotional effect over substance, nothing is. It demonstrates in spades Ted's ability to lure vulnerable women. And we can't just say DaRonch was naive. There were at least thirty or more women and girls out there that fell for his various ruses.

This is one of the mysterious factors we have to take into account when examining Ted's life. And without doubt, Ted was aware of it. Over time, as he became more successful, he must have actively exploited it. He was more than just a con-man, a trickster. There is something about him that speaks of hypnotism, a Rasputin-like power. Thompson—who it has been said was not given over to hyperbole—once said to an assembly of cops who were meeting to discuss the Ted enigma: "He's got eyes on him that you won't forget. I can't really describe them. They're piercing blue" (M&A 1983,

150). If a hardened detective can't completely escape Ted's charisma, how is a young impressionable female supposed to?

Ted obviously oozed superficial charm. He was a practiced dissembler. But his act didn't always run according to script. While he consistently fooled most people, he didn't fool everyone. Several near-miss victims are testament to that. Moreover, police and prosecutors were always quick to see through him. Perhaps Utah Highway Patrol Captain Robert "Bob" Hayward said it best. When he arrested Ted in the early morning hours of August 16, 1975 and found the infamous satchel full of "burglary tools," he remarked:

> "I couldn't put my finger on it, but there was something wrong about this guy. He shouldn't have been in that kind of situation" (*Deseret News*, January 24 1989).

Ted clearly had it when it came to conning the general public, but when it came to cops, there was something in his behavior that didn't add up. They knew it, and he knew they knew it. Even though cops might succumb to emotions, or take an interest in psychology, they remain professional most of the time (in the 70s some would say only some of the time!). They collect facts and are suspicious of coincidences. While it can be said that Ted was good at concealing his crimes, all good cops know Locard's principle, even if only intuitively: the killer invariably leaves something at the scene, and takes something away from it when he leaves. For Ted, it was just a matter of time.

References

Adams, Nathan M. (1981). 'To catch a killer: The search for Ted Bundy' *Reader's Digest*, March 1981.

Crawford, Susan. (2015) '3 close calls in Utah with Ted Bundy.' http://www.thespectrum.com/story/life/2015/07/05/close-calls-utah-ted-bundy/29742385/ (Accessed November 13, 2016), *The Spectrum*.

Crawford, Susan. (2015) 'A chance encounter with serial killer Ted Bundy.' http://www.freep.com/story/news/local/2015/03/08/meeting-ted-bundy-serial-killer/24620889/ (Accessed November 13, 2016). *Detroit Free Press*.

Darrow, L., Bertel, S. (2016). Idaho investigator speaks of interviewing Ted Bundy. Scripps Media, November 4, 2016. http://www.kivitv.com/news/idaho-investigator-speaks-of-interviewing-ted-bundy (Accessed December 3, 2016).

Fagg, Ellen, 'Utahns knew and liked U. law student.' *Deseret News*, January 24, 1989.

Florida State Archives. (1975). Aspen Seminar. A multiagency paper presented at the Aspen Seminar, November 13 & 14, 1975, Aspen.

Merrill, D., Wolf, R. & Winn, S. (1978). 'A perfect stranger, part III: End of the road.' *Utah Holiday Magazine*.

Michaud, S. & Aynesworth, H. (2000). *Ted Bundy: Conversations with a Killer* (Paperback ed.). New York: Signet.

Parsons, H. R. (2009). *The Postmortem Interval: A Systematic Study of Pig Decomposition in West Central Montana*. The University of Montana, Missoula, MT.

Smiley, Patricia (2014). 'Ted Bundy and me: One degree of separation.' http://www.nakedauthors.com/2014/05/ted-bundy-and-me-one-degree-of.html (Accessed February 15, 2015).

Schaefer, G. J. (1997). *Killer Fiction*: Feral House.

Stapley, R. (2016). *I Survived Ted Bundy: The Attack, Escape & PTSD That Changed My Life*. Seattle, WA: Galaxy 44 Publishing.

Treadway, T. (2010). 'Former Martin County deputy's killing spree in 1970s still one of most gruesome murders in St. Lucie County's history.' *TCPalm*. Retrieved from http://www.tcpalm.com/news/former-martin-county-deputys-killing-spree-in-1970s-still-one-of-most-gruesome-murders-in-st-lucie-e-345577182.html (Accessed August 27, 2015).

Thompson, Jerry. Police reports: subfolder September 26 1975, and subfolder September 13, 1978 (Florida State Archives).

Winn, S. & Merrill, D. (1979). *Ted Bundy: The Killer Next Door*. New York: Bantam Books.

First Arrest (August 16, 1975 - December 30, 1977)

The route that Hayward chased Ted on August 16, 1975. Hayward was parked outside his house at (1). Ted was parked at (2). The arrest occurred at (3). According to the 2015 map, Ted ran only one stop sign (S 3030 W and 3500 S). Map route courtesy drive-interview with Bob Hayward by Chris Mortensen 25 June, 2015. Photo insets courtesy Chris Mortensen © 2015. Bing Aerial Map image courtesy USGS Earthstar Geographics SIO © Microsoft Corporation.

Bob Hayward circa 1975. Photo public domain.

August 16, 1975: 2:30 a.m. Ted's first Arrest, Granger, Utah, by Highway Patrol Sergeant Bob Hayward. Daryl Ondrak arrives to inspect Ted's car. Ted has murdered at least 16 women and girls, and raped countless others by this time. Ted is driven down SLC County complex, downtown SLC, booked and fingerprinted. In an interview with Bob Hayward on 25 June, 2015, he had this to say:

I was parked right here, doing paper work, and all of a sudden back of me comes three cars. This is a street I know, most of these people are good Mormons, it's three o'clock in the morning and I go woah! I had all the lights off, three of 'em went by, and one pulled into that one, and one pulled into this one, and the other one went to the corner, the Volkswagen went and turned. And this was Ken Dent, lived here, and he worked for the Probation-Parole for the State, good, good friend, it looked like his Volkswagen. I says, I didn't know that was running, that broke down. So anyway, the radio comes on, and the deputy sheriff over there broke up a drinking party at 3 o'clock, he said I got people going in all directions, there's cars and motorcycles everywhere, send me some help. So I took off. Went down here (south on Hogan), came down around this corner (right into Lemay), the idea was go through where I can go straight through, that would of put me right to 'em [the drunk kids] but instead of that, I turned on this one (right into Brock), just excited, got to get over there quick. And this one

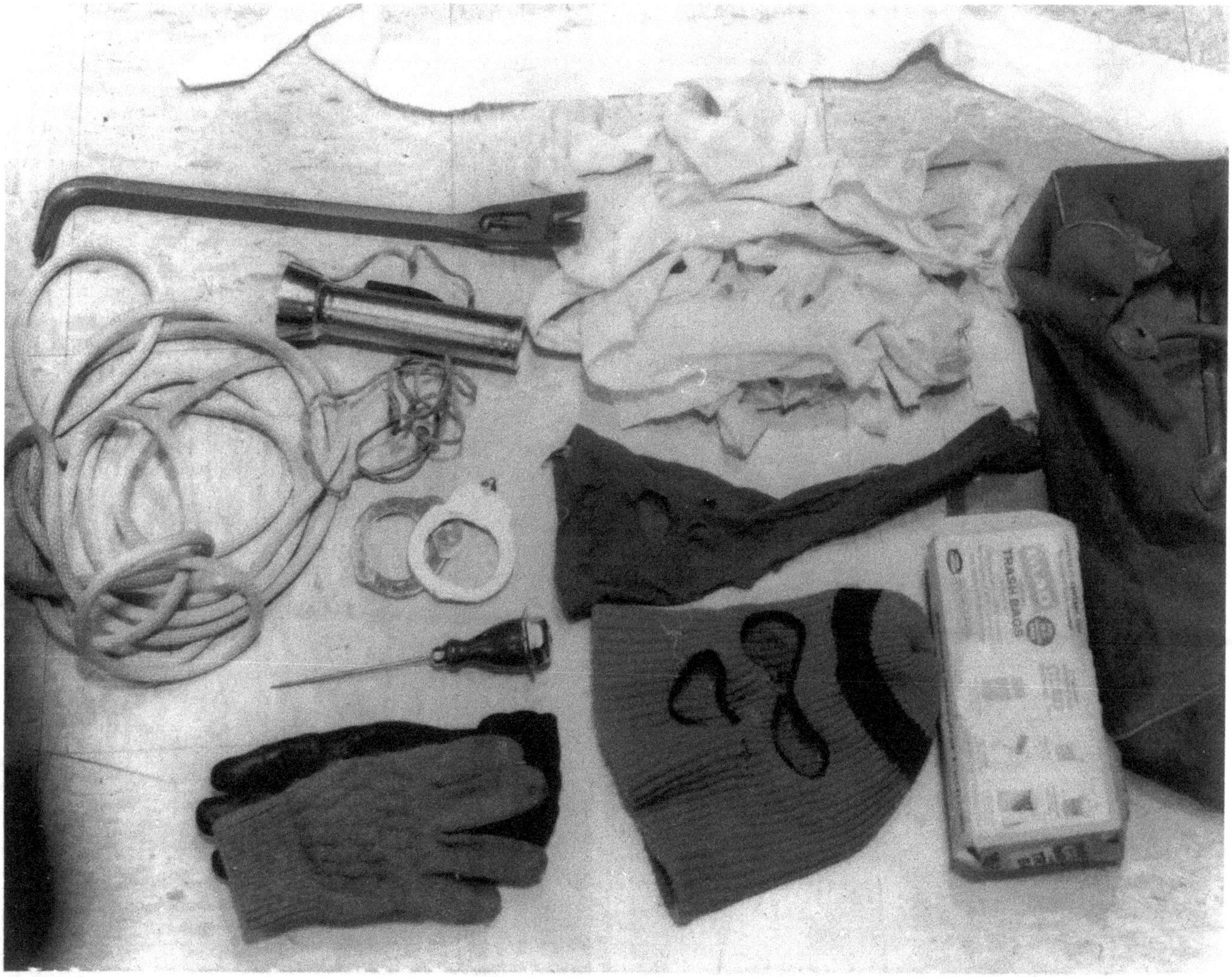

The items found in Ted's car on August 16, 1975. Bundy claimed he used the handcuffs (Jana brand) as a teaching aid in law school. Bob Hayward said, "I couldn't put my finger on it, but there was something wrong about this guy. He shouldn't have been in that kind of situation." Keppel told Thompson they found a surplus store in Seattle that sold Gerocal handcuffs, the type found on DaRonch. They couldn't ascertain if Ted bought them there, but knew he had done business with them in the past as they had return checks for purchases he made there. Note the shielded electrical wire next to the rope and flashlight. Photo courtesy KCA.

was a good friend, he's right back of me, this is where the girls lived, they had worked until midnight or something like that, or two or three o'clock and then walked home, the two of 'em worked there and they walked home, so I knew about them, but I got here, turned the corner, and threw my bright lights on and stepped on the gas, 'cause I was mad for turning on the wrong street, and he took off from here, he *squirted*. He popped out with no lights on, and stomped the gas, and I thought, what have I got here? I think it spooked him is all, I don't think he, he didn't know who I was, or what I was, 'cause I was in an unmarked car [green 1974 Plymouth], it just spooked him. He comes out and turns this corner (right on Lehi), and the race was on, I got that floodlight on him, I'm right on his butt, and we went down here (south on Lehi) down to the road that comes back around to the church (left into S 2760 W), well just as fast as he could go, I had a full-blown Plymouth, I didn't have any trouble staying with him, but when he got to those corners I thought he'd rolled several times, he'd touch the brake and make the turn (into Tess Ave), and he came through here full bore (left and south on 3030 S, crossed Lehi, and went over the gutter at Lemay) and he popped this baby (ran the stop sign at 3030 S and 3500 S), he went down to that corner (3500 S and 2700 W), and pulled right where that, he pulled in the old gas station and stopped, I stopped and opened my door and he was out and coming back towards me, and I pulled my Magnum out [357 Magnum] and just sit it in the crotch of the door and I says "Hold it right there!" I said "Stand still. Put your driver's license and registration on my hood and turn around and walk back two steps." So that's what he done, and put it on there. And I got it, and I started talking to him, and called for backup. Anyway, I had another trooper that hadn't gone home yet, he had a drunk who was just coming out of the jail. He was out here going home, so he come over, and was watching him [Ted] while I was looking in his car. And I looked in that side, and this seat was layin' in the back seat. And that's quite a space, you can stick a body in it, even for a Volkswagen, they're crumpled, you know they're unconscious, it didn't dawn on me then what was going on, but isn't that silly? He said "The seats broken I gotta get it fixed." "Okay, you mind if I look through your car?" "No go ahead." So there was a little brown, it was like a doctor's bag, sitting right here, on the floor, and I opened that up and look at it, and he had pantyhose with holes cut in it, and different kinds of little black things in there, and some little tools, jimmy tools, and stuff like that, and I said, ah, "I'm going to open your trunk" which was the front, and I looked in there, and I found some more bigger burglary tools, and as I was looking I seen, I said to myself, "What's this?" and there was a little piece of paper hanging out off it, crammed around the side, so I looked at it and pulled it out, and I looked in it, and it had brand new *handcuffs*. I says, "What do you use handcuffs for?" "I'm a law student" he says, "I use

Hayward's chase vehicle, a green 1974 Plymouth Fury. Photo public domain.

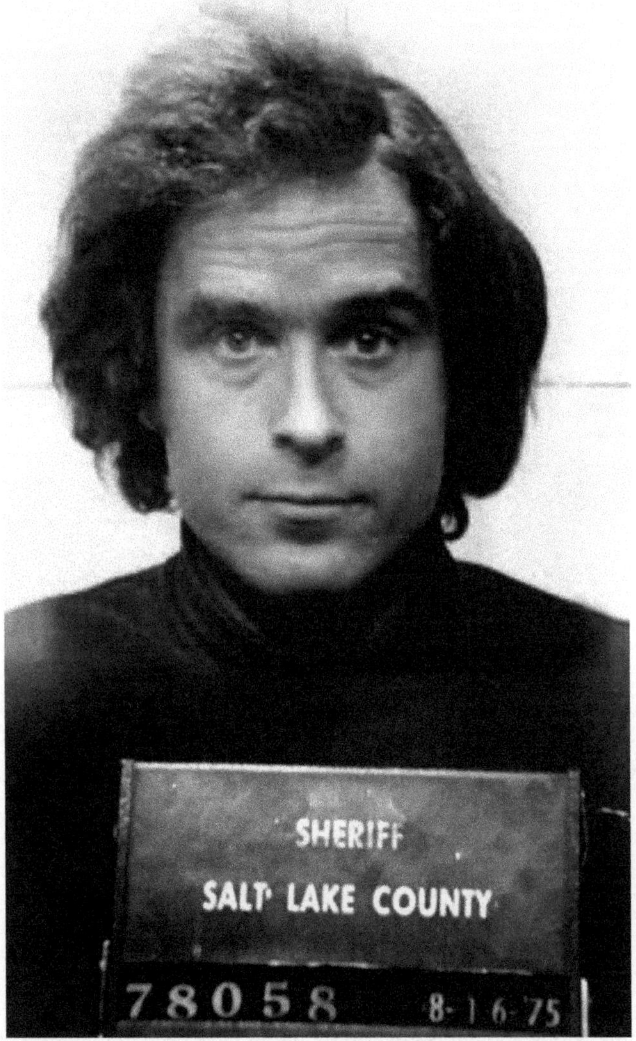

Mugshot of Ted on the night he was arrested, with bushy hair and hypnotic eyes. Can the undiscerning reader see something in that face which bespeaks of a serial killer? Photo courtesy KCA.

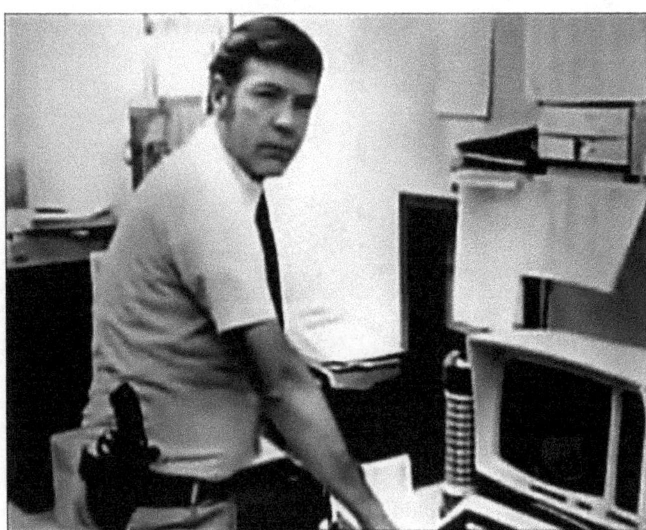

Detective Jerry Thompson circa 1975. SLC Metropolitan Hall of Justice, Police Department. Photo public domain.

them in my classes." Okay, I'll buy that too. Anyway, I called Ondrak, he was an investigator for the sheriff. I told him what we had, and he looked at everything, and I said I'm going to book him anyway on evading, and he says I'll book him on burglary tools, and we'll see what then, we'll go from there (interview courtesy Chris Mortensen, June 25, 2105).

August 17, 1975: Bailed out of jail, SLC, Utah.
August 18, 1975: 9:16 p.m. Ted on phone, SLC. Gerald "Jerry" Thompson glances at the arrest reports for the weekend. The name "Ted" catches his eye.
August 19, 1975: Morning. SLC Metropolitan Hall of

SHERIFF'S OFFICE
SALT LAKE COUNTY

col - 328-7441

Metropolitan Hall of Justice
437 South Second East
Salt Lake City, Utah 84111

DELMAR "SWEDE" LARSON
SHERIFF

KENNETH HAMMON
CHIEF DEPUTY

3214 N. 20

August 20, 1975

Detective Robert Keppel
King County Department of Public Safety
Seattle, Washington 98104

Dear Bob:

Thought you may be interested in this. On the early morning hours of 8-16-75 BUNDY was spotted by our Patrol Division prowling a residential neighborhood in his brown Volkswagen. When officers attempted to approach him, he fled in his vehicle. When officers placed him under arrest, they found in his vehicle a canvas gym bag containing the items shown in the photograph. Bundy had no reasonable explanation for being in the residential area, nor any explanation for the items in the bag. The patrol officers were not familiar with Bundy's background, and he had been released from jail before this was brought to my attention. However, we are attempting to obtain a warrant on Bundy for Possession of Burglar Tools. If we are successful in this, I will interview Bundy when he is arrested again.

Yours sincerely,

Ben Forbes

Detective Ben Forbes
Salt Lake County Sheriff's Office
Homicide

BF:jkm

Enclosure

Detective Ben Forbes' letter to Keppel, alerting him of Bundy four days after his arrest. Courtesy KCA.

Justice, 9th floor, run by Captain Pete Hayward, various Sheriff's departments and divisions do an information trade. Daryl Ondrak recounts Bob Hayward's encounter with Ted. Lieutenant Ben Forbes, a detective with the Salt Lake County Sheriff's office, called Seattle police (where the "Ted" task force had been set up since March 1975). Deputy Kevin O'Shaughnessy took the call. Forbes informed O'Shaughnessy that Theodore Robert Bundy had been arrested in the early hours of Saturday the 16th in the town of Granger and charged with evading a police officer. A charge of burglary tools possession was pending. O'Shaughnessy asked Forbes why he was sharing this information. Forbes explained that it was because Seattle police had asked for it. He then explained his telephone conversation with Hergy Hergesheimer the previous October 28, 1974. Hergesheimer had interviewed Liz Kloepfer and obtained photos of Ted. Forbes rang off promising to send a mug shot of Ted. The moment O'Shaughnessy hung up with Forbes, he went in search of the task force's Ted Bundy file. But he couldn't find it. As it happened, Kathy McChesney had taken it to her desk. It was a legal length folder with the number 7 on it – of the top 100 cases that the task force was putting through intensive review.

Captain Pete Hayward (undated). Photo public domain.

Kathy McChesney circa 1975. Photo public domain.

August 21, 1975: Buys gas in SLC. Also on this day, Ted is taken 'downtown' to be fingerprinted, photographed and booked. Jerry Thompson, Sergeant John Bernado and Detective Bob Warner take Ted to his 565 First Avenue N.E. apartment. 6:30 p.m. Thompson on his hands and knees searching Ted's apartment in Ted's presence. Finds flyer for Bountiful's Viewmont High School play *The Redhead*, and Colorado Ski Country Guide '74-'75 with 'X marks the spot' drawn next to the Wildwood Inn. Got Ted's permission to take his June 1975 telephone bill and his Chevron gas credit card bill. Notices patent leather shoes in the closet, but is unaware of the connection to the DaRonch case at this stage so does not take them into evidence. He overlooks a utility shed on west side of the house. He also overlooks a cellar at the back of the house. [Both shed and cellar still exist at the time of writing.] He takes Polaroids of Ted's VW bug. Thompson stated that he had never come across anyone who was so seemingly uninterested in such an intensive investigation.

Bob Keppel (farthest right) with two unknown colleagues working at the computer system designed to filter out potential "Ted" suspects. Photo public domain.

Also on this day, mining students entered the Willie May Mine, approximately one mile east of Berthoud Falls, Colorado, and smelled decaying material. They had inadvertently stumbled on the nude remains of Shelley K. Robertson. She had been struck in the chest, forehead, cranium, and rear of her head. Blood was found on the right side of her head. A rock was the most likely weapon.

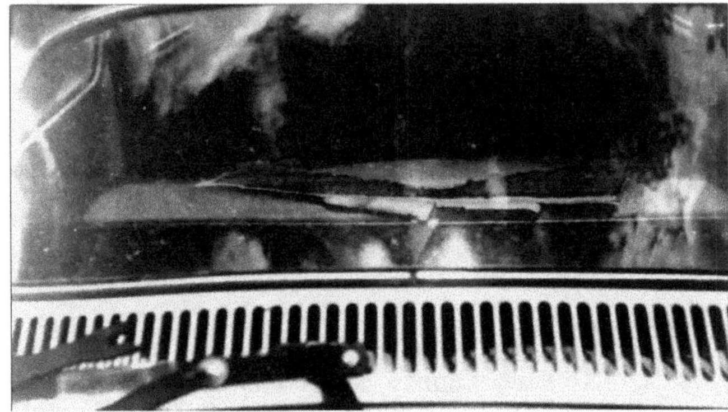

Polaroid of the tear in Ted's VW rear seat taken by Jerry Thompson, August 21, 1975. Photo public domain.

John O'Connell circa 1975. Photo public domain.

August 22, 1975: Ted appoints John O'Connell. O'Connell advises Thompson that his client will no longer speak to police.

August 23, 1975: Chief Criminal Investigator for the Ninth Judicial District State of Colorado Mike Fisher contacts Salt Lake PD, informs Thompson of his investigation into Ted. Thompson and Fisher share notes. Thompson distributes Ted information to other agencies, including Seattle PD, Bountiful PD, and Murray PD. Detectives Ira Beal and Ron Ballantyne of Bountiful PD show Raelynn Shepherd a photo line-up. Shepherd picks Ted saying "If you put a moustache on this individual, I'm sure it's probably him." They show DaRonch the photo line-up. DaRonch unconsciously picks Ted's picture, but is unsure (Jerry Thompson report, FSA).

August 25, 1975: (Early Monday morning) Jerry Thompson starts gathering Ted's documents – phone bills, law school records, bank statements, gasoline credit card records.

August 28, 1975: Assistant County Attorney Gerald Kinghorn and Thompson at Univ. Utah law school with subpoena for Ted's school records. Ted catches them by surprise as they walk from the lounge area in the hallway entrance to the registrar's office. Ted wants to talk to Thompson (to learn things), but Kinghorn forbids it.

August 30, 1975: Ted baptized into the Mormon church in SLC.

September 1, 1975 (Monday): 10:00 a.m. Outside Murray Mountain Bell Telephone company. Thompson shows Carol DaRonch Ted's VW shots, then suspects' mug shots. DaRonch pulls out Ted's picture, then hands it back. Thompson believes he now has a positive ID.

Detective Mike Fisher, circa 1975. Photo courtesy *Reader's Digest*.

Detective Ira Beal (undated) Photo public domain.

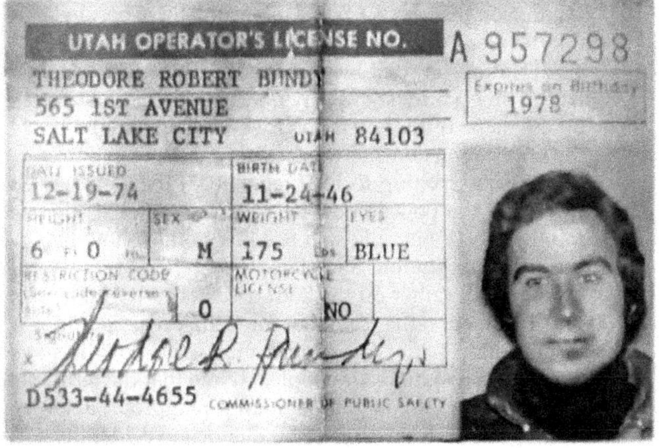

Ted's Utah driver's license. Photo public domain.

September 3, 1975: Thompson explains his case against Ted to the Attorney's Office, requests a subpoena to obtain Ted's telephone records from Mountain Bell.

September 4, 1975: Subpoena served, Thompson scrutinizes Ted's phone records. Ballantyne at Murray police station, gets handcuffs used on DaRonch, Bob Hayward's cuffs from Ted's August 16 arrest, and the cuffs key found at Viewmont High School and ships them off to the FBI for analysis. (Noon) Ira Beal takes DaRonch out on a drive looking for Ted's VW.

September 5, 1975: Beal takes DaRonch out on a drive looking for Ted's VW again.

September 6, 1975: Ted ordained to the Mormon church "lower priesthood."

September 7, 1975: Mike Fisher calls Thompson, notifies him that Ted's credit card gas purchases match the days and locations of Campbell, Cunningham and Oliverson abductions.

September 8, 1975: Beal and DaRonch at Ted's 565 First Avenue apartment, examine Ted's VW, which has new paint job (went from white or light gray on August 21, to light-brown on September 8), different hubcaps, and fresh backseat with no tear. DaRonch recognizes long creased dent on passenger side. Also, still has no front bumper or license plate.

Detective Dennis Couch (January 1989). Photo public domain.

September 9, 1975: Thompson, Beal and Detective Dennis Couch of the Salt Lake County Sheriff's Office visit Liz's father Dr. Russell Hirst in his Ogden office. Hirst initially suggests they go to Seattle and talk to Liz in person. Hirst was of the opinion that Ted "was definitely a schizophrenic." When asked to elaborate on that, Hirst said, "… at one time he is very nice, very pleasant, very helpful; then he becomes extremely moody, does not talk, gives you the opinion that he is really thinking or contemplating something" (Jerry Thompson report, FSA). Thompson obtains subpoena for Ted's credit cards.

September 10, 1975: Pete Hayward orders 24-hour surveillance on Ted. Thompson sends subpoena for Ted's credit cards to the relevant companies. Ted advertises his VW in the *Deseret News*.

September 11, 1975: Ted creeps up behind surveillance car on First Avenue and scribbles down license plate.

September 12, 1975: Police set up surveillance on a 2nd floor insurance building across First Avenue, but they're discovered by Ted's Mormon church friends.

September 13, 1975: Ted takes weekend trip to Bear Lake with Mormon friends.

September 15, 1975: Ted leads police on chase to Univ. Utah. His day "was not one of study or attending classes." Surveillance called off.

September 16, 1975: (Evening) Ted calls Liz in Seattle.

September 17, 1975: (Afternoon) Thompson, Beal and Couch fly to Seattle; Kloepfer interview. Seattle Police Department polygraph room, with two-way mirror and listening device where Ira Beal and Detective Couch could also take notes. The interview was not recorded at Kloepfer's request. She was extremely nervous. Thompson was the only person who sat with Liz face-to-face.

> At the time of the interview, Liz stated that "there is definitely not going to be a marriage now." She first became suspicious of Ted when she was shown a

composite drawing in the newspapers and on TV. Liz noticed that Ted was never with her on the particular nights that the girls had gone missing, that he was "somewhere else unknown." Then a girlfriend of Liz's went down to SLC in the Fall of 1974 and read an account of one of the missing girls there, and when she came back to Seattle said to Liz, "That's exactly the same as the girls are in Salt Lake and Ted is down there in Salt Lake now." From then on Liz started to think more strongly about him. Around this time she spoke to her father, Dr. Hirst in Ogden about her concerns. These were that she had found in Ted's apartment a pair of crutches, a meat cleaver, and a large Oriental type knife in a wooden holster type case, that was in the glovebox of her car, which he borrowed quite often. At the time of the interview Liz said that deep down she was "just not sure" if Ted was involved or not. After further questioning, she added that she had also found a roll of plaster of Paris in Ted's drawer after "snooping around." When Liz confronted him about it, Ted said, "Oh, I stole that from the medical supply place" at the university where he was working. She asked him why, and he stated, "I don't know, I guess just for the hell of it." She confronted him about the crutches and he said he used them for his landlord. She recollected that sometime in the Fall of 1973, she observed in his apartment a paper sack, and noticed that it was full and the top item was a women's bra. She believed the rest of the items were women's clothing but was "a little bit embarrassed to ask him what was in there or why he had women's clothing." She stated that during the summer of 1974, just before he moved to SLC, his sex drive reduced to almost nil, which was very unusual for him. She accused him of having other girlfriends, but he denied it, saying he was just working hard and his frustrations were up high. Before he left for SLC, she wanted to throw a party for him, and he "even refused to have sex on this deal" which was very unusual for him. She stated that in late '73 or early '74 he got a book called *The Joy of Sex*. In this book he found and read about items about anal intercourse and since that time "he heavily desired to do this." She did not relish the idea but went along with him. He also found some items in the book about girls being tied up and bound. She let him take her nylon stockings, spread eagle her on the bed and tie her legs spread eagle and her arms out and have intercourse that way, only twice, and she did not like it, it was very distasteful, and she wouldn't do it with him again. She stated that "he did not make too much comment about this but he appeared that he didn't like the idea." If she mentioned that she was going to get her hair cut he would get "very upset and told her no", that he liked her hair, liked long hair very much. She told Thompson about Ted's cars. The light brown or beige VW bug and an old white truck he bought just before going to Salt Lake. He drove her VW bug which is light green in color. Both bugs had a tear across the back seat and she figured it had something to do with the sun coming in through the back window. She didn't know that Ted' had fixed his and changed his car. She stated that she had caught him in several lies. He denied being arrested in Salt Lake. When she confronted him about it, he told her that it was a traffic violation, to which she told him he was lying, that he had some items in his car she had heard about, and he said, "Yeah, they didn't mean too much. I had a ski mask in there that I used last year when it was cold for skiing, and a couple of other things they were trying to make a big deal out of." He said he had nothing to worry about, that it was an illegal search and there was nothing to it. [In a supplementary interview that was recorded, Liz added: "... this was a long time ago but it's just weird, and he left my house late at night and then came back and I opened the door to see what he was doing and he came back to get that [taped lug wrench], and he looked really sick, you know, like he was hiding something, and I say what have you got in your pocket, and he wouldn't show me and I reached in and grabbed it and it was a pair of surgical gloves. Weird."] Thompson asked her if she knew anything about his thefts. She stated that she knew he had stolen a TV and few things in the Seattle area. She remembered one time, he said to her that if she ever told anybody about it or anything else, he told her, "I'll break your fucking neck." She said that he called her again last night and he was all "lovey-dovey", telling her how much he missed her and wanted to marry her and all these kinds of things, and then in the next breath asked her for $700.00 which he claimed he needed for his attorney. She told Thompson that Ted was an illegitimate child, that he found out from a cousin when he was 18 or 19 years old she believes, but he has never told his mother that he found out. She says this has bothered him and really upset him an awful lot. She informed Thompson that she learned from Kathy [McChesney] that he went to Colorado and that he denied telling you [Thompson] that he had ever been in Colorado. At the time Kathy showed her a picture of a woman by the name of Marguerite Christine Maughan, with the implication that Ted was having a sexual relations with her. According to Liz, Ted said in the call last night that the police knew he was coming to Seattle to sell his VW bug. Liz said she had no idea how he got that information. She stated that he went hunting with her father on the 20th of October 1974. She was aware her father called Ted a "schizophrenic." In response Liz said, "The more I think of it now he's right, he is two kinds of people." [Note that the term schizophrenic is being used totally inappropriately here, that the term should be Dissociative Identity Disorder, aka, split-personality.] They talked about Ted's use of a fake moustache. Liz smoked "exactly one full package of cigarettes" during the interview (Jerry Thompson notes, FSA, spelling corrected).

Dr. Russell Hirst. *The Ogden Standard Examiner,* Friday September 15th, 1961.

Thompson and Beal also interviewed Mary Lynn Chino (Liz's best friend) on the same day as Liz. This is when Mary told them "one night she was out late, coming home approximately 2:00 a.m. and as she entered her house she observed Ted out walking in the yards behind her house. This is in the [Seattle] University district near the area where Ted was living. She stated this occurred in 1972 and she feels he was stealing at this time." Mary said Ted loved long hair and was always running "his fingers and hands" through Liz's hair. She said the people she knew that had met Ted "saw through him as phony." She stated that if Ted called Liz and she was not home, he would call her (Mary) and be very jealous. She told the investigators that Ted steals and lies. He said that "one time when they were taking a river trip, that he likes to get down the river into the rapids area and go further than he should deliberately to try and scare the girls that are with him as he just loves to see girls scared." She finished up saying Ted comes from a poor family but likes hanging around Liz because "she has the nicer things in life that Ted desires."

September 18, 1975: In Beal's supplement to Liz' interview, he recorded that Ted follows her when she goes to various places or meetings to see who she is with or what she is doing. She stated he takes naps and sleeps a lot during the day and is out a lot late at night. She stated he used to sneak up on her when she was walking alone at night when she had no idea he was around and suddenly he would jump out of the bushes and grab her scaring the hell out of her. She stated this really made her angry.

(Deseret News, September 10, 1975)

'68 VW, sedan, very good cond. Sunroof, $800. 531-7286.

Ted's add to sell his VW.

Bryan Severson (1975). Photo courtesy Bryan Severson.

September 19, 1975: Ted sells his VW to Bryan Severson (18), a high school student at Hillcrest High, the same high school that Melissa Smith went to. According to Bryan, Ted told him not to register the car, but Bryan's father said, "No, that's your car now go register it" (interview courtesy Chris Mortensen, November 18, 2015). Ted didn't tell Bryan that in fact the title deed to the car was held by the bondsman and bail as collateral. Nevertheless, Ted forged a duplicate and passed that off to Bryan as the original. Remembering that day, Bryan said:

> I came home and [...] went and borrowed a loan from a loan company, to get the money to pay for the car, so ah, he decided to bring the car out to me, and he brought it out to Sandy [about 1 mile southeast of Fashion Place Mall], to my parent's house, and I went down to the bank to cash the check to give it to him, and they wouldn't cash it because I didn't have an account with them, so I had to wait till my mother to got home from work, so she could take me down to cash the check, well ... she ended up working overtime that night, so he had to sit here at my house for like 2 hours. We sat outside and smoked a cigarette and everything [Ted bummed one off Bryan], I was talking to ... my neighbor came home, and he was a policeman, you know, and I walked over to the fence, and I was standing there talking to him, and Ted got real, like nervous, you know, but I didn't think nothing of it, you know, because you don't – because nothing like this had happened, you know, or came out or anything. So anyway, my mother came home like 2 hours later, she took me down, we cashed the check, and we paid him, and he took off.

September 26, 1975: Moves to 364 Douglas Street, Utah, (upstairs apartment, north end). According to Ted, "... a shorter walk to campus." Same day Jerry Thompson sends a report on Ted to Mike Fisher in Colorado. He tells Fisher that the next day they will decide whether or not they will arrest Ted.

364 Douglas Street. Photo courtesy Chris Mortensen © 2015.

September 28 (on a Sunday late September), 1975: Ted calls Liz to tell her he is coming to Seattle. Says he is broke and needs to sell his VW in Seattle where he'll get more money for it. [Liz's memory correct on this date?] They hang up. Liz calls Kathy McChesney (Sex Crimes Unit), says it's an "emergency." McChesney tells Liz to play her hand to Ted. Liz calls Ted back and tells him she knows about his arrest, now six weeks past. Ted also Calls Rule asking why they're subpoenaing his law school records in Seattle, a signal to Rule that something serious is afoot as subpoenas are not issued without probable cause.

September 29, 1975: Ted buys $3.35 of gas SLC. He pays off $10.00 on his Chevron card; balance owing $251.78.

October 1, 1975: 3:30 p.m. Thompson hands Ted subpoena at 364 Douglas Street to attend line-up. When Thompson was interviewed by Al Carlisle about that event, Thompson said:

> I think he was overwhelmed and yet I think he had a sigh of relief because the arrest was not for murder. I think he was really looking for Murder One and when we charged him with kidnapping, at first he was as white as a ghost. He was trembling and rather than me telling him I handed him the paper. He read it and said, "Oh God, is that all?" I said, "You were waiting for the Murder One weren't you Ted?" I said,

Murray Police Department lineup October 2, 1975. Ted is wearing a second set of clothes beneath his outer layer. Photo courtesy KCA.

"That's next." (Carlisle 2014, p. 89. Original interview conducted by Al Carlisle, 1990).

October 2, 1975: Ted identified in line-up by Carol DaRonch, Raelynn Shepherd and Tami Tingey (Debbie Kent's locker partner who had also seen Ted at the play). 11:00 a.m. Arrested, locked up Salt Lake County Jail. Afterwards, Thompson & co. search 364 Douglas Street and find a few marijuana seeds. News breaks in Seattle that Ted has been charged with aggravated kidnapping and attempted criminal assault.

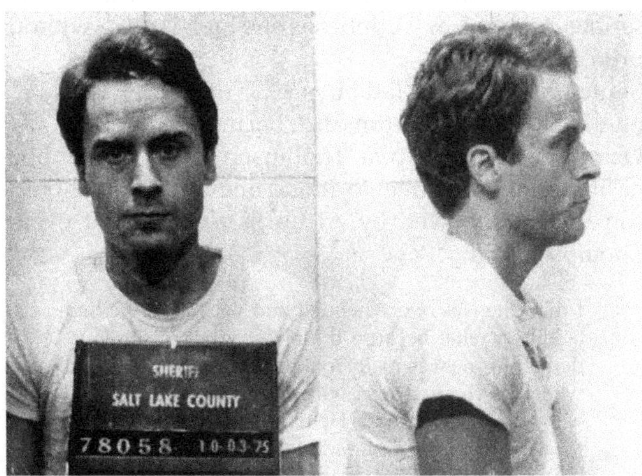

Ted's October 3, 1975 mugshot. Photo public domain.

October 3, 1975: Mug shot taken. Hair parted from right to left, the mask still on but the stiff neckedness, the neck mole, the hard gaze, the smiling Ted gone. Identified. Charged. Locked up in SLC Metropolitan (Hall of Justice and) city jail. "Utah Student Seized in Attempted Murder, Kidnapping," *Standard-Examiner*, (article written by Peter Gillins). 'U. Law Student Charged in Kidnapping,' *The Salt Lake Tribune*, (article written by Clark Lobb & Tom McCarthey). Ted sends a message through *Associated Press* to Rule: "Ted Bundy wants you to know that he is all right, that things will work out." 4:15 p.m. Thompson takes Ted's VW into possession.

October 4, 1975: Rule writes a sympathy letter to Ted in Salt Lake.

October 5, 1975: "Friends 'Stand By' Him, Kidnap Suspect Claims," *The Salt Lake Tribune*, (article written by Clark Lobb). In contrast, "Utah prisoner studied as suspect in '74 murder cases' (*Eugene Register-Guard*)

October 6, 1975: 'Utah Briefs Ted Arrest,' *The Daily Herald* (Provo).

October 7, 1975: Thompson receives a call from Keppel who had just interviewed Ted's parents in Tacoma. Keppel said he thought it was odd "they never ranted and raved or denied the fact that their son was guilty or that he had done such a thing" [ref].

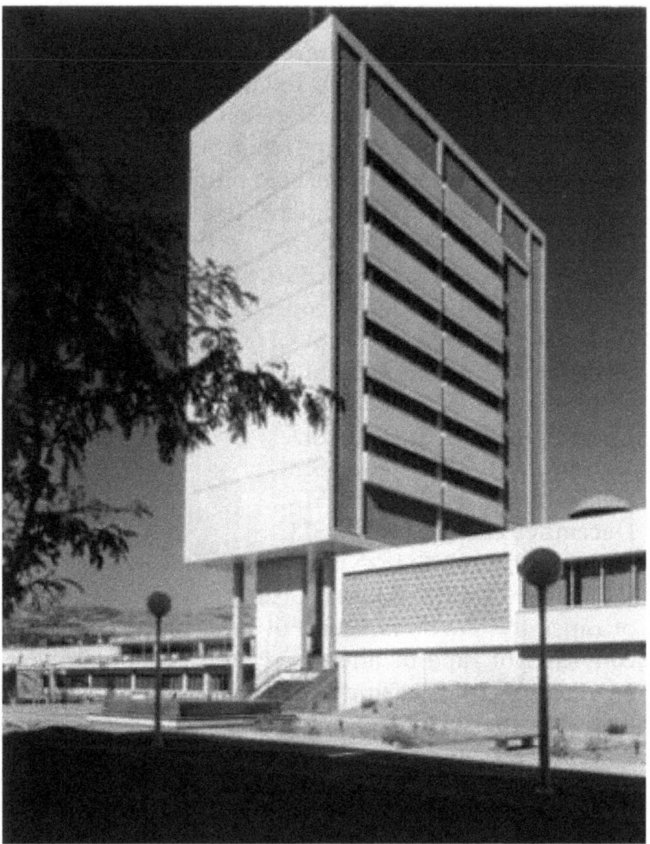

SLC Metropolitan Hall of Justice and city jail. Photo courtesy Utah State Historical Society © 2014.

October 8, 1975: Ted writes melodramatic letter to Rule ("My world is a cage").
October 10, 1975: 'Parents Defend Son in S.L. Jail,' *The Salt Lake Tribune*.
October 12, 1975: 'Utah Suspect Once Checked in 6 Deaths,' *Standard-Examiner*.
October 15, 1975: Paul Forbes (from Murray police) and Thompson take apart Ted's VW, vacuum it out and send the results to FBI for analysis.
October 16, 1975: 'Blood Sample Ordered In Law Student Case' – City Judge Robert Gibson granted the prosecution motion which was supported by an affidavit saying the girl scratched her assailant and he bled on her clothing before she escaped from his car. *The Daily Herald* (Provo). Blood taken by Dr. Henry Gibbons.
October 21, 1975: Ira Beal photographs Ted VW with 35 mm film to compare with original photos taken by Thompson on August 21, 1975.
October 23, 1975: More jail poems to Rule. "Marathon" ten-page letter to Liz. (Later at night) Ted calls Liz. She admits, "I went to the police myself a year ago." Ted told her, "It's okay."
October 30, 1975: Judge Gibson reduces Ted's bail from $100,000 to $15,000.
November 3, 1975: 9th floor SLC Hall of Justice. Captain Pete Hayward and Thompson question Ted over murders in presence of Ted's attorney John O'Connell. O'Connell intercedes, preventing any meaningful questioning from taking place.
November 5, 1975: Keppel speaks to Dr. Scott Fraser by phone. Fraser said that he thought highly of Ted as a person, that he was a very good student. He worked with him in research projects but doesn't remember if Ted and Lynda Healy were in the same projects. He said that it would seem highly probable that Ted and Lynda met at one point or other during the Camelot Program. The only thing he thought bad about Ted's behavior was his excuses for doing poor work in his early years at school. Ted said he was an orphan and had been in foster homes for a time and has had a lot of emotional problems. Fraser thought it was odd when Ted was exposed in the Rosellini dirty tricks campaign.

Professor Patricia Lunneborg (undated). Photo public domain.

November 7, 1975: Keppel received a call from Dr. Patricia Wells Lunneborg, psychology professor at Univ. Wash.. Lunneborg could not believe Ted had been charged. She was his advisor in the psychology department and said that his interest in psychology was via the political spectrum rather than child behavior, the latter which was Lynda Healy's interest. She said that even though both Ted and Lynda were in Psych 499 during Spring and Winter 1972, they were in separate groups doing independent research of each other although collectively called 499. The last she saw of Ted was in 1972 when he worked as Harborview Hospital. She didn't mention that he was suspected of stealing patients' files there. She said that she didn't recommend him for the job at the Seattle Crime Commission. She said she will do all she can for him and appear as a character witness if asked.
November 10, 1975: Keppel talks to Chuck Wilburn, who went to Junior High and High School with Ted. He had no first hand knowledge of the "shower masturbation incident" but said it was a frequent rumor across school.
November 13, 1975: Police from various states gather in Aspen to discuss Ted's case. Keppel and Thompson are among the attendees.
November 20, 1975: 6:00 p.m. Ted released on $15,000 bail paid by John and Louise Bundy. (Evening) Called Liz in Seattle. Sounded "bright." Went shopping with John and Louise in a supermarket, where he had a panic attack.
November 21, 1975: Five days of preliminary hearings begin before Judge Paul Grant. On the same day, Keppel sends a letter to Jerry Thompson:

> Please find enclosed the fingerprints of Bundy, King County Recidivism Reports written by Bundy, and Rape Papers Bundy claimed to have worked on. The two page papers were actually written by Dr. Donna Schram and Bundy claimed to have written them

on his Law School application. If he in fact wrote similar papers, they cannot be located. At this time I doubt he wrote Rape Papers since he didn't finish the recidivism project he was working on for King County Law and Justice Department. Bundy gives the impression of high ambitions but low achievements. Good luck in court (FSA).

Bundy meets the press, November 21, 1975. Ted smiles as he chats with newsmen during a break in his preliminary hearing Friday. He told newsmen his eight weeks in jail before being released on bond Thursday had "seemed like a lifetime" and that the first thing he did was to buy a pizza. Photo public domain.

November 24, 1975: Ted's birthday. Liz calls him at a house where he is staying with Mormon friends in SLC. Ted isn't home. Liz gets jealous again.
November 26, 1975: Ted formally charged with aggravated kidnapping of DaRonch; bound over to Judge Stewart Hanson's Third District Court. Ted sneaks out the back of the courtroom avoiding the media. Keppel serves subpoena on Ted's high school friend Alan Scott to show where he had hiked around Taylor Mountain with Ted. They scout out Fall City-Duvall Road, Issaquah-Hobart Road, Fall City-Preston Road. It is learned that Ted had taken Liz to the Issaquah area and North Bend.

Judge Stewart Hanson Jr (undated). Photo public domain.

November 27, 1975: Ted flies to Sea-Tac Airport, Washington State. Thanksgiving Day (fourth Thursday in November). Liz sees Detective 'Nick' Mackie in a liquor store. They don't talk. Liz no longer helping police.

Detective Nick Mackie (undated). Photo source: *The Stranger Beside Me* (Rule, 2006).

December 1-11, 1975: Ted in Seattle. Catches up with Rule.
December 2, 1975: Ted drove a VW (AQB-894) on I-5 at 320, Seattle.
December 3, 1975: 10:05 a.m. Detective Roger Dunn tracks Ted to a friend's apartment.
December 4, 1975: 12:40 p.m. Ted in Seattle. 3:00 p.m. Ted in Univ. Wash. cafeteria.
December 5, 1975: 8:30 p.m. Ted in Seattle.

Detective Roger Dunn (undated). Photo source: *The Stranger Beside Me* (Rule, 2006).

December 6, 1975: 9:20 a.m. Ted in Seattle.
December 7, 1975: 1:15 p.m. Ted in Seattle.
December 8, 1975: 4:00 p.m. Ted in Seattle.
December 9, 1975: 8:15 a.m. Ted in Seattle.
December 10, 1975: 7:47 a.m. Ted in Seattle.
December 11, 1975: 9:00 a.m. Ted purchases a bus ticket to the Sea-Tac airport. (Midnight) Ted leaves for SLC.
December 13, 1975: Ted in SLC.
December 14, 1975: Ted in court, SLC.
December 15, 1975: Ted in court, SLC.
December 16, 1975: Ted in SLC.
December 17, 1975: Ted in SLC.
December 18, 1975: Ted in court, SLC.
December 19, 1975: Ted in SLC.
December 20, 1975: Ted in SLC.
December 21, 1975: Ted in SLC.
December 22, 1975: Ted in SLC.
December 25, 1975: Liz visits Ted, SLC.
December 28, 1975: Police in Seattle received 308 reports of rapes the previous year, but only six persons were convicted of rape or attempted rape in the municipal and county courts, a study showed. The study was lead by psychologist Donna Schram (*The Milwaukee Journal*).
December 31, 1975: Ted in court, SLC.

- 1976 -

January 12, 1976: 8:00 p.m. Ted in Seattle.
January 13, 1976: 8:30 a.m. Ted seen in Seattle. 1:32 p.m. Ted drove a VW (AQB-894) Seattle.
January 17, 1976: Rule meets Ted at a Magnolia District tavern, Seattle. They spend 5 hours together. Ted denies he tried to call Rule on November 20, 1975.
January 28, 1976: 2:45 p.m. Thompson receives a call from Special Agent Robert Neill from the FBI. Two hairs from Ted's VW match victims Caryn Campbell and Melissa Smith. [The MTR has detectives receiving news of the hairs at 9:15 a.m. on January 29, 1976.]
January 30, 1976: Ted drove a VW (WA tag OPM-001), Seattle.

Debbie Smith (undated). Photo source *Salt Lake Tribune*, January 25, 1989.

Early February, 1976: Debbie Smith (17) of 2956 S 9050 West, Magna, SLC, disappears after running away from home. Ted was a free man at the time, but was under heavy surveillance. Despite this, he often managed to evade police. His whereabouts for some parts of February 1976 are not logged.
February 2, 1976: Ballantyne and Thompson go at Ted's VW again. Send off more vacuumed material to the FBI.
February 3, 1976: Ted drove a VW (Washington tag OPM-001), Seattle.
February 8, 1976: That evening, Ted has supper at James Dunn's apartment at 565 First Avenue.

February 10, 1976: Mike Fisher outlines his case, but Aspen judge says not evidence enough to warrant a murder charge.

February 11, 1976: Thompson interviews James Dunn, but Dunn is reticent in giving forth information. The only thing he says of any significance is that Ted has "an oral-anal fetish."

February 19, 1976: Charles Shearer, a 565 First Avenue apartment resident who spent evenings drinking and smoking pot with Ted, tells Utah D.A. prosecutor David Yocom shortly after Ted was arrested that Ted was in a daze and mumbled 'girls' twice and then he said 'caught.' Then he said 'Now they're trying to bust me' (Merrill, Wolf, Winn, 1978). Later, under intense questioning, Shearer slightly changes that to Ted said the cops were accusing him of abducting three girls (as opposed to it being a direct statement by Ted). He was, however, certain he'd once seen Ted wearing patent leather shoes.

February 23, 1976: Trial begins in room 310 of the old SLC courthouse. Judge Hanson presides. David Yocom prosecutes. John O'Connell (and Bruce C. Lubeck) defends. Ted waives his right to a jury trial. Midvale Police Chief Louis Smith, the father of Melissa, knew all of this and appeared at the trial. At the request of O'Connell, Yocom, and Thompson, Louis Smith has his weapon removed while in court (M&A 2000, 154).

David Yocom (circa 1976). "What still sticks out in my mind is Bundy's almost arrogant attitude," Yocom said. "You always sensed he thought he was smarter than anybody in the courtroom." Photo public domain.

February 24, 1976: John and Louise Bundy fly to SLC to attend the trial. Yocom versus O'Connell; Hanson presiding. Ted wearing light gray suit, blue shirt, bow tie in court.

February 25, 1976: Ted, John and Louise have lunch together. Ted too nervous to eat.

February 26, 1976: (Day) Ted called to the witness box. (Evening) Liz flies to SLC from Seattle.

February 29, 1976 (Sunday afternoon): Liz and Ted make love for last time.

March 1, 1976: 1:35 p.m. Ted found guilty of aggravated kidnapping, is remanded in custody.

Bruce Lubeck (undated). Photo public domain.

March 3, 1976: Donald M. Hall, investigator for the Utah Adult Probation and Parole board, interviews Ted for Judge Hanson's "presentence report." Ted angered when Hall asked him about his father. "You might say that he left my mother and me and never rejoined the family," Ted said. Hall also talked to Liz two times. The first time she

Ted arriving at court with O'Connell (March 1, 1976). Photo public domain.

expressed her doubts about Ted, the second time she became adamant that Ted was innocent. Some time in March Ted moves out of 364 Douglas into 413 "B" Street. James Dunn turns up at SLC Police headquarters and says to Thompson: "I have known Ted since about September of 1974 and he has been my closest and best friend, I thought. It was very hard for me to believe that he could possibly be responsible for the things that he's convicted of. Now that he's convicted, I don't know which way to go and which way to think. I would like to ask you personally do you truly believe without a shadow of a doubt that Ted was guilty?" Jerry told him, "That's a hell of a question to ask me. Do you think that I always investigate and sign complaints on individuals that are not guilty?" (Jerry Thompson report, FSA).

March 4, 1976: Donald Hall talks to Liz by phone. She told Hall that she wished she had not told police the things she told them about Ted on October 28-9, 1974.

March 8, 1976: *Ellensburg Daily Record* publishes article linking the dates of three victims with Ted's credit card receipts. Aspen, January 12, 1975; Dillon, March 15, 1975; and Grand Junction, April 6, 1975. Caryn Campbell, Julie Cunningham, and Denise Oliverson respectively. Also on this day, Leslie Knudson's husband Mr Knudson says he saw Ted over at Leslie's place on Redondo Street, SLC, twice; the second time he saw Bundy vacuuming the inside of his tan Volkswagen with the seats out. Mr Knudson stated that this struck him as being a little strange, because he had called Leslie a few days earlier and she told him at that time Bundy was out cleaning his car, and Mr Knudson thought to himself, on seeing Bundy cleaning his VW on the present occasion, "Why would anyone clean a ratty Volkswagen so often?"

March 10, 1976: Donald Hall talks to Louise Bundy by phone. She said Ted's life "as essentially normal lacking any excessive traumatic influences." Louise said she would like to send letters from family members and friends showing the judge a tremendous outpouring of support for Ted. She was encouraged to do so. Liz calls Hall back, and reasserts what she said to him on March 4, 1976.

March 11, 1976: Salt Lake County Jail. Mike Fisher comes to talk to Ted and O'Connell over his suspected murder of Caryn Campbell. Ted's denials are vague. Donald Hall interviews Ted again.

Q: I can't fight this loss of memory. Did you take anything with you to sleep in the car this January trip? Now that's what I'm talking about, January 10th, 11th, 12th, 13th, do you remember whether you took anything to sleep in?

A: Probably just as a precautionary measure and because I didn't have much money and didn't anticipate staying over beyond just driving, I probably took a sleeping bag.

Q: And, how would you, how would you arrange your body in a Volkswagon?

A: Sleeping in a Volkswagon?

Q: Yeah. That's got to be a trick.

A: It is. It's very uncomfortable. Hmm. Slide this, all I do to sleep in my Volkswagon, you put the back seat down, slide the front seat forward as far, maybe even off the tracks, as far forward as you can, and then that space in the back of the Volkswagon, while uncomfortable, is big enough to curl up in. Sometimes my feet would just dangle over the dropoff there, or I'd try to set the seat up in such a way that I could prop my feet (end of tape)

Excerpt of the 11 March, 1976, Fisher interrogation that may shed light on where Ted stayed during that trip. Scan courtesy KCA.

March 12, 1976: Donald Hall takes a statement from Kathy Farmer, who went to Hunt Junior High and Wilson High the same time Ted did. She said Ted was the "all American boy" even though he came from a lower socio-economic status than most of the other children at the schools. She also said that to her knowledge, she was not aware that Ted had been caught masturbating in the broom closet of his classroom at Hunt Junior High.

> Letter to Donald Hall from Linda Bundy, March 12, 1976. (1009 South Fifth Street, Tacoma, WA).
>
> I am Ted Bundy's sister, Linda. I am 23 years old and know very well what is going on. I know my brother and how interested and concerned he always has been about people and that he would never hurt anyone. I love my brother very much. I believe in him when he says that he did not try and hurt that girl.
>
> My brother worked very hard to get somewhere in life. It was not easy, going to school and working to pay his way through school. It is hard work and it takes a lot of money to be a good lawyer. My brother wants to be a good lawyer so that he can help people. He would never hurt anyone. My brother is not a kidnapper I'm sure. I know one time when he saved a little girl from drowning and another time when a man took a lady's purse and ran off and my brother caught him and got the lady's purse back. My brother is a good man. I cannot understand how you think that my brother could have kidnapped that girl. That it was no hard found evidence that proved beyond a shadow of a doubt that my brother did what you said he did. I know that he did not do it.
>
> Ted has always been very concerned about his family. I can remember one time when he was home I understand my sister was going out. My brother asked who was she going out with and where was she going because he was concerned. He has been concerned about me and my family because I live alone with my two children. Even though he was away from home and was busy with work and school he always found the time to call to see that everyone was all right. Ted has always been concerned about my brother, Glen as to what he was going to do when he was done with high school. I know that he has talked to my parents about getting Glen to get a job or to go to college. He is now in the Navy. Ted has always been a very special person to our little brother Richard. We all believe in our brother and believe him when he says that he did not kidnap a girl. We know he is not guilty because we know him better than anyone else does. I love my brother very much and believe in him. My brother has lots of friends and they all believe in him, too. Thank you for taking time to read my letter. I am sure you are a good man, too. Sincerely, Linda J. Bundy (PIR 1975).

March 14, 1976: Ted's first conviction letter to Rule.
March 22, 1976: 9:00 a.m. Judge Hanson reads, but is not satisfied with Hall's presentence report. He noted Ted denied his guilt, but when asked about the overwhelming abundance of evidence against him, Ted insisted that he was not convicted on physical evidence alone. He felt that, while he was not paranoid against the judge or police, he believed DaRonch was pressured into making a misidentification of him. Hanson orders a '90-day diagnostic evaluation.' Sentencing is set for June 30, 1976. Ted is moved to Utah State Prison, diagnostic evaluation unit. There, he is assessed by psychologist Al Carlisle for the first time.
March 23, 1976: Ted charged with fraudulent application of a motor vehicle, SLC.
March 24, 1976: Ted writes letter to "Mary" a friend of Marlin Vortman: "Today, my spirits lifted up by many letters which arrived. I have so many good friends."

Ted's address on his presentence report by Donald Hall was listed as 413 B Street, SLC. The MTR has him at this address by March 22, 1976. Photo courtesy Chris Mortensen © 2015.

April 1, 1976: Rule meets Ted at Utah 'Point-of-the-Mountain' state prison. Rule has 'demon-child' dream the night before the meeting (2006, 199). Ted continues psych-tests around this time. For the blank TAT card he tearily conjures up an image of Liz cleaning the oven. [Two years and three months since New Year's Eve 1973, when he actually surprised her in real life while she was cleaning the oven.]
April 7, 1976: Rule receives letter from Ted.
April 26, 1976: Debbie Smith's decomposed body found in a field near Salt Lake City international airport by a

"Utah Power & Light Co. lineman" (*Salt Lake Tribune*, April 30, 1976). On autopsy she was found to have been killed by three blows to the head (*Odgen Standard Examiner*, 14 May, 1976).

April 30, 1976: Seattle. Liz has dinner with Rule. Liz tearily reads shared love poems between her and Ted.

May 11, 1976: Ted writes letter to Al Carlisle complaining of his assessment of him.

May 17, 1976: Ted writes Rule a letter wherein he states his fear of losing Liz. He ended the letter with his assessment of what the psychiatrists and psychologists had determined about him:

> "... after conducting numerous tests and extensive examinations, (they) have found me normal and are deeply perplexed. Both of us know that none of us is 'normal.' Perhaps what I should say is that they find no explanation to substantiate the verdict or other allegations, No seizures no psychosis, no disassociative reaction, no unusual habits, opinions, emotions or fears. Controlled, intelligent, but, in no way, crazy. The working theory is now that I have completely forgotten everything, a theory which is disproved by their own results. 'Very interesting' they keep mumbling. I may have convinced one or two of them that I am innocent" (Rule 2006, 203-4).

June 2, 1976: Carlisle assesses Ted. In his report he wrote:

> The constant theme running throughout the testing was a view of women being more competent than men. There were also indications of a fairly strong dependency on women, and yet he also has a strong need to be independent. I feel this creates a fairly strong conflict in that he would like a close relationship with females but is fearful of being hurt by them. There were indications of general anger and more particularly, well masked anger toward women. His attempt to remain emotionally distant from others is probably a defense against being hurt by them. There were indications of a fear of being put down and of humiliation which relates to this (Carlisle report, June 14, 1976, FSA).

Al Carlisle, PhD (circa June 2012). Source: https://www.youtube.com/watch?v=9F-PRpOTtbMI (accessed June 7, 2014).

June 5, 1976: Liz spends another evening at Rule's place. Liz expresses jealousy about Ted's other woman, "a law student" in Seattle.

June 6, 1976: Rule writes to Ted telling him that Liz knows about his "law student girlfriend."

June 7, 1976: Prison psychiatrist Van O. Austin assesses Ted. Ted undergoes a full medical test battery including skull x-rays, electroencephalogram, and a brain scan (presumably CT scan). Austin finds nothing remarkable: no evidence of any mental disorder apart from some passive-aggressive features which were consistent with Ted's hostility to the testing procedure. He did note, however, that Ted had a "very pronounced tendency to rationalize and compartmentalize his behavior," and his denial for memory of the crime was "too circumspect and convenient to be real" (Austin report, June 7, 1976, FSA).

Ted's response to this Thematic Apperception Test card: "Both of them have interesting expressions on their faces. The woman's is of admiration almost and of passion. The look on the man's face is one where he looks eager and confident. He may be leaving for some—for a trip, or an adventure and she, proud of what he is about to do, wants to kiss him one more time before he leaves. He is dressed in the shirt of a working man but may not have his tie on. They're married and they haven't been married long but she appears to be very much in love with him and he appears very eager to do what he what he had to do [sic] because he had that confidence and he was ready and he came back and now with that job off his mind, he could turn to her and have the same love in his eyes that she had for him" (Carlisle 2013, 326). Photo public domain.

June 22, 1976: Ted is convicted in court for evading police in SLC on August 16, 1975.

June 30, 1976: Ted melodramatically defends himself in court against the evaluation. Judge Hanson hands Ted a sentence of 1 to 15 years in jail. Ted is sent to Utah State Prison.

A defiant Ted on his way to sentencing, June 30, 1976. Photo public domain.

Utah State Prison, Point of the Mountain. Photo courtesy Chris Mortensen © 2015.

July 2, 1976: Supreme court rules capital punishment constitutional. Ted writes a caustic letter to Rule about his psychological evaluation. Ted appears to have lied about his general IQ, which Carlisle pegged at 122, but Rule quoted was 124 (Rule 2006, 210).

July 6, 1976: Received by Utah State Prison (located near Point of the Mountain) for aggravated kidnapping. Continues to attend Mormon church services despite being excommunicated by the religion. Spends his days working in the prison printshop, ironic given that he told Carlisle about his high school ski ticket forgery scheme during his evaluation.

August 25, 1976: Ted writes to Rule. Rule has impression Ted is pulling himself together again.

August 28 – September 1, 1976: Liz visits Ted in Utah State Prison. At first kissy and cuddly, she then reveals her true motive for coming: to end their relationship (Rule believes because Ted lied to Liz about his law student girlfriend). After leaving the jail Liz visits Fashion Place Mall to replay the DaRonch's encounter:

> When Ted was out on bail he had let me read a copy of the police report on Carol DaRonch's abduction. Now I wanted to retrace her steps. I parked behind Sears, as she had, and walked through the store into the mall. The report had said something about the Walden bookstore. I stood in front of it. I tried to picture Ted approaching, wearing green slacks and patent leather shoes. No, it didn't compute. I leaned against the building and watched people walk by. There were several young, attractive women shopping by themselves. Would Ted see them as victims? Someone did. If a man came up to me right now and said he was a police officer, what would I do? Would I go with him? If he was as handsome and well mannered as Ted, I might. The way the phony police officer had led Carol DaRonch all around the mall made me think that he enjoyed toying with his victim. (Kendall 1981, 154).

September 5, 1976: Rule receives "bleak" note from Ted. "... the end of all hope, the darkening of all dreams." Rule interpreted this as Ted's reaction to Liz breaking off their relationship the previous week.

September 7, 1976: Liz receives letter from Ted. "Sunday [August 30, 1976] I think I finally recognized how powerless and weak I am."

September 26, 1976: Ted writes to Rule. Seems to have gotten through the darkness.

October 19, 1976: Ted found not returned to his cell. Discovered hiding behind a bush with an "escape kit": a social security card, a sketch of a driver's license, road maps, and notes on airplane schedules.

October 22, 1976: Ted formally charged with the murder of Caryn Campbell. [MTR dates this October 21, 1976.]

October 26, 1976: Rule receives letter from Ted's "law student girlfriend."

October 31, 1976: Halloween. Rule receives letter from Ted who is in solitary confinement for his botched escape attempt.

November 24, 1976: Ted's birthday. Rule receives letter. Relates his observations on Gary Gilmore.

December 12, 1976: Ted examined by psychologist Gary Q. Jorgensen who concluded he was "intact psychologically."

Mid December, 1976: Ted writes to Rule.

December 22, 1976: Liz visits Ted in Utah State Prison again. This time to reunite.

December 23, 1976: Rule receives letter from Ted. It seems Liz and Ted are back on the menu.

- 1977 -

January 1977: Ted writes a letter to Bruce Lubeck asking him to help him be his own counsel. Ted wants to go it alone.

January 17, 1977: Gary Gilmore executed by firing squad at Utah State Prison. His execution ends a 10-year moratorium on capital punishment in the U.S.

January 22, 1977: Liz writes love letter to Ted.

> Dear Ted
> Of course I understand your anguish over my decision not to go to Colorado and your analogy of being caught in rapids together is accurate. I try not to think ahead but I'm not very good at not doing it. In fact a vivid scenario of what's to come is a much too much real part of my emotions these days. As I see it, the most difficult part would be not being able to see you except in the controlled situation of jail. I must admit that I admire Ann Swenson's ability to cope with that situation regularly. I have found that after our visit I have been totally enraged at everything. I don't need to catalog those thoughts for you as you have expressed the identical feelings. No, I am not

Glenwood Springs jail (2015). Pretty much as it was in 1977. Photo courtesy Chris Mortensen © 2015.

> strong enough to do it. I know it is in my gut. But on the other hand, it's not totally irrevocable but I can't imagine what would make me change my mind. I am aware of your strong need for support and it makes me feel terrible that I am letting you down. All I can offer are words—but they are meant—I do love you and always will. Yes, things are make-believe in a way and reality has a nasty way of spoiling our play. But your last couple of letters about me have really been works of wonder. They're not pretend. They give me confidence and hope. They have been filled with sharing and caring thoughts and suggestions. As you said once before, you know me better than any one else in this world and I value your opinions. I feel you are giving like you've never given before. I love you. Liz (FSA).

January 25, 1977: Ted writes Rule claiming to have "never purchased" a detective magazine. Also on this day, skeletal remains of Barbara Wilcox and Collette Goodenough found at the C-24 canal located just west of the Florida turnpike, Port St. Lucie.

January 28, 1977: 2:00 a.m. Ted moved to Aspen, Colorado, to face murder charge for Caryn Campbell. His new cell lies two floors below Judge George E. Lohr's courtroom in the basement of the Pitkin County courthouse. Louise Bundy called the Sheriff's Office the week before to find out what sort of accommodation was in store for her Ted.

Judge George E. Lohr (undated). Photo public domain.

January 29, 1977: Ted charged with murder, Aspen, Colorado. Released from the Utah State Prison to Colorado under the Governor's warrant.

January 31, 1977: Locked up in Pitkin County Jail.

March, 1977: Colorado Health Department declares Pitkin County Jail a short-term facility; no prisoner should be held there for more than 30 days.

March 9, 1977: Ted composes a letter to Judge Lohr, filing a motion to conduct his own defense. Lohr told Ted to wait until after the hearing.

March 21-23, 1977: Meeting held with Thompson in SLC. Present were Mike Fisher (Aspen, Colorado), Milton K. Blakey (Chief Deputy, District Attorney's Office, Colorado Springs), Dave Yocom (Salt Lake County Attorney's Office), Sergeant Paul Forbes (Murray PD), and Brent Bullock (County Attorney's Office in Utah County).

April 4, 1977: Preliminary hearing begins, presided over by Judge Lohr.

April 6, 1977: Judge Lohr delivers his opinion. The prosecution has demonstrated "probable cause" and Ted's trial would go ahead.

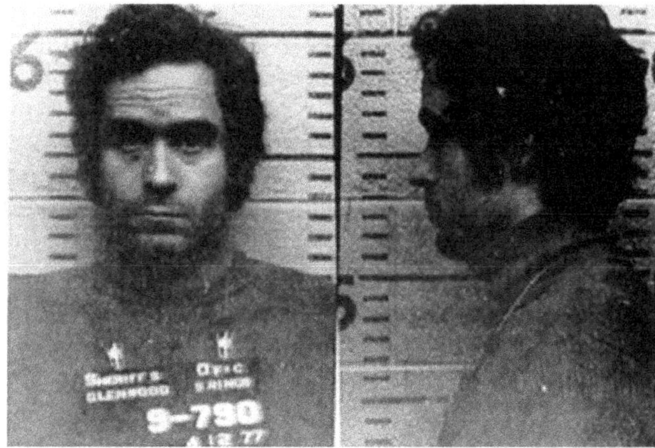

Mugshot of Ted taken on his arrival at Glenwood Springs April 12, 1977. Photo public domain.

April 11-13, 1977: Ted transferred from Pitkin County Jail, Colorado to Garfield County Jail, Glenwood Springs, Colorado, forty miles away.

May 1, 1977: Florida Chi Omega member Linda Sue Thompson (20) walked toward her Dorman Hall dormitory across Jefferson Street from the Chi Omega so-

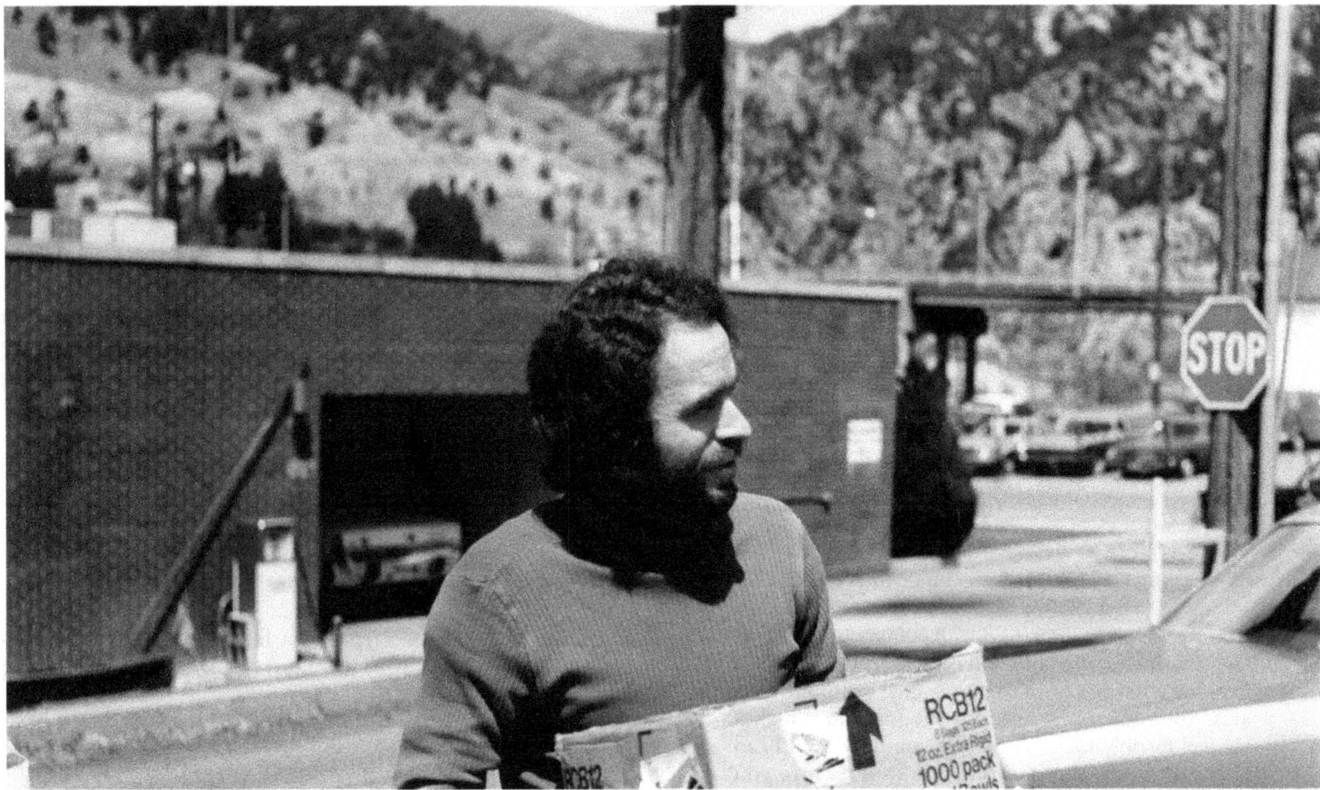

Ted walks in shackles to Glenwood Springs jail (mid-May, 1977). "My class is graduating in about a month." Photo courtesy KCA.

rority house with her fraternity date. After saying goodbye to each other, someone came up behind Thompson and struck her four times on the head with a club. The attacker then dragged Thompson to the woods beyond the 22-story State Capitol building and beat her severely. Two boys found her the next morning. Doctors said it was a miracle she lived. At the time, Nita Neary was Thompson's roommate.

May 3, 1977: Ted wrote letter to an unknown recipient: "You have probably heard that I became my own 'attorney' about two weeks ago. A recent United States Supreme Court case recognized the already existing right of a defendant in a criminal case to defend himself if his decision to do so is voluntary and intelligent and all those other good things. So I've been busier than the beer vendors in the kingdom. Up to my armpits in allegations. Things are shaping up fine."

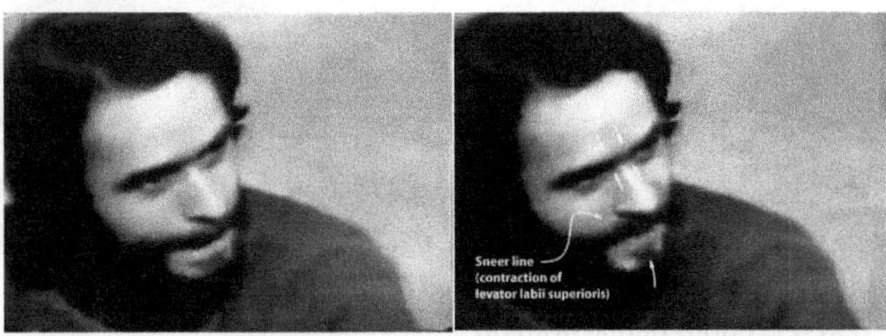

Barbara Grossman asks: "You are not guilty." Ted laughs, then replies: "I'm not guilty of the charges which have been filed against me." As soon as those words leave his lips he forms an unconscious mouth puck (image on left), suggesting he felt like he had given something away ... whereupon he checks his interviewer's response and seeing that she has not perceived his moment of weakness, allows himself a brief sneer of victory (image on right). Jerry Thompson in particular hated Ted's sneering laugh.

May 16, 1977: While in Garfield County Jail, Ted is interviewed by Barbara Grossman of KUTV. Portions of the interview are broadcast on May 16, 1977.

May 23, 1977: Enigmatic entry in Ted's 1974 diary: "FBI – now what's a nice FBI agent like you doing snooping in a book like this. Best regards, never again, ted [sic]. 5/23/77." Also on this day, Ted pleads "not guilty" to the murder of Caryn Campbell before Judge Lohr in Aspen.

May 27, 1977: Ted writes to Rule. Ted still in contact with Liz by phone. Resolves to escape.

Pitkin County Courthouse, Aspen, Colorado. Ted timed his escape down to the second. Photo courtesy Chris Mortensen © 2016.

June 7, 1977, Ted wearing two layers of clothes on his way to Pitkin County Courthouse before his escape. Photo source: AP

Ted smiles for the cameras as he is led back into court to face escape charges, June 13, 1977. "If it had been six stories, I still would have jumped." Note he is wearing a new prison outfit for his public appearance. Photo source: AP.

June 1977: Ted starts cultivating Carole Ann Boone. Letter to Boone: "Dear Carole."

June 7, 1977: (Morning) Ted is driven the 40 miles from Garfield County Jail to Pitkin County courthouse. 10:48 a.m. Ted escapes by jumping from the second story window, 25 feet (7.6 meters) above the ground, of the courthouse law library. (Evening) Rule receives 3 phone calls but no one spoke. Also on this day, Dr. Van O. Austin submits his psych evaluation of Ted to Judge Hanson.

Ted being brought back to Pitkin County Jail in the early hours of June 13, 1977. The rip in his shirt over the left shoulder suggests some sort of event occurred around his capture. Photo public domain.

June 13, 1977: 2:00 a.m. A weary Ted is recaptured after spending 5 days in the wilderness. He attempted to reach Crested Butte south of Aspen on foot but failed. MTR has Ted stealing a 1966 Blue Cadillac (CO tag ZG-1765) from 805 Bonita, Aspen, Pitkin County, Colorado on June 13, 1977. Ted tried to drive up Independence Pass but was blocked by a rockslide and had to turn back. That resulted in him being recaptured. 2:37 a.m. Ted is questioned in Sheriff Richard "Dick" Kienast's office about his escape.

June 15, 1977: Ted charged with escape, burglary and felony theft, Pitkin County.

June 16, 1977: Judge Lohr appoints Seattle lawyer Stephen "Buzzy" Ware as Ted's new counsel.

July 1977: Letter to Boone: "Beloved Boone."

July 7, 1977: Ted claims he has emerged from the post-escape recapture depression in a letter to Ware.

August, 1977: Ted finds Thompson omitted frustrating details about DaRonch as an eyewitness. Letter to Boone: "Oh My Boone."

August 11, 1977: Buzzy Ware has serious motorcycle accident, can no longer represent Ted.

August 16, 1977: Elvis Presley dead.

August 23, 1977: The United States received its first VHS-based consumer VCR – the RCA VBT200. Soon after, porn moves out of cinemas and into the home.

Mid-August, 1977: Rule writes to Ted commiserating loss of Ware. Ted replies sometime around this time with "genuine tears" for Ware.

September 1977: Letter to Boone: "Tender Apparition of Loveliness."

Carole Ann Boone (undated). Photo public domain.

September 16, 1977: Judge Lohr sets January 4, 1978 as the date for the murder trial to begin. November 14, 1977 was set for "suppression hearing" – the addition of "similar transactions" referring to other murders Ted was suspected of.

September 20, 1977: Calls Rule, asks her to send a single red rose to Liz for their "8th anniversary."

October 3, 1977: 1:10 p.m. Carlisle returns a call to Ted. Ted, it appears, originally called Carlisle to get the psychologist's impression of his June escape. "I had thought, that I was, I'm a pretty strong-willed person," Ted said, "but you know, believe or not, it's the body that was strong, the mind that was weak ...".

October 11, 1977: Request submitted to 4th District Court, Utah, by County Attorney Noall T. Wootton to exhume Laura Aime's body to obtain hair samples. He said that before the burial, hair samples were taken by the state medical examiner and given to the Utah County Sheriff, but those samples are no longer available. When asked Monday if the request indicated a break in the unsolved homicide, Wootton said, "Yes ... sure, no question about that." Wootton said he was unable to disclose what the break was (*The Ogden Standard-Examiner*).

November (sometime): Ted letter to Liz. "I have known people who, without saying a word, radiate vulnerability. Their facial expressions say 'I am afraid of you.' These people invite abuse. I don't know why but they do. Is it their self-concept? By expecting to be hurt do they subtly encourage it?"

November 2, 1977: First of the suppression hearings. Over the next two weeks starts sawing through the ceiling light fixture in his cell. Also starts shedding weight.

November 14, 1977: Judge Lohr rules "similar transactions" inadmissible, but DaRonch material permissible.

November 17, 1977: "Utah Woman Positive: Ted Was Kidnapper," (*The Daily Herald, Provo*).

November 24, 1977: Ted celebrates 31st birthday in jail.

End-November, 1977: Rule calls Ted to tell him she will move further out of his orbit due to a film script offer in Hollywood.

December 23, 1977: Judge Lohr orders the trial be moved to El Paso County, Colorado Springs. Carole Boone comes to visit Ted in Garfield County Jail, Glenwood Springs. Surprised at how fit he seemed. Even though he had a lot of trouble meeting her eyes at first, she recognized the Ted she had known at the Department of Emergency Services in Olympia. Ted's relationship with Liz is all but over.

December 27, 1977: Judge Lohr rules that the death penalty be eliminated as alternative penalty in Ted's upcoming trial.

December 30, 1977: 6:00 p.m. Calls Rule. They talk for about 20 minutes. Rule sensed Ted was saying "goodbye." 6:30 p.m. Ted escapes for the second time. The 35 pounds (16 kg) he had shed in weight allowed him to squeeze through a hole he had cut around the ceiling light fixture in his cell. Before going, he packed books and stuff under the blanket on his bunk in the shape of a sleeping person. He takes with him the $500 in donations he had received from family and friends. Once outside, he wandered around until he found an MG Midget with the keys in the ignition. It didn't drive too well, and in driving snow, he ended up getting bogged down in a snow drift 30 miles from Vail. Nevertheless, he managed to pick up a lift from a soldier on leave returning to Kentucky. They made it to Vail around 2:00 a.m. in the morning. The Vail pass was closed, so they couldn't go any further. Ted asked a cop off the freeway where they could hang out for a while and the cop said the Vail Holiday Inn. According to Keppel, Ted tried to canvas a ride inside and around outside the motel, but to no avail. By chance, Matt Lindvall happened to be working there as a night manager (whether he actually saw Ted is not mentioned).

Jailers fell for "the oldest trick in the book." Ted's jail cell after his second escape. Photo public domain.

NOTES

The dominant theme of Ted's first arrest is his steadfast denial of any involvement in the murders. It appears that for every person convinced of his guilt, there was another person convinced of his innocence. It is of interest that most of the latter group were family, friends and acquaintances. The other group, composed mostly of police and the victim's families, immediately had a sense that they had their man. One of these, Louis Smith, a police officer and Melissa Smith's father, attended court when Ted was present. Legal people from both sides specifically requested that his hand gun be removed to forestall the possibility that he might use it on Ted (M&A 1983, 154).

One person who was sure Ted was innocent was James Dunn, who lived across the hall from Ted at 565 First Avenue apartment, and who watered Ted's plants when Ted was away. Ted ended up being the best man at Dunn's wedding. When Thompson went to interview Dunn the first time on February 8, 1976, Dunn was extremely hesitant to provide any information about Ted. However, Thompson planted a seed of doubt in Dunn's mind. When Thompson asked Dunn what Ted had told him after his arrest, Dunn said that Ted told him he had been picked up for burglary tools, yet he had learned later from John O'Connell that they also found a pantyhose mask and handcuffs. Dunn then voluntarily stated: "That's the only thing that troubles me and that does make me wonder and is very suspicious to me why anyone would have pantyhose with the eyes and so forth cut out of them and a pair of handcuffs" (Thompson report February 20, 1976, FSA).

Dunn was just another one in a long list of Ted "psychological" victims. Scott Nelson was another. He lived for a brief period of time at 565 First Avenue and he later became embroiled in the police investigation surrounding Laura Aime. Ted told investigators that Scott had hung around Laura at Brown's cafe. When directly asked about that by Thompson, Nelson adamantly denied it, or any other involvement with Laura.

Bryan Severson was another victim. Not only did Ted sell him his VW with a fake title deed, but he also crossed-examined Severson in Aspen in court. In that instance, Ted got up and handed Severson three pictures of a VW bug and asked him if he could identify which car he bought from Ted. Unbeknown to Ted, during the brief two weeks that Severson had the car one of his female school friends had painted the windshield wiper water nipple with pink nail polish. Looking at the pictures he was immediately able to identify the car and said so. Whereupon, Ted turned to the court and said, "None of these are the car that I sold him" (Severson interview courtesy Chris Mortensen, November 18, 2015). Severson was flummoxed. But that is not all. Ted then went on and asked Severson how many red heads, how many brunettes, how many blonds had he screwed in that car, the inference being that he could account for Melissa Smith's hair found wrapped around the stick shift at the gear box interface. This being the case because Severson went to Hillcrest High School in Midvale, the same school Melissa Smith attended (she was a year ahead). However, this kind of questioning, trying to throw the blame on Severson was nonsensical, because Smith was murdered well before Severson was in possession of the vehicle. This display of pseudo-logic is typical of Ted and his PFC disorder; he is unable to connect the dots, but is quick to jump on isolated instances that fit his warped world view. The upshot of Ted's questioning, however, is that Severson was lumped with a shadow that would not leave him for years to come; a debt for a car he never owned, suspicion that he might have been involved in murder, and legal fees to recover the vehicle (which never eventuated).

Another victim was Bruce Lubeck, the other half of Ted's Utah defense counsel. He contended that the absence of evidence from the people who knew Ted showed Ted was "not an anti-social personality":

> There's no real explanation for beating a girl's head in and throwing her on the side of the road, except that there are monsters out there. The only way you can understand people is by what you see them do, by their actions. Everything I've seen about Ted—and I probably got to know him as well as anyone—is the same as everybody else. So, I don't think he's capable of that. You don't like to think that anybody is capable of that, but they do exist. If you've searched deep enough in his background, searched everywhere there is, and you don't see anything that indicates he beats girls over the head, then you've got to backtrack and say maybe he's not the one. I realize we're still arguing whether he is or isn't the guy. [...] And if you can't find evidence in Ted's life, then he isn't the monster the physical evidence says he is, because it would show up somewhere else and it hasn't" (Merrill, Wolf and Winn, "End of the Road," *Utah Holiday Magazine*, 1978).

Lubeck would later admit that he was fooled by Ted. As was John O'Connell. While these defense lawyers had a duty to protect their client, it also blinded them from asking the deeper questions that really needed to be answered. What was Ted doing sitting in a car at 2:30 a.m. in the morning outside a house with two teenage girls whose parents were not home, with rope, handcuffs, torch, ice pick, pantyhose mask, sheets torn in strips for bindings, gloves, crowbar, garbags ... the assemblage of items in that context requires an extraordinary explanation, and Ted did not, could not provide it.

Ruth Walsh, a television anchorwoman for Seattle's ABC affiliate, KOMO, discovered that seven other men could be linked circumstantially with some or all of Bundy's alleged crimes. "There are five possible 'Teds' in the Seattle area alone," she says. The list includes a convicted sex offender who was living in Seattle at the time of the murders there. He then moved to Aspen, where he took a job at Snowmass, the resort where victim Caryn Campbell was staying. His co-workers remember him as violent, especially toward women. He didn't show up for work on the day Campbell was murdered; the next day he picked up his paycheck and left town. (Subsequently he was given a lie detector test and passed.) Walsh also learned that another suspect in the Seattle slayings was living in Salt Lake City at the time of the DaRonch kidnapping. Later convicted of shooting a woman to death, the suspect owned a gun and handcuffs and matched DaRonch's description of her abductor – dark, slicked-down hair and a mustache. "The thing that makes me want solid proof against Bundy is that we have uncovered these other people," says Walsh. "They fit the pattern of evidence and description in an almost uncanny way (*People Magazine*, January 7, 1980).

At the time, John O'Connell did not believe that Ted tried to abduct DaRonch (this author got the impression that O'Connell still believes Ted was not responsible for DaRonch; personal email to author November 18, 2015). He felt the photo line-up by Jerry Thompson of Ted shown to DaRonch before the actual line-up at Murray police station was "suggestive" but not conclusive. He also felt that the trip from Fashion Place Mall to Viewmont High was not possible in the allotted time. In fact, due to discrepancies in the timeline, *it was possible*. O'Connell and Ted even retraced the route through Fashion Place Mall that the assailant supposedly traversed with DaRonch and found it took no more than 3-5 minutes, at least 5 minutes less than the accepted time! (W&M 1980, 152). Ted most probably would have taken the I-15 as it was the main route in 1974, a distance of around 23 miles. The trip would have taken 30 minutes at a constant speed of 45 miles an hour (72 km/p/h), within the legal speed limit in 1974 and entirely plausible. (Consider that Ted drove so fast when chased by Hayward that Hayward thought Ted's VW would tip over while cornering – so Ted was not averse to high speeds). But that is not the real clincher. Somehow, O'Connell convinced himself that Ted's explanations for the rape kit was not incriminating. Yet there were no other reports of a VW-driving crowbar wielding assailant who tried to abduct young girls in Utah for the year 1974-75. And the rape kit, for which Ted told numerous lies, when examined in context could only be interpreted as sinister, regardless whether it was the 1975 or 2015, regardless of how much background information was or wasn't available on Ted. On top of this, how many other assailants used an elaborate police officer ruse? Why O'Connell refused to join the dots is remarkable. Of course, there is a one-in-a-billion chance that it was not Ted. O'Connell could argue absence of evidence for another stalker and assailant in SLC at the time does not amount to evidence of absence. But it would take a deliberately opaque mind to ignore the more reasonable odds and circumstances of Ted's behavior. A person like Ted should not have been associated with those kind of odds. At the very least, that should have set off alarm bells, but it didn't.

On the afternoon of October 1, 1975, shortly after Jerry Thompson handed Ted a subpoena to attend a line-up at Murray Police Station for the next day, Ted visited the ward bishop and admitted for the first time details about his August 16 arrest. What explanation he offered for the crowbar and handcuffs is unknown, but he *omitted* the pantyhose mask (W&M 1980, 121). The ward bishop may have been Mel Thayne, then bishop of an LDS student branch Bundy actively attended. "All my memories of him are quite positive," Thayne said. "The girls were quite taken with him, and the fellows liked him, too. He just impressed all of us." Thayne remembers missed dinner appointments scheduled with Bundy. "He commented he would like to see what a Mormon family in our own setting was like. He had commented on what lovely girls we had." At the time, the Thaynes had four teenage daughters at home, two with long, dark hair, parted in the middle. "It kind of gives you the shivers when you think of what might have been," said Thayne's wife, Emma Lou Thayne (*Deseret News*, January 24, 1989). Those shivers were real then, but Nancy Page, administrative assistant to the Garfield County commissioners remembers how Ted would stand by the pay phone on the wall in the corridor about ten feet from her office in the courthouse, and stare at her for long uninterrupted periods - sometimes as much as 20 minutes without breaking his icy gaze. In another story, a young female dispatcher at the jail - a slender woman in her mid-'20s with brown hair - said the same thing. Ted stood by the phone

The Deseret News - Oct 9, 1986

Californian will be tried in death of woman

A California man has been bound over to district court to stand trial in connection with the bludgeoning death of a female transient on June 30.

After listening to brief arguments during a preliminary hearing, 5th Circuit Judge Michael Hutchings ruled there was sufficient evidence to bind William Michael Raine, 23, Temple City, Calif., over to 3rd District Court on charges of capital homicide.

Raine is charged with raping and killing Vivian Morse, whose seminude body was found June 30 at the bottom of a ravine near the south edge of the Pinecrest cutoff road in Emigration Canyon. She had been hit on the head with a blunt instrument about 10 times.

Salt Lake police detective Daryl Ondrak testified during the court hearing that he found a crowbar in Raine's car that appeared to have blood and hair on it.

Raine was arrested June 30 after investigators found his car parked near a canyon diner about six miles from where the body was discovered.

in the booking room and stared at her. "It was his eyes," she explained, that terrified her. She left her job unable to stand it (Merrill, Wolf & Winn 1978).

And of course, the person who should have known Ted better than anyone, Liz Kloepfer, went through numerous vacillations. Her doubts often reached their most intense when he was gone, the chief driving force her suspicion that he was having affairs with other women. As soon as Ted was back in her arms, everything was all right again, her fears subsided and hope rekindled. The evidence suggests Ted felt deeply for Liz, but for obvious reasons knew the relationship was doomed to fail. The evidence also suggests that Ted's relationship may not have been as "real" as he believed, rather, it was driven by a deeper need that he was unconscious of. During his adult years, he became involved with three women all of whom had a single child aged between 5-7 from a previous marriage. The first was Liz, the second was Leslie Knudson, and the third, Carole Boone. In each of these relationships he enthusiastically took up the role of stepfather. Could it be that he was trying to rewind the tape on the same period of his life when his mother took him across America and started a new life with Johnnie Bundy, a stepfather he never grew close to?

References

Adams, Nathan M. (1981) To Catch a Killer, *Reader's Digest*, March edition (pp. 201–239).

Carlisle, A. (2014) *I'm Not Guilty*, Genius Book Publishing, Encino, CA.

KUTV Ted Bundy interview (1977). Source: https://www.youtube.com/watch?v=AEWsxCrMM1U (accessed July 5, 2014).

McCall, C. (1980) 'The enigma of Ted Bundy: Did he kill 18 women? Or has he been framed?' *People Magazine*, Vol. 13 No. 1.

Merrill, D., Wolf, R. & Winn, S. (1978). 'A perfect stranger, part III: End of the road.' *Utah Holiday Magazine*.

Telephone call between Al Carlisle and Ted Bundy (October 3, 1977). https://www.youtube.com/watch?v=-jzRI0ga6Zw (Accessed February 11, 2016).

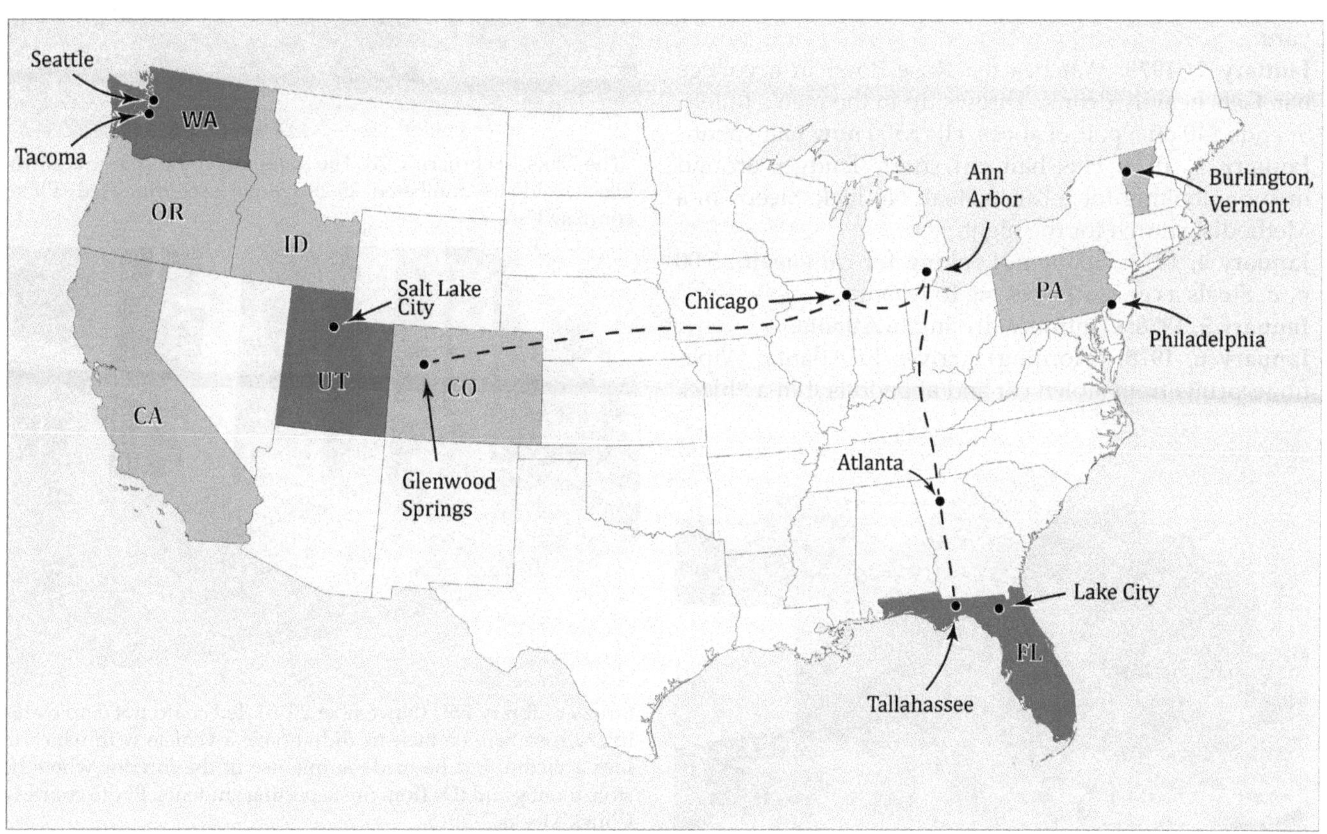

The route that Ted took on his second escape. Stolen car from Glenwood springs to Vail. Bus from Vail to Denver. Flight to Chicago. Train from Chicago to Ann Arbor. Stolen car from Ann Arbor to Atlanta. Bus from Atlanta to Tallahassee. Map courtesy © Free Vector Maps.

Escape! (December 31, 1977 - February 14, 1978)

December 31, 1977: 4:15 a.m. From Vail catches a Trailways bus to downtown Denver and the airport. 8:55 a.m. TWA flight to Chicago. 11:00 a.m. Chicago downtown. 10:30 p.m. Train to Ann Arbor. Stops in the YMCA, which lies on the western edge of the University of Michigan campus.

Ann Arbor YMCA, 350 S Fifth Ave, Michigan (May 1979). Photo © The Ann Arbor News.

- 1978 -

January 1, 1978: Ann Arbor YMCA. Shaves beard, keeps moustache. Hatches plan to work in a Gulf Coast boat yard.
January 2, 1978: Watches the Rose Bowl in a college bar. Gets heavily drunk. Throws up in the men's toilets. Spends $40 on a pair of shoes. His $500 now half spent.
January 3, 1978: Has hair cut short. Trudges around in snow looking for a car to steal. No luck. Sleeps in a Methodist church for the night.
January 4, 1978: 7:00 a.m. Looking for cars again. 5:00 p.m. Steals a car, starts driving to Atlanta.
January 5, 1978: Continues driving to Atlanta.
January 6, 1978: (Morning) Arrives in Atlanta. Wipes fingerprints from stolen car and abandons it in a "black

Atlanta Omni Center, 1978. Photo public domain.

ghetto." Steals a blue sleeping bag from sporting goods store. Goes to the Atlanta Omni Center where he takes in a movie (*The Sting*) while waiting for a bus south to Tallahassee. Later, feels a part of himself slip away like in the old movies where a ghost lifts out of the body (M&A 1983, 207).
January 7, 1978: (Morning) Arrives FSU campus. Warm thick air preceding 3 weeks of winter storms. Stores sleeping bag and extra clothes in a locker at the student bookstore. $160 left. Unwilling to go further. (Later that day) Signs rental agreement for a room at 409 West College Avenue, room 12, "The Oaks" pays $100 deposit. $ 60 left. Once settled in, the first thing he did was cruise the FSU library for an ID card to steal.

"The Oaks," February 1978. The building has since burnt down. Oaks residents numbered 25-28 people excluding Ted. Photo courtesy FSA.

Strozier Library FSU (November 2015). Ted could not employ his injury ruse here because he didn't have a vehicle with which to lure a victim. But he made ample use of the interior where he stole money and IDs from unsuspecting students. Photo courtesy Chuck Meeks © 2015.

January 10, 1978: (Daytime) Looks for work at the FSU student Employment Office. Steals Kenneth Raymond

Misner's ID card. Apparently Misner lost his ID card and someone found it. It was returned to the campus [registrar's office (W&M 1980, 242)] but the guy at the office was busy and told the person turning it in to leave it on the counter. Ted happened to be there and swiped it off the counter (Patchen interview, courtesy Chuck Meeks, October 27, 2015). He then looked around campus and stole a red bicycle. (Evening) Breaks into a 1971 Toyota and steals a Panasonic TV, a Sony transistor radio, and a Smith-Corona typewriter. Broke into a 1976 Mustang and steals a golf umbrella and a notebook. When hungry, shoplifts from local supermarkets.

January 12, 1978: 3:55 - 4:15 p.m. Ted steals a set of van

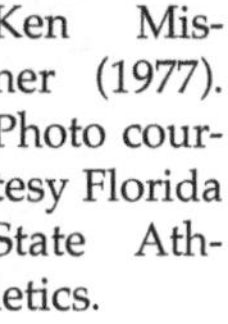

Ken Misner (1977). Photo courtesy Florida State Athletics.

FSU media center vans parked on the FSU campus (circa 1978). Photo public domain.

Ted's room at the Oaks (#12). We get a sense of how Ted lived in the room from Henry Polombo: "There was a sleeping bag, I would say light colored. [...] rolled up on top of the bed, without any sheets at all. Just bare mattress. [...] there was a t.v. and a radio" (Recorded statement to the Leon County Sheriff's Department, February 24, 1978). Tina Hopkins stated that she "never noticed a light coming from his door [...]. It was always dim TV light [...] ... he jogged a lot, [...] all the time real early in the morning [...]" (Tina L. Hopkins deposition, March 26, 1979). Leon County Sheriff's Office investigator William P. Gunter processed Ted's room and found it wiped clean, including table, chair, bedpost, closet, door and wall (*Spokane Daily Chronicle*, January 26, 1980). Photo courtesy FSA.

keys from the key hanging board at the FSU Media Center (tag 13D-11300).

January 13, 1978: Just one block from Cheryl Thomas' Dunwoody apartment, Randal Ragan, of 1002 West Street Augustine Street, notices his license plate has been stolen (13D-11300). If Randy stood at his back door, he could look directly at Cheryl Thomas' back door. He notifies the tag office and receives another tag.

January 14, 1978: Chi Omega day. The following mini-timeline depicts the main events:

(Around noon) Ted steals some chicken and potato salad from the deli section of a local supermarket [Majik Mart], eats it at a local school yard (M&A 1983, 210).

At approximately 9:00 p.m. Kathy Kratky of Reynolds Hall stated she and three other girls were walking from Reynolds Hall over to the Baptist campus ministry when they heard a strange noise. They looked behind them and observed a subject wearing a dark navy blue jacket, light pants and dark knit cap following them. They increased their speed. The subject called out "Girls, hey, girls" at which point they ran (Chi Omega Investigation Supplemental Report, January 16, 1978).

9:15 - 9:30 p.m. Ted spies on Cheryl Thomas getting ready to go out through a window. She leaves and he enters and sets things up so he can return later.

9:30 p.m. Doug Johnson arrives at Chi Omega House; he and Margaret Bowman leave in Bowman's car. They stopped at Jax's Liquors, West Tennessee Street, and attended a Phi Delta party at Westwood Condominiums, Ocala Road.

10:00 p.m. Lisa Levy, Debbie O'Brien and Melanie Nelson go to Sherrod's.

10:30 p.m. Michael Rush [pseudonym?] saw a man looking in windows of apartments and houses along West Pensacola Avenue. He was wearing a dark colored jacket, a dark colored cap, and beige pants (Sullivan 2009, 201 - no source reference provided). West Pensacola runs behind Chi Omega and down to Dunwoody. It is possible that Ted was on his way back from Dunwoody.

10:45 - 11:00 p.m. Lisa Levy leaves Sherrod's and is in bed by 11:00 p.m. (Rule 2006, 265). Ted may have seen her leave as he arrived at Sherrod's. He may have watched her from the car park at the back of Chi Omega and noticed which room she turned the light on or off.

Around 11:00 p.m. Cana Jean Nudi sees a man "walking very fast" from her 2nd floor apartment 924 West Pensacola Street (apartment A25). She sees him again about 10 minutes later walking very fast in almost the same spot (Cana Nudi deposition, March 29, 1979).

Estimated 11:00 p.m. Terri Murphy worked at Sherrod's and served Ted a drink (time unstated). She described him as being "overly polite." He was wearing a dark colored turtle neck, blue jeans, and some kind of desert or hiking boots. She got off work around 2:35 - 2:40 a.m. and returned to Chi Omega where she roomed and went to bed around 3:00 a.m. (Chi Omega Investigation Supplemental Report, June 28, 1978).

11:30 p.m. Connie Hastings saw Ted scanning the dance floor at Sherrod's; he was dressed in dark clothes, and appeared to her to be wearing other garments beneath them (M&A 1983, 211 have this occurring around 10:30 p.m.).

Midnight. Mary Ann Picano is asked to dance by Ted

Chi Omega Sorority House, 661 West Jefferson Street, as viewed from the north side of West Jefferson, showing the building that used to be Sherrod's next door (western side). Photo courtesy Chuck Meeks © 2015.

Map showing key locations where Ted was active around FSU. Map image courtesy USGS Earthstar Geographics SIO © Microsoft Corporation.

at Sherrod's. Picano describes Ted as an "ex-con" (Rule 2006, 265; M&A 1983, 211 have this occurring between 10:30 and 11:00 p.m.).

January 15, 1978:

12:10 a.m. Tom Trice, Mark Ihlefeld and Chris Kellog looking for a good time, arrive at Sherrod's. They saw some girls walk out, sorority types, not their class. They noticed a solitary male person sitting outside. Trice passed a comment to him and the person mumbled something back and they got the impression he wasn't real friendly. It was exceptionally cold, he had a dark colored "ski type hat" on, wearing a coat, had his hands in the coat pockets, light colored trousers, and a moustache. The girls walked past, and Trice noticed the guy was "actually looking straight down but he was looking kinda just spaced out" (Thomas McKell Trice, Leon County Sheriff's Office report, February 28, 1978). Incidentally, Trice believed Bowman was one of the girls that came out of Sherrod's. This can't be true if she was out with her boyfriend at a fraternity party at the same time.

12:15 a.m. Ted back checking Dunwoody. Cheryl Thomas "just got home, but the light was still on" (Nelson 1994, 291), so he heads back to the Oaks.

12:30 a.m. Tina Hopkins in her deposition said that she was going out for dinner with "Keith" from the Oaks around 12:30 a.m. and they were leaving and "he was coming back, he was coming in." When questioned further about this she said she was "real positive" she saw him, and that he might have been wearing a "plaid shirt" (Tina Hopkins deposition, March 26, 1979). Ted must have done another costume change at this point.

12:30 - 1:00 a.m. Carla Black and Valerie Stone arrive at Sherrod's. Black testified that Ted watched her for about 15-20 minutes. The last time she saw him was when she was coming out of the restroom. "He was standing up against the wall" (Carla Jean Black deposition, April 10, 1979).

1:15 a.m. Cheryl Rafferty stated that she returned to campus on Sunday morning at approximately this time and parked her car on the north side of the Longmire Building. She got out of her car and locked it. As she started to walk away a white male subject stepped out of the bushes and scared her. She began to walk very fast and the subject followed her. She then began to run and he still pursued her. She ran into Reynolds Hall (which is directly across the street from where she parked) and closed the door. She described her pursuer as wearing a dark colored button-up jacket, khaki colored pants and navy blue ski hat. She said she could definitely identify the subject as she got a very good look at his face. When shown a photo ID later on of Ted, she identified him as the pursuer (FSU Department of Public Safety and Security, January 17, 1978) (Sullivan 2009, 200-1 has this occurring around 10:15 p.m.; M&A 1983, 212-3 around midnight).

1:30 - 1:40 a.m. Bowman and Johnson leave the Phi Delta party in Bowman's car.

1:45 p.m. Bowman drops Johnson off at Phi Delta House. He tried to talk her into staying longer, but she said she was too tired and was going home.

2:00 a.m. Sherrod's closes. Bowman arrives at Chi Omega House. According to Henry Newkirk's deposition, he spoke to Melanie Nelson first. "Nelson said she came home from a date at 2:15 a.m. and noticed the rear door was unlocked. However, she did not mention it to anybody at that time. Miss Bowman walked down the stairs to see Miss Nelson when she was walking up, whereupon they both walked upstairs and into Miss Bowman's room. They talked until approximately 2:40 a.m. when Miss Nelson returned to her room" (Newkirk deposition, October 20, 1978).

2:10 a.m. Nancy Dowdy returns to Chi Omega after spending a night out. She went to bed between 2:15 and 2:20 a.m.

Approximately 2:30 a.m. Bowman loans her car to Leslie Waddell.

2:30 a.m. Greg Lowder and his friend Scott Corwin left Sherrod's at 2:00 a.m. when it closed. They drove around for an unspecified amount of time (15 – 45 minutes). They parked at the corner of Jefferson and Pensacola Street and walked to their Pi Kappa Alpha house (218 S. Wildwood). At that time they encountered a man who yelled out "Hey you", and they stopped as he crossed Jefferson Street and approached them. The man asked for directions to Missouri Street. Discussion followed, whereupon the man stated he was looking for the Holiday Inn, the "big round one." They gave the man directions and added that it was cold to be out walking around. The man said he had been walking all night and the cold didn't bother him (the temperature in fact dropped to -6 Celsius). He was wearing a dark colored knit cap with the edge rolled up, beige khaki colored pants, and a navy blue coat (nylon?) which he kept in his hands the entire time. After being shown a photo line-up, Lowder picked Ted (FSU Department of Public Safety and Security, June 21, 1978).

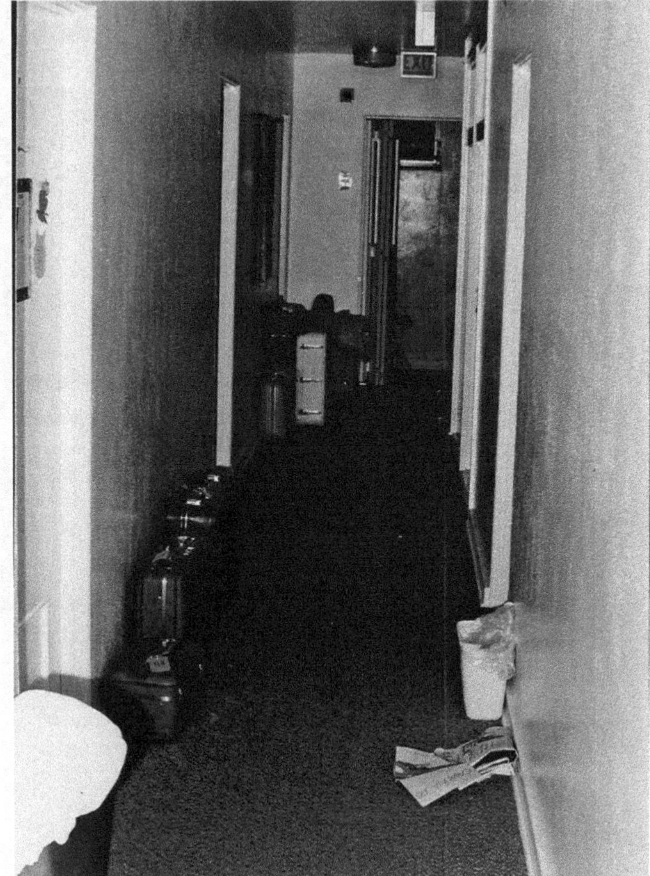

The 2nd floor corridor of the Chi Omega House (February 1978). Photo courtesy FSA.

Around 3:00 a.m. Mark Hodges was driving westbound along West Jefferson Street (on the opposite side of the road looking out of his driver's side window) and spotted a white male 5'8", 150 pounds, thin build wearing what appeared to be either blue jeans or dark work pants, a dark knit cap and blue down-filled quilted jacket "like hunters or skiers wear." The man was standing with his back toward Jefferson Street, and Mr. Hodges did not see his face. Hodges stated that he was startled by the suspicious behavior of the man because there was no other car or foot traffic around (Tallahassee police report, undated).

Some time around 3:00 a.m. Ted picks up an oak log outside the Westside ground floor entrance to the Chi Omega House, enters the building, and goes upstairs ... what happens next is not completely clear, but by the time he leaves about 15 minutes later, Margaret Bowman (21) is dead, Karen Ann Chandler (21) and Katherine Kleiner (21) sustain severe jaw injuries, and Lisa Levy (21) is dying, pronounced dead shortly afterwards. Rule rightly points out that alcohol not only affected Ted that night, but the sorority girls as well. They may have heard a thump or two, but they were too drowsy with alcohol to register fully what was going on around them.

Shortly after 3:00 a.m. Nita Neary returns home after a night out with her boyfriend at a drinking party. She had only a few drinks because she had a cold and wasn't feeling too well. She moved through the ground floor turning off the lights. Suddenly she heard a loud thump. She thought it was her boyfriend tripping on the stairs outside, but when she checked through a window she saw he was already getting into his car. A moment later she heard running footsteps in the corridor above. She moved to the doorway leading into the foyer hidden there from anyone coming down the front stairs. The foyer was lit and the double front white doors were about sixteen feet away. The sound of the footsteps gave way to the presence of a man who reached for the doorknob with his left hand. She told officers that "he had a stocking hat over his head and it was pulled down almost to his eyes. [...] he had a prominent almost pointed nose. [...] he was carrying a club that looked like it had some kind of sock wrapped around it, a dark one. He had a dark jacket on and [...] light colored pants" (Nita Jane Neary deposition, April 2, 1979). She had barely enough time to catch him in profile, and then he was gone into the night (Rule 2006, 266-7; M&A 1983, 215). Nancy Dowdy said she was woken up by Nita Neary sometime after 3:00 a.m. Neary saying a man just went out the front door. They went downstairs to check the door, then back upstairs to talk to the sorority president Jackie McGill. As they talked, Karen Chandler came out of her room and ran away from them down the hall. Dowdy brought her into room #3 alone. Chandler "had her hands over her face, and she was just mumbling." Dowdy noticed some blood on her. In the meantime, someone called the police (Dowdy deposition, October 30, 1978).

Note, it is implied that Kathy Kleiner was discovered shortly afterwards.

3:15 a.m. Christopher Anifowoshe Yommy ("Segun") was coming from a nightclub Stonehenge on 116 East Park Avenue, was on Jefferson Street, about ten yards from the Sweet Shop going West, about 2:00 a.m. went to pick up a female African-American friend "Darlene" at Frenchtown (took 5-7 minutes) outside the Clover Club 400 block West Virginia Street, stayed about 15 minutes waiting, left about 2:00 - 2:22 a.m. drove on Tennessee Street then on the street where you have Bill's Book Shop (Copeland Street) drove south and turned right on Jefferson Street, took about 5 minutes, Darlene had to be back home at 3:00 a.m., but they were going to Yommy's apartment first, this is about 2:45 a.m., when he drove by the vicinity of the Chi Omega house, when he spotted Ted walking westward (this is on Segun's left side), and he had something in his left hand, concealing something "by his side," walking fast. He was wearing a jacket and a "winter hat on his head." At first Yommy was driving about 50 m.p.h. but slowed to 25 m.p.h. when he saw Ted, thought he was acting suspiciously, "fixing to go rob somebody or something", Ted being the only person on the street at that hour. When asked what Ted was holding Yommy said "something long", thicker than an umbrella. By the time Yommy got to him, Ted was about 5-10 yards from the Sweet Shop. Yommy said the hat was above the ears, he had short sideburns, a dark colored coat and dark pants. In the end, Yommy said he stayed with Darlene at his apartment for about half an hour and got her home late at around 3:20 a.m. which placed his sighting of Ted at around 2:37 a.m. (which is clearly incorrect). Yommy had only one beer that night. They asked him if he smoked marijuana that night, and Yommy answered "No sir." (Christopher Anifowoshe Yommy deposition, March 19, 1979).

3:15 - 4:30 a.m. No information available on Ted's whereabouts or activities for this period.

3:23 a.m. Officer Oscar Brannon is first on scene at Chi Omega (W&M 1980, 228).

3:35 a.m. Officer Newkirk arrives at Chi Omega (Newkirk deposition, October 20, 1978). Officer Ray Crew discovers an unresponsive Lisa Levy. Medics begin cardiac resuscitation, but Lisa is pronounced DOA at Tallahassee Memorial Hospital. Shortly after Levy is discovered, Newkirk discovers Margaret Bowman dead from severe blows to the head and strangulation with a pantyhose. According to Diane Cossin, "A group of us are gathered in my room. And we were chatting and you know catching up on the news, and just enjoying one another, and then one by one we would turn in. My wall adjoined Margaret's wall. And her bed was up against the wall as was mine. I was roused, you know wakened, by hearing something. She [Nita Neary] saw someone coming down the stairs and then exiting through the door. There's blood everywhere, and ah, Lisa was hurt, and I just bent over to help her, um, she had just had her braces removed after wearing braces for almost a year, she had such a beautiful smile, and um, that's really the extent of what I recall until I believe it was an EMT that grabbed me by the shoulders and pulled me away." Susan Denton added, "It was a very, very cold night, and sometimes that deadbolt lock, and the combination lock would stick, and it would not retract back into the door-jam, and so, just luck" (*Murder Made Me Famous*, AMS Pictures, 2015. Season 1, Episode 5). According to one of the EMT reports: "Chandler was on the left side of the room on the floor by the bed. She was entwined with the blanket from the bed. Her knees were raised. She had been triaged by the 43/46 team. Her head was bandaged. She had been beaten about the head and face. Upper incisors broken. Her pupils were equal. [...] She did not know what happened" (Charles Norvell incident report [undated], Florida State Archives). Kathy Kleiner was treated by William Mathews. He stayed with her at the scene and all the way to the hospital. In his report he wrote that Kleiner "had two wounds to the right of the lower jaw [...] oral injury ... her tongue was also lacerated" (William Gary Mathews incident report [undated], Florida State Archives).

Approximately 4:30 a.m. Ted enters 431/A Dunwoody Street and attacks Cheryl Thomas. Thomas reported that the last thing she remembers as she was dozing off was hearing what she thought was her cat knocking a pot plant off a window sill, suggesting Ted entered through the kitchen window.

4:30 a.m. Apartment 431/B Dunwoody Street. Debbie Ciccarelli was awoken by a "real loud pounding noise." She described it as "someone was underneath the house with a hammer, just banging." She woke her roommate Nancy Young up. Together they listened. Only silence. Worried, Debbie called her boyfriend and told him what had happened. He told her to forget about it, go back to sleep. Unsure, Debbie called Cheryl's apartment. They heard the phone ring but Cheryl didn't answer. Instead, they heard whimpering sounds which they knew came from Cheryl. Debbie immediately called the police (this was logged by dispatch as having occurred at 4:37 a.m.). While on the phone to police, they heard another noise, "a loud rumbling sound in the kitchen, which [they] later thought to believe possibly was the kitchen table being moved aside" (Deborah Ann Ciccarelli deposition, October 27, 1978).

4:38 a.m. Ted climbs back out of Cheryl's window and slips back into the night.

Shortly after 4:30 a.m. Student Orley Sorrell was waiting outside his Sigma Chi fraternity house at 515 West College Avenue waiting to be picked up by a friend when he spotted a man running eastbound along West College Avenue. He "cut across the street right past the Zeta Tau Alpha house, just across the street and went to the corner, hid in the bushes, and checked out to see if there were any cars coming and then [...] waited a minute and when it was all clear, continued running down College Street and went about half a block [...] and then I didn't see him anymore." He was wearing light pants, a dark jacket, a navy pullover type thing, and a "snow cap" (FSU Police Department report, February 24, 1978).

Pre-assault photos of the Chi Omega victims. Left to right: Bowman, Chandler, Kleiner and Levy. Photos public domain.

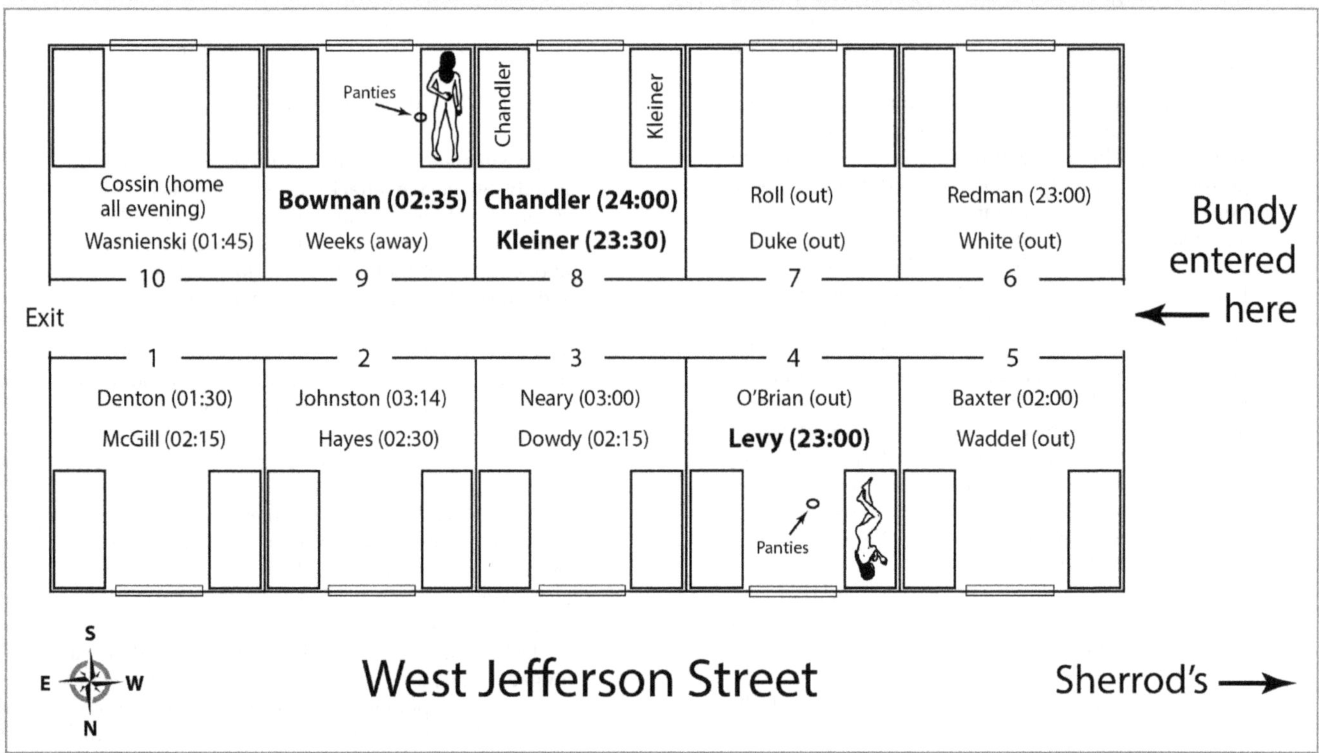

The Chi Omega first-floor layout showing room number, occupants and time occupants went to bed or arrived home. Approximately 45 girls were in the building at the time of the attack. Most were asleep. All the girls in the upper east wing, except Nita Neary and Carol Johnston, were in bed by 2:45 a.m. Neary arrived at 3:00 a.m. to find an intruder leaving the building through the front entrance foyer. From this timeline it is thought the attacks occurred within a space of 15 minutes.

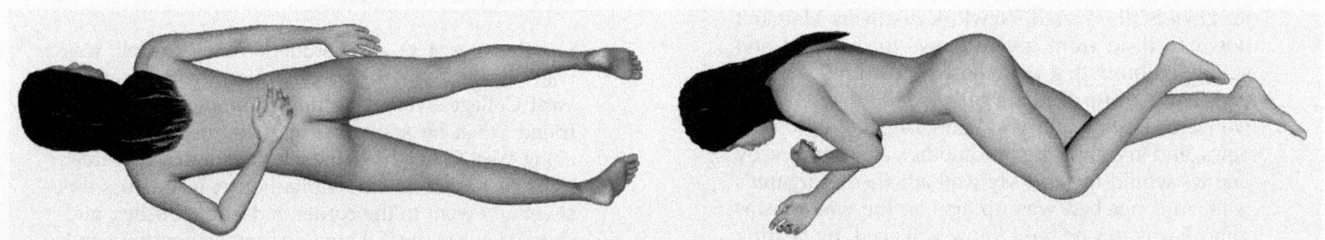

Left: Bowman as she was observed at the scene. According to Deputy Hurdle's report, there was "bark from a tree limb in her hair" [...] and "tree bark chips scattered on the floor" (Leon County Sheriff's Department, January 20, 1978). Right: Levy as she was observed at the scene. According to Dr. Mark Goldberg's report: "Large amount of swelling under both jaws, extending down to her neck. A laceration over her right nipple ... some bleeding in her [right] eardrum, severe head injury ... Also some evidence of some rectal bleeding" (Larsen 1980, 216).

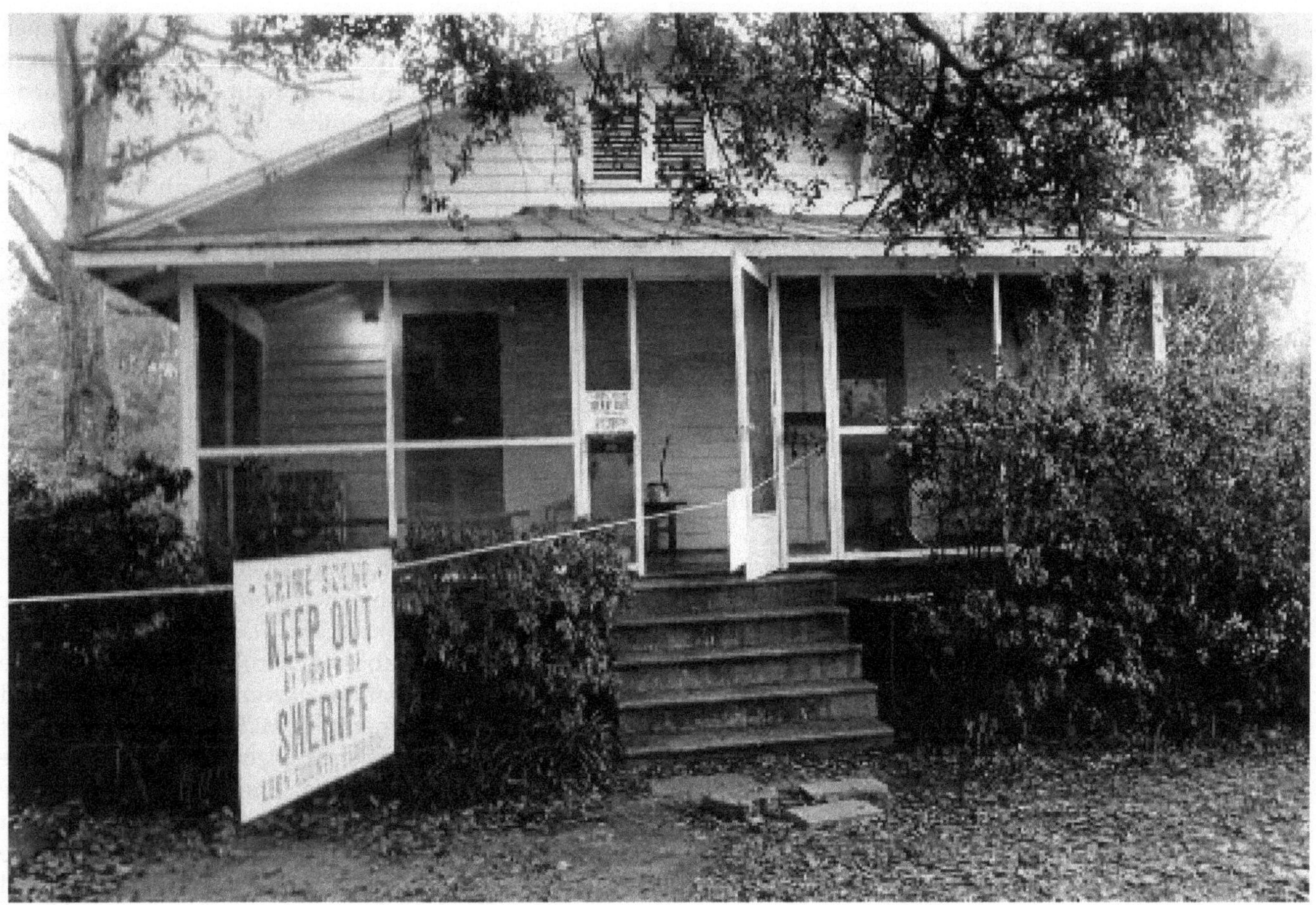

431 A/B Dunwoody with police lines in place after the assault (February 1978). Photo courtesy Don Patchen.

> 4:45 - 5:30 a.m. Henry Polombo and Rusty Gage came home to the Oaks were they lived and saw Ted inside the entrance to the Oaks at the bottom of the stairs. By the time they enter the building, Ted is at the top of the stairs. Polombo said "Hi" but Ted said nothing back ('Polombo' Leon County Sheriff's Office report, February 24, 1978).
>
> In the afternoon, Ted returns the stolen keys to the Media Center van's glove compartment.

To Dorothy Lewis, Ted admitted Cheryl Thomas was his primary target:

> Bundy.: [...] I remember on a particular night going down there, decided to do something ... watching her through the window, she was getting ... ready to go out. Her leaving the door open. And going in, going in and setting things up so that I could get in later on. And then waiting, going home and drinking some more, drinking heavily. Of course I'd been in jail for a year or two, so the alcohol was particularly potent. And then going back at midnight or so and seeing that she'd just got home, but the light was still on, and then saying I'll wait 'till she goes to sleep, I'll go back and drink some more.
> Lewis: So twice you went back there.
> Bundy: Yes, but between the place where I lived and this house, I was walking back, just happening to be walking along the road, and I was just all aroused, full of energy, you know, peaked for this. I happened to look over across the street casually and I saw a door open to the sorority house. And I just turned and walked right for the door. That's what happened (Nelson 1994, 291).

Ted makes Chi Omega sound like it was a totally spontaneous event. Based on the mini-timeline we have constructed, it clearly wasn't. So Ted is putting a spin on the truth even as late as the day before his execution. This is probably due to the fact that he still believed in his heart-of-hearts that he wasn't going to be executed – at least not yet. A news article after he was executed suggests that the efforts to delay his execution were more frantic than initially believed (Brent Kallestad, February 22, 1989).

However, his revelation that Thomas was his primary target we can take as true. Interpolating the mini-timeline, Ted first went into her apartment sometime between 9:30 - 10:00 p.m. as he was seen at Reynolds Hall at 9:00 p.m., which suggests that he was on his way from the Oaks to Dunwoody. He returned again around midnight, then went back to the Oaks for another change of clothes. Not only on the night, but in the days leading up to the attack he had ample opportunity to see girls going in and out of the back door of the Chi Omega House. Furthermore, he frequented the Tallahassee Mall where Lisa Levy worked at the Colony Shop. She was employed there part-time and usually worked nights during the week and almost every Saturday. She worked Saturday 14 January until about 5:45 p.m. (Lisa Levy Death Investigation, Florida State Archives). Incredibly, there is a report that substantiates Ted's visits to the mall. In the week leading up to the attack, Ted went into Parklane Hosiery and said to the young sales lady there that he was interested in starting a similar store of his own. Ted told her he was visiting from Valdosta. She showed him around the shop. Did he steal any pantyhose? We don't know, but the remarkable thing about this story is that later on the same day he called her up by phone and asked if she would go out with him on a date with him! She declined, saying she had a boyfriend (Pantyhose report, Florida State Archive). We can safely assume, therefore, that Ted may have seen Lisa Levy at least on one occasion as he wandered through the mall. So when Ted arrived at Sherrod's around 11:00 p.m., the same time that Lisa left the disco, there is the possibility that he saw her and watched her as she entered the Chi Omega House. All of this is pure speculation of course, but the evidence means we cannot rule it out.

In discussing Chi Omega, the issue of the order of attack remains one of the lingering questions that to this day has never been adequately resolved. Different authors arrive at different conclusions. Michaud & Aynesworth suggest Levy, Chandler/Kleiner, Bowman in that order. Their reasoning is that blood type O, Levy's type, was found mixed with type A, Chandler/Kleiner's type, on the walls and ceiling of room 8, Chandler/Kleiner's room (M&A 1983, 221). They do not provide the source for their claim that Lisa had blood type O [the Lisa Levy death report is missing pages including her bloodwork]. More importantly however, Bowman's blood type was also O (Bowman death report, FSA). Michaud & Aynesworth fail to mention this. Added to this fact is that Bowman was severely bashed releasing large amounts of blood, whereas only small amounts of blood were found on Lisa Levy's body. So blood transfer is more likely to have come from Bowman. Also, large amount of bark were found on and around Bowman, whereas significantly lesser amounts were found in the other rooms. Sullivan suggests Chandler/Kleiner were attacked first but does not state the order of Bowman and Levy (Sullivan 2009, 202). Rule proposes Bowman, then Levy, and Chandler/Kleiner as "afterthoughts" (Rule 2006, 272). Winn & Merrill do not say. Larsen doesn't say. Keppel doesn't say but the order in which he presents the girls' names suggests he believes Levy, Bowman, Chandler/Kleiner (K&B 2005, 125).

Given the possibility that Ted had seen Levy at the Tallahassee Mall and had seen her leaving Sherrod's, we propose that she was his "target" at Chi Omega. By saying target, we are drawing on our knowledge of Ted's M.O. Ted almost invariably raped and killed women that he first became fixated with. He would not attack *any* woman. She had to be just right – right age, right attitude, right body, right clothes. It wasn't that he was obsessed with girls that had their hair parted in the middle. He was more specifically obsessed with cheerleaders, dancers and athletic girls. From 1970 - 1975 Levy was listed in *Who's Who of Baton Twirling* in America (Levy death report, FSA). She was *just* right. Therefore, we propose that when Ted entered the Chi Omega house, he was searching for Levy. He didn't know which room she occupied. According to his own statement: "So I just walked in. There was nobody. Everybody was asleep. [...] I just walked upstairs and went down to the end of the corridor and went into the first room I saw. Well, I'd picked up a log from this wood pile and [...] I'd be just thinking of, like, there she is, and knocking her unconscious and going back to cover up, step by step ..." (Nelson 1994, 292). In his own words, he *went down to the end of the corridor and went into the first room*. This, then, would be Bowman's room. Bowman wasn't Levy, so he let his pent-up frustration out on her. He then moved to Chandler and Kleiner's room. Seeing that neither of them were Levy, he bashed them senseless to silence them, in case they heard the commotion next door. He then walked back into the corridor, and feeling that he wasn't having any luck on the southern side of the building, moved across to the northern side, and found her. Levy was the only victim he sexually assaulted. He bashed her, molested her, and strangled her. Therefore, he spent the most time with her. Interestingly, Ted brought "three sets of women's pantyhose with him. He had stolen them from their owners, because each, when found, showed signs of wear and laundering. He neatly cut the right leg from one pair and looped the left leg back through to form a ligature. He left this pair around Margaret Bowman's neck. A second pair, altered identically, he dropped in Bowman's room. They were found in Margaret's roommate's bed. He used the third set as a mask" (M&A 1983, 220). Bowman's roommate was Kim Weeks. The pantyhose was actually found beneath the bedcover on the sheet above the mattress. What was it doing *there*? He didn't leave it there to hide evidence. He didn't leave it there because he was disturbed and accidentally forgot it. The only feasible explanation is he entered Bowman's room and being left-handed, turned to Weeks' bed first, pulled back the covers but finding no one there, went over to Bowman and struck her. Then, as he went to strangle Bowman he excitedly (or hurriedly) pulled the pantyhose out of his pocket and in that action he may have flung the second pair onto Weeks' bed in a kind of sling-shot motion. Not realizing that he had done that, and covering up "step by step" on his way out, he pulled both Bowman's and Weeks' bed covers back over their beds when he exited the room.

Upon exiting the Chi Omega House, Ted is spotted

Top left: Cheryl Thomas pre-assault (undated). Photo public domain. Bottom left: the Dunwoody kitchen window flyscreen showing point of entry/exit. Photo public domain. Right: The flower pot that Ted knocked over as he came in. Photo courtesy FSA.

by Mr. Segun. Even though Segun's sighting according to the record occurred much earlier, we know it had to be post-Chi Omega, because he stated that he saw the suspect concealing something by his side as he walked rapidly in a westward direction, which would put him on a path to Dunwoody. However, for the next hour or so, we have no information about Ted's activities or whereabouts. Considering that he does not enter Dunwoody until about 4:30 a.m. and the oak club which he was seen carrying was never found, it is likely that he spent that time disposing of the evidence before entering Dunwoody.

Ted entered 431/A Dunwoody through the kitchen window. To do this he partially removed the mosquito screen on the outside before climbing through. His efforts weren't that successful because he half tore the curtain off its rail and knocked a pot plant onto the floor. This created enough noise to rouse Thomas from her slumber. She thought it was her cat. Ted must have moved fast, because around this time Thomas' neighbors Nancy Young and Debbie Ciccarelli heard loud banging noises followed by the sound of Thomas "whimpering" (Ciccarelli deposition, October 27, 1978). When Ciccarelli called Thomas and got no response she called 911. That call was logged at 4:37 a.m. During the call, they heard a loud rumbling sound in the kitchen which they interpreted to be someone dragging the kitchen table across the floor. It is of interest that when Bill Gunter

Left: The pantyhose mask Ted left entangled in Thomas' sheets, pulled out and laid on the floor by Leon County Sheriff's Office Deputy Mary Ann Kirkham. Right: The lath that Thomas used to prop up her bedroom window. Photos courtesy FSA.

of the Leon County Sheriff's Office processed the house for evidence on January 17 at 10:30 a.m. he reported a Formica topped table, one end of which was "directly in front of the window" (Gunter deposition, October 17, 1978). Whether the table was always there, or whether it was pushed by Ted is not clear, but we can be certain he used it to climb back out of the window and into the night. Upon arriving after the 911 call officers Wilton Dozier and Jerry Payne gained entry to the apartment; they found Cheryl "lying diagonally across the bed [...] twisting with pain and groaning. Cheryl wore only panties; her breasts were exposed; the sweater she'd worn when she went to bed had been ripped off" (Rule 2006, 276).

The most incriminating piece of evidence found at the scene was the pantyhose mask. It contained two wavy brown hairs. As for the window stick found on the floor, some authors claim it was the weapon used to beat Thomas, but her blood was not found on it. Ted more than likely took the weapon with him and disposed of it like he did the oak club.

Dancing student Thomas sustained five skull fractures, her eighth cranial nerve was severed, her jaw broken, and shoulder dislocated. She recovered but was left with profound hearing loss in her left ear and severe balance problems that effectively limited her from ever become a professional dancer.

It appears Ted was seen again on his way back to the Oaks by a student shortly afterwards. He was then seen climbing the stairs to his room at the Oaks by a couple of fellow residents. It is possible, but not conclusive, that Ted threw away his dark knit toboggan cap in the vicinity of the Oaks on his way back. The cap was found and processed but the information appears to have been lost (Fletcher Flieder deposition, October 26, 1978; Clarence Hooker deposition, January 19, 1979).

January 17, 1978: Frances Messier (cosmetology student) moves into the Oaks. Ted immediately asks her for a loan of a pair of scissors to cut a pair of shorts. Apart from this, there are no other reports of Ted's activities for this day. Presumably he laid low, listened to media reports about the Chi Omega attack and prepared his next move.

January 19, 1978: Clairol hair spray bottle used to sodomize Levy belatedly discovered in Levy's room.

January 21, 1978: Ted steals Frances Labadie's purse with her husband's credit card in it at the 1940 Monroe Street, Publix Supermarket, Tallahassee. He initially was only interested in the cash and threw the purse in a dumpster. However, he later returned and retrieved it. That night he spent $12 on dinner at the Deli restaurant. He continues using Labadie's card through till February 14.

Clairol Final Net Hair Mist bottle circa 1979. Photo public domain.

January 23, 1978: Uses Labadie's card at Phiddipide's and the Holiday Inn (food), Tallahassee.

January 24, 1978: Uses Labadie's card at the Holiday Inn (food), Tallahassee. Hanes pantyhose ligature found by Sergeant Howard Winkler on top of the mattress and under the cover Kim Weeks' bed in room #9 (Margaret Bowman's room).

January 25, 1978: Uses Labadie's card at The Deli and the Holiday Inn (food), Tallahassee.

January 26, 1978: Uses Labadie's card at the Holiday Inn (food), Tallahassee.

January 27, 1978: Uses Labadie's card at the Holiday Inn (food), Tallahassee.

January 28, 1978: Uses Labadie's card twice at the Holiday Inn (food), Tallahassee. Charged $150 worth of goods and clothing—mostly tennis gear and socks—in five stores - The Attic, D.C. Wheelers', 10 Speed Drive, The Yankee Peddler and Walden's Bookstore at the Tallahassee Mall.

January 29, 1978: Uses Labadie's card at the Holiday Inn (food), Tallahassee.

January 31, 1978: Uses Labadie's card twice at Western Sizzler, Tallahassee.

February 1, 1978: Ted receives Misner's birth certificate from Vital Records in Raleigh, North Carolina (W&M 1980, 242). Uses Labadie's card at The Pass to buy more socks and two shirts. He brazenly reappeared at Sherrod's and stole Evelyn Moore's wallet.

February 3, 1978: 3:00 p.m. First credit cards stolen at FSU campus attributed to Ted by campus security. The first belonged to Kathleen Evans' father, William Evans which Ted stole while Kathleen was at the FSU Media Center. (Afternoon) Spends $250 using Evans' card in Tallahassee. Smoker's pipe, lighter, and tobacco, at Smoker's World; luggage at Richard's Luggage; underwear, belt, shoes and socks at Nic's Toggery; washcloths, towels and sheets at Shaws Inc.; tennis gear at Rapp's Racquet Shop. (Later that evening) He stole Martha Miller's wallet at the Silver Dollar Bar, which contained her father's credit card, Ralph Miller. Uses Evans' card at the Hilton Hotel, Tallahassee; also stole two wallets at the hotel. (Later that night) Again at Sherrod's he lifted the purses of four [or was it 6?] other women.

February 4, 1978: Uses Evans' card at Nic's Toggery and Rapp's Racquet Shop. Labadie's card twice at the Hilton. Steals another credit card at Big Daddy's Lounge.

February 5, 1978: FSU Media Center personnel had frustrated Ted's efforts to steal their van. They continued blocking the van in at night with other cars. In response, Ted went to a hardware store, had copies of the van keys made, and returned the keys to the dashboard of the van. When the Media Center personnel found the keys, they stopped blocking the van in. Some time between 2:00 p.m. on this day and 6:00 a.m. the next day, Ted stole the van, replacing its tag with Ragan's tag. In between he used Evans' card at Andrews 2nd Act, and Labadie's at the Hilton, Tallahassee.

February 6, 1978: Charges $60 more on credit cards; shirts, slacks, pyjamas, and a blanket. Ted leaves Tallahassee. On the way he spent $8.58 on pastries and cookies at the Tasty Pastry Shop.

February 7, 1978: (Morning) Evans' card in Tallahassee at Tasty World, Andrew's 2nd Act, Eckerd's Drugs, J. Byrons. 11:00 - 11:30 a.m. Gulf service station at intersection of I-10 and US 441 North, Lake City, attendant identified Ted as the man driving a white van using a stolen credit card (William Evans'; $4.56). He was described as wearing a "gray sweat shirt and starting frisking around as soon as he got out of the van" and when he went to sign the credit card "his hands were shaking" (FDLE). (Mid afternoon) Gulf service station corner Roosevelt Boulevard and Saint Johns Avenue, Jacksonville, Ted used Thomas Evans' credit card. Bought 8.4 gallons at 60.9 cents a gallon. Ted headed south on Roosevelt Boulevard. 10:00 - 11:00 p.m. He stopped for a meal at the Holiday Inn at I-295 & US 217, using William Evans' credit card to pay for what he consumed: shrimp cocktail, a steak (medium rare), lobster combination plate, blueberry pie with ice-cream, totaling $13.76 with tip. He prowled around Jacksonville till midnight until he checked in at the Holiday Inn at 12:53 a.m. on 555 Stockton Street (room 134), again using William Evans' card ($19.76; FDLE).

Buck 120 General Knife. Photo public domain.

February 8, 1978: (Morning) Walked out of the Holiday Inn without checking out. Drove to the Gulf service station on Stockton & Edison Street in Jacksonville and bought a map, this time using Labadie's credit card. (Around noon) Ted entered the Green Acres Sporting Goods store at 8774 Normandy Boulevard, Jacksonville, where he bought a Buck General hunting knife from John Farhat for $26. Back in the van, Ted removed the price tag and let it flutter to the floor where it was found by forensics later when the van was recovered. 2:45-3:00 p.m. 7 miles away, Leslie Ann Parmenter (14) was walking across a K-Mart parking lot when Ted pulled the van up to her, stopped and jumped out in front of her. Posing as fireman "Richard Burton" Ted proceeded to ensnare her. He wore dark horn-rimmed glasses, a blue Navy-type uniform jacket with a badge that said "Fire Department, Richard Burton" on his chest. However, before he could abduct her, Danny Parmenter, Leslie's older brother arrived. Ted hurried back to the van and after a short verbal exchange with Danny quickly drove off. Danny followed Ted but lost the van in traffic, but not before recording his license tag. Ted headed north on US 441 pulling into an agricultural inspection station and asked for directions to a camp ground from inspector Austin Gay. 8:44 p.m. Ted checked into room 443 as Ralph Miller at the Lake City Holiday Inn at the intersection of I-75 and US 90 ($23.04). He was later positively identified by Dale Sconyers, the desk clerk, and was described as "shabby" in appearance and "doped out." That night Ted ate ($9.67) and drank alcohol (four gins and one draft beer; $6.40) on William Evans' card, possibly talking with another white male at the bar and buying him a drink.

Kim Leach circa 1978. Photo public domain.

February 9, 1978 (Thursday): Rain. (Early morning) Ted checks out of the Lake City Holiday Inn. 8:55 a.m. Abducts Kimberly Dianne Leach (12) from Lake City Junior High School, Lake City, later rapes and murders her at an unknown location.

Also on this day, Detective Steve Bodiford takes statement from Leslie Parmenter's father.

The following section of Kim's abduction from Lake City Junior High is an amalgamation of J. Victor Africano's appeal lodged for Ted on December 15, 1982 (pp. 2-3), George R. Dekle Sr.'s *The Last Murder: The Investigation, Prosecution, and Execution of Ted Bundy* (2011, 14-15), and FDLE documents.

On February 9, 1978, Kim was driven to the Lake City Junior High School, located on Duval Street (U. S. Highway 90, Lake City, Florida), by her mother, Freda Leach, at approximately 8:00 a.m. It was a cold, rainy morning. Upon crossing the street, Kim met her friend Elaine Hendricks. They bought some donuts and went into the auditorium to get out of the weather. They talked about the kind of things girls that age discuss – the Valentine Ball, Kim's plans to buy a gown, Kim's recent breakup with her boyfriend. When the bell rang, Kim went to her homeroom in John Bishop's class, located in the Central Elementary Building, a horseshoe-shaped building at the rear of the junior high campus (designated 'B' in the image below). Once there, she bought a ticket to the Valentine Ball and talked with her friend Lisa Little. The bell rang for first period and Kim left for the auditorium (designated 'C' in the image below) carrying her books cradled in her arms. After she left, Bishop noticed that she had forgotten her purse. Bishop asked Tandy Bonner, a friend of Kim's, to take a note to Juanita Caldwell, the PE instructor in the auditorium, asking Caldwell to have Kim return to get her pocketbook. Bonner took the note and walked out the south door of the Central Elementary Building (B). She then walked across the basketball courts, around some portable buildings, toward the door to the auditorium (C). As she walked across the campus, she noticed a man standing on the other side of Duval Street [we will return to this in a moment]. He was slim, looked to be 35, and had brown hair. Bonner went into the auditorium, handed the note to Caldwell, and Caldwell sent Kim back to Bishop's class (B). The two girls together retraced Bonner's steps back to the

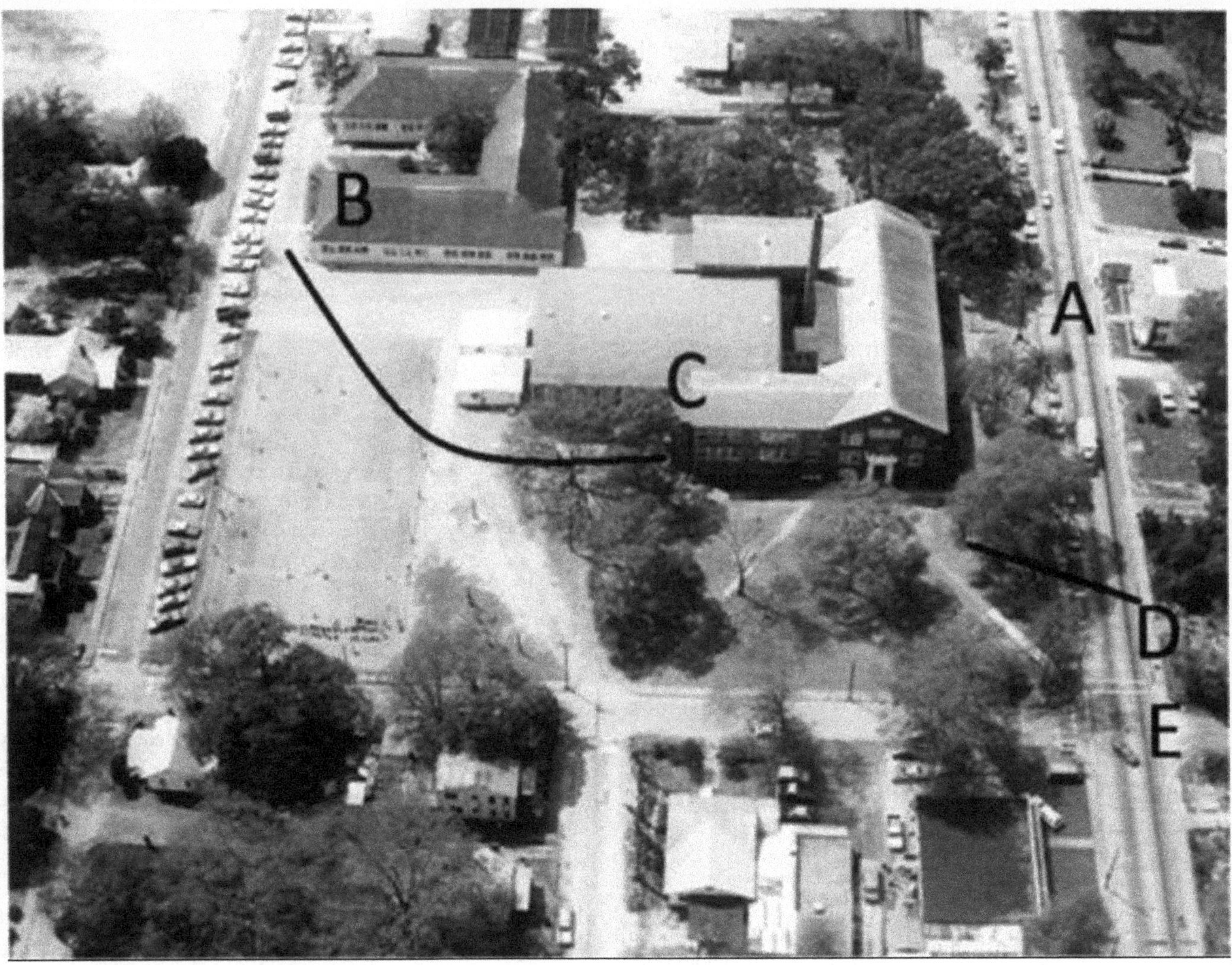

Aerial of Lake City Junior High looking west showing the path Leach took. Photo courtesy of the State Attorney's Office of the Third Judicial Circuit, Florida.

Central Elementary Building (B), and when they arrived in Bishop's class, he pointed out Kim's purse. Kim got it and left the classroom heading back across campus to the auditorium (C). She never made it.

When Kim didn't return, Caldwell assumed that Kim had simply gone on to second period class. When she exited her original homeroom classroom to return to the auditorium, it was approximately 9:20 a.m. to 9:25 a.m. This was the last time that anyone could positively identify having seen Kim Leach until her remains were found in a tin hog shed located in Suwannee County, Florida, approximately 35 to 40 miles west of the Lake City Junior High School. On the day of her disappearance, her mother said Kim was wearing Hush Puppies shoes, white cotton socks, blue denim jeans, a blue football type jersey pullover shirt with the number 83 emblazoned in red on the front, a three-quarter-length fur-trimmed coat, and she was carrying a denim purse.

Clinch Edenfield was a 71-year old Lake City Junior High school crossing guard on West Duval on February 9, 1978. Edenfield stated that he saw a man driving eastbound unusually slow around 8:00 a.m. "looking hard towards the school grounds rather than the highway" (FDLE). He saw the same man doing the same thing westbound shortly after 8:00 a.m. and then again eastbound around 8:15 a.m. In court his testimony was roundly dismantled by the defense, but there is something familiar about his description of Ted circling the school on that fateful day.

Clarence L. Anderson, an Emergency Medical Technician employed by the Lake City First Aid Rescue Department, with the rank of Lieutenant, became the State's one and only eyewitness to the abduction of Kim Leach. He testified that he was working overtime at the Fire Station on February 8, 1978, and slept there that night. At some time between 9:00 or 9:15 the next morning, he left the Fire Station to go home, shower, shave and change clothes. He traveled west on Duval Street (U. S. Highway 90), which would have taken him past the front of the Lake City Junior High School. As he approached the Junior High School, he noticed a white van stopped in the westbound lane of West Duval Street. There were two cars backed up behind the van, and then his own truck. As he waited for the traffic to clear, he noticed a young girl, approximately twelve or thirteen years old, dark hair, shoulder length, parted in the middle ("she looked very much like one of my nieces"). With her was a man, approximately early thirties, five feet seven to five feet ten, with medium brown, wavy hair, with a pullover sweater, with a shirt underneath the sweater. He got the impression that the young girl was either crying or had been crying. The man had a scowl on his face. He felt like she had gotten in trouble at the school or misbehaved in some way and had called her father to come pick her up and take her home. She was wearing dungarees and a dark blue pullover jersey with red-orange lettering "63" or "68." In her left arm, kind of clutched to her chest, was a pocketbook or a rolled-up jacket or maybe both. The man had her by her left arm, right about the elbow, and he was leading her towards the white van. The little girl was not actually resisting. It was pretty evident that she wasn't really anxious to go. He first saw them six to ten feet from the sidewalk. They crossed in front of the white van. The man opened the passenger door and helped the girl get in the van, slammed the door, and kind of jogged in front of the van, got in the passenger side, and drove off (850 F.2d 1402, July 7, 1988).

Anderson was hypnotized twice by the State to enhance his recall of events that day. Ted's defense attorneys employed the services of experts, including a Dr. Milton V. Kline, who soundly rebutted Anderson's testimony. Nevertheless, the damage was done, and the jury came to hear it as produced. Regardless of the veracity of Anderson's testimony, there are some striking observations that he made which cannot be ignored. It gives us a tantalizingly visual sequence as to what happened to Kim on that morning.

The picture we form is of Ted prowling the area and settling on the school as his target. He could not have known Kim was going to wander into his trap. But somewhere in that predatory mind of his he sniffed an opportunity. It is hard to say what cues in the environment potentiated these thoughts. Perhaps he recalled his success in Pocatello with Lynnette Culver, his second youngest known victim. Perhaps the presence of Edenfield still working the crossing that morning told him there might be some student latecomers. Maybe if he waited a little, luck would be on his side. He didn't have to wait long. First, Ted would have spotted Tandy Bonner walking alone from Kim's homeroom to the auditorium, a distance of approximately 247 feet according to Africano's report. This may have drawn him out of the van, sensing an opportunity. But before he could move on it, Tandy was already safely in the auditorium. So he

Ted would have walked across this grassy area with Leach to get to the van. Photo courtesy Chuck Meeks © 2015.

waited. Then he would have seen Tandy and Kim walking together back to the homeroom. Too risky to abduct two girls. So he waited some more. When Kim came out of the homeroom alone to return to the auditorium, he seized his chance.

No one saw the initial encounter between Ted and Kim. But Anderson's testimony provides a glimpse into what likely happened. Using the trees as cover, Ted must have crossed the open school grounds and intercepted Kim somewhere between the homeroom and the auditorium, perhaps near the portable buildings where he could surprise her, maybe even slipping in between them, like a cat burglar. We will never know what ruse he employed to overpower Kim's sense of reason. Ronald Holmes interviewed Ted for 9 ½ hours some time in September 1984. It was his first interview with a serial killer and Ted wasn't in his confessional mode yet, so Holmes' report needs to be taken with a grain of salt. Nevertheless, according to Holmes, Ted "speculated" on how Kim was abducted. He told Holmes that the kidnapper read her name off the back of her jersey and then called to her by name and told her she had to go home with him because of an accident in the family ('Author describes how Kim was lured', *Lake City Reporter*, July 2, 1986). According to Dekle:

> She dressed in a royal blue football jersey and blue jeans. The jersey bore the number 83 and had Kim's name on the back. Because of the cold, Kim wore a white long-sleeve turtleneck sweater under her jersey. She also wore a tan jacket with a fur collar (Dekle 2011, 14).

It is not clear how the "jacket" was worn, or if it was worn during the encounter. Nevertheless, if we assume Ted saw the number, then one way is he may have simply called it out. Alternatively, he may have pretended he was looking for someone and casually asked Kim her name. When she gave it to him he could have effected surprise, telling her that her father was involved in an accident, that she should come to the hospital right away. In another scenario, Ted may have impersonated a truancy officer and used that authority to haul her to his car (Dekle, personal communication, April 12, 2016). When this happened, or how, is unknown. Tandy said as she walked from the homeroom to the auditorium, she noticed a man standing on the other side of the street. "He was slim, looked to be 35, and had brown hair" (Dekle 2011, 16). She must have spotted him through the trees, it was a long shot, but it strongly suggests Ted had sepent some time there watching. The complete time frame for this sequence of events, however, is unknown.

After Anderson saw Ted taking Kim by the arm, the next sighting of Ted was on highway 90 heading west. Jackie Moore, the wife of a Lake City surgeon, was driving from the opposite direction that morning when saw a dirty white van approaching. She gasped as the van suddenly swerved into her lane, swung back, then swerved toward her again, almost forcing her off the road. She caught a glimpse of the driver. It was a man. He had brown hair and seemed to be angry. He was not looking at the road at all, but down towards the passenger seat. His mouth was open, as if he was shouting. And then the incident was over.

The rape and murder most likely occurred in the van according to the forensic evidence. We don't actually know what took place in that van, but a large blood stain was later found on the carpet covering the floor and on Kim's jersey. Combined with the knife evidence, it seems plausible to argue that Ted cut Kim's throat at some point during the encounter.

We also have Schaefer's account:

> Ted enjoyed killing women and experimented with different types of strangulation. He'd tie a cord around the captive's neck and then slip a length of doweling rod under the cord and begin to turn it slowly until the victim was strangled to death. He could control the pressure and would squeeze the windpipe closed, take the victim to the verge of death, then release the pressure. What I found most interesting was his observation that when he would do this the victim's eyes would become glassy and vacant. She would be alive and breathing, but the life force would somehow be gone. As if there was a body but lacking a soul. I figured it was simply a catatonic reaction, but Ted liked to think he had an animated corpse to play with. He progressed to a point where he would kill the woman while he was fucking her. He told me that the Leach girl, who was twelve or thirteen years old, couldn't take his cock so he rolled her over face down and went up her butt with his dick while strangling her with a belt (Schaefer 1997, 387-8).

We have no way of verifying the truthfulness of Schaefer's version. But if true, it rules out Ted killing Leach with a knife; the blood found in the van and on Leach's jersey would then be attributed to post-mortem mutilation.

6:30 p.m. Ted is drinking at Clyde's Restaurant in the Adams Street Mall in downtown Tallahassee. He calls Chez Pierre, an upscale French restaurant across the road, and books a table for 8:15 p.m. Around 8:15 p.m., an inebriated Ted eats dinner at Chez Pierre on William Evans' credit card.

February 10, 1978 (Friday): Ted is added to the list of the FBI's ten most wanted fugitives. (Sometime during the day or night) Ted stole a tag from Ragan-Roberts service station on West Tennessee Street, Tallahassee. He also stole a green Toyota parked at Firestone Tire Company on West Tennessee. Ted planned to move his stuff from the Media Center van to the Toyota. He parked both cars at the corner of Jefferson and Boulevard and waited for nightfall. (During the day) Uses Evans' card at Vivier Enterprises, Tallahassee. (Around 7:00 p.m.) Ted, wearing new Levi's, had dinner with Frances Messier, who

WANTED BY THE FBI

INTERSTATE FLIGHT - MURDER

THEODORE ROBERT BUNDY

DESCRIPTION

Born November 24, 1946, Burlington, Vermont (not supported by birth records); Height, 5'11" to 6'; Weight, 145 to 175 pounds; Build, slender, athletic; Hair, dark brown, collar length; Eyes, blue; Complexion, pale / sallow; Race, white; Nationality, American; Occupations, bellboy, busboy, cook's helper, dishwasher, janitor, law school student, office worker, political campaign worker, psychiatric social worker, salesman, security guard; Scars and Marks, mole on neck, scar on scalp; Social Security Number used, 533-44-4655; Remarks, occasionally stammers when upset; has worn glasses, false mustache and beard as disguise in past; left-handed; can imitate British accent; reportedly physical fitness and health enthusiast.

CRIMINAL RECORD

Bundy has been convicted of aggravated kidnaping.

CAUTION

BUNDY, A COLLEGE-EDUCATED PHYSICAL FITNESS ENTHUSIAST WITH A PRIOR HISTORY OF ESCAPE, IS BEING SOUGHT AS A PRISON ESCAPEE AFTER BEING CONVICTED OF KIDNAPING AND WHILE AWAITING TRIAL INVOLVING A BRUTAL SEX SLAYING OF A WOMAN AT A SKI RESORT. HE SHOULD BE CONSIDERED ARMED, DANGEROUS AND AN ESCAPE RISK.

FBI/DOJ

Ted's original FBI wanted poster. Photo courtesy FBI.

Frances Messier, a beautician student who lived at the Oaks. This photo taken shortly after Ted's second arrest, outside his Oaks room. Photo public domain.

The Spokesman-Review - Feb 21, 1978

'Compassion' felt for Bundy

TALLAHASSEE, Fla. (AP) – A college student who befriended Theodore R. Bundy while he lived here says she feels compassion for him. But she said she also feels compassion for the more than 30 women whose abductions or slayings authorities want to question Bundy about.

Bundy, 31, a prison escapee who was recently placed on the FBI's most wanted list, is in an armor-plated cell at the Leon County Jail awaiting interrogation about the bludgeoning deaths of two sorority sisters at Florida State University. Authorities in several other states also want to question him about slayings or kidnappings.

"I felt compassion for him when I read how he was treated in jail," said Frances Messier, 21, who lived across the hall from Bundy in a two-story apartment house on the fringe of the Florida State campus. "I also feel for the people who were murdered.

had moved into the Oaks on January 17 and befriended the reclusive 'Chris Hagen.' They walked from the Oaks together to Chez Pierre where they talked over a meal of steak and two bottles of champagne, paid for by Evans' card. After some cocktails on Evans' card at Clyde's across the street, they went back to Ted's room before 11:00 p.m. and watched the *Rockford Files* (Messier deposition, April 25, 1978). At this point there is a conflict in the timeline. Rule writes that Roy Dickey of the Tallahassee force sat in his patrol car near the intersection of Dunwoody Street and St. Augustine at 10:45 p.m. on the night of the 10th. He'd been there for two or three hours when he saw a man walking toward the intersection, a man who had come from the Florida State stadium and driving range area. The man was in no hurry. He walked east on St. Augustine, and then cut north on Dunwoody, before disappearing between Cheryl Thomas' duplex and the house next to it. The man wore blue jeans, a red quilted vest, a blue cap, and jogging shoes. He passed under the street light on the corner, he looked at the patrol car—briefly—and Dickey saw his face clearly. Later, when he saw a picture of Ted Bundy, Dickey would recognize him as the man who'd passed him so casually (Rule 2006, 295).

Ted can't be in two places at once. Could it be that Dickey saw someone else? Or could it be that he had the date wrong, that this incident occurred on the 11th? Because according to another police report, Ted was involved in an incident with Leon County Deputy Sheriff Keith Daws.

February 11, 1978 (Saturday): (During the day) Uses Evans' card at Vivier Enterprises. (Evening) Evans' card at Chez Pierre. 1:44 - 1:47 a.m. Daws turned onto West Jefferson near the Chi Omega House and saw a "white male fiddling with a car door" up ahead of him. Daws eased his car up to where the man was bending over the door of a green Toyota. (tag ALB 319). When he saw the deputy's car in the middle of the street, the man stood up and looked around. Rule elaborates:

> Daws identified himself and asked, "What are you doing?"
>
> "I came down to get my book."
>
> Daws saw that the man had a key in his hand … but no book. "Maybe I'm stupid or something," the deputy drawled. "But you say you've come to get your book, and you don't have no book."
>
> "It's on the dash on the other side of the car," the man answered easily.
>
> Daws studied him. He looked to be in his late twenties, wore blue jeans that looked brand new, an orange-red quilted "lining" vest. When he bent over

with the key, the deputy could see there was no wallet in the back pocket of the jeans. The brown-haired man also looked "wasted ... completely exhausted." There was a book on the passenger side dashboard, but the man said he had no I.D. He'd just come down from his room. He hadn't parked on West College Avenue where he lived because all the spots were filled. That made sense; parking on campus was tight. First come, first serve. Daws shined his flashlight into the green Toyota's interior, and saw that the seat and floorboards were covered with papers. He saw the tiny tip of a license tag under the papers on the floor.

"Whose tag is that?"

"What tag?" The man was fumbling with the papers and his hand hit the tag.

"That tag you've got your hand on."

The man in the vest handed the tag to Daws, explaining that he'd found it somewhere, and never thought that someone might miss it.

The tag read 13-D-11300.

Daws didn't recognize the number, but he routinely walked over to his car radio to check it with "Wants and Warrants" for stolen. He left the man standing by the Toyota. Daws had one hand on his microphone and the tag in the other. And then the man suddenly sprinted, running across the street, between two apartment houses, and leaping over a retaining wall. Daws was caught by surprise. The man had seemed to be cooperative. He would later ruefully describe the scene to a Miami jury. "The last time I saw him, I could have hit him with a baseball. You're talking about the width of this courtroom." The runner had leapt over the retaining wall, directly into the back yard of the Oak ... and disappeared. The tag, of course, was registered to Randy Ragan, but, when Daws went to Ragan's house, he was obviously not the same individual who had run from the deputy. The man who had "rabbited" was later picked out of a photo line-up by Daws; it was Ted Bundy. Daws, whose frustration at the near-miss was still evident when he testified in court, was even more disgusted when he read the next morning of the search for a Dodge van. There had been a white Dodge van with a flat tire parked—illegally—just behind the Toyota that the suspect was unlocking. When the detectives returned to look for it, it was gone (Rule 2006, 296-7).

After Ted "rabbited" he lay trembling for several moments in a bramble, listening for sounds of pursuit. When he heard nothing, he stumbled across the darkened yard and scurried up the fire escape to his room. He sat there in the dark, heart thumping (M&A 1983, 233). Eventually, it appears he fell asleep.

In the morning, Ted put on a tennis outfit and went down to discuss his rent arrears with the Oaks supervisor Robert Fulford. He told Fulford he was getting some money from his mother in Michigan, and even placed a fake call to Ann Arbor in front of Fulford. In the midst of this act, Ted looked down at a bowl on a table in front of him and saw a police investigator's business card in it. Despite the ominous signs of a tightening noose, Ted dallied through Saturday, riding his bike, playing racquetball. (Also during the day) He borrowed a copy of the *Democrat* from one of his neighbors at the Oaks (Larsen 1980, 223) and set down a box of cookies in front of Messier's door (W&M 1980, 245).

February 12, 1978 (Sunday): (Morning) The Media Center van was still sitting where he left it; he needed to find another car to replace the green Toyota lost to Daws. He walked across campus toward Doak Campbell Stadium looking for a car. He found an old Mazda at 312 Stadium Drive. The owner, Myrline Allen Reeves, had left her keys in the ashtray. Bundy took it, but the front end shimmied at speeds of more than 45 miles per hour. He drove north on Stadium Drive to High Road, and from High Road to Old Bainbridge Highway, where he abandoned the Mazda at an apartment complex and walked across the street to a Mormon church parking lot. In the church parking lot, Bundy spotted a 1969 souped-up VW bug belonging to Theresa Connie Shriver. The keys were in the ashtray. As he drove off in the VW, he realized it wouldn't hold up for the long drive he intended. Nevertheless, he spent the rest of the day and evening driving around in the VW looking for another car.

It wasn't until 10:00 - 10:15 p.m. that he parked Shriver's VW at 414 East Carolina Street and began prowling the area looking for a suitable car. A little more than 350 yards away, at 515 East Georgia Street, Ricky Garzaniti was parking his 1972 orange VW at his babysitter's house (tag 13D-15864). When Garzaniti and his wife went inside to get their child, he left the keys in the ignition. The Garzanitis stayed inside the babysitter's approximately 45 minutes and came out to find their car gone. Bundy had encountered so much trouble finding a good car that by the time he stole Garzaniti's car, he neglected to change the tag. This would prove to be a mistake (Dekle 2011, 31).

He hurried back to the Oaks and stuffed his belongings into the orange VW. A list of the things he packed was later compiled by investigators. Among them was 22 pairs of socks, 4 *Megaphone* cheerleader magazines, and 6 boat books (the latter attesting to his plan to get work at a boat yard along the Gulf Coast).

The FSU Media Center van as it was found. Photo courtesy of the State Attorney's Office of the Third Judicial Circuit, Florida.

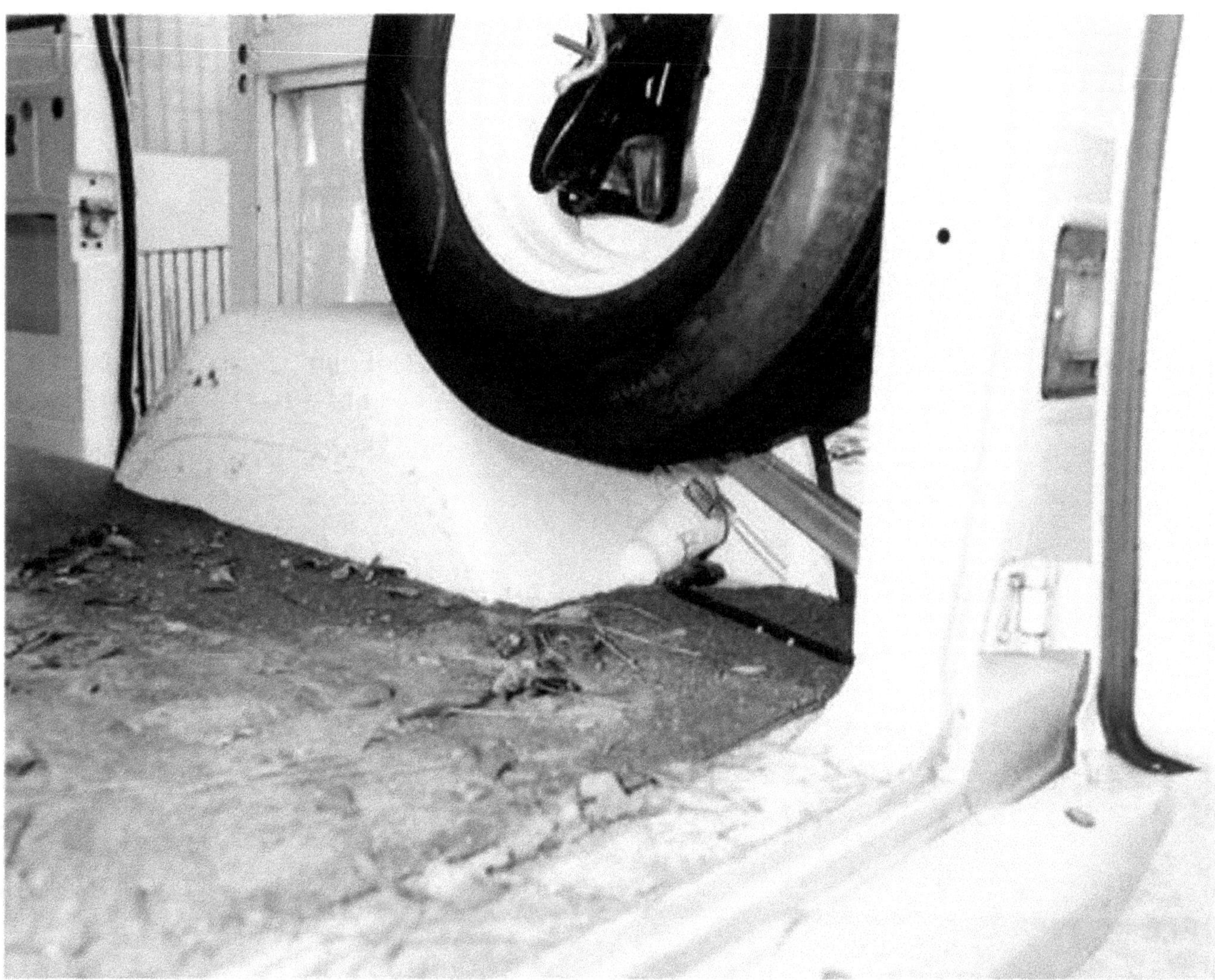

Dirt and leaves and other material found in the rear floor area of the FSU Media Center van demonstrating evidence of a cover-up. Photo courtesy of the State Attorney's Office of the Third Judicial Circuit, Florida.

February 13, 1978 (Monday): (Sometime very early in the morning) Ted finally leaves the Oaks. The state in which he left the room varies depending on which report, book, or newspaper article you read. At 11:30 p.m. on February 16, 1978, three days after Ted had vacated his room, William P. Gunter of the Leon County Sheriff's department processed it. Apart from dusting for fingerprints on all contactable surfaces, they removed shelf paper from the closet, and a Florida road map that was taped to the north side of the dresser against the east wall. Michaud & Aynesworth added that Ted also wiped "the ceiling" (1983, 234). This information was not in any newspaper or report. If Ted told them, he would be admitting to his stupidity. All he told police was that when he drove a vehicle, he wore leather gloves, "I didn't wipe my prints out" (Pensacola interview, February 17, 1978). Obviously a lie. Winn & Merrill then added, he left his room by "the fire escape" (1980, 245). This last titbit is not in any report or newspaper either. [I should add here that some authors have a fixation with Ted when it comes to fire escapes and ladders.]

Around 6:00 - 7:00 a.m. Ted parked the Media Center van in front of Beatrice Hampton's house at 806 West Georgia Street, Tallahassee (on the northern side of the university). At some point before he abandoned it, he poured a can of coke into a rag and wiped down the handles and doors (Dekle 2011, 29). The van was soon spotted by an FSU Media Center employee and secured by police forensics. They found the rear floor of the van covered in leaves and dirt. (Sometime Monday morning) Bodiford learns about Daws' encounter with the fleeing Bundy. (Between 9:00 - 10:00 a.m.) Driving off in the orange VW, Ted discovered that whenever he exceeded 50 miles per hour, one of the rear wheels would shake the entire car, forcing him to slow down. He pulled into a garage in Crestview, 129 miles west of Tallahassee. The mechanic told him he'd have to replace the tire, but didn't have a spare on hand. (Around 11:00 a.m.) Ted drove to the local Holiday Inn and had breakfast. When he tried to pay for breakfast using a credit card with a woman's

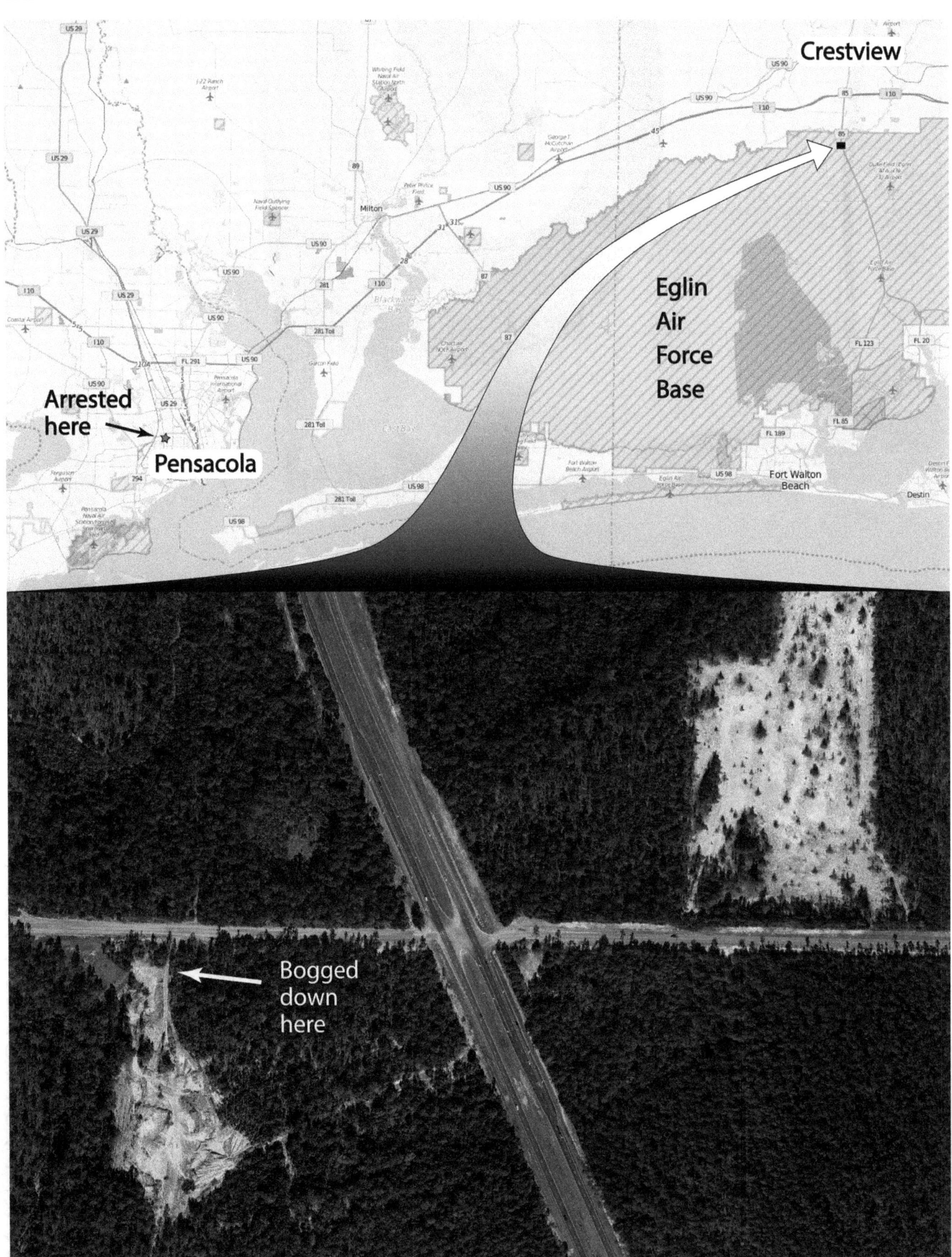

Composite map showing some of the last places Ted passed through before his final arrest. Map image courtesy OpenStreetMap contributors and USGS Earthstar Geographics SIO © Microsoft Corporation.

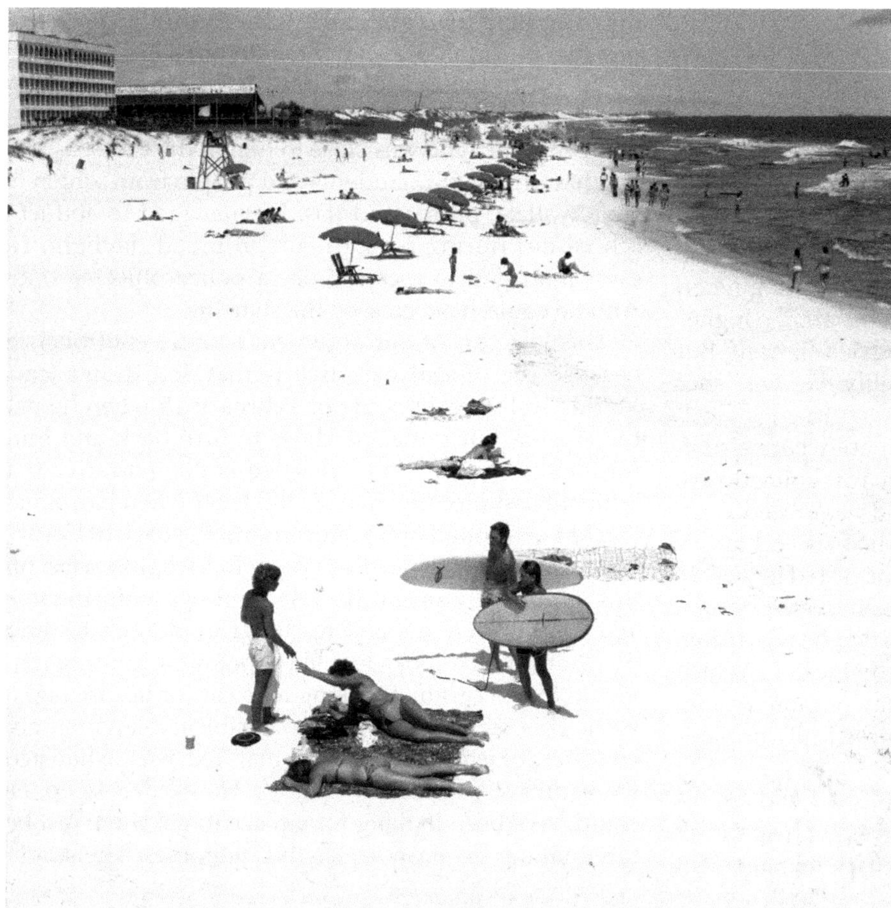

Pensacola Beach, June 1978. Photo courtesy Eric Tournay, State Archives of Florida.

name on it the desk clerk refused him. In response, Ted threw the card in the clerk's face and sped off. The desk clerk later identified the man as Ted Bundy from newspapers.

Ted drove to a deserted, sandy area a few miles down the road, part of the huge Eglin Air Force Base reserve lands. According to Winn & Merrill he bolted on a new set of license plates (1980, 247). This is incorrect; he did *not* change the tag, an error that would come back to haunt him. His intention was to wait out till dark, but when he backed the VW up a hill to park it, it wallowed in soft sand and bogged down. For the next 3 hours he clawed and dug frantically beneath the car trying to move it the sixty feet he needed to get back onto solid road. He shoved everything he could find under the rear wheels—including at one point, the rear seat—but nothing worked. Now with dark falling, and much of his clothes strewn about in the dirt, Ted retrieved his backpack and started hitchhiking for the interstate (M&A 1983, 235).

After walking a "couple of miles on foot" an airman dressed in civilian clothes picked him up and drove him the rest of the way back to Crestview. The airman dropped him off at a cluster of gas stations near the interstate at Crestview and drove on. Ted found an obliging attendant who agreed to take him back to his car and help him push it back on the road.

Back in action, Ted drove to Pensacola, found a motel, but when he tried to pay for it with a stolen credit card, he was politely refused and he continued on his way. He spent the night trying to sleep upright in his car (where is not known).

February 14, 1978 (Tuesday): 6:30 a.m. Ted woke up, had some breakfast (somewhere), and then for no particular reason drove to Pensacola Airport. (Around 9:00 a.m.) He pulled into a community college near the airport and used its men's locker room to shower, shave, and change his clothes. Refreshed, he drove to a laundromat and washed all his clothing (including his socks). Having chosen a college, perhaps he hoped the opportunity would present itself for him to do some more hunting, but he ended up spending the remainder of the day at the beach, maybe getting ideas there instead (M&A 1983, 236).

In the evening Ted ate an early dinner, noting that he was alone and isolated on Valentine's Day. It upset him. He drank heavily. He spent $23.40 on Mark F. Labadie's card. At a shopping mall he purchased more clothing and socks. Afterwards he found a bar where he intended to steal more purses and wallets. He was tired and inebriated at this stage and a waitress saw him dipping into a girl's purse. Security personnel surrounded him and took him to a back room. As luck would have it, they momentarily diverted their attention and Ted quickly stashed his cache of stolen credit cards on a shelf behind him. The security personnel questioned Ted closely about his reasons for being at the bar. They brought the woman in whose purse he had been seen rifling. She told the security personnel nothing was missing. Ted was told to leave. He accepted his $1 cover charge back and made a deft grab for his credit cards and left the building.

He got back into his stolen orange VW and headed off. It was getting late now, towards midnight. He rolled into an industrial area, lights on,* still looking for opportunities. Maybe burgle a closed business, or steal another car ... he did not see the lights of a police car following him until it was too late.

* Lee's official testimony has the lights on; Sullivan says the lights were off.

NOTES

There seems to be a general consensus among authors that Ted's final two weeks after his escape signaled the beginning of the end. If he was an airplane, he spiraled out of control into the ground. The truth is, Ted could have crossed into Alabama and got away for who knows how long. If you look at the facts, if you use the airplane metaphor, Ted at most was a plane with one engine on fire. Of course, the longer he stayed in the air, the higher the probability he would have kamikazied himself. But Ted's final arrest muted that possibility. He was shot down before he had the chance.

Ted left more clues in Florida than anywhere else in his career. That is one argument that he was going down. He used credit cards when he should have used cash. He could have broken into people's houses and apartments using gloves and rifled them for cash. He was an accomplished burglar, but he didn't exercise that option. The most probable reason for this was that he was tiring, a fugitive on the run, his resources dwindling. Which means that we have to look at his behavior more as a result of his fugitive status than him intrinsically imploding.

In support of this argument, he still had enough focus to steal the Media Center van keys, get a spare set cut and return the originals, thereby trick management into dropping their guard. He rode around on bicycle at night so he didn't draw attention to himself – except the night of Chi Omega and Dunwoody. His attacks there were brazen and shockingly excessive. He managed to fool everyone who was close to him at the Oaks, as well as a handful of FSU students and people from whom he stole wallets, purses and IDs. He managed to abduct a school girl during school hours in broad daylight. He even managed to escape from a police officer – once. And he could have crossed the state line.

This last part of our argument is more controversial because the official narrative is that Ted didn't leave Florida in the early hours or February 15 when he had the chance, but rather he chose to turn back and hunt for another victim. So entrenched is this narrative that Sullivan assumed Ted had his lights off when patrolman David Lee spotted him going around the back of Oscar's restaurant in Brownsville. When Ted's lights were off, this supposedly meant he was hunting. Unfortunately Ted's lights were on, and reading David Lee's testimony carefully, Ted looks less like a predator hunting for a victim than a car thief looking for a car (or license tag) to steal. This seems like a more plausible explanation given several factors. The first is that Ted was exhausted. He hadn't slept properly in days. He needed sleep. He could have been looking for a place to get some rest before making his dash across the state lines. The second

BUNDY: I didn't know ~~I told you what~~ it till it happened.

CHAPMAN: Right.

BUNDY: ______ the night of the capture, I wasn't looking to get caught. I was looking to get ~~away~~. away.

CHAPMAN: But you told me, the thing I can't understand is I was on the interstate, I was leaving Pensacola going west, going west, had that urge come back at 2:00 in the morning, had that urge to get back to Pensacola. Are we going to find anything in Pensacola, Ted?

BUNDY: No.

BODIFORD: Okay. And you were stopped before there was a ____________. Because Ted, you could have laid around in the National Forest over there around Eglin. You told us about that already, you did need the sleep. You told us earlier you fell asleep ___________ you told of driving, driving, driving, so ___________

BUNDY: Yeah.

One possible source of the "official" narrative surrounding Ted's final hours in Pensacola. It appears Chapman is putting words into Ted's head. Transcript excerpt from February 20, 1978, first night of interrogation at Leon County Jail after Ted was transferred from Pensacola PD, courtesy FSA.

is he just barely avoided getting turned into police for stealing out of someone's purse. He desperately needed cash. Oscar's restaurant might have looked like a good target. Break in and rifle the till. The third is that he was already going on his fourth day of possession of a stolen vehicle. He knew that if he was going to cross deep into Alabama (not just cross the border), Florida plates would highlight him as an easy target for a pesky police patrol. Thus, his priority was to find a new vehicle, or at the very least find some Alabama plates. This might explain why he snooped around the used car lot across the road from Oscar's restaurant before turning out onto North W Street. The fourth factor is Brownsville itself. By the time Ted trundled down its streets in 1978, it had already undergone terminal decline as a thriving suburb. The first pulse occurred in 1956, when business owners got enticed away to new shops at Town and Country Plaza north of Brownsville at the corner of Pace and Fairfield streets. The second pulse occurred in 1971, when Cordova Mall stole more shops and shoppers from the Brownsville strip. The third and final pulse occurred in 1978, when the Interstate 10 opened up a new more direct path to Mobile. This effectively robbed Brownsville of casual through-traffic necessary to sustain remaining businesses. The area went into terminal decline as businesses moved out to blossoming neighborhoods and malls in other parts of Pensacola (Krueger 2007). If Ted was truly hunting he was in the wrong place. At the very least he should have been 2.3 miles to the southeast, in the university district. That would have properly constituted turning back.

But all of this is by-and-by. Even if he had crossed into Alabama, his efforts would have been negated by the mountain of evidence that he left behind at his crime scenes. Even though he removed traditional evidence such as fingerprints, suggesting some attempt at a cover up, he left so much other incriminating evidence that no matter what he did, the state of Florida would eventually catch up with him.

The only moment when you get a glimpse that he acknowledged he had made a mistake was in the Pensacola interviews. Most of the time, he led his interviewers on a wild goose chase. But there was a moment, just once, when he admitted that he, and he alone, was to blame for getting himself caught. He chastised himself for it. There is a sense that he recognizes he has hit the end of the road. It was proposed that he could have escaped again—while he was getting treatment at the hospital for the superficial injuries he sustained during his struggle with officer Lee—but he didn't. Maybe he was simply exhausted. But maybe he realized that society needed to be protected from the likes of Theodore Robert Bundy.

It might be more appropriate, therefore, to consider Ted was burnt out, rather than assume he crashed and burned. The pressure of being on the run wore him down. With no money, nowhere to live, no work, and no social support system, it was inevitable that he would fail. Thus, this view paints a different picture of Ted's last days. It was the external pressures that eroded Ted's otherwise functional behavior. This contrasts against the argument that says Ted failed because of internal pressure. As if the killing unhinged him, turned him into a disorganized psychopath. The truth is, Ted *didn't* want to get caught. He wanted to go on killing. Despite not having any money, any social support system that enabled him to maintain a double life, he was prepared to run and hunt.

When officer Lee finally caught him, Ted did everything he could to get away. But as soon as he was cuffed and driven away, Lee reported that Ted mumbled suicidal thoughts. Ted would rather die than be exposed for who he really was. It shows he was not ready to reveal his true identity. Thus, Ted's last days, as much as they appear to be a downward spiral, in fact are a function of being an escapee, not a mental breakdown as has been suggested. If anything, Ted was a man who was bent on continuing down the road he set himself, right to the bitter end, if necessary.

References

Krueger, Mari s. (2007) Reviving Brownsville. *Independent News* (Vol 7. No. 10. March 8, 2007).

http://www.inweekly.net/article.asp?artID=4258 (Accessed July 2, 2016).

Second Arrest (February 15, 1978 - February 12, 1980)

February 15, 1978: (Wednesday) Ted has an opportunity to slip across state lines, but ends up prowling a Pensacola industrial area for a vacant parking lot where he can get some sleep, maybe steal another car.

1:34 a.m. Patrolman David Lee of the Pensacola Police Department spotted Ted turning into the rear of Oscar's Restaurant (Ted's headlights were on). Lee silently followed Ted while calling in the license plate (tag 13D-15864; complaint #M5308, TPD). Upon learning it was stolen, he put on his blue light. A chase ensued and ended when Ted pulled over on North W Street just north of W Cross Street. Lee got out of his car while directing his service revolver on Ted and demanded Ted get out of his car. Lee had to repeat the demand several times before Ted complied. He ordered Ted to lie down on the pavement in front of his headlights. As Ted got down, Lee directed his attention to the front passenger side of Ted's VW. With all the junk in Ted's car, Lee thought there might be someone else in the seat. Lee called out but got no response. He then asked Ted, but still got no response. As he placed the first cuff on Ted's wrist, but with his attention diverted, Ted kicked Lee's feet out from under him and struck him somewhere – Lee couldn't recall. As Lee went down and Ted came up, Lee discharged his gun in the air, more as an automatic response than with intent to hit someone. Whereupon Ted fled south on W Street and east into Cross Street. Lee got up and demanded Ted stop. Ted turned back to look at Lee, and in that moment Lee thought he could see something in Ted's hand (thinking it might be a gun). Lee later realized it was the cuff he had half gotten on Ted's wrist. Notwithstanding, Lee fired a second shot. Ted went down. There was approximately half a block between the two men at this stage. Thinking he had shot his man, Lee went

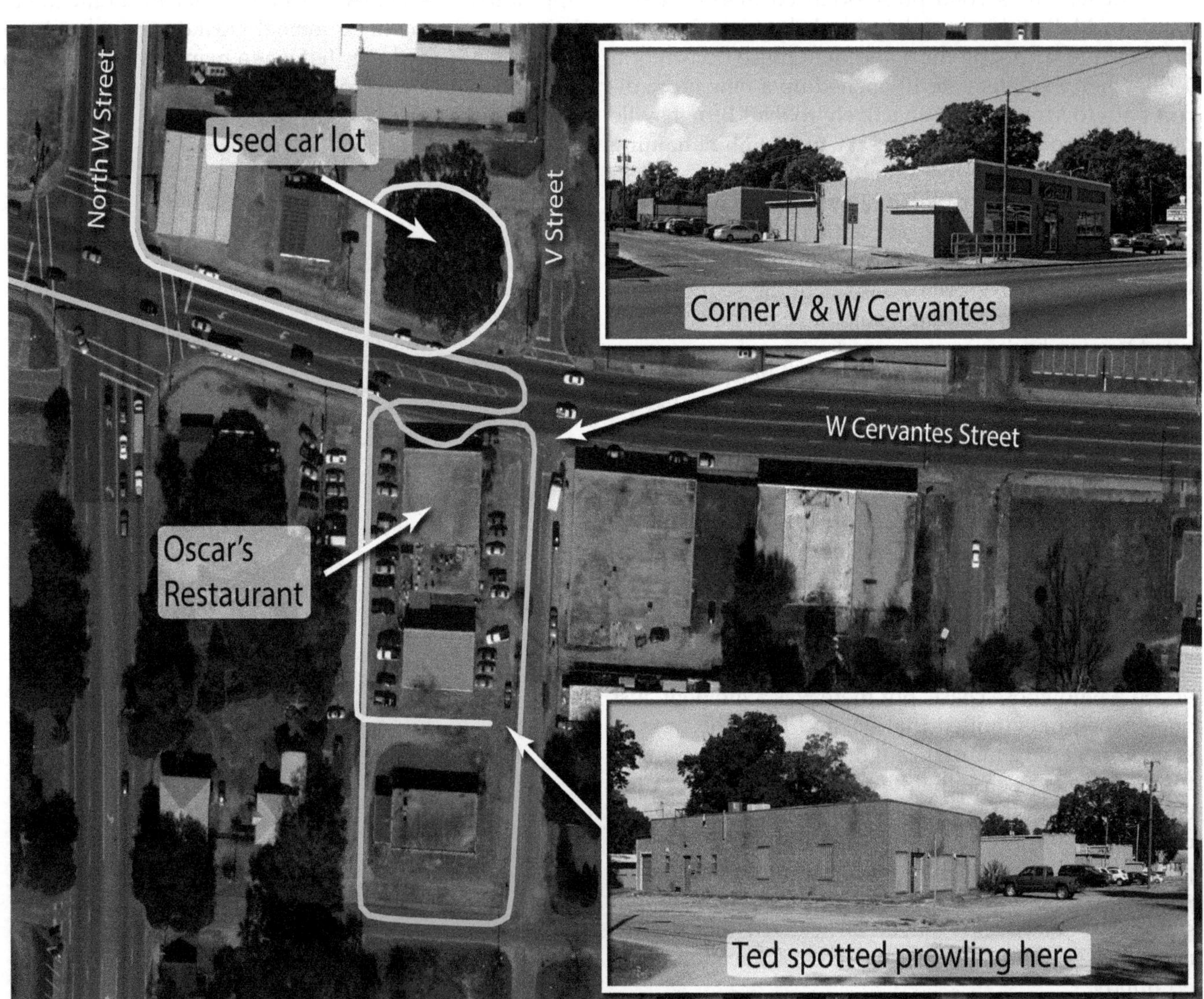

Map of events that took place around Oscar's Restaurant. The blue represents Officer Lee's path; the yellow, Ted's. Based on the historical information, it appears Ted may have either intended to burgle the restaurant or steal a car from the used car lot across the road. Map image courtesy USGS Earthstar Geographics SIO © Microsoft Corporation. Photo insets courtesy Chuck Meeks © 2015.

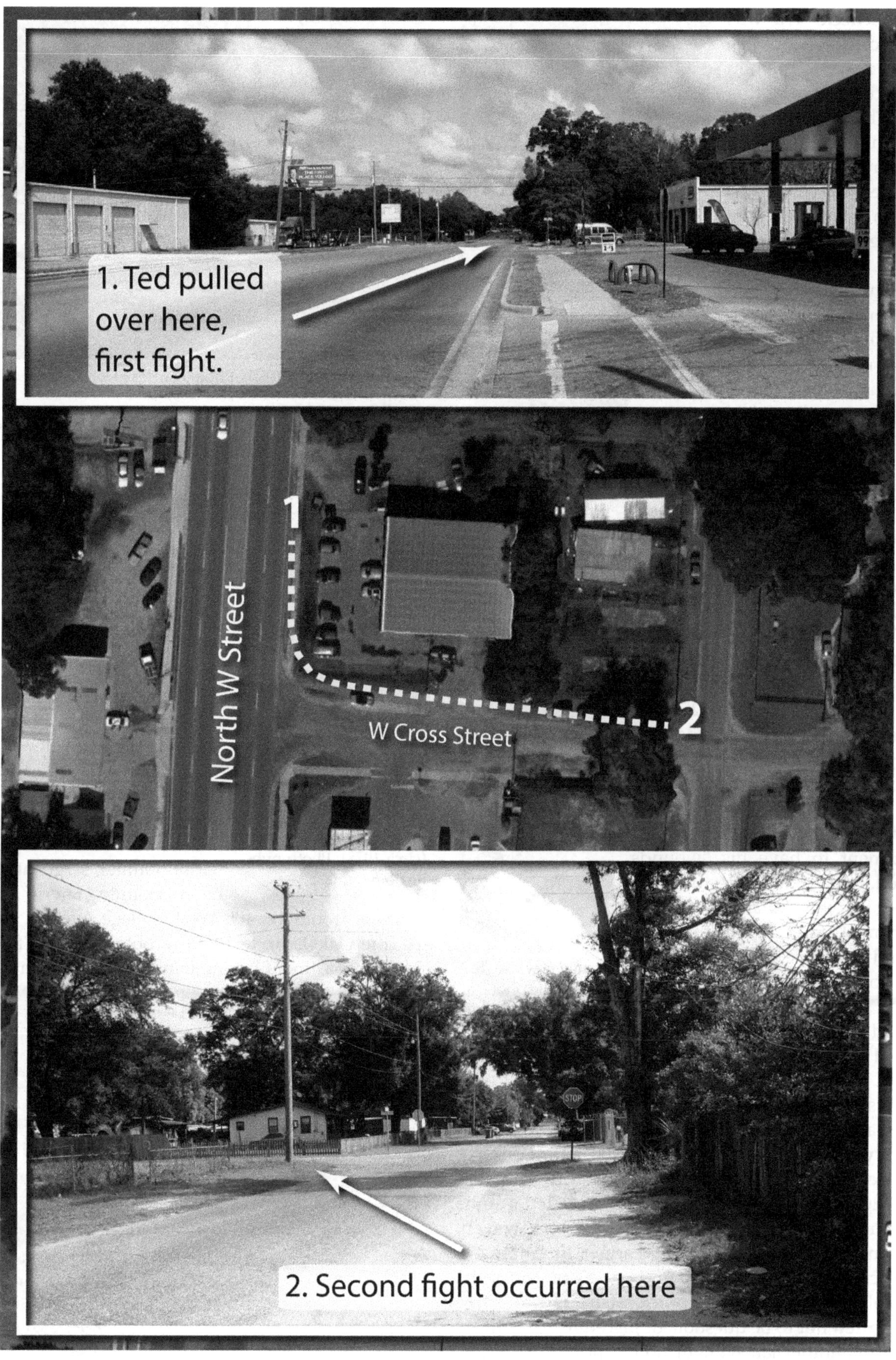

Map of where Ted stopped and fought Officer Lee. Map image courtesy USGS Earthstar Geographics SIO © Microsoft Corporation. Photo insets courtesy Chuck Meeks © 2015.

over to check. Ted was lying face down. As Lee kneeled down to roll him over, Ted started fighting again. This time striking Lee with his hands, with the handcuff that was on his left wrist. He was trying to get at Lee's gun, the same time screaming for help. At that moment a citizen came out and said something to the effect, "Why are you hurting that man?" but when he saw it was an officer doing his duty, he disappeared. Shortly thereafter, Lee got the better of Ted and fully handcuffed him. As he hauled Ted back to his vehicle, two other patrolmen arrived.

David Lee, the arresting officer. Photo public domain.

Ted's mugshot taken shortly after his arrest on February 15, 1978. Photo public domain.

Don Patchen (circa 1980). Photo courtesy Don Patchen © 2015.

When booked, Ted gave his name as "Kenneth Misner." 4:00 a.m. Detective Norman Chapman of the Pensacola Police Department arrives, and from 4:25 a.m. conducts an 8-minute recorded interview with Ted (who answers as Kenneth Raymond Misner). (Noon) Ted is escorted to Pensacola University Hospital & Clinical Emergency Department to have his "wounds checked." 4:30 p.m. Detective Don Patchen of the Tallahassee Police Department crimes-against-persons unit and Detective Steve Bodiford of Leon County Sheriff's Office arrive with a "John Doe" warrant against Ted. Ted still refuses to give his real name. The officers threaten to get an NBC news crew in and "plaster" Ted's face all over the news. Ted negotiates permission to makes some telephone calls.

This photo allegedly taken while Ted was on the phone at Pensacola PD. Photo public domain.

February 16, 1978: Approximately 6:00 a.m. Pensacola Police Department. Patchen interviews a John Doe until 7:20 a.m. in the presence of Bodiford. Ted admits to stealing credit cards, various IDs and a Volkswagen. Later on, Ted speaks to Millard Farmer in Atlanta, a capital crimes attorney. 4:30 p.m. Isaac Koran from the Pensacola public defender's office secures a protective order on Ted not to be questioned, placed in a lineup, or moved to another jail without notification of his attorneys. 5:00 p.m. Alan Holbrook negotiates Ted will reveal his true identity in exchange for telephone calls to his family and friends and no release of his name to the public until the following morning. 4:30 p.m. Ted phones John Henry Browne and Liz Kloepfer. He then states his real name. 6:00 p.m. Ted sees Father Michael Moody (or Mooney depending on sources) till after midnight. 7:00 p.m. Ted again calls Liz. (Around midnight) Chapman receives a call from a Washington State news agency asking if they have Ted Bundy in custody. Chapman is told Bundy is a suspect in 34 murders.

Norm Chapman (undated). Photo public domain.

John Henry Browne (circa 1978). Photo public domain.

Also on this day, Deputy William P. Gunter, sergeant with the Leon County Sheriff's Office, processes room 12, 409 West College Avenue, Tallahassee (the Oaks). He testified to obtaining lifts from outside the apartment but no latent lifts of evidential value

Bill Gunter (undated). Photo public domain.

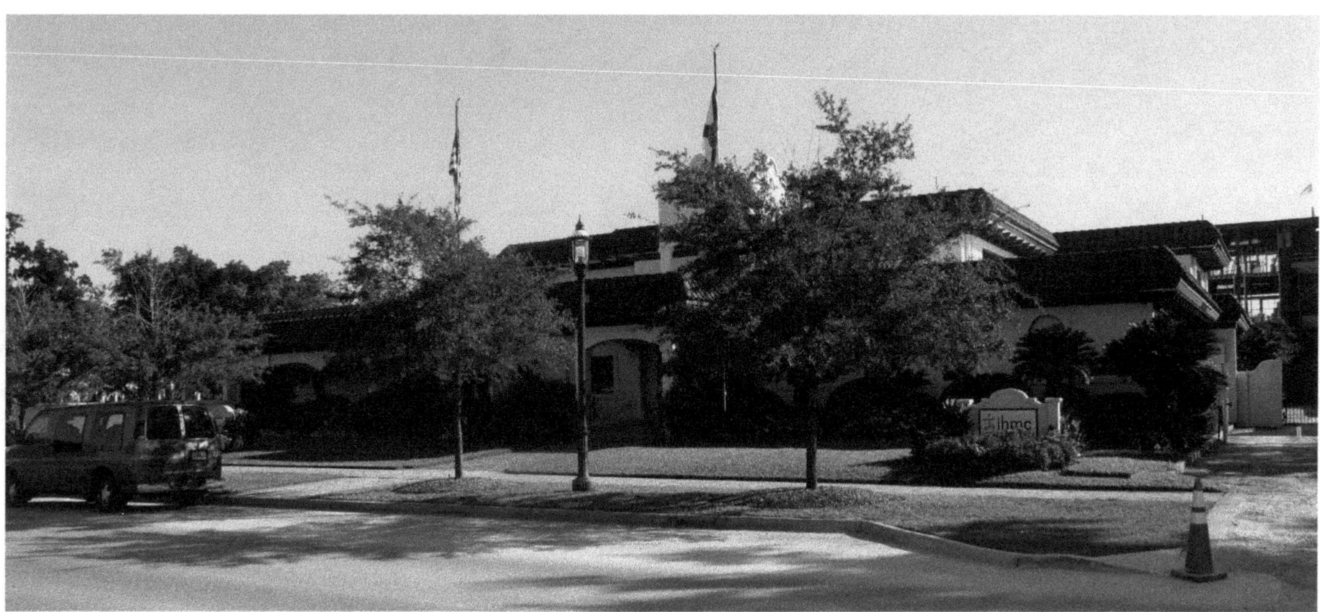

This nondescript building used to be the Pensacola Police Department, where Ted was interviewed for three days almost non-stop. Photo courtesy Chuck Meeks © 2015.

from inside, appearing to him as if the room had been wiped or cleaned. Mr. Daniel G. Hasty, FDLE latent print analyst matched the latents from the outside door panel of the Oaks apartment, 409 West College, with Bundy's. No lifts from the crime scenes compare to Bundy's.

February 17, 1978: 1:29 a.m. Pensacola City Jail. Chapman, Bodiford and Patchen start their interview with Theodore Robert Bundy. They open with "... just talk about anything you want to talk about." Ted talks about his escape from Garfield County Jail, Glenwood Springs, Colorado. Says he dropped in on a few lectures at FSU. Bought a quart of beer and drank it in his room. They don't get much else out of him. 5:00 a.m. Chapman notes he only brought 3 hours of blank audiotape, not enough to capture the full 5 hours of interview. 7:30 a.m. Liz Nicholas of the public defender's office appears demanding to see Ted but is refused. 9:00 a.m. A national press conference begins outside but Ted is still locked away with the detectives. Isaac Koran arrives and finally gets to see Ted, asking him to sign an affidavit saying Ted didn't want to talk to investigators. Ted doesn't sign the affidavit. (Afternoon) Reporters get their first glimpse of Ted as he appears in court for arraignment on charges of stolen credit cards and grand larceny. 10:00 a.m. Ted, red-eyed, about to cry, in response to the Chi Omega murders, says off-tape: "The evidence is there. Look for it." Mike Fisher from Colorado arrives with hopes of speaking to Ted.

February 18, 1978: 2:15 a.m. onwards. Ted continues his interview with Patchen, Bodiford and Chapman. Ted now tries to broker a deal. He'll tell all in exchange for no trials, but a return to an institution in Washington State where he can be kept for the rest of his natural life, close to family and friends, where psychiatrists can study him and learn lessons to prevent this kind of thing happening again. Everyone in the room knows it's an impossible deal. 4:00 a.m. Ted calls Liz again. This time talks about his "sickness" (M&A 1983, 238). (Later in the afternoon) Ted is transferred back to Leon County Jail, Tallahassee, into the care of Ken Katsaris.

February 20, 1978: Freda Leach talks to reporters from the *St. Petersburg Times*. Ted faces Circuit Judge John Rudd while the credit card charges are listed against him. Back in Leon County Jail, Joe Aloi spends time talking with Ted during the day. (Around midnight) During his interview with Chapman, Bodiford and Patchen, Ted asserts:

> Now they've got Theodore Bundy out there, master of disguise, ten most wanted list, involved in x number of things. I've got to show them that I can stand up in court of law and run these people ragged. That I'm not a fiend necessarily. But that's not, uh, all there is to me. I show them that I'm more. See I've been trying to tell you all. That's really important to me. That I'm more.

February 21, 1978: Keppel and Nick Mackie among others interview Liz to hear what Ted told her when he called her on February 18, 1978:

> [...] for years before he even met me he'd been fighting the same sickness and that when it broke we just happened to be together (M&A 1983, 238).
>
> [...] I told him that I sometimes wondered if he used me to touch base with reality, like the night Carol DaRonch was kidnapped and Debbie Kent vanished and he called me at midnight. Or taking me out for hamburgers after what happened at Lake Sammamish.
>
> "Yeah, that's a pretty good guess," he said. "It's like it's over. I don't have a split personality. I don't have blackouts. I remember everything I've done.

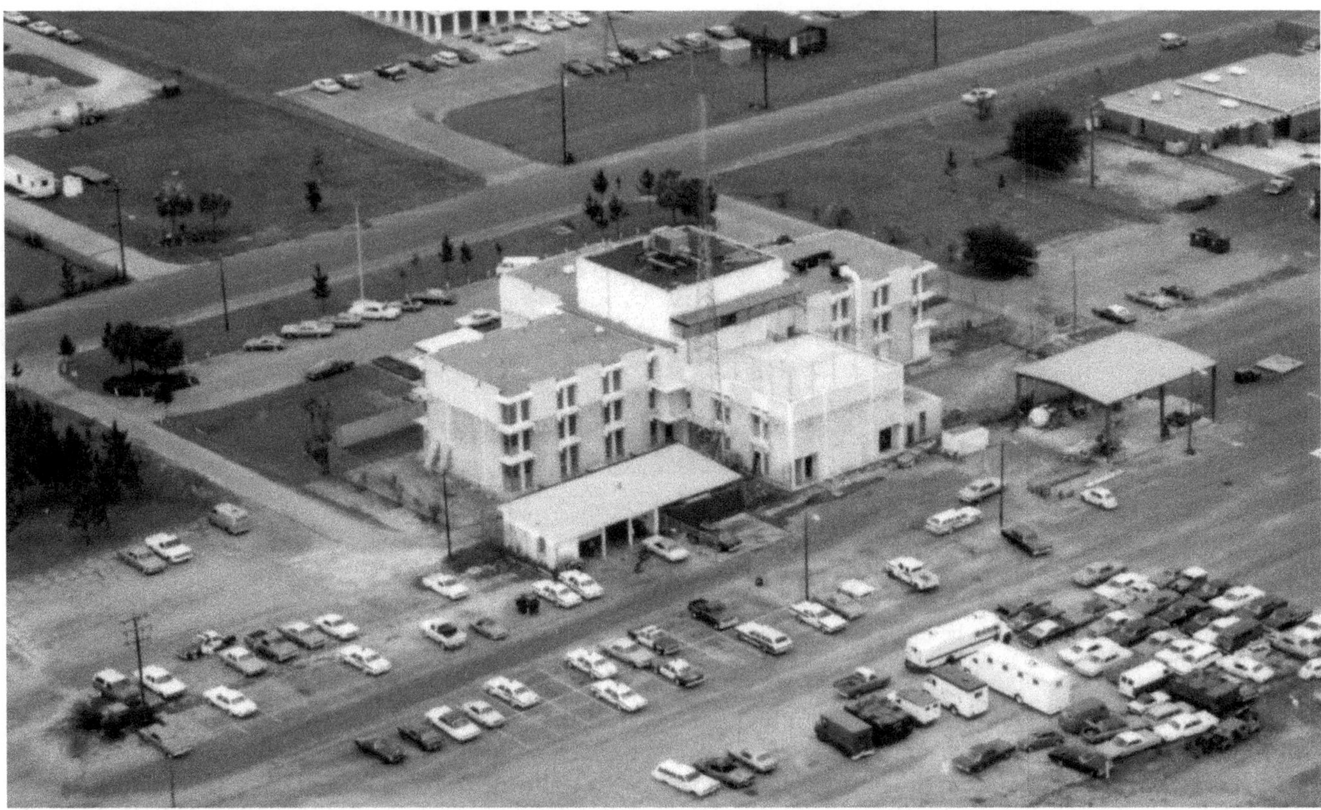

Leon County Jail (center) aerial view, May 1977. Photo courtesy State Library & Archives of Florida.

> Like Lake Sammamish. We went out to Farrell's for ice cream after eating hamburgers. It wasn't like I had forgotten or couldn't remember, but it was just over ... gone ... the force wasn't pushing me any more. I don't understand it. The force would just consume me. Like one night, I was walking by the campus and I followed this sorority girl. I didn't want to follow her. I didn't do anything but follow her and that's how it was. I'd be out late at night and follow people like that I'd try not to, but I'd do it anyway."
>
> "What about Brenda Ball? I remember you took my family and me out for pizza that night and then hurried away only to be late for Tina's baptism the next day. Is that where you were?"
>
> He mumbled something that I couldn't understand and then said, "It's pretty scary, isn't it?" (Kendall 1981, 175-6).

February 23, 1978: Pitkin County, Colorado, District Attorney Frank Tucker arrives with extradition papers, but Ted will stay in Florida.

Sometime in March, 1978: Ted writes to Carole Boone:

> I'm like a bottled up cyclone, mind spinning with memories, regrets, fears. To anchor me and calm me I conjure up fond memories of the past, but these excursions shortly turn pleasant reverie into deep sadness. I constantly attempt to avoid the reality that I failed miserably in my attempt to become a free man ... I am tired of outmanoeuvering the prosecutors and courts. I am tired of playing the news media, of staying calm and smiling for the cameras, or being stared at, of being whispered about, of being suspected and hated. I am tired of knowing what people must think, of being vilified and dehumanized. Life has always had surprises in store for me. Many of them have been pleasant. Will there be more, and will I be free again? How can I be sure, what can I do to satisfy myself I've had my ration of happiness and the rest is all pain? (W&M 1980, 267).

March 17, 1978: Five cubic centimeters of blood are drawn from Ted along with hair samples from his head, arms and legs.

April 6, 1978: Jack Pottinger interviews Nita Neary with a set of photographs, including one of Ted. Also on this day, FDLE Crime Lab fingerprint analyst Doug Barrow went through the mass of evidence submitted by the Leach search teams and found cigarette butts and a five-dollar bill that had been collected two months previously. Because it had been raining, the items had been packaged wet, and they had mildewed. The mildew process had been sped along by the fact that the evidence had been packaged in plastic. The evidence should have been allowed to dry before being packaged in paper bags. Although you can't raise latent fingerprints from mildew, Barrow thought he could do something else. Remembering the cigarette butts removed from the Media Center van, Barrow retrieved those butts and laid them beside the mildewed butts. He noticed similarities. The type of filters on the butts, the way the butts were bitten, the length to which they had been smoked, the way they had been crushed out – all these characteristics

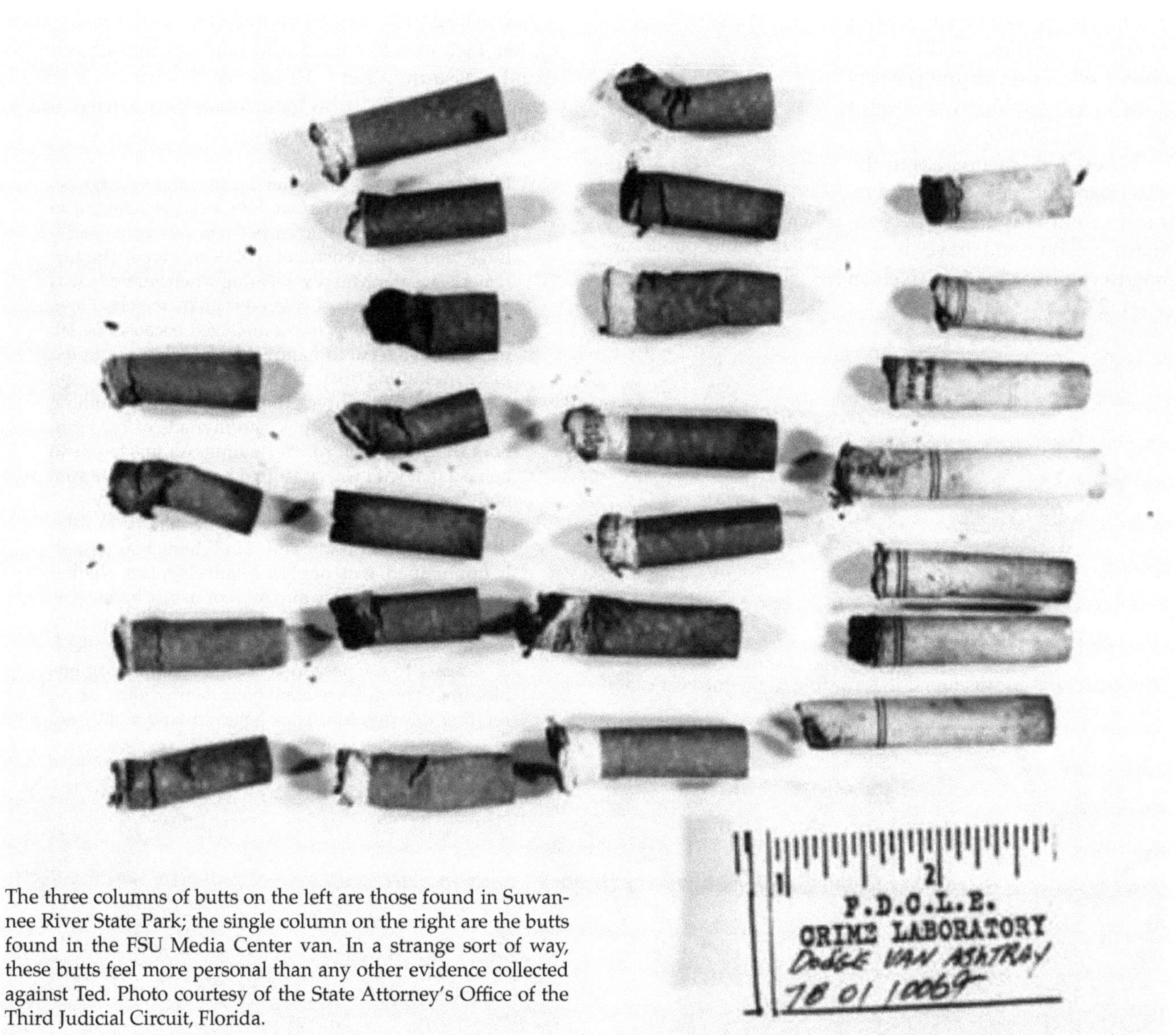

The three columns of butts on the left are those found in Suwannee River State Park; the single column on the right are the butts found in the FSU Media Center van. In a strange sort of way, these butts feel more personal than any other evidence collected against Ted. Photo courtesy of the State Attorney's Office of the Third Judicial Circuit, Florida.

were very similar. Barrow concluded that the same person smoked both sets of butts. He telephoned his conclusions to FDLE Special Agent J. O. Jackson and suggested that they return and search Suwannee River State Park. "You should consider this merely an investigative lead," he cautioned, "this is not scientifically sound enough for me to testify about in court" (Dekle 2011, 83).

April 7, 1978: (Noon) Kimberly Leach's decomposed body was found under a collapsed hog shed in Suwannee River State Park by Florida Highway Patrol trooper Ken Robinson. The Chief Medical Examiner Peter Lipkovic was called in. The only clothing item on the body was a stained, off-white appearing body shirt with a short turtleneck and long sleeves. The rest of Kim's clothing lay on the ground immediately next to the body. Crime scene analysts shortly arrived. First they photographed the pen and the parts of the body visible from outside the pen. Next they removed the roof and one wall of the shed and photographed the body in situ. Lipkovic noted

The abandoned hog shed under which Kim was found. Photo courtesy of the State Attorney's Office of the Third Judicial Circuit, Florida.

a tan leather-like jacket, denim trousers, panties, and brown shoes. What they didn't see was Kim's jersey, which was also in the pile of clothing.

When Ted learned about the discovery, he flew into a rage, ranting and raving, hyperventilating; someone gave him a bag to put over his face (Nelson 1994, 232).

Ken Robinson (January 1989). Photo public domain.

The position Kim was found in according to the medical examiner's report.

According to Robert Ressler, Ted killed Kim "by shoving her face into the mud and suffocating her while he sexually assaulted her" (Ressler & Shachtman 1993, 72). George R. Dekle Sr., who tenaciously prosecuted Ted for Kim's murder, found otherwise:

> First, my reasons for believing that the murder occurred in the van: The van had a carpet remnant in the cargo area, and the carpet remnant contained a huge bloodstain consistent with Kim's type. The turtleneck sweater Kim was wearing when her body was found had a huge rust colored stain on the chest area front. This stain was never analyzed because the lab techs were averse to handling the highly corrupted piece of clothing (they stored it on the roof of the lab). Myriads of fibers from Kim's and Bundy's clothing were found on the carpet, and myriads of carpet fibers were found on Kim's clothing. All this led us to believe that Kim was assaulted and killed in the van, and that was the way we presented it to the jury.
>
> Second, my reasons for believing that the murder did not occur as Bundy said: Kim's body was partially mummified, with her face relatively intact. Neither I nor Dr. Lipkovic saw any mud or debris in her nostrils or mouth (her throat was missing). Dr. Lipkovic testified in court that the cause of death was homicidal violence to the neck area accompanied by copious bleeding. The defense team built their whole case on refuting this opinion. They believed (and rightly so)

One of the old tracks looking east that leads to the location where Kim Leach's body was discarded beneath an abandoned hog pen adjacent to Suwannee River State Park. Photo courtesy Chuck Meeks © 2015.

Suwannee River State Park overlaid with original dirt roads (small dashed lines) from USGS 1977 map. It is not clear from which direction Ted entered the farm on which the abandoned hog shed was located. It appears he may have turned into Suwannee River State Park and then immediately right onto Stagecoach Road. Several dirt roads branch off Stagecoach Road leading onto the farm. Map image courtesy USGS Earthstar Geographics SIO © Microsoft Corporation.

> if Dr. Lipkovic's opinion were true, Kim's turtleneck would have been covered with blood. They further believed that the absence of a finding of blood on the turtleneck meant that there was no blood on the turtleneck. What it really meant was that nobody wanted to analyze the shirt because it was so soaked with putrefied body fluid. I made a point, when we got to introducing the turtleneck in evidence, to unfurl it so that the stain on the front was accentuated. The courtroom gasped, and the defense abandoned the argument that there was no blood on the turtleneck. Dr. Lipkovic's opinion stood on two legs – the complete absence of the neck and the complete presence of the eyeholes, ears, nostrils, and mouth. The bugs had entered the body through the throat, ignoring the traditional routes. This indicated that the throat provided a more attractive entrance, which led to the conclusion that the throat had been opened. I later learned from Dr. William Maples (*Dead Men Do Tell Tales* 1994) that it is a common occurrence for bugs to prefer an open wound for their invasion route instead of the more usual bodily orifices. We believed the murder weapon to have been a huge Buck General hunting knife that Bundy had bought the day before from John Farhat, the owner of a sporting goods store in Jacksonville. The knife was never recovered, but we found its pricetag in the van. Bundy was extremely agitated when Mr. Farhat positively identified him as the purchaser of the knife, to the point of blurting out that Mr. Farhat was lying (Dekle 2011, 297-8).

Ted had in fact tried to conceal the bloodstain on the carpet in the van by throwing a large amount of sand, dirt and other vegetation onto it. Dekle goes on to explain why he thinks Ted lied. Put simply, Ted needed to show he was smarter than the prosecution, that he could obscure the truth and walk away without anyone ever knowing what really happened. The truth is that Ted murdered Leach in the most heinous fashion, probably by cutting her throat with the Buck hunting knife he bought the day before. There is also the macabre possibility that he mutilated her genitals before disposing her body.

Dekle being interviewed at Suwannee River State Park on the afternoon of the discovery of the body. Photo courtesy George R. Dekle Sr. © 2015.

Richard Larsen (January 1989). Photo public domain.

April 10, 1978: Ted writes a letter (to unknown recipient) wherein he states:

> I became thoroughly disgusted with Dick Larsen some time ago (since being recaptured in February). His particular brand of sensationalism as it applied to my case struck me as being greatly lacking in taste and objectivity. The articles written by him immediately following my escape from Colorado at the first of the year revealed to me a Dick Larsen who had an interest in making me look like a bad guy. There was no pretense, no attempt to conceal his biased view in the articles he has written during the past several months. I don't need his subscription to the *Seattle Times*, nor do I think I could ever convince him to be fair in his approach to my case. I tell you this because I have let you know in the past that Larsen was someone I kept in frequent contact with. In turn, he managed to procure me a subscription to his newspaper. I always thought that it was an arrangement which did far more to benefit him than it did me. During the past couple of years he has capitalized rather handily on what became his exclusive relationship with me. But when the chips were down, I think his treatment of me was uncalled for.

April 12, 1978: Kimberly Leach is buried.
April 13, 1978: Two Tallahassee store clerks identify Ted as a credit card customer.
April 27, 1978: Dental impressions are taken from Ted by forensic odontologist Richard Souviron.

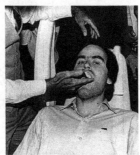

A dental impression being taken from an unhappy Ted. Photo public domain.

April - May 1978: Joe Aloi spends time with Ted in his cell. Aloi worked as an investigator for the circuit public defender's office at the time and traveled from Tallahassee to Pensacola with then Public Defender Mike Minerva to meet with their notorious new client. Describing his time with Ted to the *Tallahassee*

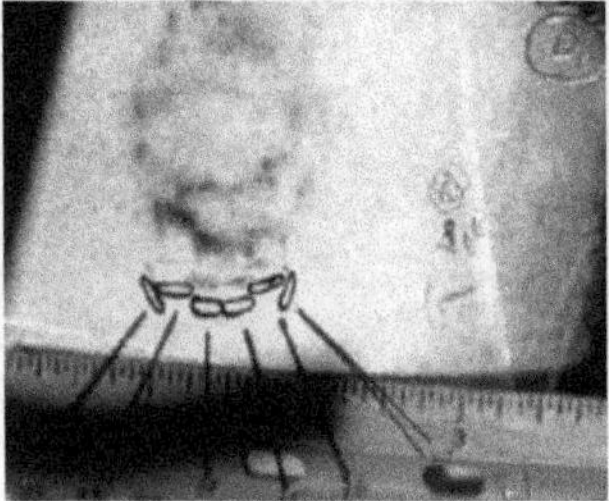

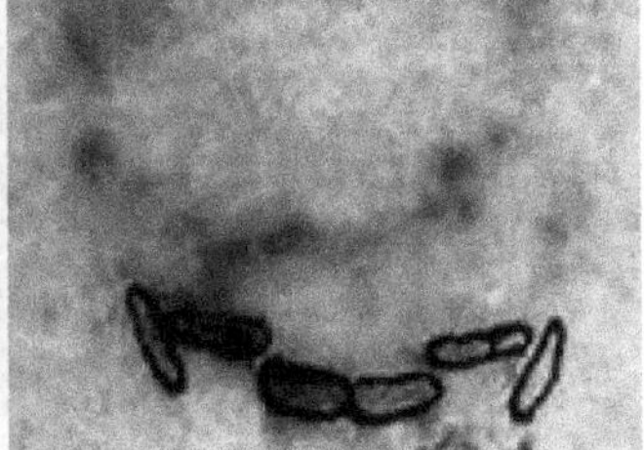

Left: Hand drawn "hollow volume" depicting Ted's lower front teeth. Right: same drawing overlaid on Levy's bite mark. Photos public domain.

Magazine, Aloi said "Ted was very irrational, which is about how he is." Aloi ended up spending several hours talking with the accused murderer. "By the time he got transported back to Tallahassee, they had me on a routine of spending almost every day with him at the jail in the top-security cell," Aloi said. "Part of my job was to try to figure out what was really going on mentally with him, and the other part of the job was to just kind of ... compartmentalize him and keep him focused on the case." Those weekday visits with Ted would last about eight months. With defense attorneys fearing that the jail cell was bugged, Aloi explained that the two would "talk" by typing messages back and forth to each other. At the end of each day, Aloi would gather the typed pages and typewriter ribbon and burn them. Ted, he says, "had the ability to turn on and turn off his murderous rage." Outwardly he appeared normal, even attractive. "I've only seen him lose control twice – only twice did he scare me," Aloi recalls. Once was when Ted was told that authorities had found another victim's body in Lake City, that of 12-year-old Kimberly Leach. "He went really nuts. I could smell him ... like an animal or a wet rug." [...] He told me everything, and I've not told people what he told me," Aloi says. "I could write a book and be very rich (telling) the things that we talked about. I really don't have the heart to tell these parents what happened to some of their daughters. They talk about closure. Closure's bullcrap. If they knew what happened to some of their daughters there would be no closure – ever" (March - April 2010).

To *The Sun Sentinel*, Aloi said:

> I spent approximately nine months straight in a cell with him, three to eight hours a day sometimes. Bundy was a truly evil person, an exceptionally sick individual and he was a master at playing games. Bundy was the purest classical form of sociopathic personality. His evil was so strong, I was with him on two occasions that I saw physical changes in him. I could smell him. I was seriously afraid of him, and I'm not the type to get afraid. One of the times was when Kimberly Leach was found. He got very weird and very disassociative. He became very irate. He gave off an odor of almost burning carpet. He was just sweating profusely, almost like a chemical scent. He told me about this before. He himself was aware of it. It was wild, just incredible. I'm not saying this to glamorize Bundy. He was just trash. Bundy told me a lot of things I didn't want to repeat. I don't want to hurt (his victims') families (August 25, 1991).

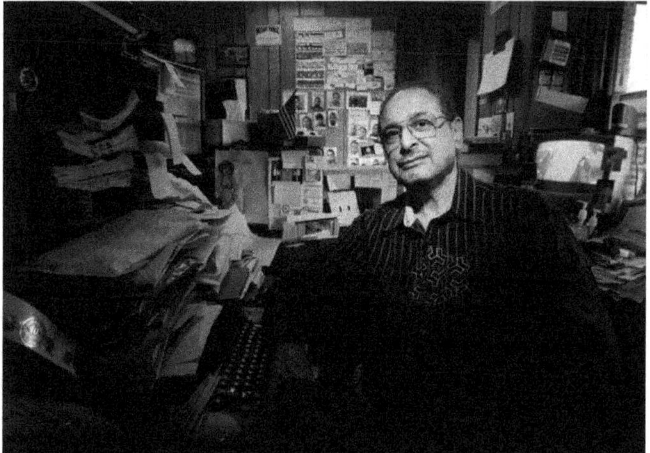

Joe Aloi, March - April 2010. Photo courtesy Rowland Publishing, Inc.

To Nelson Aloi recalled the days he spent in the cell with Ted to allow him to get things off his chest so that he would stop inviting the police into his cell to talk to him. Joe and Ted would each lie in a bunk, and Ted would talk about sex. Joe said that when he went home afterwards he'd feel dirty and find it difficult to face his wife. When asked by her co-counsel Jim Coleman whether Ted was insane, Joe said, "Oh, yeah, he was as insane as they come. But he could control it. He had a bunch of boxes in his head, see, and he could open one when he wanted to, he could open an insane one when he wanted to. He had all these boxes, see." The only time Ted couldn't control his boxes was when he underwent those transformations (Nelson 1994, 157).

May 1978: State obtains search warrant for Ted's blue blazer for fiber evidence. Ted often wore the blazer in court. It was later established he also wore it when he abducted Leach. Joe Nursey, counsel for Ted, reports that when he told Ted about a witness who could identify him driving the FSU Media Center van, he felt Ted was on another planet mentally; Nursey had wondered if he had been speaking the English language to Ted.

May 9, 1978: Remains of Warren Leslie Forrest victim Gloria Knutson found near Lacamas Lake, Washington.

May 12, 1978: Writes letter to John O'Connell & Bruce Lubeck: "What I knew was unimportant—I could live with that—it was the prospect of other people even suspecting that made me shake and sweat" (Von Drehle notes, DDA).

May 30, 1978: Richard Souviron receives photos of Lisa Levy's buttock with Ted's bite mark impressions. Souviron confers with bite mark specialist Lowell Levine to confirm that Ted's teeth fit like "a key in a lock."

June, 1978: Carole Boone visits Ted in Tallahassee. She is spending upwards of 12 hours a day working on exonerating Ted. Boone is convinced that Ted is "still just the good Republican boy he always was" (W&M 1980, 279).

June 6, 1978: Souviron writes to Larry Simpson. "Both bite marks made on the left buttocks of Ms. Levy, with reasonable dental certainty, were made by Mr. Theodore Bundy."

July 19, 1978: Mary Lynn Henson releases her interim fiber evidence report showing that Kim's and Ted's clothing came into contact with the carpet of the FSU Media Center van.

July 21, 1978: Indicted for Kim Leach kidnapping and murder.

July 27, 1978: Public confrontation with Leon County Sheriff Ken Katsaris as he is indicted for the murders of Levy and Bowman.

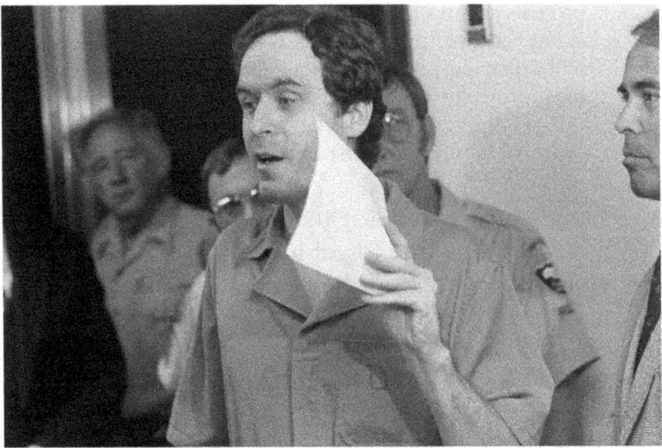

The infamous Bundy-Katsaris stand-off. "Okay, you've got the indictment, that's all you're gonna get […] I'll plead not guilty right now." Photo courtesy ©vk.com/mandsm.

Ken Katsaris, 1978. Photo public domain.

July 28, 1978: Clarence Anderson makes his first report to police on this date.

July 31, 1978: (Morning) Ted makes a plea of "not guilty" before Judge John Rudd.

Top: Newspaper drawing by Christine Elizabeth Lyttle (July 2, 1986). Millard Farmer and Ted stand before Judge Wallace Jopling. Lyttle said, "There was such an aura of evil about him. [...] He was very devious. I do believe he had a split personality." Photo source public domain.

August 14, 1978: Ted appears in Lake City with his attorney Millard Farmer and pleads "not guilty" before Judge Wallace Jopling.

October 1978: Ted pacing back and forth in his cell, according to Joe Nursey, mumbling things about people out to get him, a conspiracy and so forth. Paranoia. Ted talking about anything but the upcoming trial.

October 3, 1978: Appears alone representing himself before Judge John Rudd. Hasn't done any preparation.

On his way to the Leon County Courthouse: "I'm staying with the man I know best, and that's me." Photo public domain.

October 5, 1978: Ted arrives, escorted by sheriff deputies, at the Leon County Courthouse, for the start of the Chi Omega trial.

October 6, 1978: Floods his cell. Note of Janice Turner, RN, prison nurse, referring to District Attorney Curtis Golden – "Mr Bundy's voice was loud as he was speaking to Mr. Golden's questions, exact repetition of Mr. Golden" (Nelson 1994, 228). Lewis posits echolalia – suggestive of a psychotic state.

October 17, 1978: Ted takes the deposition of William P. Gunter. Ed Harvey is present as standby counsel while Ted is undecided whether to accept counsel. According to Harvey, at Ted's competency hearing [on October 22, 1987]: "He could look at certain issues in the case and discuss them fairly rationally one at a time, but he couldn't see the whole big picture. He couldn't see how one issue fit with another" (Nelson 1994, 193).

October 21 or 29, 1978: Richard Souviron shows the Lisa Levy bite mark evidence anonymously to the American Society of Criminal Pathologists and the Florida Medical Examiner's Commission. When Ted finds out, he calls for charges to be dropped citing prejudicial contamination of evidence. His motion is rejected.

October 26, 1978: Ted takes the deposition of Steven Bodiford at the Leon County Jail.

October 30, 1978: Ted writes letter to unknown recipient: "I've asked John Browne to come down here so that I can draw upon his legal talent and advice. I am sure he will give me much of the insight that I am currently lacking …"

November 29, 1978: Melissa Smith's father Louis Smith provides self-defense advise to young women (*Deseret News*).

- 1979 -

March – April, 1979: Mental Health Associates (421 East Call Street, Tallahassee) conduct reviews and consultations related to Ted.

April 26, 1979: Judge Edward Cowart grants funds for a poll to measure community attitudes to Ted and the impact of pre-trial publicity.

April 27, 1979: Emanuel Tanay told Mike Minerva that a pre-trial psychiatric evaluation of Ted was necessary

Spokane Daily Chronicle - Feb 11, 1980

Bundy 'Admitted 3 Murders'

LIVE OAK, Fla. (AP) — Theodore R. Bundy, who faces a third death sentence, admitted last spring to three murders but ruined his chance to avoid the electric chair by trying to outwit prosecutors, a state attorney says.

State Attorney Jerry Blair said Sunday in a telephone interview that during a plea-bargaining attempt last May, Bundy signed a statement admitting he murdered two Florida State University sorority sisters and a North Florida schoolgirl.

In a trial that ended in Orlando last week, Blair helped win a conviction against Bundy in the kidnap-murder of 12-year-old Kimberly Diane Leach of Lake City in February 1978.

Bundy, 33, formerly of Tacoma, Wash., faces sentencing Tuesday afternoon in the Leach case, following a recommendation Saturday by the jury that he receive the death penalty. He was condemned to death last July for the Tallahassee murders of sorority sisters Lisa Levy and Margaret Bowman.

In the plea-bargaining statement Bundy admitted the murders and, in return, Blair said, "the state was not going to recommend imposition of the death penalty." That, he said, would have meant no chance of parole for 75 years.

Blair said the plea-bargaining effort broke down when Bundy moved to have public defender Michael Minerva removed from his case, claiming Minerva was trying to coerce him into admitting guilt. Blair said he was sure Bundy's unsuccessful bid to drop Minerva was part of a scheme to have any guilty plea overturned on appeal.

"I'm equally sure he would not have raised the issue until the passage of several years," in hopes the state's case would be weakened by the death of witnesses and the loss of evidence, the prosecutor said.

"We obviously were not going to enter into such a plea bargain," Blair said.

He said Bundy's maneuvering "said a great deal about his personality and character," revealing another side to the attractive, well-spoken Bundy, who helped defend himself against charges.

"Obviously, the jury had no difficulty believing this bright, articulate person was capable of these things," Blair said.

even if Ted objected to it.

May 14, 1979: Pre-trial hearings begin under Judge Cowart. State prosecutor Larry Simpson, and defense attorneys Lynn Alan Thompson and Mike Minerva take center stage with Ted assisting. Bite mark evidence takes center stage. Starting on this day, Ted is prescribed and takes one tablet of Ativan at night (Ativan is a benzodiazepine; calming, sedative).

May 17-31, 1979: Ted prescribed Ativan for "anxiety" and Limbitrol for "agitated depression."

May 18, 1979: Tanay examines Ted in Tallahassee according to his book *American Legal Injustice* (Tanay 2010, 129). The Supreme Court of Florida receives his report May 21, 1979.

Emanuel Tanay (undated). Photo public domain.

May 25, 1979: John Arthur Spenkelink (30) executed by electric chair at FSP. Spenkelink shot and killed a fellow small-time criminal named Joseph Szymankiewicz in Tallahassee, Florida, in 1973.

May 28, 1979: Ted now taking two milligrams Ativan in the morning.

May 31, 1979: Ted takes 2 mg Ativan in the morning. According to a nurse, "He was depressed and needed to talk to someone" (Nelson 1994, 244). Later in the day he was placed on suicide watch. Ted rejects guilty plea (which would have saved his life). From this point on he is doomed.

June 1, 1979: "He was extremely agitated with symptoms of depression" (Nelson 1994, 244). A plan is made to take him off Ativan and try other medication. Placed on suicide precaution.

June 7, 1979: Hervey Cleckley examines Ted for 2 hours and finds that "the defendant is capable of understanding the charges against him and of participating in his defense" (*Sarasota Herald-Tribune,* June 12, 1979).

June 8, 1979: Ativan stopped. Chlorhydrate (sedative, hypnotic) started.

June 12, 1979: Jury selection begins. Initial trial proceedings in Tallahassee, but a change of venue is granted. The trial is reset to begin in Miami on June 25, 1979.

June 14, 1979: Mary Lynn Henson releases her final fiber evidence report.

June 24, 1979: The following list of people were granted access to see Ted in preparation for his trial: Ed Harvey, Margaret Good and Lynn Thompson (lead attorneys); Phil Spiellman (consultant); Joe Aloi (investigator); John Morris, David Marcus (law clerks); Eloise Clary (secretary); Bob Haggard, Mike Minerva (attorneys).

June 25, 1979: Dade County Courthouse (73 West Flagler Street, Miami) – Bowman-Levy trial.

June 30, 1979: Jury selection continues.

July 1, 1979: Carole Boone fired from the Washington state Energy Office "for cause" effective this day.

Left: Ted inspects the license plate he stole from Randy Ragan with Lynn Alan Thompson and Vic Africano. Right: Margaret Good, July 1979. Photos public domain.

July 2, 1979: Margaret Good, an appellate specialist, begins her pretrial motions for Ted with the aim of suppressing evidence.
July 3, 1979: Nancy Dowdy, Nita Neary pre-trial testimony.
July 5, 1979: Ted's defense team stand Ted next to Ronnie Eng.

Former Chi Omega sorority houseboy Ronnie Eng stands profile-to-profile for Bundy's defense team and trial judge Edward Cowart (far left). Photo courtesy AP images.

July 6, 1979: Ted takes the witness stand in an attempt to make evidence seized from the August 16, 1975 search of his VW inadmissible.
July 7, 1979: Bowman and Levy trial opening statements commence.
July 16, 1979: Patricia Lasko presents hair and fiber evidence against Ted.

Ted in the witness stand in the Dade County Courthouse, Miami, July 6, 1979. Photo public domain.

July 17, 1979: 1:00 a.m. Jailers report that Ted broke a light near his cell by throwing an orange at it, then stuffed toilet paper into the lock on his cell and refused to prepare for court. Ted was taken before Judge Cowart to whom he complained that officials at Dade County Jail were trying to "coerce me and wear me down" (*New York Times*). In court, Nita Neary recounts her testimony against Ted. "I was at the entrance to the foyer and I saw a man at the door ... he was leaving. [...] He was standing right at the door with his hand on the doorknob." In his hand was "a club or a log. [...] It was sort of rough in texture, like maybe a branch" (*St. Petersburg Times*, July 18, 1979).

Top left: Nita Neary looking over to Bundy's table as she testifies in court, July 1979. Photo public domain. Top right: Drawing made by police sketch artist based on Neary's eye-witness report. Photo courtesy FSA.

Richard Souviron presenting bite mark evidence in court, a landmark in the history of the science and art of bite mark identification. Photo courtesy AP images.

July 18, 1979: Richard Souviron presents his dental evidence against Ted in court.
July 21, 1979: Ted is granted access to the telephone "for the rest of the evening."
July 24, 1979: Found guilty of the murders of Levy and Bowman.
July 25, 1979: Ted's mother visits him in jail. She is photographed with Jamie Boone.
July 31, 1979: Sentenced to death for the murders of Levy and Bowman.

Mugshot post Chi Omega death sentence. Photo courtesy Florida Department of Corrections.

August 1, 1979: Mugshot taken.
September 7, 1979: Supreme Court of Florida receives another report from Tanay in which he describes Ted as a typical psychopath or someone who suffers from a personality disorder.
September 14, 1979: Pasted magazine pictures on cell wall; violation of prison rules. Privileges revoked.
September 26, 1979: Appeals to the Florida Supreme Court.
October 30, 1979: The Leach trial originally arises in the Circuit Court of the Third Judicial Circuit, Columbia County, Florida, but is changed to the Circuit Court of the Third Judicial Circuit, Live Oak, Suwannee County, Florida
November 4, 1979: Ted writes first letter to Stephen G. Michaud and Hugh Aynesworth, about five months after the two authors began investigating him.

November 19, 1979: The venue for the Leach trial is changed from Live Oak, Suwannee County, to Orlando, Orange County.

- 1980 -

Stephen Michaud (January 1989). Photo public domain.

January 7, 1980: Leach trial starts in Orlando.

January 9, 1980: Stephen Michaud and Hugh Aynesworth start their interviews with Ted, resulting in *The Only Living Witness*, (published 1983) and *Ted Bundy: Conversations With A Killer* (published 2000).

Hugh Aynesworth (January 1989). Photo public domain.

January 23, 1980: Ted talks about his sock fetish:

> One of my fondest dreams, [he told Carole Boone], is to have all the underwear and socks I ever could conceivably use. It's one of my fantasies. To be able to wear new socks every day! And I must admit, I have had three or four dozen socks, all purchased on [stolen] credit cards. [...] I have always felt deprived of underwear. I always felt that I would have really made it if I had all the socks and underwear I could ever use. Even in Pensacola, I went to a shopping mall and bought some socks. I was buying socks everywhere. [...] This is for real. I mean, I've got a sock fetish. No question about it. I must have six or seven pairs right here with me in my cell. [...] I am really sick when it comes to socks. These are some of the things for people who really want to know what makes Ted Bundy tick. They're parts of the combination to the deepest, most secret recesses of my mind. [...] I'm very close to my feet. Right now. I'm lying on my back with my foot propped up on the bars. And I'm studying my toes. For a good portion of the night. They're probably the most attractive feet you've ever seen. [...] I'm sure all these law-enforcement officers around the country are looking through their unsolved crimes for anything to do with the presence or absence of socks. [...] Socks are such a serious part of my life. They're so very important to me. They kept reading the list of socks and all [in court] and I felt proud. Honestly, it didn't even begin to occur to me that people might wonder why I had all those socks. I just felt proud that I owned all those socks. Like a man who stands at the back of his ranchhouse and looks out over the range and sees all them cattle. [...] The only time I began to have a little bout of sheepishness was when I read about a white sock with a blue band and green stripe on the toe. Those are odor eaters – and that was getting too personal (M&A 2000, 36-7).

Ellensburg Daily Record - Feb 12, 1980

Dekle says Bundy looks at magazines featuring pictures of cheerleading competitions. His fingerprints were found all over a pile of such magazines in the car he was driving when he was arrested in Pensacola on Feb. 15, 1978.

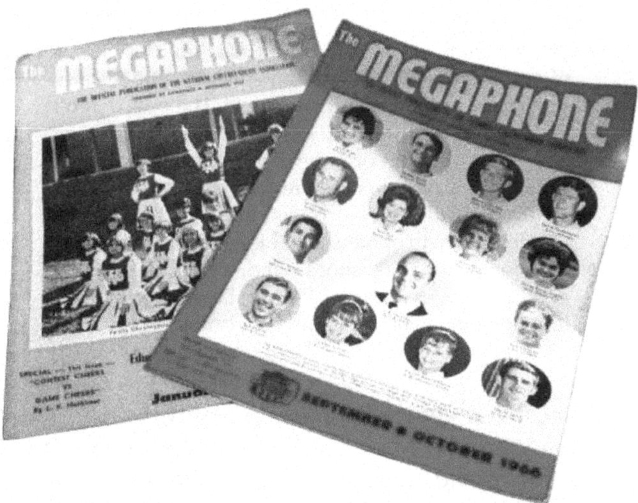

Four *Megaphone* cheerleader magazines were found in a briefcase in Ted's stolen 1972 orange VW. Photo public domain.

February 7, 1980: (Noon) Found guilty of the Leach murder.

February 9, 1980: Marries Carole Ann Boone in the courtroom. According to Michaud & Aynesworth, she was the architect behind the charade.

Carole Ann Boone: "I do." Photo public domain.

February 11, 1980: *Spokane Daily Chronicle* explains how Bundy first contemplated signing a guilty plea-bargaining deal then reneges.

February 12, 1980: Sentenced to death for Leach's murder. Gets life for her kidnap. David Kuypers, a psychologist who had helped Ted through his two murder trials, commits suicide. Wakulla County Sheriff David Harvie said, "He was upset over the verdict. He had other pressures – including domestic and job related ones – but the guilty verdict against Bundy at Orlando hit him hard" (*Spokane Daily Chronicle*).

NOTES

It has been said that Ted was railroaded at the Chi Omega trial, that the evidence was shaky at best. Nita Neary's eyewitness description had gone through so many renditions that by the time it came to court it was so far removed from the actual event that it was at best a contrivance. The club weapons he used were never found, nor were any fingerprints ever found matching him to the crime.

But evidence *was* found. Ted left a pantyhose stocking around Margaret Bowman's neck, and another in Kim Weeks' bed. He left another at Cheryl Thomas' apartment, and possibly semen stains. The mask from Cheryl Thomas' apartment contained hairs that were for all intents and purposes indistinguishable from Ted's. He also left a bite mark on Lisa Levy's buttock. In addition to this, there were multiple eye-witness sightings of Ted on the night, each one placing him in proximity to the crime. The bite mark evidence can be criticized, but taken in conjunction with Nita Neary's account and the pantyhose masks, once again the odds that it was someone else is vanishingly small when one considers Ted's M.O. and his presence in Tallahassee.

The thinness of Ted's Chi Omega case is contrasted with the Kim Leach murder. In that prosecution the evidence against him was overwhelming. Fiber evidence triangulated Ted with Leach and the Media Center van. Since Ted was categorically identified as being in the van, the presence of his clothing fiber there *and* on Kim's clothing reduces the chances of a false positive to almost zero. In the words of fiber evidence expert Mary Lynn Henson: "I have never seen anything like the combination of fibers which is present in this particular case in any other case. I have never seen so many fibers which were similar to the standards in any other case" (Dekle 2011, 272). Yet this is what Ted said to Hugh Aynesworth in response to the fiber evidence:

> The conclusions you can form based on those kinds of examinations are so general and so vague that we don't know what the probability is. The police don't know what the probability is of finding any given fiber or set of fibers or any hair or given set of hairs if they're in a location where there is a lot of opportunity for hairs to be dropped and left there for an indefinite length of time. Hair blows. Fibers blow, and they're tracked in on shoes – and on clothing. So you just can't say with any certainty how, I mean, how long a fiber has been in a given location (M&A 2000, 236).

Typical Ted generalizations. In reality, Leach's jersey was made from a fiber that had a faulty thread. It had thirty-one threads (or strands) instead of the usual thirty-three (M&A 2000, 236). The statistical chance that it was not the same thread is vanishingly small. Since numerous fibers from Ted's clothing were also found in the van, the fiber evidence essentially slam-dunked Ted's case.

One wonders what Carole Boone thought about all this. Michaud & Aynesworth provide an interesting snapshot of her mental state throughout the trials. According to them, Carole was continually in search of "irrefutable physical evidence" of Ted's innocence (1983, 262). No such evidence of course would ever be found. So why did Carole pursue it? Larsen got a quote from her, just after Ted's first arrest and imprisonment, referencing how they first met at the Washington Department of Emergency Services in the summer of 1974. "His desk was just across from mine. He was a great friend to me at a time when I desperately needed a crutch. For her, the summer of 1974 was a period of turmoil, going through a divorce. Ted "guided me through that summer ... got me going again. He was the sort of person I would have trusted my life with" (Larsen 1980, 87). Carole, however, left Ted in August 1986, unable to bear the stress of his death warrants.

The standard narrative is that Ted didn't start confessing until the last few days before his execution, but in fact he began confessing in April 1988. This was part of his long-range planning to delay his execution. His idea was to give up information on the whereabouts of his victims in return for three additional years of life. He had in fact already broached a similar idea during his Pensacola 1978 interviews. In those sessions he tried to preempt a confession in return for a life in a Washington mental hospital close to family and friends:

> Now, if I had my choice, and I don't necessarily (indiscernible) again I can't, I'm not, I can't force anything but if I were to sit back and think about how I would like the thing to resolve itself, everybody being satisfied to the degree they would be satisfied to getting all the answers they want to all the questions they want to ask, then after that was all over I would like to be back in Washington state, because that's where my mother is, that's where my family is and that's where I'm from (Pensacola Police Department interview, February 18th, 1978, 12:15 a.m.).

Was Carole unaware of this attempted confession? The transcripts of the Pensacola police interviews were deemed inadmissible to the Chi Omega court by Judge Cowart. However, the circus behind the scenes did become public when Ted's Chi Omega lawyers managed to negotiate a guilty plea bargain in return for a life sentence. All Ted had to do was sign the document. On the day it was supposed to happen, Ted reneged, and the whole thing fell apart. He chose execution over life. In that instance Carole wrote to Ted: "Poops, check to see if you're part of the problem" (M&A 1983, 258). Yet her faith in him remained steadfast, right through Chi Omega and right through the Leach trial. We might be tempted to put her behavior down to the Bundy groupy phenomenon. But we would be wrong.

Ted was able to insinuate himself into her life because he had a knack of playing roles. He made her feel like they were soul mates right off the bat. The superficial charm at work which she interpreted as a deep emotional connection. She can't be faulted for that. Many people fall for that. The problem is, it took her an awful lot of time to see the truth. Love can blind, especially if it is formed in a codependent manner that psychopaths are good at eliciting in unsuspecting victims. All of this to say that Ted's empathy system was very much intact, but was deviously bent to his narcissistic and destructive self.

References

Dekle, G. R. (2011). *The Last Murder: The Investigation, Prosecution, and Execution of Ted Bundy*. Santa Barbara, California: Praeger.

Michaud, S. G. & Aynesworth, H. (1983). *The Only Living Witness: The True Story of Serial Sex Killer Ted Bundy*. Irving, TX: Authorlink.

Michaud, S. G. & Aynesworth, H. (2000). *Ted Bundy: Conversations with a Killer*. Irving, TX: Authorlink.

Michaud, S. G. & Hazelwood, R. (1998). *The Evil That Men Do*. New York: St. Martin's Press.

Nelson, P. (1994). *Defending the Devil*. New York: William Morrow and Company, Inc.

Ressler, R. K. & Shachtman, T. (1992). *Whoever Fights Monsters: My Twenty Years Tracking Serial Killers for the FBI*. New York: St. Martin's Paperbacks.

Tanay, E. (2010). *American Legal Injustice: Behind the Scenes with an Expert Witness*. Plymouth, U.K.: Jason Aronson, Inc.

Execution (March 27, 1980 - January 24, 1989)

March 27, 1980: Ted begins his third-person account of how he became a serial killer to Michaud & Aynesworth.
April 22, 1980: Appeals Leach sentences (kidnap & murder) to the Florida Supreme Court.
End of June 1980: Ted mails last letter to Liz Kloepfer; several weeks later phones her. Last contact between them (Rule 2006, 429).
October 4, 1980: Ordered to pay for a food tray he burned a hole in with a cigarette.

- 1981 -

March 30, 1981: John Warnock Hinckley (26) attempts to assassinate United States President Ronald Reagan, 69 days into Reagan's presidency. Three others were shot and wounded by Hinckley. One of them died decades later of related injuries. Hinckley's motivation for the attack was driven by his erotomanic obsession with actress Jodie Foster.

John Hinckley, Jr. circa 1980. Photo public domain.

September 30, 1981: Boone is reported pregnant with Ted's child. According to a former correctional officer: "He was very cordial, quiet, kept to himself. If you didn't know what he had done, you'd never guess. [...] If you called him 'Theodore' he would blow up! It would make him instantly furious." According to the same officer Bundy ejaculated into a contraband condom just prior to Boone's regular visit, and tied off the condom to hide in his mouth. During visitation, Bundy passed the semen-filled condom to Carole via a kiss, as a kiss was allowed. Carole immediately departed the prison, the condom in her mouth to keep it warm, and drove quickly to a clinic to be artificially inseminated. The result was the birth of a daughter in October. "She probably passed him the condom the same way [in a kiss]" during a prior visit (*Examiner.com*, December 7, 2014).

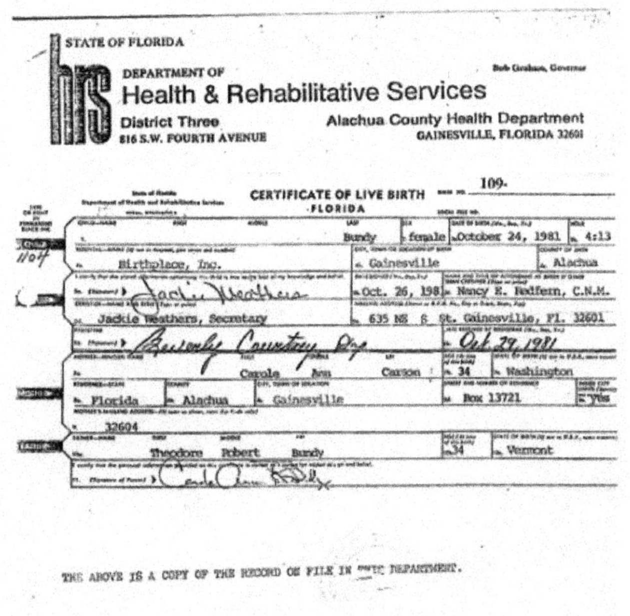

STATE OF FLORIDA
DEPARTMENT OF
Health & Rehabilitative Services
District Three
816 S.W. FOURTH AVENUE
Alachua County Health Department
GAINESVILLE, FLORIDA 32601

CERTIFICATE OF LIVE BIRTH 109-
FLORIDA

Bundy · female · October 24, 1981 · 4:13
Birthplace, Inc. · Gainesville · Alachua
Oct. 26, 1981 · Nancy E. Redfern, C.N.M.
Jackie Weathers, Secretary · 635 NE 8 St. Gainesville, Fl. 32601
Oct. 29, 1981
Carole Ann Carson · 34 · Washington
Florida · Alachua · Gainesville · Box 13721 · Yes
32604
Theodore Robert Bundy · 34 · Vermont

THE ABOVE IS A COPY OF THE RECORD ON FILE IN THIS DEPARTMENT.

Document pertaining to Rosa's birth. Photo public domain.

October 1981: Liz publishes *The Phantom Prince* under the pseudonym "Liz Kendall" in which she reports Ted admitted to being a murderer.
October 24, 1981: Boone gives birth to a baby girl "Rosa" at The Birthplace, a private birthing center near the University of Florida campus.

- 1982 -

March 30 1982: Ted's new attorney Robert Augustus Harper Jr. files a petition to Florida Supreme Court to overturn Ted's Chi Omega conviction.
October 6, 1982: Florida Supreme Court listens to his arguments for new trial in Chi Omega case.
October 7, 1982: Assistant Attorney general David Gauldin: "I think he got a fair trial and I think the jury was untainted."

- 1983 -

February 2, 1983: Disorderly conduct. Repeatedly flushed toilet, flooding cellblock. Privileges revoked.
April 8, 1983: The court listens to his arguments for new trial in Kim Leach case.
June 26, 1983: Larry Voshall dies of an apparent heart attack aged 39. At the time he was communications director for the Republican caucus in the state senate, Washington (*Ellensburg Daily Record*, June 28, 1983).
December 19, 1983: Samuel F. Cowell (DOB: September 23, 1898) dies aged 85 in Lafayette Hill, Montgomery County, Pennsylvania.

- 1984 -

May 21, 1984: Writes letter to "Diane": "I find that I have more than enough to keep my days full from 5 in the morning to 11 at night."
June 1984: Robert "Eddie" Blackwelder, chair of the Political Science and Paralegal Studies Department at Wallace Community College, Cullman, teaches a course on serial-killings. He meets Bundy with one of his students. They sit at a table for three hours and talk about football, abortion, and the death penalty.
June 21, 1984: Supreme Court upholds its ruling. Robert Harper's appeal fails.
July 18, 1984: Prison officials find cell bar sawed through,

concealed with putty and paint. Privileges revoked.
September 1984: Ronald M. Holmes, of Louisville University, interviews Ted for 9 ½ hours.
September 6. 1984: Letter to unknown recipient: "I have stopped writing to Carole for a while ..."
September 24, 1984: Florida Supreme Court denies request for rehearing of Chi Omega case.
October 2, 1984: Keppel receives first letter from Ted offering his help in solving the Green River serial murders. Keppel says he can see Ted in Florida in the "middle of November" [1984].
October 15, 1984: Keppel receives second letter from Ted offering his help in solving the Green River serial murders.
October 16, 1984: Keppel writes to Ted, agreeing to see him.
October 27, 1984: Keppel receives third letter from Ted showing he has a grasp of the challenges in the Green River case.
November 8, 1984: Ted writes letter to "Mary":

> Rosa has changed so much in the four weeks since I last saw her. The major difference is that she is really talking now. She won't stop. She's like a beautiful little parrot. All day it was "Daddy" this and "Daddy" that. She was very much into talking to me and generally trying to keep me to herself. "You stay here, Daddy" she'd say when I'd tell her to get back to Carole ...

From left, Carole, Rosa, Ted (circa 1986). Photo courtesy © vk.com/mandsm.

November 17, 1984: Keppel and Dave Reichert visit Ted in Florida State Prison.

- 1985 -

May 9, 1985: The court affirms sentence in Kim Leach case.
June 1985: ViCAP inaugurated.
July 11, 1985: Florida Supreme Court denies request for rehearing of Kim Leach case.
December 18, 1985: Clemency denied by Florida Board of Executive Clemency.

- 1986 -

January 1986: Ted asks U.S. Supreme Court to overturn his conviction and death sentence in the Chi Omega case.
February 5, 1986: Governor Bob Graham signs first death warrant – for the Chi Omega case. Execution date: March 4, 1986.
February 13, 1986: U.S. Supreme Court denies request for stay of execution for Chi Omega case.
February 19, 1986: Polly Nelson takes on Ted's case (Mello 1991). Jim Coleman supervises. Ted writes letter to unknown recipient:

Polly Nelson. Photo source *Defending the Devil*, 2011.

> I must let you know that I'm doing just fine. Things are not nearly as bleak as they may seem. There's progress being made on the legal issues. I have a lot to work with. There's no reason to worry. I am able to see Carole for a couple of hours five days a week and everything is about the same for me except I don't get to go outside. [...] I will write [...] once I'm off this warrant.

Jim Coleman (circa 1988). Photo courtesy State Archives of Florida, Mark Foley Collection.

February 21, 1986: U.S. Supreme Court denies second request for stay of execution in Chi Omega case.
February 22, 1986: Nelson talks to Ted for the first time by phone.
February 24, 1986: First Hinckley letter to Ted. An excerpt reads:

> ... I hope I'm not being rude, but I just saw the article about you in the *Post*, and I thought you could use a friendly word from someone who truly knows firsthand how tough it can be to stand up and tell the world, "Look, I'm really sorry, but I just went totally apeshit." The paper talks about how you didn't want to plead insanity at your trial. (Hey, who does?) Like that means you weren't nuts? (If you ask me, it proves it!) And how you were only doing it on appeal to es-

> cape the death penalty. (Duh.) Ted, I heard that same exact baloney, and I got so bummed that I tried to commit suicide three times. So what I really wanted to tell you is, don't let the bastards get you down. You have as much right to appeal as anyone else, even if you killed and fucked a hundred dead girls. (But why am I telling you that? You went to law school!) (*GQ*, January 1997, Edited by Scott Raab, Published by Alfred A Knopf).

February 25(26), 1986: U.S. Supreme Court grants stay of execution for Chi Omega case. Argues it needs time to consider his appeal.

March 4, 1986: Execution is set, then postponed. Christian Evangelists John and Marsha Tanner enter Ted's life. According to John Tanner: "We were watching the evening news and they showed us a picture of Ted, and she [Marsha Tanner] looked at me and said, 'John, the Lord just told me you're going to have a dramatic influence over his life'" (August 16, 2006, *Ted Bundy: Natural Porn Killer*). The two met on the eve of Ted's first postponed date with the electric chair. Tanner, then a private defense attorney in Daytona Beach, and his wife, Marsha, had been writing to Ted, as had many other Christians. When Ted's March 4, 1986, execution date was set, he asked the Tanners, who lived less than two hours from the prison, to visit him on his last night. They did. The execution was postponed. Three months later, Ted wrote and asked for them to visit him. This time, as part of a prison ministry program, they continued seeing him every few weeks. They talked about each other's families, friends and interests. They talked about how he thought pornography had satisfied, then intensified his hunger for sexual violence. The three-hour sessions also included much prayer and Bible study. The one thing conspicuously missing was any discussion of his crimes. "John told him at the very beginning that he wouldn't be his lawyer," Marsha said. John said Ted never confessed to him about any murders, and he didn't ask him to. He was there to steer Ted toward salvation, not to interrogate him, Tanner said.

While it may be true that pornography has the potential to foster warped views on sex in some vulnerable individuals, other industries, such as the advertising industry are just as much to blame for the objectification of the human body. Despite the widespread and increasing availability of sexually explicit materials, according to national FBI Department of Justice statistics, the incidence of rape declined markedly from 1975 to 1995. This was particularly seen in the age categories 20–24 and 25–34, the people most likely to use the Internet. The best known of these national studies are those of Berl Kutchinsky, who studied Denmark, Sweden, West Germany, and the United States in the 1970s and 1980s. He showed that for the years from approximately 1964 to 1984, as the amount of pornography increasingly became available, the rate of rapes in these countries either decreased or remained relatively level. Subsequent research has shown parallel findings in every other country examined, including Japan, Croatia, China, Poland, Finland, and the Czech Republic (Kutchinsky, 1991). Not lost on this argument is the role that violence in the media also plays in shaping young minds. Moreover, relatively little is known about the mixing of the two, as in Ted's case. Basically, it doesn't follow that just because porn inspires lust, it also inspires blood lust.

John and Marsha Tanner. Photo source *Ted Bundy: Natural Porn Killer*, August 16, 2006.

John Tanner also said, "In the beginning, Ted felt guilty after seeing the pictures and reading the books [porn]. But eventually, he used them several times a week. Then it was every day except Sunday. 'I still had a moral side to me' Ted said. 'I felt I shouldn't do it on the Sabbath. It sounds foolish, but I tried to keep some decency'" (Nobile 1989, 43). Well, we can easily blow that one out of the water. Ted abducted Ott, Naslund, Campbell, and Oliverson all on a Sunday. It would appear he was just telling Tanner what he wanted him to believe, and Tanner was only too happy to go along with it.

March 5, 1986: Ted writes to Rule. Chides her for her misunderstanding the true nature of serial murder.

March 13, 1986: Rule writes to Ted. Gives him *her* list of serial killer traits in a ploy to get Ted talking. He doesn't respond.

March 15, 1986: Ted replies to Hinckley's first letter. A short excerpt reads:

> ... I must ask that you refrain from profanity in any future letters. On that day two years ago when I accepted Jesus Christ as my personal Lord and Savior, I took the trash out of my life. I can't undo my past – I am sorry; I did go non compos mentis – but today I am His lamb. Look to Him, John. There are no loners in His flock (*GQ*, January 1997, Edited by Scott Raab, Published by Alfred A Knopf).

March 21, 1986: Second Hinckley letter to Ted. A short excerpt:

> ... You think you're so smart, but who's going to Yale? Jodie Foster (*GQ*, January 1997, Edited by Scott Raab, Published by Alfred A Knopf).

March 30, 1986: Ted gives an interview to Jon Nordheimer of the *New York Times*. "If anyone considers me a monster, that's just something they'll have to confront in themselves ... For people to want to condemn someone, to dehumanize someone like me is a very popular and effective understandable way of dealing with a fear and a threat that is incomprehensible."
April 2, 1986: More of Jon Nordheimer's March 30 interview leaked: "... whatever precipitated that act of violence that resulted in a murder ... er ... How should I put it? ... that part of them ... er, of themselves is only a small, small part." (*Gainesville Sun*, p. 12A). Same day Ted writes a reply to Hinckley's second letter:

> I don't know what they're putting in your pill cup, old boy, but one snide joke – for which I now hasten to beg your forgiveness – is no reason to unholster your .22 automatic and strafe a crowd of suits. Take it from a fellow who on more than one occasion bit off more nipple than he could chew: Let go of the anger (*GQ*, January 1997, Edited by Scott Raab, Published by Alfred A Knopf).

April 6, 1986: Nelson meets Ted for the first time.
April 9, 1986: Third Hinckley letter to Ted. A short excerpt:

> You're so right about needing to let go of our anger. When we lash out, we don't just hurt other people, we also hurt ourselves. The therapists tell me this all the time, but it means a lot more coming from you (*GQ*, January 1997, Edited by Scott Raab, Published by Alfred A Knopf).

April 21, 1986: Ted's last letter to Hinckley. A short excerpt:

> I received some most disheartening news this week – yet another ruling that I was competent at my trial and thus deserving of the death sentence. It's always the same: The judge sees my grades, my Boy Scout merit badges, the pamphlet on rape prevention I authored when I served on the Seattle Crime Prevention Advisory Committee, and finds that I was sane. That these aged, black-robed cretins can't grasp that a sane man could not have performed such unspeakable acts just slays me (*GQ*, January 1997, Edited by Scott Raab, Published by Alfred A Knopf).

https://en.wikipedia.org/wiki/File:The_Deliberate_Stranger.jpg

May 4, 1986: A 4-hour mini TV series based on Richard Larsen's *The Deliberate Stranger* airs on US TV for the first time. Nelson writes extensively about her reaction to the mini-series. She quotes Ted as saying:

> I've seen myself in the media enough over the years. I know how I'll be portrayed – it'll be the same old thing. I'm not going to watch it. I've worked too hard to put all that behind me. I'm another person now. It would only make me angry, and I can't afford to get angry (Nelson 1994, 66).

May 5, 1986: Supreme court turns down Nelson's Chi Omega appeal.

Florida State Prison R-wing (death row). The door at the end of the hall leads to Q-wing and the execution chamber. Photo courtesy State Archives of Florida, Mark Foley Collection.

May 22, 1986: Governor Bob Graham signs second death warrant – Chi Omega case. Execution date: July 2, 1986. Additionally signs Gerald Stano's death warrant. Same day Ted appeals to U.S. Supreme Court in the Kim Leach case. Meets with prison Superintendent Richard Dugger. Bundy: "We've got to stop meeting like this" (*The Birmingham News*, May 23 1986). Carole Boone starts daily two-hour visits, waiting nervously while the death warrant is drawn up, one time arriving with a green plastic bag over her head to thwart photographers (*Spokane Chronical*, July 3, 1986).
June 28, 1986: Trial judge denies stay in Chi Omega case.
June 30, 1986: Ted Bundy asks U.S. District Court in Miami for stay of execution in Chi Omega case. Florida Supreme Court denies stay in Chi Omega case. Detectives Dennis Couch, Garth Beckstead (Salt Lake County), and Ira Beal visit Starke but Ted refuses to speak to them.
July 1, 1986: U.S. Circuit Court of Appeals grants temporary stay in Chi Omega case. U.S. District Judge William Zloch says he wants to give the attorneys time to appeal Bundy's case to the 11th U.S. Circuit Court of Appeal in Atlanta.
July 2, 1986: 11th Circuit Court grants permanent stay of execution fifteen minutes before he is scheduled to die.
August 1986: Carole Boone returns to Seattle permanently. Ted loses permanent contact with Rosa.

September 1986: First Ted-Lewis interview.
September 10, 1986: Psychological evaluation by Marilyn Feldman M.A.
September 15, 1986: EEG evaluation by Dr. Leslie S. Prichep. Found pattern "similar to that seen in endogenous depression" (Von Drehle notes, DDA).
October 9, 1986: Arthur Norman, a forensic psychologist, introduces civil attorney Diana Weiner to Ted. Around this time Norman taped several interviews with Ted wherein he recorded Ted saying he did the Somers Point double homicide of Susan Davis and Elizabeth Perry. Norman told Rule, "I have never encountered an individual who could move from one relationship to the next so easily, being seemingly deeply involved with someone, and then dropping them completely and moving on" (*The Forensic Examiner,* Fall 2013, 18-25).'

Diana Weiner, 31 January 2012. Photo public domain.

October 14, 1986: U.S. Supreme Court denies new trial in Kimberly Leach case.
October 21, 1986: Governor Bob Graham signs first death warrant for Kim Leach case (Ted's third warrant). Execution date: Nov. 18, 1986.
October 23, 1986: 11th Circuit Court hears oral arguments in Chi Omega case.
November 1986: Second Ted-Lewis interview.
November 4, 1986: Uses profanity when moved to another cell. Privileges revoked.
November 7, 1986: Trial judge denies stay in Leach case.
November 10, 1986: Ted files request in state court for stay in Leach case.
November 11, 1986: U.S. Circuit Court of Appeals denies stay in Leach case.
November 17, 1986: John and Marsha Tanner visit and counsel Ted before his execution. Florida Supreme Court denies Ted's appeal in Leach case. He is denied stay of execution by U.S. District Court in Orlando.
November 18, 1986: 11th U.S. Circuit Court grants request for stay in Leach case at 12:40 a.m., less than 7 hours before he is scheduled to die. 11th Circuit wants to give Bundy's attorneys time to present their arguments that he had been mentally incompetent to stand trial and act as his own attorney.

The three circuit judges, Robert Vance, John Godbold and Frank Johnson, confer by telephone and decide there isn't time to decide. The issues are too complex, they've never seen the case before, there would hardly be time to turn the pages of the relevant documents—without even reading them—before the current would flow through Ted. At 12:40 a.m., the judges issue this order, sent to court headquarters in Atlanta: "The limited period of time remaining until the scheduled execution is insufficient to allow this Court to fully consider petitioner's claim. For that reason, a stay of execution is mandated." An indefinite stay is ordered. Tuesday, about 1:00 a.m.: A clerk at the 11th Circuit, Angela Bickers, calls the Florida State Prison in Starke, and tells officials the execution has been stayed. Bickers also calls the U.S. Supreme Court, " ... so those folks can go to sleep. The public seems to think that if a guy is convicted, and he's pretty scummy, and his crimes are the sort you can't even talk about at dinner, well, then a judge should do the right thing and cook the guy. However, when judges consider death penalty appeals, they hardly think about the man to be executed at all. They think about him no more than they think about his crimes. They think about the law" (*The Sentinel,* October 11, 1987).
November 24, 1986: Ted implicitly confesses to the murder of Kim Leach to Nelson.

- 1987 -

January 15, 1987: 11th U.S. Circuit Court sends Chi Omega case back to U.S. District Court for hearing on whether Bundy was competent to stand trial in 1979. The court says that the district judge erred by not requiring the state to respond to the defendant's petitions and by not having the case's 10,000-page state record before him.
February 5, 1987: Ted has first panic attack.
February 10, 1987: Writes letter to unknown recipient: "There is a reason why I am still alive. God is not finished with me yet."

Psychiatrist Dorothy Otnow Lewis (circa 1987). Photo public domain.

April 4, 1987: Nelson meets Dorothy Lewis for the first time in Washington. Lewis feels that Ted's crimes were most likely "committed during depressive phases, which he had attempted to end through the stimulus of stalking and capturing victims" (Nelson 1994, 152).
April 12, 1987: U.S. Circuit Court of Appeals orders hearing on Bundy's competence to stand trial.
April 14, 1987: Ted-Hinckley letters leaked. Dekle heard an unverifiable rumor that Ted was gang-raped by other prisoners sometime before the first Hinckley correspondence (February 24, 1986) (Dekle 2011, 216). Ted denied it. Around this time, Ted also talked to Bill Hagmaier from the FBI. Bill had given Ted a questionnaire on serial killers the FBI was developing. Ted honed in on one specific area: he thought the authors of the questionnaire had only touched in passing on whether an offender returns to the place where the body is left, not fully examined the offender's post murder behavior at the body location. He went as far as significantly expanding that section in his own hand-writing:
April 18, 1987: Ted says to Ronald Holmes: "A large number of serial killings [are] an attempt to silence the

This section should be expanded to include data from offender about place where body was found. Among areas to be explored include:

1. Reason for selecting site where body disposed (check all which apply)
   a. to conceal crime
   b. to facilitate post mortem activities with body (i.e. sexual molestation)
   c. to display victim's body
   d. to facilitate discovery of body
   e. impulse
   f. convenience
   g. no reason
   h. other ______________
2. Picked site prior to time made contact with victim
   □ yes □ no
3. Return to site after body placed there
   □ yes □ no
4. Number of times
   □ 1 □ 2 □ 3 □ 4 □ 5 □ 6
   □ more than six ______ (no.)
5. Time lapse between visits to site (days)
   Between original disposal of body and
   first visit ______
   first and second visit ______
   second and third ______
6. Time of day usually returned to site
   □ early morning □ midnight to 4:00
   □ midday □ 4:00–8:00
   □ evening (after dark) □ 8:00–4:00
   □ late night □ 4:00–12:00
   □ variable □ time varied
7. Manner in which offender returned to site
   □ drove by site only without stopping
   □ approach site on foot but kept distance from body
   □ approach site on foot and came right up to body
8. Reason(s) for returning to site (check all that apply)
   □ To check for and retrieve evidence
   □ to retrieve personal belongings of victim
   □ to observe body
   □ to mutilate body
   □ to further conceal (bury, decapitate, etc.) body
   □ to engage in sexual activity with body
   □ other (photograph, general curiosity, etc.) ______
9. When you were returning to site, did you ever think that the police might be watching the site?
   □ yes □ no

The first two pages of the FBI questionnaire. Photo source *Defending the Devil*, pp. 168-9.

victims, an extreme but simple form of elimination" (H&H 2008, 23).

May 23, 1987: Kenneth James Parks (23) got up from his bed, still asleep, drove roughly 23 km to his in-laws' home, broke in, assaulted his father-in-law, Dennis Woods, and stabbed his mother-in-law to death. After careful investigation, specialists discovered he suffered a sleep disorder, and he was eventually acquitted in 1992.

June 1987: More panic attacks. Talks to Lewis on phone about it. Sometime around this period Nelson learns that Dr. Art Norman "was out in Tacoma and had burst in on Ted's mother […]. Apparently he had attempted to interview her, but ended up browbeating her, telling her she must have been a bad mother not to have seen the signs in Ted as he was growing up" (Nelson 1994, 172).

June 6, 1987: Tried to mail letter to Hinckley's family. Privileges revoked.

July 7, 1987: Article suggests Ted will be around for years (*Seattle Post-Intelligencer*).

July 26, 1987: Ted writes letter "to a woman who knew Bundy in Seattle, WA before the rest of the world had heard of him." Talks about the possibility of Carole and Rosa moving back to Florida.

August 2, 1987: Judge Edward Douglas Cowart (62) dies after suffering a heart attack the day before.

October 22, 1987: Ted competency hearing starts. 4:30 a.m. Ted was taken out of his cell for a short period of time to the District Court in Orlando as part of the process. He was not allowed to shower or shave (Nelson 1994, 177). "The slim, pale Bundy, now 40, was dressed casually and looked as if he had been interrupted en-route to the local country club, instead of being outside Florida State Prison for the first time in seven years" (*Boca Raton News*, October 23, 1987; no doubt deliberate irony). "Ted was in the courtroom in Orlando, listening to Mike Minerva testifying that Ted wasn't competent at his Chi Omega and Kim Leach trials. He wore a blue and white striped sports shirt and white pants. His wavy hair was close-cropped, but the short cut didn't hide the gray hair that wasn't there seven years earlier" (Rule 2006, 465).

October 28, 1987: Kathleen Parker of *The Sentinel* saw Ted sitting in court. She wanted to find out if "I would have gotten in the car with him." She reported that: "As I watched him in the courtroom I thought, he's not so good-looking. But then, we've all aged. He's 40 now. And pale the way people are who have been institutionalized for a long time. Last week was the first time he'd left death row in seven years and it showed. He was gaunt, hollow-eyed, sallow. He also had a two-day beard. Still, it was easy to imagine the man's physical appeal, especially if he were tanned, smiling and confident."

October 30, 1987: Dr. Charles Mutter and Dr. Umesh Mhatre testify Ted competence to court.

November 1987: Nelson persuades Louise Bundy to see Lewis in New Haven (Connecticut). The law firm paid for her trip. Lewis and Nelson confronted Louise with Ted's crimes. Louise insisted he was innocent.

November 6, 1987: Florida rapist Tommie Lee Andrews is first person in the United States to be convicted on DNA evidence for raping a woman during a burglary. Sentenced to 22 years.

December 2, 1987: James J. Aime, father of Laura Aime dies circa this date. Mr. Aime was hospitalized for depression after Laura's murder. On one occasion, while

Mr. Aime and Jim Massie, a Kentucky parole officer, were driving through Timpanogos Cave area, Mr. Aime said: "My little baby was up there by herself, and there was nothing I could do to help her" (H&H 2008, 265).

December 12, 1987: Nelson takes Dr. Emanuel Tanay's deposition. According to Nelson, Tanay "obviously thought that Ted was a despicable psychopath" (Nelson 1994, 201).

December 17, 1987: U.S. Circuit Court of Appeals Federal District Judge G. Kendall Sharp rejects Bundy's appeal that he was incompetent to stand trial.

- 1988 -

February 11, 1988: Ted writes to Keppel again, inviting him back to Florida for another conversation.

February 22, 1988: Keppel visits Ted in Florida prison again.

March 30, 1988: Eleanor Rose buries a dress, a rose, and other remembrances of Denise Naslund in a casket as a symbolic gesture.

July 7, 1988: 11th U.S. Circuit Court denies request for new trial in Leach case.

July 26, 1988: Ted asks the same court for a rehearing in the case.

- 1989 -

January 16, 1989 (Monday): Second death warrant in Leach case drawn up (Ted's fourth and final warrant).

January 17, 1989 (Tuesday): U.S. Supreme Court denies appeal in Leach case; Governor Bob Martinez signs Leach case death warrant. Ted moved to Q-wing cell to start his deathwatch. Notifies authorities that he is willing to talk. Additionally notifies authorities that he will only give a solo press conference to James Dobson; he will forgo his right to answer questions from a pool of journalists.

Governor Martinez, January 18, 1989. Who mentioned 3 years? "That was Mr Tanner." Do you have any sympathy for those family members, survivors of victims, who may have questions in their own minds, and outside by other states, who would like to have this resolved, that he would come forward and make a confession? "For him to be negotiating for his life over the bodies of victims is despicable." Photo public domain.

January 18, 1989 (Wednesday): Jim Coleman advises Ted against confessing. Governor Bob Martinez holds a press conference confirming that Ted's execution will go ahead as scheduled. Ted changes his mind; he will give a pooled press conference on Monday, the day before his execution.

January 19, 1989 (Thursday): Weiner calls Keppel in Seattle 3:00 a.m. Washington State time. Florida Circuit Court denies stay and appeal in Leach case. Jamey Boone (Ted's stepson through Carole Boone) visits Ted and learns that his stepfather is a murderer. Begs Ted not to publicly confess. "Carole has already been hurt enough" (M&A 1983, 318).

January 20, 1989 (Friday): Florida Supreme Court denies appeal in Leach case. Keppel scheduled by Hagmaier to see Ted from 11:00 a.m. - 2:30 p.m. Keppel loses 30 minutes getting a briefing from Weiner and Tanner. Another "visitor" intervenes, Keppel doesn't get to see Ted until just before noon. Ted starts confessions. He says he can articulate what is going on inside him a lot better than most; the why is important to him, not just the where and how, which is all Keppel is interested in. He wants 60, 90 days, a few months reprieve so he can play his last fiddle. Tears flow. He's saying a couple of months are not going to make a difference. Keppel claims Ted completely misjudged the will of the state to execute him. In any case, the timing was wrong; all the body locations were buried under snow.

The Spokesman-Review - Jan 24, 1989

"I don't understand what makes him tick at all," Keppel said.

January 21, 1989 (Saturday): U.S. District Court judge denies appeal in Leach case; 11th U.S. Circuit Court of Appeals refuses to hear appeal in Leach case. First radio broadcasts of Ted's confessions. Ted admits to Mike Fisher that he murdered Julie Cunningham, but will not discuss the Caryn Campbell or Denise Oliverson murders (M&A 1983, 320). Carole Boone leaves devastated upon hearing confessions.

January 22, 1989 (Sunday): 7:30 p.m. – 9:30 p.m. Utah confessions to Dennis Couch. Gives him tidbits of Kent and Wilcox. When Couch shows him pictures of Smith and Aime, Ted feigns memory loss. Denies abducting Nancy Baird when Couch shows a photo of her [Utah confession tapes]. Ted meets with Russell Reneau and Randy Everitt. Confesses to two Idaho victims: the Boise hitchhiker and Lynnette Culver. (Later that night) Ted has one last meeting with Hagmaier. They go over the victim numbers state-by-state. 7 States; 30 in all.

Hagmaier said he first started meeting with Ted in 1986. He had asked Ted for assistance with his research on serial murders for the National Center for the Analysis of Violent Crime. "I think he agreed to talk to me out of curiosity. When he realized that I wasn't writing a book or trying to influence him in any way, he started to trust me" (*The Free Lance-Star*, February 28, 1989). Ted

Bill Hagmaier and Ted Bundy (around January 23, 1989). Photo public domain.

told Hagmaier just before his execution that the correct number of victims was 30. When asked about that, Hagmaier said, "I think it would be fair to say I believe him, but I would be open to the possibility that he did more" (*The Spokesman-Review*, February 28, 1989). Hagmaier schedules Ted's confessions to law officials over the final days of his life. Hagmaier said his attitude to Ted was somewhat different from that of the others. "Law enforcement people are human" he said. "Some had to work these cases for 14 years and would be very suspicious of anything he had to say." But Hagmaier said his relationship with Ted was built on trust and respect. "He trusted me and respected what we were trying to do," said Hagmaier. Ted was different from most other serial killers because "he would select a place to deposit the body beforehand" (*The Tuscaloosa News*, May 17, 1989). Most killers choose the victim then select the site. He selected the site previously because it was part of his long range planning. He perceived it as an intellectual approach. "He said going about killing someone is like going about any other task in life: you prepare yourself for it, you plan, you consider the consequences, the dangerousness of it and the thrill of it. All of it was part of a conscious decision he made in killing another (human being)." Hagmaier said most of the 30 murders Ted confessed to were planned, while five or six were committed impulsively. As Ted related it to Hagmaier, the serial killer sought "worthy prey" – young, attractive women from good homes. Ted knew some of the victims came from good homes and probably were reared in an environment where they were raised to be Good Samaritans and help others. Ted said those children "became my victims." Ted told Hagmaier he started killing in May 1973, killed about 30 victims, buried about 10 of those, severed about half a dozen heads, stresses that he is not really a mutilator, that if he did lash out at a victim after killing them it would be because it was accompanied by a high degree of intoxication and a lot of anger and frustration that had built up in the weeks preceding the murder and it was more out of an attempt to conceal the body than anything else, and finishes up by describing biting as a unique form of aggression.

On the night before his execution, Bundy talked of suicide. "He did not want to give the state the satisfaction of watching him die. We had some discussions about morality and the taking of another life and his concerns about trying to explain to God about his actions." After helping Bundy draft a will and letters to his mother, wife and daughter, Hagmaier said there was one more thing the killer wanted. He wanted to rehearse his execution. "I talked him through it, the mechanics of it." "I'm afraid to die," Bundy told Hagmaier (*The Seattle Times*, January 24 1999).

January 23, 1989 (Monday): Salvador Dali dies aged 84. 9:00 a.m. - 1:00 p.m. Nelson and Lewis talk to Ted for the last time. Ted describes how he became a serial killer. 1:00 p.m. - 2:00 p.m. Fisher, Lindvall (and Mike Sexton, Colorado attorney general's office) see Ted but get very little. 2:30 p.m. - 3:00 p.m. Public interview with James Dobson. 3:00 p.m. Andrea Hillyer, Governor Martinez' special liaison assistant with the state department of corrections whom Weiner approached about postponing the execution arrives. Ted demands one last contact visit from Weiner. Hillyer tells Ted she cannot do anything for him; she is under strict orders from the governor not to interfere (M&A 1983, 322). Ted writes his will with Hagmaier's help. 8:00 p.m. Signs release form James Dobson gave him. 8:00 p.m. - 10:00 p.m. Legal visit with attorneys. 10:00 - midnight. Visit from James Boone and a Methodist minister from Gainesville (Fred Lawrence). John & Marsha Tanner visit starts. (Near midnight) Ted connected by phone to Coleman and Nelson, learns of Supreme court turn-downs. Is visibly shaken. Cancels pooled interview.

January 24, 1989 (Tuesday): Midnight - 1:00 a.m. Final contact visit with John Tanner and James Boone. "When

Dobson: "… do you remember where you decided to throw caution to the wind?" (20:44). Ted: "It's a very difficult thing to describe ..." Photo permission limited to only showing Ted. Photo courtesy Focus on the Family © January 23, 1989.

his last evening came, Ted was composed, calm and repentant," Tanner said, who along with his wife visited from Monday 10 p.m. till Tuesday 1:20 a.m.; they prayed and talked about forgiveness, God's grace, Christ's resurrection and death. They had communion together. "We broke bread and we took it," Tanner said. "A soft drink took the place of wine." 2:00 a.m. Places two phone calls to his mother. 4:47 a.m. Ted is given his last meal; drinks a glass of water, refuses the rest. 5:00 a.m. Witnesses arrive. Hagmaier is not allowed into the execution chamber. Just before 6:00 a.m. Ted is prepared, showered, and conducting gel is applied to his head. Prison superintendent Tom Barton carries a tape recorder. Final confessions: Oliverson and Curtis. 6:57 a.m. Ted is led from his cell. 7:04 a.m. Strapped into the chair. Last words: "Jim [Coleman] and Fred [Lawrence], I'd like you to give my love to my family and friends." 7:06 a.m. Electricity switched on. 7:10 a.m. No pulse. 7:16 a.m. Pronounced dead (Robert Macmaster, FSP January 24, 1989, post-execution pre-written statement to media). 7:35 a.m. Body transported by Doyle Archer Funeral Home of Lake Butler, Florida, where an autopsy was performed. When state representative Randy Mackey was asked: Did he go in under his own power, or was he carried in or what? The reply was:

Sketch by Christine Elizabeth Lyttle. Photo public domain.

> He needed assistance ... but he regained that composure once he was placed in the chair ... his coloration was not good when he was first brought to the room, but once he sat down, all his color came back and everything else ... he even recognized people across the glass from him, he knew who they were, people who worked on the case all this time ... he spoke to them, he acknowledged their presence and said hello ... I see you, I know who you are ... we're all getting this behind us ... let's get it on, let's do it, let's get it over.

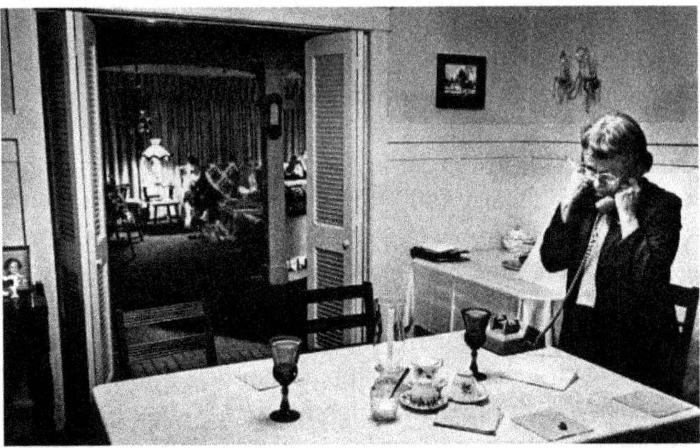

Five hours before his execution, Bundy was allowed to make two brief phone calls to his mother. He told her of his regrets, that he was really two people: "I'm so sorry I've given you all such grief ... but a part of me was hidden all the time ... but the Ted Bundy you knew also existed" (*The Spokesman-Review*, January 25, 1989). 2:12 a.m. Louise told her boy: "You'll always be my precious son" (*The Telegraph*, January 24, 1989). Photo by Russ Carmack, *The News Tribune*.

James C. Dobson (January 23, 1989) shortly after he obtained Ted's signature on the release form for the interview. "Did I believe Ted Bundy in his expression of remorse? Yes, I did believe him. I think it's genuine." Photo public domain.

Rule wrote: "Reportedly calmed by massive tranquilizers" (2006, 492). Von Drehle's notes contradict this. While the guards were cleaning Ted's cell after his execution, an old photo fell out of one of Ted's Law books. The photo had been carefully folded and discreetly tucked between the bindings of the book. The photo was of a rather plain looking woman. She had cherry blossoms intertwined in her long, long, light brown hair and wore a Mexican Blouse. Her childlike smile had lit up her large brown eyes as she held up a baby rabbit for the camera. The photo was dated 1969. On the back, in Ted's handwriting it was written "You will always be the love of my life. I thank God for your love ..." The ink was still fresh, indicating Ted had written this a few hours before his execution. The guard asked the Superintendent if he recognized the woman in the photo. "Oh yeah, simple," replied the Superintendent. "That's Bundy's old lover ... Elizabeth Kloepfer ... I think was her full name." He shrugged "He always just called her Liz" [ref].

Ted's body was subsequently transported to Williams-Thomas wake home in Gainesville where he was cremated.

1:00 p.m. (10:00 a.m. Seattle time) Louise Bundy via telephone link talks to Vivian Rancourt who appears via satellite link on *Northwest Afternoon*, a Seattle daily afternoon television talk show hosted by Dana Middleton Silberstein. "We don't know why this happened. We feel so desperately sorry for you. We didn't want our son to do these things. We have two beautiful daughters of our own, and we know how we would feel. I am sorry," Louise said (Silberstein 2015).

Some of the victims and victims' family members:

> Kathy Kleiner: "I used to hate his guts, and I used to be scared of him. I really now feel sorry for him.

His life isn't easier now; I want it to be over" (*Sarasota Herald-Tribune*, January 24, 1989).

Dale Rancourt, father of Susan Rancourt: "I suspect it will trouble us the rest of our lives." Vivian Rancourt, mother of Susan Rancourt: "It's a bag of mixed emotions when we find relief in a man's death. We all feel justice has been done. All of his escapades – it was like a sharp knife twisting at us. It was being done to all of us – all his victims. If anything good comes of this, we won't allow this to happen again" (*The Spokesman-Review*, January 25, 1989).

Edie Hawkins, mother of Georgeann Hawkins: "I haven't thought about forgiving him. How could you forgive somebody who hurts your child? I'm not that gracious an individual" (*Green Valley News*, June 11, 2014).

Donald E. Blackburn, father of Janice Ott: "It's too soon to really digest this" (Moscow-Pullman Daily News, January 24, 1989). "I view him pretty much as a cancer that (has) to be removed" (*The Telegraph*, January 24, 1989). "Would you like to hear the story of what happened to your daughter?" (*New York Times*, February 13, 1989).

Eleanore Rose, mother of Denise Naslund: "I feel kind of numb in a way. My daughter's murderer was taken care of. He paid for what he did. It seems like I was sentenced to a lifetime of waiting. Now there's really nothing to wait for" (*The Spokesman-Review*, January 25, 1989).

Connie Wilcox, mother of Nancy Wilcox: "I was shocked when he confessed. I just wasn't ready to hear it. Nancy was such a sensitive person, so kind. If she were alive today, she'd probably feel pity for Bundy for being such a sick person" (*People*, February 6, 1989)

Louis Smith, father of Melissa Smith: "Melissa's murder ruined [our] lives and that of [our] younger daughter, Jolene. Joan [Melissa's mother] keeps emotions to herself. She became deaf in one ear." [Louis] seemed to age overnight and his dark hair turned gray (*Deseret News*, June 7, 1978).

Dean Kent, father of Debbi Kent: "I had anticipated a much different feeling than I had. I'd felt some of the bitterness would be relieved, but that isn't the case. I think I'll carry it to my grave" (*Boca Raton News*, December 24, 1989).

Robert Campbell, father of Caryn Campbell: "You never really forgive someone for something like that. You just try to put it behind you. It's not important to me now. The thing I'd like to have back, I can't have." (*The Harvard Crimson*, January 25, 1989).

Edward Culver, father of Lynnette Culver: "He may have deprived the world of something exceptional. Every single person in this country may have lost something when that kid was killed. I suppose you can say that there is a 99 percent chance that it's over. But I'm hesitant to write it off, period. There's always that 1 percent chance" (*People*, February 6, 1989).

Robert Nicholson, father of Denise Oliverson: "We're just happy he's been executed because it should have happened a long time ago" (*The Spokesman-Review*, January 25, 1989).

Roberta Robertson, mother of Shelley K. Robertson: "Killing Ted Bundy won't make me feel better ... and it won't bring back Shelley. [...] A lot of people seem to want it out of vengeance. But it gives people a false sense of security, and it's terribly expensive" (*The Telegraph*, January 24, 1989).

Since their daughter's funeral, Tom and Freda Leach have refused to discuss the Bundy case publicly. They mostly keep to themselves. Leach runs a wrecking service. His wife long ago sold her beauty salon business and cuts hair a few times a week at a friend's shop. Leach has lost weight from working so hard, Elwood Tyre, 58, a close friend of Tom Leach said. "One thing to be said for Tom Leach is he did not do what a lot of men in his situation have done – become an alcoholic," Tyre said. "This made him a workaholic. He works day and night. We had to tell him to 'slow down, boy'" (*Orlando Sentinel*, January 22, 1989).

Richard Dugger, Secretary of the Florida Department of Corrections during the Bundy execution. He also knew Bundy personally because he had previously been the Warden (then called Superintendent) at Florida State Prison, where Bundy was housed: "Ted Bundy was a perverse, demented serial rapist and murderer. He was arrogant and clever but did not seem particularly brilliant or articulate as some reports have suggested. His murderous crime spree and avoidance of early capture was likely more attributable to his geographical mobility rather than his 'intellect' or 'charm.' During my tenure as Warden at FSP, my most vivid recollection of Bundy's case was the occasional sad and haunting phone calls and letters from the mother of a victim seeking my personal reassurance that Bundy would be executed and justice served in the murder of her only daughter (Florida Department of Corrections, 1989).

Paula Tully Bryant, Governmental Operations Consultant II: "What I remember most about that time is that our two phone lines never stopped ringing from the moment the warrant was signed by Governor Bob Martinez until after the execution. Even afterwards, when Bundy's autopsy photos surfaced in the tabloids, the ringing continued. (A reporter had told me days earlier that tabloid reporters were offering large sums of money to anyone who could get a picture of Bundy after the autopsy. It appears someone took them up on their offer. Bundy was no longer in the Department's custody when those pictures were taken.) [...] I found out from a reporter that Bundy had canceled his group press interview. (Inmates about to be executed are entitled to a one-on-one interview with the journalist of their choice and a group interview with a pool of journalists.) For the past several years, Bundy had refused all media requests, so we didn't really expect him to agree to any now. I think everyone was surprised that he decided to do a one-

> on-one interview, and with whom he chose to do it. He picked James C. Dobson, Ph.D., president of Focus on the Family, a nonprofit organization that produces a syndicated radio show. My notes from that time indicate that he is from Pomona, California and that he brought with him cameramen Steve Stiles and Charlie Barth, and soundman Tom Wheatley. (It's interesting to note that in the book mentioned at the beginning of this article*, Bundy talks about how much he loves listening to radio talk shows.) The gist of the interview is that Bundy said pornography greatly influenced his life of crime. I got the sense there was a lot of skepticism about Bundy's sincerity, and some just viewed it as Bundy manipulating 'the system' for his own purposes one last time. {...} At 7 a.m. Barton nodded to the executioner and Bundy's back arched tight against the wood chair as the hum of the transformer kicked in. Ten minutes later, we were walking out to the drive behind the prison [...]. Before noon, Barton approached me with a sealed manila envelope and asked if I could drop it by the Governor's Office when I returned to Tallahassee. I said sure, tucked it into my black briefcase and headed for home shortly after. I later learned that the envelope contained some of Bundy's last recorded words. Barton had expected Bundy to try talking his way out of this. As Bundy was being readied for his walk to the chair, he had offered to tell about more killings, more bodies, and where they could find them, if only they would give him a little more time. Barton reached into his pocket, switched on the tape recorder, and said something like: "OK, talk. You've got 15 minutes." (Florida Department of Corrections, 1989).
>
> Robert Macmaster, Management Review Specialist: "I remember the look on Bundy's face as he was escorted to the well-worn oak chair, his head shaved clean, his steps faltering, and his eyes looking more desperate than they had the day before. They seemed to be searching in vain for a way out where there was none" (Florida Department of Corrections, 1989).

January 30, 1989: Keppel initiates a meeting at the Issaquah site in an effort to find Donna Manson's remains. Some preliminary digging is done, but stopped when it is decided that the use of heavy machinery would improve progress.

February 4, 1989: Weiner attacks Bob Martinez for lying to the press about Ted's final weeks. Ted actually agreed to confess before his final death warrant was signed. Weiner had in fact organized it.

February 6, 1989: *The Weekly World News* publishes first photos of Ted post-execution.

February 15, 1989: Keppel & co. digging at Issaquah with heavy machinery commences. The area dug measured approximately 58 feet by 23 feet, and was dug to an approximate depth of 4 feet. Nothing was found and the dig was terminated.

February 28, 1989: Trash magazine *Weekly World News* releases pictures of a dead Ted post-autopsy.

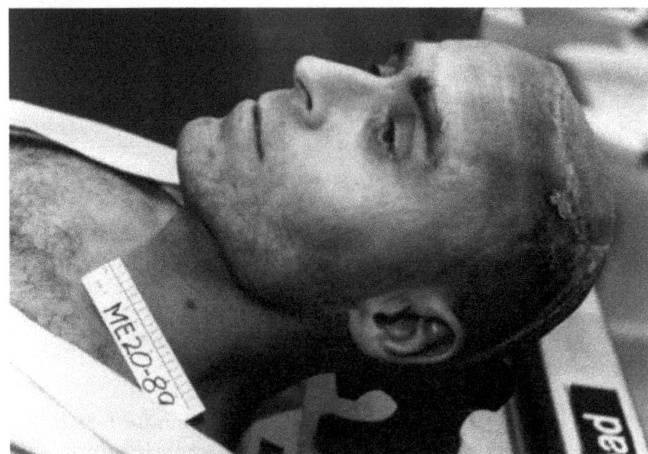

Ted lying dead on the gurney. Photo original source: *The World Weekly News*.

Early May: A single unverified human patella was found near a road leading into Fairview Canyon, Utah. It was where Ted said he buried Debbie Kent (*Deseret News*, December 27, 1989).

- 1990 -

February 14, 1990: Thomas L. Leach, father of Kim Leach dies.

- 1995 -

December 3, 1995: Gerard Schaefer was found stabbed to death in his cell at Florida State Prison. Killed by fellow inmate Vincent Rivera.

Sarasota Herald-Tribune - Feb 4, 1989

Weiner also disputed Martinez's assertion that Bundy had asked for his execution to be delayed up to three years in exchange for cooperation with investigators.

"That was a flat-out misstatement from the governor's office," she said. "What Mr. Bundy was asking was to have 30 days to make his confessions. He understood he would be executed."

Forget 'Moral Compulsion,' It's Time For Florida To Do Justice To Ted Bundy

SunSentinel

January 22, 1989 | By STEVE WELLER, Staff Columnist
COMMENTARY

In a move that should serve as a chillingly appropriate farewell con job, Bundy is asking for a two or three year reprieve so that he can come clean about all of the crimes he committed during the 1970s.

According to Nelson, Ted originally demanded 3 years in the spring of '88, but faced with the reality of his impending doom, whittled that down to 30 days as his execution date approached (as per Weiner's statement). Ted didn't want to die, there is ample evidence of that, but he knew the state was going to kill him whether he liked it or not. While it is generally accepted Ted momentarily went weak at the knees before he walked to the chair, he also gave them the look, once strapped in, to get it over with.

* Original reference is M&A 1983.

- 1998 -

March 23, 1998: Gerald Stano executed by electric chair, Florida State Prison.

- 1999 -

1999: Louise Bundy expresses shock that anyone would connect her son to the 1961 death of 8-year-old Ann Marie Burr. She told local media:

> "I resent the fact that everybody in Tacoma thinks just because he lived in Tacoma he did that one, too, way back when he was 14. I'm sure he didn't" (*The News Tribune*, January 9, 2013).

- 2000 -

- Born Feb 18. 1949. in Utah
- Moved to south King County when he was 11.
- In his mid-teens, stabs 6-year-old boy in the liver. Boy survives, but spends weeks in a hospital recovering.
- Graduated from Tyee High School in 1969, after being held back two grades.
- Joined the Navy in July 1969, honorably discharged July 1971
- First marriage in August 1970, ended in divorce, January 1972.
- Started working as a painter for Kenworth Truck Co. in August 1971.
- Second marriage in December 1973. Son born Sept. 5, 1975. Marriage ended in divorce May 1981.
- July 15, 1982, body of first known Green River victim, Wendy Lee Coffield, 16, of Puyallup, found in the river south of Seattle.
- Ridgway comes to attention of Green River task force in 1984 disappearance of Marie Malvar.
- In April 1987, detectives search Ridgway's house and take a saliva sample.
- Third marriage, June 1988.
- Arrested Nov. 30, 2001.
- Legally separated from third wife September 2002.

Judith Lorraine Lynch, third wife of Gary Ridgeway with Gary circa 1990s (married June 12, 1988; divorced September 5, 2002). Photo public domain.

2000: Eleanor Rose, mother of Denise Marie Naslund dies.

- 2001 -

April 19, 2001: Richard W. Larsen, author of *The Deliberate Stranger*, dies aged 73.

November 30, 2001: Gary Ridgeway, the Green River serial murderer and necrophile, is finally apprehended.

- 2005 -

August 20, 2005: Carole Ann Boone dies in Texas according to United States Social Security Death Index. The index has her age as 58 (DOB: 30 July, 1947). Note: a 60 Minutes report found that Social Security wrongly labels at least nine thousand living Americans as deceased every year, while millions of long-dead Americans are mistakenly listed as still alive, leading to IRS fraud and other problems (Diamond 2015).

September 19, 2005: Detective Raphael Crenshaw (a veteran of the Green River killer investigation) writes letter to University of North Texas asking for tests to be done on some "recently" located remains related to Ted's Taylor Mountain victims. The remains are of at least two victims, unidentified [ref].

- 2006 -

March 28, 2006: Jerry Brudos dies in Oregon State Penitentiary infirmary from liver cancer.

- 2007 -

March 4, 2007: John "Jack" R. Cowell dies of a heart attack. Dr. Cowell was born to a musical household in Springhouse, Pennsylvania in 1920, youngest of seven siblings. He left behind his wife of 63 years, Eleanor G. Cowell, daughter, Edna Martin and son-in-law, Don Martin of Seattle, son, John DeCoville of Tucson, Arizona, granddaughter, Anna Martin Siadek and grandson-in-law, Steve Siadek, and sister, Virginia Bristol of Kennett Square, Pennsylvania.

May 17, 2007: Johnnie Culpepper Bundy dies in Tacoma, Pierce County, Washington, according to official records.

- 2008 -

May 28, 2008: Proxy rites for Bundy, consisting of a baptism and an "endowment" ceremony, were performed in the Jordan River Utah Temple, a Mormon temple in South Jordan, a suburb 16 miles south of downtown SLC.

- 2011 -

June 3, 2011: First report of the discovery of Kerry May Hardy's body buried in a shallow grave at Suncadia Resort, Washington State.

- 2012 -

December 2012: Louise Bundy dies aged 88 after a long illness.

- 2015 -

July 26, 2015: Ann Rule dies aged 83.

NOTES

Michaud & Aynesworth open the penultimate chapter of *The Only Living Witness* with: "Ted in 1980 felt a contentment not unlike that of a retired suburban squire" (M&A 1983, 293).

In the spring of 1979, Millard Farmer had worked diligently behind the scenes (with his assistant Joe Nursey) to steer Ted towards a guilty plea. He had to persuade Louise Bundy and Carole Boone who both staunchly believed in his innocence ... Millard flew to Seattle where both were, and somehow convinced them. The three then flew to Tallahassee where they in turn worked on Ted. Ted appeared to comply, but then on May 31, 1979, he rejected the guilty plea. Millard said: "I've only got so much time, I'm going to spend it on people who want to live" (Von Drehle 2006, 318).

This is against the backdrop of Ted's veiled confessions at the Pensacola police station in February 1978.

But then in 1981 Carole Boone gives birth to a daughter. Dead man walking becomes father. In 1984 Ted offers help in solving the Green River killer case. In 1986, a 4-hour TV mini-series is aired about his life: *The Deliberate Stranger*. Carole departs and the platonic Diana Weiner steps in.

What happens next unfurls like a slow motion car accident. Maybe it was the three death warrants signed against him by Governor Bob Graham in 1986. Maybe it was him getting off cannabis. Maybe it was the religious influence. It seemed like he had talked about his murders for nearly a decade without ever admitting to them, but he finally starts openly confessing. He had an upcoming competency hearing that was being prepared by Nelson. At the time, Ted would have agreed with Vic Africano, his Leach trial attorney: "He was no trouble to me at all. He was perfectly competent in every way. More than competent, even" (Nelson 1994, 125). Nelson took Ted on in April 1986. More than half a year would go by before Ted would implicitly give her his first admission of guilt – on this occasion, the Kim Leach murder (November 24, 1986). It comes as a shock to Nelson. From this point on it is just a little over two years until his execution. Von Drehle rightly pointed out that Ted was actually on a fast track to the chair (Von Drehle 2006, 320).

After Ted's first arrest, all he gave out was blanket denials. After his second arrest, he started squeezing through the cracks. There was a marked shift between these two points. We would like to think that even Ted realized he should be kept off the streets – this is in stark contrast to him quipping in a May 1977 interview that he would love to be out on the streets, where he can put to practice all the new things he had learned (in prison). Well, then came Florida, where he metaphorically bit off more than he could chew. If he was a retired suburban squire, he also had a bad case of serial killer indigestion.

Von Drehle concluded that Ted, like all mass murderers and serial killers, suffer from a monstrous case of narcissism (*Time*, April 26, 2007). Technically, Von Drehle is right. More specifically, mental illness, because of its insular and circular nature, turns people into insightless narcissists. Put simply, inner speech has *that* much power over what people experience. Many of the human reactions to social situations and events occur beneath the level of conscious awareness. These unconscious responses *bias* inner speech towards perceiving the world in one way or another. If there is a negative bias in unconscious responses, and if the mechanism that interprets inner speech (the PFC) is faulty—fails to gate certain responses—then the individual may experience deviant thinking patterns, including thought insertion, and this experience, because of its overwhelming nature, draws all attentional resources to itself, resulting in a cognitive behavioral style that is predominantly self-centered. The individual now increasingly references themselves rather than objective external markers. They begin to superimpose their reality *onto* reality more so than the average well-adjusted person.

This doesn't rule out snatches of cognitive dissonance. A murderer cannot help but bump into reminders of their behavior. It is the way memory works. A murderer doesn't go around hermetically sealed from the past. The justification process draws a lot of ego energy. It takes away from ongoing acts of kindness, pro-social behavior. Each good act now takes on the quality of a small miracle. But gradually the bank runs out of money. At this juncture there are two paths. One is seek out sexually and violently explicit images, to raise the level of arousal, which partially replenishes the ego so it can keep bank-rolling those little miracles, or let it go, and regress, and unleash socially dominating behavior, make someone feel small so the deviant can feel more powerful. The frustration at this point is explosive.

The fact is, normal individuals show in miniature (both ethically and objectively) what happens when their ego is depleted. If you subject a normal individual to a period of forced abstinence of the thing they crave, when they are let free they immediately go on a binge of that substance or behavior. Sugar (salt and fat) is an interesting case. Most people deprived of it soon crave it and seek it out. When they do get it, as they imbibe it they slip into a mild trance. Afterwards, when they are sated, they appear calm again. The agitation is gone. However, if they are put back in a situation where they are deprived, the pattern repeats. If we extrapolate this to killing, we can see that it is much more complex, encompassing, and ultimately destructive. But the basic pattern is the same.

We note that after a murder, the individual is less agitated for a period of time. But slowly, as the pressure builds up, as more time and distance between them and the murder elapses, they begin to seek out triggers again. It starts with little things, the looking for stimuli in the environment that excites the urge. The phase before this happens is quite complex. There is a possibility of recrimination. Not for what they did, but how they did it. Was all the evidence removed? The cleaning routines are all important here. Once the murder has been "cleaned" away, the individual feels calm again for a while. But then daily chores and responsibilities, all those little miracles which have to be sustained, drag the mood down again. Getting drunk momentarily eases the low. Cannabis and masturbation to pornography also works for a period of time. But after a while neither of these is enough. Stealing offers a solution. The behavior turned inward is now turned outward. The increased risk brings with it increased excitement. But it also threatens to destabilize the whole process. Get caught for stealing and the game is up before it even starts. The mind turns to new strategies. How about indulge in some licentious behavior? That's the ticket. Uh-oh. Embarrassment. Better get away. Be alone. Keep a lid on that boiling pot. All the while knowing there is only one thing that can bring on that high. The one thing that guarantees a result ...

And so ... the planning begins in earnest. The boredom that was once there begins to fade. It is replaced by an itchy feeling of anticipation. Acts of kindness are possible but better if they could be dispensed with altogether. They take away energy from the goal. The solution is to retreat from society, get more deeply into the planning, work out the exact steps that will make it better, more exciting, more powerfully overwhelming *this time*. The alternative is to fall into a screaming heap.

Narcissism is obviously part of the picture, but there is clearly much more. Having slowly strangled the life out of his victims, Ted knew that when his time came, it would be over in a flash. He had absolutely nothing to worry about. So why did he confess in the end? Why did he open up, if only a crack? There is an assumption it was due to the company he kept in the last years of his life. Tanner. Weiner. The groundwork laid by Keppel. The discussions with Hagmaier. Maybe Ted was able to partially rewire some of his brain. He claimed prison offered absolutely nothing in terms of rehabilitation. What he proved is that rehabilitation depends on the individual's desire to change. Ideally, in a punitive world, we would want the individual to suffer for this growth. We do not want it to come easily. Yet no amount of punishment could ever repair the suffering he caused. He is just one man against 30+. The counter argument to this might be the 2008 French-Canadian film *Martyrs*. But in the real world ...

We could dispute the neural rewiring hypothesis. The fact is that suppressing anti-social instant gratification in exchange for prosocial delayed gratification requires improving the performance of the PFC. How would this happen given Ted's PFC deficit? It suggests that in the end, whatever behavior he displayed, was situationally driven; it did not come from a deep intrinsic change. Which means the Dobson interview was a charade. The proof is that after his confessions, nothing substantial was ever found. Perhaps this is a function of not looking hard enough, but more than likely it was a combination of insufficient map detail and not enough information. Had Ted been kept alive he could have been brought to the sites where he claimed he buried his victims.

We lost not only that opportunity, but also his brain. Weiner made the monumental error of convincing Ted not to donate it to science. Lewis tried to convince him otherwise, but it never came about. So we have to assume he was listening to Weiner, not Lewis. There are CT scans (apparently), but this author enquired without luck. A technique was developed in the late 90s that enables researchers to estimate a schizophrenic diagnosis from CT scans (Smith et al 1997), and if Ted's scans are ever found, it might constitute a step forward. The same applies to his DNA, if the legal issues surrounding it can be resolved (Asplen 2011).

What this amounts to is that the last chapter on the Theodore Robert Bundy story is still waiting to be written.

References

Asplen, C. (2011). Ted Bundy vs. Arrestee DNA Databasing. Retrieved March 26, 2016, Web Address http://www.forensicmag.com/articles/2011/10/ted-bundy-vs-arrestee-dna-databasing.

Diamond, D. (2015). 'When Your Government Thinks You're Dead.' Forbes. March 15, 2015. (Accessed 18 Dec 2016) http://www.forbes.com/sites/dandiamond/2015/03/15/60-minutes-reveals-nightmare-of-social-security-death-list/#221a2ff8605f

Dobson, J. (1989). Fatal Addiction. http://www.focusonthefamily.com/media/social-issues/fatal-addiction-ted-bundys-final-interview

Von Drehle, D. (2006). *Among the Lowest of the Dead: The Culture of Capital Punishment.* East Lansing, MI.: University of Michigan Press.

Florida Department of Corrections (1989). http://www.dc.state.fl.us/oth/timeline/1988-1990a.html (accessed February 15, 2016).

Holmes, S. T. & Holmes, R. M. (2008). *Sex Crimes: Patterns and Behavior: Patterns and Behavior* (3rd ed.). Thousand Oaks, CA: SAGE Publications.

Kutchinsky, B. (1991). Pornography and rape: Theory and practice?: Evidence from crime data in four countries where pornography is easily available. International Journal of Law and Psychiatry, 14(1), pp. 47-64.

Lynn, A. (2013) 'Ted Bundy's mother, Tacoma resident Louise Bundy, has died.' *The News Tribune* (January 9).

Mello, M. (1991). On metaphors, mirrors, and murders: Theodore Bundy and the rule of law. *Review of Law and Social Change,* XVIII(3), pp. 887-938.

Silberstein, D. Mrs. Bundy. *The Morning News,* September 3, 2015. http://www.themorningnews.org/article/mrs.-bundy.

Smith, G., Flynn, S., Kopala, L., Bassett, A., Lapointe, J., et al. (1997). A comprehensive method of assessing routine CT scans in schizophrenia. *Acta Psychiatrica Scandinavica,* 96(5), pp. 395-401.

Ted Bundy interview – Utah confession full, remastered. https://www.youtube.com/watch?v=zMTEzcTUmz8 (Accessed Jan 24, 2016).

Yates, J. (2014) 'Former correctional officer tells how Ted Bundy impregnated Carole Boone,' *Examiner.com,* http://www.examiner.com/article/former-correctional-officer-tells-how-ted-bundy-impregnated-carole-boone (accessed July 6, 2015).

1·21·89 -1-
notes

5. Eat.
Keep strong
take Bible
pray
meditate

Must get it together today!!!

6. Families

1·22-89 -1-
notes

1. Will

2. Meet w/ Bill, John, Diana
(see p. 2)

3. Draft letter for investigators to sign

4. Do Utah today
need maps of Cedar City to Green River
need ~~Colorado~~ Utah representative
contact Kent family
Bill and John should ~~do~~ do it.

5. Fischer and Keppel
What have they done
What are they doing

Extract of Ted's to-do-list written three and two days prior to his execution respectively. Items 5 & 6 of January 21st highlight the sense of urgency Ted felt. Item 1 of January 22nd refers to his Will; item 4, obtaining maps covering Ceder City to Green River, and contacting the Kent family. Scan courtesy DDA.

Epilogue

Bundy: `Well, you gentleman knew that you're getting involved with a pretty strange creature ...`

Leon County Jail, February 20, 1978. 12:47 a.m. FSA.

"... even after twenty or thirty [...] it's the same thing, because you're the *last* one there" (M&A 1983, 317).

Now that our story has come to an end, what can we say? Do we know Ted any better? Maybe. We've debunked some myths. But we haven't yet synthesized all the data. The goal of this chapter is to do just that.

Introduction: Ted's evolution

Readers who suspect Ted of earlier murders will be disappointed by this trajectory. However, it is time to put unsubstantiated claims aside. One of the more serious problems for proponents of Ted-the-teenage-murderer is aligning that behavior with his adult trajectory. The reality is, a person does not wake up one day and suddenly kill, not unless something extraordinary happens to them that pushes them to do so, and in Ted's case, the evidence for this is simply lacking. The path to murder is typically sign-posted with clear evolutionary steps. Moreover, once the killing starts, it is extremely rare for it to stop. Some killers have indeed cooled off for lengthy periods between murders, but these periods are *not* without behaviors that are allied to killing in some way, such as continued fantasy activity and lesser crimes such as theft and rape.

The model we propose is that Ted progressed along each part of the trajectory in small steps, each one building on the next. So for example, he first tried rape before he tried abduction. Abduction itself has several steps, where the first attempts were non-instrumental, which rapidly progressed to becoming instrumental (i.e., use of a weapon to render the victim compliant, e.g., knife, crowbar, wooden club etc.). The level of violence during each rape then escalated until eventually he committed his first murder. This may have occurred as early as June 1972, citing the Kerry May Hardy case. We cannot say

Year	Age	Behavior	Moral boundary crossed
1950	3-4	Exposure to pornography	Lying
1959	12-13	Deviant autoerotic activity	Theft
1961	14-16	Rape fantasies start	
1964	17-19	Voyeurism starts	Psychological rape
1968	21	Switches to being the actor in his rape fantasies	
1969	22	First attempted rape	Assault (rape)
1970	23	Meets Liz Kloepfer	
1971	24.5	Progresses to instrumental rape	Assault (battery & rape)
1972	25	Attempts first home invasion rape	
1972	25.5	Possible first murder due to loss of control	Murder
1973	26.5	Decision to actively start killing	Mutilation
1974	27 +	Necrophilic behavior emerges	Necrophilia

with any certainty that Ted murdered Hardy, but she fits many of the parameters. She disappeared from an area in Seattle that Ted had frequented at one time or another. She was found in Suncadia, about 45 minutes west of Ellensburg along the I-90 axis. Interestingly, she was clothed when buried in a shallow grave. One explanation for this is that Ted panicked and buried her in a hurry. If true, this reflects the generally accepted observation that a premeditative killer's first murder is a nervy affair, one which demands a steep learning curve. Shock and remorse are likely to be highest at this point of the trajectory compared to later killings. So too awe. To Aynesworth Ted said: "And when he's fifteen, I mean, it'd be a much more mystical, exciting, intense, overwhelming experience ... than when he's fifty" (M&A 2000, 186). Those who want to believe Ted did Ann Marie Burr use this quote as an indirect reference to her, however in the context of the conversation Ted was talking about hunting and he was clearly referring to the typical age that parents usually allow their children to first hunt game using a rifle (i.e., early teens). The fact is, Ted was an extremely organized killer. Teenage murderers are without exception generally disorganized and suffer from significant emotional problems, including anger and delusion. Ted's personality type was first and foremost centered around secrecy. He was intelligent and organized enough to know that if he made a mistake any possibility of him continuing on his trajectory would be terminated. It is for this reason that he approached killing methodically in step-wise fashion. He knew that to succeed, he needed transport, knowledge how to role play, money, and a private apartment. He had none of these things, except perhaps some paper-round money, when Ann Marie disappeared.

Still, proponents will argue that Ted could have abducted Ann Marie as a special one-off case. For example, the typical romanticized scenario is he might have just wanted to interfere with her sexually but she struggled and he accidentally killed her. If true, then at this early stage he would have almost certainly made some mistakes. Panic would have played an important role in the post-crime cover up. He might have even sustained some injuries such as scratch marks during the rape. But there were no reports of any disturbance or otherwise out-of-the-ordinary behavior in Ted at this time that could be construed as circumstantial evidence linking him to Ann Marie's disappearance. The perpetrator in all probability knew the victim through the family, or was a neighbor, and for all that has been written, at age 14 Ted lived far enough away not to be familiar with the Burrs. Take your local suburb. It is hard enough to keep track of one's immediate neighbors, let alone the whole block. Any other connections that have been reported have more to do with wish-fulfillment than reality. A final illustrative point is the issue of coincidence. What are the odds that an infamous serial killer happened to live only a few miles from the location of an unsolved abduction when he was a teen? Very low some would argue. In fact, it is not unusual at all. Ann Marie Burr is not the only person to disappear near where Ted lived. Heidi Peterson disappeared from Capitol Hill, a suburb that Ted frequented, on February 21, 1974. Ted had already killed by this time, but no one ever talks about Ted and Heidi. It could be argued this is because she was too young (aged 4). But do we really know that? A case could be mounted because all the dates of Ted's activities align with her disappearance and discovery a year later, including her skull, which appeared to have suffered trauma. But no, we will not speculate about Ted and Heidi.

Ted's M.O.

Based on what we know, it appears Ted divided up his abductions and murders into discrete stages, each one involving its own set of tasks. The first stage was the planning. Ted only spontaneously abducted about 5 of his 30 or so victims. It all began when he became obsessed with a certain individual. He stalked them to learn where they lived and what their habits were. He gathered the paraphernalia for the ruse that he would employ to abduct them. He identified the abduction location, a separate rape & murder location and oftentimes, an additional separate body disposal location, and lastly, a strategy for disposal of crime scene evidence. All of this took a lot of time and work.

He sometimes performed dry runs at the abduction location to gain confidence in his ruse. This might include entering the victim's house or apartment while they were away to set it up in advance. As a rule, he generally chose a rape and murder location that was as close to the scene of abduction as possible to limit the amount of time that he had to transport a live victim and satisfy his urges, which by the time he obtained the victim would usually have reached fever pitch. These locations would invariably possess several key attributes, such as a looped side road (powerline roads were his favorite), a crossing of some sort (railway line, small bridge), trees or shrub cover, proximity to water if possible, isolation from random passersby, and proximity to a major highway for ease of access. If he could not find a spot that met all these criteria, he would bind and gag the victim during the rape to prevent noise.

Based on what we know, Ted generally raped then murdered his victims in a combined phase before transporting them to a separate body disposal site. Sometimes the rape and murder site also served as the body disposal site, but this was the exception, not the rule. At some point between these two sites, Ted separated all clothing and other items of identification from the victim. If he did leave something with the victim, it would usually be a piece of jewelry and a pantyhose ligature. We do not know why he did this, but it plausibly served two purposes: crime scene staging for the purpose of satisfying a fantasy; later identification of the victim after other signs of the victim had decayed.

In some cases, victims were never found. Ted said that in these cases it was because he buried the victim, or because animal predation had done his work for him.

Pornography

Ted supposedly was exposed to pornography at a young age. Early exposure, as discussed in the introduction, will have altered his threshold of excitement to explicit material, making him more likely to accept extreme images of female subjugation as time went on. Detective magazines, with their racy covers depicting rape and blood lust would have only added fuel to the fire.

Voyeurism

Masturbation to macabre and sexually deviant material could only take him so far; eventually Ted wanted to experience it in the flesh. It was at this point that he decided to sneak around and peer into windows. It was not like he had not done this before. As a pre-teen, he had almost certainly prowled around his neighborhood. But now he specifically wanted to hide beneath a window and peer at the naked female form. Voyeurism is rightly regarded as a gateway to acting out, because like all addictions, the individual wants to see more, do more. The first successful clandestine observation of a partially naked female is a thrill, but that scenario eventually loses its excitement value. No one knows, but it has been estimated that about one-half to two-thirds of voyeurs go on to rape. Voyeurism is also associated with other paraphilias. In Ted's case, socks was one of his confessed fetishes, but because of his detective magazine exposure he would have also gone on to develop some macabre fetishes as well. The period when Ted transitioned from voyeurism to sexual assault was without doubt the most nervy period of his life, however, there are no police records of Ted having ever been charged with sexual assault, even though police suspect he was involved in a number of cases. The closest Ted ever came to being spotted as a voyeur was in September 1972, by Liz's best friend, Mary Chino.

Rape

Having the sex addiction that he had, it was inevitable that Ted's voyeurism would lead to rape. By his own admission, his rape fantasies began during early adolescence (e.g., the sun-baking female in the woods). Of course, his fantasies at this time were still immature; he would have lacked knowledge of the mechanics of rape at that age. It is interesting that his rape fantasies switched from passive to active around the age of 22, and coincides with when he said he lost his virginity to an older woman while inebriated. Shortly after this he said he attempted his first rape (in New Jersey). That attempt failed and he retreated back to Washington. Not long after that he embarked on a systematic trajectory towards achieving his goal of obtaining a female so that he could do what he wanted to her and get away with it.

Nowadays rape is defined as penetration (oral, vaginal, anal) against the victim's will. It is a sub-category of the more general "sexual assault." Since Ted also battered many of his victims, he also engaged in sexual assault "with battery." Rape statistics are incredibly hard to define, but it is generally accepted that about 80% of all rapes are by acquaintances. The remainder are usually defined as "stranger rape." Nicholas Groth has proposed three subtypes of rapist: anger, power and sadistic (Groth & Birnbaum, 1979). The Massachusetts Treatment Center (MTC) proposes four subtypes: opportunistic, pervasively angry, sexual gratification and vindictive. According to the MTC typology, the sexual gratification subtype is comprised of men who have extensive sexual fantasies, are preoccupied with them, many of which they incorporate into the rape act itself. They may or may not be sadistic. The non-sadistic type can be further differentiated according to their level of social competency (Knight, 1999). Ted draws some striking resonances with the MTC sexual gratification subtype. Approximately 15% of Ted's rapes were of the acquaintance type; the remaining 85% were stranger type. About 25% of Ted's abductions were non-violent in nature, the remainder involved battery, and in two known cases, he used a knife.

> As he came up behind her, she heard him. She turned around and he brandished a knife and grabbed her by the arm and told her to do what he wanted her to do. You know, to follow him (M&A 1983, 133).

This encounter echoes similar reports such as the following from the Australian Institute of Family Studies:

> I was coming home from the pub near my place. It was late in the evening, I was walking home and listening to music. I live in, like, a really safe neighborhood. I was walking down my street, and I do it all the time. No one was following me ... then, all of a sudden, I just felt this weight on my shoulders. It was a guy, and he was grabbing me from behind. He then took a blade and held it to my throat. He dragged me into the park next to where I was walking and then he came and stood in front of me. He said, "I'm going to rape you and kill you." He made a fist and he started hitting me on the left side of my face.

Thus it would appear that Ted was just your regular garden variety violent rapist, but the following passage reveals he was a lot more than that:

> What should he do with her? He'd have to debate a considerable amount. There had been an illegal act of rape. Yet he refrained from harming her physically and left the scene and returned to his car and drove home. Had it occurred a few weeks later, he wouldn't have acted in the same way. Or a few days later. But he did not want to create a great amount of public furor because it would reduce the opportunity for victims later on and it would increase the possibility of eyewitness reports. And he knew enough about these circumstances that, in all likelihood, it wouldn't be reported. Or if it was reported, nothing much would be done about it. They wouldn't necessarily link it to the other crimes. It would have been a simple act of rape of the type that is fairly common (M&A 2000, 144).

Ted studied criminal law. He had access to police rape reports sometime between October 1972 and March 1973. So he knew the terrain. This enabled him to come to the conclusion that there are "types" of rapes, some of which are fairly common (so he had a sense of statistics, something he would have learned studying psychology). He also had a sense of the zeitgeist. He knew that the vast majority of rapes went unreported. He then reveals his more sinister motive, Ted the Fisherman, making sure he doesn't fish out his pond. It reveals his long-range planning. He went out of his way to make sure he didn't kick up a "furor." Beneath the hood of this dark engine his use of language shows us that he has a good concept of morality. He knew that what he did was wrong, but he is emotionally disconnected from it. Like when he says: "... he refrained from harming her physically," he minimizes the physical and psychological suffering he inflicted on the victim, paints a portrait of himself as a gentleman rapist, if that term could be used. The truth, unfortunately, is more prosaic. As a life-long rapist, Ted inevitably grew more violent over time. Thus, while he may not have started out as a sadistic rapist, by the time he finished his career, he had thoroughly turned into one. Note, this is in contrast to someone like Gerard Schaefer, who started out as a sadistic rapist from day one.

If we were to delve a little into his "style," then we could compile the following list of behaviors extracted from things he said about himself or were reported of him by others: he preferred his victims to undress in front on him (to satisfy his voyeuristic tendencies); he called women "bitches" when intoxicated with alcohol; he once joked publicly to a victim that he was going to rape her (suggesting that he probably verbalized his intentions to other victims once he had them in his control); he issued threats of bodily harm if the victim didn't comply with his requests; he bound and gagged victims if he was forced to rape them close to public areas; at least two of his girlfriends reported that he choked them during sex, he was not averse to raping victims that he had severely injured, or were close to death or had just died.

Assault

It appears Ted initially employed assault as an operational method to obtain victim compliance. Later on, this appears to have evolved into hurting women for sexual gratification in and of itself. As he explained to Michaud and Aynesworth, he started out with voyeurism, but over time was driven to "active" stimulation and started shifting from "psychological rape" as Hagmaier defined it, to active rape. His first attempts at securing a victim involved tampering with victims' cars – removing the rotor device out of their motors' distributors or deflating their tires (M&A 1983, 110). For various reasons these efforts failed. He needed a more reliable approach. This led to his first experiments with instrumental assault (use of clubs, knives). It seems that from these first clumsy experiments he learned that the best approach was to attack the victim ninja-style; either from behind unawares, or while they slept in their beds. Invariably the bashings were so severe that those who experienced them usually ended up with life-threatening penetration wounds to the skull and brain.

During rape, control of the victim is paramount to the rapist, and Ted was no exception. Thus, in those cases where the victim was sufficiently under his psychological control, he had them undress in front of him so that he could satisfy his voyeuristic tendencies, or if they resisted, he handcuffed them or bound them with rope or strips of material. In about half of all his cases, he rendered the victim semi-comatose during the abduction. This allowed him to perform his devious acts on the victim without resistance. These acts included sodomy and foreign object insertion into vaginal and / or anal orifices. In the other half, he employed a ruse to lure the victim to a location where he could gain control over them, oftentimes handcuffing them before they had time to react. Once the victim was restrained, they had little choice but to comply with his demands.

Murder

No one knows why Ted was driven to murder, nor when he first murdered. However, there are enough clues to paint a reasonable picture. According to Hagmaier, Ted's first murder came as a result of displaced aggression. Displaced aggression occurs when someone builds up frustration over an incident in one encounter and releases it on a secondary target in separate encounter. The classic case is kicking the dog at home after an argument with the boss at work. All it takes is for the dog to do one small wrong thing and that serves as a trigger for the release of the pent-up frustration and anger. As much as we would like to agree with Hagmaier on this assessment, we find Hagmaier's claim to be something of a smoke screen. It may be true that Ted lost control during the rape and the situation then escalated to murder, however, the fact that Ted went on to commit multiple murders suggests a deeper undercurrent of motivation behind his behavior than a simple case of displaced aggression would have us believe, even for the first murder.

We know Ted was fascinated with death from a relatively young age. We also know that thoughts of murder generally develop in serial killers around adolescence. This is when the brain undergoes massive upheaval due to hormonal processes, when the body crosses the threshold into adulthood. It would be fair to say that the first simmerings of sexual desire that arose in Ted's brain were not your average thoughts on the matter. He had already primed his brain with multitudinous images gleaned from pornos and detective magazines by this time, so these would have colored those first sexual stirrings with deviant and macabre themes. At first, they may have merely arisen as a set of kinky ideas about sex and death. But for reasons that we still do not know, they became more and more oriented towards violent sex and death, eventually reaching the status of obsession. The apparent similarity of this process with the development of addiction in individuals has made the *addiction theory of serial murder* one of the most plausible theories that explains their behavior. On the surface, indeed, there is nothing to distinguish Ted's addiction to murder from any other addiction, whether it be alcohol, gambling or sex-addiction.

At the core of Ted's addiction, of course, is the pervading fantasy process. Fantasy is so central to sexual murder that it could be argued that Ted was primarily addicted to the fantasy process *itself*. The problem with the fantasy theory of serial sexual murder, however, is that it fails to explain the physical reality of the murderous act and its aftermath. Increasing addiction to fantasy by its very nature is supposed to distance the individual from reality. Arguably, murder, more than any other activity, is the quintessential existential act, and could not be further (phenomenologically at least) from inward turning fantasy. Or is it? How can we redress this contradiction? One way that fantasy theorists have attempted to patch over this problem is argue that the killer attempts to perfect his fantasy with each murder, but because murders are anything but perfect, the killer is left dissatisfied and eventually starts planning the next murder in order to achieve that perfection, learning from his mistakes as he goes. Evidence for fantasy addiction in Ted comes from the things he said about the aftermath of a murder, that it was like coming out of a bad dream, a night sweat and so forth. He would have us believe that during the commission of the murder he was in some sort of altered state and only afterwards did he snap out of it and see the stone cold reality of what he had done. Unfortunately, Ted himself busted that theory: "Yeah, I try to get away with split personality" (Pensacola bug tape, February 18, 2:15 a.m., FSA). The day before his execution, he made it very clear to Lewis that he did not have split personalities, or multiple personality disorder: "... the malignant portion of my personality or consciousness, call it what you will—the entity—is more or less directing the mood and the action, I'm still on another level conscious of this, I'm not totally unconscious of, or unaware of it (Nelson 1994, 287). Indeed, to Hagmaier, Ted said he just "liked to kill." From this we can conclude that we have to be careful when arguing that Ted killed because he was addicted to fantasy, that killing served the function of maintaining the fantasy.

Despite this, it cannot be denied that fantasy plays a key role in the evolution of a serial killer. Here it may help us to operationalize our definition, since all healthy normal individuals engage in fantasy on a daily basis (and much more frequently and unconsciously too, if neuroscience is correct). Obviously fantasy is not hallucination. But what is its relationship to ordinary cognitive activity, such as day dreaming, active imagination (visualization in the mind's eye to solve problems, inventing things), forgetting a train of thought (because we were interrupted by a reverie or flashback), eidetic imagery, or illusions to name some of the phenomena that could fall under the heading of fantasy activity? It would appear that when we use the word "fantasy" in relation to serial killers, we are specifically talking about violent sexual fantasies, their frequency, intensity, and most important of all, the crossing of the threshold between purely thinking them and acting them out.

Perhaps Ted came closest when he gave us the phrase "as if seen through a motion picture screen" (M&A 1983, 124). The acting out of a fantasy appears to be a kind of superimposition phenomenon whereby the individual projects visual forms onto an external object through active imagination. In the very simplest of analogies, seeing a female in a detective magazine wearing a particularly revealing blouse, then projecting that image onto a victim during an abduction even though she may not be wearing the same blouse. Ted may have even taken it so far as to bring clothes and props he had seen in magazines and made his victims wear them, to turn them more closely into the images he had seen and rehearsed in his mind.

What makes acting out so difficult to nail down is that it is *not* an all-or-nothing process. There are many small gradations. It can start with something as simple as fixating on the hair of a sibling. It can progress to scaring a girlfriend by jumping out at her from behind a bush. The next step might be to pick up a piece of two-by-four and carry it with the intention of striking someone, but not actually do it. The perpetrator could rationalize their behavior by arguing that there is no differences between them and a builder carrying a piece of wood out of a hardware store. Except the perpetrator knows that the context has determined their act to be criminal. They have crossed a threshold not necessarily in behavior, but in *intent*. At the same time, the physical act of carrying the wood has allowed them to become habituated to that behavior. It is not unlike a child using training wheels on a bicycle. There will come a time when the wheels are no longer needed, but in the interim some important skills have to be learned. When it is time for the training wheels to come off, it is like a ratchet falling into place. It is not that this cannot be reversed due to a physical barrier (the wheels could be put back on) but because a psychological threshold has been crossed (the exhilaration of riding without wheels has ample attractive value in itself to make going back to riding with training wheels undesirable). Thus, when the first murder finally takes place, it springs forth from the culmination of these small steps, not some singular act of displaced aggression. This paints a picture of a willful individual who has resolved to behave in a certain way. It does not answer the question why Ted chose to kill. Whether he hated women, loved them, was obsessed by them, or wanted to possess them, or most likely, needed to cover up his rapes ... or all of the above, we shall forever speculate and this is one of the reasons why these individuals are so fascinating (even as we detest their behavior).

Necrophilia

Ted was a self-confessed necrophile. There are claims, however, that Ted engaged in necrophilia with bodies that had undergone significant putrefaction. It is difficult to find a direct quote by him in the archives saying he did that. Nevertheless, it is reasonable to assume that if he did return to a body that had decayed, we cannot rule out some sort of non-contact auto-erotic behavior. This is apart from removing the aforementioned heads. This kind of close contact with a partially skeletonized body would involve a degree of habituation to putrefaction odors that would repel ordinary people. When he said he buried Cunningham after leaving her on the surface for weeks, that meant digging a hole and putting her in it, which implies man-handling a decayed cadaver.

The other contentious issue is whether Ted specifically murdered in order to obtain a dead body for the purposes of post-mortem sexual molestation. Once again, this is unconfirmed. He did make the comment to Lewis that he sometimes lamented that he killed his victims too quickly and would have liked to have spent more time with them while they were alive, suggesting that his primary motive for necrophilia was not an end in itself, but an opportunity he took advantage of after having gone through all that trouble of getting a victim in the first place. Thus, we cannot say he could only ever achieve orgasm with a dead individual, as he had normal sexual relations with women who generally reported mostly normal sexual contact with him. We also cannot assume he had an aversion to being gazed upon intimately by the victim during the sex act, as in the case of the suspected Seattle rape victim where he taped over her eyes. It would appear that he taped over her eyes so that he could remove his ski mask while he raped her and not be identified. This would allow him to use his mouth, as has been observed in the Chi Omega case. Thus, concealment appears to be his primary motive.

Mutilation

There appears to be as many fantasies about Ted as Ted had himself when it comes to what he did with his victims after he murdered them. Ted admitted that he transported around "half a dozen" of his victims' heads post-mortem to a different location to obfuscate crime scene evidence (in once case he admitted using a hacksaw to decapitate a victim's head). Since he knew the importance of fingerprints, we could argue that he must have therefore also amputated hands and transported them to a separate location as well but no hand or finger bones have ever been recovered from Taylor Mountain and as far as this author was able to ascertain, none were recovered from Issaquah either.

Ted's admission that he cut up victims is somewhat constrained by his embarrassment about this aspect of his behavior. Obviously post-mortem dismemberment and decapitation serves the purpose of crime scene obfuscation, but investigators would like to believe Ted derived some sort of macabre satisfaction out of these acts as well, not to mention having oral sex with decapitated heads. The truth is we don't know that. Ted alludes to "frenzied" states where he lashed out at some victims because he was particularly intoxicated with alcohol at the time and had built up a lot of anger and frustration in the weeks preceding the murder. It is impossible to say wheth-

Bill: I am not sure how many, but you opted to sever the heads from the victims and, how many was that do you recall of thirty?

Bundy: Oh, that's

Bill: I realize it's a difficult question because you are a different person now than you were then. But to search back and

Bundy: Oh perhaps half a dozen.

Bill: So approximately twelve of the thirty had their heads severed. Were there any other body parts severed?

Bundy: Again, it was extremely rare and it was not, it was not I know with some people I have heard it is their kind of signature but it was not something like that for me, but in those occasions when it occurred it was almost, outside of those couple of occasions, I was sort of frenzied, lashing out, it was more of an attempt to transport, conceal, uh, their remains more than anything else.

Interview excerpt altered to fit format. Note Hagmaier exaggerates the number of decapitations. Date of interview: January 22, 1989.

er this kind of lashing out was targeted at that particular victim, or whether that victim had simply been in the wrong place at the wrong time.

The fact that Ted severed heads and transported them prompted Keppel to ask him whether he ever kept body parts in the refrigerator. Ted denied getting into that sort of behavior. In fact, when you look at the Issaquah and Taylor Mountain crime scenes, evidence of post-mortem mutilation is extremely vague. Hawkins' head was never found, despite extensive digging at Issaquah. Ott & Naslund appeared to have been disarticulated more by animal than human activity. The skulls at Taylor Mountain without exception were missing all their vertebrae which led one medical examiner to conclude that they must have been *pulled from already skeletonized remains elsewhere*, and as for the remaining found victims, Smith, Aime, Campbell, Bowman, Levy and Leach, they were all intact, with only Leach perhaps showing signs of post-mortem mutilation, but because of decomposition it could not be conclusively determined one way or the other. The one case where Ted gave away some detail about post-mortem activity was Cunnigham, and he described her as intact except she had mummified by the time he returned to her.

Thus, the post-mortem mutilation scenarios that have been ascribed to Ted appear to be tenuous at best. The evidence, if anything, points more towards Ted leaving bodies whole above ground for animal predators in some cases, and in others, complete burial. If he did return to the bodies at a later date, it would appear that he only did this for the above-ground cases, and only then to remove body parts (such as heads) once they had already undergone significant skeletonization, the purpose of which was to further obfuscate crime scene evidence. It doesn't rule out multiple visits to some bodies, but the frequency of these would be low. We could estimate an average number of visits post-mortem, but that rule would only apply to some victims, not others.

Mythbusting

According to Hagmaier:

> Serial killers used to get ideas from detective magazines, which we called "the serial killer's Bible." As you may recall, on the cover of almost every detective magazine, there would be an adult male in a menacing stance over a female who looked terrified but still sexy, with part of her breast or leg exposed. There was a chemistry of sex and violence together—pleasure and power—which appealed to certain marginal members of our society. When Ted Bundy killed his victims, he was basically reenacting the covers of detective magazines. (Something that is still not generally known about Ted Bundy is that some of his victims were found wearing nail polish that wasn't theirs or with their hair styled or dyed differently than was their habit, because he had kept them sometimes for days, not alive but dead. He was into necrophilia, as a number of serial murderers have been.) So killers such as Bundy got ideas from the fiction on the covers of detective magazines; today's criminals watch television and movies (Hagmaier, 1997).

Well, not even Hagmaier is immune to distorting facts. None of Ted's victims had their hair dyed a different color; unless that fact was treated as special information which was withheld and only given to police; no mention of it is made in the available coroner's reports. The two victims that have been associated with post-mortem activity of this type are Smith and Aime, and no mention of hair dye is made in official reports that can be found in the archives. Hagmaier's claim that Ted kept live victims for days is also unsupported. In the first edition of this book we argued the same, however, careful examination of the timeline and all the available evidence leads us to believe that it is extremely unlikely that Ted kept live victims longer than he had to.

However, from Hagmaier, we also learn that:

> ... after a while, murder isn't just a crime of lust or violence. It becomes possession. They are part of you. After a while, when you plan these, that person becomes a part of you and you are forever one [with them]. [...] even after twenty or thirty that it's the same thing, because you're the last one there. You feel the last bit of breath leaving their body. You're looking into their eyes and basically, a person in that situation is God! You then possess them and they shall forever be part of you. And the grounds where you kill them or leave them become sacred to you, and you will always be drawn back to them (M&A 1983, 317).

We trust Hagmaier paraphrased Ted to a reasonable degree of accuracy. Here Ted talks about possession and the mystical aspects of murder. The line, "You're looking into their eyes ..." goes back to how Ted must have become a reasonably good observer of vital signs: pulse, pupil dilation, breathing, any physical movement of the body, post-mortem twitching, etc. We know that in a handful of cases he did not spend much time with the body, but mostly he had plenty of time after killing the victim to linger over them. It didn't always happen after the midnight hours, but that was the general pattern. To check some of the vital signs required light. He had the option to use his car headlights, or a flashlight. The reference to "God"and the "sacred" raises obvious connotations with religion, however, as we shall discover, it has drawn some strange attractants.

The following paraphrased quote is supposedly Ted talking to a victim and is posted by Daniel Mann on his blogspot under the title 'Ted Bundy and Atheism.' The quote is a complete fabrication; Ted never said anything of the sort, but here it is anyway:

> Then I learned that all moral judgments are "value judgments," that all value judgments are subjective, and that none can be proved to be either "right" or "wrong." I even read somewhere that the Chief justice

> of the United States had written that the American Constitution expressed nothing more than collective value judgments. Believe it or not, I figured out for myself what apparently the Chief Justice couldn't figure out for himself: that if the rationality of one value judgment was zero, multiplying it by millions would not make it one whit more rational. Nor is there any "reason" to obey the law for anyone, like myself, who has the boldness and daring—the strength of character—to throw off its shackles. I discovered that to become truly free, truly unfettered, I had to become truly uninhibited. And I quickly discovered that the greatest obstacle to my freedom, the greatest block and limitation to it, consists in the insupportable "value judgment" that I was bound to respect the rights of others. I asked myself, who were these "others"? Other human beings, with human rights? Why is it more wrong to kill a human animal than any other animal, a pig or a sheep or a steer? Is your life more to you than a hog's life to a hog? Why should I be willing to sacrifice my pleasure more for the one than for the other? Surely, you would not, in this age of scientific enlightenment, declare that God or nature has marked some pleasures as "moral" or "good" and others as "immoral" or "bad"? In any case, let me assure you, my dear young lady, that there is absolutely no comparison between the pleasure I might take in eating ham and the pleasure I anticipate in raping and murdering you. That is the honest conclusion to which my education has led me after the most conscientious examination of my spontaneous and uninhibited self (*Christian Research Journal*, Vol 33, No 2, 2010).

To track down where the original quote came from, we turn to the *Christian Research Journal* and to the article authored by Chad Meister (pp. 23-35). Meister writes:

> A statement by Ted Bundy, paraphrased and rewritten by Harry V. Jaffa, Homosexuality and the National Law (Claremont Institute of the Study of Statesmanship and Political Philosophy, 1990, pp. 3–4).

So we go to Jaffa's book, which is available at Amazon.com and read one of the reviews of his book:

> "... he provides an imagined conversation between serial killer Ted Bundy and one of his victims. Though professional philosophers do occasionally like to dramatize their arguments, or even present them in fictionalized form, Jaffa's evocation of Bundy is ill-advised" (David Walters, March 29, 2012).

A polite way of saying it was stupid to try and put words in Ted's mouth when you don't know what you're talking about. The funny part is that there are numerous instances of people blogging on the web that refer to this fictional quote, many of which are aligned to religion, showing that religion and Ted do not mix. Philosophers have also been caught out. Louis P. Pojman & James Fieser have a book out in 6th edition where they continue to peddle this quote as true even when they reference Jaffa's article. The book is on ethics, so go figure the ethics of representing fabrication as fact!

In another example you have Pamela Lillian Valemont who has written a numerological analysis on Ted. The book is 104 pages in length and the list price is US $74.00. It's enough to make you scratch your head. Obviously there is an entire Freak Show out there dedicated to creating myths about the man. For example, the following person claims to be Ted's great-grandnephew (going by the name of Michelle Cowell; see Creepypasta reference). Putting aside the obvious clanger (or are we to assume intersex?), we find this person claiming to have found a chest about the size of a shoe box in her grandmother's attic containing a "letter, a small mirror, and what appeared to be a sapphire amulet." The letter reads (in part):

> Dear Samantha,
>
> [...] One night I was walking home from a play, and as I walked I came across a necklace and a mirror, and a note, all banded together. My curiosity made me take these items home. When I did I found that the note said if I put the necklace on and wished for something in front of the small mirror, it would come true. [...] I put the necklace on and wished for the ability to have any girl I wanted. Immediately the mirror glowed a bright green and I swore I saw some eyes in the mirror too. I felt a jolt go through my body. Next thing I knew I woke up in my bed like normal. I went and did everything I would do on a normal day, but when I was walking outside every girl would look at me with lust. Surprised I decided I would try something. Later that day I visited a woman I had the hots for, and I asked if she would like to go on a date, to my surprise she said yes! But after the date when we left the club I blacked out. The next day I woke up and she was laying next to me in bed, but when I looked at her she was beaten bad. Her jaw was shattered, she was bleeding everywhere, most of her bones were broken, some poked out of her skin, skin was torn off, it was horrifying. I jumped out of the bed and vomited. Something kept me from calling the police. I left her body there; I was so shaken up but for some reason I continued to do my daily activities. I seduced a woman into letting me stay at her house, but when I woke she was dead too; even worse this time. It was horrible. I ran home and wished into the mirror for people to stop dying, This time the mirror glowed red, blood red. The eyes came back except this time they spoke. "You have made your wish Theodore. And nothing is going to stop your thirst for blood. Good Luck, I will help you evade the police until your 30th murder, in which case you're on your own." Then he faded away with a deafening evil laugh. Do you see now?? It wasn't me. I did research and this demon's name is [the words here were smeared with what appeared to be blood]. I mailed you the necklace and mirror a couple months ago; destroy them, and if you can't, bury them in the middle of a forest or woods. You must get rid of these demonic items. Good bye Sam. I am sorry.
>
> Uncle Ted

We're not going to explore the provenance of this piffle, but we have to treat it with some seriousness, because it brings back the claim by the unknown source who quoted Ted saying he was possessed by a "Beast." We brushed the religious connotations of that aside at the time, but here we shall explore it a little further for sake of fulfilling the breadth and depth of our research brief.

Demonic possession is as old as the hills, however modern neuroscience places it firmly in the domain of mental illness. Epilepsy, specifically petit mal seizures, are considered the most likely explanation. Either that or trance drugs. However, Ted's EEG showed no trace of epileptic-type patterns, so it would appear we can rule out "possession" in the orthodox sense. This didn't stop Lewis from hypothesizing the possibility of altered states. She was exceptionally driven to find evidence of petit mal-type phenomena in Ted:

> I reviewed [...] some papers that Mr. Bundy had written [...] around the time that he was in college [...] and there is a drawing that he did and there is an interesting kind of metamorphosis in the drawing and also in the writing on the page. [...] When I asked Mr. Bundy about it, first of all, he said, "Did I do this?" He said this is my writing, which I think is quite interesting because certain individuals when they are in an altered state or whatever write differently from the way they do at other times. And here is a picture where, first of all, there is a head, a person of some sort, and then the head enlarges and the head has teeth like Dracula. And there also seems to be a change in the writing right within the page itself. It looks as if he became less organized or whatever on the page. [...] When I showed this to Mr. Bundy, his first reaction was did I do it, that he didn't remember it, and then he said "Was I on drugs." I don't know, but this was at college and as far as we know he was not into drugs. And this seems to be sort of a visual representation of perhaps what happens with him when he goes into these states (Lewis testimony. December 15, 1987, pp 227-8).

What are we to make of this analysis given the drawing in front of us? We recall he supposedly referred to himself as a "vampire" during the Pensacola interviews. The context of the quote is that he stayed up during the night and slept during the day. There is no explicit reference to the more macabre connotations of vampirism.

The implicit assumption is that vampirism denotes a physical metamorphosis. We know Ted has been associated with such changes on a number of occasions. Stephen Michaud remembers his experience vividly:

> Early on when we started talking in the third person [...] I remember, at one point I finally got him to talk about one of the murders we both knew he was involved with [...] he grabbed the tape recorder and started talking, [...] under his right eye I saw this white line start to develop, [...] it was like a lash mark, [...] it had nothing to do with the character or the contour of his face, [...] like a scar, and it stood

Ted's college drawing of a vampire with writing about the "fundamental essentials of freedom." Photo source: *The Miami Herald*, December 11, 1986.

> out, and it got really [...] distinctive as he was talking about what he did to the girl, what he did to her afterwards, [...] and then he finally stopped and he looked up at me, it was the first time our eyes had actually locked together in fifteen minutes, and he was exhausted, he was sweating (Michaud 2015).

Joe Aloi as we recall witnessed the change. He described it as an odor, like an animal or a wet rug (*Tallahassee Magazine*, March - April 2010). Then we have Virginia Bristol's account from around 1968 (presumably when Ted first returned to the east after breaking up with Diane Edwards). In that version she said that after a very pleasant evening at a concert as they waited in a train station Ted suddenly started to ramble, he made no sense and he looked crazy, and she felt that he was not in touch with her (Lewis testimony. December 15, 1987, p. 225). Finally we have Liz's accounts. For example, the time he pushed her into the icy waters of the Yakima River (July 6, 1974). In that instance, when she surfaced and their eyes locked, she said his "face had gone blank, as though he was not there at all. I had a sense that he wasn't seeing me" (Kendall 1981, 52). Liz's father, Russell Hirst, an M.D., stated that if he was going to give an opinion of the individual, "[Ted] was definitely a schizophrenic." When asked to elaborate on that, he stated that "at one time he is very nice, very pleasant, very helpful; then he becomes extremely moody, does not talk, gives you the opinion that he is really thinking or contemplating something" (Jerry Thompson report. Russel N. Hirst interview, September 9, 1975).

These reports are too numerous and consistent to dismiss as figments of people's imaginations. It seems that during these episodes Ted momentarily fell under the spell of the "Beast." Neurologically, we posit a PFC decompensation event caused by ego-depletion. This leads to a gating malfunction, where the dark and sinister contents of his fantasy-world spill into his conscious stream and take it over. In the words of Schaefer: the "ghoul" has come out. The original Arabic ġūl (derived from the late 18th century) describes a person who robs graves to prey on corpses. From what we know, Ted was not a grave robber—at least there are no reports of him robbing graveyards for corpses—but he did create his own graveyards from the corpses of young females he abducted and murdered. The witnesses' descriptions of weird facial transformations, of foul odor, strongly suggest that during these episodes Ted's necrophilic fantasies may have become engaged. And even though he may not have verbalized these thoughts, they may have leaked out in his behavior and people have an uncanny sense when it comes to these kinds of things. They sense that something out of the ordinary is happening, and it triggers an unconscious reaction. We cannot say with absolute certainty that Ted stunk, or had a lash mark across his face; people may have projected these things into him out of their own fearful imaginations, even though they are not without foundation (i.e., they may be exaggerations of real things).

BUNDY: I know that what it comes to that ________ there is something wrong with me [don't you understand that,] I can't go any further ______

Voice: Why? You can to Ted.

BUNDY: I'm as cold as a mother fuckin __ ever that you've ever put your fucking eyes on. ________ I don't give a shit about those people.

CHAPMAN: So!

BUNDY: I do ______________

CHAPMAN: Tell us about it, Ted.

BUNDY: It's just so strong ____ [in me] ~~and meaningless~~

The context of this statement as was reported in newspapers was that police were exhorting Ted to tell them where he left Kim Leach's body. In fact, the context is the Carol DaRonch case, and police were losing their grip on Ted and were desperately trying to get him to open up, but Ted had already abdicated (First night Tallahassee, 12:47 a.m. February 20, 1978, p. 53).

Neuroscientifically, much more work still needs to be done to elucidate the neural signatures that comprise ghoulish experiences. It is not a case of entertaining ghosts and spirit worlds. Rather, a more mundane explanation can be found in out-of-body experiences (OBE) and "shadow" phenomena. The temporo-parietal junction (TPJ) has been identified as a key brain area that subserves these phenomena. Katherine Ramsland has tentatively put forward the suggestion that Ted's sense of an "other" within himself may have stemmed from a TPJ problem (2013). Research has shown that the TPJ is important for binding ongoing sensory experience with sense-of-self (Blanke & Arzy, 2005). If there is asynchrony between the sense-of-self and incoming spatial and temporal data, this can result in the experience of phantom projections such as OBEs, doppelgängers, or other weird bodily states. Often, the cause of TPJ asynchrony is epilepsy, but it can also come about as a result of drugs or brain trauma (e.g., a stroke or head injury). Ted, as we know presented a "slightly" abnormal EEG profile suggestive of depressive-like neural patterns. We do not know if more extensive tests would have uncovered evidence of an epileptic disorder. It may be that his use of cannabis and alcohol exacerbated a vulnerability. Cannabis in particular has been associated with trance-like states and may have triggered an abnormal neural firing pattern in Ted's brain that caused more of the deviant thought patterns to emerge – not necessarily taking over his personality, but changing his mood.

Sadism

As commented on earlier, Ted may not have started out as a sadist, but he almost certainly became one by the time he killed his last victim. In his final interview with Lewis the day before his execution, Ted was contradictory about his sadistic behavior. On the one hand, he admitted that his "need, the thought, the feeling, the excitement of harming, of getting some sort of sexual gratification at harming someone, was absolutely paramount" (Nelson 1994, 293). Then, about a minute later, he says, "there were many times the girls were conscious, but—and I'm quite serious about this—I never got off, never was aroused or excited in any way by the women being scared" (Nelson 1994, 294). What are we to make of this? It would appear he is making a distinction between getting sexual gratification out of physically harming someone and getting off on the fear response of his victims. The most generous interpretation we could make of this is that while they were conscious he liked to role play his ruse right up until the moment he harmed them physically. The victim might be terrified at being raped, but they would be of the belief that once they got through that they would be free. Moments later, Ted would strangle them to death. At least this accords with what he told Nelson on a different occasion when describing one of the hitchhikers he killed:

> He drove across the state line to a secluded place in the woods that he was already familiar with. He led the girl out of the car, assuring her that no harm would come to her. He made her strip and kneel on her hands and knees while he took Polaroid pictures of her. [...] She cried. He could see the look of terror

> in her eyes, her eyes begging for mercy. He kept reassuring her. He didn't like to see their hurt, he said, he didn't like to see his victim as a person – he wasn't the kind of person who would harm another. [...] not the kind of person who would hurt a fly. [...] Then he got behind her, slung a noose around her neck, and strangled her as he raped her. He'd continued to reassure her he would let her go, and she seemed to believe him. He said he felt a little sad that he could not let her go, that he had to kill her, but she would be able to identify him, of course (Nelson 1994, 258-9).

There are so many clues in this passage, the use of a secluded area, the demands that the victim pose for his pleasure, the terror in the victim's eyes, the maintaining of the surface validity of the encounter, then the noose, which seems to conveniently materialize from a pocket ready-to-hand, and the insistence that he was a rapist only, even as he strangles his victim to death, as if he needed to keep that part of his behavior hidden away from the victim so as not to sully the image of himself as the gentleman rapist. Apart from the callous premeditated plan to kill the victim, there appears to be no evidence that he did get off on seeing the terror in the victim's eyes. This of course clashes with the statement he gave to Hagmaier, that he would look into the victims' eyes as the life drained from their bodies. Perhaps that statement of Ted is Hagmaier's interpretation. Because Hagmaier also reported that Ted liked to strangle his victims from behind – which has a stronger ring of plausibility about it:

1. it allows the killer to bring out a noose without the victim's awareness
2. it is easier to strangle a victim from behind as they cannot defend themselves as well from that position
3. it allows the killer to maintain the surface validity of the encounter in their eyes; the victim does not see the rapist transform into the killer
4. it allows the rapist to perform the sex act anonymously, while keeping the victim depersonalized

Brent E. Turvey in his examination of Ted found a lack of evidence supporting claims that Ted was a sexual sadist (Turvey 2011, 469-70). He found three instances of authors conflating the evidence:

- "Ted Bundy, in addition to being a serial killer, must be viewed a serial sadistic rapist" (Holmes 1991, 81).
- "Far from being the Rudolph Valentino of the serial killer world, Ted Bundy was a brutal, sadistic, perverted man" (Ressler and Schactman 1992, 63).
- "Clinically speaking, Ted Bundy was a sexual psychopath who enjoyed killing women in the context of expressing his sadistic sexual fantasies" (Geberth 1996, 798).

We also find psychiatrist Robert Simon latching onto the bandwagon:

> With his arm in a cast, he would get them into his car, or to some isolated spot, and then bludgeon them with a short crowbar concealed in the removable arm cast. While the women were unconscious or semiconscious, he would then commit gross sexual acts, including anal assault. Bundy bit various body parts, sometimes biting off a victim's nipple or leaving bitemarks on her buttocks. He killed the victims by strangulation. Bundy mutilated and decapitated their bodies, and severed their hands with a hacksaw. He would leave the bodies in secluded spots and return to them after several days to commit necrophilic acts such as ejaculating into the mouth of a disembodied head (Simon 1996, 259)

Passages such as these reveal more about the author's own fantasies than anything authentic written about Ted. Nowhere in the forensic literature on Ted does it say he secreted a crowbar in his arm cast, or that he cut victims' hands off with a hacksaw, or that he routinely mutilated them, or that he ejaculated into the mouths of decapitated heads. Ted may have actually done much worse things than these acts, but the reality is *we don't know*. It seems that most authors cannot help themselves; they simply cannot limit themselves to the evidence. They have to inject their own tepid imaginations into Ted.

If we do limit ourselves to the evidence, then the most authentic iteration possible is that Ted was first-and-foremost a rapist concerned with concealing his identity, and to this end he worked very hard to remove any and all evidence that connected him to his crimes. Was he a sadistic rapist? It would appear from the evidence that it was not his primary motive. That the victims were terrified is unquestionable, but did Ted specifically engineer that terror, ratchet it up to the maximum degree possible to get the gratification he desired? That part of the story is open to interpretation. In this book, we have used Gerard Schaefer as a comparison to put Ted into context. When we examine Schaefer's crimes, and his writings, what we find is a man whose fantasies specifically revolve around sadistic torture. He was also far more deviant than Ted:

> He wasn't familiar with the basic chemistry of human putrefaction. I'd been a hunter, so I know how to prevent spoilage of meat in the field. I'd listen to him whine about how a girl would turn rotten on him so fast, then I'd clue him in on how to keep her fresh as long as possible. I told him to string the girl up by the ankles and cut off her head to exsanguinate her. Blood rots fast, and so do brains. So it's best to cut off the head and drain the blood. He wanted to know

> what I'd do with the head, and I said I'd put it on a stick so she could watch me make love to her body. He'd almost come in his shorts listening to this stuff (Schaefer 1997, 228)

And ...

> He added the practice of killing and mutilating livestock according to his doctor. Not only did he kill and behead them, he had intercourse with them. The strange part of his "confession" about the killings of livestock was he told the doctor he had not remembered it before when he had talked to other doctors, but he had an epiphany with this particular one. There were reports in the town of Davie 15 miles west of Ft. Lauderdale of livestock being killed, beheaded and human seamen left on them. It is highly probable that Schaefer was indeed telling the truth. When the doctor asked Schaefer why he remembered this incident at this point, Schaefer told him he was crazy. He told the doctor he was not normal and that he badly needed help for his hostility (Mason 2011, 700-1).

Obviously, we would not associate Ted with this kind of depravity. Schaefer seems to be pretty much the bottom of the barrel. Ted by comparison *was* a Boy Scout.

A. I'M NOW TRYING TO SUMMARIZE ABOUT TEN OR FIFTEEN YEARS OF WORK.

WHAT IT HAS SHOWN, AND THIS IS, NOT ONLY WHEN WE COMPARED MORE VIOLENT INDIVIDUALS AND MORE VIOLENT OFFENDERS WITH LESS VIOLENT OFFENDERS, BUT ALSO WHEN WE HAVE COMPARED LET'S SAY INCARCERATED DELINQUENTS WITH ORDINARY NON-DELINQUENTS, WHAT YOU FIND IS THAT WHEN YOU HAVE A COMBINATION OF SOME KIND OF INTRINSIC VULNERABILITY, BE IT BECAUSE OF A NEUROLOGICAL KIND OF DISORDER OR BECAUSE OF A PREDISPOSITION TO A PSYCHOTIC DISORDER SUCH AS SCHIZOPHRENIA OR MANIC DEPRESSIVE ILLNESS, AND WHEN YOU COUPLE THAT WITH AN UPBRINGING IN A HOUSEHOLD THAT IS VIOLENT, YOU OFTEN CREATE AN INCREDIBLY VIOLENT INDIVIDUAL.

Evidentiary hearing, Dorothy Lewis court transcript, December 15, 1987, case number 86-968-CIV-ORL-18.

Conclusion

In the preface to this book we accepted the proposition that an inherited vulnerability and family modeling played a significant role in Ted's etiology, but we said it wasn't sufficient. We have argued that the vulnerability was his PFC deficit and that this directly impacted Ted's management of ego-depletion. It is probable that, like Jerome Brudos, Ted became fixated on a fetish object early in life (e.g., socks). How this came about is not clear, but there is plenty of scope for speculation, ranging from super-stimulus imprinting (Aronsson, 2011) to trauma (Freud & Strachey, 1975). Ted's sock fetish foreshadowed his later sexual deviancy, and likely involves a compulsive component. The compulsive component is probably directly linked to his PFC deficit, much the same way that Asperger's syndrome and other autistic spectrum disorders involves compulsive (and obsessive) behavior (Bejerot, 2007; Haskins & Silva 2006; Kristiansson & Sörman, 2008; Reaven & Hepburn, 2003). While none of this explains Ted's motivation to seek out sex and violence, it lays the groundwork for the association between sex and violence. One way this could have happened was through compulsive masturbation. If Ted was masturbating repeatedly to images of violent sex and death, then this would have reinforced the association between pleasure and those images. Repetition strengthens the neural circuitry that underpins the behavior, in effect creating a positive feedback loop, much the same way that drug addiction is formed. Compulsive masturbation also causes distress and feelings of social inadequacy, which compounds the problem, making the individual prefer to withdraw into loneliness where they feel less out of control. However, this only leads to insularity and a decline towards deviant thinking. By the time Ted became a young adult and added cannabis and alcohol to his routine, the stage was set for the killer to emerge through the twin forces of fantasy elaboration and PFC disinhibition. Here, his "voices" played a causative role by amplifying his deviant thinking. The impact of this was to make him more susceptible to empathy failure. The process began when his ego depleted in the face of social and cognitive challenges (which in turn was potentiated by his PFC deficit). When this happened, his go-to response was to turn to the thing that gave him the most comfort: masturbation to sexually violent material. Later, as he became habituated to this activity, he engaged in voyeurism to achieve the same arousal levels that solo masturbation provided. Voyeurism in turn led to acting out. Once that happened, there was no going back. The first murder opened a whole new world of possibilities, the most deviant of which was necrophilia and mutilation. Make no mistake, Ted tried to "de-escalate" his actions, however, given that he had a fixed PFC deficit and a categorical unwillingness to seek help for his "sickness" (because of a fear of being permanently institutionalized), he eventually chose to became a Macbeth-like figure:

> I am in blood
> Stepped in so far that, should I wade no more,
> Returning were as tedious as go o'er.
> (Act 3, Scene 4, p. 7.)

Ironically, after his final capture in Florida in 1978, when he knew that the likes of Theodore Robert Bundy should never be allowed on the streets again, he asked to be institutionalized in a Washington facility close to family and friends. The only problem—and he knew it—was that it would never work in practice. He would try to escape again, just like he tried to escape from Florida State Prison maximum security. There is no permanent cure for addictive behavior, only eternal vigilance.

References

Aronsson, H. (2011). *On Sexual Imprinting in Humans*. Stockholm University.

Australian Institute of Family Studies (2010). Insights into sexual assault perpetration. Giving voice to victim/survivors' knowledge. Research Report No. 18 – December 2010. https://aifs.gov.au/publications/insights-sexual-assault-perpetration/chapter-3-victimsurvivor-narratives (accessed August 14, 2016).

Bejerot, S. (2007). An autistic dimension: A proposed subtype of obsessive-compulsive disorder. *Autism*, 11(2), pp. 101-10.

Blanke, O. & Arzy, S. (2005). The out-of-body experience: Disturbed self-processing at the temporo-parietal junction. *Neuroscientist*, 11(1), pp. 16-24.

Freud, S. & Strachey, J. (1975). *Three Essays on the Theory of Sexuality:* Basic Books.

Geberth, V. J. (2013). *Practical Homicide Investigation: Checklist and Field Guide* (4th ed.). Boca Raton, FL: CRC Press.

Groth, A. N. & Birnbaum, H. J. (1979). *Men Who Rape: The Psychology of the Offender*. New York: New York: Plenum.

Hagmaier, W. (1997). Combatting child abduction and serial killers. *International Society of Barristers Quarterly*, 32(4), pp. 435-41.

Haskins, B. G. & Silva, J. A. (2006). Asperger's disorder and criminal behavior: forensic-psychiatric considerations. *Journal of the American Academy of Psychiatry and the Law Online*, 34(3), pp. 374-84.

Holmes, R. (1991) *Sex Crimes*. Sage Publications: London, England.

http://creepypasta.wikia.com/wiki/Ted_Bundy%27s_Letter (accessed February 8, 2016).

Knight, R. A. (1999). Validation of a typology for rapists. *Journal of interpersonal violence*, 14(3), pp. 303-30.

Kristiansson, M. & Sörman, K. (2008). Autism spectrum disorders: legal and forensic psychiatric aspects and reflections. *Clinical Neuropsychiatry: Journal of Treatment Evaluation*, 5(1), pp. 55-61.

Mann, D. (2010) Ted Bundy and atheism. http://mannsword.blogspot.com.au/2010/07/ted-bundy-and-atheism.html, July 8, 2010 (Accessed April 2, 2016).

Mason, Y. (2011). *Silent Scream*: Lulu.

Meister, C. (2010). Atheists and the quest for objective morality. *Christian Research Journal*, 33(2), pp. 28-35. October 26, 2015.

Michaud, S. (2015). *100 hours behind bars with Ted Bundy*. https://www.youtube.com/watch?v=gSAnIp4C-6c (Published on Oct 26, 2015; accessed December 21, 2015).

Nelson, P. (1994). *Defending the Devil*. New York: William Morrow and Company, Inc.

Pojman, L. & Fieser, J. (2011). *Cengage Advantage Books: Ethics: Discovering Right and Wrong* (6th ed.): Cengage Learning.

Reaven, J. & Hepburn, S. (2003). Cognitive-behavioral treatment of Obsessive-Compulsive Disorder in a child with Asperger Syndrome: A case report. *Autism*, 7(2), pp. 145-64.

Ramsland, K. (2013) Bundy's demon: Part I. Several killers have described a driving force they could not control. https://www.psychologytoday.com/blog/shadow-boxing/201309/bundys-demon-part-i. Posted September 01, 2013 (Accessed March 2, 2015).

Ramsland, K. (2013) Bundy's demon: Part II. Several killers have described a driving force they could not control. https://www.psychologytoday.com/blog/shadow-boxing/201309/bundys-demon-part-i. Posted September 04, 2013 (Accessed March 2, 2015).

Ressler, R., Schactman, T., (1992). *Whoever Fights Monsters*. St. Martin's Press: New York, NY.

Schaefer, G. J. (1997). *Killer Fiction* (Susan London Ed.): Feral House.

Simon, R. I. (2008). *Bad Men Do What Good Men Dream: A Forensic Psychiatrist Illuminates the Darker Side of Human Behavior* (Updated ed.). Arlington, VA: American Psychiatric Publishing, Inc.

Turvey, B. E. (2011). *Criminal Profiling: An Introduction to Behavioral Evidence Analysis* (4th ed.). Oxford, UK: Academic Press.

Valemont, P. L. (2013) *Numerology Serial Killer Ted Bundy*. Lulu (1st edition).

Index

C

This appendix contains a list of about 70 missing females age and region appropriate between 1963 and 1975 primarily for Washington State, Oregon and California. British Columbia victims, the so-called Highway of Tears victims, have been omitted on the grounds that they are not feasibly related. There are very few victims in this list that can be associated with Ted with any confidence, if at all, however, since the list was disseminated to authorities shortly after Ted was arrested in 1975, it represents an interesting snapshot of how authorities were thinking about him at the time. In retrospect, it is obvious that other killers (e.g., Zodiac) could be reasonably suspected as the perpetrator of some of these cases, but as killers in their own right have been omitted as not relevent as the focus of this list is victims that fit Ted's demographic. Data (images and text) in this section have been extracted and weaved together from the King County, Google Newspaper Archives and other newspapers. In many cases, images have been enhanced due to poor condition of the source material. The reader is advised to remember that the victims listed here were real people that had honor despite the circumstances they found themselves in.

Judith Gail Williamson (18).
Missing: October 29, 1963.
Found: April 1966.
Albany: suburb of greater San Francisco, CA.

Williamson was a coed at Berkeley University who went missing early in the morning near her home in Albany while posting a letter. On November 12, 1963, two bloodstained books belonging to Judith were found at Berkeley University in a garbage bin. Shortly afterward, a pool of blood was found in the university campus garage, matching Judith's blood type. She was eventually found in a ravine near Santa Cruz. Mostly upper portion bones. Her breastbone had been pierced. Also found were her blouse, skirt, stockings and slip. Her blouse had 15 tears in the fabric. Apparently stabbed to death based on cuts in her clothes. A paring knife was found near her body. Another report said she was wearing a black cardigan. The ex-Mayor's son, Joseph Egenberger (33), turned himself in to Oakland police in November 30, 1977 and confessed to the murder. Was her schoolmate at Albany High School and at UC Berkeley. He was described as "a brilliant student." He had sometimes driven her to the university. According to his testimony, she had resisted his vows of love, he got angry. Convinced by his lawyer to plead not guilty despite his confession, he was convicted of second-degree murder, sentenced to five-to-life and was eventually set free to live with his conscience. [JOSEPH EGENBERGER confirmed].

Barbara Jane Morritz (18).
Missing: February 9, 1964.
Found: February 11, 1964.
Monterey: about 75 miles (120 km) south of San Francisco., CA.

Morritz worked as a motel maid. She was last seen at a Salinas bus station. Her body was found lying off the shoulder of a dead-end country road between Salinas and Monterey. Her clothing was bunched around her mid-riff, her panties were around her ankles and her bra was twisted around her neck. It was established that she had been raped.

Cheri Josephine Bates (18).
Missing: October 30, 1966.
Found: October 31, 1966.
Riverside: suburb of greater Los Angeles, CA.

A 1966 graduate of Riverside's Ramona High School, Bates was beaten and stabbed multiple times with a short-bladed knife. There was no evidence of robbery or sexual molestation. There were no witnesses. Bates had been studying in the Riverside Community College library prior to the attack. She left the library at 9:00 p.m. to head home in her VW bug. She was found 6:30 a.m. in the morning face down fully clothed in a dirt alley on Terracina Drive between two unoccupied houses on campus. Her throat was slashed and she had several stab wounds in her back. Her car was found intentionally disabled approximately 100 yards from the alley. A men's Timex watch with a band suggesting a seven-inch wrist was found at the scene, along with a military-style heel print indicating a size 8-10 shoe. The origin of the watch was eventually traced to a military post, possibly in England. The shoes could have been sold at nearby March Air Force Base. Investigators established the watch was ripped from the attacker's wrist during the struggle. Although the watch stopped at 12:24 a.m., it's believed the crime occurred a few hours earlier and that Bates died very quickly. [ZODIAC is one suspect].

Nikki Alexandra Benedict (14).
Missing: May 1, 1967.
Found: May 5, 1967.
Poway is a suburb of greater San Diego, CA.

Poway, late afternoon. Benedict was hanging out with her friend when they see a strange man looking at them. The surviving teen takes note of the man's face and the make of the vehicle. 6:00 p.m. Benedict leaves her friend's home located on Halper Road (12784 off Pomerado Road) and heads to her home on Olive Tree Lane. Much of the path was through open fields—typical in Poway those days—from Pomerado and

Carriage roads, extending to Community Road. She was attacked near an access road located 75 yards west of where she was initially found. Ron Fisk (11) was riding his bike when he spotted Benedict injured on the ground less than 100 yards from the intersection of Poway and Carriage roads. Benedict apparently crawled after being stabbed in the chest and neck, seeking help. Fisk rode to his father's nearby shop, told his dad and the elder Fisk called the Poway Fire Department for assistance. The fire department's Lewis "Pat" Wills told the Poway News Chieftain he recalls arriving with the ambulance. He noticed the girl's shallow breathing, then bandaged two stab wounds in her chest before transporting her to Palomar Medical Center, where she died about 30 minutes later. A coroner's report indicates there was no sexual assault, but the stab wounds were likely from a short knife, causing the fatal injury.

Susan Marie Cardwell (18).
Missing: May 19, 1967.
Found: May 25, 1967.
San Martin is a small town about 248 miles (400 km) south of Portland, OR.

Cardwell was formerly of White City, Oregon. Her body was found near San Martin, somewhere along the highway near San Jose adjoining a prune orchard. Her clothes were pulled up around her neck, her underclothes down below buttocks. She was shot 15 times above the waist, her jaw was broken, and her skull was fractured. The coroner's deputies said she had been dead a week and there were indications of a sex attack.

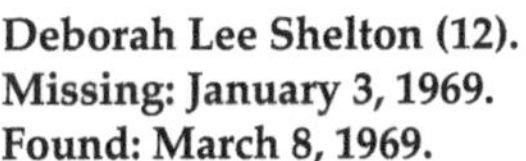

Deborah Lee Shelton (12).
Missing: January 3, 1969.
Found: March 8, 1969.
Aptos is a coastal town about 62 miles (100 km) south of San Francisco, CA.

Shelton was last seen approximately 10 a.m. in front of Farmer's Market, Soquel Drive, Aptos, Santa Cruz. Her family received an extortion call. Her decomposed body was found in a wooded area about 100 yards from the Aptos Bridge. It was established that she had ben strangled with her own panties after her hands were taped and her clothing pulled up. The tape that had covered her mouth had slipped down around her neck during decomposition of the body.

Laura Lee Asynithe Flink (21).
Missing: February 21, 1969 [Ted in New Jersey around this date].
Not found.
Aberdeen is a coastal town of Washington State, about 50 miles west of Olympia, WA.

Flink was last seen in Aberdeen, WA, at approximately 4:00 p.m. She was driving her live-in boyfriend's red 1967 Ford Ranchero with WA license plates numbered U23307 on County Road 101 towards Moclips, WA, to pick up some furniture and children's clothing. She never arrived at her destination and has never been seen again. Flink's brown leather jacket was found on a sidewalk in Hoquiam, WA, on February 23, and mailed to her post office box in Aberdeen, but she never picked it up. The car she was driving was found in the 700 block of J Street in Hoquiem on February 24. Shortly before he disappearance, Flink received legal custody of her 16-month-old son. She was employed as a waitress in 1969, and had no other source of income. She may have been three months pregnant at the time of her disappearance.

Judy Gail Lattaker (22).
Missing: April 10, 1969.
Found: April 10, 1969.
Oakland is a city of greater San Francisco, CA.

Lattaker was found between Alameda and Oakland, near the waterfront on gravel road. Her skull was crushed. There were several recent needle marks on body. When found she was nude below waist. Rape was undetermined.

Kathleen Marie Butts (19).
Missing: date unknown.
Found: August 29, 1969.
Long Beach is a coastal suburb of greater Los Angeles, CA.

Butts was discarded behind a Long Beach store in some brush. Her body had partially decomposed. She was strangled and her ankles and hands were bound with yellow cord. Her clothing was found 1 mile from the scene.

Elaine Louise Davis (17).
Missing: December 1, 1969.
Found: December 19, 1969
Walnut Creek is a suburb of greater San Francisco, CA.

Davis was abducted through a sliding rear window while baby-sitting her 3-year-old sister at the family's Walnut Creek home. Police found no evidence of a struggle at the scene. A button Davis had been planning to sew onto her coat was found in a field behind her house two days later; the coat was found by a motorist on Highway 17 near Santa Cruz.

Authorities found the body of a female floating off Light House Point near Santa Cruz, CA, about two weeks after Davis' disappearance. In 2000 it was identified as Elaine Davis. Davis' body showed some signs of cartilage damage in her neck, indicating that she might have been strangled. No information about clothing was reported when she was found. A shoe, however, was found on I-680 which is believed to have belonged to her. [PHILIP JOSEPH HUGHES / ZODIAC suspected].

Leona LaRell Roberts (16).
Missing: December 11, 1969
Found: December 28, 1969
Rodeo is a suburb of greater San Francisco, CA.

A Napa Valley beauty college student, Roberts disappeared from her boyfriend's apartment in Rodeo as she waited for him to return from work. A neighbor said she heard a scream just minutes after Miss Roberts arrived. A man was seen speeding off in a station wagon. Her smock was found on a sofa and a Christmas tree was overturned. Her nude body was discovered on a beach near Bolinas Lagoon, Marin County. Death was apparently caused by aspiration from a virus and there was a suggestion of ligature marks on her wrists and ankles. The exact time of death was undetermined but put at around 10 days prior to the time of discovery. She had been on the beach 5 days by one estimate. Clothes not found. [PHILIP JOSEPH HUGHES/ZODIAC suspected].

Cindy Lee Mellin (19).
Missing: January 20, 1970.
Not found.
Ventura is a coastal suburb about 50 km north of Los Angeles, CA.

Mellin was employed by the Broadway Department Store in the Buenaventura Shopping Center, Ventura. She left work shortly after closing and was last seen standing next to her car in the shopping center parking lot while an unidentified male changed her tire. Her vehicle found with rear flat tire caused by sharp instrument that punctured the sidewall.

Cosette Ann Ellison (15).
Missing: March 3, 1970.
Found: January 1, 1971.
Moraga is a suburb of greater San Francisco, CA.

Ellison was a sophomore at Campolindo High. She was last seen about 3:30 p.m. in the driveway of her Canyon Road home in Moraga, after getting off a school bus (in front of her Canyon road home). Found in a ravine (or creek bed) off of Morgan Territory Road, nude, partially decomposed. Her clothing was found 1 mile from the scene. [PHILIP JOSEPH HUGHES suspected].

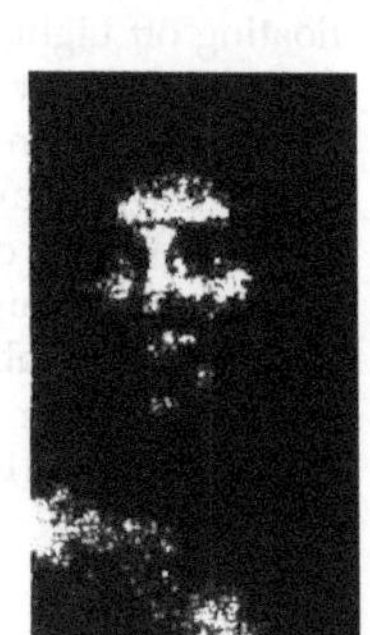

Patricia Ann King (20).
Missing: March 5, 1970.
Found: March 6, 1970.
Pleasant Hill is a suburb of greater San Francisco, CA.

Patricia left a dance class at Diablo Valley College, Pleasant Hill. Her body, which was nude below waist with her bra pulled up, was found in the Diablo Stadium by a "construction"

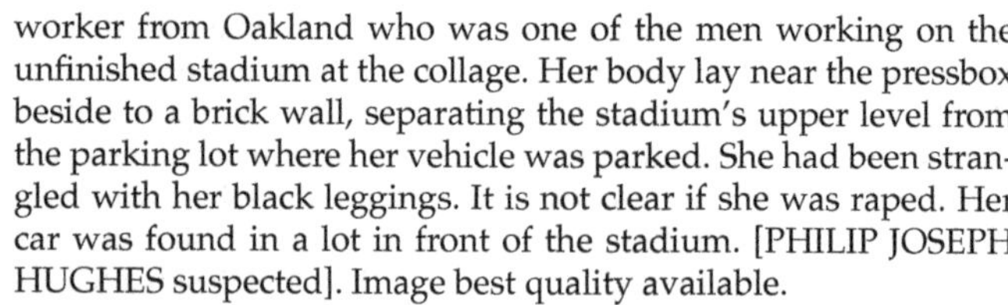

worker from Oakland who was one of the men working on the unfinished stadium at the collage. Her body lay near the pressbox beside to a brick wall, separating the stadium's upper level from the parking lot where her vehicle was parked. She had been strangled with her black leggings. It is not clear if she was raped. Her car was found in a lot in front of the stadium. [PHILIP JOSEPH HUGHES suspected]. Image best quality available.

Judith Ann Hakari (23).
Missing: March 7, 1970.
Found: April 25, 1970.
Sacramento is an inland city about 62 miles (100 km) northeast of San Francisco, CA.

Hakari worked her usual shift at Sutter General Hospital, getting off work at 11 p.m. She was last seen leaving the hospital parking lot around 11:30 p.m. Her fiancé, who was waiting for her at her Markston Road apartment, on the corner of Markston and Alta-Arden Way (then called Glendale Ave), became alarmed when Judith did not come home. He found her car parked in her assigned parking stall in the apartment building parking lot. She must have been immediately seized, either at gun point or simply knocked unconscious and abducted because her car was found unlocked and her keys were on the floorboard. A couple was hiking about Weimar on Highway 80 on the way to Reno and Lake Tahoe, on Ponderosa Way, looking for an old mine, when they found see a human knee protruding from the ground. According to a Sacramento Bee article she had been buried in a white sack. Under the body was a gray zip-up sweatshirt with a pocket on either side of the zipper. Other sources said that she was buried in her nurse uniform, which was open in front and her underwear was found beneath her. Strangled by a stocking (her hyoid bone was crushed), face crushed with a rock to the point where she was unrecognizable. Some reports say she was raped, others not. Her watch and purse were off her body.

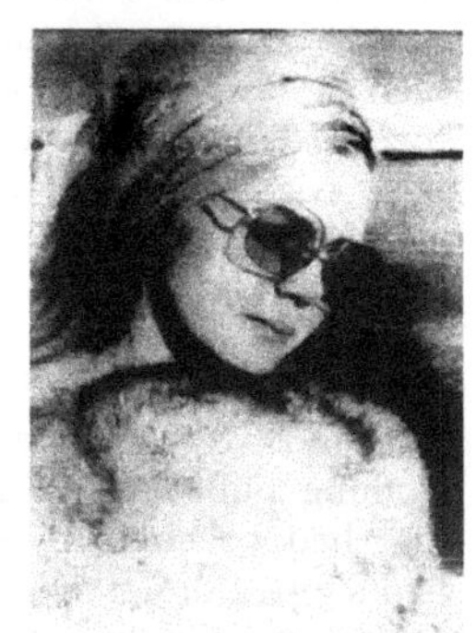

Marie Antoinette Anstey (24).
Missing: March 13, 1970.
Found: March 21, 1970.
Vallejo is a suburb of greater San Francisco, CA.

Last seen in parking lot at Coronado Inn, city of Vallejo. Found lying off isolated road in some heavy brush. Nude. Blow to head followed by drowning. No clothes found. Suspected drug overdose (later pronounced accidental death).

Lois Jean Reicher (21).
Missing: September 27, 1970.
Found: September 28, 1970.
Redlands is a far western suburb of Los Angeles, CA.

Reicher was last seen leaving the University of Redlands Library en route to her dormitory. Her nude body was found in an orange grove on university property. She had been raped. Death was caused by head injuries as a result of aspirating her own stomach juices.

Nancy Marie Bennallack (28).
Missing: October 25, 1970.
Found: October 26, 1970.
Sacramento is an inland city about 62 miles (100 km) northeast of San Francisco, CA.

Sacramento. She was stalked. The killer jumped the fence, climbed up the gas meter and onto her second story apartment balcony in order to get in. She must have jumped out of bed and met her fate. She was stabbed or sliced over 30 times, her throat being cut as well. She was found in her underwear, some of her clothes beneath her. Cuts on her hands indicate she struggled with her killer, and a trail of blood leading from her apartment indicate she wounded her attacker. A court reporter for four years, she was engaged to Chief Public Defender Farris Salamy. They were to be married November 28, 1970. Salamy said he last saw Bennallack about 11:30 p.m. Sunday at her apartment. A neighbor said she heard what sounded like someone crying about 1:30 a.m. Bennallack's body was discovered after she failed to show up for work on Monday.

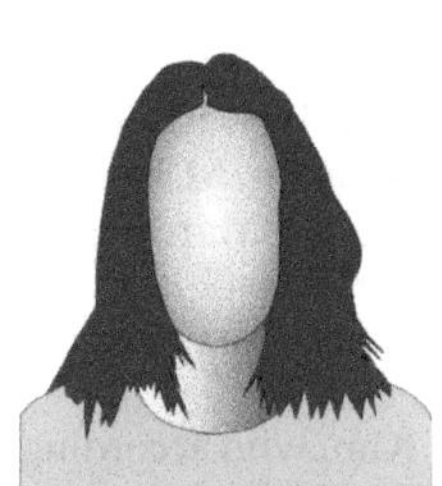

Wachalain Marmlarnil (20).
Missing: October 27, 1970.
Found: October 28, 1970.
Hawthorne is a suburb in southwestern Los Angeles.

Marm-larnil was visiting California from her native Thailand. She was enrolled at a local school where she was taking a course in hotel management. Apparently abducted from a bus stop, school children found body on the grounds of Cimarron Elementary School, 11559 Cimarron Ave., Hawthorne. She was nude below the waist, her skirt pulled up and her bra pulled down. Her panties and hose were not found.

Carol Beth Hilburn (22).
Missing: November 13, 1970.
Found: November 14, 1970.
Sacramento is an inland city about 62 miles (100 km) northeast San Francisco, CA.

Nurse's assistant. On the night she disappeared she was visiting Sacramento from Sonoma County where she worked at the Sunlight Royal Convalescent Hospital. Late that Friday night she visited an old bartender friend at the The Zodiac Club on West Capitol Avenue (a biker's hangout). From there she went to Lloyd Hickey's Forty Grand Club on Del Paso Boulevard, Sacramento. She had once worked there and chatted until the early morning hours. After she left (around 5 a.m. Saturday morning), nothing was seen of her until her body was found several miles north in the rural Rio Linda area. She had been dragged naked from a car and dumped in the open area at the corner of Ascot and 4th Street. She was only wearing one suede boot/sock. Her face and skull had been beaten to a pulp. She might also have been strangled. She had not been sexually molested.

Robin Ann Graham (18).
Missing: November 15, 1970.
Not found.
Santa Monica is a coastal suburb of Los Angeles, CA.

Graham was last seen by California Highway Patrol officers at approximately 2:00 a.m. beside her car on the shoulder of the southbound Hollywood Freeway near the Santa Monica off-ramp, LA. She was in the presence of a dark-haired white man estimated to be in his mid-twenties who drove a late 1950s model Chevrolet Corvette C1, pale blue or green with primer. Graham used a call box to ask that a CHP emergency operator let her parents know she had run out of gas. Graham's younger sister took the call and relayed the information to her parents upon their return home at approximately 2:30 a.m. They went immediately to the location where they found Robin's car, but she was not there. The case remains unsolved.

Christine Marie Eastin (19).
Missing: January 18, 1971.
Not found.
Hayward is a bay suburb of San Francisco, CA.

Eastin borrowed her former boyfriend's 1969 Ford Maverick in the evening. She was going shopping with a friend and promised to wash the car before returning it later that night. She bought a pair of boots while shopping, dropped her friend off, and then continued to Charlie's Car Wash, a self-service wash on Mission Boulevard in Hayward. The Maverick was located at the wash during the early morning hours of January 19 the following day. Eastin had apparently completed washing the vehicle's exterior before she vanished. The car was locked and papers from the interior were laying on the pavement outside of the driver's door. There was no sign of Eastin and she has never been seen again.

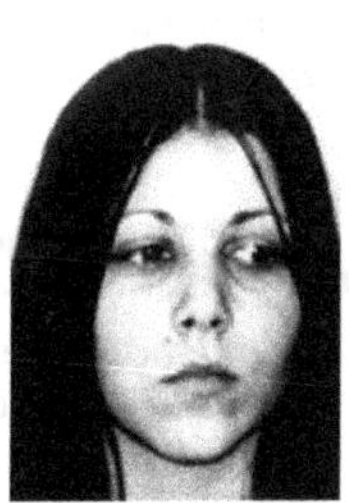

Lisa Smith (17).
Missing: March 16, 1971.
Not found.
Santa Rosa lies about 62 miles (100 km) north of San Francisco, CA.

From Petaluma, Smith was last seen hitchhiking along Hearn Avenue in Santa Rosa. Little else is known about her.

Debra T. Pscholka (12).
Missing: June 5, 1971.
Not found.
Corona is a southwestern suburb of greater Los Angeles, CA.

Debra was last seen in Corona, Riverside County, LA, at approximately 8:15 p.m. She went to the now-defunct Corona Theater on 6th Street with friends. The staff caught her smoking and asked her to leave the theater. She left alone, telling friends she was going to the park. She has never been heard from again.

Elizabeth Marie "Betty" Cloer (22).
Missing: June 19, 1971.
Found: June 19, 1971.
Sacramento is an inland city about 62 miles (100 km) northeast of San Francisco, CA.

Cloer was last seen departing a Sacramento bar with a suspect. Her nude body except for a bra was found the same day at the end of a dead-end road in the remote foothills of Cameron Park. All other clothing except her purse was located at scene. She was shot 3 times with 0.32 caliber automatic. Her head was also crushed to a pulp with a large rock. There was no evidence of a sexual attack. She had a five-year-old son. In October 30, 2003, PHILIP ARTHUR THOMPSON was charged with her murder.

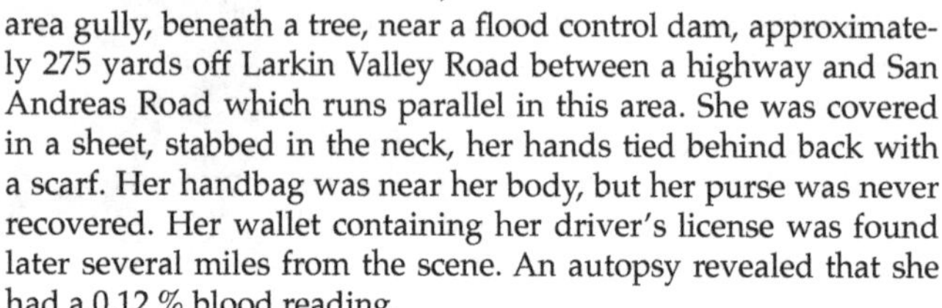

Rosa Linda Cantu Zuniga (18).
Missing: July 10, 1971.
Found: July 26, 1971.
San Jose is a suburb of greater San Francisco, CA.

Zuniga, who hitchhiked, partied and took drugs, was last seen on 1300 East Williams, San Jose. Her decompoased body was found on La Selva Beach, in a rural area gully, beneath a tree, near a flood control dam, approximately 275 yards off Larkin Valley Road between a highway and San Andreas Road which runs parallel in this area. She was covered in a sheet, stabbed in the neck, her hands tied behind back with a scarf. Her handbag was near her body, but her purse was never recovered. Her wallet containing her driver's license was found later several miles from the scene. An autopsy revealed that she had a 0.12 % blood reading.

Susan Marie Lynch (22).
Missing: July 29, 1971.
Found: July 31, 1971.
Santa Cruz is an ocean-side suburb about 62 miles (100 km) south of San Francisco, CA.

Lynch was last seen hitchhiking from Santa Cruz to Nevada City, Northgate area. Her body was found in a shallow grave near a drainage ditch in Rio Linda. She was wearing her blouse and shoes but her bra had been removed. Her cut-off pants were also removed and left in the grave. It was established that she had been rendered unconscious via blow to the face and buried alive. The only injury found in an autopsy was a dislocated jaw. Accordingly, it appeared that she had died of suffocation as a result of inhaling sand. It was also established that she had been raped.

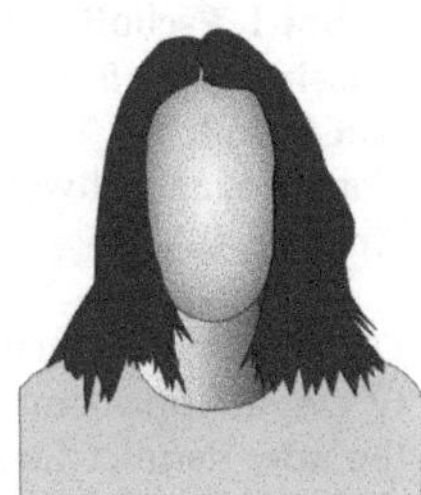

Linda Susan Dudley (22).
Missing: August 22, 1971.
Found: August 27, 1971.
Lake Merced is a freshwater lake in the southwest corner of San Francisco, CA.

Dudley was known to work as a prostitute. Her nude body was found lying in some brush on the bank of Lake Merced, stabbed 3 times in the chest and abdominal area. No clothing was found.

Yvonne Lisa Weber (13, top).
Maurine Louise Sterling (12, bottom).
Missing: February 4, 1972.
Found: December 28, 1972.
Santa Rosa lies about 100 km north of San Francisco, CA.

Both girls attended junior high school, but according to police were into the dope scene. Sterling was cited as being sexually experienced. Both would hitchhike from the Redwood Empire Ice Arena to Howarth Park, which is across town, and hitchhike back before their mothers would be at the ice arena to pick them up. On the day they disappeared they were dropped off at the ice arena around 4:00 p.m. They were last seen hitchhiking on Guerneville Road, northwest of Santa Rosa. Their bodies were found 2.2 miles north of Porter Creek Road on Franz Valley Road, down a steep embankment approximately 66 feet off the east side of the roadway. A single earring, orange beads and a 14-carat gold necklace with a cross were found at the scene. The cause of death could not be determined from their skeletal remains.

Kim Wendy Allen (19).
Missing: March 4, 1972.
Found: March 5, 1972.
San Rafael lies about 12 miles (20 km) north across the Golden Gate Bridge, CA.

Kim, who according to police was sexually immature and did not partake in the dope scene, was given a ride by two men from her job at Larkspur Natural Foods to San Rafael. They last saw her at approximately 5:20 pm hitchhiking to a school near the Bell Avenue entrance to Highway 101, northbound, carrying a large wooden soy barrel with red Chinese characters on it. Her nude body was found the following day down an embankment in a creek bed twenty feet off Enterprise Road in Santa Rosa. She had been bound at the ankles and wrists, raped and strangled with a clothesline. There were cuts on her chest. Semen was recovered from her body and a single gold loop earring was found at the site. Markings at the top of the embankment and a possible leg impression in the loam indicated the assailant likely slipped or fell while throwing or transporting the body. The two men who gave her a ride, one of whom was given and passed a polygraph test, were ruled out as suspects.

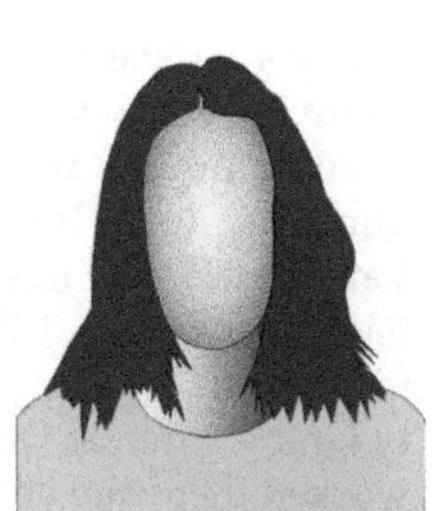

Jane Doe (?).
Missing: ?
Found: March 22, 1972.
Ensenada lies about 62 miles (100 km) south of San Diego, CA.

A body was found at Ensenada Beach, Baja California.

Jeanette Kamahele (20).
Missing: April 25, 1972.
Not found.
Santa Rosa lies about 62 miles (100 km) north of San Francisco, CA.

Kamahele was last seen hitchhiking on the Cotati on-ramp off Highway 101 in Santa Rosa. A friend of hers was going to stop and pick her up, but before she could, another vehicle pulled over and Kamahele stepped into a faded brown 1970-72 Chevrolet pickup truck driven by a 20 to 30-year-old Caucasian male with an Afro-type hairstyle.

Sandra June Peters (17).
Missing: April 29, 1972.
Found: April 30, 1972.
Carmel Valley lies about 125 miles (200 km) south of San Francisco, CA.

Peters was last seen in Sambos restaurant in the company of a white male at 7:30 p.m. Her body was found 2.5 miles east of Carmel Valley Village in a secluded brushy area near Carmel River. Her body located 30 feet from roadway and was nude from the waist down except for socks. She was clutching her torn panties in one of her hands. Other clothes wer found in the vicinity. Zig Zag cigarette papers were found in her pocket. She had been shot twice in the head with a 0.25 caliber weapon. Police believe that her death was a possible drug-related crime.

Beverly May Jenkins (16).
Missing: May 25, 1972 [Ted cannot be ruled out for this date].
Found: June 5, 1972.
Springfield is a suburb of Eugene, Oregon. It lies about 93 miles (150 km) south of Portland, OR.

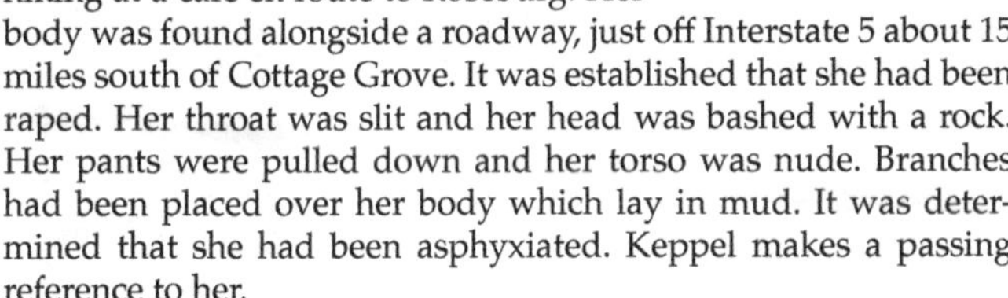

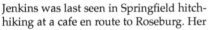

Jenkins was last seen in Springfield hitchhiking at a cafe en route to Roseburg. Her body was found alongside a roadway, just off Interstate 5 about 15 miles south of Cottage Grove. It was established that she had been raped. Her throat was slit and her head was bashed with a rock. Her pants were pulled down and her torso was nude. Branches had been placed over her body which lay in mud. It was determined that she had been asphyxiated. Keppel makes a passing reference to her.

Jane Pellett (28).
Missing: June 7, 1972 [Ted cannot be ruled for this date].
Found: June 26, 1972.
Salem lies about 37 miles (60 km) south of Portland, OR.

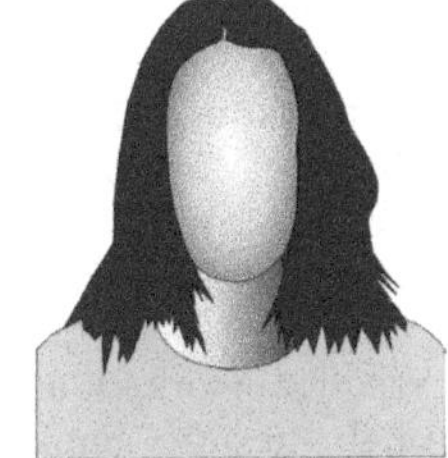

Pellet was last seen in a Salem restaurant at 8:05 p.m. She was found on a busy roadside. A grave had been prepared nearby, but was unused. Instead, brush was placed over her body. Only her rosary was found. Robert E. Oliver confessed to Pellet's murder in 1978.

Geneva Joy Martin Irvin (19).
Missing: June 10, 1972 [Ted cannot be ruled out for this date].
Found: June 16, 1972.
Salem lies about 37 miles (60 km) south of Portland, OR.

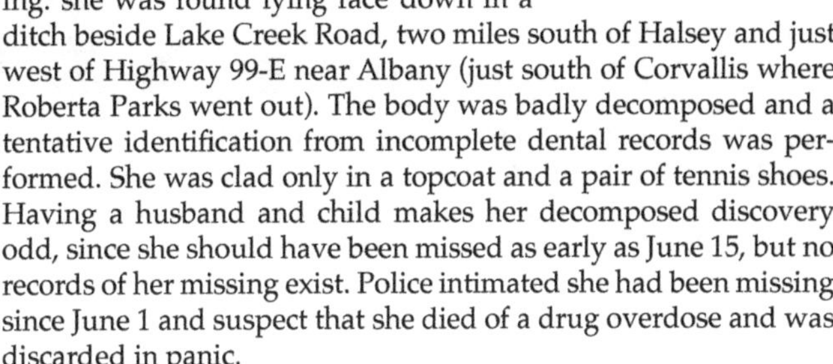

Wife of Harvey N. Irvin. Mother of Dahphina Joy Irvin. Possibly hitchhiking. she was found lying face down in a ditch beside Lake Creek Road, two miles south of Halsey and just west of Highway 99-E near Albany (just south of Corvallis where Roberta Parks went out). The body was badly decomposed and a tentative identification from incomplete dental records was performed. She was clad only in a topcoat and a pair of tennis shoes. Having a husband and child makes her decomposed discovery odd, since she should have been missed as early as June 15, but no records of her missing exist. Police intimated she had been missing since June 1 and suspect that she died of a drug overdose and was discarded in panic.

Maureen Patricia Field (19).
Missing: November 14, 1972.
Found: February 15, 1973.
Pleasant Hill is a suburb of greater San Francisco, CA.

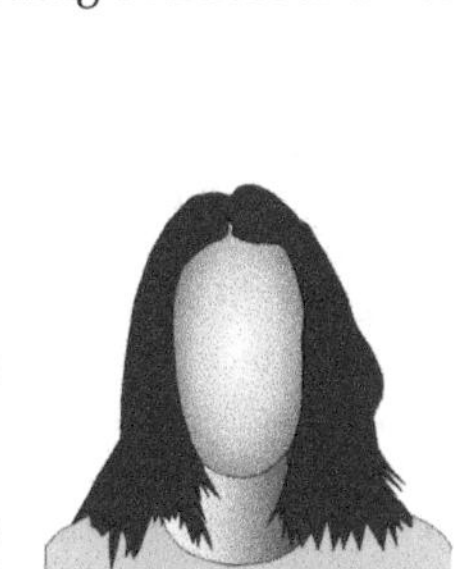

Last seen leaving work at K-Mart store in Pleasant Hill. Body found at foot of Mount Diablo down a roadside embankment near a creek in a brushy area. Decomposed. Nude. Possibly stabbed to death. [PHILIP JOSEPH HUGHES suspected].

Lori Lee Kursa (13).
Missing: November 20, 1972.
Found: December 14, 1972.
Santa Rosa lies about 62 miles (100 km) north of San Francisco, CA.

A Lawrence Cook Middle School student, Kursa was reported missing by her mother on November 11, 1972 after disappearing while they shopped at a U-Save Market, Santa Rosa. Apparently Kursa ran away. She was last seen on November 20 or 21 in Santa Rosa while visiting friends. She had been known to hitchhike occasionally. Her frozen remains were located in a ravine approximately fifty feet off Calistoga Road, northeast of Rincon Valley in Santa Rosa. The killer had thrown the body at least thirty feet over an embankment. The cause of death was a broken neck with compression and hemorrhage of the spinal cord. Kursa had not been raped and likely died one to two weeks prior to discovery. A possible witness to her abduction later came forward stating that on an evening somewhere between December 3 and 9, while on Parkhurst Drive he saw two men push a girl fitting Kursa's description into the back of a van driven by a Caucasian man with an Afro-type hairstyle. The vehicle then sped north on Calistoga Road.

Barbara Jean Stroud (18).
Missing: January 7, 1973.
Found: January 10, 1973.
Willits lies 137 miles (230 km) north of San Francisco, and about 80 miles (130 km) north of Santa Rosa, CA.

Approximately 11:30 p.m. Stroud dropped her boyfriend off at his residence within Willits city limits, then traveled north on Highway 101 towards her residence. Approximately 2 miles north of Willits city limits, evidence showed her vehicle was forced off the roadway. Coincidentally, approximately 30 minutes after leaving her boyfriend's residence, a Mendocino County Sheriff's Deputy was en route to a call for service in Laytonville when he observed Stroud's vehicle parked alongside Highway 101 and noticed it was unoccupied. After handling the call in Laytonville the Deputy returned to Stroud's vehicle and noticed her personal belongings inside. The Deputy checked the vehicle's registration and learned that it was not wanted or stolen. The Deputy then left the area. Approximately 2:00 a.m. Stroud's parents phoned the Sheriff's Office and reported her missing. A search was conducted but she was not located. Her nude body was located in a remote area within 2 miles of where her vehicle was located. Her clothing was later found approximately 1 mile away from where her body was discovered. Her glasses, a ring and panties were missing. An autopsy revealed she had been sexually assaulted and strangled to death.

Leslie Marie Perlov (21).
Missing: February 13, 1973.
Found: February 16, 1973.
Palo Alto is a suburb of greater San Francisco, CA.

Perlov worked as a legal secretary in the North County Law Library in Palo Alto. Co-workers there were the last to see her alive. Perlov's car, an orange Chevrolet was first spotted parked at the gate of a dead-end road on Stanford land near the intersection of Page Mill Road and Junipero Serra Boulevard in the afternoon by a passing off-duty Palo Alto policeman, who said he saw her talking to a young man with long blond hair. A beige auto was parked nearby. Perlov's Chevrolet Nova was found abandoned at the gate in the evening. Her body was found in a clump of bushes in an area of rolling oak-tree-covered hills south of Stanford University (at the site of the Old Quarry near the intersection of Stanford Avenue and the Foothill Expressway). Her skirt had been pulled up around her waist and her pantyhose stuffed in her mouth. Scarf knotted around neck, coat pulled up over shoulders, blouse unbuttoned, bra pushed up over breasts. Boots found in stream 80 feet from body. Purse missing. Captain Frank Mosunic said "she had to walk there. She wasn't dragged". It appeared she had not been sexually molested. If Ted was responsible for Perlov's murder, she may be the most likely candidate due as there is no information of Ted's whereabouts between February 10–27 of 1973. Ted has "County Council" penned in his 1973 diary for February 13.

Susan Gail McLaughlin (20).
Missing: March 2, 1973.
Found: March 3, 1973.
Sacramento is an inland city about 62 miles (100 km) northeast of San Francisco, CA.

McLaughlin was last seen en route to Sacramento, hitchhiking from Berkeley to Oakland. Her body was found in mountains two miles east of Kyburz, near Highway 50 in El Dorado County, 150 yards north of Highway 50, nude from waist down except for boots. Her Levi pants were found nearby with the front completely cut out and her bra was cut in several pieces. She may have been bound with adhesive tape. Her backpack was later found on top of a restroom in Alder Creek campgrounds, 6 miles from where her body was located. She had alcohol in her blood at the time of death. Bryan Lee Gelenaw, who is incarcerated in Clallam Bay Corrections Center for a different murder, is currently a person of interest.

Kathleen Edna Rodgers (16).
Missing: March 3, 1973.
Not found.
Oroville lies about 150 miles (240 km) north of San Francisco, and about 70 miles (112 km) north of Sacramento, CA.

Rogers was last seen by her stepmother Elda Stevens after an argument at approximately 12:00 p.m. at their residence at 1512 Keko Street in Oroville. She was reported missing the same day. Nothing else is known about her case.

Rosa Vasquez (20).
Missing: May 26, 1973.
Found: May 29, 1973.
San Francisco, CA.

Vasquez worked at Letterman General Hospital, Presidio, San Francisco. Her nude body was found lying in shrubbery in San Francisco Golden Gate Park. It was established that she had been strangled. Only a bra was found around her neck. Semen was discovered in her vagina, mouth and rectum. Her image was constructed from an IdentiKit and is unverified.

Yvonne Quilantang (15).
Missing: June 8, 1973.
Found: June 9, 1973.
San Francisco, CA.

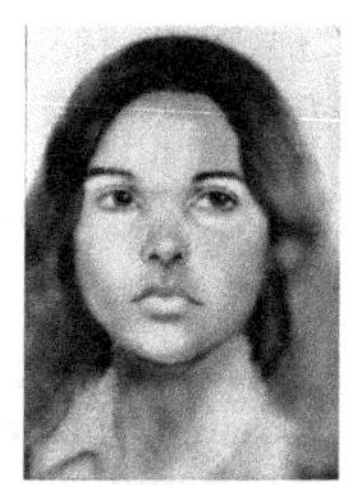

Quilantang was last seen in San Francisco. Her nude body was found in some bushes on a Bay-view District vacant lot. It was established that she had been raped and strangled. None of her clothes were found. She was seven months pregnant at the time of her death. Her image is from a drawing and is unverified.

Allison Lynn Caufman (15).
Missing: June 20, 1973 [Ted cannot be ruled out for this date].
Found: June 21 1973.
Portland is the northernmost city of Oregon and sits south across the border from Vancouver, Washington State, OR.

Caufman went missing from Portland. Her nude body was found by swimmers near Blue Lake Park between North Marine Drive and Columbia River (just east of Portland). It was established that she had been strangled.

Rose Lena Cole (15–16).
Missing: July 1973
Not found.
Oakland is a suburb of greater San Francisco, CA.

Cole ran away from home in Flint, Michigan, around the fall of 1972 and moved to the west coast scene where she got involved in drugs. A judge sentenced her to a rehabilitation program operated by Synanon (at the time a cult-like organization). In late 1972, Cole began writing letters and poems to her family from the Synanon compound, telling them that she wished to come home. She then escaped from Synanon and wrote more letters, telling her parents that she was living in a large house in San Francisco's Chinatown area with an older couple. She said she was afraid of being sent back to Synanon, and wouldn't contact them again until she was legally considered to be an adult. The fourth and last letter was sent in early 1973. She hasn't been heard from since.

Laurie Lea Canaday (18).
Missing: July 1973 [Ted cannot be ruled out for this period].
Found: July 1973.
Portland is the northernmost city of Oregon and sits south across the border from Vancouver, Washington State, OR.

Canaday went missing from Portland. It was established that she died of head injuries sustained after she fell or was pushed from a speeding car. Very little else is known about her case.

Angela Thomas (16).
Missing: July 1, 1973.
Found: July 2, 1973.
San Francisco, CA.

Thomas was last seen leaving friend's house in San Francisco. Her nude body was found lying in the schoolyard of Benjamin Franklin Junior High, San Francisco. It was established that she had been murdered by asphyxiation. No clothing was found.

Linda Ann O'Keefe (11).
Missing: July 6, 1973.
Found: July 7, 1973.
Corona del Mar is a suburb in Orange County, California, about 45 miles (62 km) south of Los Angeles, CA.

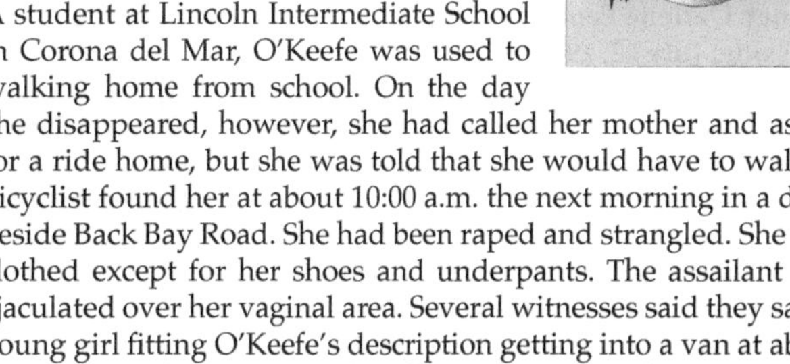

A student at Lincoln Intermediate School in Corona del Mar, O'Keefe was used to walking home from school. On the day she disappeared, however, she had called her mother and asked for a ride home, but she was told that she would have to walk. A bicyclist found her at about 10:00 a.m. the next morning in a ditch beside Back Bay Road. She had been raped and strangled. She was clothed except for her shoes and underpants. The assailant had ejaculated over her vaginal area. Several witnesses said they saw a young girl fitting O'Keefe's description getting into a van at about 1:15 p.m. on the afternoon that she disappeared. The van was described as a 1969 to '73 turquoise-colored vehicle of an unknown make and model, with windows on both of the rear double doors, no windows on the left side, and the license plate mounted on the left rear door. The driver was a male Caucasian, about 24 to 30 years old, with brown, curly, medium-length hair, small or droopy eyes, and a deep tan.

Nancy Patricia Gidley (24).
Missing: July 12, 1973.
Found: July 15, 1973.
San Francisco, CA.

Gidley was last seen leaving the Rodeway Inn at 895 Geary Street, San Francisco. Her nude body was found lying in a parking lot of George Washington High School in the Richmond area, although it was believed she was murdered elsewhere. It was establishd that she had been raped and strangled. No clothing was found. She was previously stationed at Hamilton Air Force Base for four years, until the early months of 1972, when, as an X-ray technician, she arrived in San Francisco in mysterious circumstances, supposedly invited to be the maid of honor at a wedding (which apparently nobody was able to verify). Before leaving her home in Idaho, she also told close friends her intention was to work as a freelance writer at the *Chronicle* newspaper, but staff at the *Chronicle*, again, had never heard of her.

Caroline Nadine Davis (14).
Missing: July 15, 1973.
Found: July 31, 1973.
Garberville lies about 200 miles (320 km) north of San Francisco, and about 150 miles (240 km) north of Santa Rosa, CA.

Davis ran away from her home outside Anderson in Shasta County on February 6, 1973, but disappeared on July 15 after being dropped off by her grandmother at the Garberville Post Office. She was last seen hitchhiking that afternoon near the Highway 101 ramp, southbound, in Garberville. Her body was discovered just three feet from where the remains of Sterling and Weber had been recovered seven months prior. The cause of death was determined as Strychnine poisoning 10–14 days before her body was found. It could not be established if she had been raped. Investigators postulated that her body had been thrown from the road as the hillside brush appeared undisturbed.

Nancy Darlene Feusi (23).
Missing: July 22, 1973.
Found: July 22, 1973.
Sacramento is an inland city about 62 miles (100 km) northeast of San Francisco, CA.

At the time of her death Feusi was living with her five children in a hotel room after separating seven months earlier from her husband over abuse and unfaithfulness. She was last seen in the 3000 block, 42nd Street, Sacramento, at a dance hall, accompanied by adult a number of African-American males. It was established that she had sexual intercourse with an African-American male on the evening of the dance. She was found on a roadside at Riego and Pleasant Grove Road, in a rural area clad in a miniskirt and bikini-type briefs. A blouse was found nearby. She was stabbed 29 times in the stomach, chest and arms.

Jane Doe (15-20).
Missing: ? [Ted cannot be ruled out for this victim].
Found: July 27, 1973.
Lake Desire lies south of Lake Washington, Seattle, WA.

At Lake Desire, King County, dogs found a lower left leg and foot encased in blue denim pants as well as a separate right femur. The ankles had been tied and the bones may have been pared down.

Martha Joan Stevens (19).
Missing: August 19, 1973.
Found: August 29, 1973.
San Francisco, CA.

Stevens was last seen hitchhiking to San Francisco. She was dropped off near Hollywood Bowl by the person she rode with from Colorado to LA. Her decomposed body was found 6.5 miles past 1/2 Way Inn in Gorda, 50 yards up Soda Springs Creek in a National Wilderness area. Her head was bashed in with an axe-shaped rock. She was lying on her back with her knees up and legs spread wide apart and was nude except for a T-shirt pulled up to her neck area. It was established that she had been strangled to death. A bathing suit was located around her left ankle and had been slit from top to bottom. All other clothing articles were left at scene.

Corrine June Groenenberg (14).
Missing: November 1, 1973.
Not found.
Compton is a suburb between Los Angeles and Long Beach, CA.

Groenenberg was last seen departing her family's residence in Compton, California, on November 1, 1973. A friend told authorities they saw Groenenberg walk to a nearby highway and hitchhike. The friend saw her enter a blue or green pick-up truck with an unknown male driver. She has not been seen since, and her case remains unsolved.

Laura O'Dell (21).
Missing: November 4, 1973.
Found: November 7, 1973.
San Francisco city, CA.

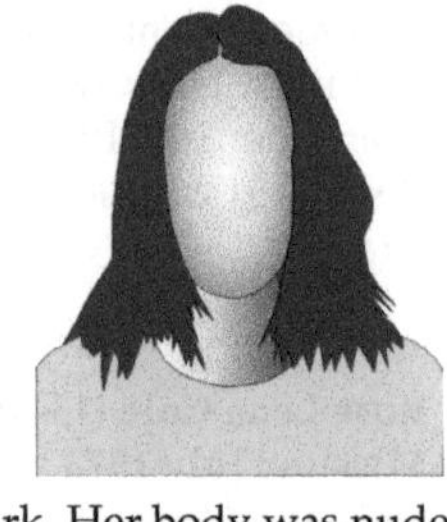

O'Dell was last seen leaving a halfway house for the mentally ill while en route to her home on a bus around 8:30 p.m. (She had a past history of mental illness). She was found in shrubbery in Golden Gate Park. Her body was nude from the waist down, and her hands were bound behind with a strap from her shoulder bag. It was established that she had been beaten with a thin blunt instrument, raped and strangled. The location where her body was found is directly opposite 1252 15th Ave, San Francisco, where Ted stayed some time during 1970 according to the Ted Bundy Multiagency Investigative Team Report 1992.

Therese Diane Walsh (23).
Missing: December 22, 1973.
Found: December 28, 1973.
Malibu is an ocean-side suburb of Los Angeles, CA.

Walsh was last known to be hitchhiking on Highway 101 from the area of Malibu Beach to her home in Gaberville intent on joining her family for Christmas. She wore a silver handmade cross around her neck, and a fire-opal ring and a copper-banded ring on her fingers. She carried ten dollars of colored beads she used for making bracelets in her backpack. Her partially submerged body was located under a log in the water of Mark West Creek in Santa Rosa, near the spot where Kim Wendy Allen's body was found. She had been hog-tied with one-quarter-inch nylon rope – her hands bound in front of her and pulled down between her legs, her feet tied and pulled back by the rope that was also tied around her neck, strangulating her. She had been sexually assaulted. No clothing found. Due to recent heavy rains in the area, high water marks suggested the body could have drifted several miles.

Lulaida Morales Sejalbo (17).
Missing: November 25, 1973.
Not found.
Santa Clara is a suburb of greater San Francisco, CA (near Palo Alto where Ted had previously studied and temporarily lived)

Sejalbo disappeared on her way home from work at a McDonald's, Santa Clara, CA. Her car was recovered a month later with her purse, work uniform, keys and other personal belongings still inside. Nothing else is reported about her case.

D-Ann Kathleen Hammond (27).
Missing: January 19, 1974.
Found: January 26, 1974.
Sunnyvale is a suburb of greater San Francisco, CA.

Hammond, a nurse at Kaiser Hospital Los Altos, disappeared from her home in Sunnyvale. Her nude body was found washed ashore on a beach near Piedras Blancas Lighthouse, west by northwest of San Simeon, California. She died as a result of a blow to the head and had a broken back. It was possible she fell from a nearby low cliff. Her vehicle, purse, and clothing was not recovered. Authorities revealed she had knowledge of a crime committed by a suspect and had received threats by phone. It was also repoted she had suicidal tendencies. She had an eight-year-old child.

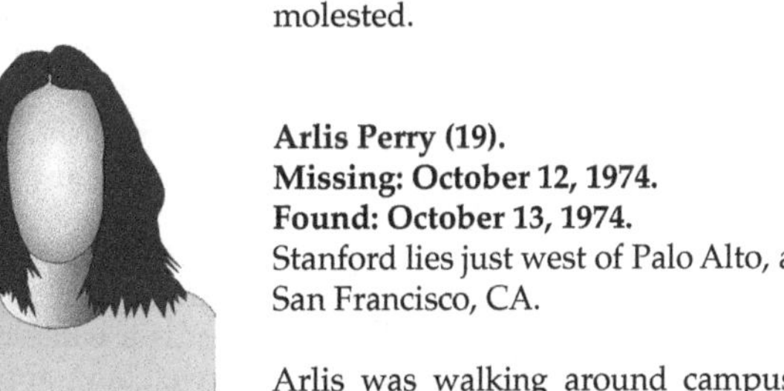

Lisa Ann Beery (15)
Missing: January 26, 1974.
Found: July 1979.
Montclair is a suburb of the San Francisco Bay Area, CA.

Hughes and Perrin kidnapped Beery, a choir girl, at knife-point near her Montclair home and took her to an Oakland home where Hughes stabbed and raped the her to death. Police found her body five years later buried on a Moraga (Rheem) hillside. [PHILIP JOSEPH HUGHES convicted].

Barbara Ann Barry (18).
Missing: Mid February, 1974 [Ted cannot be ruled out for this period].
Found: March 29, 1974.
Highway 14 traverses east out of Vancouver, WA, before heading to northeast Goldendale.

Barry was last seen hitchhiking on Highway 14 to Goldendale. When found, post-mortem was estimated at 6 weeks. The cause of death was established as stabbing. She was known to be promiscuous with any male aged 16-55. Her body was badly decomposed and missing a bra. Evidence at the location was hampered due to U.S. Army from Fort Lewis bivouacking in the same area and policing it before leaving. One soldier remembers finding a bra and throwing it in a creek.

Janet Ann Taylor (21).
Missing: ?
Found: ?
Stanford lies just west of Palo Alto, a suburb of San Francisco, CA.

Taylor, pretty and auburn-haired, was last seen near the Stanford campus hitchhiking. Her body was found 2 miles away near the intersection of Mayfield Ave. and Junipero Serra Blvd. in a ditch off Sand Hill Road near Searsvllle Lake in the rolling hills behind Stanford University campus (beside a rural road). Her neck was broken and she had a bruise on her chin. Death was estimated to have occurred 15 hours prior. She had been manually strangled but not raped. All her clothes were found except for her shoes. Her purse and bracelet were missing.

Donna Marie Braun (14).
Missing: September 29, 1974.
Found: September 29, 1974.
Greenfield lies about 140 miles (225 km) south of San Francisco, CA, and about 35 miles (56 km) inland.

Braun was found floating in Salinas River near the city of Greenfield, Monterey County. She had ben strangled and dumped nude. No clothing was recovered. She was still relatively warm when found. It was not established if she had been sexually molested.

Arlis Perry (19).
Missing: October 12, 1974.
Found: October 13, 1974.
Stanford lies just west of Palo Alto, a suburb of San Francisco, CA.

Arlis was walking around campus with her husband (then a sophomore pre-med student) disputing the air pressure in their car's tires. They parted ways, and she went to pray at Stanford Memorial Church on the grounds of Stanford University, a frequent place of meditation for the two. "It wasn't unusual for her to be at church, except that she was killed," Bruce Perry said. He reported her missing at 3 a.m. and again at 6:55 a.m. Around 5:45 a.m., Arlis' body was found near the altar, half-hidden under a pew, by a security guard opening the church for services. She lay face up on the floor of the east transept, nude from the waist down and violated by two-foot-long candles carefully removed from the candle-holders. There was no sign of a violent struggle and, except for the missing candles. Dean of the Chapel, Robert G. H. Kelly, said that the church's pulpit had not been disturbed. The coroner's report revealed that Arlis died around midnight, following ice pick wounds to the back of her head. She had not been raped. The case is still unsolved. A 2004 San Jose Mercury News article noted that Santa Clara County sheriff's detectives worked on the case for hundreds of hours. Bruce Perry was ruled out as a suspect, along with various individuals who had access to the church at the time of Arlis' murder. The couple, married fewer than two months before the crime, lived in an Escondido Village apartment. Arlis Perry had been working as a receptionist at a Palo Alto law firm for two weeks before her death.

Janna Marie Hanson (13).
Missing: December 26, 1974 [Ted can be ruled out for this date].
Found: August 2, 1975.
Edmonds is a bayside suburb about 19 miles (30 km) north of Seattle, WA.

Hanson went to school in Edmonds, but was last seen leaving her Mount Terrace home. Her skull was later found prompting a wider investigation. Searchers later found two earrings, part of a scarf, and strands of hair. King and Snohomish county authorities said that there was no evidence linking Hanson's death with the Taylor Mountain findings earlier in the year (*The Spokesman-Review*, August 7, 1975). Someone fitting Hanson's description was seen hitchhiking early March 1975 on Lake Paradise Road, two miles distance from where her skull was found (*The Spokesman-Review*, August 19, 1975). Kenneth M. Burke (39) was identified as a suspect but was later found dead due to an apparent suicide on October 16, 1975.

Loralee Sue Lhotka (19).
Missing: January 1975 [Ted can be ruled out for this period].
Not found.
Seattle, WA.

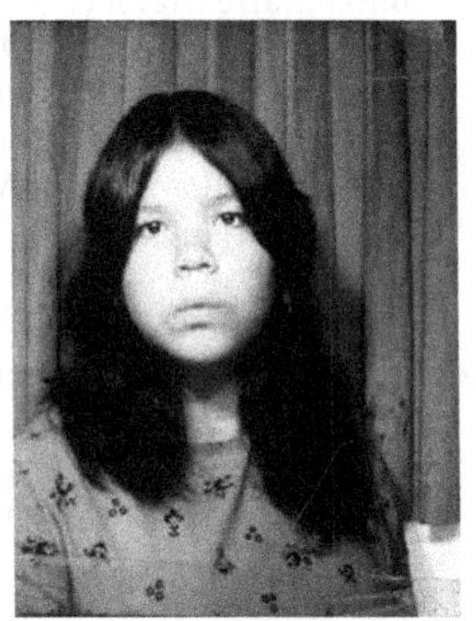

Lhotka was last seen in Seattle after leaving home to go to a doctor's appointment. She never made it. She was supposed to take the bus, but she may have hitchhiked instead. Her wallet was found in the Wenatchee National Forest sometime in 1978.

Letitia Fagot (25).
Missing: March 19, 1975.
Found: March 19, 1975.
Walnut Creek is a suburb of greater San Francisco, CA.

PHILIP JOSEPH HUGHES Jr, then a Pleasanton janitor, broke into the Walnut Creek house of Fagot on Los Cerros Ave, just a few blocks away from San Pedro Ct. Fagot worked at the French Bank of California in San Francisco with Hughes' wife (Suzanne Perrin), who suggested that he ought to target her. Hughes strangled Fagot with a cord and beat her with a hammer. Police arrested Hughes on July 16, 1979 (aged 31) after his wife gave him in. Hughes is suspected of at least three other killings:

- Lisa Dickinson, 9, disappeared September 5, 1976 while riding her bike from her home on Los Cerros Ave. in Walnut Creek toward Heather Farms Park. Her bike was found leaning against a tree inside the park, but the girl has never been found. Louis Fresquiz is currently the prime suspect in her disappearance.

- Lou Ellen Burleigh, 21, of Walnut Creek vanished September 11, 1977, on her way to a job interview at a Pleasant Hill shopping center on Contra Costa Boulevard.

- Tara Cossey, 9, was last seen while walking to the Pirelli's Liquor store in San Pablo to purchase a bag of sugar for her mother on June 6, 1979.

Mona Jean Gallegos (22)
Missing: June 19, 1975.
Found: November 28, 1975.
Alhambra is an inner east suburb of Los Angeles, CA.

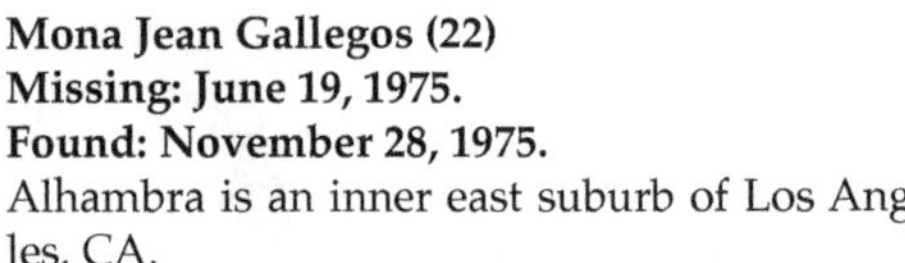

A waitress at Coffee Dan's in West Covina, Gallegos was last seen leaving a friend's house around 1:00 a.m. She was returning to her Covina home from Alhambra when she vanished. Her 1970 Pontiac was later found on the San Bernardino Freeway at the Santa Anita Avenue off-ramp in El Monte around 4:45 a.m. It was locked and out of gas and had body damage on the right front fender and was inoperable. There was a 24 hour gas station near the off-ramp where her car stalled out, and detectives believe someone offered her a ride to that gas station. She was last seen wearing a red and white pantsuit and white shoes. Six months later, her skeletal remains were found in a Riverside ravine.

Tina Michelle Migis (17).
Missing: October 3 1975.
Found: October 7, 1975.
Salem lies about 37 miles (60 km) south of Portland, OR.

Migis was last seen boarding a bus at Yreka, California, en route to Portland at about 1:00 p.m., She was not on that bus when it arrived in Portland late in the evening. It was determined she remained on the bus at least as far as Roseburg, Oregon. A witness reported seeing Migis hitchhiking at a Eugene, Oregon, ramp to northbound I-5 on the afternoon of October 6, 1975. She was reported to be wearing a heavy-knit cream-colored sweater that had a two-inch horizontal stripe, calf-length brown lace-up boots, and possibly blue bell-bottom pants. The witness observed Migis enter an older (perhaps mid-1960s) dirty green or blue Ford or Chevrolet van with covered windows that may have had areas of primer paint on the body. The driver was a white male in his mid-twenties, approximately 6 feet tall, weighing approximately 165-175 pounds, sporting light brown hair and a mustache. A second occupant of the van was described as a slender white male with shoulder-length black hair. It is not known whether the second occupant was an associate of the driver or was another hitchhiker.
Migis' nearly nude and decapitated body was found beside River Road North, north of Salem, Oregon on October 7, 1975. The following morning, her severed head was found in a field adjacent to Labish Center Road northeast of Salem.

Book versions consulted

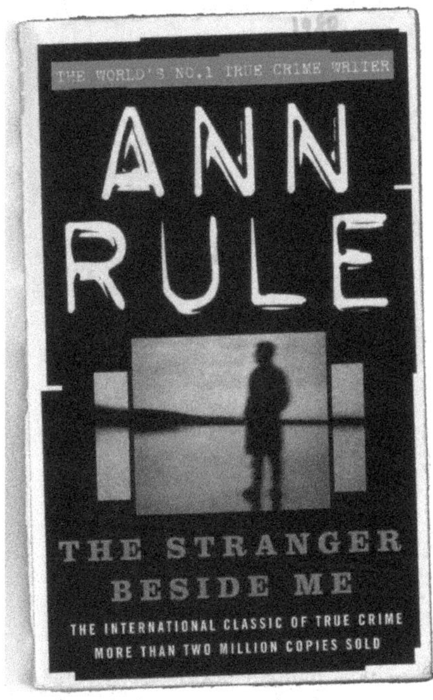

2006, Time Warner Books. Original published 1980.

1980, Bantam.

1980, Prentice-Hall.

1981, Madrona Publishers.

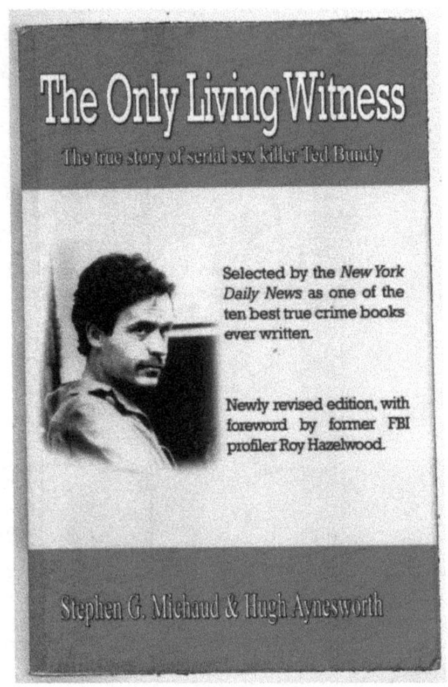

1999, Authorlink Press; first published 1983.

KILLER FICTION

BY

G.J. SCHAEFFER

AS TOLD TO

SONDRA LONDON

FOREWORD BY COLIN WILSON

INTRODUCTION BY SONDRA LONDON

FERAL HOUSE

1997, Sondra London & Feral House.

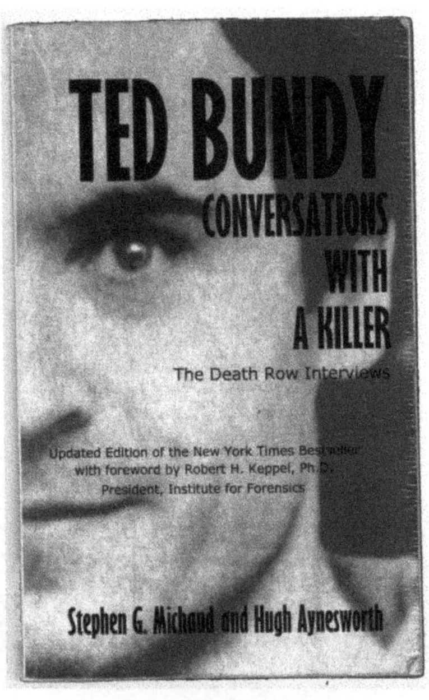

2000, Authorlink Press.

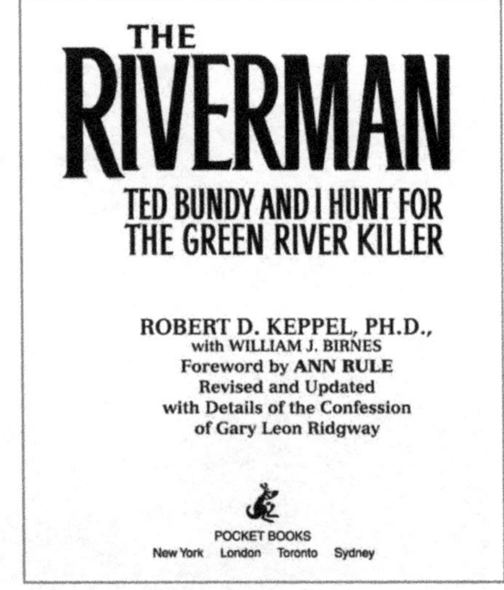
THE RIVERMAN

TED BUNDY AND I HUNT FOR THE GREEN RIVER KILLER

ROBERT D. KEPPEL, PH.D.,
with WILLIAM J. BIRNES
Foreword by ANN RULE
Revised and Updated
with Details of the Confession
of Gary Leon Ridgway

POCKET BOOKS
New York London Toronto Sydney

2005, Pocket Books.

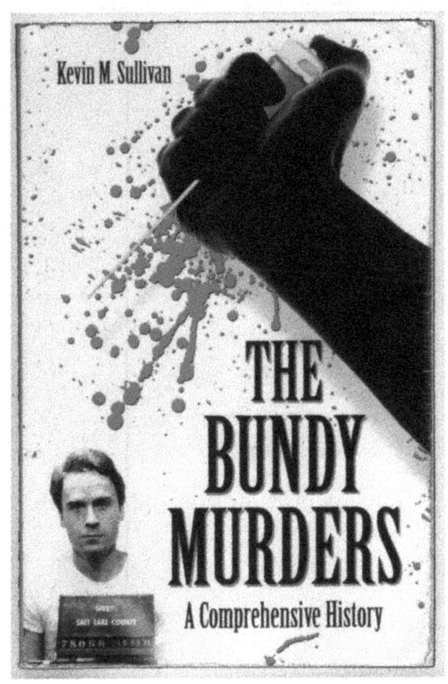

2009, McFarland & Company, Inc.

2011, Lulu.

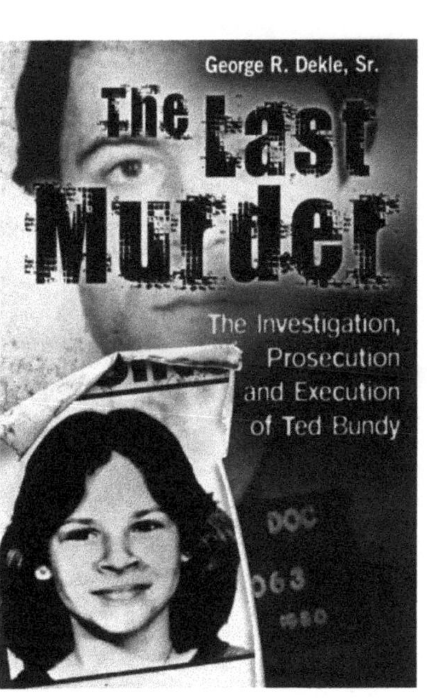

2011, Praeger.

Terrible Secrets
2012

(Placeholder – unable to show image due to copyright protection)

2012, MT7 Productions.

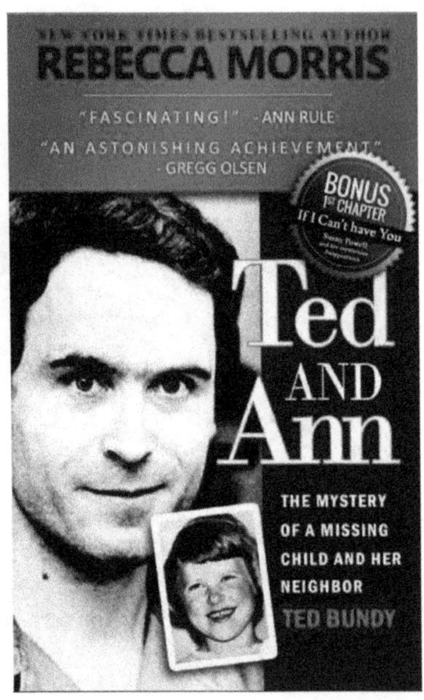

2013, True Books.

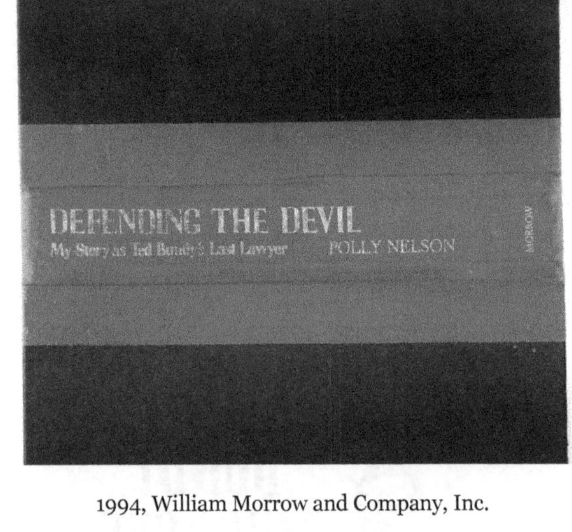

1994, William Morrow and Company, Inc.

2014, Genius Book Publishing.

Dr. Rob Dielenberg was born in Melbourne. He played in rock bands until his mid-20s, then earned a BA (Psychology) and Ph.D. (Neuroscience) from the University of Sydney. In between his degrees he did a year of clinical psychology, a year of TAFE sciences, and a 2-year fiction writing course. He retired as a post-doctoral fellow and went freelance in 2005. For the last decade he has diversified into areas such as neuroanthropology and criminology. He is also a co-director of Motion Mensura which develops tracking software and UAVs for high resolution mapping. He is married without children. His hobbies are tennis and cross-country mountain bicycle riding. He currently resides in Newcastle, Australia.

Chris Mortensen is married and lives in Salt Lake City, working as a high school teacher, with a BS in Severe Needs Special Education from the University of Utah, and a M.Ed. in Reading Literacy from Belhaven University. Born and raised in Sonora Ca, he moved to the Roaring Fork Valley area of Colorado in 1992. Moving to Salt Lake City in 2001, Chris has always been fascinated with local Utah history, and has spent many hours researching local criminology and urban development, conducting many interviews with local policemen and longtime residents. Chris enjoys playing multiple instruments with various bands which he has continued since his teen years, and loves exploring the Western United States by car in his free time.

Charles "Chuck" Meeks grew up in Pocatello, Idaho, and is retired from the United States Air Force. During his 22 year career in the military, he was a nuclear weapons specialist and later an imagery analyst. While on active duty, he was fortunate to have been stationed at various bases throughout Europe and able to experience many different cultures. He is currently a full time graduate student working on an MS in Clinical Counseling, having also earned a BS in Business Information Systems and an AS in Munitions Systems Technology. His hobbies include target shooting, board gaming, and photography. He is married with no children and currently resides in Bellevue, Nebraska.

Lightning Source UK Ltd.
Milton Keynes UK
UKHW051949070219
336840UK00007B/91/P